Library of Congress Cataloging-in-Publication Data

McGee, John S.
  Industrial organization

    p. cm.
  Includes index.
  ISBN 0-13-464207-4
  1. Industrial organization (Economic theory)   I. Title.
HD2326.M39 1988
338.6—dc 19   87-32623

Editorial/production supervision
  and interior design: Sonia Meyer
Cover design: Wanda Lubelska Design
Manufacturing buyer: Barbara Kelly Kittle

 © 1988 by Prentice-Hall, Inc.
A Division of Simon & Schuster
Englewood Cliffs, New Jersey 07632

Printed in the United States of America
10 9 8 7 6 5 4 3 2 1

ISBN   0-13-464207-4

Prentice-Hall International (UK) Limited, *London*
Prentice-Hall of Australia Pty. Limited, *Sydney*
Prentice-Hall Canada Inc., *Toronto*
Prentice-Hall Hispanoamericana, S.A., *Mexico*
Prentice-Hall of India Private Limited, *New Delhi*
Prentice-Hall of Japan, Inc., *Tokyo*
Simon & Schuster Asia Pte. Ltd., *Singapore*
Editora Prentice-Hall do Brasil, Ltda., *Rio de Janeiro*

INDUSTRIAL ORGANIZATION

JOHN S. McGEE
University of Washington

Prentice Hall
Englewood Cliffs, New Jersey 07632

To my mother and
to the memory of my father

CONTENTS

10   THE THEORY OF PRODUCTS
AND MONOPOLY   229

11   MEASURING CONCENTRATION
AND MONOPOLY   244

12   ECONOMICS OF VERTICAL INTEGRATION   272

PREFACE

In the 1930s, industrial organization emerged as a specialized field in economics. It is not surprising that the field has changed in the many years since it began. What is remarkable is how *much* it has changed. Changes in the last few years, especially, can fairly be called revolutionary. Many of the older theories, facts, and public policy conclusions about industrial organization have been overturned; some others are tottering.

This book integrates and clearly presents the economic theory, empirical evidence, and public policy analyses needed to understand how industrial organization has evolved, and to appraise it as it stands today.

More than other industrial organization books, this one traces the history of the theories and inferences that have proved most important to the field. Knowing where we've come from can help us understand where we are and where we're going. This book is also unusual in explicitly recognizing that institutions matter. Law and liberty are as much a part of civilization as are art, music, and literature. The quality and robustness of civilization, as well as economic efficiency, are profoundly affected by competition and the restraints placed on it. Much of what we call civilization consists of defining and limiting the kinds of competition that are acceptable. These definitions and limits are embodied in constitutions, laws, and culture.

Most people come into economics with a strong interest in public policy,[1] and this book emphasizes public policy issues. In analyzing them, I have hoped to do two things. First, I have worked with law and government regulations for years and want to pass along what I have learned about their substance. Second, I have learned something about analytic tools that can help us understand what institutions and public policies do and—in

[1] A fascinating survey demonstrates this, among other things. David Colander and Arjo Klamer, "The Making of an Economist," *The Journal of Economic Perspectives*, I (Fall 1987), pp. 95–111.

the interest of helping others reach their own conclusions—have illustrated how to use the tools.

Although it is possible to learn some of the same economics by working problems carefully chosen from price theory texts and workbooks, it is more direct and economical, as well as more interesting, to work on important real problems. Besides, real problems are good for us. Because they can be difficult, real problems teach us respect and humility as we grapple with them.

I have tried to be as direct and clear as possible without sacrificing substance, and have developed the theoretical tools and analyses step by step. Although standard English is by far the most important expository device used here, diagrams and numerical examples also help mark the way at various points. I use a little basic algebra and calculus at a couple of places in the text and in a couple of optional appendices. The appendices are truly optional. You do not need them to understand what is going on; but they are there for anyone who wants to *do* economic studies as well as to understand and evaluate them. As suits their purpose, the appendices are more like demonstration lessons than workbook drills.

Those who believe that public policy and real industrial performance are more important and interesting than pure theory should be pleased to learn that this is not just another price theory book in disguise. It selects theories that are most relevant to appraising economic performance and public policy, treats those theories as a tool kit rather than adornment, and shows how to use the tools. This book does not slight theory, though, and can help those who are interested in theoretical as well as empirical and policy problems.

As we go along, I will point out a number of puzzles and problems that I hope readers will try to solve. If they do, they may decide to do some research on their own, and, more important, begin to look at business and government practices more closely and to ask questions about them.

Those who are interested professionally in the kinds of policies and problems this book discusses can pick up the specific economics they need more quickly here than by plowing through unspecialized theory textbooks. Lawyers, consultants, and business executives will find that this book can help in much of what they do.

I have already mentioned some of the unusual features of this book, such as showing how institutions matter and presenting appendices that can help those who want them without imposing on those who do not. There are also some novelties in topics covered, including new material in Chapter 9 about what I call *compound pricing*, and predatory pricing; and in analyzing the problem of externalities, Chapter 17 discusses airport noise, lighthouses and bees, buffalo hunting, commercial fishing, and crude oil production. A short section in Chapter 14 shows how to read and interpret the regression equations that now commonly appear in empirical works on industrial organization.

Seattle, Washington

1 INTRODUCTION

WHAT IS INDUSTRIAL ORGANIZATION?

Industrial organization studies how the performance of an industry is related to its structure; that is, to the number and size of firms it contains. How can industry performance and structure be measured or appraised? Concentrated industries are those in which the leading firms do a relatively large share of the business. Do concentrated and unconcentrated industries perform differently? How does the performance of individual firms affect the structure and performance of the industries in which they operate? If there is a substantial causal relationship between performance and structure, does it go both ways, with structure affecting performance and performance affecting structure? And, if industrial performance seems deficient but remediable, which government policies are likely to help more than they cost?

Answering questions such as these is what this book is about.

Systematic study of industrial organization started at Harvard University in the 1930s, during the Great Depression, a time of political and intellectual ferment everywhere. It is hard to pin down why specific schools of thought started where they did. Edward Mason, the Harvard professor of economics who practically fathered the new field, later wrote that the influence of Edward H. Chamberlin had been "profound."[1] In Mason's words:

Chamberlin's theoretical insights were developed by his Harvard colleagues in the messier areas of industry statistics, studies of particular firms, and antitrust policy. I had some hand in this along with younger colleagues and graduate students of whom Donald H. Wallace and Joe S. Bain deserve particular mention. . . . we had some hope of developing an operational classification of market structures that would not only go far toward explaining the behavior of firms but also provide normative standards of performance of use to antitrust policy. Although this goal was never reached, a substantial contribution, I believe, was made in shaping the field of industrial organization.[2]

The last two sentences of this quotation refer modestly to one of the things for which Professor Mason and Joe Bain are famous. It came to be known as the Structure-Conduct-Performance Paradigm, which dominated the field of industrial organization for many years and is still popular.

In the beginning, most economists seem to have believed that the structure-conduct-performance relationship was largely or altogether one way: to a significant degree the *structure* of an industry determines the *conduct* of firms in it; and how firms behave to a significant degree determines how well the industry *performs*. The major hypothesis was that a highly concentrated industry—one with a few large firms—was more prone to collude or act as though it had, resulting in high prices, high profits, and perhaps laggard technological innovation and other deficiencies as well.[3]

Naturally enough, different writers used somewhat different ingredients in their versions of the same basic model. In some versions, for example, structure included concentration on both the seller side and buyer side of markets; the degree of vertical integration; product characteristics, including whether the goods are durable or nondurable, principally used by consumers or producers; and whether entry is easy, hard, or "blockaded." Behavior, or conduct, included such things as advertising, product differentiation, price discrimination, predatory and exclusionary tactics, collusion, and quasi-independent price determination. Performance included production efficiency, optimum sizes of firms and how fully economies of size had been realized, excess capacity, margins between price and cost, profits, price flexibility, and "excessive" advertising and other selling costs.

Many studies of specific industries—so-called industry studies—used this paradigm to judge whether specific industries were effectively competitive, or needed government intervention to improve their performance.[4]

Like most theories, the structure-conduct-performance paradigm proved to have problems. One was that industrial structure did not seem to determine performance as reliably or in quite the same way as had been theorized. A related problem was that causality, if any, might run in the opposite direction: the superior performance of some firms could lead them to grow large, creating the very concentration that the earlier paradigm led us to fear. In this case, however, concentration would lead to, or would have been produced by and symptomize, superior performance in such industries. Or perhaps, overall, causality ran in both directions; or sometimes one way and sometimes another.

Information about such relationships, and confidence in them, changed greatly over the years, as we will see in subsequent chapters.

THE ROLE OF THEORY AND SCIENTIFIC METHOD IN POLICY STUDIES _____

Industrial organization might conceivably have developed as a purely scientific field, avoiding normative conclusions and policy proposals altogether. If it had, it would have used theory to collect and organize information about real firms and industries, tested and modified the theory to explain new facts as they came along, and let it go at that. Such an approach is not trivial: it helps explain how the world works and why it works that way—a major accomplishment. Nor is scientific method brutal. It need not crush out compassion or force conformity. As physical science and medicine show, scientific method probably will never eliminate disagreement about even ''the facts,'' which change over time. And important differences in values and goals will surely remain, more perhaps in some fields than in others.

Pure theory and pure science are not enough to satisfy everyone: many want at least as much to improve the world as to understand it. Most who major in economics came to that field largely because they are interested in public policy.[5] Many of even the best economists were attracted to economics because they hoped to do good. Alfred Marshall, the great English economist, is an illustrious example of one who retained his interest in understanding and combating poverty.[6] In industrial organization, as in other fields of economics, scholars have seldom hesitated to make policy proposals, even when their theories and facts were weak.

For several reasons, industrial organization tends to be even more policy oriented and controversial than some other fields. It attracts those who are interested in policy and who like policy debates, then teaches them skills useful in controversies that pay well. Antitrust laws and other regulations employ industrial organization economists in business, government, and courtrooms.

Economic theories and quantitative analyses offer precise answers to some public policy questions. It is dangerous, however, to worship precise answers for their own sake. First, it is clearly better to be approximately correct than precisely wrong.[7] And, as John von Neumann, a world-famous mathematician, is supposed to have said, it makes no sense to be precise about something when you do not even know what you are talking about.

Second, one reason to ask what any theory covers is that cold arithmetic tends to drive out values that are difficult to measure. But we must also be leery of analyses that depend crucially upon the unmeasurable or upon an analyst's personal values. For one thing, charlatans have a field day when we permit them to be vague. Diviners want to be able to take any side of all questions and hate to be bound by logic, consistency, or empirical tests. They relish the freedom to sound judicial and wise, and to treat each case as a unique phenomenon.

Third, precise quantitative answers sometimes come from analyses more complicated and demanding than our data and understanding can support. When data are poor, analysis that is hypersensitive to what we feed it can drag us far off track. And, as Alfred Marshall warned, long chains of reasoning and reckoning can go wildly wrong even when our intentions are good. On top of that, complexity can be used purposefully to obscure a trail and confuse the hounds.

Dangerous though bad theory is, there is no substitute for what good theory can do. No finite human mind can cope with all the facts; facts do not speak clearly for themselves. Theory helps organize the facts we have and directs the search for others not yet in view. Clear, explicit theory can improve communication by showing what is at issue and by keeping us talking to one another about the same things, one at a time. Since tractable theory must simplify, however, it can never be completely realistic. As Milton Friedman put it:

> A hypothesis is important if it ''explains'' much by little, that is, if it abstracts the common and crucial elements from the mass of complex and detailed circumstances surrounding the phenomena to be explained and permits valid predictions on the basis of them alone. . . . the relevant question to ask about the ''assumptions'' of a theory is not whether they are descriptively ''realistic,'' for they never are, but whether they are sufficiently good approximations for the purpose at hand.[8]

Joan Robinson, by contrast, claimed that the assumptions of a theory should be realistic enough to communicate and keep a decent reputation with ''the practical man,'' if for no other reason. When answering a question, she said, the economist should:

> . . . make clear what assumptions about the nature of the problem are implicit in his answer. If those assumptions are near enough to the actual conditions to make the answer serviceable the practical man can accept it, but if the assumptions are very abstract the economist will only bring the practical man into confusion and himself into disrepute by allowing him to suppose that the question which is being answered is the same as the question which is being asked.[9]

It is often hard to decide which of competing theories is most consistent with the facts. And sometimes even the best theory does not explain or predict very well. Chapters 14 to 20 discuss these problems.[10]

THE ORGANIZATION OF THIS BOOK

This book provides what we need to answer the central questions of industrial organization and to evaluate studies such as those Professor Mason mentioned in his historical summary. The industrial organization economics developed here has three major themes: theory, measurement, and policy.

Much of this book is about resource allocation in a market system. Earlier chapters lay necessary theoretical foundations. Chapter 2 discusses competition in nature, war, and games; outlines functions performed by all economic systems, from individual households on up; defines efficiency; and presents the traditional and still popular theory that the efficiency of resource allocation depends upon whether industry is competitive or monopolistic. It also discusses institutions and how to appraise them.

Chapter 3 inquires whether the theory of atomistic competition is a reliable and wholesome pattern from which to tailor public policy.

Industries in which relatively few firms do most of the business are called "concentrated." Their structure is very different from the atomistic industries pictured in theory texts. Chapters 4 and 5 cover theories about how firms in concentrated industries behave if they do not agree to limit competition. Chapter 6 discusses cartels, which result when firms *do* agree to suppress competition.

Chapters 7, 8, and 9 discuss what determines the number and sizes of firms in an industry. Chapter 7 shows how costs and demands affect industrial structure. Chapter 8 is about patents. Chapter 9 analyzes business practices that have been denounced as "barriers to entry" and "monopolizing" devices.

Chapter 10 defines monopoly and monopoly power, and Chapter 11 explains how economists measure these factors. Chapter 12 analyzes vertical integration, which occurs whenever a firm operates at two or more different "levels" of an industry.

Chapter 13 appraises criteria for judging industrial performance. Chapters 14 and 15 summarize empirical findings about how industrial concentration is related to profits, pricing, and innovation. Chapter 16 discusses empirical findings about advertising.

Chapters 17 and 18 study the rationale for and effects of detailed government regulation of outputs, prices, and profits. Chapters 19 and 20 explain and evaluate U.S. antitrust policies.

QUESTIONS

1. What *is* industrial organization?
2. How does industrial organization differ from pure price theory?
3. Why is industrial organization more controversial than, say, zoology?
4. Over the years many have complained that theory is unrealistic and irrelevant, cold and unfeeling. What is good about theory? What are its limitations?
5. What kind of "realism" should a good theory have?
6. What is the structure-conduct-performance paradigm? At this point, how would you decide whether it is true?

NOTES

1. Chamberlin wrote one of the most famous economics books of this century. Edward Hastings Chamberlin, *The Theory of Monopolistic Competition* (Cambridge, Mass.: Harvard University Press, 1933).
2. Edward S. Mason, "The Harvard Department of Economics from the Beginning to World War II," *Quarterly Journal of Economics*, 97 (August 1982), pp. 383–433, at pp. 423–24.
3. A textbook influential in the 1960s used this paradigm as its central principle and major theme: ". . . eight chapters (4 through 11) constitute the core of the book, analyzing, on an

empirical level, market structure, conduct, performance, and their interrelations in American industries.'' Joe S. Bain, *Industrial Organization* (New York: John Wiley & Sons, Inc., 1959), p. ix.

4. An early industry study that became famous began as a 1931 Harvard Ph.D. thesis: Donald H. Wallace, *Market Control in the Aluminum Industry* (Cambridge, Mass.: Harvard University Press, 1937). Other well-known examples are Jesse W. Markham, *Competition in the Rayon Industry* (Cambridge, Mass.: Harvard University Press, 1952); and M. A. Adelman, *A&P: A Study in Price-Cost Behavior and Public Policy* (Cambridge, Mass.: Harvard University Press, 1959).

5. An unpublished survey is David Colander and Arjo Klamer, ''The Making of An Economist,'' March 1986.

6. Alfred Marshall (1842–1924), author of *The Principles of Economics* (1890) and founder of the Neo-Classical and Cambridge schools of economics: ''. . . I read Mill's *Political Economy* and got much excited about it. . . . Then, in my vacations I visited the poorest quarters of several cities. . . . looking at the faces of the poorest people. Next, I resolved to make as thorough study as I could of Political Economy.'' John Maynard Keynes, ''Alfred Marshall,'' in *Essays in Biography* (New York: W. W. Norton & Co., Inc., 1951), pp. 125–217, at p. 137. Indeed, although his biographical essay on the great man is reverential, Keynes nevertheless remarks that ''Marshall was too anxious to do good,'' *Essays in Biography*, p. 175.

7. Compare Tom Parker, *Rules of Thumb* (New York: Houghton Mifflin Company, 1984).

8. Milton Friedman, ''The Methodology of Positive Economics,'' in *Essays in Positive Economics* (Chicago: University of Chicago Press, 1953), pp. 3–43; reprinted in William Breit and Harold M. Hochman, *Readings in Microeconomics* (New York: Holt, Rinehart & Winston, Inc., 1971), pp. 23–47, at p. 30.

9. Joan Robinson, *The Economics of Imperfect Competition* (London: Macmillan and Co., Limited, 1946), pp. 1–2. The first edition of this classic was published in 1933. It was reprinted in 1934, 1936, 1938, 1942, 1946, and perhaps subsequently as well. References in this present volume are to the 1946 edition.

10. See Edward Leamer, ''Let's Take the Con Out of Econometrics,'' *American Economic Review*, 73 (March 1983), pp. 31–43; and the introduction to Chapter 14 of this book.

2 COMPETITION AND EFFICIENCY

INTRODUCTION

This chapter discusses competition in nature, games, and war, and then briefly reviews functions that every economic system, from the family on up, performs. How well an economic system does these things determines how well it performs. In the theory of atomistic competition, sellers and buyers are so numerous and small that none can affect price and each takes price as given. A further section of the chapter shows how an atomistically competitive economic system would, in theory, perform the basic economic functions. Building on the theoretical results of atomistic competition, the next section defines economic efficiency, a concept often used to judge industrial performance in the real world.

In principle, at least, the economic, political, and cultural qualities of economic systems can be discussed separately. The last section argues that differences in constitutions, laws, and other institutions matter. Among other things, the choice of institutions affects economic efficiency and performance.

COMPETITION IN NATURE, GAMES, AND WAR

Scarcity is a fact of life that inevitably engenders competition of one kind or another. There is competition between two animal species whenever an increase in the population of one reduces the maximum viable population of the other. If two species use the same food, water, nesting sites, and so on, they are competitive over ranges in which population presses upon these resources. It is as though each species tries to maximize its numbers; each organism, its own descendants. There is competition among different families of the same species and among different members of the same family.

Competition in nature relentlessly selects, substitutes, and eliminates. Natural niches are created, filled, and held by species and individuals that—looking backwards—were not only able to do it, for that is obvious, but were arguably also best suited to do it, at least given local circumstances that governed at the time. In this kind of competition, the "consumers" serve themselves.

Natural evolution goes so far back that it is impossible to know about all the competitors in detail and figure out how they interacted. Many interesting questions remain unanswered and may be unanswerable. Some decisive and apparently irreversible shocks produced relatively quick evolutionary steps. Did the timing, kind, and amount of actual evolutionary responses really maximize something? If so, what is it? Over what time does maximization take place?

Humans seemingly come to this world aware of self and prepared to exercise their will. Confronted by scarcity, as we always are, we compete. When scarcity is acute, or a prize is great, we compete with everything we have, which on average is considerable. We compete with brains, production skills, and, as occasion suggests, force. Human beings are tool-users and their tools have included weapons from earliest times. Aggression and predation are ingredients of evolution. Among animals and unarmed people, even a single person with primitive arms is a commanding presence. Teams of heavily armed people are more like a plague.

Humans have some power to influence how natural competition turns out, as medicine and agriculture show. Which characteristics survive and prosper in any natural or economic system depends upon the rewards and costs associated with those characteristics. In parts of the world, cattle look poor to western eyes. It is as though the characteristics of cattle had evolved to maximize the *number* of cows, given the constraints they face. These characteristics change when people want meat and milk and are permitted to produce and market them. And much of what we call civilization, law for example, attempts to limit how we compete with each other.

Whether we conclude that the kind of competition we have is good or bad depends upon the standards we use to judge it, the alternatives that we face, and the costs of getting to the alternatives from where we are. Any purposeful policy assumes some objective. Different policies can be judged on how well they achieve the objective. If, for example, we want to maximize the quantity of meat produced from a given habitat, one technique may clearly be best. If we seek maximum human *satisfaction* from that habitat, different prescriptions may be better, among other reasons because humans like some foods better than others and also want more things than food.[1] If the object is to maximize, say, the number of people, or zebras, still other plans may be better.

Competition occurs in sport and spectacle as well as in nature. Because rules and rewards affect performance, it makes sense to seek rules that get us the kinds of performance we want. Outcomes are affected by how participants are permitted to compete. When statistical records were poor, agents of the king could choose elite military archers by holding "competitions." Many were called; fewer were chosen. Some won; some lost. When it pays to win and competition is recurrent, more and better resources will flow into the field. Paying successful competitors well will raise archery standards generally, which may be worthwhile in itself.[2]

Depending upon the rules and the object of the game, "scores" will rise for several reasons. Training pays, and skills of current participants will improve. It will pay potentially skillful archers now in other trades to become archers; and equipment can be refined. The kind of performance you get also depends upon the criterion for winning. It may be average or best distance, best or average accuracy, or the number of arrows shot into a broader target area within a short period. Or it could be the greatest penetration into an armored target, a criterion that would encourage new designs of arrows and bows, or other weapons altogether.

On the other hand, if entertainment values are dominant, and if observers prefer closer contests rather than higher scores, some form of handicapping may make sense. A simple technique is to make superior competitors stand farther from the targets, or carry heavier burdens. The first is done in modern trapshooting; the second, in horse racing. In the long run, handicapping may alter overall performance levels and the ranks of individual performers.

Most rules eventually come under pressure and, in the long run, at least, may change. Aesthetic values, morals, and law can affect demands for different kinds of events and for similar events presented under different rules. In undertakings that are primarily commercial, enterprisers and players have an incentive to respond to the market and will encourage rule makers to help them do it. If participants run a sport for their own enjoyment, they can try for rules that maximize it.

Sports involve more than one kind of competition. Take racing, for example. Since there are fewer winners than participants in each event, one's gain is someone else's loss. This is competition among those already in the "field." In addition, there is competition to get into the field.[3] And, when resources used in one activity cannot at the same time be used in another, different activities compete for them.

Rules can encourage or prohibit equipment and appurtenances that alter performance qualitatively or measurably. Examples are younger and faster bulls for bullfighting; livelier balls for golf and baseball; and soft cushions, instead of sand, for vaulters and jumpers to land on. These are examples of competitive substitution in production. Ingenious and unexpected competition sometimes occurs even when the rules sound rigid.

Finally, the same and different kinds of contests compete for consumers' limited income and time. This is competitive substitution in consumption.

Consider carefully each of the games just discussed. Rule changes may increase both spectator satisfaction and measurable technical accomplishment; increase one and reduce the other; or reduce both. The sense of a game, and of the rules of the game, must be judged by the object and results of the game.

This discussion leads to three main points. First, within limits, rules of the game matter and can be changed. Second, there is competition beyond that among direct rivals that are trying to do the same things in the same way. Doing different things, and doing the same things differently, can also compete. Third, there is no way to decide in the abstract which rules and types of competition are best. That depends upon the goals, and upon the costs and effectiveness of alternatives.

Though to this point the discussion may not seem to be about economics, it can help us appraise economic models and economic performance. We turn now to textbook theories about competition in markets for ordinary goods and services.

WHAT DO ECONOMIC SYSTEMS DO?

No matter how much their institutional frameworks differ, all economies share certain general features. First, whether through the impersonal operation of free markets or through detailed government planning, all economies perform the same basic classes of functions. They must reconcile what consumers want with what it is possible to produce. They allocate resources to produce the goods. They divide (distribute) the resulting output among consumers.

Second, competition of one kind or another is at work in all economic systems, as it is in all life. Third, modern economies use prices and rewards. Fourth, there is always someone to claim powers over resources, including human resources. Property rights are powers to exclude others from using resources, and are exerted even in communist states—whatever their written constitutions may claim.[4] Important questions, therefore, are who can exclude whom from using each resource; what kinds of competition are at work; and who determines prices and other terms.

Different economic systems, operating within different institutional arrangements, perform these functions differently. As economists see it, the central economic problem in all such systems is to maximize benefits, net of costs. Most nontotalitarian economists believe that benefits are to be measured in terms of individuals' preferences. Governments as such have no preferences; people do. In private-property market systems, individuals have rights to themselves and to other things they own. As Robert Nozick points out, goods and services do not spill into our hands from a heavenly cornucopia: they arrive in this world attached to individuals. That is, *people* produce the goods.[5] Reasonable and just though this may sound, rulers of much of the world consider such notions heretical and subversive.[6]

THE MODEL OF ATOMISTIC COMPETITION

Introduction

Economists use several theoretical models to show how resources would be allocated and priced under different sets of assumptions. These models have been used for scientific (positive) analysis, as in explaining or predicting how real markets respond to changes in demand and costs. They have also been used normatively, as in judging whether specific firms and industries or the economy as a whole perform as well as they "should"; or deciding whether we "should" pass or rescind certain government regulations.

Using economic theory to understand how things work ought also to help improve policy and law. For example, will a specific law, contract, or business practice raise price or lower it? Will it raise price but, by improving quality, increase consumer satisfaction? Could the price and output patterns observed in a certain industry have been produced under competition? What *kind* of competition? Or could the data have been produced by a group of competitors who fix prices by agreement, that is, by what is commonly called a *cartel?*[7] Which hypothesis fits the facts better?

Positive and normative theory have been commingled in economics from the start. Early economists used theory to demonstrate that private property and competition maximize the value of an economy's output; that certain kinds of governmental interferences reduce national output; that competition in markets for factors of production distributes income fairly, as well as efficiently; and so on.

This chapter presents the theory of atomistic competition. Later chapters discuss other models.

Atomistic Competition with Identical Firms

The standard model of atomistic competition is the most refined and complete that economists now have. Although it does not predict or explain a number of common business practices, over the ground it does cover, the atomistic model is less ambiguous than other theories.

The traditional atomistic model predicts the direction in which price will change when demand increases and decreases, and when costs rise and fall. In most monopoly and other price-searcher models, by contrast, a fall in demand might raise price, lower price, or leave price unchanged. In those models, even the direction of effects depends upon the size of demand and cost parameters, about which we know relatively little.

The most influential classical economists, including such giants as Adam Smith, John Stuart Mill, and David Ricardo, were vague about what they meant by competition.[8] Mathematical economists, starting with Cournot, made competition a much more precise idea. Chapter 4 discusses Cournot.[9] McNulty says the classical economists' conception was better than what came later. They thought of competition as a force—like gravity—rather than as a state—like a vacuum.[10]

It may be even better to think of competition as a *process* that determines the number and qualities of competitors. In the abstract, at least, competition tends to maximize values for given costs and to minimize the costs of accomplishing given results.[11]

The present-day standard model of atomistic competition commonly assumes that each of many *identical* firms sells a homogeneous product. None can significantly affect the prosperity of the others, and each assumes that the others are indifferent to what it does. Because in this model each assumes that changing its own output has no perceptible effect on market price, each seller is called a price-taker: it takes the market price as a datum. A price-searcher, by contrast, has some power to choose price and searches for one that produces the largest profit.

Each price-taker firm maximizes its profit, R_i.[12] Its total cost, $C(q_i)$, is a function of its own output, q_i. Its marginal cost, $C'(q_i)$, is the first derivative of its total cost: $\delta[C(q_i)]/\delta q_i = C'(q_i)$.

$$R_i = Pq_i - C(q_i),$$

and

$$\delta(R_i)/\delta q_i = P - C'(q_i) = 0.$$

To maximize its profits, each price-taker firm produces at a rate for which marginal cost and price are literally equal:

$$P = C'(q_i).$$

This is the familiar textbook rule for profit-maximization under competition: set price and marginal cost to equality. As Chapter 4 and 5 show, some models in which a relatively few price-searchers compete also approximate these results.

An individual consumer's demand for a good is derived from his tastes, money income, and the prices of other goods and services. To achieve maximum satisfaction, each consumer allocates his limited income so as to get equal marginal benefit (also called *satisfaction* or *utility*) per dollar spent on each of the goods he buys. That is, the contents of a consumer's market basket are just right when all goods in it provide equal marginal benefits per dollar spent.[13] Consumers adjust the kinds and quantities of goods they buy until that equality is established.

The consumer demand functions we typically use are schedules showing the dollar value of marginal benefit from consuming each of various quantities of a specified good, as Figure 2-1 illustrates, for a hypothetical good, X. A consumer's demand for X shows how much X he will buy at each of various prices, P_x. In atomistic competition, no consumer can influence P_x, the price he pays. A necessary condition for maximum net consumer benefit is that the marginal cost of consuming the good, which is its market price, is equal to marginal benefit from the good, which is its demand price. Unable to affect the prices of goods he buys, each consumer adjusts his purchases so that his demand for a good is brought to equality with its market price. In Figure 2–1, this occurs when he consumes Q_x. The dollar price of each good is then equal to (and therefore *measures*) marginal satisfaction from each good.

Analogously, producers must maximize wealth as producers if they are to maximize their satisfaction as consumers. To maximize wealth, they must minimize the cost of each output. The cost function of a firm is derived from the technology it uses and prices of the factors it buys. Assuming, as this model does, that no firm can affect the prices it pays for factors of production, each takes factor prices as given. For each level of expenditure, the firm chooses the combination of factors that maximizes output. The optimum quantity of each factor is that which brings the dollar value of that factor's marginal product (VMP) to equality with its price, as Figure 2–2 shows.

In "pure" atomistic competition, knowledge is limited and costly to some unspecified degree. In "perfect" atomistic competition, by contrast, it is often said that

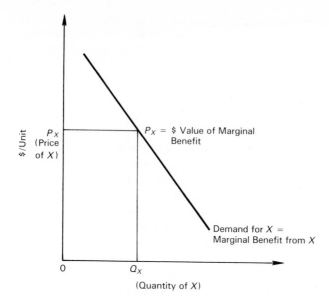

Figure 2-1 Consumer Demand Is a Dollar-Measure of Marginal Consumer Benefit

knowledge is perfect; but it is better to say merely that firms know all about *current* prices, costs, and so on.

With the notable exception of Cournot, economists do not specify how many and what sizes of firms are necessary to insure that none can affect the prices of inputs and

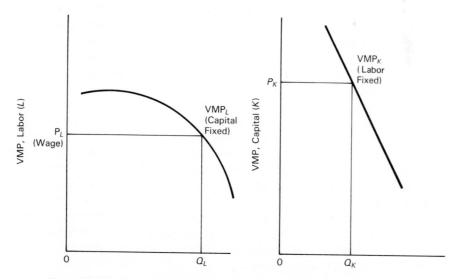

Figure 2-2 A Producer Brings Each Factor's Value of Marginal Product (VMP) To Equality With Its Price

outputs. Cournot says it would require an infinite number. As we will see later, some others believe that as few as two, or even one, will do that job.

To explain the number of firms in competitive, oligopoly, and monopoly pricing models, we need to consider several things: the level of costs; the size of firms at which production costs are lowest (the so-called optimum size); the size of demand; and the rules firms use to determine their outputs. Chapter 7 discusses these factors in greater detail. In textbook atomistic competition, cost functions of all present and (marginally) prospective firms are relevant. Optimal firm size and the level of average and marginal costs are crucial. If an industry has a constant long-run supply function, the level of minimum average cost determines long-run market price. At that price, Q is the industry production rate that satisfies total market demand. If all firms have identical U-shaped average cost functions, their average costs reach a minimum at the same output rate, q. The number of firms is, then, simply Q/q.

Rather than trying to specify the number of firms required to guarantee a certain kind of behavior, it is tempting simply to *assume* that behavior from the start. But pricing models ought to be able to explain the number and characteristics of firms rather than assuming them. For the most part, however, economists have not been very clear about what determines the number of firms.[14] This is one respect in which many models fail to provide reliable policy guides, as we will later see.

The number of consumers is usually left vague. For atomistic competition, consumers in each market are assumed to be numerous and small enough so that each takes all prices as given.

Let's see how the standard textbook theory of atomistic competition has been used to portray economic outcomes in an idealized world. The usual assumptions are as follows. All firms are alike. All produce the same product; each has one plant; costs and outputs are identical for all. The whole *industry* is small enough relative to markets in which it buys that it does not affect prices of factors it uses. As a result, cost *functions* of firms do not change as the industry expands or shrinks. In equilibrium, each firm employs the amount of each factor at which the value of its marginal product equals its price. (Remember Figure 2–2.)

In an atomistically competitive world, no seller can affect market price. It faces a perfectly elastic demand: it can sell all it wants at the market price; nothing at a higher price. The only choices are whether and how much to produce. The wealth-maximizing output is that for which marginal revenue—the change in total receipts per unit change in output—is equal to marginal cost—the change in total cost per unit change in output. For each firm, marginal revenue and market price are equal: market price is a constant for each seller.

Look more closely, now, at what marginal cost means. With perfect competition in the markets for labor and other factors of production, no firm can influence the price of any factor it buys, and no factor owner can influence the price at which he sells. Each firm faces a perfectly elastic supply of each factor it buys: it can buy all it wants at the market price, none at any lower price. Each factor owner faces a perfectly elastic demand for its factor: it can sell all it wants at the market price; none at a higher price.

To maximize wealth, a firm must produce as cheaply as possible. It therefore organizes production so that a dollar's worth of each factor of production it uses contributes equally to output. Since, to each firm, the market price of each factor is fixed, the firm minimizes costs by adjusting the quantities of factors it uses. Competition then forces the price of every factor to equality with its contribution to output; and both the price of each factor and its contribution to total output will be forced to equality in every use to which they are put. Factors used in any industry must be paid what they can earn elsewhere, and what they earn elsewhere is equal to what they contribute to production elsewhere.

In such a world, marginal costs measure the value of what must be given up to produce another unit of any particular good. For example, if the marginal cost of a typewriter were $500 and the marginal cost of a computer were $2,500, we could get five typewriters by doing without one computer. Relative marginal costs would, then, properly signal real costs, namely, the least that must be given up to obtain more output of any specific good.

In a world in which no consumer can affect market price, each maximizes satisfaction by allocating a fixed money income among divisible goods and services until he receives equal satisfaction per dollar from all things he buys. The consumer takes market prices—however determined—as his real costs. Prices are important signals, showing how much of any one good he must give up if he purchases one unit of any other.

Economic analysis works best by proceeding from one equilibrium situation to another. For some purposes, it is crucial to distinguish between short-run and long-run equilibria.[15] In the long run there is full-adjustment equilibrium, sometimes called *full competitive equilibrium*. Figure 2–3 shows a full long-run atomistic equilibrium for a firm and the industry of which it is a part. SRMC is the firm's short-run marginal cost, its supply function in the short run, when the quantity of one or more factors of production is

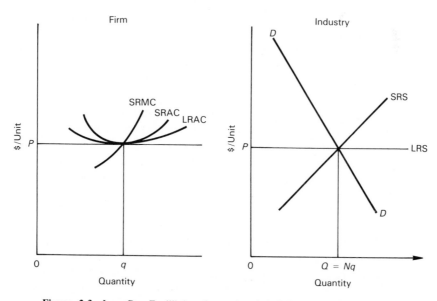

Figure 2-3 Long-Run Equilibrium for an Atomistic Industry with Identical Firms

fixed. SRAC is short-run average cost. SRS is the industry supply function in the short run, in which the number of firms is fixed. LRAC is the firm's average cost in the long run, when it can vary the quantity of all factors. LRS is the industry supply function in the long run, when the number of firms can change. Q, total industry output, is equal to Nq, where q is the output of one firm and N is the number of firms.

Note that product price equals marginal cost for each firm. That is a necessary condition for profit maximization. The relevant costs are opportunity costs, and include a "normal" competitive return to capital. For each firm, total revenues equal total costs.

What do economists think is so good about all this? First, each firm minimizes its own costs. A dollar spent on each of the inputs used increases output the same amount as a dollar spent on any other.

Second, costs for the *industry* are the lowest achievable for each output rate. For each firm, $P = MC$, and price is the same to each firm. Because things equal to the same thing are equal to each other, marginal cost is brought to equality amongst firms. Marginal cost is the change in total cost accompanying a one-unit change in output. Suppose that one firm has a marginal cost of $20 per unit and another's marginal cost is $28. Reducing output from the second firm by one unit and increasing the output of the first firm by one unit would leave output unchanged while lowering total cost by about $28 - $20 = $8. When the marginal costs are brought to equality, as price-taker competition would do, the total costs of production are minimized. Any change in the allocation of output amongst firms, by king, congress, or politburo, would raise total costs of producing that total output.

Third, if all *other* industries are also in competitive equilibrium, total net economic benefits are maximized. When all industries are competitive, supply and demand are brought to equality in all of them. Each industry supply function measures the value to consumers of other goods that might have been produced, and is therefore the marginal opportunity cost of supplying that good. And the demand function in each industry measures in dollar terms the marginal benefits from that good as consumers perceive them. No reallocation of resources amongst industries can increase net benefits. For the whole industry, $P = MC$, and *price* is the dollar value of the marginal benefits, as evaluated by consumers.

Figure 2-4 illustrates the notion of consumer surplus. The difference between income (1) and (2) is a money measure of how much more income the consumer would have to be paid to be as well off with none of good X rather than the quantity, X_1, he now buys. That is a money measure of consumer surplus. As Stigler shows, the price consumers pay is their *marginal* valuation, and—under carefully defined conditions—the *area* under the demand curve approximates the relevant total valuation.[16] Many economists believe that a reasonable goal is to maximize the *sum* of consumer surplus and producer surplus. Producers must be counted in: they are human and consumers, too.

Marginal cost is money cost in terms of alternative outputs forgone. A necessary condition for maximum net benefits is that marginal cost equal marginal benefit. That is true when price equals marginal cost. Thus, pure competition is said to be both production-efficient and utility-efficient.

It is production-efficient since, by implicit assumption, every output is produced as

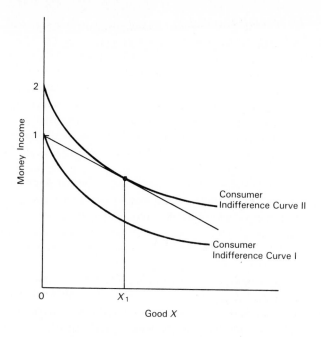

Figure 2-4 Consumer Surplus
from Good X

cheaply as atomistic competition can do it, which, *by assumption*, is cheaper than any other industrial structure could manage. It is utility-efficient since consumer benefits are maximized, as is the sum of consumer surplus and profits.

There are other ways of saying all of this. For a given distribution of income, and when social costs and benefits correspond to private costs and benefits,[17] this imaginary mechanism would maximize economic welfare, in the essentially equivalent senses of creating the largest sums of consumer and producer surplus everywhere, or of maximizing the value of output; or of making it impossible to improve any individual's position without worsening that of someone else.[18] Economic efficiency is analyzed in greater detail later in this chapter.

The sort of competition pictured in formal atomistic models is not the only kind that matters in the real world, and models are sometimes vague about what kinds of competition they do cover. In nature, empty biological niches are scarce and temporary: plants and creatures tend to fill them up. In atomistic economic models, consumers fill up niches in their consumption by adjusting amongst existing goods and by signalling or confirming signals that they have unsatisfied wants. Similarly, enterprisers try to find and fill up gaps left by deficiencies in the quantities or qualities of goods now produced.

Atomistic Competition with Differences Among Firms

There are models of atomistic competition for both constant-cost and increasing-cost conditions. Perhaps because it is convenient and simple, the constant-cost case dominates textbook and classroom discussions. It is easier to deal with large numbers of firms by assuming that they are all alike and that their cost functions do not change with the size of the industry of which they are a part. In general, however, it is dangerous to assume either that long-run industry supply functions are flat or that all firms are alike.

Two different cases of increasing costs need to be distinguished. In the first, all firms in the industry use the same technology and qualities of production factors. Firms are identical in every way, including costs. But the industry faces an upward-sloping supply function for some factor of production. The price of that factor rises as the demand for it rises, and falls when the demand for it falls. As a result, the cost functions of all firms in this industry, though identical, *change* as the industry expands or shrinks. This case is analyzed in some price theory texts.

A second case is more important for industrial organization economics. In this case, firms are *not* identical. This recognizes facts of life the truth of which every business journal and business executive takes for granted. Some factors of production, some firms, and some people are simply better than others at some things; some are better at one thing and worse at another. Such differences are commonplace in business and other trades, professions, and occupations.

Early in the history of economics significant differences were also observed in agriculture. In the nineteenth century, David Ricardo recognized that land rents (and farm costs) differ amongst farms because of differences in land fertility, location, climate, and so on. Farms with lower costs do better, and may also be much bigger. Besides differences in land itself, farmers and farm managements are not equally good at hiring and using workers, guessing about future prices for various crops, deciding what to plant, or reading weather signs. More generally, differences in the costs of firms generate an upward-sloping supply function for an industry. See Figure 2–5. Firms such as Firm 1, with AC lower than P, earn profits. Firms such as Firm 2 earn no profits and are marginal firms. In atomistic models that recognize differences in firm costs, market price equals

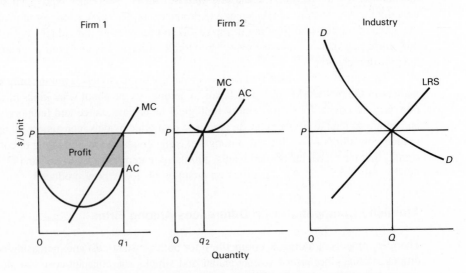

Figure 2-5 Competitive Equilibrium When Firms Have Different Costs

short-run and long-run marginal cost of *every* firm and equals the average cost of the *marginal* firm, in long-run equilibrium.

Although there is no doubt that such cost differences arise, it matters how big they are and how long they persist. Much depends upon what causes the difference; whether whatever causes it can be quickly and cheaply identified; and, then, upon how cheaply and quickly the source of superiority can be bought and effectively transferred. But profits—or rents—might persist indefinitely; or at least until the firm ''capitalizes'' them by increasing the accounting value of the assets responsible for the superiority. And that may never happen unless the *source* of the rents is actually sold.[19]

A closer look at the parable about farms and land quality is worthwhile. Suppose that differences in the qualities of a fixed factor—land—explain why one class of farms has much lower costs of production than another. If it were costless to discover this, the price of superior land would tend to be bid up until using such land affords no cost advantage at all. Or, alternatively, people who own such superior land might keep it, but, as economists say they ought to do, would capitalize the additional earnings attributable to superior land by writing up the land value, on their mental accounting records if not on the real ones. If they did, they would realize that they are earning only average profits on their superior land, the natural scarcity of which generated the rents.

In the real world, this process of equalizing costs is neither simple, sure, nor fast. In general, more than superior fixed factors of production like land are involved. Rents may also arise from superior teams of superior or ordinary people; different ways of doing things; product and production innovations; economies of size, including those from learning, that are realized by some firms but not all; and from differences in management effectiveness. It is costly to uncover these sources of superiority, evaluate them, and transfer rights to them by purchase and sale. Information and transactions costs affect the precision with which bundles of factors are brought together, the identity of those who retain the fruits of unusual efficiency, and whether the reported costs that economists use in empirical work come to capitalize the value of superior resources.[20]

Modern farms are not nearly as simple as economics textbooks make them seem and many manufacturing concerns are even more complex. Some firms produce better results than others. The best performance of different firms is not equally good. In a complex firm, it is even more likely that much of the returns attributable to special qualities and talents, and all or most of the greater return from superior meshing of teams and functions, will remain with the superior firm in the form of profits and not be bid away. Part or most of it will be reflected in a high going-concern value not easily attributable to anything in the firm that can be transferred, certainly nothing that is transferable piecemeal.[21]

This is not because of monopoly or market failure. It is not because of temporary disequilibrium. It is a characteristic of real-world equilibrium, given significant costs of information, evaluation, and change.

Chapters 4 to 7 discuss in greater detail how such differences influence industry structure, and other chapters also discuss their implications.[22]

Models in which all firms are alike and in which long-run equilibrium comes quickly mislead by ignoring phenomena that are important in real industries. For example, when firms *do* have different costs, their market shares and profit rates differ significantly. And assuming that we quickly reach or are always in long-run competitive equilibrium leads us to expect zero profits when there is competition and to conclude that there is monopoly whenever we find that profits are not zero. When it takes some time to establish a new long-run equilibrium, profits—and losses—can be very large indeed, even under atomistic conditions. Profits are not a reliable symptom of monopoly.

Atomistic Competition: A Tentative Summing Up

As Stigler pointed out, competition means different things to different people. Some think of competition as a specific kind of industrial structure, from which zero profits and equalities of marginal costs and price are likely to emerge. Clearly, though, consumers' welfare rests on economic performance, which is not the same thing as a particular industry structure, or marginal cost-price equalities, or zero-profit equilibria. Sensible real people want the largest benefits they can reasonably expect to get in this imperfect world.

ECONOMIC EFFICIENCY

The last section explained why atomistic competition is supposed to be efficient and why efficiency is supposed to be desirable. As originally used in English, however, *efficient* meant *effective* or *causative*,[23] which is more neutral and less laudatory. Economists have made the word into something else altogether. An outcome is production-efficient, we say, if the same output could not be produced more cheaply. Efficiency in consumption requires production efficiency, plus more. It depends not only on what something costs, but also upon what it is worth to consumers. The basic notion is that efficient solutions maximize the amount by which benefits exceed the cost of producing them. It is usual to say that efficient solutions maximize the sum of producer surplus and consumer surplus.

Although many technical writings about consumer surplus are very complicated, some intermediate textbooks have excellent discussions.[24] Stigler's definition is all we need to start: consumer surplus is "the amount over and above the price actually paid that a man would be willing to pay for a given amount of a commodity rather than go without it."[25]

Following this line, we estimate consumer surplus as the area underlying the demand function for a good, minus what consumers are spending on it. For present purposes, we use economic profit as a measure of producer surplus.[26]

These concepts are brought together in Figure 2–6 to illustrate the most popular ideas about economic efficiency. Concepts illustrated there are a foundation stone of industrial organization economics and remarkably influential in other fields as well. *DD* is the total market demand for a good, and MC = AC is the marginal (and average) cost of producing it. MR is marginal revenue, the change in total revenue accompanying a unit change in output. A monopoly maximizes profit by setting MR to equality with MC.

One crucial assumption in Figure 2–6 is that production cost is identical under single-firm monopoly and atomistic competition.[27]

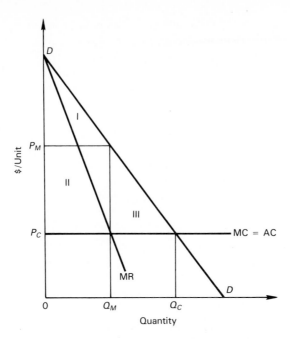

Figure 2-6   Economic Efficiency

The last section showed that price will be P_C and output will be Q_C if the market is atomistically competitive. Consumer surplus is the sum of areas labeled I, II, and III. Profit is zero; but the sum of consumer surplus and (zero) profit is the largest that those demand and cost conditions can generate.

By contrast, P_M and Q_M would result if the good were sold by a profit-maximizing single-firm monopoly producing at the same cost. Profits, area II, are greater than zero, and consumer surplus is smaller than with atomism. Monopoly profit is labeled II, which, since profits are zero in long-run atomistic equilibrium, also measures how much producer surplus increases under monopoly. Those who buy this product lose consumer surplus equal to the profits that the monopoly gains. Because owners of producing firms are also consumers, however, total consumer surplus is not reduced by profits that the monopoly earns. That amount is transferred from one group of consumers to another, and is not a net loss to consumers as a whole.

But matters do not end there. Consumer surplus is also reduced by the area labeled III—the dead-weight loss. The monopoly does not gain this part of the real income that consumers lose. According to the diagram, therefore, consumers lose more than the monopoly gains, shrinking the *sum* of consumer and producer surplus. The monopoly solution is said to be inefficient because the total surplus is smaller than competition could achieve. The competitive solution is efficient because, by the standards applied to the circumstances assumed, it yields the highest dollar value of satisfaction obtainable.

Confusingly enough, economists do not always use "efficient" in that sense. Go back to Figure 2–6. Suppose we were starting from scratch and could, without bias, handicap, or preferential cost, choose whether the industry pictured will be competitive or monopolistic. If they could make a fresh and even start—a scratch start—consumers would prefer that industry to be competitive rather than monopolistic, and a government representing their interests perfectly would, if necessary, help them get it. Given the assumptions and welfare standards already discussed, competitive organization of that industry would be efficient and monopoly organization would not. This is an example of what will here be called scratch-start efficient, or scratch-start preferred.[28] In this book, the term *efficient* means scratch-start efficient, unless some other meaning is explicitly specified.

Although this is where the story about Figure 2–6 usually stops, the diagram suggests some troubling questions. First, by assumption, an atomistic industry could produce as cheaply as a monopoly. How, then, could a monopoly arise; or endure if it did? If that kind of monopoly were created by private agreements or mergers and not sustained by government, it could last only as long as it would take new firms to enter the industry, which might not be very long.

But, second, what if such a monopoly *were* established by government franchise and preserved by law? Compared with the competitive solution, this would cost consumers more than the monopoly gains. If they cannot prevent government from doing that to them, why don't consumers reduce the monopoly's sting by making private contracts? For example, suppose that consumers agree to pay the monopoly the same yearly profit as area II, plus, say, $1. That would leave the monopoly a little better off. In return, the monopoly would contract to produce the competitive output, Q_C, and to sell it at the competitive price, P_C. Consumers would be worse off than they would have been under atomism; but they would be better off than Figure 2–6 leaves them.

A popular explanation of how monopoly dead-weight losses occur and persist is that it costs too much for consumers to inform themselves, organize, and put things right. If that is correct, any such government-supported monopoly already in place would continue to do what it's doing in Figure 2–6. The monopoly, though scratch-start inefficient, could persist.

But why would government create or sustain such monopolies? That is part of the larger problem discussed in the next section.

THE CHOICE OF CONSTITUTIONS, RULES, AND LAWS

In the Western democracies, we tend to believe that individuals matter and that we can choose the kinds of rules we have, altering history as we improve our lives. Not everyone thinks we are free to change institutions in order to improve economic welfare. On the contrary, in believing that economics is prime mover, some think that institutional changes *follow* economic changes, rather than the other way around. In this vision, economic processes have a life of their own. Like rivers in full flood, economic forces erode away and push aside whatever institutions stand in their way, creating new institutional topography by redeposition and accumulation. This vision locks economics, history, and institutions together ineluctably, making everything inevitable. Marxians tend to view the world this way.

The purest, simplest forms of each of these very different theories have begot near-religious enthusiasms, even animating national ideologies and international conflicts. For analytic purposes, though, it is better to avoid pure dogma if we can. We adopt here the weaker working hypothesis that institutions and economic processes affect one another, influencing economic outcomes in the process. One of the objects of this book is to analyze some ways in which they do so.

Although some cool heads decry all subjective value appraisals and advise economists to avoid such questions like the plague, most of us have continued to plunge in. It is doubtful that all institutions are equally benign. Some people try to distinguish agreements arrived at by individuals from those broader and more formal institutions that seem to come from the "outside," possibly overriding significant resistance in the process. Some present-day libertarians argue that all voluntary transactions and agreements are sacrosanct, and that "involuntary" restraints are evil. In part, this argument rests on sentiments and moral values that economics has no competency to judge. But this position rests on claims about how the world actually works as well as on value judgments about how it ought to work. One view of the facts is that although some voluntary transactions are not economically beneficial, it is not feasible to attack the few that are hurtful without discouraging or killing the preponderance that are good.

Although we may doubt whether all voluntary arrangements are economically beneficial, there is no doubt that it is costly to determine which ones help and which ones hurt. To demonstrate definitively that a specific institutional arrangement is beneficial, we need to show what it actually does as compared with what alternative arrangements could do. To do that, we need—among other things—standards for judging and summing up several effects, not all of which go in the same direction.

To avoid the costs of such difficult evaluations, some use economic logic rather than empirical estimates to claim that voluntary arrangements are beneficial in and of themselves. Because voluntary arrangements are voluntary, the story goes, they must be beneficial. Otherwise, they would not be agreed to.

This ignores that credentials of some voluntary arrangements are clearly suspect because they damage third parties who are not willing participants and whose interests were not well-represented in the negotiations. Collaborative price fixing by competitors is an example. As Chapter 6 shows in detail, such price-fixing cartels can hurt consumers. But it is undeniable that an anticartel policy would cost something, and we might even conclude that effective laws against these and other kinds of monopolies would cost more than they would gain us. It is quite another thing to claim that all voluntary arrangements are necessarily good, and that restrictions on voluntary arrangements are necessarily bad.

Law is a major source of restrictions on voluntary arrangements made by individuals and firms. Law is part pedagogy and part coercion. Anarchist extremists argue that a significant coercive component is enough to make law bad, in and of itself, though some accept small doses as a practical necessity. That argument is not completely convincing. If we judge government and law by the same standards we apply to voluntary arrangements among individuals, we will usually turn up benefits as well as costs. Prejudging which side is heavier is not good science.

Although property rights, moral and legal commandments, contracts, and agreements are meant to restrain and exclude, some restraints liberate.[29] By substituting humane restraints for a brutish state of nature, some civilizations increased material benefits at the same time that they increased personal security and freedom.

It would be a mistake, therefore, to denounce a specific institution merely because it restrains, for that is exactly what institutions are meant and bound to do.

Unless we define as good whatever exists, however, it is surely possible that some restraints are detrimental. Some restraints accomplish some good but go too far; others follow mistaken objectives or incorrect factual assumptions. Still others may even have had evil objectives and results. It seems fair, therefore, to ask what effects specific restraints have. Chapters that follow outline ways to attack that very difficult question.

What Is the State?

Economic theories, including those about competition, implicitly assume something about rules and law, property, contracts, and so on. By implication, they also assume something about force. For an allocation of income and rights is not stable if it gives people less than they can seize and hold by force, or by threatening force. Much of what even benevolent governments do simply recognizes that force needs to be balanced by force. It is a commonplace that states claim a monopoly of the legal use of violence. States use force not only to establish and maintain themselves, but also to encourage some kinds of behavior and discourage others.

In economic markets, we exchange and contract piecemeal, dealing with goods whose quantities are variable and divisible. We can completely ''secede'' from Safeway, Eastman Kodak, and Campbell Soup by buying nothing from them; we can withdraw partially by buying less. Seceding from a state is not so easy. The state coerces us to remain members and sends us bills for what it claims we ordered. We can flee its territories, leaving our goods behind; or we can stay on as outlaws. Both are practically all-or-none decisions. We can not secede from a state piecemeal.

Historically, various theories about the nature and origins of the state evolved.[30] We will consider four theories here. All of them match the claims of one or more governments now in existence. A number of governments have justified themselves with two or more of these theories simultaneously.

According to the divine right theory, the state acts for God, which is a stable situation so long as enough citizens believe in the same God and accept the state's interpretation of God's will. Iran under Ayatollah Khomeini comes to mind. Marx, Lenin, and Mao have also been raised as gods by governments claiming to speak for them. And, with or without explicit gods, totalitarian theories are in effect closed theological systems that are used to reconcile or bury all facts and counterarguments. In any case, those who put such theories into practice can fall back on physical force in a pinch. That brings us to the next theory of the state.

The brute force theory says government comes from the power to seize and retain control, or—as Mao put it—comes out of the barrel of a gun. The theory has been used by a startling variety of political thinkers and practitioners: by anarchists to oppose government per se, and by both communists and absolute monarchists to explain and retain governments they like. *Ultima Ratio Regum*, the final argument of kings, was the explanation that Louis XIV of France cast into his cannons. "How many divisions does the Pope have?" and "Does the British Navy have wheels?" exemplify the rhetoric one comes to expect from such states. Force also has a role to play in other sorts of government, even the most benign democracies. Those who have and use brute force often seek other explanations for government, including the next one.

The organic state, like a person, is supposed to have tastes and interests and objectives, to which those of mortal individuals are inferior and subordinate. Believers in this theory of government sometimes cite specific virtues of subservient obedience. Like bees or baboons, for example, humans have survived partly because they will subordinate narrowest self-interest to broader interests of family, tribe, and country. The effect of such subordination can be seen in war and, with few exceptions, only those groups that are competent in war survive. It is true, however, that famous real examples of organic states have not relied solely upon persuasion through parable, preachment, and exhortation. Such states have commonly forced their subjects to obey state commands.

The voluntary compact theory appeals to many who admire Western democracy. According to this theory, rational individuals voluntarily subordinate themselves to a constitutional contract. Among other reasons, they do so to discourage certain kinds of competition, including foreign invasions and domestic anarchy, force, and violence.

Once entered into, however, the voluntary compact is not force-free. For a capacity to use force is necessary to limit force. Take, first, the capacity to repel invasions and win wars. Even if all citizens benefit from defense, government typically finances and provides it. It is difficult to get people to pay for defense voluntarily, because it is difficult to keep those who do not pay from enjoying the defenses provided by those who do. As a result, so few would pay voluntarily that little or no defense could be bought. This is the so-called public goods problem that is used to justify much of what governments do.

So long as government formed by voluntary contractual agreement provides individuals larger total benefits than the total costs it imposes on them, they remain loyal subjects. Following this theory of rational individual choice, it has been argued that ideal competition in the economic sphere is like ideal democracy in the political sphere. In each case, some kind of acquisitive competition is the disciplinary force that keeps everything in line.[31]

A Basic Economic Rationale for Law

An individual can improve his economic status in any of several ways. First, he can simply take from someone else. This is roughly what happens if someone steals your car. It looks like a simple redistribution of wealth. Economic output has not increased. Indeed, if theft is common, the total economic pie will actually shrink. Too many resources will be devoted to taking whatever has already been produced; too few to producing.

Second, it is possible for an individual to benefit while taking *more* from you than he gains. This is roughly what happens if someone steals your car and, without joy, maims you in the process. The total pie has clearly shrunk. Finally, an individual can benefit economically while receiving only a part of the larger gains produced when he engages in voluntary transactions with you. Voluntary transactions between individuals make both of them better off. That is, he and you can both gain by participating in voluntary transactions and arrangements that increase the total size of the pie.

These are very important matters, since in a brutish state of nature—without law—there are incentives to take rather than to produce. Voluntary trade, on the other hand, is productive. Such questions lead directly to examining what anarchy appears to offer and analyzing the appropriate role and size of the state.[32]

One of the great accomplishments of history has been the rise of institutions that encourage producing, rather than taking. Various institutions, including effective private property, facilitate trade. These institutions protect against political tyrannies, large and small, at the same time that they increase the size of the pie.

Governments are responsible for the grossest horrors in history, and our enlightened twentieth century has had its share.[33] So far we have had various regional and two world wars; large-scale slave-labor camps; millions murdered by the state in Russia, Germany, China, and Cambodia; and large numbers starved as a result of national policies, in Russia and Ethiopia, among other places. Nevertheless, government has not disappeared from those places or from the earth in general, partly because government produces benefits as well horrors.

At all events, anarchists, who claim we would be better off with no government at all, are rare even where they are tolerated. Also scarce are those claiming that unregulated private markets for goods and services *always* produce the best conceivable results for consumers. The majority view in the West probably is that most markets usually work tolerably well; but that some kinds of government regulations help.[34]

The Choice of Institutions

Economic activities take place within a framework of institutions. What kind they are presumably matters. As Nobel Laureate George Stigler put it, ''The basic role of the scientist in public policy . . . is that of establishing the costs and benefits of alternative institutional arrangements.''[35] More than some other subjects, industrial organization ought to be concerned with the origins, rationale, and operation of institutions, none of which is a trivial concern.

Rather than calling for anarchy, proponents of the eighteenth century philosophy labeled *laissez faire* advocated a working principle for limiting the size and functions of governments: anyone seeking to extend state authority and regulation should demonstrate that it would increase benefits more than costs. In short, they said—for theoretic and historic reasons—the rebuttable presumption should be that private property and voluntary exchange generally produce good results when not interfered with.[36] Philosophies such as Adam Smith's relied on several elements from theory and history, as well as upon some bald assertions. First, private property, competition, and free voluntary trade tend to maximize national income and well-being. Second, states tend to grow at the expense of individual liberties. Third, even when they are not dangerously tyrannical, states tend to be inefficient at much of what they undertake to do.

But Adam Smith was no anarchist. He claimed that the state must be active in several ways. It must protect its citizens from the violence of both internal and foreign aggressors. It must establish and maintain a system of law and justice that would, among other things, enforce beneficial contracts and punish crime. And so on. And, in performing these and other functions, the state would have to provide certain public works, public goods, and institutions.

The question of government is partly a matter of what functions government is permitted to perform, and partly a matter of how they will be permitted to perform them. The variety of institutions we see among countries, and within a country over time, is consistent with the hope that humans have some power to choose their institutions, altering both the size and scope of government as a result. Observation suggests that the choice matters.

Economic and political outcomes are very different in Hong Kong, Taiwan, and the People's Republic of China, which nevertheless have much in common. They share, for example, a common gene pool and a long history of great accomplishments. It looks as though their vastly different institutions explain their vastly different performance. It is possible to reach similar conclusions by comparing East and West Germany, and North with South Korea. And, it is clear, economics and politics differ greatly on either side of the border between Texas and Mexico. Mexico has more oil and other natural resources, a much better natural climate, and a resourceful and hard-working population capable of making much out of little. But Mexico also has profoundly different cultural, legal, and political institutions.[37] Argentina, one of the world's ten richest countries in the 1920s, has been going downhill since.[38]

By consumer-benefit standards, it is doubtful that the rules of the game are equally efficient among the Chinas; between East and West Germany, and North and South Korea; and between Texas and Mexico. Even if there were no other evidence that consumers fare better some places than others, patterns of human migration strongly support the hypothesis.

Although humans spend much time trying to better themselves, it would not be rational for them to make changes that increase costs more than benefits. It is tempting to conclude therefore that existing institutions and laws must be more "efficient" than alternative arrangements simply because they have survived. That is, given the costs of obtaining information, forming political coalitions, and so on, it was evidently not worth changing the institutions we see. In fact, it has become moderately fashionable to say that *all* political institutions, including laws and constitutions, are efficient in that sense.

In trying to apply the everything-is-efficient argument to such things as the Bolshevik revolution and the rise and crimes of Hitler, one might argue that people mistakenly did not vote right or fight early enough, owing to poor information and false prophecy. And, the argument continues, what citizens knew about the theory and practice of government, and about communists and nazis, must have been optimal: otherwise it would have paid them to learn more about them. Once it was clear where mistakes had got them, it was too late. Costs of change were too high, including as they did costs of overcoming machine guns and tanks.

Or perhaps "rational" economic choice was the problem, rather than ignorance. Unless bolstered by a strong ideology or love of the community to which he belongs, each individual may decide that it is dangerous for him to oppose evil on his own, and, in any case, recognizes that his lone opposition will not be enough to stop it. As a result, few—perhaps none—stand up. Evil prevails.

In any case, it is not very comforting to say that whatever Russia and Germany got was efficient, simply because the costs of altering outcomes seems to have been larger than the perceived benefits of doing so.

That argument may be a better explanation of what happened than a certification that the result was usefully efficient. Economists, historians, and people in general are better at explaining past events than at predicting what's to come. But neither explanation nor prediction is as easy as it sounds.[39] In any event, explaining malaria is not equivalent to demonstrating that it is efficiently beneficial to people.

There are reasons not to call institutions and outcomes "efficient" unless they are scratch-start efficient. We tend to think that efficient means "good." Even if we call it efficient, some of what exists is clearly bad enough that we should stop to marvel at it and ponder the costs of reform. What has been accomplished within one set of institutions may be so bad that, unless we take it for granted, we may decide to change the rules; or, at least, decide never to accept them in our own time. Anyhow, what is efficient and good can change, and it may pay to re-evaluate from time to time what we see. A list of situations that are probably not scratch-start efficient hints at what is likely to be worth reassessing. Many economists believe that economic analysis can help in preparing the list.

If we divert our attention away from scratch-start inefficiencies merely by defining them away, we may succumb to terminal stoic passivity. We would disregard some lessons that history can teach. Not all past failures are unique. Some have common causes and characteristics that we may learn to recognize and avoid in the future.

By traditional economic standards, some rules are more efficient than others. We would presumably get the best ones if political markets for rules were competitive, costless, and frictionless; if adjustments could be made piecemeal; and if foresight were perfect. For, then, the most efficient rules would be chosen. Although no theory can be completely realistic, assuming that information is perfect and transactions are costless can cause lots of trouble. As Coase pointed out in a classic article, the nature and placement of rules do matter when transactions costs are significant. For, if the wrong rules are chosen to start, it may be too costly to replace them.[40] That is, given free choice at the beginning, the choice of rules matters.[41]

Differences and Relationships Between Political and Economic Markets

The survival of certain outcomes and institutions does not guarantee that they are scratch-start efficient, in either economic or political markets. A crucial question is, however, whether survival is more reliable evidence of efficiency in economic than in political markets. In other words, is inefficiency likely to be a more serious and long-lived problem in political markets?

Classical economists certainly thought so. Their theory was that inefficient arrangements and outcomes are more likely to be created and to persist in government and political markets than elsewhere.

What is the rationale for such a theory? First, certain kinds of inefficiencies are inherent in political markets. Because voters must delegate decision making to the people they elect to political office, several tendencies come into play. First, consumer preferences tend to get expressed in relatively few large clots, not in many small and continuous flows, and the adjustments that follow are discrete and large. Take-it-or-leave-it, and all-or-none are the stuff of politics and law.

Second, the mechanics of governmental institutions and processes are inherently biased towards certain kinds of inefficiencies. As well-established theories of choice demonstrate, legislative and committee votes produce inherently inefficient or inconsistent results.[42]

Third, competition may be a less precise and reliable force for reform in the markets for rules and laws than in economic markets generally. Constitutions, politicians, and laws are more complex and difficult to appraise than are most of the ordinary products that consumers buy. This opens the way for mistakes and fraud. Rules tend to develop a life and force of their own. This is partly because those who command the machinery for rule making can raise the transactions costs of those who later seek to change inefficient rules.[43] That problem is acute when revolutions, invasions, or mass imprisonments not only root out existing rules but also capture and may change the rule-making machinery itself.

A specific example, monopoly creation, illustrates the more general problem. As the efficiency analysis showed, both private and government monopoly have the theoretical power to hurt consumers. Does it make any practical difference whether government is itself the source of monopoly power?

From the beginning of recorded history, people have tried hard to create monopolies for themselves. To be worth that much effort, prospects for profitable monopoly have to look pretty good. This seems to suggest (but surely does not prove) that monopolies hurt consumers. For, according to Figure 2–6, monopoly hurts consumers even more than it profits monopolists, and prospective profits have been high enough to encourage monopolizing attempts. Even so, it might cost us more to prevent or destroy monopolies than we could help consumers by doing so.

An important issue, therefore, is whether consumer losses due to monopoly are great enough to justify the costs of doing something about them. That depends upon what kind of monopoly it is, which is related to how it was achieved. A highly profitable monopoly achieved through superior efficiency, through cost reduction or product innovation, for example, is very different than the monopoly portrayed in Figure 2–6. Chapters 7, 9, 13, and 17 to 20 discuss these extremely important issues at length.

This brings us to an important question that did not get answered at the end of the last section. Why and how do governments create and sustain clearly inefficient arrangements, including tariffs and monopolies? When they come to government asking favors as a bloc, producers ascertain and stress their common interests. Tariffs, price supports, and government franchises demonstrate that narrowly focused special interests can outbid consumers in political markets. Though the special interests to which political and legal favors are worth most tend to get them, this need not maximize the sum of consumer and producer surplus.

Suppose that a city government wants to award a monopoly franchise to sell food and drinks at sports events held in the municipal stadium. Not surprisingly, the results depend upon how the city chooses the franchisee and upon how it restricts operations in the stadium.

Figure 2–7 assumes that the franchisee will sell only one product in the stadium, and shows costs and demand facing one of several identical applicants. The franchisee will enjoy a limited local monopoly in the stadium, and will be permitted to charge whatever price it chooses. All applicants will face stadium demand DD, and costs AC = MC. As is common in such cases, the city awards an exclusive franchise to the firm making the highest bid in a sealed-bid auction. If there are two or more identical high bids, the franchise is awarded by drawing lots.

Assume that the firms seeking the franchise do not get together to rig their bids. A franchisee could maximize profits by charging the monopoly price P_M and selling output Q_M. Profits equal to the area R_M would result, and that is the absolute maximum amount any firm would bid to get the franchise, for, at that bid, the franchise would earn only a competitive rate of return. In some respects, the result seems anomalous. Competitive bidding to get the franchise generates the largest amount of money for the city authority, which is pleased of course. But the kind of competitive bidding used here eventuates in consumers paying the monopoly price in the stadium.

A law granting a monopoly franchise only to whoever guarantees lowest prices to consumers could produce drastically different results. Competition among those seeking the franchise could force down prices to consumers, approximately to average cost. It

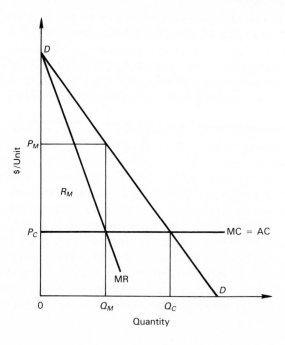

Figure 2-7 Awarding a Government Franchise

should not surprise us if politicians oppose such a scheme. Politicians and bureaucrats who benefit by selling or trading favors collect more from lump-sum bidding than by selecting those who offer lowest prices to consumers. No one will pay as much for a right to sell at cost as for a right to sell at a profitable monopoly price.

When a constitution permits government to grant and protect monopoly franchises, or award other favors, people in government will exercise their biases when they award them. If they award a franchise to whoever bids the highest lump-sum for it, for example, the low-cost producer will get it. But it will charge customers the monopoly price. Consumer benefits depend upon the dimensions on which competition is allowed.[44] The sort of competition shown in this example has been popular in political markets, and it tends to produce scratch-start inefficiency.

It is easier to show that favors can be got by outbidding consumers in political markets than to explain why constitutions permit it in the first place. One reason is that it is not easy to write a constitution that will prevent it, partly because it is people who write constitutions. If the constitution permits it, special interests will get favors that consumers cannot effectively oppose. Each consumer typically loses little from even the most outrageous political favor that the state gives to some special interest. Total consumer losses may be enormous; but costs of forming politically effective consumer coalitions are often even larger.

A constitutional prohibition of monopoly franchises, tariffs, and so on, would produce different results.[45]

If, on the other hand, government permits them to compete freely, sellers in ordinary markets for goods and services will compete for consumers' business on all relevant dimensions, including price. Consumers need no special bidding rules to get that result. In political markets, including those for laws and rules, governments trade on different dimensions. Bidding in political markets seems inherently biased.

When they stand before consumers as competitors, members of the same industry have adversary interests, and many economists believe that even a modest government program can keep them from hurting us seriously by ganging up.

Instead, governments have sometimes held consumers down while special interests bled them. It is usually too costly for consumers to use political markets to prevent it. Perhaps, as economists have been saying for centuries, government franchises and legal barriers to entry do explain how the most serious monopoly problems arise and persist. Can changes in or limits on government solve this problem? And, starting from where we are now, are deficiencies in market performance serious enough to call for government intervention? How much good does government regulation do for what it costs?

Ignorance, fraud, and mistakes surely exist. So does monopoly. But alternatives, including government regulation, have problems and costs, too, as Chapters 17 to 20 suggest.

Cartels and wholesale mergers of competitors can produce economic harms similar in kind, if not in duration and magnitude, to those caused by the franchises, import restrictions, and other favors that industry, farm, and labor groups buy in political markets. Classical economists believed that monopoly will not endure unless it has significant efficiency advantages or government protection. Even without efficiency advantages of the sorts that benefit consumers, however, government-franchised monopolies have endured, preserving scratch-start inefficiency. Indeed, for more than two hundred years there have been economists claiming that government franchises and other legal barriers are by far the most important source of durable monopoly. It may be, as classical economists claimed, that the most significant and efficient antimonopoly policy would simply be to prevent governments from granting such favors and creating such barriers.[46]

A presumption of efficiency may be less dangerous in private markets for goods and services than in political markets, though it can be carried too far there, too.[47] Scherer criticized what he characterized as the "extreme view . . . that whatever happens in the market-place must be for the best."[48]

In the spirit of positive science, there is work enough to do just analyzing, predicting, and describing causes and effects. For example, we could investigate whether and in what respects economic and other effects differ in private and government markets. If we find different results in the market for law and rules—politics—than in open markets for goods and services, we will have made an important start.

To solve all these difficult problems we could use a genius with a universal mind to do for earthly affairs at least as much as Laplace did with his celestial mechanics. Such a system may comprise interrelated economic, political, and military mechanisms, each with its own efficiency properties and conditions. At issue is how these mechanisms work and interact and how they affect consumers. How do consumers fare when the rules governing each mechanism change; or when resources are shifted from one mechanism to another? From the start, the classical economists were interested in questions like these.

By this point, you may have concluded that atomistic competition is grand and that monopoly, whether created privately or by government, sounds pretty bad. For many economists, indeed, atomistic competition is the ideal, which has caused a number of problems in itself. It may seem odd, then, that atomistic competition does not even *sound* very good to a some people. Chapter 3 discusses criticisms of and objections to the theory of atomistic competition. The objections to it are partly objections to the theory as pure theory and partly to using it as a standard for policy formulation, especially since other industrial structures often perform better.

Using an abstract model as the working standard for judging economic performance raises important questions, including whether and to what extent atomistic competition exists, and whether other forms of industrial organization and competition are better, in principle or in fact. Chapter 3 discusses those questions at length.

SUMMARY

Scarcity is with us always and inevitably engenders competition of one kind or another. Various kinds of competition occur in nature, games, war, politics, and economics.

Whether we conclude that the kind of competition we have is good or bad depends upon our objectives; the alternatives we have; and the costs of getting to each alternative from where we are now.

For a given distribution of income, atomistic competition would maximize economic welfare, in the essentially equivalent senses of creating the largest sums of consumer and producer surplus everywhere; maximizing the value of output; or of making it impossible to improve any individual's position without worsening that of someone else. This means that, for the narrow conditions assumed, atomistically competitive solutions are what this book calls scratch-start efficient. Starting from scratch, they are the best that consumers can get.

Economic competition means different things to different people. Some see it as a specific kind of industrial *structure*, from which, for example, zero profits, and equalities of marginal costs and price, are likely to emerge. If we are interested in what different kinds of competition *do* for us, however, we are interested in performance rather than in structure, marginal cost-price equalities, or zero-profit equilibria for their own sake.

When we come to compare the performance of atomistic competition with that of other structures, we do not want to assume that efficiency requires zero profits, prices equal to marginal costs, and other of the equilibrium conditions from the theory of atomistic competition. Even in atomistic competition, firms earn profits when they have lower costs. And all firms can earn profits in short-run equilibrium.

In studying economics, we must not lose sight of the role that institutions play. One of the great accomplishments of history was to evolve institutions that encourage producing, rather than taking. These institutions protect against political tyrannies, large and small, at the same time that they increase the size of the pie.

Given free choice at the beginning, the choice of rules matters. If inefficient laws and rules are chosen to start, it may be too costly to replace them.

An old theory argues that inefficiency is likely to be a more serious and long-lived problem in political markets than in markets for ordinary goods and services. If the constitution permits it, special interests can institutionalize political favors that consumers cannot effectively oppose. Each consumer typically loses little from even the most outrageous tariff, franchise, subsidy, or tax break. The sum of consumer losses from such things may be enormous; but so are the costs of forming politically effective consumer coalitions to prevent or remove them.

Even without efficiency advantages of the sorts that benefit consumers, government-franchised monopolies have endured, preserving scratch-start inefficiency.

On the other hand, from what we have discussed so far it is not obvious how a business monopoly can endure unless it has significant efficiency advantages or government protection.

QUESTIONS

1. Show that changing the equilibrium output allocation among firms in an atomistic industry raises costs. Hint: Demonstrate that costs can be reduced whenever the marginal costs of different firms—dollars/day/bushel—are *not* equal.

2. Explain the concept of consumer surplus.

3. Show how the aggregate supply function of a competitive industry is derived from the marginal cost functions of all the firms in the industry.

4. Given the cost functions of one firm, and the total market demand function, show how N, the number of firms, is determined in atomistic competition.

5. Show how atomistic competition maximizes the sum of consumer and producer surplus, while a monopoly operating under the same cost and demand conditions does not.

6. What does *scratch-start efficient* mean? How does it differ from survivability or viability?

7. Briefly state an economic rationale for law.

8. During and before the reign of Elizabeth I, Queen of England, sovereigns sold (or gave) monopoly grants to a chosen few. This apparently gained a lot of money (or loyalty) for the crown. In 1623, however, Parliament took away the sovereign's right to grant such monopolies, and arrogated the same right to itself!

   Show how such favors affect consumers.

   Why do you suppose the Crown, and later Parliament, raised money this way instead of through general taxation, or otherwise?

9. What case, if any, is there for assuming that government activity is likely to be less efficient than private?

NOTES

1. For an interesting recent study, see Eugene Silberberg, "Nutrition and the Demand for Tastes," *Journal of Political Economy*, 93 (October 1985), pp. 881–900.

2. It was decisive at the battle of Agincourt, France (1415) and its precursors, Crecy, France (1346) and Aljubarrota, Portugal (1385). For a splendid analysis of Agincourt, see John Keegan, *The Face of Battle* (New York: The Viking Press, 1979).

3. Harold Demsetz, "Why Regulate Utilities?" *Journal of Law & Economics*, 11 (April 1968), pp. 55–65.

4. Gary D. Libecap, "Property Rights in Economic History: Implications for Research," *Explorations in Economic History*, 23 (1986), pp. 227–52, at p. 227.

5. Robert Nozick, *Anarchy, State, and Utopia* (New York: Basic Books, Inc., Publishers, 1974).

6. Compare the arguments encountered in Koestler's *Darkness at Noon*. An "I-versus-we" debate led Rubashov, the aging Bolshevik hero, into a fatal "grammatical fiction." It led him to ask whether an individual equals a mass of 200 million people divided by 200 million—or whether the mass is 200 million individuals. Arthur Koestler, *Darkness at Noon* (New York: The Macmillan Company, 1941).

7. A cartel is a group of firms limiting competition by explicit agreement. Chapter 6 analyzes the phenomenon, and Chapter 19 discusses its legal implications.

8. Adam Smith (1723–1790), Scots university teacher and author of *The Wealth of Nations* (1776), is the most famous of all economists and in many ways the first modern economist. David Ricardo (1772–1823), English banker, speculator, and amateur (though publishing) economist, made a fortune in his youth. His reputation was next to Smith's. He is best known now for a theory explaining the nature and causes of land rents. John Stuart Mill (1806–1873) was a child prodigy whose father was a famous economist. A masterly expositor, Mill wrote books that sold widely. Antoine Augustin Cournot (1801–1877), a mathematician, teacher,

and academic administrator in France, may be the most original of all economists. His books did not sell at all.

9. George J. Stigler, "Perfect Competition Historically Contemplated," *Journal of Political Economy*, 65 (February 1957); reprinted in *Essays in the History of Economics* (Chicago: University of Chicago Press, 1965), pp. 234–67.

10. Paul J. McNulty, "Economic Theory and the Meaning of Competition," *Quarterly Journal of Economics*, 82 (November 1968), pp. 639–56.

11. Compare William W. Baumol, "Contestable Markets: An Uprising in the Theory of Industry Structure," *American Economic Review*, 72 (March 1982), pp. 1–15.

12. Wealth is the discounted stream of profits through time, and it is appropriate to talk of wealth maximizing in multiple-period models. For present purposes, we may take wealth maximizing and profit maximizing to be equivalent.

13. When a consumer buys N goods in number, and MB is marginal benefit,

$$\text{MB}_1/P_1 = \text{MB}_2/P_2 = \ldots = \text{MB}_N/P_N.$$

14. For a fuller discussion, see Chapter 7.

15. This is what Brozen means when he talks about disequilibrium. Yale Brozen, *Concentration, Mergers, and Public Policy* (New York: Macmillan, Inc., 1982), for example, at pp. 101, 229.

16. George J. Stigler, *The Theory of Price*, 3rd ed. (New York: Macmillan, Inc., 1966) pp. 78–81.

17. See Chapter 17.

18. The last condition is called the Pareto Optimality Condition, after Vilfredo Pareto, the economist who formulated it. One problem with Pareto optimality is that it does not distinguish between scratch-start efficient and scratch-start inefficient. In what follows, we will see Pareto optima that are *not* scratch-start efficient. For excellent discussions of this and related matters, see David D. Friedman, *Price Theory: An Intermediate Text* (Cincinnati, Ohio: South-Western Publishing Co., 1986), pp. 350–64.

19. Rents are total revenues minus total variable costs. Milton Friedman once argued that accountants and capital markets should follow economic theory and capitalize profits and rents. Milton Friedman, "Comment," in *Business Concentration and Price Policy*, ed. George J. Stigler (Princeton, N.J.: Princeton University Press, 1955), p. 235. But accountants do not write up capital values, though on occasion they write them down. William W. Alberts, "Do Oligopolists Earn 'Noncompetitive' Rates of Return?" *American Economic Review*, 74 (September 1984), pp. 624–32, at p. 630, note 29. Because, for good reasons, accountants do *not* alter asset values as economic theory would have them do, the profit rates that accountants report and economists analyze *may* indicate something about differences in the efficiency of real firms.

20. Chapter 11 and Chapters 14 to 16 discuss this and other measurement problems.

21. See John S. McGee, *In Defense of Industrial Concentration* (New York: Praeger Publishers, 1971), p. 42; Harold Demsetz, "Industry Structure, Market Rivalry, and Public Policy," *Journal of Law & Economics*, 16 (April 1973), pp. 1–9; and Armen A. Alchian and Harold Demsetz, "Production, Information Costs, and Economic Organization," *American Economic Review*, 62 (December 1972), pp. 777–96.

22. See Chapters 9, 13, and 14.

23. One dictionary includes the following in its definitions of *efficient*: "Making, causing to be; that makes (a thing) to be what it is; chiefly in connection with *cause*. . . . Productive of effects; effective; adequately operative. Of persons: Adequately skilled. . . . 'The cause which makes effects to be what they are'. . . Obs., but in 17th C. very common." *The Compact Edition of the Oxford English Dictionary* (New York: Oxford University Press, 1971).

24. There are excellent discussions in David D. Friedman, *Price Theory*, pp. 80–82, 93–95, 246–50, 365–77, and 518–20.

One extremely popular article about consumer surplus is Robert D. Willig, "Consumer Surplus without Apology," *American Economic Review*, 66 (September 1976), pp. 589–97. For evidence on its popularity, see David N. Laband, "Article Popularity," *Economic Inquiry*, 24 (January 1986), pp. 173–80.

25. Stigler, *The Theory of Price*, p. 78.

26. Economic profit is the amount by which total revenue exceeds total opportunity cost.

27. Chapters 9, 11, and 12 explain monopoly.

28. It is tempting to apply the term *first best* to such situations. Some other term seems preferable, since that one is by implication related to *second best*, a term used in a famous article about rather different problems, and therefore heavily freighted with different context and implications. R. G. Lipsey and Kelvin Lancaster, "The General Theory of Second Best," *Review of Economic Studies*, 24, no. 1 (1956), pp.11–32.

29. It may have been Schumpeter who observed that automobiles achieve higher operating speeds *because* they have brakes.

30. For example, see Jack Hirshleifer, *Price Theory and Applications* (Englewood Cliffs, N.J.: Prentice-Hall, Inc., 1976), pp. 465-88.

31. See Gary Becker, "Competition and Democracy," *Journal of Law & Economics*, 1 (October 1958), for example.

32. For example, see R. H. Coase, "The Choice of the Institutional Framework: A Comment," *Journal of Law & Economics*, 27 (October 1974), pp. 493–96; and Robert Nozick, *Anarchy, State, and Utopia* (New York: Basic Books, Inc., Publishers, 1974).

33. For statistical estimates of death tolls from twentieth century horrors, see R. J. Rummel, "War Isn't This Century's Biggest Killer," *The Wall Street Journal*, July 7, 1986, p. 10. For stories of some earlier horrors, see Barbara W. Tuchman, *A Distant Mirror: The Calamitous 14th Century* (New York: Ballantine Books, Inc., 1978). For a broader historical sampler, see Barbara Tuchman, *The March of Folly* (New York: Alfred A. Knopf, Inc., 1984).

34. For example, see John S. McGee, *In Defense of Industrial Concentration* (1971); and McGee, "Efficiency and Economies of Size," in *Industrial Concentration: The New Learning*, eds. H. J. Goldschmid, H. M. Mann, and J. F. Weston (Boston: Little, Brown & Company, 1974), pp. 55–97; and F. M. Scherer, *Industrial Market Structure and Economic Performance*, 2nd ed. (Chicago: Rand McNally College Publishing Company, 1980), p. 290.

35. George J. Stigler, *The Citizen and the State: Essays on Regulation* (Chicago: University of Chicago Press, 1975), p. 39.

36. "Laissez faire has never been more than a slogan in the defense of the proposition that every extension of state authority should be examined under a presumption of error. The main tradition of economic liberalism has always assumed a well-established system of law and order designed to harness self-interest to serve the wellfare of all. The institution of private property—at least since Hume—has always been defended on this ground. . . . It has always assumed that there were some economic results which cannot be attained at all or attained only in inappropriate amounts if left to the free market.

"The tradition has always been hostile to private monopolies, whether contrived by enterprise or by labor. . . . Special reference should also be made to the recognition that a suitable monetary framework cannot be provided by competition and that it constitutes one of the requisite legal institutions." Aaron Director, "The Parity of the Market Place," *The Journal of Law & Economics*, 7 (October 1964), pp. 1–10, at pp. 2, 3.

37. "One time they asked Milton Friedman, the Nobel laureate in Economics, what he thought of governments as enterprisers and he replied: 'If you give a government the Sahara desert to manage, within five years there will be a shortage of sand.' Though this comment caused laughter, it seems that the Mexican government has accomplished something similar. In 1938, they gave it a country full of oil to manage and in a few years there was a shortage of oil in Mexico." Luis Pazos, *Mitos y Realidades del Petroleo Mexicano* (Mexico City: Diana Publishing Co., 1979), p. 53. Translation by John S. McGee.

   The following observation has been attributed to Mancur Olson, Professor at the University of Maryland: "Success doesn't depend on natural resources and location as much as on the degree of stupidity of the policies and institutions of the country," *The Wall Street Journal*, 19 August 1986, p. 26.

38. Roger Cohen, "Struggling Back," *The Wall Street Journal*, 12 November 1986, pp. 1, 26. Also see Roger Cohen, "Brazil Vote Precedes Economic Overhaul," *The Wall Street Journal*, 13 November 1986, p. 32; and June Kronholz, "Power Struggle [with India's Bureaucracy]," *The Wall Street Journal*, 7 November 1986, pp. 1, 25.

39. Edward Leamer, "Let's Take the Con Out of Econometrics," *American Economic Review*, 73 (March 1983), pp. 31–43, at p. 31.

40. R. H. Coase, "The Problem of Social Cost," *Journal of Law & Economics*, 3 (October 1960), pp. 1–44.

41. Many seem to forget what Coase said about the spark-emitting locomotives. When transactions costs are significant, it *does* matter whether railroad companies are liable for damages.

42. Classic foundations for the modern theory of public choice include James M. Buchanan and Gordon Tullock, *The Calculus of Consent* (Ann Arbor: The University of Michigan Press, 1962); and Kenneth Arrow, *Social Choice and Individual Values*, 2nd ed. (New Haven, Conn.: Yale University Press, 1970).

   Voting paradoxes and inefficiencies are explained clearly in David Friedman, *Price Theory*, pp. 358–61. For an interesting real example, see Robert J. Mackay, "The FTC Budget Process: Zero-Base Budgeting by Committee," Working Papers in Political Science no. P-86-2 (Stanford, Calif.: Hoover Institution, January 1986, unpublished).

43. Charlotte A. L. Twight, *Government Manipulation of Constitutional Level Transactions Costs: An Economic Theory and Its Application to Off-Budget Expenditure through the Federal Financing Bank* (unpublished Ph.D. thesis, University of Washington, 1983).

44. Demsetz, "Why Regulate Utilities?"

45. In a delightful and powerful article on public policy, Milton Friedman suggested that we should "influence policy by changing institutional arrangements so as to make it in the self-interest of legislators to behave in a way that is in the public interest." Milton Friedman, "Economists and Economic Policy," *Economic Inquiry*, 24, no. 1 (January 1986), pp. 1–10, at p. 8.

46. Aaron Director, so one of his students said, distinguished between removing rent controls and imposing them in the first place. He was against imposing them; but declined to urge that

they be removed. See Edmund W. Kitch, ed., "The Fire of Truth: A Remembrance of Law and Economics at Chicago, 1932–1970," *Journal of Law & Economics*, 26 (April 1983), pp. 163–234, at p. 182.

47. For example, see McGee, *In Defense of Industrial Concentration* (1971), and his "Efficiency and Economies of Size," in *Industrial Concentration: The New Learning*, eds. Goldschmid, Mann, and Weston pp. 55–97.

48. F. M. Scherer, *Industrial Market Structure and Economic Performance*, 2nd ed. (Chicago: Rand McNally College Publishing Company, 1980), p. 290.

3 | CRITICISMS OF ATOMISTIC COMPETITION AS THEORY AND AS POLICY GOAL

INTRODUCTION

Chapter 2 stated the case that, theoretically and within the limits of its assumptions and system of values, perfect competition allocates resources ideally.[1] Popular and useful though the model of perfect competition is, it has suffered its share of criticism. One objection is that atomistic models are unrealistic and unachievable dreams. And some would add that the dreams would not satisfy us even if they could be realized. Another criticism is that such theories glorify selfishness, materialism, and other base human drives. Yet another objection claims that atomistic industry structures would be too costly even where they could be achieved.

Altogether, then, there are reasons to doubt that atomistic competition is a reliable standard by which either to judge real-world performance or to improve public policy. This chapter discusses these criticisms and what they imply for policy formulation.[2]

The next section of this chapter discusses objections that perfect competition is an irrelevant guide to policy because it is simply unachievable. The following section notes various reasons why we might want to alter perfectly competitive outcomes even if they could be achieved. Such alleged deficiencies include poverty, inequality, and distortions owing to external effects. Then there are objections that, even judged by static standards, atomistic competition is often more expensive than alternative industrial structures would be; and that, according to the theory of second best, reducing concentration in one industry can decrease total welfare because of bad indirect effects it has on other industries. Policies altering industrial structures should take these total effects into account. The last section inquires whether the dynamic superiorities that more concentrated industrial structures actually have are more important than the static advantages that atomistic competition is often claimed to have.

PERFECT COMPETITION IS UNACHIEVABLE

Although economics textbooks have made perfect competition into a demigod, some economists and many noneconomists find it hard to take the model that seriously. They say, for example, that no industry or economy really works that way or could be made to work that way. Information in the real world is neither perfect nor free. The model overlooks gross blemishes and distortions, including cartels and monopolies, which cannot be eliminated; and externalities, which are ubiquitous.[3]

We do not live in a perfectly competitive world. *Perfect* competition does not exist and we cannot create it anywhere. Indeed, departures from even pure competition are commonplace. Apart from some farmers, virtually no real-world firms face perfectly elastic demand curves. If, mistakenly, we decide that there is monopoly whenever prices exceed marginal costs, "There are virtually no industries in which there is no monopoly power, there are many industries in which monopoly power is inappreciable, and a rapidly decreasing number at each higher level of monopoly power."[4] Economists disagree about what causes these departures from atomistic competition; how great they are; how long they last; and where the largest of these discrepancies are to be found. For now, however, it is enough to note that literally millions of sellers charge prices that are not equal to marginal cost.

After studying 37 cost functions estimated empirically for a wide variety of industries, John Johnston concluded that pure competition is often quite impossible because of cost conditions, if nothing else. In his words, "Constant short-run marginal cost and an L-shaped long-run cost curve were incompatible with any determinate output under perfect competition and indeed with the very existence of the perfect competition of the textbooks."[5] Thus, it can be argued, perfect competition is an unrealistic goal, since there is little or none of it, and we cannot remake the whole world.

This is serious criticism from any standpoint. It is neither scientific nor fair to pit real alternatives against unachievable ideals. That the ideals will always win is both obvious and irrelevant to judging how good the real alternatives actually are.

THE INVISIBLE HAND NEEDS HELP

Even if we believed that much of the world works as the theory of competition suggests, we might deny that the results it produces are even attractive, let alone the best we can expect to get. Adam Smith praised self-interest and private property because, like an "invisible hand," they lead us to serve consumers although we seek only to serve ourselves.[6] Critics say, however, that the results of competition, even atomistic competition, are not so good as that. One criticism is that competition nourishes and may even compel the basest human values rather than inspiring and elevating us. Another is that self-interest and competition need substantial refinement or government regulation before they can accomplish what theory suggests they do unaided.

Objections to Competitive Values and Goals

In some versions of the theory of competition, consumer tastes are almost sacred, the ultimate source of power—an unmoved mover, like a god. And in almost all versions, consumers are pre-eminent and in control. Consistently with humanist tradition and philosophy, this gives consumers power as a group and dignity as individuals. Yet consumer sovereignty does not set very well with everyone, either in specific instances or as a general principle. It is common to disapprove of what's in someone else's market basket.

One objection to the principle of consumer sovereignty is that it would let individuals make serious mistakes that we should not be permitted to make. Cynical dictators as well as sincere consumer advocates tell people what is good for them and what they "need," rather than encouraging them to buy what they want.

Ethical and philosophical objections include that, although it may raise our money income,[7] competition makes us aggressively bad-mannered and materialistic and, in the end, leaves us alienated and unhappy. Usually economists evade questions such as these on the grounds that the study of economics does not include them. Critics might reply that this is so much the worse for economics, and is exactly what their criticism is about.

We should admit the obvious: economics cannot cover everything. Even if we decide to limit our claims about ideal outcomes to narrowly economic matters, we can nevertheless respond to these criticisms broadly. First, whereas competition exists in all economic systems, it seems plausible that manners, ethics, and values may indeed differ in different institutional systems and for different kinds and degrees of competition. It is also possible that intellectuals and the rich benefit more from and are therefore more interested in such things than are ordinary people, who have clearly benefitted historically from consumer-driven market competition. It also appears that these so-called higher classes have historically used, and are still using, the preservation of standards and values as one excuse for restraining both competition and the poor. Second, however, to appraise the manners and ethics of different economic systems, we need a factual record. But we have no data for perfect competition and the other Utopias, for they have never existed. As for mean-spirited competitive values, if that is what they are, a free and tolerant private-property market system to a remarkable degree allows us to keep our own values, if we are willing to pay for them. In any case, this highly productive system has generated so much output that many of us manage to survive reasonably comfortably without competing very hard.

Inequality and Poverty

Competition is sure to produce an unequal distribution of income. Income depends partly upon what we have when we come into the world, including intelligence, health, physical aptitudes, and family wealth, none of which is distributed equally. In competitive theory, we earn as much as we produce, and some can produce more than others. This is one reason for criticisms based on equity. Cynics say that such criticisms really spring from envy and jealousy.[8] Third, not only will some earn less than others, but some may be very poor, indeed. This leads to criticisms that competition causes poverty, or at least does not completely eliminate it. We are told, for example, that huge agricultural support programs are necessary to correct equity and poverty problems that competitive markets dump on farmers.[9] We do know, however, that equity is a slippery concept to put into practice and that curing poverty has also proved difficult.[10]

In any case, like it or not, we simply cannot eliminate competition. To blunt competition in the market place, we substitute competition in political arenas. One politically popular way to alter income distribution has been to regulate market processes and outcomes in detail, as we have tried to do with rent ceilings, legal wage minima, and price supports. Many economists now believe, however, that we can do better than that if we maximize output first, then reduce inequality and poverty via direct income transfers.

Externalities

The existence of spillover effects—externalities—is not only used to attack the theory of competition but also as a rationale for government regulation or ownership. Imagine, for example, a factory that emits smoke, grime, and unpleasant odors. These emissions impose costs on many other firms and households outside the factory's walls. Part of the total costs of what that factory does are therefore *external* to the production going on within its walls. The image of this factory is striking, even though its pollution may be no more than a nuisance, and the language used to describe and analyze it is strong stuff, too. When pollution kills people—as it did in 1984 at San Juan Ixhuantepec, Mexico and Bhopal, India, and in 1986 at Chernobyl in the USSR—image and language become stronger still.[11]

These actual examples are more serious degrees of the same economic problem that our hypothetical factory pictured. The costs that the polluter imposes upon the rest of us are often called *social costs*, which sounds noble and important.[12] Costs that the factory bears itself are often called *private costs*, which sounds parochial and petty by comparison. To humanists, the distinction is troubling and misleading. *All* relevant costs are private: individual human beings bear them.

Unless law compels him to do so, the story goes, a factory owner will not indemnify outsiders on whom he has imposed spillover costs. That sounds unfair. Nor will he include such costs in his profit-maximizing calculus, an omission that pains economists even more: it distorts resource allocation. When the prices of goods produced by polluters do not include all the costs incurred to make them, they sell too cheap and consumers buy too much of them. Too many resources will be used in industries that pollute and too few in industries that do not. As a result, we are told, competition cannot maximize consumer welfare when externalities are present, as they often are.

Following this logic, economists for many years taught that those responsible for spillover costs should be taxed or fined in the amount of the damage caused; or that spillovers should simply be prohibited outright. Apart from anything else, either approach calls for an expanded government role.

In 1960, however, Ronald H. Coase challenged all those claims in one of the most famous and influential articles ever written in economics.[13] Coase's paper is about both economics and institutions. Professor Pigou, and everybody else, had claimed that externalities distort resource allocation unless they are internalized by taxes, by damage payments, or by legal prohibitions.[14] Coase reanalyzed the whole problem from the ground up, starting with the example of a farmer and rancher whose properties share an unfenced property line. The rancher's cattle do not respect property lines and eat or damage the farmer's crops as they stray.

Table 3-1 shows the simple arithmetic that Coase used as his starting point. As the numbers show, crop damage is greater when the rancher's herd is larger. For such cases, Pigou's analysis was reasonably clear: if the rancher is not liable for damages, he will ignore the farmer's crop loss and run too many cattle. The farmer will raise too few crops. Resources are misallocated and consumers are ill-served. But are they?

Coase begins by noting that damages are only one part of the economic problem. The economic objective is not to minimize damage; it is to maximize total net benefits. Spillovers are, in general, part and parcel of useful and productive activities. It would be wasteful to reduce those activities to zero merely to avoid small damages. A sensible objective is to get the *right* amount of damages and gains—costs and benefits. If a rancher is liable for what his cattle do, he will include damage settlements as part of the costs of raising cattle, and not raise too many of them. But what if the rancher is *not* liable?

It is difficult to negotiate agreements unless it is clear who owns rights to what. But once the property rights are clearly specified, it may be possible to achieve the right results by contract, whatever the strict legal liability may be. It would usually cost something for the farmer and rancher to negotiate, sign, and enforce contracts. Coase calls the total of such costs "transactions costs." Suppose that transactions costs are literally zero.

The famous Coase Theorem says that, even if the rancher is not liable at law, negotiation under zero transactions costs will produce the efficient solution. For a payment forgone *is* a cost. If the rancher is not liable, the farmer would, nevertheless, be willing to pay to get him to run fewer cattle. The farmer would, for example, be willing to pay the value of crop damage avoided by reducing herd size: the value of four tons to reduce the herd from four steers to three; the value of three tons to reduce it from three steers to two;

TABLE 3–1   Coase's straying cattle

Size of Herd	Annual Crop Loss (tons)	Marginal Crop Loss (tons)
1	1	1
2	3	2
3	6	3
4	10	4

Source: Adapted from R. H. Coase, "The Problem of Social Cost," *Journal of Law & Economics*, 3 (October 1960), p. 3.

and so on. In deciding to run more rather than fewer cattle, a rational rancher would include in his total costs of raising cattle the loss of payments that the farmer would otherwise make.

As a result, the rancher *will* include crop damages in the costs of raising cattle, even if he is not liable at law. It thus appears that the right quantities of cattle and crops will be produced whether the rancher is liable or not, a result that nobody before Coase appears to have seen.

Coase did not stop there. In the real world, it is clear, transactions costs are not zero. What happens to resource allocation then? Look at the case in which transactions costs are so high that contracting is out of the question. Assume, first, that the rancher is not liable. Law does not compel him to include crop damage in his cattle-raising costs. Because it is no longer practical for rancher and farmer to contract, negotiations cannot produce a better solution, either.

The obvious alternative is to make the rancher liable. Unfortunately, that might not be better and could be worse. One trouble is that the rancher would pay for the part of the crop that his cattle ruined, and the farmer would sell the rest on the market. The farmer would then be paid for his whole crop, damaged or not, and have no incentive to reduce damage to it. If the rancher were not liable, the farmer might plant crops that are less attractive to or more resistant to cattle; reduce plantings in fields that cattle prefer to stray through, or that are otherwise more liable to damage; or fence some or all of the farm.

There are other possible ways to deal with the problem, including forbidding farming and ranching in the same areas; compelling ranchers (or farmers) to fence; or encouraging or compelling mergers of all adjoining farms and ranches. None of these solutions is trouble-free; all may cost more than they are worth.

Coase studied many English common law cases to see what judges had actually done with problems like these. His delightful history suggested to him that judges have tried to interpret nuisance and torts law so as to maximize net output.

What can we conclude from all this? First, if transactions costs were zero (or very low) it would not matter where liability is placed, so long as the parties know what the rule is. These findings can be applied more broadly to laws and regulations generally, as well as to liability principles.

Second, when transactions costs are prohibitive, however, some rules may produce larger net output than others. The economic objective is to find rules of the game that permit the largest output. In general, the solution we want produces the same result as would a merger of the interests and activities involved in the externality.

Spillovers take on different dimensions when the effects or sources of the effects are difficult to discover; are deliberately concealed; or are physically dangerous. For example, it takes a long time for the effects of some toxic substances to become obvious, and by that time it may be hard to find out where they came from. Transactions costs are so high in such cases that simple negotiations among the parties are not a practical remedy. Some sort of regulation or liability rule may be desirable. It is one thing if *nobody* realizes that a substance or activity will, with substantial delay, do great harm. The result is rather like a fault-free accident. It is quite another thing when people who cause the harm know it will occur and seek to cover it up. That is fraud at best. It sounds reasonable to punish extremely harmful activities severely when the chances of detecting a harm *and* successfully punishing whoever did it are low. Lethal or maiming spillovers, such as toxic wastes, are especially serious. To maximize net outputs, it seems reasonable to impose liability on those who know what is going on and can most cheaply do things right.

Third, prohibiting activities outright removes all (nonpolitical) possibilities to negotiate and contract. Fourth, Pigou's rules and principles are generally shaky and often simply wrong. In general, simple taxes on spillovers will not do the job. Solving airport noise problems by taxes, for example, seems to require taxing those who benefit from reduced noise as well as those who make noise.[15]

It is striking how many remember Coase's rule for zero transactions costs, but forget what he said about the problems that arise when those costs are large. For then it matters which rules and regulations apply. Under those circumstances, rules once applied are hard to modify or remove.

External effects are practical as well as theoretic concerns. When property rights are badly defined—as they were for game animals such as buffalo, for fish, and for crude oil—costly spillovers tend to produce unfortunate scratch-start inefficiencies. In fish and game, the typical result was overexploitation, at excessive cost, and sometimes extinction. Wastes in crude oil arose because firms drilled too many wells and produced from them too fast. Reservoir energies were ill-used and dissipated; costs of production were much too high; and too much oil was left in the ground.

But how do externalities affect industry structure, competition, and economic performance? The answer depends upon law and institutions, among other things. In cases such as fisheries and oil reservoirs, externalities tend to increase the size of firm or control unit that is needed to minimize cost—the so-called optimum size of firm. In the limit, if law permits, this might lead to a single firm (or operating unit) in each fishery and oil field. Government regulation or ownership are other possibilities.

Chapter 17 discusses commercial fishing and crude oil production as examples of these problems and analyzes government regulations historically used to solve them. Among other things, Chapter 17 suggests that regulation often creates externalities of its own.

COMPETITION MAY COST MORE

Competition May Be Ruinous

Early in the chapter J. Johnston's cost evidence was cited. According to Johnston, price-taker competition is simply impossible in many industries. Other theories claim that price-taker competition is, on the contrary, all too likely to occur, even with costs like that. And, if competition does break out, it would be ruinous and grossly inefficient. J. M. Clark may have been the first academician to develop this notion in detail; but, disinterred and refurbished, it has enjoyed recurrent waves of popularity since.[16]

Revised versions of this old theory rely on several assumptions, which proponents say match the facts of life. First, in many industries, efficient plants and firms are large relative to the markets they serve. That is, firms are like large lumps in a pitcher of butter-milk, as an English economist once put it, rather than fine grains of sand on a large beach. Adding or removing even one firm can therefore have significant price and output effects. Second, until a firm's output reaches limits set by plant capacity, its marginal cost is much lower than average cost. Both marginal and average cost climb abruptly at or around ca-pacity output.

There is supposed to be wreck and ruin whenever competition is strong enough to force identical firms such as these to sell at marginal cost. Equilibrium is a precarious balance on the razor's edge, if it occurs at all. For, if firms were identical and there were not just the right amount of capacity to clear the market and cover both marginal and average cost, the industry would not be in full long-run equilibrium. If the price were lower than that, firms would go broke; if higher, they would earn profits and attract more entry. If entry occurs, losses ensue and capacity is wastefully redundant.

Competition under these circumstances causes trouble unless it is slowed down and tamed by market frictions and costs, or by at least a little downward slope in the firms' demand functions.[17]

There are several versions of what might happen in such a world. One theoretic possibility is that there is no equilibrium at all, which may mean only that this theory does not tell us what will happen. Or perhaps there would be wide and wild fluctuations, with periods of great profits following periods of great loss. Productive capacity might never be even close to the amount needed to minimize costs over time, and consumers might be worse off as a result. But what arrangement would be better? Price-searcher competition of some kind, perhaps;[18] private monopoly by merger or agreement; or perhaps a government-regulated cartel.[19]

According to such visions, an imperfectly competitive world can be much better than a purely competitive one.

Any of several possible helps could save us from all this ruin. In spite of some em-pirical evidence, maybe firms' cost functions are not really like that. Or firms might actu-ally face demand functions that slope downward enough to preserve them while generating enough competition to serve us. Or *differences* in firms' costs could—as in Ricardo's theory—permit adjustments in the number of firms and bail us out.

If these or other factors could not prevent ruinous competition, policy remedies are not so easy to formulate.

But useful industries are not likely to evaporate if we don't permit them to cartelize, which is a dangerous cure anyway.[20] A lot depends on how much ruin competition would heap on us if we do not civilize it. There tends to be as much capacity as enterprisers believe can earn a competitive rate of return. Sometimes they suffer losses; sometimes they make profits. If bad times last too long, some go broke, perhaps to be recapitalized and reborn. This backing and filling may not give us precisely the ideal amount of capac-ity, but it need not leave us shoeless in the snows.

On the other hand, we should not suppose that a cartel would content itself with prices that are just high enough to pay for the optimal amount of capacity. The power to set a price may lead them to choose the price that best serves themselves but hurts consumers. Finally, consumers may be less interested in minimizing production costs than they are in minimizing the present value of *prices* over time.

It is not clear how well these and some other recent theories mix and where they leave us. For example, one theory suggests that the world is biased toward too little competition rather than too much. This is supposedly because expensive and specialized production factors required in some industries give resident firms a decisive cost advantage—they already own these factors—and can bar entry. The result is too little competition, and monopoly resource misallocation.[21]

On the other hand, even the *prospect* of entry might force monopolies to price competitively.[22] Hit-and-run or unregulated entry against a regulated, multiproduct natural monopoly might even produce more competition than is best for consumers.[23]

The theory of ruinous competition can lead us astray by inducing us to substitute one unachievable goal for another. In any case, however, this theory is an important criticism of competition as an ultimate good and goal. We should keep it in mind.

Though Not Ruinous, Competition May Be Too Expensive _____

We don't need complex theories to recognize another important possibility. Costs under atomism may be much higher than those under some other nonatomistic industrial structure, including monopoly; or under government ownership or regulation. If costs for this "natural" nonatomistic structure are the lowest achievable, atomism could be accomplished only through government intervention and would tend to be expensive and unproductive.[24]

Atomism is not natural for many industries because demand is too small to support swarms of efficient-size firms. Differences in consumers' tastes are one cause of this condition. Relative to the sizes of efficient firms, demands are smaller than if all consumers were alike. If we rank consumer sovereignty high, this is not necessarily an evil. Cost conditions are not always compatible with atomism. Simple marginal cost pricing is infeasible when marginal cost is always less than average cost.[25] In addition, the superior performance of some firms can make industries even more concentrated than economies of pure size or scale require. Chapter 7 discusses this process in detail.

For whatever cause, efficient atomism is not a universal option. The efficient structure for some industries is concentrated. In some industries, in short, the choice is between fewer firms with lower costs and more firms with higher costs.

Under some demand and cost conditions, even an unregulated single-firm monopoly will charge *lower* prices than an atomistically competitive industry would. It is difficult to see how atomism would benefit consumers under these circumstances. Furthermore, even if an atomistic industry produces lower prices than a concentrated one, its costs could be higher. In such cases, compelling atomism by policy may be antieconomic. Assuming lower *prices* under atomism is not sufficient to sanctify such a policy. For, when concentrated industries have lower costs, the prices consumers pay must be weighed against enhanced efficiency and profits. Chapters 7 and 13 discuss these matters at length.

Piecemeal Policy and the Theory of Second Best _____

The theory of policies towards monopoly would be simpler if only a single industry were monopolistic. That is the usual textbook assumption, pictured earlier in Chapter 2, Figure 2-6. Actually, however, firms in *many* industries face downward-sloping demand functions. As a consequence, improving competition by compelling or inducing marginal cost pricing in some industries, but not in all, could do more harm than good. Real-world policy is necessarily piecemeal, and industries may be so interdependent in demand or costs that "improving" things a little in one or a few industries—but not simultaneously in all—can make things much worse in other industries.[26]

For example, forcing marginal-cost pricing in one previously monopoloid industry increases its output, which can drive up prices of inputs it uses. That would contract output in other monopoloid industries using the same inputs. By standards of perfect competition, outputs in those industries are already too small and improving the situation in the first industry worsens the situation in these industries: rising costs there reduce both consumer and producer surplus. Consumers may either gain or lose on balance. This theory is not popular among those who seek change through government policies: "Because it indicates that maintaining competition wherever possible is not necessarily optimal but offers no guidance toward improved policies in the absence of information seldom if ever obtainable, the theory of second best is a counsel of despair."[27]

DYNAMIC CONSIDERATIONS _____

On top of the objections aired to this point, we can add that the real world is dynamic, not static. It is common to hear that competition produces excessive instability over time. Though that evil is usually not defined clearly, it might have something to do with excessive adjustment costs, including inequities, poverty, and other human costs. Anyhow, the claim itself is highly debatable. And what is instability to one taste is merely flexibility to another.

With dynamics comes change. Tastes and technology change, and change unpredictably, over time. Consumers appear to have a taste for change. In such a world, imperfectly competitive industries may produce larger consumer benefits over the long haul than purer competition could, even though their prices *always* exceed marginal costs significantly. This could occur if more concentrated industries perform better over time with respect to costs and product qualities.

Some say that pure competition is an inferior vehicle for change and progress, or that progress and change are basically incompatible with it.[28] There is little in theory to tell us whether atomistic or concentrated industries have the edge in adjusting to externally induced changes in demand and cost. The theory seems clearer with respect to *producing* changes in contrast to adjusting to them. In producing random discoveries, atomism offers statistical advantages: if more people search, it is more likely that they will find something. Otherwise, atomistic competition appears to be a less favorable organizational form for producing new ideas, products, or techniques. The argument is well known: change, too, is a business, subject to profit incentives. For discovery to be a profitable business, it must more than cover the costs of search. But if it is easy for everyone to quickly to exploit a discovery that one pioneer makes, as seems plausible under atomistic competition, returns expected from new discovery will be smaller than if imitation lags. In this respect, imperfect competition and monopoly seem to offer more to pioneers and therefore to have an edge in encouraging dynamic improvements.

Property rights in new ideas and techniques can be provided through patents, for example; but this does not remove doubts about how compatible discoveries and atomism really are. A patent system encourages discoveries, including those made by atomistic industries; but it offers exclusive claims on whatever is discovered. Patents can concentrate old industries and create new industries that are concentrated from the start.

Even with a patent system, however, many things are not patentable. And some that are patentable in principle remain unpatented in fact. Imperfectly competitive or monopolistic environments seem to offer greater incentives to discover things that will not be patented. Chapter 8 discusses patents; Chapter 15 discusses empirical evidence relating industrial structure to invention and innovation.

It thus appears that monopolistic or imperfectly competitive industries may be more efficient mechanisms for producing change; and that institutions—such as patents—that are meant to encourage invention may themselves create monopoly elements.

Even when new techniques greatly concentrate a previously unconcentrated industry, it is premature to claim that competition is eclipsed, monopoly is ascendant, and consumers are hurt. That evaluation of competition and monopoly is not as solid as it sounds. For the old unconcentrated industry and the new concentrated industry have different costs, or different product qualities and demands, or both. New ways win out over the old in a competition governed by costs and tastes.[29] Much the same analysis applies when the efficient sizes of firms increase because of technological or managerial changes within or outside of the affected industry.

Schumpeter claimed that this new and broader competition is more important than the old. In his words,

> . . . in capitalist reality as distinguished from its textbook picture, it is not that kind of competition which counts but the competition from the new commodity, the new technology, the new source of supply, the new type of organization (the largest-scale unit of control for instance)—competition which commands a decisive cost or quality advantage and which strikes not at the margins of the profits and outputs of the existing firms but at their foundations and their very lives. This kind of competition is as much more effective than the other as a bombardment is in comparison with forcing a door, and so much more important that it becomes a matter of comparative indifference whether competition in the ordinary sense functions more or less promptly; the powerful lever that in the long run expands and brings down prices is in any case made of other stuff.[30]

Schumpeter may be right; but whether one kind of competition is more important or more valuable than another is a question of fact that is very hard to answer.[31] The theory, though, is clear enough. With or without patents, changes in costs or tastes can increase industrial concentration substantially. Suppose that an industry contains many firms, all using the same simple but efficient small-scale methods to make the same product. Entry to the field is not artificially limited, and price approximates long-run marginal cost. Suppose that a revolution in technology or management now occurs, so that there is room in the market for only a few firms using the new and more efficient methods. Whether transformed quickly through merger or gradually through bankruptcies, an atomistic industry will be turned into what some will call a monopoly, albeit one selling the same product at a lower price than before.[32] Price will exceed the new (and lower) marginal cost of surviving firms; but it is incomplete and misleading to characterize the result as a decline of competition.

What happened was that consumers naturally preferred the new industrial organization, with its lower price. Competition from the new ways of doing things proved decisively more valuable to consumers than competition among larger numbers of the old-style firms had been.[33]

One view is that the new industry can charge no more than the marginal costs of old-style firms, whose higher cost then becomes the relevant long-run opportunity cost. That the new-style firms may earn large profits does not justify dissolving or ejecting them, or prohibiting the new techniques. For, on the whole, processes like this benefit consumers. Some claim that there is an even better solution: regulate the more efficient industry to compel marginal cost pricing.[34] That idea is not as good as it sounds. First, static comparisons between equal-cost competitive and monopoly industries are clearly suspect when the monopoly is both the creator and the creation of major dynamic improvements. Second, government regulation has probably stifled more innovation than it has encouraged. One danger is that this sort of government intervention will discourage improvements within precisely those industries that show an innovative flair. Another danger is that government intervention will also stifle innovations that could challenge the regulated industry in the future. For example, when competition from trucks threatened the railroad industry, the Interstate Commerce Commission, the federal agency that regulated railroads, obtained authority to regulate trucking, too. Finally, history shows that regulations tend to persist long after the original justification for them has disappeared. Railroad regulation is one of many examples.

In sum, it is dangerous to use government regulation to achieve marginal-cost pricing just because the formal requirements of pure competition have not been met. That policy undermines incentives to improve and innovate. It could also transform much of the economy into essentially government enterprise, with far-reaching political as well as incentive effects.

The history of diesel-electric railroad locomotives puts some flesh on these ideas, which may sound arid in the abstract. Before General Motors (GM) entered the locomotive business, steam locomotives were king. Three companies sold most of the steam locomotives in the U.S.: Alco, Baldwin, and Lima. All were "stubbornly wedded to steam."[35] Since the 1920s, GM's Charles F. Kettering, and the GM Research Laboratories, had been studying high-compression internal combustion engines, including diesels. High-compression engines squeeze more useful energy out of a drop of fuel. One reason for GM's interest in high compression was a fear that the world was running out of oil.

In 1933, GM developed a new lightweight two-cycle diesel engine as a prototype for use in submarines, where weight- and space-savings are valuable. The engine weighed

20 pounds per horsepower, compared with 60 pounds for the lightest of its contemporaries, and was much smaller.

In 1935, GM built a diesel-electric locomotive plant at La Grange, Illinois and entered the locomotive business. At first, U.S. railroad executives doubted that diesel-electric locomotives were suitable for general use and bought them only for the limited applications in which steam engines could clearly not do as good a job.

It usually takes a while to convince customers that a new product is really superior. The Aluminum Company of America (Alcoa) had trouble convincing manufacturers that aluminum was good for making a wide range of products, including electrical transmission cable; pots and pans; and pistons, cylinder heads, and other parts for cars. That was one reason that Alcoa began manufacturing such goods itself. GM's approach to the same problem was to provide demonstrator locomotives, complete with diesel-electric engineers, so that railroads could try them out.

In 1939, GM built its first diesel *freight* locomotive. They reasoned that if diesels could compete with steam locomotives in line-haul freight service, steam was finished. For diesels completely dispensed with expensive appurtenances like roundhouses, watertowers, coal chutes, ashpits, and turntables.

Because the diesels were designed for mass production, major parts were interchangeable and repairs were quick and cheap. Steam locomotives, by contrast, were highly varied and practically custom-built. Major parts were heavy and many were not interchangeable. GM designed diesel locomotives so that older models could be upgraded by fitting improved parts rather than scrapping whole units.

Each diesel locomotive was versatile. It was no longer necessary to have a large stable of different, complex, and specialized steam locomotives. Parts interchangeability within a fleet of diesels reduced inventories, downtime, and costs. Diesels permitted long hauls with minor service and delays. Diesel trains could cross the continent without changing locomotives.

The *total* costs of operating diesels were less than the variable costs for steam locomotives, and the price per diesel-electric horsepower declined steadily. The effective market price of a new steam locomotive would have had to be *negative* to compete.

From 1940 on, U.S. railroads rapidly converted to diesel-electric locomotives. Apparently nobody but GM had ever believed that the diesel would win out so dramatically. GE and Westinghouse both had experience with straight-electric locomotives. Except for Lima, the steam locomotive builders had experimented with diesels. There were no fundamental locomotive patents and all necessary components were available to anyone. A GM executive said that, in the beginning, the crucial competitive advantage had been that everyone else thought GM was crazy. Only GM developed, invested, and plunged in.

After World War II, railroads concluded that GM diesel-electric locomotives were best; but any diesel was better than steam, and all locomotives were in short supply. In 1920, 60,000 steam locomotives had been in service in the U.S. By 1971, only 13 were left. Each diesel was doing the work of four steam locomotives.

GM created a new industry and came to have 75 percent of the market. Steam locomotive manufacture died.[36] In the early 1960s, the U.S. Department of Justice brought civil and criminal antitrust suits against GM, claiming that it had monopolized the locomotive industry. By 1967, it dropped both suits.

In cases like this, it is quixotic to lament the death of the old industry, however unconcentrated it may have been and however concentrated the new industry became. To call this a decline of competition is old-fashioned orthodoxy in industrial organization; but that is small reason to attack innovators or to restructure a new and more productive industry by force of law.

More detailed discussions of the theory and facts of trade-offs between structure and economic welfare are deferred to Chapter 13 and Chapter 14.

SUMMARY

Perfect competition is unrealistic and nonexistent, as all abstract ideals are, and it is doubtful how relevant it is either to appraise real situations or to propose policies that can effectively improve the results we actually enjoy. Indeed, some critics claim that it is deficient even as theory, partly because of what it leaves out. They claim that, left to its own devices, competition falls short. It creates income inequalities and will not eliminate poverty. It encourages materialism and alienates individuals from one another. It does not produce the miracles of efficient resource allocation claimed for it, because of spillover effects among other things.

Any system that pays people for what they produce will generate significant income inequalities, and it cannot guarantee to eliminate poverty, either. Nor will such a system pay back wages to those who once were slaves or who have been disadvantaged by other historical handicaps. Those criticisms apply to monopoly, atomistic, and other models as well. Nor are they confined to private-property market systems. They apply also to the USSR and other totalitarian systems.[37]

In addition to other complaints about competition, some theories claim that we are in at least as much danger of having too much competition as too little. For, they say, too much competition can be ruinous to economic efficiency.

It is even clearer that concentrated industries may be more efficient than less concentrated structures, including atomistic ones. In that case, atomism may be too expensive to contemplate.

Finally, second-best and dynamic considerations cast even more doubt on policies that are hostile to concentrated industry structures just because they *are* concentrated. From a consumer's standpoint, it is economic *performance* that counts, not structure for its own sake. The history of diesel-electric locomotives illustrates these contrasts and apparent paradoxes.

The total effect of alternative structures, and policies toward them, should be assessed if consumer interests are to be served. Rather than equating it with an atomistic *structure*, it is useful to think of competition as an evolutionary *process* involving selection, substitution, and displacement. A rational goal is maximum economic benefits, whatever the structure of industry turns out to be. On this view, achieving unconcentrated industries is simply not the dominant objective.

Theoretic differences between monopolistic and competitive performance are often used both to criticize how real industries perform and to rationalize government regulation. Though critics claim that markets often fail in one way or another, at least some of the market failures they cite offer money-making opportunities to those who would correct them. There is disagreement about how serious such market failures are, how quickly private profit-seekers will correct them, and whether government correctives work faster or more cheaply than market forces. How well market processes work depends partly upon how much we permit markets to do and how much we allow enterprisers to profit.

Government regulation has costs and deficiencies, too. Many government policies claim to prevent or reform monopoly. Chapters 17 and 18 suggest, however, that a good deal of governmental intervention has nothing to do with correcting monopoly; and some of the rest ends by creating monopoly. Furthermore, whatever else is claimed for them, many government policies simply redistribute income, by design or accident, not necessarily in favor of consumers, at that.

This is far enough to go with these questions until the sources and types of efficiency can be discussed in greater detail. Chapter 7 does that. And Chapter 13 shows rational trade-off analyses that might be made to encourage industrial efficiency.

QUESTIONS

1. Professor John Johnston concluded that the cost functions of real firms are incompatible with price-taker competition. Why?
2. Explain Adam Smith's invisible hand.
3. What is the theory of ruinous competition? In principle, how could we tell whether competition is ruinous or just right?
4. Define *external effect*.
5. What is the Coase Theorem? Does it suggest that the appropriate policy towards externalities is to ignore them?
6. Suppose that there are serious external effects that raise the costs of all firms producing in a large oil field. Think of several methods that might be used to cure this problem. (Chapter 17 analyzes this case thoroughly, but a rough, general approach is fine for now. You may want to compare the answer you write to this question now with the one you give after reading Chapter 17.)
7. What is the theory of second best?
8. Is it possible for a single-firm monopoly to perform better than an atomistic industry, even though the monopoly price exceeds marginal cost and earns large profits? Illustrate with a diagram, and explain.

NOTES

1. It is common to call competition *pure* rather than *perfect* if, though all firms are assumed to face perfectly elastic demand functions and are price-takers, knowledge is imperfect and there are frictions, costs, and lags in market adjustments. Atomism is said to make the best out of even these imperfections.

2. Many complaints about the atomistic models would, in one degree or another, apply to *any* theory. For example, in the 1920's, when Frank H. Knight listed the underlying assumptions, people began complaining that the theory is "unrealistic." The same complaint is popular today. George J. Stigler, "Perfect Competition, Historically Contemplated," *Journal of Political Economy*, 65 (February 1957), pp. 1–17; reprinted in Stigler, *Essays in the History of Economics* (Chicago: The University of Chicago Press, 1965), pp. 234–67, at p. 256.

    There are several masterly defenses of assumptions traditionally made about rationality, information, and external effects. For example, see Gary S. Becker, "Irrational Behavior and Economic Theory," *Journal of Political Economy*, 70 (February 1962), pp. 1–13; Armen A. Alchian, "Uncertainty, Evolution and Economic Theory," *Journal of Political Economy*, 58 (June 1950), pp. 211–21; Ronald H. Coase, "The Problem of Social Cost," *Journal of Law & Economics*, 3 (October 1960), pp. 1–44; and G. Warren Nutter, "The Coase Theorem on Social Cost: A Footnote," *Journal of Law & Economics*, 11 (October 1968), pp. 503–7.

3. For a further discussion of externalities, see the section "The Invisible Hand Needs Help," in this chapter.

4. George J. Stigler, "Competition in the United States," in *Five Lectures on Economic Problems* (London: Longmans, Green, 1949), pp. 46–65. Also see R. G. Lipsey and P. O. Steiner, *Economics* (New York: Harper & Row, Publishers, Inc., 1966), p. 309; P. A. Samuelson, *Economics*, 6th ed. (New York: McGraw-Hill Book Company, 1964), p. 472; *Report of the Attorney General's National Committee to Study the Antitrust Laws* (March 31, 1955), p. 316; E. T. Grether, "Public Policy Affecting the Competitive Market System in the United States," Reprint no. 15, Institute of Business and Economic Research, University of California (reprinted from *Proceedings, American Marketing Association*, September 1–3, 1965); Edward Mason, "Workable Competition versus Workable Monopoly," *Business Practices Under Federal Antitrust Laws*, Symposium of Section on Antitrust Law, N.Y. State Bar Association (1951), pp. 67–72, reprinted as Chapter 18 of Edward Mason's *Economic Concentration and the Monopoly Problem* (Cambridge, Mass.: Harvard University Press, 1957), pp. 382–88; Paul J. McNulty, "Economic Theory and the Meaning of Competition," *Quarterly Journal of Economics*, 82 (November 1968), pp. 639–56.

5. John Johnston, *Statistical Cost Analysis* (New York: McGraw-Hill Book Company, 1960), pp. 168, 193.

6. ". . . every individual necessarily labours to render the annual revenue of the society as great as he can. He generally, indeed, neither intends to promote the public interest, nor knows how much he is promoting it. . . . he intends only his own gain, and he is in this, as in many other cases, led by an invisible hand to promote an end which was no part of his intention." Adam Smith, *An Inquiry into the Nature and Causes of the Wealth of Nations* (New York: The Modern Library, 1937), p. 423.

7. In an unpublished paper, Bruce Johnsen analyzes a related controversy between two legal scholars. D. Bruce Johnsen, "Wealth *Is* Value: A Comment on Posner and Dworkin," citing Richard A. Posner, "Utilitarianism, Economics and Legal Theory," *Journal of Legal Studies*, 8 (1979), p. 103; Ronald M. Dworkin, "Is Wealth a Value?" *Journal of Legal Studies*, 9 (1980), p. 191; Richard Posner, "The Value of Wealth: A Comment on Dworkin and Kronman," *Journal of Legal Studies*, 9 (1980), p. 243.

8. See, for example, Robert Nozick, *Anarchy, State, and Utopia* (New York: Basic Books, Inc., Publishers, 1974).

9. Chapter 18 discusses agricultural programs.

10. See, for example, Charles Murray, *Losing Ground* (New York: Basic Books, Inc., Publishers, 1984).

11. Spillovers can occur in concentrated as well as atomistic industries. A plant owned by Pemex, a government monopoly, caused the disaster in Mexico. Lethal gas from a chemical plant caused the disaster in India. Union Carbide, a private U.S. corporation, owned it. A state nuclear plant caused the Chernobyl disaster in the USSR. For a discussion of spillovers from oil and gas operations, involving large-number industries operating over large geographic areas in Louisiana, see *The Wall Street Journal*, 23 October 1984.

12. A. C. Pigou, *The Economics of Welfare*, 4th ed. (London: Macmillan Co., 1932), Part II, Chapter 9.

13. R. H. Coase, "The Problem of Social Cost," *Journal of Law & Economics*, 3 (October 1960), pp. 1–44. The following summary, including Table 3-1, is by permission of the University of Chicago Press, publisher of *The Journal of Law & Economics*.

    The genesis of Coase's article and the skeptical reception it initially got are described in Edward Kitch, ed., "The Fire of Truth: A Remembrance of Law and Economics at Chicago, 1932–1970," *Journal of Law & Economics*, 26 (April 1983), pp. 211–12, 214, 215.

14. *Internalize* has become popular jargon. It often means forcing whoever causes a spillover to pay for it, thereby bringing external costs back home to their source. But, as Coase pointed out, it takes both a receiver and a source to make an external effect.

15. Coase, "The Problem of Social Cost" (1960), pp. 41–42.

16. John M. Clark, *Studies in the Economics of Overhead Costs* (Chicago: The University of Chicago Press, 1923); Clark, "Toward a Concept of Workable Competition," *American Economic Review*, 30 (June 1940), pp. 241–56; Clark, "Competition: Static Models and Dynamic Aspects," *American Economic Review*, 45 (May 1955), pp. 450–62. See also Lloyd G. Reynolds, "Cutthroat Competition," *American Economic Review*, 30 (December 1940), pp. 736–47.

    For much-modernized versions, see William W. Sharkey, *A Study of Markets Involving Increasing Returns and Uncertain Demand* (unpublished Ph.D. dissertation, University of Chicago, 1973) ; Sharkey, *The Theory of Natural Monopoly* (New York: Cambridge University Press, 1982); Lester G. Telser, *Competition, Collusion, and Game Theory* (Chicago: Aldine-Atherton, 1972); Telser, *Economic Theory and the Core* (Chicago: The University of Chicago Press, 1978); Lester G. Telser and William W. Sharkey, "Supportable Cost Functions for the Multiproduct Firm," *Journal of Economic Theory*, 18 (June 1978), pp. 23–37; and George Bittlingmayer, "Decreasing Average Cost and Competition: A New Look at the Addyston Pipe Case," *The Journal of Law & Economics*, 25, no. 2 (October 1982), pp. 201–29.

17. Bittlingmayer, "A New Look at the Addyston Pipe Case" (1982). When there are cost differences among firms, some of the shock of price changes is absorbed by putting higher-cost firms into or out of operation. Not all need go broke or close down, for example, to establish an equilibrium.

18. See Chapter 4 and Chapter 5.

19. Bittlingmayer, "A New Look at the Addyston Pipe Case" (1982). See also William Baumol, "Contestable Markets: An Uprising in the Theory of Industry Structure," *American Economic Review*, 72 (March 1982), pp. 1–15; Sharkey, *A Study of Markets Involving Increasing Returns and Uncertain Demand*; Sharkey, "Existence of Sustainable Prices for Natural

Monopoly Outputs,'' *Bell Journal of Economics*, 12 (Spring 1981), pp. 144–54; Sharkey, *The Theory of Natural Monopoly*; Lester G. Telser, *Competition, Collusion, and Game Theory*, especially pp. xiii–xix, 3–4, Telser, *Economic Theory and the Core*; Lester G. Telser and William W. Sharkey, ''Supportable Cost Functions for the Multiproduct Firm,'' pp. 23–37.

20. See Chapter 6.

21. W. J. Baumol and R. D. Willig, ''Fixed Costs, Sunk Costs, Entry Barriers, and Sustainability of Monopoly,'' *Quarterly Journal of Economics*, 96(August 1981), pp. 405–31.

22. William J. Baumol, ''Contestable Markets: An Uprising,'' pp. 405–31.

23. W. Baumol, E. Bailey, and R. Willig, ''Weak Invisible-Hand Theorems on the Sustainability of Prices in a Multiproduct Natural Monopoly,'' *American Economic Review*, 67 (June 1977), pp. 350–65. On the other hand, see Lester G. Telser and William W. Sharkey, ''Supportable Cost Functions,'' pp. 23–37.

     For a spirited argument that potential competition does not produce price-taker behavior in concentrated industries, see W. G. Shepherd, '' 'Contestability' vs. Competition,'' *American Economic Review*, 74 (September 1984), pp. 572–87. Although Shepherd's complaint is that competition is *less* intense than it ought to be, refugees from ''ruinous'' competition may find comfort in that.

24. Chapter 13 analyzes this and other theoretical possibilities in detail. Chapter 14 and Chapter 15 discuss some empirical evidence.

25. Chapter 18 discusses the policy choices this situation presents: compulsory marginal cost pricing plus subsidies, which is not without difficulties; certain kinds of price discrimination under regulation, which more nearly approximates the statically optimal output; or unregulated monopoly, whose price will exceed marginal cost and whose profits may be high.

26. This is the main point in the theory of second best. R. G. Lipsey and K. Lancaster, ''The General Theory of Second Best,'' *Review of Economic Studies*, 24, no. 1 (1956/1957), pp. 11–32.

27. F. M. Scherer, *Industrial Market Structure and Economic Performance*, 2nd ed. (Chicago: Rand McNally College Publishing Company, 1980), p. 28.

28. Chapter 15 discusses these questions in detail.

29. J. S. McGee, ''Patent Exploitation: Some Economic and Legal Problems,''*Journal of Law & Economics*, 9 (October 1966), pp. 135–62.

30. Joseph A. Schumpeter, *Capitalism, Socialism, and Democracy* (New York: Harper & Row, Publishers, Inc., 1947), pp. 84–85.

31. Chapter 16 presents empirical evidence.

32. If price should rise and stay high, the old methods and perhaps even the old facilities could be used again. One problem is whether anyone would dare rely on the old methods. Firms adopting the inferior method could be ruined if a firm using best techniques cut price enough. Whether, and the circumstances under which, this is likely to happen are debatable. See further discussions of this point in Chapter 9 and Chapter 13.

33. ''It would be arbitrary to attribute to competition among firms using the same productive techniques greater economic virtue than is attributed to competition among different methods of doing things.'' J. S. McGee, ''The Decline and Fall of Quantity Discounts: The Quantity Limit Rule in Rubber Tires and Tubes,'' *Journal of Business*, 27 (July 1954), pp. 225–34.

Henry Ford's model "T" and GM's locomotives are interesting stories to contemplate. Locomotives are discussed later in this chapter.

34. See Chapter 18.

35. For more details, see General Motors Corporation, *The Locomotive Industry and General Motors* (New York: Bar Press, Inc., May 1973).

36. Unlike dinosaurs, dead industries sometimes rise again. A good deal of money has been wagered on the rebirth of steam locomotives. Daniel Machalaba, "Diesels Watch Out, The Old Iron Horse May Derail You Yet," *The Wall Street Journal*, 30 January 1985, p. 1. And even without any return to steam, the diesel-electric industry declined dramatically for other reasons. "GE Plans to Idle 500 at Locomotive Plant," *The Wall Street Journal*, 14 January 1987, p. 17.

37. Manuela Hoelterhoff, "The Upper Crust in Mother Russia," *The Wall Street Journal*, 29 August 1985, p. 18. This is a review of David K. Willis, *Klass* (New York: St. Martin's Press, Inc., 1985).

4

CLASSICAL THEORIES OF OLIGOPOLY AND DOMINANT FIRMS

INTRODUCTION

Models of atomistic competition and large-number cartels are interesting and important; but those are not the only industry structures that matter. As Chapter 7 shows, for example, it is sometimes more efficient to have relatively few firms in an industry, or to have only a few firms producing most of the output.

For this or other reasons, most U.S. manufacturing industries are not atomistic, as even the grossest measures suggest. The U.S. Census of Manufactures periodically calculates the percentage of business done by the four largest firms operating in each of about 450 industries. That percentage is the industry's concentration ratio, measured for four firms. Weighted by industry size, the weighted-average industry concentration ratio was 35 percent in 1947 and about 39 percent in 1972, 25 years later.[1]

In April 1986, Census published 1982 concentration ratios for 441 industries, the unweighted average concentration ratio for which was about 38 percent. Some U.S. industries are much more concentrated than that; others, much less. Industries with relatively low concentration included the women's and girl's dress industry (6 percent), and blouses (8 percent); and wood pallets and skids (5 percent). Industries with relatively high concentration included chewing gum (95 percent); household refrigerators and freezers (94 percent); motor vehicles and car bodies (92 percent); and breakfast cereals (86 percent). What, if anything, such numbers imply for economic performance is an important question that is debated heatedly, as we will see in subsequent chapters.

In any event, however, it is a fact that much of American manufacturing does not have the kind of atomistic structure that most textbooks associate with pure and perfect competition. And concentration, it is often said, raises efficiency, welfare, and regulatory questions of its own.

The purpose of this chapter is to discover what classical economic theories say about relationships between industrial structure and performance. Several famous theories are discussed: the oligopoly theories of Cournot, Bertrand, Edgeworth, and Bowley; and the dominant-firm theories of Forchheimer and von Stackelberg.

The next chapter reviews still more theories, several of which are more recent. Empirical tests of some of these theories will be summarized and evaluated later, in Chapter 14.

To answer questions about concentrated industries, it is reasonable to start with theories of oligopoly, of which duopoly is a special case. Oligopoly literally means few sellers; duopoly means two sellers. And in spite of popular opinions about what differences the number of sellers makes, taken together, the theories turn out to be rather ambiguous.

The public policy question about concentrated industries is not usually whether *large* numbers of sellers would be more competitive or otherwise perform better than the relatively few that are there. Usually the question is whether somehow slightly increasing the number of firms would help.[2] Whether we are talking about deconcentrating an industry a lot or only a little, however, we need to know how structure affects performance, and how efficiency requirements affect structure.

Oligopoly theories posit that each of relatively few firms can significantly affect the relevant market price. Every oligopoly theory must specify how each firm behaves and how it assumes the others will behave. It should also explain how many firms there are. Noncollusive theories assume that each firm maximizes its own profits, and does not agree with its rivals to fix price or output. To this extent, the firms compete, by searching for the profit-maximizing quantity or price.

CLASSICAL THEORIES ABOUT THE EFFECTS OF NUMBERS _____

How each rival *assumes* the others will behave is one thing that distinguishes different oligopoly theories, and there are a variety of possibilities. Another distinction is whether each firm assumes that the others' prices or outputs change because of what it does. In the first theory discussed here, output quantity is the decision variable. Each firm assumes that others will not change their outputs in response to changes in its own.

Cournot _____

Published in 1838, Cournot's theory was the first systematic treatment of oligopoly. Though the earliest, it does not mess around: it asserts precisely how differences in the number of firms affect market performance.[3] It is remarkable how popular Cournot's logic still is for both theoretical and empirical work. But much of the contemporary work that follows Cournot closely does not even cite him, for whatever reason. Instead, it usually cites an article by J. F. Nash, a modern mathematician, whom Cournot anticipated by 113 years.[4]

In its simplest form, Cournot's theory applies to homogeneous output for which production costs are zero, and to a linear final demand function. His assumptions about zero costs, demand linearity, and undifferentiated products turn out not to be crucial.[5] In Cournot's theory, as in all subsequent oligopoly theories of the classical persuasion, what is crucial is the treatment of rivals' response. Rival reaction is the essence of oligopoly, whereas it is absent from simple monopoly and pure competition. That is what makes oligopoly such a tough problem to analyze. As Hurwicz put it:

> There is no adequate solution of the problem of defining "rational economic behavior" on the part of an individual when the very rationality of his actions depends on the probable behavior of other individuals: in the case of oligopoly, other sellers. . . . Thus, the individual's "rational behavior" is determinate *if* the pattern of behavior of "others" can be assumed *a priori* known. But the behavior of "others" cannot be known *a priori* if the "others," too, are to behave rationally. Thus a logical impasse is reached.[6]

Detailed specification of rival reaction is what distinguishes classical oligopoly theories from their modern counterparts. The classical theories simply *postulate* both how oligopolistic rivals behave and how each assumes the others will behave. The modern theories assume a *goal*—whether it is maximizing total industry (joint) profits or seeking the most profitable of the worst outcomes that can occur—then infer what kind of behavior is best suited to reach the goal. In principle, these are very different things.

Although Cournot recognized this difference, his discussion of oligopoly excludes joint-profit maximization achieved through either collusion or merger. He separately considered single-firm monopoly and the attempts of two or more firms to achieve monopoly power through agreement. Dealing as he did with a homogeneous product sold in a perfect, centralized market, Cournot took output as the variable to be manipulated by each rival: price will necessarily be the same for all sellers. Each seller, acting independently, seeks maximum profits. At any moment each rival knows his own cost function, the total commodity demand, his own and his rivals' output, and the market price. In short, he knows the present situation.

It is probably best to view Cournot's model as the *simultaneous* solution of a system of equations. In addition to increasing the subjective comfort with which such a model can be used, a simultaneous version has other support. Citing Samuelson as his authority, Waterson observes, "many authors suggest only local stability (in the vicinity of equilibrium) is of interest rather than, say, the movement between equilibria."[7] As we will see in Chapter 5, game theory shows how oligopolists *rationally* reach Cournot's equilibrium precisely.[8] On this view, sequential or dynamic adjustments need not be incorporated into the model.

Many have not been content to leave Cournot's model at that. Instead, they have tried to make it dynamic, or at least sequential, having one firm move, the other adjust, and so on, until equilibrium is reached. Given Cournot's assumptions about behavior, the model and the equilibrium still hold together. But this transformation of Cournot's simultaneous model into a sequential model does make things look a little peculiar. Starting the sequential-adjustment version off at some nonequilibrium position reveals the problem. Except at equilibrium, the story goes, each seller should learn that he has been seriously wrong about how his rival behaves. But he is myopic and does not learn.

Now let us look more closely at Cournot's models. In the simplest case of oligopoly, two firms sell exactly the same product. Call the sellers firm 1 and firm 2. Each seeks maximum profits. C_1 and C_2 are the total cost functions of firms 1 and 2, and TR_1 and TR_2 are their total revenue functions. Each firm's revenue function depends upon the quantity sold by *both* firms. They compete: market price depends upon the sum of their outputs; and, at any price, given the total market demand, a larger quantity sold by one firm leaves less for the other. In a well-specified theory, each firm must assume something about whether and how the other will react to changes in its own output rate, and there are a number of possibilities.

In Cournot's system, each seller assumes that the sum of his rivals' output will not change because he changes his own. Each seller takes as his own that part of the industry demand curve not satisfied by rivals. As a consequence, equilibrium comes through the sum of output decisions independently made, which is brought to equality with industry demand. In equilibrium, the market clears on price and no seller can unilaterally improve his position, given what his rivals are doing.[9] For years critics have complained that, although Cournot's system reaches a unique equilibrium, to which it returns if moved away, it gets there by assuming short-sighted seller behavior—myopia. Except at equilibrium, the argument goes, each seller is seriously wrong about how rivals behave, and ought reasonably to change his assumptions about it. But he does not learn; he does not improve.

Only two firms sell the homogeneous product that we are interested in. Given the market demand function for this product, price is some function of the total output produced by firms 1 and 2:

$$P = F(q_1, q_2).$$

And, for each firm, total revenue is market price *times* its own output rate:

$$TR_1 = q_1 F(q_1 + q_2); \text{ and}$$
$$TR_2 = q_2 F(q_1 + q_2).$$

Profit for each firm, R, is total revenue minus total cost, C:

$$R_1 = TR_1(q_1, q_2) - C_1(q_1); \text{ and}$$
$$R_2 = TR_2(q_1, q_2) - C_2(q_2).$$

Although each firm can directly determine only its own output, changes in its own output rate might induce the other firm to change its output rate. Any serious theory must specify how all this works, and—at least as important—how the firms assume that it works. To find each firm's profit-maximizing output and determine the market equilibrium, we differentiate (and set to zero) the profit function of each firm with respect to its own output rate:

$$\delta R_1 / \delta q_1 = [\delta TR_1(q_1, q_2) / \delta q_1] + \{[\delta TR_1(q_1, q_2) / \delta q_2] [\delta q_2 / \delta q_1]\}$$
$$- \delta C_1(q_1) / \delta q_1 = 0.$$

$$\delta R_2 / \delta q_2 = [\delta TR_2(q_1, q_2) / \delta q_2] + \{[\delta TR_2(q_1, q_2) / \delta q_1] [\delta q_1 / \delta q_2]\}$$
$$- \delta C_2(q_2) / \delta q_2 = 0.$$

For each firm, the second term has two elements. In the second term, the second elements, $\delta q_2/\delta q_1$ and $\delta q_1/\delta q_2$, show how each firm's output is *assumed* to alter the output of the other. In 1933, Ragnar Frisch called these kinds of derivatives *conjectural variations*. The first element in the second term shows how any conjectural variation in the other's output could affect this firm's revenues.

There are many different theories of oligopoly, including duopoly. One of the important ways the theories differ is in what they assert about the conjectural variations— $\delta q_2/\delta q_1$ and $\delta q_1/\delta q_2$ in the duopoly versions. In Cournot's 1838 version, for example, firms act as though $\delta q_2/\delta q_1$ and $\delta q_1/\delta q_2$ are both equal to zero. That is, each firm sets its own output on the assumption that the other's output will remain unchanged. Because both conjectural variations are zero, the value of the second term in each firm's output equation is zero, and we have:

$$\delta R_1 / \delta q_1 = [\delta TR_1(q_1, q_2) / \delta q_1] - \delta C_1(q_1) / \delta q_1 = 0, \text{ and}$$

$$\delta R_2 / \delta q_2 = [\delta TR_2(q_1, q_2) / \delta q_2] - \delta C_2(q_2) / \delta q_2 = 0.$$

Putting these functions into shape to solve for q_1 and q_2, respectively, gives two reaction functions, one for each firm. The Cournot equilibrium solution is then got by solving the reaction functions simultaneously.

Let's make the problem more concrete by specifying a linear market demand function and a linear cost function for each firm. This illustration assumes that the firms have identical cost functions; but the same procedure also works if cost functions differ. Lower-cost firms get larger shares, a relationship worth recalling when we get to Chapters 7, 13, and 14.

Market price is determined by the sum of outputs produced by the first firm, q_1, and by the second firm, q_2:

$$P = 200 - q_1 - q_2.$$

For simplicity, assume that the total cost functions of both firms are identical:

$$C_1 = 10q_1; \text{ and}$$

$$C_2 = 10q_2.$$

For each firm, total revenue—TR—equals market price *times* the output it produces. Profit—R—equals total revenue minus total cost, C.

$$TR_1 = (200 - q_1 - q_2)q_1;$$

$$C_1 = 10q_1; \text{ and}$$

$$R_1 = (200 - q_1 - q_2)q_1 - 10q_1$$

$$= 200q_1 - q_1{}^2 - q_1q_2 - 10q_1$$

$$= 190q_1 - q_1{}^2 - q_1q_2.$$

$$\delta R_1/\delta q_1 = 190 - 2q_1 - q_2 = 0.$$

Similarly, for firm 2,

$$TR_2 = (200 - q_1 - q_2)q_2;$$

$$C_2 = 10q_2; \text{ and}$$

$$R_2 = 190q_2 - q_1q_2 - q_2{}^2.$$

$$\delta R_2/\delta q_2 = 190 - 2q_2 - q_1 = 0.$$

We now have two profit-maximizing equations, for $\delta R_1/\delta q_1 = 0$; and $\delta R_2/\delta q_2 = 0$:

For Firm 1,

$$-2q_1 - q_2 = -190. \text{ And,}$$

$$q_1 = (190 - q_2)/2 = 95 - 0.5q_2.$$

For Firm 2,

$$-q_1 - 2q_2 = -190 \text{ And,}$$

$$q_2 = (190 - q_1)/2 = 95 - 0.5q_1.$$

Each of these reaction functions shows how one seller reacts to any output decision the other may make. For equilibrium to be stable, the sellers' reactions must be compatible. To find such a point, we solve the two reaction functions simultaneously, graphically, or otherwise. This gives:

$$q_1 = 63.33$$

$$q_2 = 63.33,$$

which satisfy the first-order and second-order conditions for maximum profit. Figure 4-1 shows these two reaction functions, the intersection of which produces the equilibrium solution.

From the *market* demand function we obtain

$$P = 200 - 63.33 - 63.33 = 73.33.$$

Figure 4-2 illustrates the equilibrium solution for firm 1. In this case, the corresponding diagram for firm 2 would be identical. The market demand and cost functions need no further explanation. Firm 1's average revenue and marginal revenue functions are derived from its total revenue function, TR_1, evaluated at $q_2 = 63.33$:

$$TR_1 = 200 q_1 - q_1{}^2 - q_1q_2.$$

$$AR_1 = 200 - q_1 - q_2. \text{ At equilibrium, } q_2 = 63.33, \text{ and}$$

$$AR_1 = 136.67 - q_1.$$

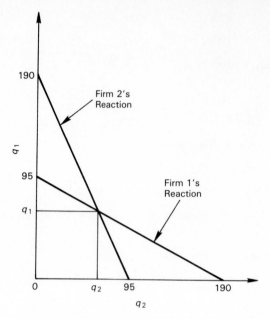

Figure **4-1** Cournot Duopoly Reaction Functions

$MR_1 = 200 - 2q_1 - q_2$. At equilibrium, $q_2 = 63.33$, and

$MR_1 = 136.67 - 2q_1$.

$MC_1 = 10$.

The relationship between market-demand and firm-demand elasticities is interesting. At this equilibrium, the elasticity of total market demand—the genus demand—is about $-.58$. But each firm faces at equilibrium a (species) demand with price elasticity of -1.16. When Cournot duopolists have identical costs, each faces a demand whose price elasticity is *twice* as great as that of the market demand. This relationship extends to cases of larger numbers of sellers, as we will see.

What does Cournot equilibrium look like for cases in which there are more than two sellers? Each behaves as before; but there are more of them. As before, assume the same market demand and cost functions. Suppose there are four sellers. We derive a system of 4 equations:

$$P = 200 - q_1 - q_2 - q_3 - q_4$$

$$C_1 = 10q_1$$

$$TR_1 = (200 - q_1 - q_2 - q_3 - q_4)q_1$$

$$= 200q_1 - q_1^2 - q_1q_2 - q_1q_3 - q_4q_1$$

$$R_1 = 200q_1 - q_1^2 - q_1q_2 - q_1q_3 - q_4q_1 - 10q_1$$

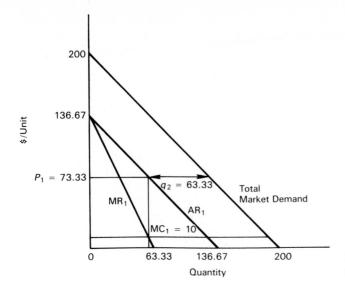

Figure 4-2 Demand and Costs for a Cournot Duopolist

$$= 190q_1 - q_1^2 - q_1q_2 - q_1q_3 - q_4q_1$$

$$\delta R_1/\delta q_1 = 190 - 2q_1 - q_2 - q_3 - q_4 = 0.$$

Equations for the other three sellers are derived in the same way, and we end up with:

$$-2q_1 - q_2 - q_3 - q_4 = -190$$

$$-q_1 - 2q_2 - q_3 - q_4 = -190$$

$$-q_1 - q_2 - 2q_3 - q_4 = -190$$

$$-q_1 - q_2 - q_3 - 2q_4 = -190.$$

Solving these simultaneous equations gives us $q_1 = 190/5 = 38$. Since all firms are alike, $Q = 4(38) = 152$.[10]

It should be clear by this point that there is nothing collusive in all this: these firms are not agreeing to do anything.

Although Cournot was a genius, his model is not foolproof and it is easy to get in trouble with it. For example, Cournot was not talking about *converting* an industry of two sellers into one of four: He was talking about alternative natural states. He *explained* the number of firms[11]; so far, this discussion has not. Too many economists and government employees have since assumed that they can somehow costlessly *choose* alternative states of the same world, an unacceptable proposition about which more will be said later.

Although, for reasons discussed later, it is a dangerous practice, many economists give high marks to industries in which price is equal to or close to the marginal cost of some or all sellers and give bad marks to industries in which price significantly exceeds the marginal cost of some or all sellers.

Cournot's analysis predicts that the relationship between price and marginal cost is related to the number of firms.[12] We showed that each of Cournot's firms contemplates the following relationship, where $\delta C_i / \delta q_i$ is marginal cost of the i-th firm:

$$R_i = Pq_i - C_i.$$
$$\delta R_i / \delta q_i = P + q_i(\delta P / \delta q_i) - (\delta C_i / \delta q_i) = 0.$$

In profit-maximizing equilibrium, MR = MC:

$$P + q_i(\delta P / \delta q_i) = \text{MC}.$$

Using N to denote the number of firms and Q to denote the total industry output,

$$q_i N = Q, \text{ and}$$

$$NP + Q(\delta P / \delta Q) = N(\text{MC}).$$

$$P + (Q/N)(\delta P / \delta Q) = \text{MC}.$$

$$P = \text{MC} - [(Q/N)(\delta P / \delta Q)].$$

The elasticity of total market demand, ϵ, is defined as $(\delta Q / \delta P)(P/Q)$, and is negative. Because

$$1/\epsilon = (\delta P / \delta Q)(Q/P)$$

$$(Q/N)\,\delta P / \delta Q = (1/N)(1/\epsilon)(P/1) = P/N\epsilon, \text{ and}$$

$$P = \text{MC} - (P/N\epsilon).$$

Since ϵ is negative, price falls closer to MC the larger the number of firms, or the more elastic is the total market demand at equilibrium, or both. The larger the number of firms, the closer price approaches marginal cost, whatever the elasticity of market demand. Similarly, whatever the number of firms, price approaches marginal cost as the elasticity of market demand grows. In Cournot, however, no *finite* demand elasticity, or finite number of firms, can make price *precisely* equal to marginal cost.

Although many have objected because Cournot's behavioral assumptions are unrealistic, his model yields unambiguous predictions that are testable in principle.[13] In addition, Cournot's analysis can handle larger numbers of firms without relying on other troubling assumptions. For example, we need not assume either that demand elasticities are literally infinite or that marginal cost is rising over the relevant range. As a result, Cournot's analysis can more comfortably explain various kinds of real-world price and nonprice competition, at the same time that it is compatible with outcomes close to those of pure competition.[14]

In Cournot, output and price are clearly related to the number of rivals. If changing the number of sellers does not change the firms' cost functions, market price declines continuously as the number of sellers increases, approaching marginal cost in the limit. And the net effect on price can, furthermore, be easily shown if increasing the number of sellers does raise the cost functions of each. The net effect on consumers depends upon whether the unfavorable cost effect outweighs the favorable numbers effect.

Furthermore, for a given number of Cournot oligopolists, price will more closely approximate marginal cost as the market demand elasticity is higher. Thus, for even one seller, price will tend toward marginal cost (i.e., toward the purely competitive solution) as demand elasticity tends toward infinity. This is consistent with monopoly theory in general and with common sense: a misallocation effect from even single-seller monopoly requires relatively poor total substitutability from other products. A monopoly of something for which demand elasticity is infinite has no monopoly power, and its price and output will be at competitive levels.

In general outline, these conclusions seem so reasonable that many economists would embrace them, especially if they were not attributed to old Cournot. It is not clear whether this is because many economists learned Cournot's conclusions and may remember them; or that many economists share Cournot's view of how the world actually operates.

Whereas many economists have adopted Cournot's general conclusions, most would probably deny their precision. For Cournot *is* precise. As Chamberlin's arithmetic explanation shows for linear market demand, single-firm monopoly produces one-half as much as a purely competitive industry; Cournot's duopoly output is two-thirds the competitive output, triopoly is three-fourths, and so on.[15] In short, going from monopoly to duopoly makes a big difference, whereas further increases in the number of sellers have progressively smaller and smaller effects. Reducing the number of sellers from, say, four to three would only lower output from 80 percent to 75 percent of the competitive level, *if* costs were not changed at all in the process.

Putting these results less precisely confirms how prevalent Cournot's vision has become: duopoly is very different from monopoly; other things equal, mergers are especially dangerous when sellers are very few and relatively innocuous when they are numerous; and practically competitive results can emerge even when the number of sellers is not really very large. Cournot's conclusions could be couched and conceivably even tested in terms of Herfindahl indexes of concentration; for that index has a numbers equivalent.[16] Five firms of equal size would yield a Herfindahl index value (calculated in the old style) equal to .20; equal-share duopoly, an index of .50.[17]

If Herfindahl concentration values were perfectly correlated with monopoly, equal values should yield the same outcomes even though the structures from which they were derived are different. If empirical tests show that Herfindahl indexes *are* inversely related to competitiveness, Cournot's predictions of the effects of an increased number of sellers would be confirmed in a general way. Chapter 5 returns to this comparative implication, in discussing modern oligopoly theories, especially Stigler's.

Bertrand and Edgeworth

After Cournot, Bertrand and Edgeworth developed various oligopoly models using different decision rules than Cournot's. In general, they show that if each duopolist assumes that his rival's present *price* will remain unchanged, it will pay each to undercut. Price therefore tends to fall to the atomistically competitive level.[18] In homogeneous-product versions of these theories, small changes in the number of sellers affect prices abruptly and a lot, rather than gradually. If we ignore the effects that different industry structures can have on costs and product varieties, increasing the number of sellers from one to two transforms the single-firm monopoly price into one equal to the atomistically competitive price. Further increases in the number of sellers, however, would have virtually no effect. Two firms provide all the competitiveness there is.[19]

Although the models so far discussed have been criticized for using simple and unrealistic assumptions, so do all tractable economic theories. What bothers critics most is that in these theories sellers seem to hold to incorrect assumptions about what their rivals will do even after experience shows they are wrong. This feature makes many economists uncomfortable, and they accept it grudgingly.

But it would be unwise to write off Cournot and Bertrand before finding better theories to substitute for them. And, uncomfortably or not, economists use such theories regularly, often without explicitly mentioning the features that make them uncomfortable or noting names of the old economists whose theories they really are. For one thing, there continues to be intelligent methodological debate about the relevancy of realistic assumptions. According to the positivists' view, predictive or explanatory power is the real test of a theory, and the realism of assumptions is irrelevant. On that view, the question is whether actual behavior refutes or confirms the theory. For example, do sellers act as though they were using Cournot decision rules? That is an empirical question.[20] Until there has been more empirical testing, it may be wise to reserve judgment.

Furthermore, as we will see, assumptions that look absurd when price and output information are good may not seem so strange when information is poor.

Dominant-Firm Theories

This section discusses two theories about the dominant firm: Forchheimer's, and von Stackelberg's.[21] Though dominant firm is the misleading name usually associated with a famous model attributed to Karl Forchheimer (1908), Stackelberg's theories include a dominant firm that is even more dominant.[22] Stackelberg's leader-follower theory, which is usually discussed as an oligopoly theory pure and simple, is a dominant-firm theory by any standard.

For easy direct comparison with Cournot's results, we discuss Stackelberg first. Though discussed here as a duopoly theory, Stackelberg's model is more flexible than other dominant-firm theories: it works with any number of fringe firms, and can cope with a wide variety of cost conditions.

Although those who use Stackelberg's model do not usually explain what determines which firm is leader, one could, for example, assume that the dominant or leader firm has a cost advantage. To permit direct comparisons with the Cournot examples given earlier, assume that leader and follower have equal costs. Cost differences are easy to incorporate.

Stackelberg's Leader-Follower Theory.   Assume that two firms with identical costs sell a homogeneous product. One firm is the leader; the other follows. To make comparisons easier, use the same cost and market demand functions used earlier for Cournot.

In Cournot duopoly, the conjectural variation terms are zero for both firms: each takes the other's output as given, a constant. In Stackelberg, the *follower* acts exactly like a Cournot duopolist. That the *leader* firm does not is an example of the asymmetric behavior common to dominant-firm theories.

As before, market price is a function of the sum of output produced by the leader—q_L—and the follower—q_F:

$$P = 200 - q_L - q_F.$$

For simplicity, assume that leader and follower have identical total cost functions:

$$C_L = 10q_L$$

$$C_F = 10q_F.$$

TR, the total revenue of each firm, equals market price *times* the output it produces. Profit, R, equals TR $-$ C. For the follower,

$$TR_F = (200 - q_L - q_F)q_F;$$

$$C_F = 10q_F; \text{ and}$$

$$R_F = 190q_F - q_L q_F - q_F^2.$$

$$\delta R_F/\delta q_F = 190 - 2q_F - q_L = 0, \text{ and}$$

$$2q_F = 190 - q_L$$

$$q_F = (190 - q_L)/2 = 95 - 0.5q_L.$$

This last equation is the follower's reaction function. It gives the quantity that maximizes the follower's profit *for any output that the leader chooses to produce*. It is precisely the same kind of function we saw *both* Cournot duopolists using. Here, however, the leader's outlook is different. It assumes, correctly, that the follower always takes the leader's output to be a constant, therefore assuming that $\delta q_L/\delta q_F = 0$. The leader knows that is how the follower will behave and takes it into account. Since by choosing its own output the leader can (indirectly) determine what output the follower will produce, the leader chooses so as to maximize its own profit. To do so, the leader enters the follower's reaction function into its own profit function, substituting it for the q_F term that appears there.

Before substitution, the leader's profit function is

$$R_L = (200 - q_L - q_F)q_L - 10q_L$$

$$= 190q_L - q_L^2 - q_L q_F.$$

Substitute the follower's reaction function for q_F:

$$R_L = 190q_L - q_L{}^2 - q_L(95 - 0.5q_L)$$

$$R_L = 190q_L - q_L{}^2 - 95q_L + 0.5q_L{}^2$$

$$= 95q_L - 0.5q_L{}^2.$$

This substitution makes the leader's profit solely a function of its own output, because by choosing its own output the leader firm leads the follower to choose the output that maximizes the leader's profit.

$$\delta R_L/\delta q_L = 95 - q_L = 0$$

$$q_L = 95.$$

When the leader produces at a rate of 95 per period, the follower maximizes its own profit by producing

$$q_F = 95 - 0.5q_L = 95 - 47.5 = 47.5.$$

$$Q = q_L + q_F = 95 + 47.5 = 142.50.$$

$$P = 200 - q_L - q_F = 200 - 142.50 = 57.5.$$

Table 4-1 compares results for the Cournot and the Stackelberg solutions, assuming that cost and market demand conditions are identical in both cases. Some of these results may seem a little odd. First, giving a little more knowledge to one duopolist than to the other seems to benefit consumers. With the same cost and market demand functions, price is lower in the Stackelberg solution than in Cournot duopoly. Many seem to believe that only naive oligopoly behavior produces results that differ from "the monopoly solution," and that the more clearly oligopolists recognize that they *are* interdependent, the more monopolistic the results will be. That is not what the table shows. Indeed, recent work suggests that making conjectural variations consistent does not in general make for a less competitive outcome. As one recent article puts it,

> A conjectural variation is consistent if it is equivalent to the optimal response of other firms at the equilibrium defined by that conjecture. When the number of firms is fixed, we find that competitive behavior is consistent when marginal costs are constant, but that when marginal

TABLE 4–1   Comparison of Cournot and Stackelberg solutions

	Cournot Solution	Stackelberg: Firm 1 Is Leader
Output, firm 1	63.33	95.00
Output, firm 2	63.33	47.50
Total Output	126.67	142.50
Price	73.33	57.50
Profit, firm 1	4,011.11	4,512.50
Profit, firm 2	4,011.11	2,256.25

costs are rising, the consistent conjectural variation will be between competitive and Cournot behavior. Finally, if we allow free entry and redefine consistency to account for such, then only competitive behavior will be consistent.[23]

Second, although the leader firm is better off, total profits are lower in the Stackelberg model. The follower is much worse off than a Cournot oligopolist, which suggests that no one would want to play the follower role unless compelled or compensated to take it. Because total industry profits are lower in this case, however, it is not clear how the leader could compensate the follower, and there is nothing in this example—cost differences, for example—that explains why the follower got stuck with that role. Stackelberg also showed that if *both* firms try to be leader, things degenerate into warfare and both are worse off yet.

Forchheimer's Dominant-Firm Model. According to Cohen and Cyert, clear expositors of this theory, "One way of avoiding an assumption about the values of the conjectural variation terms is to create a model in which one of the firms is clearly so *powerful* that it is the leader. Such is the case in the dominant-firm model."[24]

This is a strange way to put it. In what sense is the dominant firm "so powerful?" Whenever it has no cost advantage, the dominant firm is so powerful that it earns a lower rate of return than the less powerful fringe firms, whose facilities enjoy a higher rate of utilization. Some power! An investor would be better off investing in fringe firms than in the allegedly more powerful dominant firm.

Cohen and Cyert are misleading about something else. The dominant-firm model does *not* dispense with conjectural variation terms; no well-specified theory can. It merely makes a different, and special, assumption about them.

One nice thing about Cournot and Stackelberg is that they work equally well with a wide variety of cost functions. That is not true of Forchheimer's dominant-firm theory. Constant short- or long-run average and marginal cost functions, for example, cause trouble. With constant costs, the so-called fringe firms take everything whenever their costs are equal to, let alone lower than, those of the so-called dominant firm.[25]

Assume that, for the industry in question, one type of industrial plant, with a U-shaped average-cost curve, achieves a lower average cost than any smaller plant can achieve; but that there are neither cost savings nor penalties if a firm operates one, few, or many such plants at the same rate per plant. Assume, further, that all firms operate identical plants. The fundamental difference between the dominant firm and each fringe firm, we assume, is that the dominant firm has several plants, while each of the many fringe firms has only one. The (assumed) result is that, over the relevant output ranges, the dominant firm's aggregate (multiplant) marginal cost function is therefore flatter than that of each fringe firm. Unless the fringe comprises a larger total number of plants than the dominant firm has, the dominant firm's marginal cost will be flatter than the supply function for all the fringe firms taken together. This is the same phenomenon observed in comparing the short-run supply functions of competitive industries that have different numbers of firms.

Costs are part of the story. Behavior and demand are the rest. Here, as in other models, specifying behavior comes to the same thing as *not* "avoiding an assumption about . . . the conjectural variation terms," to twist Cohen and Cyert. Like Stackelberg, the dominant-firm model assumes asymmetric behavior. The fringe firms do not collude or merge. Each is relatively small and assumes that market price is a given datum. Each maximizes profit by choosing an output for which $P = MC$. Each fringe firm acts like an atomistic competitor. Taken together, the fringe has a supply function, just as an atomistic industry does. Total output of all the fringe firms taken together brings their supply price and the market price to equality.

But what about the dominant firm? It behaves differently. It assumes, correctly, that the total fringe supply quantity is a unique function of market price: they are price-takers, each and all. In effect, the fringe reaction function is its supply function, which is a function of market price. In turn, because market price is also a function of how much the dominant firm chooses to produce, the quantity supplied by the fringe depends upon how much the dominant firm sells. The dominant firm, by contrast, is a price-searcher. It is assumed to take as its own demand any part of the total market demand that the fringe does not satisfy. If price were set so high that the fringe supply equaled the total market demand quantity, the dominant firm would have nothing to call its own—except for its own disused plants. If price were set low enough, the fringe would produce nothing and the dominant firm would face a large, but unremunerative, demand.

In this model, the dominant firm seeks the output and market price that maximize its profits, given the presence and behavior of the fringe and the behavior assumed for the dominant firm itself.

Take a simple, specific example. Designate dominant firm variables with subscript D and those of the total fringe with subscript F. Call the supply price (marginal cost) of the fringe sP_F:

$$sP_F = MC_F = 18 + 6q_F.$$

We convert this to a reaction function for the fringe by noting that

$$6q_F = sP_F - 18,$$

from which we get

$$q_F = (sP_F - 18) / 6 = (sP_F / 6) - 3.$$

This is the fringe's reaction function: it is the rule by which the dominant firm predicts how the fringe will behave.

Turn, now, to the dominant firm itself. Assume that the total market demand function is $P = 200 - Q$, where Q is the total output sold by both the dominant firm *and* the fringe. That is, everyone sells the same good, and market price is determined by the total quantity produced by the fringe and the dominant firm.

The dominant firm derives its own (residual) demand function by subtracting from total quantity demanded the amount that the fringe will offer at each price.

According to the fringe reaction function, $q_F = P/6 - 3$. The total market demand is $Q = 200 - P$. Therefore, the demand function faced by the dominant firm becomes:

$$q_D = Q - q_F = (200 - P) - P/6 + 3.$$

$$q_D = 203 - 7/6 \, P.$$

Partly because it is convenient to write MC_D as a function of q_D rather than P_D, we will take the inverse of this residual demand, expressing P_D as a function of q_D. We can then solve for the dominant firm's profit-maximizing quantity.

$$7/6 \, P_D = 203 - q_D.$$

$$P_D = (203 - q_D) / (7 / 6) = (203 - q_D)(6 / 7).$$

Total revenue, TR, equals $P_D(q_D)$:

$$TR_D = (203q_D - q_D{}^2) \, (6 / 7)$$

$$MR_D = \delta R_D / \delta q_D = (6 / 7)(203 - 2q_D).$$

We assume that $MC_D = 18 + 2q_D$. Profit maximization requires that

$$MR_D = MC_D:$$

$$(6/7) \, (203 - 2q_D) = 18 + 2q_D$$

$$174 - 1.714286q_D = 18 + 2q_D$$

$$3.714286q_D = 156$$

$$q_D = 42$$

$$P = 138$$

$$q_F = P/6 - 3 = 20$$

$$q_F + q_D = 62$$

$$P = 200 - Q$$

$$= 200 - 62 = 138.$$

Figure 4-3 graphs this solution. Since q_F, derived above, shows how much the fringe firms will sell at each price, q_F *is* their supply function, labeled s_F. At each price, the quantity given by s_F is deducted from the total market demand to give the dominant firm's residual demand function. Quasi-rent is the amount by which total revenue exceeds total *variable* costs. So long as quasi-rents exceed zero, a firm is better off to stay in business. Note that the quasi-rents, quasi-rents per unit of output, total profits, and return on invested capital (ROI) can be computed for the fringe and dominant firm.[26] Assume that the (daily) costs per plant, (for rates measured in thousand pounds daily) are:

$$TC = 30X^2 + 18X + 18$$

$$AC = 30X + 18 + 18 / X$$

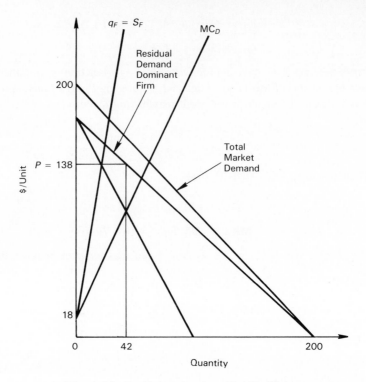

Figure 4-3 Forchheimer Dominant-Firm Equilibrium

$$MC = 60X + 18$$

$$FC = 18.[27]$$

Table 4-2 shows AC and MC for such a plant, and Figure 4-4 graphs them. The (linear) MC of each plant has a minimum value of $18 per thousand pounds and rises at the rate $60 per thousand pounds (or $6 per 100 pounds).

Assume that there are no (net) economies of multiplant operation. The MC function for multiple plants has the same $-intercept, but has a smaller slope: X/N, per thousand pounds of daily output. For 10 plants, this gives an aggregate marginal cost function of:

$$MC_{10} = 6X + 18.$$

At a total output rate of 20 thousand pounds per day, 10 plants have a MC of $138 per thousand daily pounds. For 30 plants

$$MC_{30} = 2X + 18.$$

At a total output rate of 20 thousand pounds per day, a thirty-plant dominant firm has MC = $58 per thousand pounds. And, at 42 thousand pounds per day, MC = $102 per thousand pounds.

Now, in the spirit of the graph, suppose that the dominant firm (with 30 plants) sets

TABLE 4–2 Plant costs: TC $= 30X^2 + 18X + 18$

Output (000's Pounds per Day)	AC ($ Per 000 Pounds)	MC ($ Per 000 Pounds)
0.0	Undefined	18
0.1	201.00	24
0.2	142.20	30
0.3	87.00	36
0.4	75.00	42
0.5	69.00	48
0.6	66.00	54
0.7	64.71	60
0.7[a]	64.48	64[b]
0.8	64.50	66
0.9	65.00	72
1.0	66.00	78
1.1	67.36	84
1.2	69.00	90
1.3	70.85	96
1.4	72.86	102
1.5	75.00	108
1.6	77.25	114
1.7	79.59	120
1.8	82.00	126
1.9	84.47	132
2.0	87.00	138

[a]0.774596669.
[b]64.48.

price at $138 per thousand pounds. It produces 42 thousand pounds per day. Each of 30 plants produces 1.4 thousand pounds per day, and each plant has the following daily operating results:

$$TC = 30X^2 + 18X + 18$$

$$= \$102/\text{day}.$$

$$AC = \$72.86 \text{ per thousand pounds.}$$

$$TR = (1.4)(138) = \$193.20/\text{day}$$

Daily $R = \$91.20$, or—say—91.20/180 = 51 percent ROI.[28] And average profit, $R/X = \$65.14$ per thousand pounds.

Each of the 10 fringe plants faces the same cost function as each plant owned by the dominant firm, but produces at a higher rate (and higher value MC). Each produces 2 thousand pounds a day. For each fringe plant, daily operating results look like this:

$$TC = 30X^2 + 18X + 18 = (30) 4 + 36 + 18$$

$$= \$174 \text{ per day.}$$

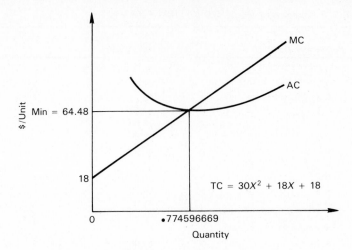

Figure 4-4 Plant Cost Curves: Dominant-Firm Model

AC = 174 / 2 = \$87 per thousand pounds.

TR = (2)(138) = \$276 per day.

R = 276 − 174 = \$102 per day, or \$51 per thousand pounds, which is a lower R *per pound* than the dominant firm earns. But each fringe plant produces 2 thousand rather than 1.4 thousand pounds.

Each fringe plant thus earns 102/180 = 57 percent ROI. The dominant firm earns 51 percent. A one-dollar investment in fringe firms would have earned 12 percent higher returns—assuming that someone else had formed a dominant firm in the first place.

What about quasi-rents? For each plant,

$$TC = 30X^2 + 18X + 18$$

$$ATC = 30X + 18 + 18/X$$

$$TVC = 30X^2 + 18X$$

$$AVC = 30X + 18.$$

Producing at a rate of 2,000 pounds, each fringe firm has total daily revenues of \$276, and TVC of \$156. Daily quasi-rents are \$120.

Each of the dominant firm's plants has total daily revenue of \$193.20 and daily TVC of \$84. Daily quasi-rents per plant are \$109.20. Fringe plants earn 10 percent higher quasi-rents. Measured either way, the dominant firm does worse.

Why, then, would anyone want to be a (Forchheimer-type) dominant firm? Perhaps the dominant firm assumes no one else will play that role. If it shoulders the burden, it will profit, even though, relative to capacity, the fringe will profit even more. What happens to the dominant firm once additional entrants have made it even less dominant can be very sad. For, so long as it holds price above average costs of entrants they will keep piling in, earning positive profits even when the dominant firm earns competitive-level ''profits''—or less.

It is an interesting and difficult problem to show how many plants the dominant firm would buy, for any number of fringe plants assumed. The answer depends upon how much it has to pay for the plants, of course, and that figure tends to rise once sellers figure out what is going on. Another possibility is to buy the plants very quickly, using options or cash. Yet another, is simply to form a new company and pay for it with shares in the dominant firm. Some of these routes might reduce the problem of firms holding out to get top dollar for their plants.

Some suggestions are in order. Note that there are at least two ways of looking at the preceding dominant firm example. First, perhaps a firm that completely monopolized a 30-plant industry unexpectedly finds itself confronted by ten single-plant entrants.[29] Or second, perhaps a firm merged 30 out of 40 plants to form a dominant firm. Three-fourths of the total industry capacity is close to the shares that some leading firms actually reached by merger between 1895 and 1904. Looking at the example in this way, however, does raise several questions. If the total number of plants was expected to remain at 40, why did the dominant firm content itself with only 30 plants rather than merging them all? Or, at least, why not merge a few more, since that would, arguably, reduce average and flatten marginal cost and increase its power to set price. Would it?

Other Conjectural Variation Theories. Various economists attempted to broaden the Cournot-Bertrand models by including different kinds of conjectures about rivals' responses. Bowley is an example.[30] Unlike what happens in the Cournot model, these variations make each seller aware that his rivals will not remain inert, but will react. For each seller, such theories specify his (often incorrect) appraisal of just how the others will react. In duopoly, for example, the total (expected) output change resulting from a change in one seller's output is the sum of his own output change and the (expected) change in the rival's output that will occur in response to his own moves. These (expected) induced effects might just neatly offset, reinforce, or more than offset his own direct effect, with different consequences.

For two reasons, these more complicated models have impressed some economists. First, when each seller is an important part of the market for relatively close substitutes—i.e., when sellers are few—it seems plausible for each to assume that rivals will react. In that respect, conjectural variation theories look more realistic. Second, because various symmetric and asymmetric rival reactions can be assumed, such theories offer a wide variety of possible outcomes. They include various competitive outcomes (one being warfare); essentially complete monopoly solutions; and indeterminacies of different sorts.

Unfortunately, the attractiveness of more complex models may be superficial gloss. On a logical level some are open to the same criticism that has been so lavishly heaped on Cournot. Why would sellers retain and act on even the most complex assumption about rival reactions once it is proved incorrect? And, on a practical or policy level, these theories are neither easily testable nor very useful. In the first place, what each version predicts will happen depends upon the particular subjective expectation that is modeled. It is impossible to reject such a prediction without both quantifying undiscoverable private conjectures *and* proving that the results thereby predicted do not actually occur.[31] Second, since everything depends upon what sellers believe their rivals will do, by varying such beliefs, models of this kind can be made to generate practically any outcome. This produces what some call a *rich* theory. In the hard sciences, that indicates impoverishment. The richness results because we don't really know how things work.

Even if costs do not differ among sellers, prices in such models can be lower than under either pure competition or Cournot oligopoly; higher than Cournot predicts, but less than the simple monopoly level; precisely the same as under competition, simple monopoly, or Cournot oligopoly; may be indeterminate; and, perhaps, may even be higher than the simple monopoly level. Taken as a whole, these theories furnish no clear guide for appraising different industrial structures or reforming them. The effects of dissolution or mergers would depend upon the kinds of conjectures that these changes create or suppress, and upon interactions among them. Even if costs were not affected, dissolution of large firms might raise, lower, or not affect prices. The same is true of mergers.

The theories do not clearly tell us what changing the *number* of sellers will do. Stackelberg's bewildering array of possibilities emerged even for duopoly, and he apparently made only unsystematic and gratuitous assertions about three or more sellers.[32] According to Fellner, however, "there is a presumption that the addition of more firms increases the likelihood of Stackelberg disequilibrium." "Disequilibrium" in this sense is a euphemism for indeterminacy at best, or for the combative pursuit of incompatible objectives that leads to stalemate or warfare of undetermined character and duration. Since Stackelberg's theory predicts a high probability of disequilibrium even under duopoly, the outlook with more sellers is clearly unclear.

Finally, even if the theories predicted unambiguously, there are other crucial problems in adapting them to real-world policy making. For example, they assume that there is no entry, without explaining why; and they do not investigate the relationship between costs and different structures of industry.

Rightly or wrongly, believers in theories that predict indeterminate results need not adopt a hands-off policy position. Stackelberg, for example, thought the probability of duopoly impasse was high enough, and its results so distressing, as to justify comprehensive state controls. On the other hand, anybody who believes in Stackelberg, admires rivalry, and thinks that the social advantages of rivalry increase the more closely chaos is approached, might argue that any increase in the number of sellers is likely to be a good thing.

SUMMARY

This chapter presents and analyzes Cournot's classical oligopoly model in detail and briefly outlines models by Bertrand, Edgeworth, and Bowley. It also presents the dominant-firm models of Forchheimer and von Stackelberg.

Such models predict that firms with lower costs will achieve larger market shares, a hypothesis that will surprise no one in business. It is important to remember this hypothesis when we come to analyze industry performance, in Chapters 13 to 16.

Differences in the number of firms, which none of the models seriously attempts to explain, have different effects in different models. In Cournot, results with larger numbers of firms rapidly approach competitive results, though price always exceeds marginal cost with any finite number of firms. That general tendency also appears in the orderly versions of von Stackelberg, and in Forchheimer, though warfare and ruin occur in Stackelberg's world if two or more firms each try to be leader.

In all these models, one firm gives monopoly results, but in both Bertrand and Edgeworth, two firms are enough to produce (approximately) purely competitive results.

QUESTIONS

1. Most economists have worked on the oligopoly problem. Their success in solving it may seem modest. Oligopoly is not easy to figure out, or economists are not very smart, or both.

   What makes oligopoly a difficult problem even in theory? Hint: put Professor Hurwicz's statement into your own words.

2. In the theories discussed in this chapter, what determines the number of firms? What do the theories say about the entry of new firms? What difference does their treatment of entry make?

3. The prices and outputs resulting in all these theories differ from those that single-firm monopoly would produce. Take Cournot, for example. Given identical firms and linear demand and cost functions, there is a simple arithmetic relationship between the number of firms and their total output measured as a fraction of purely competitive output, at which price is literally equal to marginal cost. What is that relationship?

   Suppose the total market demand function is

   $$P = 200 - Q,$$

   where Q is total industry output and P is market price. Suppose each firm has a constant marginal cost, MC $= 10$. At $P = $ MC, output rate would be 190 and consumer surplus would be $[(190)(190)] / 2 = 18,050$. What would P, Q, and consumer surplus be with six Cournot-type firms? With one?

4. How do the profits of the dominant firm and fringe firms compare? What causes this?

5. Is it reasonable to suppose that follower firms act as von Stackelberg assumes? Discuss.

6. Consider the short-run Forchheimer equilibrium solution derived in this chapter. Market price was 138. Suppose you have money to invest and can quickly build a plant exactly like those the fringe and dominant firms have. What would you do? What are other investors likely to do?

   At what values of daily fixed costs and total capital investment would the dominant firm in the text example just break even? How about a fringe firm?

NOTES

1. Each industry is weighted by its *value added*, which is roughly equal to industry sales minus materials and energy. Chapter 11 explains and critically evaluates concentration measures in detail.

2. Eugene Singer, "The Concept of Relative Concentration in Antitrust Law," *American Bar Association Journal*, 52, no. 3 (March 1966), pp. 246–50. For example, he says, the choice in *Continental Can* (1964) "was not between unconcentrated or concentrated market structures, nor oligopoly or pure competition, but between two highly concentrated market structures." Ibid., p. 249. See *U.S.* v. *Continental Can Co. et al.*, 378 U.S. 441 (1964).

3. A. A. Cournot, *Researches into the Mathematical Principles of the Theory of Wealth* (1838), trans. Nathaniel T. Bacon (New York: Augustus M. Kelley, 1960), Ch. 7.

4. J. F. Nash, "Non-Cooperative Games," *Annals of Mathematics*, 64 (September 1951), pp. 286–95. Cournot equilibrium satisfies Nash's requirements. It *is* a "Nash-point equilibrium."

5. William Fellner, *Competition Among the Few* (New York: Alfred A. Knopf, Inc., 1949), p. 69; Josef Hadar, "Stability of Oligopoly with Product Differentiation," *The Review of Economic Studies*, 33 (January 1966), pp. 57–60; F. T. Dolbear, and others, "Collusion in Oligopoly: An Experiment on the Effect of Numbers and Information," *Quarterly Journal of Economics*, 82 (May 1968), pp. 240–59.

6. Leonid Hurwicz, "The Theory of Economic Behavior," *American Economic Review*, 35 (1945), pp. 909–25; reprinted in G. J. Stigler and K. E. Boulding, *Readings in Price Theory* (Homewood, Ill.: Richard D. Irwin, Inc., 1952), pp. 505–26.

7. Michael Waterson, *Economic Theory of the Industry* (New York: Cambridge University Press, 1984), p. 32.

8. "Critics have pointed out the naivety of this sequential process in which each firm's underlying assumptions are continually falsified. More recently, though, attention has focused on the equilibrium independent of the path." Waterson, *Economic Theory of the Industry*, p. 22.

9. This is basically how Nash equilibrium is defined.

10. Each of 8 firms would produce 21.1111, for a total quantity of 168.8888. If it were possible to get perfect competition with a finite number of firms, the $P = MC$ solution would give a total industry output of 190. And $152/190 = 4/5 = .8$. This confirms the assertion that Cournot equilibrium output is $N/(N + 1)$ times the total competitive Q.

11. In Cournot's basic formulation, there can be only one firm per artesian well, and costs are zero.

12. What follows is derived from George J. Stigler, "Perfect Competition, Historically Contemplated," *Journal of Political Economy* 65 (February 1957), reprinted in Stigler, *Essays in the History of Economics* (Chicago: University of Chicago Press, 1965) p. 243.

13. Making conjectural variations more realistic or consistent does not necessarily produce more monopolistic effects. See Martin K. Perry, "Oligopoly and Consistent Conjectural Variations," *Bell Journal of Economics and Management Science*, 13 (Spring 1982), pp. 197–205.

14. It might also cure some of the problems that Telser, Sharkey, and Bittlingmayer raise. So might E. H. Chamberlin's large-group Monopolistic Competition model. Edward H.

Chamberlin, *The Theory of Monopolistic Competition*, 5th ed. (Cambridge, Mass.: Harvard University Press, 1946), especially Chapter V. However useful it may be, Chamberlin's "tangency solution" is one of the most famous pictures (and notions) in microeconomics.

See G. C. Archibald, " 'Large' and 'Small' Numbers in the Theory of the Firm," *The Manchester School of Economics and Social Studies* (1959), pp. 104–9; reprinted, with a useful addendum, in Yale Brozen, ed., *The Competitive Economy* (Morristown, N.J.: General Learning Press, 1975), pp. 48–52.

Also see Chapters 3, 7, and 19 of this book.

15. Chamberlin, *Monopolistic Competition* (1946), pp. 32–34.

16. Chapter 11 discusses such indexes in detail. Originally, the (full) Herfindahl index was computed by summing the squares of individual firms' market share expressed as decimal fractions. That is, a 15 percent share became .15, which was squared and summed with the others. Values of that index could range from 0 to 1. This is the version used here. The same index value could emerge for an industry with a very few large firms and a lot of very small ones, and from an industry of a smaller total number of identical intermediate-sized firms. The equal-sized number equivalent is the reciprocal of the Herfindahl value: $.2 = 1/5$, or the value for an industry of five equal-sized firms. Plotted against its number equivalents, the Herfindahl index falls very rapidly as we move from pure monopoly to duopoly, then at a decreasing rate, since the product of index and number equivalents is always 1.

More recently, the Federal Trade Commission and others altered the method of computation, presumably to spread out the index, like the band spread on a short-wave radio. In this new scheme, a 15 percent share becomes 15, which is squared and summed with the others. Calculated this way, the index can have values ranging from 0 to 10,000.

17. The new-style values for those same structures are 2,000 and 5,000. See Chapter 11.

18. Modern summaries of the Bertrand and Edgeworth models include William S. Vickrey, *Microstatics* (New York: Harcourt Brace Jovanovich, 1964); Chamberlin, *Monopolistic Competition*; Cliff Lloyd, *Microeconomic Analysis* (Homewood, Ill.: Richard D. Irwin, Inc., 1967), pp. 211–15; George J. Stigler, *Essays in the History of Economics* (Chicago: University of Chicago Press, 1965), p. 248; Stigler, "Perfect Competition Historically Contemplated," pp. 1–17; and Fellner, *Competition Among the Few*, pp. 77–91. Fellner also discusses some implications of introducing product differentiation into the Bertrand framework. Ibid., pp. 87–90.

19. Compare Chamberlin, *Monopolistic Competition*, pp. 36–37.

20. Baumol, for one, claims to find some favorable evidence from his own consulting experience. William J. Baumol, *Business Behavior, Value and Growth* (New York: Harcourt Brace Jovanovich, 1959), p. 27.

21. Stackelberg's book was published in German: Heinrich von Stackelberg, *Marktform und Gleichgewicht* (1934). The discussion that follows relies on secondary sources, in English: Fellner, *Competition Among the Few*; Vickrey, *Microstatics*; Kalman J. Cohen, and Richard M. Cyert, *Theory of the Firm: Resource Allocation in a Market Economy* (Englewood Cliffs, N.J.: Prentice-Hall, Inc., 1965), pp. 236–39.

22. F. M. Scherer, *Industrial Market Structure and Economic Performance*, 2nd ed. (Chicago: Rand McNally College Publishing Company, 1980), p. 233.

23. Martin K. Perry, "Oligopoly and Consistent Conjectural Variations," *Bell Journal of Economics and Management Science*, 13 (Spring 1982), pp. 197–205, at p. 197.

24. Cohen and others, *Theory of the Firm*, 2nd ed., p. 245. Italics not in the original.

25. But the model will work, mechanically, if we assume that the fringe firms, individually and collectively, have an upward-sloping supply function. Given that, we could if we want assume that only the dominant firm has an (unexplained) constant AC = MC function, or a constant MC function.

26. Needless complications can be avoided by assuming that each plant faces a total cost function such as $TC = AX^2 + BX + C$. See R. G. D. Allen, *Mathematical Analysis for Economists* (London: Macmillan and Co., Limited, 1947), pp. 119, 120, 156. This cost function avoids a range of downward-sloping MC, and kinks and flat spots in a multiplant aggregate marginal cost function. For the messy alternative, see Don Patinkin "Multiple Plant Firms, Cartels, and Imperfect Competition," *Quarterly Journal of Economics*, 61 (February 1947), pp. 173–205.

27. At \$18/day, fixed costs are \$6570 per year per plant, with capital valued, say, at \$65,700 per plant.

28. With daily value of investment put at \$180: daily fixed cost = \$18. At 10 percent, capital = \$180 per day.

29. "Unexpectedly," since if it had known what was going to happen it might have altered its scale of operations.

30. A. L. Bowley, *The Mathematical Groundwork of Economics* (New York: Augustus Kelley, 1924).

31. The problem is comparable to testing the kinked demand curve hypothesis. Lloyd, *Microeconomic Analysis*, pp. 216–17.

32. Fellner, *Competition Among the Few*, pp. 102–3, and 115, note 19.

<table>
<tr><td>

5

</td><td>

MODERN
OLIGOPOLY MODELS

</td></tr>
</table>

INTRODUCTION

The next six sections of this chapter discuss additional theories of oligopoly, some of which are more recent than, and all of which differ markedly in spirit from, those covered in the preceding chapter. The next section deals with theories of E. H. Chamberlin, which Edward Mason said had influenced industrial organization economics at Harvard from the start[1]; and with theories later propounded by William Fellner. Some versions of these theories assert that oligopoly and collusion differ little, if at all. After this comes a summary of Stigler's theory of oligopoly, in which imperfect information makes collusion much less effective, and therefore much less likely, as the number of firms rises above one. The following section discusses something that most oligopoly theories leave out: actual and potential entry. This section includes theories by Demsetz, Day, and Baumol, among others. The next two sections discuss the theory of games and what could be called games about theories—the stuffier professional names for which are experimental economics, and economic simulation.

CHAMBERLIN AND FELLNER

The oligopoly and dominant-firm theories discussed in Chapter 4 suggest that even as few as two competitors do not act like a single-firm monopoly. In the 1930s, however, theories asserting that oligopoly and monopoly are virtually identical became popular. By the 1960s they had become part of the conventional wisdom, although some thought them wrong.[2] These theories began to lose ground around 1970; but they are still popular.

Such theories seem to have grown out of a proposition that sounds plausible enough: sellers with large market shares know that what they do affects what rivals do, and vice versa. From this proposition, it may have seemed natural to infer that oligopolists could then, somehow, achieve monopoly results merely by recognizing how interdependent they are. Two popular sources of these kinds of doctrines were works by Chamberlin and Fellner.[3]

Chamberlin

Chamberlin offered two or more rather vague theories about how the number of firms affects industrial performance. The first assumes perfect knowledge. Given perfect knowledge, and that each seller is big enough to affect the market significantly, "If sellers have regard to their *total* influence upon price, the price will be the monopoly one."[4] And, "If the sellers are three or more, the results are the same, so long as each of them looks to his ultimate interest. There is no gradual descent to a purely competitive price with increase in numbers, as in Cournot's solution. The break comes when the individual's influence upon the price becomes so small that he neglects it."[5]

Anyone who thinks this theory is relevant to real-world policy should not oppose mergers in industries that are already concentrated or propose industrial deconcentration that falls short of atomization. For if the number of firms is relatively small, further reductions (or increases) would not appear to matter.

Chamberlin treats uncertainty and time lags separately. His general conclusion is that uncertainty makes the outcomes indeterminate: price may be at the monopoly level, competitive, or somewhere in between. At only one point does the number of firms seem to have anything to do with how things turn out, and even there Chamberlin is vague:

> If numbers are fairly small, any one seller can be *certain* that his incursions upon the others by a price cut will be large enough to cause them to follow suit; and therefore no one will cut. If they are very large, he can be certain that his incursions will be such a negligible factor to each other seller that no one will "follow suit" (i.e., cut *because* he did); and therefore everyone will cut. But in between there is a range of doubt. . . . Between these limits the result is unpredictable.[6]

That is not very helpful, because "few" and "many" are undefined; or, at best, are defined in terms of attitude rather than arithmetic; and because real policy questions are usually about what *small changes* in the number of firms will do. In short, if small changes in the number of firms leave the number still "small," it apparently makes no difference. If we take Chamberlin literally, changes in number do not matter unless, for example, "fewness" were changed into the undefined intermediate number case in which anything may happen.

What does all of this imply for merger and dissolution policy? According to Chamberlin, in a world of perfect knowledge only extreme atomism will suffice to produce competitive results. Otherwise, the monopoly solution will emerge; and there seems to be no real room for improvement through antimerger or dissolution policy. In an uncertain world, however, results may lie at the monopoly or competition poles, or anywhere in between. This revelation, too, affords little support for dissolution or merger policy: Results from fewness may be very good or even perfect without any policy; and, bad or good, it is not clear that antitrust policy will have any effect, let alone whether it is likely to be desirable. For somewhat obscure reasons, Chamberlin does assert that—even under uncertainty—*extremes* of concentration will tend to produce some sort of monopolistic results, while extreme atomism will tend to the competitive solution. But between the extremes, for the usual kinds of cases, anything can happen and small changes in concentration do not matter.

Chamberlin's doctrines therefore furnish little or no policy guidance. This is particularly strange, since much academic and judicial support for deconcentration and anti-merger policy comes from Chamberlin's theory that, with perfect information, fewness is practically equivalent to monopoly. All in all, Chamberlin contributes surprisingly little to policy making with respect to industrial concentration. This may reflect his emphasis on other market structures than oligopoly. In particular, he was introducing his theory of monopolistic competition, to apply to such markets as restaurants, bars, and shops, in which relatively large numbers of firms sell somewhat different products.

Fellner

Unlike Chamberlin, Fellner did emphasize oligopoly. He theorized that noncollusive oligopolies *partially* achieve joint-profit maximization. In principle, maximizing total profits for the industry sounds like a sensible goal: it should be possible to make every competitor better off by first getting, then dividing, the largest possible total pot.

In many cases, however, even *colluding* firms have failed to maximize their joint profits. Some of the impediments to joint maximization that Fellner discusses plague both cartels and oligopolies: arguments about how to divide the profits; uncertainties and mistakes; cost and product differences that can be reconciled perfectly only by pooling and reallocating profits, which is generally infeasible; interfirm differences in risk appraisal; difficulty in harmonizing preferences of shareholders and managers; infeasibility of perfectly coordinating the type and rate of innovation and other nonprice variables; and so on. As a result, price competition—even price warfare—often breaks out.[7] Noncolluding oligopolists are likely to miss the goal still further. Nevertheless, Fellner claims that oligopolies are very like cartels except in degree.

But *nearly* maximizing profits is a vague standard: a folk philosopher once said that whoever coined the term *near beer* was a poor judge of distance. In this and other respects, Fellner's analysis is not a clear policy guide. Although he asserts that larger numbers make perfect joint maximization even less likely, he does not really analyze the problem of numbers.[8] Even so, he strongly recommends increasing the number of sellers, presumably by forcible dissolution. He asserts, without evidence or even explicit theoretical support, that increasing the number of sellers will increase competition in a static sense, and will increase technological progress over time enough to outweigh such static cost increases as are likely to result from increasing the number of sellers by law.[9] He prescribes these strong medicines without support from either his theory or empirical evidence.

Although Fellner did not do it, it may be possible to link his policy recommendations to his theories. In Fellner's scheme, it is *differences* among firms (and their managers) that inhibit joint-profit maximization most. And perhaps variations among firms will rise with their numbers. But it is still not clear how *much* effect should be expected as numbers vary. Furthermore, as Fellner recognizes, raising the number of firms can raise costs.

STIGLER'S THEORY OF OLIGOPOLY

Chamberlin and Fellner are highly indefinite about how the number of firms affects competition. More definite and otherwise very different theories can be built from the proposition that, because rivalry pulls profits below the levels that collusion theoretically offers, firms will collude when they can, and collusion ought to be easier when there are only a few of them. Take Stigler's 1964 theory, for example.[10]

Stigler's theory generates wide-ranging economic hypotheses largely from statistical laws and a theory about information. His major hypotheses are quantitative and testable, and he confronts them with some empirical evidence.[11] He starts by accepting "the hypothesis that oligopolists wish to collude to maximize joint profits."[12] Wishes and accomplishments are different things, however, and Stigler's theory is "a systematic account of the factors governing the feasibility of collusion, which like most things in this world is not free."[13]

Whereas his argument is framed for collusion, Stigler neither assumes nor concludes that profit maximization by oligopolists guarantees monopoly results even with collusion. And noncollusive oligopoly is likely to differ from monopoly even more.

Assuming that information is imperfect, Stigler investigates how the incentive secretly to cut price changes with changes in the size and number of buyers; number of sellers; and the probability that customers who buy from a given seller in one period will do so in the next in the absence of price cutting.

When price exceeds marginal cost, there is an incentive for each cartel member to cut it. By definition, secret price cutting occurs when information is imperfect, and will be less attractive the more quickly or certainly it will be found out. If buyers are small, a seller has to cut prices to more of them to attract a given volume of business. And the larger the number of buyers to whom price cuts are offered, the more likely it is that competitors will find out that prices are being cut.[14] For this reason, the number and sizes of customers affect how attractive price cutting is and therefore how much of it there will be.

For a given volume of industry sales and number of customers, increasing the number of sellers reduces the absolute number and proportion of buyers that each seller serves. If sellers do not pool their data on sales and prices, and if it is too costly for sellers to collect such data independently, each can only infer what is going on by studying his own sales over time. By assumption, even in the absence of price cutting there is some random fluctuation in the number of customers served by a single seller. The number of customers served by any seller in one period is the sum of old customers who buy again, plus other sellers' customers who switch, less old customers who switch to other sellers.[15] Given a specific probability that customers in one period will repeat in the next—i.e., a loyalty probability—each seller expects his volume of business to fluctuate around some *average* volume even in the absence of "chiseling."

Since the sales of any seller can fall below his average because of chance variation as well as because someone is chiseling, it is hard to be sure whether price cutting is going on. Within limits, therefore, chance variations in sales afford a shelter behind which price cutters can hide. The degree to which they can do so influences their incentive to do so.

Stigler quantifies a price cutter's incentive to cut price as the percentage increase in sales that he can get away with. It depends upon what rule sellers use to decide whether price cutting is going on; the number of buyers; the number of sellers; and the probability that a buyer will keep buying from you in the absence of price cutting. According to Stigler's computations, the incentive to cut prices secretly "increases roughly in proportion to the number of rivals. . . . falls as the number of customers per seller increases. . . . [and] rises as the probability of repeat purchases falls, but at a decreasing rate."[16]

A single-firm monopoly has *no* incentive to chisel. There is a significant incentive to chisel when there are only two sellers; this incentive increases as we go from two to three sellers. Thus it is that some of Cournot's most important propositions are supported by a theory about imperfect information, even though the support comes from a very different model than Cournot's.

Stigler's theory, like all others, rests on specific assumptions. It ignores entry, and its policy implications are somewhat ambiguous. The number of firms is only one of the ingredients that could be influenced by policy, and in a world like Stigler's it might not be the best one to influence. For example, since departures from the collusive solution arise from ignorance, it may even be fruitful to tax information, as by prohibiting firms from posting prices publicly, instead of requiring them to do so. Repealing laws against price discrimination would encourage chiseling, for the same reason. This might be more helpful than trying to raise the number of firms by dissolution, which can raise costs. Mergers of buyers might lower, rather than raise, prices of those who supply them. But, since sellers are also buyers, and vice versa, it is not clear whether increasing their size and reducing their number would help or hurt, considering total effects on both sides of the market.

In Stigler's theory, oligopoly seems to hurt consumers only if it results in successful collusion. Particularly if costs are influenced by the number of firms (but in principle even if they are not), it can be argued that enforcing laws against collusion makes at least as much sense as trying to change the number of firms.

Finally, Stigler's theory says that in two otherwise comparable situations, markets with more sellers or fewer buyers or both will tend to have lower prices. It does not advocate changing the number of buyers or sellers by artificial means, including public policy.

This is not only because all policy has direct costs. In addition, product types and variety, and firms' cost functions may all be related to the number of firms.[17]

THE PROBLEM OF ENTRY, ACTUAL AND POTENTIAL

In formulating either theories or policies, we should distinguish increases in the number of firms due to *entry* from those produced by forcible dissolution. Unlike most of his successors, Cournot had an explicit, though ad hoc, explanation for the number of firms whose activity he modeled. The number of firms is determined by an absolutely limited natural resource: the number of free-flowing artesian wells. Each firm must have a well, and no firm owns or operates more than one well. Given the cost functions he assumes, oligopoly simply will not endure if there is open entry. The most obvious potential explanations of permanent oligopoly in such cases seem to be governmental restrictions or ownership of some absolutely fixed resource. In Cournot's theory, there can be more firms if there are more wells of a given quality.

In general, however, this kind of explanation will not do: many oligopolies do not seem to fit the bill. Although most modern oligopoly theories simply ignore the problem, one really must ask what determines the number of firms that a model applies to. This raises two questions: (1) What about entry of new firms? (2) What about efficiency explanations of the number of firms?

Firms enter an industry if they expect prices to exceed their average costs. If there *are* more firms it is because fewer firms would produce prices higher than the relevant costs—which most theories assume to be equal among firms and unaffected by the number of firms. If resident firms set price above cost despite having no cost advantage, entry would occur. In such cases, there is a *natural* efficiency explanation for the number of firms.

Efficiency explanations include the usual sorts of economies of size as well as some firms' growing larger than others because they have lower costs or better products. These are two different things. First, economies of size require that firms must be large to *be* efficient. That is, lowest achievable costs occur at a relatively large size. The second explanation is that some firms get larger *because* they achieve lower costs or better products at the same cost. Chapter 7 discusses these questions at length.

At this point, however, note that the outcomes depend upon whether entry is closed or open. In closed entry, the number of firms is absolutely fixed, and Figure 5-1 shows the result of Cournot-type decision rules under that assumption.[18] In equilibrium, the demand facing each firm has the same slope as the industry demand. This is the kind of equilibrium explained in Chapter 4. Cournot's solution differs significantly from that for a single-firm monopoly or a cartel.[19]

Figure 5-2 shows the "perfect cartel" solution, which maximizes total profits earned by *N* identical firms. The demand facing each firm has the same *elasticity*, at all prices, as the *industry* demand. In such a case, the price would be the same—for any number of firms—as for a single firm having identical marginal cost over the relevant

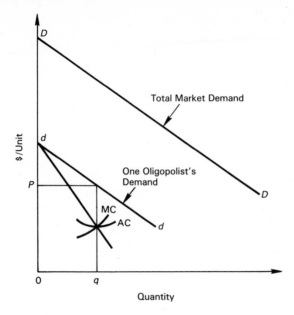

Figure 5-1 Closed Cournot Oligopoly

range. Whether several firms would actually have the same aggregated cost function as a single firm is another matter.[20]

Profits tend to induce entry. In Cournot, the demand facing each firm has the same *slope* as the total market demand. Firms enter until each earns zero profits; until (even if firms have different costs) there are zero profits at the margin; or until profits are as close to zero as the "lumpiness" of relatively large firms permits. Figure 5-3 shows (ideal) open-entry results for a Cournot model. Figure 5-4 shows open-entry results for a joint-

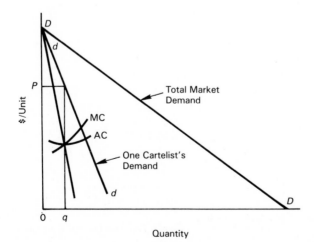

Figure 5-2 Perfect Cartel: Closed Entry

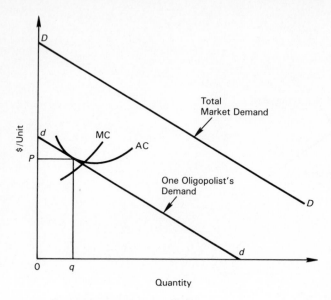

Figure 5-3 Open Cournot Oligopoly:
Tangency Solution

profit maximizing cartel, which all new firms are assumed to join when they enter the industry.

In both cases, prices exceed marginal cost; but total revenues equal total costs. Profits are zero. For given costs, industry demand, and number of firms, price would be higher with joint-profit maximizing than in Cournot's model.

Dissolution is a very different matter. Because it is produced forcibly by government, we cannot assume that the resulting structure will be cost determined and efficient.

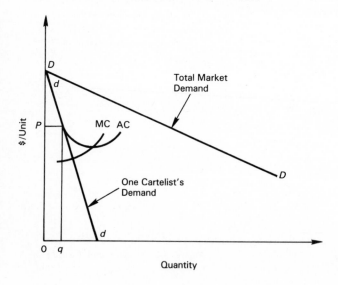

Figure 5-4 Open Cartel: A Different
Tangency Solution

Dissolution obviously has direct costs of its own and in addition may very well create a less efficient industrial structure. The cost functions and product varieties of individual firms are likely to be affected by dissolutions of various kinds and degrees. These influences, which may be static and dynamic, are discussed later in greater detail.[21]

Starting from an antique argument that had almost been forgotten, Demsetz argued in 1968 "that the asserted relationship between market concentration and competition cannot be derived from existing theoretical considerations and that it is based largely on an incorrect understanding of the concept of competition or rivalry."[22] Size economies in some industries may produce natural monopoly, which means that there is room in the market for only one efficient producer at a time. Nevertheless, there could still be rivalry to determine which firm will serve that market. If, as Chapter 2 noted, sellers are permitted to compete through product price, and if the average cost differences between the most efficient and next-most-efficient producers be small, price and profit should approximate the competitive level.[23]

Demsetz makes the case that, even under natural monopoly, this kind of competition differs from unregulated monopoly and could approximate the results of average-cost public utility regulation as practiced in the U.S. Indeed, it approaches the purely competitive solution. The precise outcome depends upon information, costs of obtaining bids, whether bidders collude, and the costs of the prospective entrants, none of which is related in a simple way to any given number of present producers. And, in a later but closely related theory, Baumol argues that, under certain conditions, "hit-and-run" competition—or the prospect of it—can produce essentially perfectly competitive results even in the face of high concentration.[24]

According to Richard Day's abstract model, "Competitive equilibrium obtains even with a sole surviving low-cost producer."[25] The crucial assumptions seem to be ignorance both of the industry demand curve and of rivals' responses; and that each seller acts as a price-taker. Results are competitive no matter how many sellers are in the market at any given time. By permitting entry, Day's theory achieves Edgeworth-Bertrand results even though we would observe only a single surviving firm in the market.

By considering potential and actual entry squarely, these theories of Demsetz and Day partially redress a common weakness of oligopoly theories, in most of which entry is simply ignored. In the Demsetz and Day theories, the number of actual sellers is neither here nor there: approximately competitive outcomes result even when we see only a single firm producing. So far as public policy is concerned, both theories are consistent with punishing collusion and avoiding closed entry. Neither furnishes support for "trustbusting."

THE THEORY OF GAMES[26]

Strategy derives from a Greek word meaning *generalship*. It denotes grand, high-level plans for waging war against adversaries who have strategies of their own and will react to what you do. A complete strategy would map responses for every conceivable contingency, which would be an awe-inspiring accomplishment. *Tactics*, by contrast, concerns techniques used by lower-level officers once they have brought their particular forces into contact with an enemy.

For centuries people have made war and theorized about how best to wage it. They have also played strategic games such as chess, that—though fairly complex as board games go—are drastically stylized set-piece battles.

In the 1940s, John von Neumann and Oscar Morgenstern developed the first formal theory of strategic games.[27] Game theory analyzes games played by two or more players, whose fortunes are interrelated and each of whom has a strategy. Each responds to what the others do. It therefore sounds like just the kind of tool we need to crack a variety of strategic problems. Over the last forty years, the theory of games has been applied to a variety of fields, including economics, business, and international politics. Though applied in several different disciplines, the theory of games also became a specialized field with a distinctive language and concepts of its own,[28] which we can only briefly summarize here.

The theory of games embraces both noncooperative and cooperative games. Such games are incorporated in game-theoretic models. In noncooperative games, players cannot make agreements; in cooperative games they can. Noncollusive oligopoly is treated as a noncooperative game. Cooperative games include collusion as well as other types of contracts and coalitions.

Every such game has a specific number of players, each of which has a specified strategy. Each player's strategy tells what he will do in response to anything the other player(s) may do. In full-information games, players know what everybody's strategic alternatives are. And for every move and response to it, there is a specific gain or loss (payoff) to each player. Payoff values depend upon what strategies are assumed to exist and which of them players choose, which among other things depends upon their criteria of choice. Payoff values also depend upon the specific demand and cost functions assumed.[29] Games can permit each player to make one or a series of moves. Supergames model a finite or infinite *series* of games.

Table 5-1 sets up a noncooperative duopoly game in which each firm uses output as its strategic choice variable. In principle, firms can have any number of alternative strategies, and different firms may have different strategies. For simplicity, assume here that each firm has four alternative output strategies, from which it chooses one, and that the firms are identical in all respects. Outputs for firm 1 are called q_1. Outputs for firm 2 are called q_2.

Output strategies for firm 1 are listed across the top of the table, from left to right: $q_1 = 30$; $q_1 = 47\text{-}\frac{1}{2}$; $q_1 = 63\text{-}\frac{1}{3}$; and $q_1 = 70$. Changing firm 1's strategy moves us horizontally, from one vertical *column* to another. The output strategies of firm 2 (which, in this game, are the same as firm 1's) are listed *vertically* at the left side of the table. In consequence, a change in firm 2's strategy moves us vertically, from one horizontal *row* to another.

Assume, as most such games do, that players rank alternative strategies according to how good their worst possible result is. The best strategy is assumed to be the one that offers the best of all the worst-possible outcomes. Once both firms put their chosen strat-

TABLE 5–1   Profit matrix for a duopoly game

| Firm 2 Strategies | Firm 1 Strategies | | | | Row Minima for Firm 2 |
	Col. 1 $q_1 = 30$	Col. 2 $q_1 = 47 - 1/2$	Col. 3 $q_1 = 63 - 1/3$	Col. 4 $q_1 = 70$	
Row 1	3900	5344	6122	6300	
$q_2 = 30$	3900	3375	2900	2700	2700
Row 2	3375	4512	5014	5075	
$q_2 = 47 - 1/2$	5344	4512	3760	3444	3444
Row 3	2900	3760	4011	3967	
$q_2 = 63 - 1/3$	6122	5014	4011	3589	3589
Row 4	2700	3444	3589	3500	
$q_2 = 70$	6300	5075	3967	3500	3500
Column Minima for Firm 1	2700	3444	3589	3500	

egy into effect, the game is over and players get the payoffs that the interaction of their choices produced.

To proceed, we need information about the total market demand function and the costs of each duopolist. Assume, for example, that the market demand is

$$P = \$200 - q_1 - q_2, \text{ and}$$
$$MC_1 = AC_1 = MC_2 = AC_2 = \$10.$$

For these demand and cost assumptions, Table 5-1 shows 16 outcomes that the strategic alternatives of firms 1 and 2 might conceivably produce. In the language of game theory, Table 5-1 is a four-by-four payoff matrix. Each cell displays the profits that the two firms would gain if they should choose one specific pair of strategies. The first figure in each cell is firm 1's profit. The second is firm 2's profit. Values in the table are calculated from the prices and costs that each strategy produces. If, for example, firm 1 and firm 2 each choose to produce 30 units per period, we would be in the upper left-hand corner. A total production of 60 units (30 + 30) clears the market at a price of $140 per unit. Firm 1's profits would be $3,900 per period. So would firm 2's. On the other hand, if firm 1 should choose to sell 47-½ units per period and firm 2 should sell 70, firm 1 would make $3,444 and firm 2 would make $5,075.

What strategies will these two firms choose? With what results? In evaluating its strategies, firm 1 looks at its profits one *column* at a time, since each column shows how the results of one of its strategies vary with different strategies that its adversary might choose. Firm 1's expected profits from choosing $q_1 = 30$, for example, vary from a low of $2,700 to a high of $3,900, depending upon what output strategy firm 2 chooses. A q_1 = 30 strategy will therefore earn firm 1 $2,700, at worst. Proceeding to the right, column by column, we see that a $q_1 = 47$-½ policy would earn no less than $3,444; $q_1 = 63$-⅓, $3,589; and $q_1 = 70$, $3,500. The strategy $q_1 = 63$-⅓ yields the largest of these minimum expected profits, $3,589 per period, and this is the one that firm 1 will choose.

Firm 2 looks at each *row* of Table 5-1 to find the lowest profit expected for each strategy *it* can choose. These row minima range upwards from \$2,700. The largest of these row minima is \$3,589, which is the worst that firm 2 expects to do if it chooses $q_2 = 63\text{-}\frac{1}{3}$ as its output strategy. And, when each firm chooses to market 63-⅓ units, each earns \$4,011 per period, as row 3, column 3 of the payoff matrix shows. By assumption, firms 1 and 2 have identical cost functions and face the same market demand function.

Thus it is that, without either colluding or exchanging information, the duopolists arrive at a mutually compatible strategic equilibrium. Remarkably, it is *identical* to the 1838 Cournot duopoly equilibrium analyzed earlier, in Chapter 4. And it also satisfies Nash's (1951) criterion for stable equilibrium: given the strategies each firm chose, in the absence of collusion neither could do better than it is doing at this equilibrium.

This brings us to what Table 5-1 says about collusion and "the prisoners' dilemma," a famous topic from game theory. Suppose that two partners in a homicide are arrested on flimsy circumstantial evidence and jailed in separate cells, from which they cannot communicate with one another. The authorities offer each accomplice the same deal separately: if only one prisoner confesses, he will get one year's probation and send the other to the gallows. If both confess, each will get three years at hard labor. Though the police do not mention it, it is clear that both prisoners will go free if neither confesses. Given the incentives, however, it is rational for each prisoner to confess, and both go to the penitentiary for three years.

In many circumstances, a similar dilemma confronts those who try to achieve monopoly results, through collusion or otherwise. Look at row 2, column 2. If each firm were to sell 47-½ units per period, joint profits would be maximized. In principle, both could gain by choosing that strategy. But, unfortunately for them, neither can count on the other. Because a firm that sells 47-½ units while the other does not would be much worse off than it is at the Cournot equilibrium, neither sells 47-½ units. They do not reach the monopoly equilibrium position.

In recent years, basic game-theoretic models such as this one have been expanded and complicated enormously in trying to deal with entry, differentiated products, and the different paths that firms might take through time en route to a dynamic equilibrium. For example, in basic supergames the same players replay the same game repeatedly, in long series. To game theorists it apparently matters whether the series is finite, which seems a reasonable assumption, or infinite, which does not. It is impossible or unlikely, for example, that players in a *finite* supergame can reach or sustain joint-profit maximizing equilibria such as that just described for the single-period game. The reason is that, even if retaliation were effective in general, fear of retaliation will not inhibit what a firm does in the last period of a finite game. For there is, then, no later period in which retaliation could be applied.

It would pay the firm, and hurt its sometime associate, therefore, to cheat this one last time by departing from any joint-maximizing solution that might have been accomplished by that time. That settles what happens in the last period. What about the next-to-last? The same thing happens in that period; and so on, backwards to the beginning of the whole finite series.[30]

However that may be, it appears that introducing dynamics and displacing certainty with probabilistic expectations greatly expands the range of possible outcomes. According to Waterson, for example,

> . . . the interesting feature clearly demonstrated by game-theoretic methods, is that mutual self-interest may not require explicit agreement to bring about the desired quasi-cooperative result. One caveat should immediately be noted. If the equilibrium considered is not unique, then at least verbal assent will be required on which equilibrium . . . will be chosen. Such discussion might be considered tantamount to collusion even if no explicit coordination is needed after that preliminary decision.[31]

This brief introduction necessarily leaves out many variations and complications that can be found in the theory of games. Recent work attempts major improvements and extensions of the theory, as well as (fewer) attempts to use the theory to explain the real world. Much work is being done, for example, on models that comprise more firms; on dynamics, including entry; and on game-theoretic models in which the products are differentiated rather than homogeneous.

Game theories of oligopoly are, paradoxically, both lineal descendants of and reactions against the classical theories. Game theories, by promising determinacy in complex cases, inspired much optimism.[32] At this point, however, after more than forty years, the contribution of game theory is still being debated. Has it significantly improved our understanding of how economic structure and performance are related?

Martin Shubik, an early and famous proponent, remains enthusiastic[33]; most price theory texts say something about it; and some professional surveys of oligopoly theories give game theory a prominent place.[34]

On the other hand, many economists are not enthusiastic. As two distinguished British economists put it, for example, ". . . the main outcome of the literature of game theory is that there are few analytical solutions to the perennial problems of bargaining. Generally, the theory of games has not served as a fruitful source of hypotheses on the behavior of monopolies and small groups; it has provided interesting puzzles rather than valuable insights or testable hypotheses."[35]

In reviewing Shubik's recent books, Mordecai Kurz noted that "One of the great promises of game theory was to fill the broad scientific territory between the models of perfect competition and those of perfect monopoly. . . . the lack of progress in this area is not due to the unavailability of mathematical tools or an opposition to their use. Rather, . . . we simply do not understand how these markets function."[36]

EXPERIMENTAL ECONOMICS: GAMES OF THEORY

In experimental economics, paid subjects actually play complex, well-specified economic games, the moves and end results of which are meant to simulate and shed light on real-world problems. Each game is played under detailed rules and within specified market institutions, and postulates specific values of economic variables, including costs, demands, and the numbers of buyers and sellers. Those who win the game earn more real money than losers do.[37]

In 1968, Dolbear and his associates reported results from an early but sophisticated oligopoly game.[38] In these experiments, the number of firms did affect price and profits, as in Cournot. With complete information, four firms produced 9 percent lower prices and 14 percent lower profits than two firms. With incomplete information, four firms produced 7 percent lower prices and 9 percent lower profits than two firms; and 16 firms produced 12 percent lower prices and 20 percent lower profits than two firms.

In a 1982 article, Charles R. Plott summarized the large literature about experimental economics.[39] According to Plott, "Three models do well in pedicting market prices and quantity: the competitive equilibrium, the Cournot model, and the monopoly (joint maximization) model. Experiments help define the conditions under which each of these alternative models apply."[40]

Similarly, from the simulations that they made, Coursey, Isaac, and Smith conclude that "There is clear evidence not only that contesting duopolies exhibit behavior more competitive than theoretical monopoly predictions, but also that they actually perform up to the standards of the competitive model."[41]

SUMMARY

As in Chapter 4, the theories discussed in this chapter do not all point in the same direction. Far from it: instead of having a single coherent theory of oligopoly, we have several conflicting theories. Predicted behavior depends crucially upon the assumptions made.

For example, those who favor reducing concentration by law—trustbusting—may want simply to *assume* (or assert) that there are no significant economies of firm size, and deny that firms grow large because they are more efficient. They could then choose theories—such as equal-cost Cournot models—to urge that government deconcentrate industrial structures by law. On the other hand, the more recent of the modern theories discussed in this chapter—Day's, Stigler's, Demsetz's, Baumol's, and the simulations—suggest that oligopoly behavior and performance are likely to be significantly different than those of single-firm monopoly. Performance may be equally or more competitive than less concentrated structures, and, in the presence of superior efficiency, can serve consumers better than less concentrated structures do.

That other assumptions and other theories yield other results is really the point. Depending upon which theory one chooses, increasing the number of firms may increase prices (even above the single-firm monopoly level),[42] may lower prices, or may leave prices unchanged. As Demsetz put it, "We have no theory that allows us to deduce from the observable degree of concentration in a particular market whether or not price and output are competitive."[43] In free Western economies, the public policy choice is rarely between single-firm monopoly and atomistic competition. The usual policy question is whether a few more firms in a concentrated industry would produce better results than a few less. To answer this question one must analyze oligopoly—in other words, markets of few sellers. At least since 1838 economists have approached the oligopoly problem by various routes, all of which have since been very heavily traveled by distinguished people.[44]

The next chapter is about cartels.

QUESTIONS

1. Why doesn't *every* industry collude all the time?

2. Chamberlin advanced (at least) two theories about oligopoly. What are they? What accounts for their differences?

3. Briefly explain what Stigler's theory predicts. How does this theory differ from Chamberlin's? From Fellner's?

4. If Stigler is right, reducing the cost of information and increasing the amount of it that sellers have could make consumers worse off. Does that make sense? Why?

5. A theory that does not consider entry or explain why the number of firms is what it is can mislead us about how well industry actually performs. How?

6. Suppose you have lots of good information about economies of size, and about the costs, market shares, and profits of individual firms. You might discover that larger firms have higher profits, lower average costs, and equal (or lower) marginal costs. What would you make of that? Why?

7. Show that noncolluding price-searcher firms, as well as colluding firms, would charge the same price if they have identical marginal cost functions and demands that are equally elastic at equal prices.

8. Suppose that Cournot and Stigler are right: other things equal, an industry with more firms will price closer to costs. Nevertheless, a policy of forcibly deconcentrating industries may hurt consumers. How? Why?

9. When, as in Demsetz's theory, firms compete to get a monopoly position, price will not precisely equal marginal cost except in a special case. Show what it is. (Hint: draw a simple diagram showing a bidder's average and marginal cost and the monopoly demand it would face if successful.)

10. In your own words, describe one or more hypotheses that the theory of games contributes to oligopoly theory. Do any of the other oligopoly theories discussed in this or the preceding chapter advance those same (or similar) hypotheses?

NOTES

1. See Chapter 1.

2. Although the Temporary National Economic Committee (TNEC) had presented data on and complaints about industrial concentration, and sought to relate them to monopolistic performance, empirical support for these theories was mostly anecdotal and casual in the 1930s.

Joe Bain published the first systematic quantitative study, also crude by present standards, in 1951. Joe S. Bain, "Relation of Profit Rate to Industry Concentration: American Manufacturing, 1936–1940," *Quarterly Journal of Economics*, 65 (August 1951), pp. 293–324.

Chapter 11 discusses the conceptual and measurement problems involved in formulating and testing such theories. Chapter 14 discusses the empirical evidence.

3. Edward H. Chamberlin, *The Theory of Monopolistic Competition*, 5th ed. (Cambridge, Mass.: Harvard University Press, 1946), pp. 46–51, 53–54; William Fellner, *Competition Among the Few* (New York: Alfred A. Knopf, Inc., 1949).

4. Chamberlin, *Monopolistic Competition*, p. 54.

5. Ibid., p. 48. Compare George J. Stigler, *Essays in the History of Economics* (Chicago: The University of Chicago Press, 1965), pp. 260–61.

6. Chamberlin, *Monopolistic Competition*, pp. 52–53.

7. For a theory of "warfare" see R. L. Bishop, "Duopoly: Collusion or Warfare," *American Economic Review*, 50 (December 1960), pp. 933–61.

8. Examples of Fellner's broad assertions appear at Fellner, *Competition Among the Few*, pp. 34–35, 102–3, 185, 189.

9. For examples of his dicta, see *ibid.*, pp. 283, 286–88, 291–92, 294, 297–98, 310. But also see p. 306.

10. George J. Stigler, "A Theory of Oligopoly," *Journal of Political Economy*, 72 (February 1964), pp. 44–61. An earlier paper is helpful for background: Stigler, "Economics of Information," *Journal of Political Economy*, 69 (June 1961), pp. 213–25. See also the brief summary in Stigler, *The Theory of Price*, 3rd ed. (New York: The Macmillan Company, 1966), pp. 216-20; and Ronald I. McKinnon, "Stigler's Theory of Oligopoly: A Comment," *Journal of Political Economy*, 74 (June 1966), pp. 281–85.

11. See Chapter 14.

12. Stigler, "A Theory of Oligopoly," p. 44.

13. Ibid., p. 44.

14. Ibid., p. 47.

15. Stigler also considers customers entering the market for the first time. This inessential complication is ignored here.

16. Stigler, "A Theory of Oligopoly," p. 51.

17. For Stigler's later views on oligopoly theory and facts, see Stigler, *The Theory of Price*, pp. 217, 219, 220; and Stigler, "The Economic Effects of the Antitrust Laws," *Journal of Law & Economics*, 9 (October 1966), pp. 225–37. Compare J. T. Wenders, "Entry and Monopoly Pricing," *Journal of Political Economy*, 75 (October 1967), pp. 755–60.

18. Donald Dewey, *The Theory of Imperfect Competition: A Radical Reconstruction* (New York: Columbia University Press, 1969).

19. See Chapter 6 of this book.

20. See Dewey, *Imperfect Competition*.

21. Suggestive analyses for entry, but not dissolution, are William S. Vickrey, *Microstatics* (New York: Harcourt Brace Jovanovich, 1964), pp. 314–34; Harold Hotelling, "Stability in Competition," *The Economic Journal*, 39 (1929), pp. 41–57, reprinted in *Readings in Price Theory*, eds. G. J. Stigler and K. E. Boulding (Homewood, Ill.: Richard D. Irwin, Inc., 1952), pp. 467–84; Arthur Smithies, "Optimum Location in Spatial Competition," *Journal*

of Political Economy, 49 (1940), pp. 423–39, reprinted in Stigler and Boulding, eds., *Readings in Price Theory*, pp. 485–501; E. H. Chamberlin, *Monopolistic Competition*, pp. 100–104.

22. Harold Demsetz, "Why Regulate Utilities?" *Journal of Law & Economics*, 11 (April 1968), pp. 55–65.

23. If only a single price is charged, this price will equal marginal cost only if the product demand curve cuts long-run average cost precisely at its minimum point. Whether, in cases for which this is not true, price discrimination or "ideal" marginal-cost pricing regulation are still better are questions that involve cost and other welfare indicators that Chapter 18 discusses.

24. William J. Baumol, "Contestable Markets: An Uprising in the Theory of Industry Structure," *American Economic Review*, 72 (March 1982), pp. 1–15, and sources cited there. But see William J. Baumol and Robert D. Willig, "Fixed Costs, Sunk Costs, Entry Barriers, and Sustainability of Monopoly," *The Quarterly Journal of Economics*, 96 (August 1981), pp. 405–31.

25. Richard H. Day, "A Note on the Dynamics of Cost Competition Within an Industry," *Oxford Economic Papers*, 20 (November 1968), pp. 369–73.

26. Helpful introductions to this subject are Leonid Hurwicz's review article, "The Theory of Economic Behavior," reprinted in Stigler and Boulding, eds., *Readings in Price Theory*, pp. 505–26; and Vickrey, *Microstatics*, pp. 342–67. A critical and disappointed reaction to game theory is found in Carl Kaysen's review of Shubik's 1959 book, in *American Economic Review*, 50 (December 1960), pp. 1039–40.

27. John von Neumann and Oskar Morgenstern, *Theory of Games and Economic Behavior* (Princeton: Princeton University Press, 1944).

28. For example, see Martin Shubik, *Game Theory in the Social Sciences*. Vol. I, *Concepts and Solutions*, Vol. II; *A Game-theoretic Approach to Political Economy* (Cambridge, Mass.: MIT Press, 1982; 1985).

29. Here, the total market demand is assumed to be $P = 200 - q_1 - q_2$. The total cost functions are $C_1 = 10q_1$; and $C_2 = 10q_2$.

30. R. D. Luce and H. Raiffa, *Games and Decisions* (New York: John Wiley & Sons, Inc., 1957).

31. Michael Waterson, *Economic Theory of the Industry* (New York: Cambridge University Press, 1984), p. 46.

32. Von Newmann and Morgenstern, *Theory of Games*.

33. Martin Shubik, *Strategy and Market Structure: Competition, Oligopoly, and the Theory of Games* (New York: John Wiley & Sons, Inc., 1959); Shubik, "A Curmudgeon's Guide to Microeconomics," *Journal of Economic Literature*, 8 (June 1970), pp. 405–34; Shubik, *Game Theory in the Social Sciences*. Vol. I, *Concepts and Solutions*. Vol. II, *A Game-theoretic Approach to Political Economy*.

34. For example, see James Friedman, *Oligopoly Theory* (New York: Cambridge University Press, 1983); and Michael Waterson, *Economic Theory of the Industry* (New York: Cambridge University Press, 1984), especially Chapter 3.

35. P. T. Bauer and A. A. Walters, "The State of Economics," *Journal of Law & Economics*, 18 (April 1975), pp. 1–23, at p. 3.

36. Mordecai Kurz, untitled book review in *Journal of Political Economy*, 94 (June 1986), pp. 688–89.

37. For a good nontechnical introduction, see Jerry E. Bishop, "Field Work," *The Wall Street Journal*, 25 November 1986, pp. 1, 24.

38. F. T. Dolbear and others, "Collusion in Oligopoly: An Experiment on the Effect of Numbers and Information," *Quarterly Journal of Economics*, 82 (May 1968), pp. 240–57.

The title of this paper is somewhat misleading: it is not about collusion, since the student participants did not collude. This is "closed" oligopoly: there is neither potential nor actual entry in this game.

Costs are identical among firms and independent of industrial structure. The authors recognize that the limited number of price choices probably biases the results.

Although the products are differentiated, product is not a variable, nor is the mode of production. The own elasticity of demand faced by each firm is independent of the number of firms, but—apparently—the cross elasticities for all pairs of firms decline systematically with the number of firms. The implication is that, as the number of firms is increased, each substitute is now a correspondingly more remote substitute.

39. Charles R. Plott, "Industrial Organization Theory and Experimental Economics," *Journal of Economic Literature*, 20 (December 1982), pp. 1485–1527.

40. Ibid., p. 1523.

41. Don Coursey, R. M. Isaac, and V. L. Smith, "Natural Monopoly and Contested Markets: Some Experimental Results," *Journal of Law & Economics*, 27 (April 1984), pp. 91–113.

42. According to Machlup, for example, "There may be instances in which the risks of 'rocking the boat' are so high that oligopolists keep their prices above the price that would maximize their joint profits." Fritz Machlup, "Oligopoly and the Free Society," *Antitrust Laws and Economic Review*, 1 (July–August 1967), p. 18.

43. Harold Demsetz, "Why Regulate Utilities?" pp. 59–60.

44. Anyone wondering whether, in spite of the variety of theoretic possibilities, there is, or used to be, general agreement about concentration and oligopoly should compare the following sources: Morris A. Adelman, "Effective Competition and the Antitrust Laws," *Harvard Law Rev.*, 61 (September 1948), p. 1303; Joe Bain, "Price and Production Policies," in *A Survey of Contemporary Economics* (Homewood, Ill.: Richard D. Irwin, Inc., 1948), pp. 159, 169; and Bain, "Conditions of Entry and the Emergence of Monopoly," in *Monopoly and Competition and Their Regulation*, ed. E. H. Chamberlin (New York: St. Martin's Press, Inc., 1954), p. 240; E. H. Chamberlin, "Product Heterogeneity and Public Policy," in *Readings in Industrial Organization and Public Policy*, eds. R. B. Heflebower and G. W. Stocking (Homewood, Ill.: Richard D. Irwin, Inc., 1965), pp. 237, 243; Clare E. Griffin, Testimony, June 9, 1955, Hearings Before Senate Subcommittee on Antitrust and Monopoly of the Committee on the Judiciary, 84th Cong., 1st sess., pt. I, "A Study of the Antitrust Laws," pp. 375–402, especially pp. 383–85, 387, 389, 393, 395, 398–99; J. M. Clark, "Competition: Static Models and Dynamic Aspects," reprinted in Heflebower and Stocking, eds., *Readings in Industrial Organization*, pp. 246, 254, 255; Richard H. Leftwich, *The Price System and Resource Allocation*, 3rd ed. (New York: Holt, Rinehart & Winston, 1965), p. 212; George W. Stocking, *Workable Competition and Antitrust Policy* (Nashville, Tenn.: Vanderbilt University Press, 1961), pp. 182, 272, 276–77, 368; R. B. Heflebower, "Monopoly and Competition in the United States of America," in Chamberlin, *Monopoly and Competition and Their Regulation*, p. 111; Paul M. Sweezy, "Demand Under Conditions of Oligopoly," Stigler and Boulding, eds., *Readings in Price Theory*, pp. 404, 409; J. R. Hicks, "Annual Survey of Economic Theory: The Theory of Monopoly," in Stigler and Boulding, eds., *Readings in Price Theory*, p. 374; Vickrey, *Microstatics*, pp. 212–13, 367; Gideon Rosenbluth, "Measures of Concentration," in *Business Concentration and Price Policy* (Princeton: Princeton University Press, 1955), p. 57; Tibor Scitovsky, "Economic Theory and the Measurement of Concentration," ibid., p. 112; Carl Kaysen, "Comment [on Scitovsky], ibid., p. 118; Shorey Peterson, "Antitrust and the Competitive Model," in Heflebower and Stocking, eds., *Readings in Industrial Organization*, pp. 329, 331–32; Almarin Phillips, "Corporate Mergers, Industrial Concentration, and Public Policy," *Wharton Quarterly*, 3 (Winter 1968), pp. 21–24; Edward Mason, "Market Power and Business Conduct: Some Comments," *American Economic Review* (May 1956), p. 480; Joel Dean, Testimony, *Economic Concentration*, Hearings Before the Subcommittee on Antitrust and Monopoly of the Committee on the Judiciary, U.S. Senate, 89th Cong., 1st Sess., pt. 4 (1965), p. 1697; John Blair, ibid., pt. 2, p. 578; J. K. Galbraith, "Monopoly and the Concentration of Economic Power," in *A Survey of Contemporary Economics*, ed. Howard S. Ellis (Homewood, Ill.: Richard D. Irwin, Inc., 1948), Vol. I, pp. 102, 127; Jesse W. Markham, "Market Structure, Business Conduct, and Innovation," *American Economic Review*, 55 (May 1965), pp. 323–32.

6 | COLLUSION AND CARTELS

INTRODUCTION

Collusion is secret agreement to deceive or defraud. It includes covert agreements to fix prices. A cartel is an organization of individuals or firms that fixes price, output, or product qualities; allocates markets or customers; or otherwise limits competition.

By definition, collusion is secret. Some cartels, the Organization of Petroleum Exporting Countries (OPEC) for example, have operated brazenly in the open. Arrangements to which the term was applied in Europe suggest that cartels also tend to be more formal, detailed, and sophisticated than run-of-the-mine collusion. Legal status is another possible distinction. Whether used to suppress competition, defraud insurance companies or shareholders, or to do something else, most collusion is technically illegal and the term itself has a nasty sound. Some cartels are legal and aboveboard. Many foreign cartels, including OPEC, are for practical purposes beyond the reach of U.S. law; and some domestic cartels, including labor unions and agricultural marketing arrangements, were established and protected by law. Nevertheless, most union executives, business people, and farmers in the U.S. would deny that *cartel*, let alone *collusion*, applies to anything they do.

Collusive price fixing is evidently an old practice. Aristotle recorded it; ancient kings tried to outlaw it. And, in a famous (though undocumented) empirical generalization, Adam Smith asserted that collusion was widespread in the eighteenth century:

> People of the same trade seldom meet together, even for merriment and diversion, but the conversation ends in a conspiracy against the public, or in some contrivance to raise prices. It is impossible indeed to prevent such meetings, by any law which either could be executed, or

would be consistent with liberty and justice. . . . [but] law . . . ought to do nothing to facilitate such assemblies; much less to render them necessary.[1]

Collusion and cartels are harder to define than one might think. Do they include a group of land owners and crude oil producers who try to lower costs by coordinating drilling and production in a single oil reservoir?[2] Or a group of computer firms reducing costs by sharing basic research efforts and results? Or a group of lawyers or doctors or engineers who form a firm? Or a single firm that allocates territories to its dealers, or sets their resale prices? Where do our definitions leave joint ventures, and partnerships in general? Where, indeed, do they leave even a single firm considered in isolation? Can we devise reliable empirical tests for distinguishing between collusion and competition? Between arrangements that hurt and those that help consumers?

Questions like these enchant and employ many economists and lawyers, benefits with which they are naturally pleased. Even more important, sensible answers to such questions are necessary if such policies as antitrust are to serve consumer interests. Lawyers say that private cartels in the U.S. are illegal in and of themselves (per se) because, to use antitrust jargon, they restrain trade. In some cases, participants in alleged cartels have been fined, imprisoned, and forced to pay heavy damages. Yet it is often hard to decide whether they were operating a cartel or doing something else innocuous or beneficial.

This ambiguity poses two serious problems. First, an objective of any civilized legal system should be to punish only the guilty and leave innocents alone. If transgressions are ambiguously defined and diagnosed, innocents get stuck. Second, rules can simply be wrong, even though clear, discouraging institutions and practices that could make consumers better off. To choose sound policies, we need to understand what business arrangements do before deciding which of them should be discouraged. In principle, at least, we could decide on the basis of their economic effects.

This chapter analyzes several types of cartels, in each case studying their symptoms as well as economic effects. The next section shows how to build a cartel when member firms have different costs. After that there is an analysis of bid rigging with two famous examples: *Addyston Pipe* and *GE-Westinghouse*. The following section is about basing-point systems as used in the U.S. steel and cement industries. Exclusive sales agencies such as that found in the *Appalachian Coals* case are studied next. The last section analyzes buyers' cartels, as illustrated by the U.S. and Spanish sugar industries.

THE BASIC MODEL: A CARTEL OF FIRMS WHOSE COSTS DIFFER

Cartels have a long history and much has been written about them.[3] Real cartels face several practical problems. Among other things, they need to define the product; fix output, or price, or both; allocate output amongst their members; distribute earnings; and decide what to do about open defection, secret cheating, and new firms entering the industry.[4]

Assume that an unconcentrated industry comprises three groups of firms. Within each group, firms have the same cost functions. Costs differ significantly among groups, as in Figure 6-1. The supply function of each firm is its marginal cost function, and the industry supply function sums the production of all these firms at each price. Industry supply is the SRMC function shown in Figure 6-1. In short-run equilibrium, competitive market price is P_C; quantity is Q_C. Firms with lowest costs produce and profit most; firms with highest costs produce and profit least. P_C equals marginal cost for each firm. By specifying different fixed and average costs, a variety of different cases could be illustrated. Class III firms, for example, might be suffering losses. If that situation persists, they would go out of business in the long run and the industry would shrink. Similarly, in some cases high-cost firms may already be shut down, producing nothing even in the short run.

As drawn, however, Figure 6-1 shows all the firms earning rents even under competition: total revenue exceeds total variable cost. A cartel pays either by increasing profits or reducing losses, taking the costs of cartelization into account. For our purposes, achieving smaller losses is equivalent to increasing profits. There is evidence that many, if not most, cartels have been formed in bad times, reduced losses, but suffered negative economic profits. Successful cartelization does not necessarily imply positive accounting or economic profits.

Suppose that all firms in this hypothetical industry enter into a cartel, with objectives that are simple and clear. They neither seek nor achieve greater efficiency or better product quality. Their sole objective is to maximize total wealth of the member firms by reducing output and raising price. The cartel equates members' summed marginal cost, SRMC, and marginal revenue, MR; producing a much smaller output, (Q_M instead of Q_C), and charging a much higher price, (P_M instead of P_C).[5] To minimize cost, the cartel allocates output among members so that marginal costs are equal for all firms that are allowed to produce anything at all. Sometimes, as in this case, profits can be increased by shutting down the least efficient firms, those in class III. To accomplish that, however, the cartel will have to pay them something. Otherwise, no matter how high the cartel price is, shut down firms would get zero output and zero market revenue. Such money transfers are called side payments, and cartels that use them in this way are said to pool profits. Pooling is a sophisticated but difficult trick, especially when it is illegal.

In general, a member firm will not remain loyal if it earns less than it could get by breaching the cartel agreement and increasing output. But the other members would not be willing to pay a firm more to remain loyal than it could reduce cartel profits by defecting. Determining whether any such payment will work in specific circumstances is an interesting exercise. In some cases, no such solution exists.

Contemplating this tricky balancing act, we see a fundamental obstruction to forming a cartel in the first place: small firms become important. It is hard to cartelize an industry of many small producers. For a relatively small firm stands to gain by staying out of the cartel from the start, or by defecting from it (secretly or openly) after it starts. *If* the cartel will be formed and operate even if such a firm does not participate, defection is very tempting. A defector can increase its output while the cartel props up the price by keeping its own output low.

The problem could be solved if everyone believes the cartel will not be formed unless all firms join and remain loyal; or if firms could be forced to join and punished if they

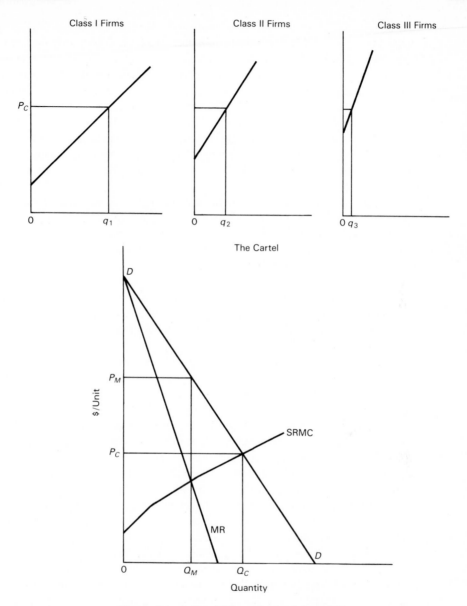

Figure 6-1 A Cartel Whose Members' Costs Differ

defect. Damages could be collected if cartel contracts were legally enforceable, as they used to be in Europe. Some cartels have required members to deposit with the cartel cash or negotiable securities that would be forfeited if they cheat or defect. When law permits them, such arrangements are reasonably effective private enforcements.

As a practical matter, direct government participation or policing and enforcement may be necessary to turn large-number industries into profitable and durable cartels. And "large numbers" may be fewer than commonly supposed. With varying success, governments have cartelized large-number industries. Trade unions, farmers, and certain professions are examples. In many cases, joining the cartel and observing the rules are mandatory and breaches are punished by law. This happened in the U.S. from 1933 to 1935, when the National Industrial Recovery Administration (NRA) compelled many industries to cartelize, and fined price cutters.

On the other hand, it is a mistake to assume that a cartel needs loyal participation by every firm to be worthwhile. Reasoning from a simple economic model, Akerlov and Yellen conclude that "For the noncheaters to gain they must be at least half the industry."[6]

Figure 6-1 offers interesting findings about market shares. Under the conditions assumed, the more efficient firms get larger shares and profits—under either competition or the cartel. The competitive case shown in Figure 6-1 has some features like Ricardo's rent theory, discussed in Chapter 2. The share of low-cost competitive firms rises when market demand and industry output fall. Their share falls when market demand and industry output increase. When this cartel reduces industry output to raise price, the market share of the lowest cost firms will soar, even though the market demand did not shift. In some cases, it is possible to confirm a cartel diagnosis with relationships like that. Much can also be inferred from the entry of new firms and from the changes in shares (and other things) that it causes.

On the other hand, some popular diagnoses fail. Many say that stable shares are a sure sign of cartel activity. In this profit-pooling cartel, however, shares are *not* stable as market demand shifts. On the contrary, shares are extremely unstable.[7] Most cartels today are, however, pale beer as compared with the ring illustrated in Figure 6-1. Most private U.S. cartels do not pool profits, and many settle for rough approximations, rules of thumb, and infrequent adjustments. Stable market shares (or stable prices) may be a more reliable symptom under such circumstances.

A notably profitable cartel will attract entrants if, like most, it is unable to repel them. Whether new entrants to the industry join the cartel or operate outside of it, entry will eventually increase the number of firms in the industry and reduce industry concentration; tend to reduce the market shares of cartel members or the cartel's share overall; or both. Entry and declining concentration are ambiguous symptoms, although it is common to hear that they are sure signs that a trade is competitive. They are signs that entry was not barred and that the trade may be getting closer to long-run competitive equilibrium. But they may also indicate that a cartelized trade is becoming more competitive. These are rather different diagnoses.

BID-RIGGING CARTELS

Bid-rigging cartels started long ago and continue even now.[8] They range from simple to extremely sophisticated schemes. The simpler ones typically allocate business among members in rotation. In its turn, each "low" bidder gets the business with an artificially inflated price while its confederates submit even higher bids by agreement. Much can be learned from two famous examples, one antique and one modern. The old case is *Addyston Pipe* (1898); the modern one is *GE-Westinghouse* (1961, and following).

Addyston Pipe[9]

This landmark case is about a secret bid-rigging cartel of six firms that in the 1890s sold cast-iron pressure pipe to water and gas plants in many cities and towns. Cast-iron pipe is heavy and freight commonly accounted for a significant proportion of its delivered cost. Two of the conspirators' mills were located on the Ohio River and the others were south of the Ohio and east of the Mississippi. Within that large area, cartel mills had a substantial freight advantage over nonmember mills elsewhere.

Such a cartel has two objectives. First, on each contract it seeks, it wants to bid as high as it can while underbidding such competitors as there are outside the cartel. Second, it wants to produce and deliver each order as cheaply as possible. How could it accomplish these tasks?

The first thing is to determine the highest price at which the cartel can get an order it wants. Suppose a city notifies the trade that it wants to buy 1,000 tons of cast iron pipe for its gas or water system. Since firms in the cartel are familiar with the cast-iron pipe business, they can estimate the probable low bids from the outside competing mills that are most likely to bid for that contract. To make these estimates, the cartel needs to know the location of noncartel mills making that type of pipe, the costs of shipping it, and the approximate costs of producing that order in mills likely to be serious rivals. Beginning in 1887, ICC regulation eased this task by making railroad rates "open" and "stable." Of course, production costs depend not only upon the general relationships between costs and output rates, that is, upon the cost *functions*, but upon rates of plant output expected at the time the products are to be made.

In sum, for each prospective piece of business the cartel determines a point (or narrow range) on the relevant demand curve. Having collectively determined a price above which they will not get the order and at which they will, the cartel now decides which of its members will win the contract and produce the pipe.

This determination and allocation might be done by a separate specialized staff in a central cartel office, though that would require incorruptible experts who are intimately familiar with each participant's cost curves and present and prospective plant schedules. One naive alternative is simply to *ask* cartel members about their costs and outputs, in response to which, unfortunately, they have reason to lie. There is a simpler and more reliable way to go about it: use the familiarity of each participant with his own costs plus his own inclination to make as much money as possible.

The solution was to participate in *two* auctions. The first was a secret auction *within* the cartel. It determined which cartel member could produce and deliver an order most cheaply. Once the cartel agreed to the maximum price at which the city's contract can be bid for and won, the internal secret auction proceeded. Each cartel member knew the following: (1) the rigged bid price that members had agreed to charge the city for the pipe; (2) the type and quantity of pipe; (3) destination and delivery date; (4) its own costs and production schedules. As a consequence, each knew (a) the incremental costs of producing the order (total costs with the order *minus* costs without it); and (b) the incremental revenues (total revenues with the order *minus* revenues without it).

The firm that bid highest for the order in the secret auction was permitted to produce it. The amount of this winning secret bid was deposited, together with the highest internal bids on other orders, in an escrow account and subsequently divided among the members according to shares previously agreed upon. It is clear that the absolute maximum amount anyone would bid internally to get an order is the difference between incremental costs and incremental revenues attributable to the order, plus the share of its own bid that it will get later, when the escrow account is divided among the members. Thus, the firm to which the order is worth most will bid the most, thereby buying the right to get the contract at an agreed-upon monopoly price.[10]

Even if, contrary to fact, cartel members had identical production-cost *functions* and transport costs to the city, we should not expect identical internal bids. For it is unlikely that firms will have identical mill schedules and output when they make their bids. Furthermore, all are bidding for future delivery, and their expectations are likely to differ. Identical internal bids are extremely unlikely, just as it would be extremely unlikely that six firms genuinely competing on bids to the same city would bid identically.[11] This suggests that even a few firms will not bid identically or price like a cartel unless they are colluding. *Addyston* supports that inference: the internal bids were not identical.

The hypothetical data in Table 6-1 show how all this worked. Firm 1 can deliver this order at the lowest total incremental production-cost-plus-freight, $18,600. That is $6,400 less than the revenues that this order would add. In addition, it will get a 7 percent (.07) share of all internal bids, including its own. Ignoring that rebates were not instantaneous—in fact, bids were divided frequently—firm 1 would not bid more than $6,881.72—shown as 6.88 (thousand) in the table—for the right to sell that order at $25 a ton, the agreed monopoly price.[12] If it bids that much, it would be just as well off having won the order as it would have been without it. Its rebated share of that bid is (.07)(6,881.72), or about $481.72, reducing its net bid to about $6,400. That plus its total incremental production and freight costs equals the $25,000 revenue that the order would add.

If cartel members know everything shown in Table 6-1, firm 1 will not bid more than about $6,706, slightly more than firm 2's maximum bid. And firm 2 better not try to bluff by bidding more than its own top-maximum bid ($6,705.88). If firm 2 bluffs, firm 1 can let it take the order—and the loss. Note another temptation. Cartelists who expect to have lowest costs for a particular order may be tempted to form a (secret) cartel-within-a-cartel to cheat the broader membership by reducing their own internal bids and splitting what is saved by doing so. If firms 1 and 2 collude before bidding internally, firm 1 could get the contract by bidding a bonus of only $5,488—a little more than firm 3 will bid—and the two lowest cost firms would split the bonus saved. This would reduce the bonuses that higher cost cartelists get and increase the share of lower cost cartelists. But it would still achieve minimum production and freight costs.

The second auction was the one in which cartel members and outsiders individually submitted sealed bids for a city's contract. If the cartel's estimates were good, the chosen cartel firm would submit the lowest bid and get the contract. Other members of the cartel

TABLE 6–1   Hypothetical data for a $25/ton, 1,000 ton bid-rigging scheme

Firm	Incremental Revenue ($000)	Freight ($000)	Incremental Production Cost ($000)	Total Incremental Cost[a] ($000)	Net Incremental Revenue[b] ($000)	Share of Internal Bids	Top Bid[c]
1	25	1.6	17.0	18.6	6.4	.07	6.88
2	25	1.8	17.5	19.3	5.7	.15	6.71
3	25	2.0	18.5	20.5	4.5	.18	5.49
4	25	2.2	19.0	21.2	3.8	.20	4.75
5	25	2.3	22.0	24.0	1.0	.20	1.25
6	25	2.5	28.0	30.5	−5.5	.20	0

[a]Total incremental cost = incremental production cost + freight.
[b]Net incremental revenue = incremental revenue − incremental cost.
[c]Top bid = (incremental revenue − incremental cost)/(1-share).

submitted fraudulent bids, nonidentical and all higher than the successful bid, to suggest that they are competing. Nonmember firms submitted higher legitimate bids, reflecting their cost disadvantage in serving this market.

In this scheme, the cartel firm to which an order was allocated bid a rigged monopoly price. Its fellow members "protected" it by bidding higher delivered prices. This gave the false appearance of active competition among the membership. Cartel correspondence and records indicated that a net foundry price of $15 per ton, or somewhat less, typically covered incremental cost and left a firm better off with the contract than without it.

If any firm or cartel is to hold price above its own costs, outsiders must be unwilling to add enough supply to drive price down to that cost level. In cases like *Addyston*, it is the total of each outsider's costs that matters, not just freight. Suppose, for example, that outsiders have less efficient mills, or must use more expensive pig iron or other inputs. They are thereby at a delivered-price disadvantage, even if freights are equal.

In *Addyston*, the low bid takes the whole order. To exclude an outsider means undercutting the sum of its production and freight costs. If your low bid earns you profits or quasi-rents, it is because the sum of your costs and freights is even lower than that. That the secret internal bids were significantly higher than zero shows that the prices fixed were higher than they otherwise would have been.

But sealed-bid competition is not the only kind of competition there is. In many other kinds of markets, production and purchases are continuous, with several to many buyers transacting. Assume that several producers are serving the same market, within which they have significant freight advantages. Although they will enjoy some rents even under competition, they may do even better if they collaborate. This situation is analogous to *Addyston*.

Two collaborating low-cost firms can raise price somewhat above their costs when other competitors are unwilling to supply enough output to drive price down to the lower cost level. This is analogous to some features of Forchheimer's dominant-firm model, which was discussed in Chapter 4.

Because systematic, persistent price discrimination requires monopoly power or poor information, it is often taken as a symptom that a cartel is at work. Figures 6-2 and 6-3 picture two useful models for analyzing price discrimination. Figure 6-2 shows demands for each of two markets. In the domestic market, the cartel has significant monopoly power and faces a downward-sloping demand function, *DD*. In the world market, this cartel has no monopoly power and faces a perfectly elastic demand function, P_w.

Assume that identical products are sold in both markets. Costs at the factory gate are identical for sales to either market. (Any transport or other cost differences could be dealt with by adjusting the demand functions.) To maximize wealth, the cartel equalizes marginal revenues in all markets served, and chooses the total output for which aggregate marginal revenue and marginal cost are equal. The cartel can sell as much as it wants on the competitive world market, at a price of P_W. P_W is also the value of marginal cost at Q_T, the total cartel output that maximizes joint profits. For profit maximization, therefore, the value of marginal cost is P_w. The amount to be sold in the cartelized domestic market must bring MR and P_w to equality. This occurs at output Q_D. Thus, Q_T is the total cartel output, of which Q_T *minus* Q_D is dumped on the competitive world market and Q_D is sold in the cartelized home market. Price, P_D, is much higher in the domestic market, where demand elasticity is much lower. This model captures some features found in *Addyston*. It also recreates the foundations of the government-enforced Spanish sugar cartel, some aspects of which are analyzed in the Appendix to this chapter.

Figure 6-2 teaches important lessons. First, unless an artificial barrier separates the two markets, the home market price cannot long exceed the world price by more than transport cost. In Figure 6-2, the barrier is a prohibitive tariff. Second, even with that same tariff, *competing* sellers in the domestic market could not get anything like as high a

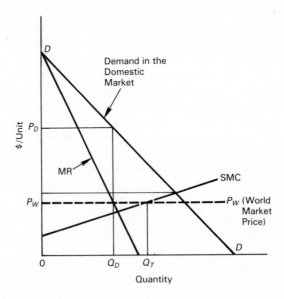

Figure 6-2 Simple Price Discrimination: Dumping

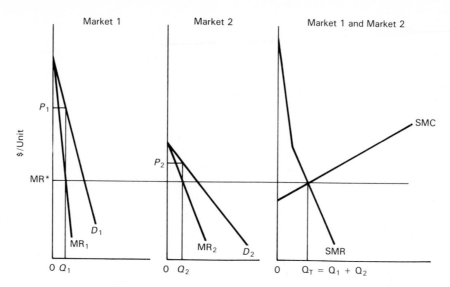

Figure 6-3 Complex Price Discrimination Model

price as P_D. Given the conditions shown in Figure 6-2, the domestic market would clear at a competitive price only slightly higher than that in the outside world market. Third, under price-taker competition no seller would be willing to dump in the outside market at a lower price than he can get at home. If the cartel of Figure 6-2 collapses, restoring price-taker competition, sellers would export less to the outside market and increase sales in the home market, beating down domestic prices in the process. Given the costs and demands shown in Figure 6-2, they would withdraw from the outside market altogether.

Interestingly enough, Judge Taft's *Addyston Pipe* decision used this same kind of analysis in 1898, though without mathematics or diagrams. Taft noted that the pipe cartel extracted monopoly prices where it had significant freight advantage and dumped where it did not. Indeed, he argued, the large differences between net prices in these two market classes measured, as well as symptomized, the cartel's effectiveness—just as it does in Figure 6-2.

Figure 6-3 illustrates price discrimination when a cartel faces downward-sloping demand functions in both markets. To maximize wealth, the discriminating cartel equalizes marginal revenues among all markets served. That is, at each dollar value of marginal revenue, the summed marginal revenue function (SMR) sums the quantities that can be sold in both markets. Per-unit costs of producing for and serving both markets are identical. The summed marginal cost function (SMC) is the cartel's relevant MC function. At each dollar value of marginal cost it sums the quantities cartel members can produce. The wealth-maximizing output is Q_T, at which SMC = SMR. At Q_T, marginal revenue is MR*, the value of marginal revenue at the profit-maximizing output. At MR*, Q_1 is produced in market 1, and Q_2 in market 2. P_1 is higher than P_2, because—at given prices—demand elasticities are significantly higher in market 2. In market 1, therefore, the total substitutability of competitive suppliers of these or other goods is lower. Market 1 offers a stronger monopoly position.

Success of the cast-iron pipe cartel depended upon members' having significant delivered-cost advantages in some areas. At least part of their advantage was in freights. Since the maximum prices the cartel could get varied with geography, geographic price discrimination resulted. Significant, persistent price discrimination requires bad information, or monopoly elements, or both. In a competitive market, no buyer will knowingly pay more when he can get the good for less, and no seller will persistently take less when he knows he can get more. In *Addyston*, the cartel engaged in significant geographic price discrimination.

This analysis of cost advantages suggests something that defenders of basing-point and other delivered-price systems tend to neglect. Only if the low cost producers do not compete can they collect the *maximum* rents their advantages could earn them. This is obviously relevant to appraising schemes such as basing-point pricing, which is analyzed later.

Although lower freights are not the only kind of advantages relevant to market definition, stable ICC rail rates were easy for the cartel to use and helpful for price fixing. They can also help us diagnose the presence of a cartel. Tariff rates on imports are also easy to obtain. It is often possible to decide whether domestic prices are higher than tariffs alone would permit if there had been competition among domestic producers. But when it is hard to measure some of the cost advantages that a cartel has, it is harder for outsiders to diagnose collusion.

It was not until 1948, 50 years after *Addyston*, that the Department of Justice again filed suit against the defendants' successor companies and other firms, charging restraint of trade and monopoly. Among other things, the resulting consent decrees established royalty-free patent licensing and suspended a Birmingham-plus basing-point system.[13]

GE-Westinghouse[14]

This case is famous for cloak-and-dagger procedures, large damage settlements, and debates (to this day) about how effective the collusion was. During the 1950s, and perhaps earlier than that, 30-odd U.S. manufacturers of electrical equipment began conspiring to fix prices. Annual sales of such equipment totalled about $2 billion.

As it bought electrical equipment, the Tennessee Valley Authority noted and questioned identical sealed bids, rapidly rising prices, and a British manufacturer's underbidding the delivered price of an expensive turbine generator by one-third. In 1959, the Department of Justice (DJ) commenced investigations.

Although it is not clear how much they profited from it, there is absolutely no doubt that the firms colluded. Their employees attended many secret meetings and used procedures reminiscent of spy novels. A grand jury handed down criminal indictments in 1960. Allis-Chalmers, one of several defendants, pleaded guilty and turned state's evidence.

Several corporate and individual defendants were found guilty of violating Section 1 of the Sherman Law and fined a total of more than $1 million. Some individuals received jail sentences. In 2,000 or more damage suits, private utility companies and state and local governments also collected $150 to $200 million. Chapter 19 puts the law of this case into historical perspective.

Ralph Sultan's 1974 and 1975 studies had concentrated on one product—turbine generators— and concluded the conspiracy had little or no effect.[15] The FTC's *Assessment* studies how the conspiracies affected eight of the twenty products that had been involved: steam turbine generators, steam surface condensers, power transformers, distribution transformers, power circuit breakers, power capacitors, insulators, and demand and watt-hour meters. FTC had data about these products for the period 1950 to 1970. They partitioned this whole period into subintervals accordingly as the firms were colluding, not colluding, or actively signalling their intentions and desires to collaborate. For each period, FTC tried to separate the influence that other factors might have had on profits. FTC assumed that conspiratorial meetings were suspended in about January 1955, then resumed from 1956 to 1959; and that none was held during the 1960s.

In 1963, following the conspiracy cases, FTC claimed, GE and Westinghouse started signalling each other. GE issued a revised price book and openly announced major changes in its pricing policies. It guaranteed not to raise prices on orders delivered within 36 months. GE also promised that, if it increased the discount to any buyer, it would do so on *all* orders placed during the six months preceding. Customers could determine whether they were getting the same discounts by asking GE's accounting firm to audit the records and accounts. GE also published all orders and quotations in effect when it announced these policy changes. It did so again when it later announced price increases.

In 1964, Westinghouse published a similar price book, adopted a price-protection policy like GE's, and published its own list of outstanding orders and quotations. DJ was not amused, claiming both that GE had signalled to Westinghouse that it was abandoning secret price cutting and that Westinghouse had received the signal and reciprocated. DJ argued that the new pricing books and a percentage multiplier applied to list prices made it much easier to calculate and match prices for complex, custom-built products. It also claimed that the retroactive discount policy chilled price competition, because it greatly increased the cost of cutting price on even a single order and, by notifying its competitor, nullified any advantage that a secret cut would have gained. Offering the customers price audits eliminated secrecy and any incentive that secrecy may have offered to price cutters. One question is whether this price signalling raised turbine generator profitability from 1964 to 1970, after which the practice was under attack.

DJ challenged this situation, and—in December 1976—GE, Westinghouse, and DJ agreed to modify the 1962 turbine generator consent decree, which had grown out of the original conspiracy cases. This agreement went into effect in the spring of 1978. According to the FTC,

> The new decree prohibits public statements of pricing policy intended to signal an invitation to eliminate competition, the price-protection policy. . . , publication of outstanding quotations or information from which a pricing policy could be inferred, and examination by one seller of documents from which a rival's pricing policy could be inferred.[16]

The FTC staff report concluded that conspiracy from 1957 to 1959 increased the ratio of before-tax profits to sales by at least 2 percentage points (10.5 percentage points for circuit breakers); and that signalling between 1964 and 1970 increased turbine generator profitability from 7 to 10 percentage points.[17] This makes it sound as though signalling is more effective than explicit agreements, which seems strange. It is not so strange if what we have here is a price reporting system used to enforce prices established collusively.

Overall, the FTC staff report said, conspiracy from 1950 to 1959 may have raised profitability by 4 percentage points or more. Oddly enough, and contrary to Sultan's findings, the pre-"whitesale" meetings—1950 to 1954—increased profits most—by more than six points. Conspiratorial meetings to fix prices apparently did not raise profits significantly except in the case of insulators and circuit breakers.

Some companies did not participate in the conspiracies. According to the FTC, conspiracy profited nonconspirators as well as the conspirators, which seems reasonable. We should remember this when, in Chapter 13 and Chapter 14, we ask whether higher profits in concentrated industries come from monopoly or from the superior efficiency of larger firms. Nonparticipants appear to have benefitted more from signalling than the signalers did. Theory suggests that a nonmember firm will produce at a higher rate and earn a higher profit rate than an equally efficient cartel member. Members help keep prices up by holding their own output down.

The FTC staff's inferences are incomplete as well as debatable. It ought to be added, for example, that even in product lines where a few firms did most or all of the business, achieving anything close to monopoly-level pricing seems to have required explicit collusion. This suggests that there would have been substantial competition otherwise, a suggestion confirmed by behavior during periods in which FTC claims that the firms did *not* collude.

BASING-POINT SYSTEMS

Mechanics

Many firms at least occasionally quote delivered prices, including freight.[18] Firms that quote prices in no other way can be said to use a mandatory delivered-price *system*, and a variety of such systems have been used. They include postage-stamp pricing (a uniform delivered price applies to the whole nation); zone-pricing (prices differ among specified geographic areas and are uniform within each such area); single basing-point pricing; multiple basing-point pricing; and plenary basing-point systems (every plant is a basing point).

The following discussion concentrates on basing-point systems, an historically important species of delivered pricing. Assume for now that such a system is applied perfectly, without deviation. If the whole industry uses the system, all sellers quote the same price to the same destination. There are spectacular instances in which several firms quoted identical delivered prices, to several decimal places; but there is no doubt, either, that every basing-point system suffered periods in which price uniformity broke down. Nothing works perfectly, of course, and it is not clear how much actual prices must differ at the same destination before we decide that we do not have a delivered-pricing system.

An even more important question is whether systematic delivered pricing reduces competition or hurts consumers or both.[19]

In a single basing-point system, the delivered price to any destination is the *base price* quoted at one specific location (the *basing point*) *plus* a formula *transportation* charge from that point to the destination. The most famous example is steel pricing in the United States from about 1900 to 1924—"Pittsburgh-plus."[20] A system with two or more basing-points is called a *multiple basing-point system*. In that case, the price at any destination is the *lowest* base-price-plus-transport-charge to that destination. The most famous multiple basing-point systems are steel (from 1924 to 1948) and cement (until 1948).[21] Plants located at basing points are called *base mills*; those not located at basing points are called *nonbase mills*.

Figure 6-4 is a simple map showing how a single basing-point system works. For clarity, the map ignores all but three destinations (out of perhaps hundreds). In this case all three of the consumption points shown also happen to be production centers. (P), like Pittsburgh in the old days, is the only basing point, at which the recognized base price is $40 per ton. Nonbase mills produce at points (C) and (B). From (P) to (B), transport charges are $5 per ton; from (P) to (C), $10 per ton. The delivered price quoted for customers at (B) is therefore $45 per ton, whether the stuff is delivered from mills at (P) or from mills located at (B) itself. The delivered price at (C) is $50 per ton, whether delivery is from (C) or from (P).

If the formula freights are the same as actual transport costs between (P) and (C), and between (P) and (B), base mills at (P) receive, net of transport costs, $40 a ton for deliveries at all three destinations, (P), (C), and (B). They are said to realize identical *mill nets* at all three destinations. Nonbase mills at (C) enjoy a higher mill net—$50—on de-

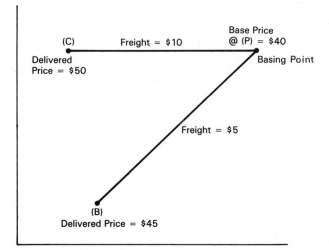

Figure 6-4 Map of a Single Basing-Point System

liveries at (C). If they ship to (P), however, they get only $30—$40 less $10 actual freight from (C) to (P). Similarly, nonbase mills at (B) get a $45 mill net on deliveries at (B) itself, and only $35 on deliveries to (P).

Mill nets in multiple basing-point systems also varied systematically at different destinations, for example when base mills delivered to destinations freightwise closer to other basing points.

It is important to recognize not only that mill nets differ at different destinations, but that they can vary for different reasons. Customers at Chicago complained that Chicago steel mills charged them ''phantom freight,'' just as though their orders had come all the way from Pittsburgh rather than from next door. Without more, that is not necessarily uncompetitive or hurtful. It happens even in atomistic competition, where producers nearer large markets enjoy rents owing to their superior location.

Figure 6-5 pictures the situation in a large market for, say, wheat. There is a demand for wheat (including necessary transport charges) and a supply of wheat (including necessary transport charges). For simplicity, assume that there are three wheat-growing zones, within each of which all producers are subject to the same transport costs, but among which freight charges differ substantially. Zone 3 is closest to the market and is

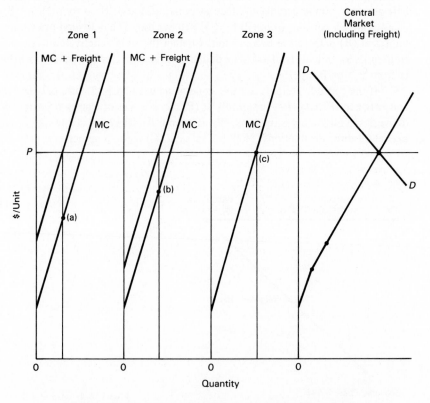

Figure 6-5 Three-Market Equilibrium, Competitive Wheat Industry

assumed to have zero transport costs. Zone 1 is farthest. The industry is competitive. The costs among zones differ only because of transport charges. In Figure 6-5, (a), (b), and (c) are the *net* prices that farmers in zones 1, 2, and 3, get after deducting transport costs to the market.

Flour millers located at the large market in effect pay phantom freight to growers in zone 3 (who pay no freight); and could get wheat more cheaply if all growers were located in zone 3 and if all had as low costs as now prevail there. They also pay more for wheat than if they were located in zone 1, any small miller in which could buy local wheat by paying a net price to growers of not less than (a). But the cost of wheat is only one factor in deciding where to locate a mill, or bakery, or anything else. Another is the cost of transporting the finished product to market. And it is largely irrelevant to the degree of competition in flour milling that millers pay different net prices to growers in zones 1, 2, and 3.

The long and short of it is that growers in zone 3 earn "locational rents" as compared with those in zones 1 and 2. The difference in net prices paid to growers in zones 1, 2, and 3 is irrelevant to the issue of competition amongst flour millers, who are free to locate where they will, and who will pay the same price as their rivals at any given location. Yet, given similar price relationships in other cases, FTC and the courts complained that processors in the large market pay relatively higher prices to zone 3 farmers; and millers in zone 1 will be able to pay absolutely lower prices for wheat. But nothing short of forcing farmers in zone 3 to sell at as low net prices as those in zone 1 receive will eradicate that problem. The legal theory seems to have been that a seller should not be permitted to enjoy benefits of its favorable location, but that buyers should be able to.[22]

Look at the same problem from the standpoint of the wheat farmers. Suppose you own three farms, one each in zones 1, 2, and 3. On sales to the large central market, you would obtain three different net prices, as you would if you sold to millers located in each of the growers' zones.

So a simple rule that goes against systematically different mill nets among different plants (or farms) seems defective, unless you want to compel pricing arrangements that would not efficiently allocate scarce resources even under competitive conditions. Defective, too, is the argument that purchasers are necessarily injured whenever net prices differ at different locations. Observe Chief Justice Stone's statement that "Petitioners' pricing system results inevitably in systematic price discriminations, since the prices they receive upon deliveries from Kansas City bear relation to factors other than actual costs of production or delivery."[23] Look at the farmers located in our hypothetical zone 3. Where do they stand under such a rule? In fact where does anyone stand who sells at a uniform price from plants whose costs differ?

What would a sensible theory be? Basing-point systems, uniformly adhered to, are relatively simple tools for suppressing price competition when freight cost is relatively significant. Professor Stigler's theory is that geographic instability of demand is the most important factor making conspirators choose a basing-point price system.[24] However that may be, with basing-point pricing, individual plants for long periods received systematically different net prices on sales made in different markets. But we would not expect to find one farmer located in zone 3 persistently selling at price P in zone 3 and in the large central market, and at the same time happily selling at price (a) in zone 1 and price (b) in zone 2. Why? Because he could sell all he wants at the higher net price of zone 3, and will do so. If he is systematically and persistently discriminating from his zone 3 farm, this may indicate something important: monopoly.

Suppose that nonbase mills such as those at (C) and (B) (in Figure 6-4) routinely ship to various destinations, including those toward (P). Their mill nets will then vary destination-to-destination. That is, they realize significantly more on sales freightwise closer to home and away from (P) than they do from sales towards (P). Why would they do that rather than reducing price a bit around their own locations? Systematic differences in mill nets were also a feature of *multiple* basing-point systems. On deliveries to destinations that were closer (freightwise) to other basing points, even base mills got lower mill nets. How could such discriminatory price patterns *persist* as they did, in the absence of collusion?

The steel industry faced a much more complicated pricing problem than Figure 6-4 even hints at. There are thousands of different qualities and dimensions of steel products, for which a single base price would not do. Instead, steel producers used the same base prices for broad product classes, plus a list of extra prices for product variations, and adopted a rule for quoting prices on specifications that fall between two extra-book price listings.[25] Base-price changes were commonly announced in trade journals or trade association communications.

If all sellers use the same basing points and prices, and calculate freight charges in the same way, they can all quote identical prices to any destination, regardless of how complex the product is and no matter how far the destination is from their own plants. If all sellers in the industry did that, they would quote identical delivered prices, and the system could, in that respect at least, be said to work "perfectly."[26]

In summary, a basing-point system can eliminate price differences among firms, increase price stability, or neutralize competitive advantages stemming from geographic location. Where collusion is illegal, as it is in the United States, such a scheme may have been the best alternative available, imperfect though it was. Reciprocally sharing of markets, openly deprecated by industry leaders when it leads to costly cross-hauling of products, may result both from geographical demand instability and from sales rivalry remaining when, though conspiring, an industry has not been consolidated within one ownership unit. [27]

Steel[28]

Some of its critics (and even some of its supporters) claim that basing-point pricing did a remarkable job of stabilizing steel prices. According to a United States Labor Department study, actual prices paid by consumers for various types of steel remained relatively unchanged during periods when the steel industry's rate of operations fluctuated widely.[29] Between the second quarter of 1939 and the fourth quarter of 1941, the steel industry's rate of ingot capacity utilization climbed from 51 percent to 98 percent. But during the same period, actual delivered prices of hot-rolled sheets rose only 8 percent. Cold-rolled sheet prices rose only 5 percent. Prices of structural shapes rose by only 3 percent.

Whether the industry used its facilities fully or had tremendous idle capacity, the prices consumers paid for steel varied relatively little.[30]

Critics also claim that steel prices were too high as well as too rigid, especially, perhaps, during the Great Depression. From 1933 to 1935, the NRA Steel Code enforced basing-point pricing. And, in 1938, even without the NRA and in a very bad year for steel, prices were still high enough so that the U.S. Steel Corporation could break even with 55 to 60 percent of its total steel-making capacity idle.[31] The ability persistently to maintain prices at levels permitting profits (or, at worst, minimal losses) when roughly one-half of an industry's capacity is idle suggested to critics that competition was not very effective.

It is not necessary to admire delivered-pricing systems to conclude, however, that the quality of economic analysis used to attack them was not very good. As we have seen, regional chauvinism and catchy, loaded terms—phantom freight, for example—played a role in the political and legal campaigns against basing-point pricing. More relevant criticisms include that basing-point pricing was a reliable way to fix prices and that collusion would have been much harder without it.

As is often true, it is not clear whether antitrust victories against basing-point systems accomplished much in steel. Indeed, it is not clear to what extent the legal commandments laid down have actually been obeyed.

Cement

The Federal Trade Commission (FTC) charged that some 80 cement firms (operating a total of 150 plants) had collusively used a multiple basing-point system to suppress price competition.[32] The case generated an enormous volume of evidence and claims: 99,000 pages of testimony and exhibits; 176 pages of findings and conclusions by the FTC; and 4,000 pages of legal briefs.

The Cement Institute, organized in 1929, succeeded a long line of similar trade associations purporting to protect and promote the interests of member cement producers.[33] The Lehigh Valley of Pennsylvania— cradle of this industry in the U.S.—began producing cement in 1872. Because freight charges made up a large part of its delivered cost, and because materials necessary to make the new Portland cement were widespread, the industry dispersed as it grew. Before 1902, cement plants sold F.O.B. mill.[34] For a time F.O.B. pricing coexisted with delivered pricing. But from the early 1900s on, cement manufacturers allegedly acted in concert to create more "orderly" methods of selling their product.[35] As early as 1910 cement appears to have been sold in the midwest on a Lehigh Valley base. This method assertedly developed through joint action on the part of the industry. By the 1930s, the multiple basing-point system was in use over practically the entire United States.[36] At least one famous economist claimed that this system had evolved spontaneously, rather than collusively.[37]

The National Recovery Administration (NRA), a remarkable New Deal innovation that lasted from 1933 to 1935, in the middle of the Great Depression, did not explicitly require basing-point pricing in cement. But the NRA Cement Code helped enforce it. Before that period and after, according to the *Cement* case, the industry used the basing-point system to suppress competition. They were held to have conspired to prepare and use uniform freight-rate books for quoting delivered prices; to eliminate truck delivery; to remove individualistic managers from plants; to standardize cement specifications or give the appearance that cement is a standardized commodity; to standardize credit and discount terms; to prepare and disseminate statistics divulging the production and capacity of individual cement firms; to boycott dealers who sold imported cement; and otherwise to eliminate competition.

According to Mr. Justice Black's U.S. Supreme Court opinion,

> It seems impossible to conceive that anyone reading these findings in their entirety could doubt that the Commission found that respondents collectively maintained a multiple basing point delivered price system for the purpose of suppressing competition in cement. . . .

> We cannot say that the Commission is wrong in concluding that the delivered-price system as here used provides an effective instrument which, if left free for use of the respondents, would result in complete destruction of competition and the establishment of monopoly in the cement industry. . . .

> . . . for many years, with rare exceptions, cement has been offered for sale in every given locality at identical prices and terms by all producers. Thousands of secret sealed bids have been received by public agencies which corresponded in prices of cement down to a fractional part of a penny.[38]

As "one among many" examples of identical price quotations, Justice Black chose the now-legendary case of Tucumcari, New Mexico, to which, in 1936, 11 different cement producers offered to deliver 6,000 barrels of cement for $3.286854 per barrel, an identical price to six decimal places. To discourage identical pricing, Secretary of the Interior Harold Ickes reputedly formulated the following rule for government purchases: when delivered prices are identical, buy from the mill farthest from the destination. That rule yields sellers the lowest *net* price and largest transportation bill. Railroads, if not consumers, would benefit.

Basing-Points: Collusion or Competition?

Cases that U.S. courts decided from 1945 to 1948 climaxed a long campaign by the FTC (and some economists) to outlaw basing-point systems. By 1949, antitrust authorities were in a position to win almost any basing-point case they chose to bring. This situation caused a political backlash.[39] As a result, FTC pulled in its horns and stopped attacking delivered-pricing systems on purely formalistic grounds such as that mill-net variations technically violated the Robinson-Patman anti-price discrimination act. Antitrust cases against basing-point systems stopped.

By that time, though their interest in delivered pricing had faded, most economists probably were still suspicious of the practice. John M. Clark, long an exception, persisted in his theory that basing-point systems in the steel and cement industries were not products of collusion but had evolved spontaneously and competitively. Although Clark may have been right, cases such as *Cement Institute* (1948) had convinced many that he was wrong. And, as in the 1930s and early 1940s, most industrial organization economists probably still believed that delivered-pricing systems had collusive origins and effects.

Much later, private antitrust suits against plywood manufacturers eventuated in enormous damage settlements that made the news.[40] This may explain the recent flurry of articles about delivered-pricing matters.[41] Economists' cruelest critics say this is just more proof that we always ride toward the sound of clinking coins; but perhaps it is just that we are interested in topics of the day.

Virtually by definition, an industry that collectively fixes and adheres to base prices for each variety of product, and quotes the same freight and other charges to each destination, succeeds in fixing prices at every destination. Less clear are whether what look like symptoms of monopoly pricing are symptoms of competition or something else; or whether and under what conditions other cartel techniques would be more effective. According to David Haddock, for example,

> My analysis implies that statutory restrictions against collusion still ought to require direct evidence of collusion; the use of freight-absorbing basing-point prices may arise in a competitive industry at least as readily as in a poorly cartelized one. In contrast, a well-cartelized industry will almost surely not use such arrangements. If freight-absorbing basing-point prices are used in an industry, then collusion is either weak, or it is non-existent.[42]

This conclusion goes too far, even if we ignore the substantial factual record about such things and concentrate on theoretical problems. In Haddock's model each of a group of actively competing firms located at the basing point sells at marginal cost plus (actual) freight. A single-firm local monopoly located at a non-base point sells at base price plus freight from the basing point, discriminating in price by absorbing freight to destinations that are freightwise closer to the basing point.

He calls this a case of *noncollusive* basing-point pricing. We can agree that *noncollusive* does include single-firm monopoly; but it should include *competitive* as well. Haddock is not clear about what competition means to him. It appears, however, that the competition he envisions must be intense enough to produce marginal cost pricing, yet weak enough to permit *persistent and systematic* price discrimination (freight equalization) and price matching by firms located both at non-basing points and basing points in a multiple basing-point system.

It also appears that it would not take many noncolluding firms to produce the kind of competition Haddock is talking about. Assume that is so. It is also true that there are often two or more firms at or near enough to a producing point to affect and be affected by it. If so, how *could* they discriminate in price and forbear to compete unless they collude? And when there are not two or more firms at such a point, why not? Haddock says it is because natural monopoly makes entry impossible.

Under competition, perhaps including the kind that Haddock is talking about, the spatial relationships among prices would reflect *real* transport costs—the lowest-cost alternatives, actually. In real basing-point systems, it was apparently common for buyers to pay formula freights that differed from real freight costs.

Finally, by *effective* cartel, Haddock seems to mean a *perfect* cartel. Even single-firm monopolies maximize profits subject to constraints, and cartels are often narrowly constrained. *Any* monopoly profit is better than none, and the best solution achievable in practice is the one to choose, however imperfect someone may say it is. As Stigler showed, a basing-point cartel can adjust flexibly to marked changes in regional demand, without using more obvious monopolistic arrangements such as profit pools or simply assigning exclusive markets by agreement. It also avoids the tortures of trying to change collusive prices frequently without either exposing the cartel or losing its coherence. For a long time, delivered-pricing systems were effectively antitrust-resistant, seemingly immune. Such a record is impressive, especially if such systems were actually collusive all along. Impressive, even though imperfect.

SALES AGENCIES

Exclusive sales-agency cartels have been popular where law permitted them. Figure 6-6 illustrates how they work, using the same cost functions used earlier in Figure 6-1. Costs differ among three classes of firms that belong to a cartel of bituminous coal producers. Members of the cartel create a sales agency and each of them contracts to market all output through it. Each member's ownership in the agency is proportional to its agreed share in cartel profits or rents. SRMC is the aggregate cartel marginal cost function. To calculate net coal revenue, costs of running the sales agency must be deducted from the final market demand for the cartel's coal. Let agency costs be AC = MC, as shown in Figure 6-6. The net demand and net marginal revenue, ND and NMR, are used to determine cartel selling prices and the profit-maximizing buying prices that the agency offers to the cartel members who own the agency.

    If all goes well, the sales agency purchases the cartel members' coal at the purchase price PP*. The profit-maximizing final price is FP* and final quantity is Q*. The sales agency nominally earns profits of R_A, which it distributes to member firms in proportion to their ownership share. No explicit output ceilings or quotas need be assigned: the purchase price is set at $PP*$, the value of cartel marginal cost at the profit-maximizing output. High-cost producers sell less than the others, and members that produce and sell nothing are compensated by what they earn as shareholders in the sales agency.[43] Under competition, the purchase price is PP_C and final price is FP_C.

    Of course, not all exclusive sales agencies are cryptocartels. Some no doubt reduce the costs of information, transactions, and so on, thereby benefiting producers and consumers alike. How can we tell which kind we've found?

    If what we have is a cartel arrangement, the price at which the agency purchases should be lower than it was before or otherwise would be. Total net revenue per ton (including profit redistribution) that coal producers receive will rise. If this vertical integration into coal sales increases efficiency, the net coal price should, it is true, rise even if the sales agency is *not* a cartel scheme. Second, however, if it *is* purely a cartel, final market price will be higher than it was before or otherwise would have been. This is easiest to detect when no such combinations have been formed in other similar markets, for they offer a noncollusive outcome for comparison. Third, if the sales-agency business were generally competitive, a cartel sales agent should look abnormally profitable as compared

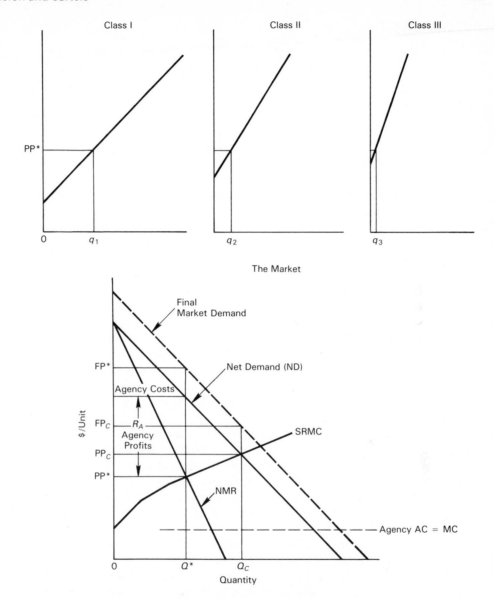

Figure 6-6 Cartel Sales Agency

with bona fide agents. Fourth, if some producers do *not* enter into cartels, the market share of producers that own a cartel sales agency should decline. The net returns to coal producers should also rise if their sales-agency arrangement lowers costs rather than increasing monopoly. If it is not a cartel, though, the market share of the producers involved should rise, and the final market price should fall.

BUYERS' CARTELS _____

Buyers' cartels are interesting in their own right, and not much analyzed. One reason is that they may be rare, as Posner claims.[44] Another reason is that analyzing monopsony can get complicated.

Perhaps, as Posner suggests, few monopsony cases have been brought because monopsony is rare. Yet there are important instances of factors of production (inputs) that are used by only one industry. Minerals such as bauxite, iron ore, and crude oil seem to qualify, for example, and they are not trivial. In cases like that, monopsony might pay well if members of the purchasing industry manage to collaborate.

Monopsony literally means one buyer, and there are not very many examples of that. Usually, economists apply the term to cartels of buyers, for which it may be a reasonably good fit; or to markets that are merely concentrated on the buyers' side, for which it is likely to be a poor fit. These cases are buyer-side analogies to monopoly, sellers' cartels, and oligopoly—the counterpart jargon for the last of which is *oligopsony*.[45]

History of the Spanish sugar industry illustrates some complexities that arise when a monopsony buys different qualities of a good. Assume that a number of sugar manufacturers are located in the same region and are the only buyers of sugar beets produced in it. These refiners sell their finished sugar over a much wider area, in competition with many other producers. Under competition, an input is worth what it contributes, at the margin, to the *net* value of output. Output is valued at market prices.[46] The value of a factor's gross marginal contribution is its physical marginal product *times* the market price of the product. Because the beets must be processed in expensive machinery, we evaluate the market value of sugar beets by deducting processing costs from the gross addition that beets make to revenue.

The simplest theories of market organization and structure are models of extreme or polar cases. For monopsony, that means a single buyer. Take the simplest monopsony case first. Assume that the refineries produce only sugar from the sugar beets.[47] Beets are used in fixed proportions with the other inputs, one ton of beets with each dose of refining services, as in Figure 6-7. We derive the net market demand for *sugar beets* by deducting beet processing costs from the market demand for *beet sugar*. This yields DD, shown in the diagram.

There can be no monopsony control over price of an input if its supply function is perfectly elastic: any reduction in price would dry up supply altogether. As the diagram assumes, the overall market supply of sugar beets—SS—is *not* perfectly elastic. Given the supply and demand conditions shown, sugar beets will sell for P_C under atomistic competition. Q_C will be produced and sold. Suppose that these same refiners form a beet-buying cartel, but must continue to sell their sugar on competitive markets. They maximize profits by buying beets up to the point at which the marginal net revenue added by beets equals the *marginal* expenditure on a ton of beets, ME rather than the *price* of beets. That is, refiners recognize **that** they now control the price of local beets. If they buy only a few beets, the price is low. If they buy heavily, they drive up the price. The marginal expenditure is defined as the change in total expenditure resulting from a unit-change in the quantity bought. As the diagram shows, the marginal expenditure on beets (ME) is no longer

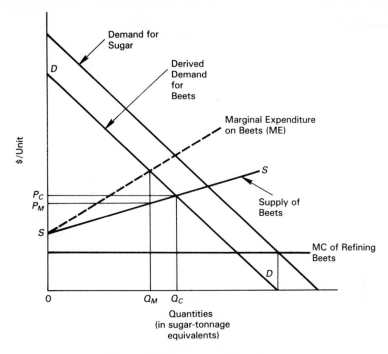

Figure 6-7 Monopsony of Sugar Beets

equal to the market price of beets. As a result, the buying cartel buys fewer beets—Q_M—at a lower price—P_M.

Because diagrams for multiple-product and multiple-input price discrimination get complicated, we'll use an arithmetic example instead. We now assume that Spanish beet-sugar refiners produce and sell two products monopolistically, sugar and wet beet pulp; and buy two different qualities of beets monopsonistically, class 1 and class 2. Table 6-2 shows hypothetical data derived from the Appendix. The product yields are fractions of tons of products got from refining a ton of beets. Prices are in Spanish currency, pesetas per ton. Revenues and costs are per ton of beets refined.

A ton of class 1 beets increases *gross* revenues by about 970 pesetas per ton. No one will pay more for class 1 beets than that amount *minus* processing cost, i.e., about 820 pesetas per ton. Under competition, no one can get them for less. The same logic applies to class 2 beets. Under competition, they will fetch 522 pesetas per ton.

Under conditions of monopoly plus monopsony, however, we are in a different world. Prices of both types of beets are much lower and the ratio of their prices much altered. Product prices are much higher. Beet prices are much lower than their net contribution to revenues. The model developed in the Appendix, for example, gives beet prices of 463 and 419, and product prices of 10,547 and 584. That model incorporates an upward-sloping marginal cost of refining.

One reason why so few cases have been brought against monopsony may be that it

TABLE 6–2 Beet-sugar yields

	Class 1 Beets	Class 2 Beets
Sugar yield	.1500	.1000
Sugar price	6295.3650	6295.3650
Revenue from sugar	944.3048	629.5365
Pulp yield	.0600	.1000
Pulp price	428.9054	428.9054
Revenue from pulp	25.7343	42.8905
Total revenue, sugar and pulp	970.0391	672.4270
MC of refining beets	150.0000	150.0000
Net addition to revenue	820.0391	522.4270

is hard to detect. Unless we understand the economics of monopsony, we will not recognize its symptoms. Viewed in the large, however, the symptoms of monopsony are analogous to those produced by monopoly. Price discrimination, for example, can crop up in either case, though it is harder to find and measure when different qualities of inputs are involved. And difficulties arise when the inputs are used to make several products. We then need to know something about process costs and the amounts of different products that different qualities of an input can produce. In fact, as a listing of information required to draw even Figure 6-7 reveals, it often takes more information to solve monopsony problems. Even more information is required to solve multiple-product problems, as the example (and Appendix) show.

As a practical matter, however, suggestive analyses can be made with relatively scanty information, once the economic principles are understood. Something can be accomplished, for example, by calculating changes in differences between input prices and the revenues got from goods that the input is used to produce.

SUMMARY

Diagnosing cartels is not only an interesting scientific problem. It is also important to justice and to economics whenever law punishes those convicted of colluding. For several reasons, we are likely to be plagued by conflicting diagnoses. The first problem is how to use economic theories to improve law and justice. From the tangle of oligopoly theories, we can choose theories predicting all manner of different outcomes. To be consistent, people who believe as a scientific matter that noncollusive oligopoly is pretty much the same as monopoly should believe that only direct attacks on market concentration per se will do much good. On the other side are people who believe that even a few firms will produce competitive outcomes *unless* they collude. To be consistent, they should, as a scientific matter, be willing to infer collusion from symptoms of sorts found in collusive arrangements rather than requiring direct evidence of explicit collusion. Consistency is relatively rare on both sides of that debate. Concentration is not a criminal offence under U.S. law; but collusion is. Both of these bloodless scientific positions neglect important issues of crime, punishment, and justice. Humane justice seems to demand that whichever "scientific" position we take, we have clear evidence of explicit collusion before deciding that an illegal *cartel* had been at work and imposing criminal penalties on anybody who happened to be standing around.

A second problem is getting *cartel* theory into shape before using it to diagnose actual industrial histories. Building workable models and tests is the problem. Economic theory is at its best when put to *maximizing* simple objective functions, minimizing costs in the process. When law is hostile and seriously punitive, however, we should not expect to find many cartels that maximize quite so simply as textbooks suggest. Covert cartels are trying to maximize profits all right, but within constraints set by the probability and costs of detection and punishment. Outsiders know little about the number, type, and weight of such constraints.

Significant cost differences among firms cause problems unless a cartel can set individualized quotas, allocate territories, make side payments to shut down high-cost plants and firms, and so on. Many real cartels did just that, when laws permitted.[48] When law is hostile, however, profit maximizing is constrained and compromises must be struck. Compromises do not work as well as arrangements that can be made in a hospitable legal climate. But even rough compromises may be better for the industry than competition is. The most profitable of those compromises is what cartels are typically looking for. Fellner's main conclusion, discussed in Chapter 5, may have been backwards. Perhaps it is the real cartels, rather than noncollusive oligopolies, that look like watered-down, imperfect versions of the cartels pictured in textbooks.

When untidiness beclouds the theory, there is room for honest error, as well as refuge for scoundrels and sophists. We observe industries doing some things that resemble what a textbook cartel might do; but doing other things that a perfect textbook cartel would not do. This causes serious trouble for both cartel theory and anticartel law.

If we compromise simple profit-maximizing economic theory too much, we will brand as cartelists some who are not. The limiting case is to brand as cartel monopoly anything that differs from atomistic competition. If, on the other hand, we diagnose as cartels only those arrangements that closely match the theory of joint profit-maximizing cartels, we will acquit some cartelists who are injuring consumers significantly. The limiting case is acquitting all who do not function just like *perfect* joint-maximizing textbook cartelists would.

Many economists believe that cartels will not endure unless they tightly control some indispensable input or get government support. For, if a cartel earns profits, entry will occur. Even if a cartel is formed when the industry is depressed, as perhaps most have been, and earns less than normal profits as a result, new entry would occur if good times return. Furthermore, cartels tend to erode even in the absence of entry by new firms, because secret or open defection often pays. What it comes down to is that, from birth, cartels spread existing economic niches wider and may open up new ones. It often pays someone to put resources into them. In the process, cartels tend to lose their ground.

Histories of cartels reveal something else important. Many law cases involve cartels with only a few members, from two firms on up. Many had few enough members to qualify as highly to moderately concentrated oligopolies. Since cartelization costs something, collusion among small groups seems inconsistent with assertions that nonconspiratorial oligopoly is equivalent to or very close to monopoly. If these assertions were right, why would oligopolists have needed to cartelize in the first place? As Posner put it, ''The prevalence of small-number express collusion cases . . . casts some doubt on the practical importance of tacit collusion.''[49]

As far back as historic records go, sellers and buyers have displayed great ingenuity and persistence in trying to fix prices through agreements with their competitors. Most, and perhaps all, of these schemes have hurt consumers, though nobody knows how much. It is tempting to urge harsh punishments to keep such practices at optimal levels; that is, to pursue and punish them until the marginal consumer benefits from punishment are brought to equality with the marginal costs of imposing punishment. It is not clear how to apply that rule, partly because we know little about what the benefit and cost functions of such a policy look like. Who knows, for example, whether we now spend too little or too much on anticollusion policies?

Classical liberals of the eighteenth and nineteenth centuries recognized the policy problem. Adam Smith opposed collusion, but believed that policies strong enough to be effective against it would jeopardize ''liberty and justice.'' Smith had a point. This chapter showed how cartels work and proposed various diagnostic tests for deciding whether a cartel or competition is at work in specific instances. It is well to recognize, however, that law and economics are not precise laboratory sciences. And our data are not very good. The theories and diagnostic tests our courts use have often proved to be ambiguous or worse. As a result, unless we fortuitously catch conspirators red-handed, anticollusion laws will inevitably punish some beneficial practices and innocent people, and acquit some who are guilty. More than eighty-five years after basing-point systems appeared, for example, economists are still debating whether such systems are collusive or competitive, hurtful or beneficial.

This chapter said little about any good effects that cartels might produce. In discussing U.S. antitrust policies, Chapter 19 says more about that problem.

What reasonably realistic policy alternatives do we have? First, like the classical liberals, we could try to discourage *governments* from establishing and propping up cartels. We could, like the classicals, encourage open interstate and international trade, because cartels are less effective in broader markets. Second, with or without misgivings about justice and liberty, we could continue or even enlarge our relatively modest antitrust programs against collusion. Anticollusion may be the easiest part of our antitrust policy to defend. Its direct costs, at least, are relatively modest.

QUESTIONS

1. Is OPEC a success or failure? Discuss.
2. How does profit pooling work? How does it help when the costs of cartel members differ? Why don't all real cartels pool?

3. Discuss: "In the theory of atomistic competition, all sellers charge the same price. Why, then, claim that 11 producers have colluded because they merely quoted the same delivered price per barrel of cement, down to the sixth decimal place?"

4. What does *Addyston* suggest about the likelihood of identical sealed bids?

5. "To prevent fraud and collusion by their own purchasing officers, governments at all levels publicize how much everyone bid when they open sealed bids and award contracts. This is one reason bid-rigging works as well as it does." Explain and discuss.

6. Economists may seem to have things both ways: differences in prices charged by the same seller, and price differences among sellers, have been used both as symptoms of collusion and as evidence that competition is alive and well. So have uniform prices. Discuss.

7. Since even a *competitive* industry may charge higher prices when its domestic markets are protected by a high tariff, how can a higher price in the domestic market be used as a symptom of collusion?

8. In principle, how could you decide whether an exclusive sales agency is a cartel or a beneficial cost-reducing business form used competitively?

9. What, if anything, do conspiracies among relatively few firms suggest about oligopoly theory?

10. Present a theory of how collusive monopsony works. In principle, how could we diagnose one?

APPENDIX: MORE GENERAL MONOPSONY MODELS

Small systems of linear equations, which even inexpensive microcomputers can now handle, permit us to do simple analyses that are very powerful.

Though the task at hand is to analyze a known monopsony, the real job often includes *diagnosing* monopsony. That is, could the prices observed have been produced competitively? Or by Cournot-style price-quantity searchers who are not colluding? Or do they look like prices that would be produced under collusive or single-firm monopsony?

Answers to questions like these require comparative analyses, for which we need models of competition as well as monopsony. Start with atomistic competition, using a model with five variables and five equations:

$$dP_1 = \text{demand price for class 1 beets.}$$

$$dP_2 = \text{demand price for class 2 beets.}$$

$$P_S = \text{price of sugar.}$$

$$P_P = \text{price of pulp.}$$

$$C(\text{Ref}) = \text{MC of Refining Services.}$$

PURE COMPETITION

Product Prices

Assume that sugar beets are only used to produce two products: (1) sugar; and (2) pulp. These goods are unrelated in demand: cross-elasticities are zero. The demand functions are:

$$P_S = 15,000 - 30Q_s.$$

$$P_P = 750 - 2Q_p.$$

Quantities are measured in thousands of tons per year. There are two kinds of beets: type 1 and type 2. Type 1 yields more sugar and less pulp. Each type of beet is homogeneous, and a ton yields fractional tonnages of products as shown in Table 6-3.

The total quantity—and therefore price—of each product is determined by the type and quantity of beets refined. Take the price of sugar—P_S—for example. Q_1 is the total quantity of type 1 beets refined; Q_2 is the quantity of type 2 beets refined. The quantity of sugar produced from type 1 beets is the yield per ton *times* the tonnage of type 1 beets refined; similarly for type 2. The price of sugar is determined by total quantities refined from both type 1 and type 2 beets:

$$P_S = 15,000 - 30(0.15Q_1) - 30(.10Q_2).$$

$$15,000 - 4.5Q_1 - 3Q_2.$$

The price of pulp is derived the same way:

$$P_P = 750 - 2(.06Q_1) - 2(.10Q_2).$$

$$= 750 - 0.12Q_1 - 0.2Q_2.$$

We can now prepare the first two equations, for the demand prices of the two products. The first equation—for the price of sugar—is:

(1) $$P_S + 0P_P + 4.5Q_1 + 3Q_2 + 0C(\text{Ref}) = 15,000.$$

The second equation—for the price of pulp—is:

(2) $$0P_S + P_P + 0.12Q_1 + 0.20Q_2 + 0C(\text{Ref}) = 750.$$

The Quantities of Beets Refined

We can determine the quantity of beets refined by using the demand and supply functions for beets. This model assumes that the two types of beets do not compete on the *supply* side. This might be true, for example, if they do not grow in the same areas.

The most anyone would pay for a ton of beets is the value of products got from them *minus* the costs of extracting those products. In the case of type 1 beets, for example,

TABLE 6–3 Tons of products yielded per ton of beets

	Type 1	Type 2
Sugar	0.15	0.10
Pulp	0.06	0.10

$$dP_1 = 0.15P_S + 0.06P_P - C(\text{Ref}).$$

The supply of type 1 beets is

$$sP_1 = 100 + 0.5Q_1.$$

Since $dP_1 = sP_1$ in equilibrium,

$$0.15P_S + 0.06P_P - C(\text{Ref}) = 100 + 0.5Q_1,$$

from which we get the third equation:

(3) $$0.15P_S + 0.06P_P - 0.5Q_1 + 0Q_2 - C(\text{Ref}) = 100.$$

Turn now to the supply and demand for beets of type 2:

$$dP_2 = 0.10P_S + 0.10P_P - C(\text{Ref}).$$

$$sP_2 = 300 + 0.3Q_2$$

$dP_2 = sP_2$:

$$0.10P_S + 0.10P_P - 0.3Q_2 - C(\text{Ref}) = 300.$$

This yields equation (4):

(4) $$0.10P_S + 0.10P_P + 0Q_1 - 0.3Q_2 - C(\text{Ref}) = 300.$$

The Marginal Cost of Refining, C(Ref)

Because all beets are refined, and one "unit" of refining services is applied to each ton of beets,

$$Q(\text{Ref}) = Q_1 + Q_2.$$

In this five-equation model, $C(\text{Ref})$ need not be constant. Assume that the supply function of refining services is:

$$C(\text{Ref}) = 75 + .034380(Q_1) + .034380(Q_2),$$

which yields

$$C(\text{Ref}) - .034380Q_1 - .034380Q_2 = 75;$$

or

(5) $$0P_S + 0P_P - .034380Q_1 - .034380Q_2 + C(\text{Ref}) = 75$$

Under these assumptions, atomistic competition produces the following values:

$$P_S = 6295.370$$
$$P_P = 428.906$$
$$Q_1 = 1440.080$$
$$Q_2 = 741.425$$
$$C(\text{Ref}) = 150.000$$

From either their demand or supply functions, we derive the prices of class 1 and class 2 beets. Using demands, we get:

$$dP_1 = 0.15P_S + 0.06P_P - C(\text{Ref}) = 82\ 0.0399$$
$$dP_2 = 0.10P_S + 0.10P_P - C(\text{Ref}) = 522.4276.$$

Using supplies, we get:

$$sP_1 = 100 + 0.5Q_1 = 820.0400$$
$$sP_2 = 300 + 0.3Q_2 = 522.4275.$$

Close enough.

MONOPSONY SOLUTIONS

How do competition and monopsony compare? We could compare competitive results with those for monopsony in sugar *plus* monopsony in beets. Or we could assume, as most of the text does, that there is competition in sugar and monopsony in beets. Here, we assume that there is monopoly in the sale of sugar and pulp *and* monopsony in the purchase of beets.

To obtain maximum profits, the monopoly-monopsony calculates *marginal* revenues for products and *marginal* expenditures (or *marginal* factor costs) for inputs.

But we must be careful. An integrated monopsonist, who *owns* and operates sugar refineries as well as sugar beets, and is not merely a specialist intermediary who buys and resells beets, will not exploit his own refinery—and himself—by relying on some function that is "marginal" to his own marginal refining costs. *That* would not maximize his total profits.

Marginal Revenues from Products

Instead of using product prices to evaluate marginal products, a monopolist-monopsonist uses marginal revenues. These linear marginal revenues are twice as steep as the linear demand functions from which they are derived:

$$MR_S = 15,000 - 60Q_S$$
$$= 15,000 - 60(0.15Q_1) - 60(0.10Q_2)$$
$$= 15,000 - 9Q_1 - 6Q_2.$$

From this, we derive equation 1:

(1) $MR_S + 0MR_P + 9Q_1 + 6Q_2 + 0C(Ref) = 15,000.$

The marginal revenue from pulp is derived the same way:

$$MR_P = 750 - 4Q_P$$
$$= 750 - 4(.06Q_1) - 4(.10Q_2)$$
$$= 750 - 0.24Q_1 - 0.40Q_2.$$

This yields:

(2) $0MR_S + MR_P + .24Q_1 + .40Q_2 + 0C(Ref) = 750.$

The Quantities of Beets

The (net) marginal revenue products and marginal factor costs of beets determine the rate at which beets are refined. The marginal factor cost functions slope upwards twice as steeply as the competitive supply functions from which they are derived.

Under monopsony, the marginal factor cost of class 1 beets is:

$$MFC_1 = 100 + 1.0Q_1.$$

Because, in equilibrium, $MFC_1 = MRP_1$, we can derive equation (3) as follows:

(3) $0.15MR_S + 0.06MR_P - Q_1 - 0Q_2 - C(Ref) = 100.$

Similarly,

$MFC_2 = 300 + 0.6Q_2$. And, because $MFC_2 = MRP_2$, we derive equation (4) as follows:

(4) $0.10MR_S + 0.10MR_P + 0Q_1 - 0.6Q_2 - C(Ref) = 300.$

C(Ref)

This model assumes that $C(Ref)$ *varies* with the quantities of beets processed:

$$C(Ref) = 75 + .034380(Q_1) + .034380(Q_2),$$

which yields,

$$C(Ref) - .034380Q_1 - .034380Q_2 = 75.$$

TABLE 6–4 Competitive and monopoly plus monopsony solutions, beets and products

	Atomistic Competition	*Monopoly + Monopsony*
P_S	6,295.370	10,547.10
P_P	428.906	583.74
Q_1	1,440.080	725.581
Q_2	741.425	395.971
$C(Ref)$	150.000	113.559
P_1	820.0400	462.7905
P_2	522.4275	418.7913

As a result, we derive equation (5) as follows:

(5) $\qquad 0MR_S + 0MR_P - .034380Q_1 - .034380Q_2 + C(Ref) = 75.$

Solving the five−equation market system yields the following equilibrium solution-values:

$$MR_S = 6093.940$$

$$MR_P = 417.472$$

$$Q_1 = 725.581$$

$$Q_2 = 395.971$$

$$C(Ref) = 113.559.$$

Table 6-4 compares results under atomistic competition with those for a combination of monopoly *and* monopsony. Monopoly increases the price of sugar more than the price of pulp because the demand for sugar is less elastic with respect to price. Monopsony drastically reduces the prices of both types of beets, reducing that of type 1 more severely because its supply is less elastic with respect to price.

One useful thing about these models is that they can produce all the comparative static results we want. For example, we can change, separately or in combination, sugar demand; pulp demand; cost of refining (long- or short-run); supply functions of class 1, or class 2 beets, or both; and so on.

TABLE 6–5 Comparative statics: monopoly + monopsony

		New Results	*Previous Results*	*Percentage Change*
P_S	=	7,576.720	6,295.3700	+ 20.4
P_P	=	325.854	428.9060	− 24.0
Q_1	=	1,767.680	1,440.0800	+ 22.7
Q_2	=	1,060.120	741.4250	+ 43.0
$C(Ref)$	=	172.220	150.0000	+ 14.8
P_1	=	983.840	820.0400	+ 20.0
P_2	=	618.036	522.4275	+ 18.3

One example is enough to show how we can get and compare as many static results as we want. Suppose that the demand for sugar unexpectedly increases by 50 percent at each price.[50] The price intercept of the demand function remains unchanged. So do all other parameters. Table 6-5 shows some results for short-run competitive equilibria.

Untrained intuition can fail when even so few variables as these are involved: several of these results are not so obvious as first appears.

NOTES

1. Adam Smith, *The Wealth of Nations* (New York: Modern Library, 1937), Chapter X, Part II, p. 128.

2. Chapter 3 discussed spillover effects in general and mentioned crude oil production as an example. Chapter 17 analyzes the crude oil problem (as well as other spillovers) in detail.

3. For some basic theory, see Don Patinkin, "Multiple-Plant Firms, Cartels, and Imperfect Competition," *Quarterly Journal of Economics*, 66 (February 1947), pp. 173-205. Most of the complications that Patinkin wrestles with are due to the kind of cost function he assumes. He uses traditional U-shaped marginal cost functions, which he approximates with linear segments. A simpler cost function avoids all that. Define total cost as $AX^2 + BX + C$, where X is the firm's output rate. It yields a linear, upward-sloping marginal cost function and a U-shaped average cost function. See R. G. D. Allen, *Mathematical Analysis for Economists* (London: Macmillan and Co., Limited, 1947), pp. 120, 156.

4. John S. McGee, "Ocean Freight-Rate Conferences and the American Merchant Marine," *The University of Chicago Law Review*, 27, no. 2 (Winter 1960), pp. 191–314.

5. Dead-weight loss triangles can be drawn and measured, just as discussed for Figure 2-6, in Chapter 2.

6. G. A. Akerlov and J. L. Yellen, "Can Small Deviations from Rationality Make Significant Differences to Economic Equilibria?" *American Economic Review*, 75 (September 1985), pp. 708–20, at p. 719.

7. Recently Mills and Schumann theorized that demand fluctuations produce large differences in the variability of market shares of large and small firms, even in highly competitive industries. D. E. Mills and L. Schumann, "Industry Structure with Fluctuating Demand," *American Economic Review*, 75 (September 1985), pp. 758–67. Their analysis of COMPUSTAT data "suggests that the market share effect is not due primarily to market power. We believe it supports our hypothesis that small, flexible rivals absorb a disproportionate share of industrywide fluctuations." At p. 766.

8. Some recent examples are discussed in "Busting a Trust: Electrical Contractors Reel Under Charges that They Rigged Bids," *The Wall Street Journal*, 29 November 1985, pp. 1, 10; "Grand Jury Indicts 2 Electrical Firms for Rigging Bids," *The Wall Street Journal*, 7 July 1986, p. 6.

9. *U.S.* v. *Addyston Pipe & Steel Co.*, 85 F.271 (1898). A modern analysis that praises restraints on competition, given the cost and demand conditions in this industry, is George Bittlingmayer, "Decreasing Average Cost and Competition: A New Look at the Addyston Pipe Case," *The Journal of Law & Economics*, 25, no. 2 (October 1982), pp. 201–29.

   Addyston is a masterpiece in antitrust law and economics. It is the first major case to rehabilitate and reconcile British and U.S. common law cases dealing with restraints of trade; establish broad jurisdiction for the Sherman Law, under the Commerce Clause; develop legal and economic grounds for a per se rule against "naked" price fixing, which is supposedly without redeeming benefits; analyze in detail the functions and economic effects of a cartel; and establish net economic effects as a general antitrust criterion.

10. Note the analogy with auctions to grant government monopoly franchises, discussed in Chapter 2.

11. George J. Stigler, "Administered Prices and Oligopolistic Inflation," *The Journal of Business*, 35 (January 1962); reprinted in Stigler, *The Organization of Industry* (Homewood, Ill.: Richard D. Irwin, Inc., 1968), pp. 235–51. From time to time, governments have published data on identical bids. See for example, *Identical Bidding in Public Procurement*, Report of the Attorney General Under Executive Order 10936, Department of Justice, Washington, D.C., July 1962; and *Identical Bidding*, Second Report, July 1964.

12. The maximum bid for any member can be calculated with the following formula:

$$\text{Max. bid} = (\text{inc. rev.} - \text{inc. cost})/(1 - \text{share})$$

where share is the bidder's proportion of internal bids, which was agreed to when the cartel was formed.

13. Simon N. Whitney, *Antitrust Policies: American Experience in Twenty Industries* (New York: The Twentieth Century Fund, 1958), vol. II, pp. 9–13.

14. Final Judgment, *U.S.* v. *General Electric Co., et al.*, Civil No. 28288 (October 1, 1962); *Ohio Valley Electric, et al.* v. *GE, et al.*, 244 F. Supp. 914 (1965); *U.S.* v. *GE & Westinghouse* (1976), Plaintiff's Memorandum, Civil No. 28288. There are several other sources: John Fuller, *The Gentlemen Conspirators* (New York: Grove Press, Inc., 1962); John Herling, *The Great Price Conspiracy* (Washington, D.C.: Robert B. Luce, Inc., 1962); Clarence C. Walston and Fred W. Cleveland, Jr., *Corporations on Trial: The Electric Cases* (Belmont, Calif.: Wadsworth Publishing Co., Inc., 1964); U.S. Senate Committee on the Judiciary, Subcommittee on Antitrust and Monopoly, Hearings on Administered Prices, *Price Fixing and Bid Rigging in the Electric Manufacturing Industry*, pts. 27 and 28, 87th Cong. 1st sess. (1961); D. F. Lean, J. D. Ogur, and R. P. Rogers, *Competition and Collusion in Electric Equipment Markets: An Economic Assessment*, Bureau of Economics Staff Report to the Federal Trade Commission (Washington, D.C.: July 1982), hereinafter referred to as FTC, *Assessment*.

15. R. G. M. Sultan, *Pricing in the Electrical Oligopoly* (Cambridge, Mass.: Harvard University Press, vol. I, 1974, vol. II, 1975).

16. FTC, *Assessment*, p. 78.

17. FTC, *Assessment*, p. 47.

18. American industries that used delivered-price systems at one time or another include steel, cement, corn syrup, nonferrous metals, fertilizers, clay pipe, rigid steel conduit, building tile, raw porcelain enamel, oil, gasoline, sugar, lumber, lime, book paper, linseed oil, welded chain, bolts and nuts, milk and ice cream cans, malt, salt, firebrick, farm equipment, and snow fence. See Frank A. Fetter, *The Masquerade of Monopoly* (New York: Harcourt Brace Jovanovich, Inc., 1931), p. 242; Fritz Machlup, *The Basing-Point System* (Philadelphia: Blakiston Co., 1949), p. 17; Arthur R. Burns, *The Decline of Competition* (New York: McGraw-Hill Book Company, 1936), pp. 298, 328; Federal Reserve Bank of Philadelphia, *The Business Review* (September 1948); "Basing Point: The Great Muddle," *Fortune* (Sep-

tember 1948), p. 79; Vernon Mund, *Open Markets* (New York: Harper & Row Publishers, Inc., 1948), p. 213.

19. Most, if not all, of the antitrust cases about delivered pricing involve industries with a history of price-fixing conspiracies. Joseph E. Sheehy, "The Legal and Factual Content of Recent Geographic Pricing Cases," 37 *Georgetown Law Journal* 199 (January 1949).

20. C. R. Daugherty, M. G. de Chazeau, and S. S. Stratton, *The Economics of the Iron and Steel Industry* (New York: McGraw-Hill Book Company, 1937), vol. I, pp. 533–44; George W. Stocking, *Basing Point Pricing and Regional Development* (Chapel Hill: The University of North Carolina Press, 1954); George J. Stigler, "A Theory of Delivered Price Systems," *American Economic Review*, 39 (December 1949), pp. 1143–54; *U.S.* v. *United States Steel Corporation*, 251 U.S. 417 (1920), and *In the Matter of the United States Steel Corporation*, 8 FTC 1 (1924). The last case was a *legal* victory for the Federal Trade Commission; but for various reasons its order never got enforced. See Machlup, *The Basing-Point System*, pp. 66–71.

21. See *Federal Trade Commission* v. *Cement Institute, et al.*, 333 U.S. 683 (1948).

22. *Corn Products Refining Co.* v. *FTC*, 324 U.S. 726 (1945); *FTC* v. *A. E. Staley Mfg. Co., et al.*, 324 U.S. 746 (1945).

23. *Corn Products Refining Co.* v. *FTC* (1945), p. 732.

24. George J. Stigler, "A Theory of Delivered Price Systems," *American Economic Review*, 39 (December 1949), pp. 1143–54. By geographic demand instability, he means that "the proportion of national or regional sales made in each consumption center is subject to substantial fluctuations."

Under such conditions, a cartel may adopt a scheme such as basing-point pricing rather than meeting and changing prices so often that secrecy and stability are both jeopardized.

25. To insure that all sellers quoted the same price to any destination, the industry collectively compiled and distributed freight-rate and extra books and sought to use them consistently. The rule for qualities between two extra quotations was to quote the *higher* extra price. Sellers used their "official" freight-rate books to quote delivered prices even when they knew actual freight rates were different. Although actual weights per lineal foot of rigid steel conduit differed, sellers used a formula to translate different product weights into identical freight charges.

26. In 1936 Robert Gregg, vice president of the United States Steel Corporation, conceded that "if that plan were universally followed there would be no competition insofar as one element of competition is concerned, namely price." United States Congress, Senate, *Hearings Before Committee on Interstate Commerce on S. 4055*, 74th Cong., 2nd sess. (Washington, D.C.: United States Government Printing Office, 1936), p. 207.

Also see *United States* v. *United States Steel Corporation*, 251 U.S. 417 (1920); and George W. Stocking, "The Economics of Basing-Point Pricing," *Law and Contemporary Problems*, 15 (Spring 1950), p. 167.

27. Compare Stigler, "A Theory of Delivered Price Systems," and John S. McGee, "Cross Hauling: A Symptom of Incomplete Collusion Under Basing-Point Systems," *Southern Economic Journal*, 20, no. 4 (1954), pp. 269–79. Stigler's theory predicts that there will be little or no cross hauling under a basing-point system. McGee concludes that there was a lot of it.

28. *U.S.* v. *United States Steel Corp.*, 251 U.S. 417 (1920); *In the Matter of the United States Steel Corp.*, 8 FTC 1 (1924).

See also *Triangle Conduit & Cable Co., Inc.* v. *FTC*, 168 F.2d 175 (1948).

29. Willard Fazar and Fay Bean, "Labor Department Examines Consumers' Prices of Steel Products," *Iron Age*, 157 (26 April 1946), pp. 118–45, cited by Stocking, "The Economics of Basing-point Pricing" (Spring 1950), p. 173 n. This study analyzes *actual* transactions prices, not merely *official* or *formula* prices. It therefore indicates that even when price concessions are taken into account, steel prices were relatively stable.

30. See the testimony of George W. Stocking before the Celler Committee: U.S. Congress, House Committee on the Judiciary, *Hearings Before the Subcommittee on Study of Monopoly Power of the Committee on the Judiciary*, 81st Cong. 2nd sess., serial no. 14, pt. 4A, 1950, p. 973.

31. United States Steel Corporation, *Temporary National Economic Committee Papers* (Privately printed, 1940), vol. II, p. 57; and in *TNEC Hearings*, pt. 26.

32. *FTC* v. *Cement Institute*, 333 U.S. 683 (1948).

33. See, for example, *Cement Manufacturers' Protective Association* v. *United States*, 268 U.S. 588 (1925).

34. F.O.B. means "free on board," a price that does not include transport costs from mill to destination.

35. United States Steel's cement-producing affiliate may have introduced or popularized basing-point pricing in the cement industry.

36. In southern California, producers added a complicated zone-pricing system.

37. J. M. Clark, "Basing-Point Methods of Price Quoting," *Canadian Journal of Economics and Political Science*, 4 (November 1938), pp. 477–89.

38. *FTC* v. *Cement Institute*, 68 S. Ct. 793, at p. 809.

39. See Corwin D. Edwards, *The Price Discrimination Law: A Review of Experience* (Washington, D.C.: The Brookings Institution, 1959), Chapter 12.

40. *In Re Plywood Antitrust Litigation*, 655 F.2d 627 (1981); *certiorari granted sub nom. Weyerhaeuser Co.* v. *Lyman Lamb Co.*, 456 U.S. 971 (1982).

41. For example, see D. Haddock, "Basing-Point Pricing: Competitive Versus Collusive Theories," *American Economic Review*, 72 (June 1982), pp. 289–306; Dennis W. Carlton, "A Reexamination of Delivered Pricing Systems," *The Journal of Law & Economics*, 26 (April 1983), pp. 51–70; J. Greenhut, M. Greenhut, and S. Li, "Spatial Pricing Patterns in the U.S.," *Quarterly Journal of Economics*, 94 (March 1980), pp. 329–50; and T. Gronberg and J. Meyer, "Spatial Pricing, Spatial Rents, and Spatial Welfare," *Quarterly Journal of Economics*, 97 (November 1982), pp. 633–44.

42. Haddock, "Basing Point Pricing," p. 293.

43. This may be the kind of arrangement that Chief Justice C. E. Hughes confronted in *Appalachian Coals, Inc.* v. *U.S.*, 288 U.S. 344 (1933). If so, he misdiagnosed it.

44. Richard A. Posner, "A Statistical Study of Antitrust Enforcement," *The Journal of Law & Economics*, 13 (October 1970), pp. 365–420, at p. 403.

45. For details of a sugar-beet monopsony and beet-sugar monopoly established by law, see J. S. McGee, "Government Intervention in the Spanish Sugar Industry," *The Journal of Law & Economics*, 7 (October 1964), pp. 121–72.

46. The same analysis is used on patents, in Chapter 8.

47. If they produce more products, at the margin the gross value of beets is the total revenue from

all the products made from beets. From that total, the costs of processing would then be deducted. The Appendix analyzes such a case.

48. Taft's *Addyston* opinion, for example, briefly mentions a number of early pooling cartels that sound sophisticated.

49. Richard A. Posner, "A Statistical Study of Antitrust Enforcement," pp. 399, 402.

50. Equation (1) becomes: $P_S + 0P_P + 3Q_1 + 2Q_2 + 0C(\text{Ref}) = 15{,}000$.

7

COSTS AND DEMAND AS DETERMINANTS OF THE NUMBER AND SIZE OF FIRMS

INTRODUCTION

In free atomistic competition, the number of firms is determined by market demand and by the costs of firms capable of entering the industry. Until costs are minimized, it seemingly would pay firms to reallocate outputs among themselves by entry, exit, or otherwise. Until maximum consumer values are created out of given resources, it seemingly will pay existing firms to adjust, and for firms to enter (or leave) the industry. Whenever the gap between consumer values and costs widens, it pays existing or prospective firms to put more resources into the niche, until it fills up. Though constrained by information and transactions costs, as everything is, these powerful forces move industries toward production- and utility-efficiency.

These forces and tendencies are at work not only in atomism, but in *all* industrial structures. Costs and demands can obviously help explain every industrial structure and, if defined right, should explain it completely. Name calling explains little or nothing. It does little good to claim, reflexively, that we have found ''barriers to entry,'' or that markets have ''failed'' or ''broken down,'' whenever market structure and performance seem worse than ideal. We can make more progress by investigating specifiable causes, including some that are natural or benign. Start with costs and demands.

If efficient firms are large relative to the market they serve, it is only natural for there to be few firms.[1]

The next section of this chapter talks about various economies of pure size, defined as those that are, in principle, available to any firm achieving a certain size. In discussing such economies, textbooks commonly measure size by output *rate*; but for many purposes, total model *volume* is a better measure. This section discusses two important

140

sources of size economies: technological advantages of processes and equipment that make mass production pay; and lowering costs through learning.

The following section, on the other hand, notes that pure size efficiencies are not the only kinds that matter. Differences among firms account for important differences in their efficiency; and differences in their efficiency account for much of the difference in their size. The next section argues that efficiency is not an ''entry barrier'' in any sense that should trouble consumers or a government interested in their welfare. The last section narrows in on a specific cost component long denounced as an entry barrier: the large dollar-size of investment necessary for efficient production in many fields.

ECONOMIES OF SIZE

Rates and Volumes

Textbooks use a concept called *economies of scale* to analyze relationships between efficiency and firm size. There are two problems with this approach. First, a change in scale means a proportionate change in the rate of *all* input services, which are assumed to be homogeneous and divisible. This means proportionate changes in entrepreneurship and management teams; in the space needed to move goods in and out, and to work and breathe; and in all other relevant factors. Under these assumptions, it is hard to see how returns to scale could be anything *but* constant.[2] There is constant returns to scale if increasing all inputs proportionately increases output in the same proportion: doubling inputs doubles output.

If all factors were supplied at constant prices, firms' long-run average costs would then also be constant: unit costs are equally low no matter what size the firm is. This creates some unfortunate implications including that the number and size of firms are indeterminate and that there are no limits on the size of a firm.

To avoid such problems, economists contrived ad hoc escapes. One is to assume that each firm can have only one unit of entrepreneurship.[3] But then we cannot talk about returns to *firm* scale anymore, since, with one factor fixed even in the long run, no firm can vary all factors proportionally. In a sense, then, economists have had it both ways: to wring out certain welcome results (including marginal productivity and output distribution conditions), constant returns to scale simplifies life; but for some other purposes the implications are embarrassing, and are then bent into ''better'' fit. In fact, few of a real firm's problems are scale problems.

Second, traditional economies-of-scale analysis ignores important differences among products and firms. In analyzing efficiency problems, most textbooks ignore product variety and differences in total volumes produced over the lives of various models. Instead, they picture firm size as, say, the annual production rate of some (relatively) homogeneous product, VW Beetles, say. One million Beetles per year is a rate of output. If they are produced at that rate for twenty years, 20 million is the model volume.[4] It is one thing to produce one million Beetles per year, for one year, at which point the plant is converted or sold off; it is quite another to produce one million per year for twenty years.

The organization of the firm, the tooling, and the costs, will be very different. Yet the rates of output are the same, and most textbooks do not distinguish between these profoundly different output programs. This fixation is not only troublesome logically; it clogs communications with engineers and business people, and makes it harder to understand how real firms and industries work.[5] Empirical and policy problems often hinge on the costs of supplying different models using different techniques and different production periods.[6]

The variety of feasible products and techniques, and differences in the ability of managements to choose amongst them, help explain why some firms flourish while others fail. On this view, there are two principal explanations of how costs relate to industrial structure. First, in some industries firms must be large if they are to become efficient. This is a question of economies of pure size that are in principle available to any large firm. Second, firms that are more efficient than others will become larger, whether the industry is atomistic or concentrated, and whatever economies of pure size may be. Chapters 2, 4, and 5 showed how that works.

From a consumer's standpoint, efficiency means something more than lowest cost. Product quality, variety, and change are at least as important. We begin with economies of pure size, which is all that most textbooks consider, and will explore later why costs differ among firms.[7]

What economists call *technical economies* show up most obviously in production. It is paradoxical that economists, who have yet to demonstrate a comparative advantage in production engineering, emphasize production economies, which involve hardware and techniques, and have commonly ignored, denied, or feared the other kinds. In fact, of course, firms perform several functions, including production, accounting and control, finance, marketing, research, management, and risk taking.[8]

Economies of Expensive and Durable Machines

The classic example of technical economies is Adam Smith's pin factory.[9] It relies primarily upon economies from labor specialization. If there is little or no market for pins, each person or family must make for itself such pins as it wants. If there is a broad market, it pays to divide the process into many subprocesses, each completed by one or more workers. In Smith's words,

> I have seen a small manufactory . . . where ten men only were employed, and . . . some . . . performed two or three distinct operations . . . . Each . . . making a tenth . . . of forty-eight thousand pins, . . . four thousand eight hundred pins in a day. But . . . separately and independently, ... they certainly could not each of them have made twenty, perhaps not one pin in a day . . . certainly, not the two hundred and fortieth . . . part of what they are at present capable of performing, in consequence of a proper division and combination of their different operations.[10]

In such a case, there are several sources of economies. Human interests and talents differ, and a better fit for these peculiarities can be had if one worker need not do it all.

Less time is lost setting down one task and tools and taking up others. Learning and physical skills are acquired by concentrating on a smaller range of tasks. And—when technology is primitive—a simple and efficient machine may be designed to take over one or more subtasks, even when there is no machine that can economically undertake them all. As a consequence, said Smith, a relatively small, specialized team work force was able to turn out many times more pins than a corresponding number of isolated workers, each forced to perform all the tasks.

But there is much more to size economies than the specialization and division of labor. There are also economies of the large machine (which often has as real-world counterpart the absolutely expensive, durable, or highly productive machine or process). It is well known, for example, that the capacity of pipelines, storage tanks, blast furnaces, and ships rises more or less with physical *volume*—that is to the third power or cube of the dimensions. Costs, on the other hand, rise more or less with the *areas* of materials used, that is with the second power or *square*. Engineering and economic literature are filled with examples showing that, in general, productive capacity increases faster than cost.[11] A nontrivial example is the production of automobile bodies.[12] Equally good automobile bodies can be made using any of a variety of production techniques. Most, however, are now made from metal stampings, parts formed by pressing sheet metal between dies under heavy load. Stamping processes enjoy decreasing average costs over a wide range of output rates.[13]

Economies in stamping arise for several reasons besides learning, which is discussed later. First, the more durable dies that are used for long model runs cost less per part produced. Second, in the rare cases in which duplicate dies are needed to reach high *rates* of output, two identical dies cost less than twice as much as one. Third, by interchanging different removable sections in the same parent dies, manufacturers can produce several car models without raising costs proportionally. Fourth, given the different kinds of presses and dies that are appropriate for different rates and volumes of output, average costs decline with volume. Fifth, at higher rates of output, both dies and presses can be used more fully, lowering costs.

Beyond some rate, not yet approached in automobile press shops, the tendency of higher production rates to raise costs overtakes the tendency of higher volumes to lower costs, and unit costs rise. So far, however, body outputs have not been large enough to exhaust technical economies in press-plant operations. Similar forces are also involved in assembling the panels into finished body shells. In the auto industry so far, higher rates and volumes have lowered average cost. The firm that sells the most can sell for less, *if* it was prepared for the larger production program.

But volume economies and technical efficiencies will come to naught if a model does not sell. And even if its product does sell well, the company will not prosper unless its car is reasonably well designed for production, its tooling well conceived and executed, and its final production reasonably efficient.

On top of that, production is only one of several basic business functions. Economies and talent matter in the other ones as well. In the first place, someone must judge the market. This requires forecasting three or more years ahead. Second, someone must determine the physical characteristics of all parts and how they will fit together. Third, someone must decide how to tool to produce each of the parts. Fourth, someone must schedule production so as to minimize costs. And, finally, someone must sell enough of the cars at prices that make the whole venture worthwhile.

Mistakes at *any* stage can ruin everything. Technically good designs can fail to provide what consumers really want. A design may be good, but fail because parts and tools were designed poorly for production. It is easy to make mistakes about the size or duration of a market, and under- or over-tool. In short, technical economies matter, but they are not everything.

As varied as automobile demands have been, however, concentration within major car-producing countries has increased persistently for many years. This suggests that mass-production cost savings of the sort discussed here have been important in practice. This section discussed a specific example of technical volume economies that are in principle available to all managements that are good enough to realize them. The next section uses economic theory to show more generally how volume economies can affect industrial structure and competition.

The Effects of Volume on Costs and Industry Structure _____

Alchian posited that cost functions have several dimensions, including the rate of production and the total volume produced over time. For given volumes (i.e., for a given total serial production of a given model), at some point higher output rates cause marginal cost to rise. For given output rates, however, increasing total *volume* reduces average cost.

There are various explanations for this volume effect, which has been observed and documented many times.[14] One reason is learning: management and labor become more efficient as they accumulate experience from producing larger serial-volumes.[15] Technical economies such as we saw in the case of auto-body production are another reason.

Technology and the Period of Production. How does total production volume affect costs and industrial structure?[16] For such time as a given industry demand curve persists, the number and size distribution of firms will differ with the relative strength of the cost effects of rate and volume, and with differences in their relative strengths among firms. Take the case of a new product the total demand for which continues for a number of periods, then disappears forever. Assume that all output must be sold at the same price. If at any price the total revenues obtainable exceed the total costs necessary to capture them, some quantity of the product will be produced. Any prospective firm could produce any given volume at a low rate for a longer time, at a high rate for a shorter time, or at any combination of production rate and length of run that yields the same total volume. According to Alchian, total cost will be lower, for a given volume, if it is produced at a lower rate per unit time. Since factors of production cost something no matter how knowledgeably they are used, there are limits to how much the volume effect can cut costs.

A few examples will clarify the problem. Remember that the demand for the product remains the same for several periods, then disappears altogether. The *total* volume demanded at any price is, then, the quantity demanded per unit time *times* the number of time periods during which the product is demanded. Assume for simplicity that the interest rate is zero. Further, abstract from inventories, and assume that demand in one period is not influenced by demand or price in other periods.

The question is how the most efficient structure of industry changes with different durations of demand, and with stronger or weaker cost savings from volume production. Assume that each potential producer of the product has access to the long-run total cost function used in Table 7-1:

$$C = .5X^3 - 6X^2 + 70X + 400 \, (MX)^{2/3},$$

where C is total cost, X is the rate of output per unit time, and M is the length of production period. Since, by assumption, so long as *any* output is produced, production rates are constant through time, the total volume produced is simply MX. Average cost is total cost divided by total volume, that is, C/MX. The exponent in this example is two-thirds, corresponding to the famous two-thirds rule that engineers often use to estimate costs.

For each volume, at a given rate, the only relevant C is always the minimum achievable total cost,[17] which means—for each rate of output and period of production—that the best information, most appropriate equipment and techniques are used. This minimum cost cannot be achieved, of course, unless the planned X and M are *actually* achieved. And, since there is no total fixed cost term in the total cost function just shown, we would have to specify the fixed cost applicable to each production program *if adopted* before we can specify actual costs for cases in which the actual and planned rates and volumes dif-

TABLE 7–1   Average Cost Related to Output Rate, Production Period, and Volume

Average Cost $= (.5X^3 - 6X^2 + 70X + 400(MX)^{2/3}) / (MX)$

Output Per Year	Production for 1 Year		Production for 2 Years		Production for 5 Years	
	Vol.	Aver. Cost	Vol.	Aver. Cost	Vol.	Aver. Cost
1	1	464.50	2	349.73	5	246.82
2	2	377.48	4	322.40	10	197.66
3	3	333.84	6	244.39	15	173.49
4	4	305.98	8	227.00	20	158.16
5	5	286.42	10	211.91	25	147.30
6	6	272.13	12	200.71	30	139.13
7	7	261.60	14	192.22	35	132.78
8	8	254.00	16	185.73	40	127.76
9	9	248.80	18	180.88	45	123.76
10	10	245.66	20	177.36	50	120.58
11	11	244.36	22	175.00	55	118.08
12	12	244.72	24	173.68	60	116.17
13	13	246.62	26	173.27	65	114.78
14	14	249.97	28	173.72	70	113.84
15	15	254.69	30	174.98	75	113.35
16	16	260.73	32	176.99	80	113.23
17	17	268.06	34	179.80	85	113.47

fer. For a *given* production period, average cost declines with greater output rates, reaches a minimum, then rises. In that respect, at least, this cost function looks like a typical textbook case.

Table 7-1 shows how average cost changes with the rate of output, for production periods of 1, 2, and 5 years.

If all firms have identical U-shaped cost-functions, it is sometimes argued that the "proper" number of firms can be determined by comparing average cost for the firm and demand for the industry. Note how the argument applies to Table 7-1. Assume that production and demand last one year, after which demand disappears and output stops; and that the cost function is identical for all potential producers. Average cost reaches a minimum at a production rate of 11 units per year, at which rate average cost is $244.36 per unit.

Suppose that marginal cost equals average cost at the output rate that minimizes average cost, and that price equals marginal cost. How many units will be demanded at a price of $244.36? If the quantity demanded at that price is 11 units, there is just room in the industry for one firm of "optimal" size. For a demand of 33 units, there is room for 3 firms; for 110 units, 10 firms; and so on.

For the cost function underlying Table 7-1, observe what happens, alternatively, if demand and production should last 2 years. For given rates of output, average cost would be lower than before. Average cost is minimized at a *higher* rate of output, in this instance at 13 units per year. Assuming that the *annual* demand curve has not changed, at any given price the total volume demanded is simply twice as much as before. But since the value of minimum average cost is $173.27, which is lower than before, the total volume demanded would be more than twice as great at prices that would just cover minimum average costs. Consequently, whether there will be room for more, the same number, or fewer firms depends upon the percentage change in the optimum size of firm; the percentage change in the value of minimum average cost; and the (arc) elasticity of demand.

The cost-minimizing annual output rate for a two-year demand increased from 11 to 13, or 18.18 percent. For there to be room for precisely as many "optimum size" firms as before, the quantity demanded per unit time (and the total volume demanded) must rise by the same percentage. If it should rise by a larger proportion, there would be room for more firms; if by a smaller proportion, there would be room for fewer firms. In this case, doubling the demand period reduced minimum average costs about 29.09 percent, a proportion by which it would be "possible" to lower price and still cover costs. If the (arc) elasticity of industry demand were about .625, there would just be room for the same number of firms having minimum average cost.[18] If the elasticity of demand were smaller than that, there would be room for fewer firms. If it were larger, there would be room for more firms. Now compare the situation for one-year and five-year production periods. If the price elasticity of demand is less than about 1.3, there will be room for fewer firms to satisfy a five-year demand than a one-year demand.

For the form of total cost function analyzed here, the period of production (and true volume effect) figures only in the last term,[19] which in general could be expressed as $D(MX)^Y$.

Examine what happens in Table 7-2, for given values of the other parameters, at

TABLE 7–2 Minimum average cost related to value of D coefficient[a]

	Production for 1 Year		Production for 2 Years		Production for 5 Years	
Value of D	Output Rate for Minimum AC	Value of Minimum AC	Output Rate for min. AC	Value of Minimum AC	Output Rate for Minimum AC	Value of Minimum AC
			For $Y = 1/2$			
200	9	123.20	10	74.70	12	39.82
400	11	185.10	12	116.70	14	64.61
700	13	270.60	15	174.10	17	98.43
			For $Y = 2/3$			
200	9	152.60	11	103.60	13	65.05
400	11	244.40	13	173.20	16	113.20
700	13	374.10	15	271.50	19	180.70

[a] $AC = ((.5X^3 - 6X^2 + 70X + D(MX)^y))/(MX)$.

different values of D. For a given production period and value of Y, increasing D increases both the output at which minimum average cost is reached and the level of that minimum average cost. For a given value of D and Y, increasing the production period decreases the level of minimum average cost, but increases the rate of output at which the minimum occurs. For given production periods and values of D, increasing Y raises the value of minimum average cost and may increase the rate of output at which the minimum occurs. Note that *two* kinds of forces are involved in the whole problem: those altering the duration, magnitude, and elasticity of *demand*; and those determining the *cost function* itself. These two sets of forces might be correlated.

These arithmetic exercises lead to some important propositions. First, the length of time over which a given product is demanded—which is, in turn, a function of tastes, income, and the prices of other goods—can influence the "optimal" or viable structure of industry. Second, the strength and even the direction of that influence depend not only upon what happens to the optimum size of firm, but upon the direction and extent of cost change and upon elasticity of demand as well. If each one-period demand curve is *independent* of the number of periods, there seem to be two unambiguous cases: If the volume effect not only reduces costs, but either (1) reduces optimum scale or (2) leaves it unchanged, increased volume—as through an increase in the period of production—will leave room for more firms. But of course there is no reason to believe that tastes, for example, work only one way: in response to consumer demand, the period of production can decrease as well as increase. In this case, too, whether the tendency is to concentrate or deconcentrate industry depends upon cost and demand.

For shorter periods of production, there are two unambiguous cases: if reduced volume raises costs but (1) *increases* or (2) leaves the average cost minimizing output unchanged, there will be room for fewer firms. For, with unchanged demand in *each* period, a higher price will yield smaller quantities demanded per unit time. If the efficient size of firm should *fall* with the period of production, we need additional information to know whether the industry will naturally concentrate or deconcentrate.

Things get more complicated if the demand in *each* period changes together with changes in the number of periods. If per-period demand *falls* with the number of periods, and costs rise, an even smaller efficient firm size, or smaller demand elasticity, would be needed to avoid concentration. If per-period demand *rises* as the number of periods falls, an even greater increase (if any) in efficient firm size, or smaller elasticity, would be required to resist deconcentration. Similar considerations apply to cases in which the production period *rises*, accordingly as per-period demand rises or falls.

Suppose for example, that the industry demand function each period is of the form $Q = RP^n$, in which R is related to the period of production, M; P is price, and n is the price elasticity of demand. What happens to N, the maximum number of efficient-size firms, now depends upon average cost (which is related to M—the period of demand and production); Q (which is related to M); and the elasticity of demand. The issues are revealed by using the cost function underlying Table 7-2, and by assuming, alternatively, four different demand functions of the forms

(1) $$Q = CMP^{-.5}$$

(2) $$Q = CMP^{-2}$$

(3) $$Q = CM^{-1} P^{-.5}$$

(4) $$Q = CM^{-1} P^{-2}.$$

The same assumptions will be continued for M, the period of production. It will be, alternatively, 1, 2, or 5 years. Table 7-3 shows how N, the maximum number of efficient firms, varies as these demand assumptions vary. For different cost and demand relationships, results differ, which is the whole point.

Learning.   A firm that produces a product in large total volume ought to learn how to do it better. Beginners' costs tend to be higher than those of experienced, seasoned firms. Two important questions then naturally arise: whether and in what sense entry is "barred" as a consequence, and, if so, whether that is "bad."[20]

When, as we assume now, newcomers have higher costs than established firms, prospects look especially bad for entry. To see how bad things can be, assume an extreme case: learning keeps lowering costs for all increases in volume, though eventually the rate at which it lowers cost must diminish. As a result, firms with large past output will always have lower costs than those with less experience. When newcomers can never catch up, isn't entry barred and competition reduced? The question has two parts. First, what does a significant learning effect do to the speed of entry once the possibility of creating such an industry is first perceived, and how fast do firms produce when they do enter? Second, what happens when some enter before others see the opportunity?

Expectations of substantial learning effects precipitate early entry and fast produc-

TABLE 7–3 Maximum number of efficient firms for different demands
(When $C/MX = (.5X^3 - 6X + 70X + 400(MX)^{2/3})/MX$)

M	X *at Which* C/MX *is Minimum*	*Value of Minimum* C/MX	*For* Q = 1,000MP$^{-.5}$	*For* Q = 1,000,000MP^{-2}	*For* Q = 1,000M^{-1}P$^{-.5}$	*For* Q = 1,000,000M^{-1}P^{-2}
1	11	244.36	Q = 63.97	Q = 16.74	Q = 63.97	Q = 16.74
			N = 5.82	N = 1.52	N = 5.82	N = 1.52
2	13	173.27	Q = 151.94	Q = 66.60	Q = 37.98	Q = 16.65
			N = 11.69	N = 5.12	N = 2.92	N = 1.28
5	16	113.23	Q = 469.88	Q = 389.95	Q = 18.80	Q = 15.60
			N = 29.37	N = 24.37	N = 1.17	N = 0.97

tion. Firms will tend to "sell below (present) costs" to minimize discounted costs and maximize discounted profits. Michael Spence put it this way in a 1981 article: "There is a payoff to early entry. If . . . there were no other constraints, all firms would enter immediately or at the start."[21] The second question is what happens when some enter earlier or produce faster than others. Suppose experience is the only thing that distinguishes newcomer and oldtimer: starting from scratch, their roles could have been interchanged with no net change in the cost situation. Furthermore, assume that learning comes solely from summed output, and not merely from the passage of time. Several inferences emerge. First, knowledge is valuable. But it costs something to get it. By assumption, the established firm had to pay as much to learn as the newcomer would.

Second, in fact it would take time for any new industry to reach full competitive equilibrium and some never reach it. And the most common case is that some firm enters a new industry first, sometimes much earlier than those that come afterwards. New goods are introduced before anyone can really be sure whether they will succeed. The demand for something new is tested only when someone actually tries to make and sell it. If it passes the test, the firm is first in a field. If it fails, it becomes the latest to go into the boneyard, unnoticed by most and lamented by only a few.

Third, under our assumptions, entry will occur if discounted revenues are expected to exceed discounted costs. Since we assume, at this point, that all firms offer the same product, they get the same prices. Just as we saw before, when costs were assumed to be identical among firms, much again depends upon the duration, size, and elasticity of industry demand and upon the costs of new and seasoned firms. Look first at the time of entry relative to the duration of demand. As Table 7-1 showed, a firm anticipating that demand will stay the same for five annual periods (and then disappear) could achieve the lowest possible average costs ($113.23, at a yearly production rate of 16). Any other firm that makes the same correct prediction could achieve the same costs. The *maximum* number of most-efficient firms would then be given by the quantities demanded per year at a price of $113.23, divided by 16, the minimum-cost output rate.

Suppose that fewer firms than this actually get into production.[22] For first-wave firms, average costs over the five-year period will not be lower than $113.23. In practice, they may be higher, since average cost is U-shaped, and markets clear on prices that can exceed minimum average cost in the short run. Assume there are fewer first-wave entrants than would be needed to drive price down to minimum average cost. As a result, price is higher than $113.23, and profits are positive. Assume also that no one else plans to enter before the beginning of the fifth year of the total five-year demand period.

With a cost function like that, later entrants can never reach an average cost as low as $113.23, the lowest they could have achieved by entering at the very beginning and adopting the most efficient program for five-year production. Potential fifth-year entrants will not come in unless they expect price to be higher than $244.36, the lowest long-run average cost they can achieve for a one-year production run, which is the best that they can now accomplish. If the quantities demanded at going prices are large relative to the output that minimizes newcomers' average cost, (one or more) newcomers will enter if they expect prices to remain even a little higher than $244.36. If the efficient firm size is relatively large, entry-attracting prices may need to be somewhat higher than that; but that depends upon the output response of present producers. Although this looks a little complicated on the surface, it is really quite familiar: the equilibrium number of firms in an industry depends upon costs and the size of markets; price is related to demand and costs, including those of potential entrants; and profits, under competition or monopoly, are related to demand, the costs of insiders, and the costs of all outsiders producing or capable of producing substitutes.

Economists offer different appraisals of the kind of situation just analyzed. According to Spence, for example,

> The learning curve creates entry barriers and protection from competition by conferring cost advantages on early entrants and those who achieve large market shares. These cost advantages are not permanent. But with moderately rapid declines in unit costs, they have significant impacts on market shares and profitability. The effects are similar to (though more pronounced than) those caused by economies of scale.[23]

Joe Bain made the term *entry barriers* famous a long time ago.[24] Bain, Spence, and others, have applied that label to efficiency and its sources as well as to obstructions that injure consumers.

Neither as concept nor diagnosis does *barrier to entry* help us formulate policies that help consumers.[25] How, for example, could we remove or ameliorate the barrier caused by learning? It would not help consumers if we discourage learning, though that is what raises the standards for entry at a late date. It would not help consumers if, following Spence, we conclude that someone had "conferred" knowledge and efficiency on "early entrants," instead of noticing that they had worked hard and risked much to earn those advantages themselves. Nor would it help consumers if we denounce economies of large size, again on the grounds that they are a barrier to entry. And it would not help to denounce consumers themselves, on the grounds that their demands were not large enough to support swarms of efficient firms, and dwindled away completely in five years rather than lasting forever.

But calling such conditions barriers neither informs public policy nor helps consumers. We should recognize that coral reefs are not the same as mine fields; and that driving skill and luck differ from dumping oil on the road during a motorcycle race. In the example analyzed, there are no bad practices to punish.

If the effects of learning and early entry displease us, what remedial policies could we cook up if we were dictators? We could forbid the production of *anything* until a pleasingly large number of producers of suitably close substitutes at least promise to start. Of course, some things might then never get produced at all, and others with greater or lesser delay. Alternatively, we could force firms having valuable knowledge to give it away to all applying newcomers if it can be transferred; or to subsidize all comers if it cannot. In addition to raising formidable administrative difficulties, such a policy blunts the incentive to be first and tends to slow things down. Or, if radical surgery appeals to us, we could break up any firms whose cost advantages and profits persist beyond, say, the end of the fourth year. In the short run, for production plans already undertaken, we could try to impose whatever combination of cost raising and firm dissolution is required to produce a pleasing number of firms and zero profits; or that would raise the costs of established firms sufficiently to produce what we regard as an appropriate amount of entry.

In the long run, of course, policies that tax success may rid us of the problem everywhere: if superior knowledge will not be permitted to pay, who will strive to get it? Choosing the more expensive four-year or one-year production plans, or none at all, may now make more sense than plowing hard new ground. If none of these suggestions seems ideal, other possible programs, like a complex taxation and subsidy program to tailor all industry demands and costs to a master plan for the ''right'' number and efficiency of ''equalized'' firms everywhere, can easily be engineered—on paper. But they would be highly subjective and cause problems of their own.

When all is said and done, the question is whether to choose fewer low-cost firms or a larger number of high-cost firms. It is not a choice to be made lightly.

OTHER DIFFERENCES AMONGST FIRMS

Costs differ among firms for other reasons besides economies of pure size and early or late entry. Suppose, for example, that two firms could manufacture similar products by operating on identical cost functions. Even if both adopt identical production programs, they will not incur equal unit costs if they *realize* different output rates and volumes. For example, one firm sells more because consumers prefer its product.

Or suppose that, although two firms could produce identical products at the same cost by choosing identical production programs, they choose different production programs, because of different sales forecasts, for example. Depending upon the precise circumstances, both firms may end up with identical realized unit costs; the first firm may have lower unit costs than the second; or the second may have lower unit costs than the first. Such differences arise even though both firms could, in principle, produce identical products equally cheaply. The rub is that they made significantly different choices.

Some would say that firms are equally efficient if, in principle, they could climb onto the same cost function. That is not enough. Actual results also depend upon whether firms are equally efficient in making choices: choosing the right product designs and timing, the right sales forecasts, the right tooling, the right plant layouts and locations, and so on. Those who make better choices are more efficient, no matter what their costs for identical choices might be.

Economists have theorized about whether larger firms are better able to cope with risk. Although this is fine so far as it goes, it distracts us from another aspect of the risk problem, and it leads the unwary to improper tests of riskiness. It is conceivable that a firm may try hard to start life large, on the conviction that risk demands large size. To get large, of course, a firm must somehow sell what a lot of people want. On the other hand, some firms start small, prosper, and grow large simply because over the years they have adjusted better to such risks as there are.

Low-cost mass-production techniques are risky, because, among other reasons, they commonly involve long-term commitments to apparatus and organization that are highly specialized. If the plans prove to be wrong, highly specialized processes and skills are expensive to convert and very burdensome.

In the real world, then, how well a firm does is partly determined by the degree and kind of risk it faces, and partly by how well it adjusts to such risk as it faces. It is very difficult to separate these factors empirically. It will not do to infer that some larger firm has not been exposed to much risk because its earnings have been relatively stable and high over time. Such studies usually do not count how many other firms failed, and it is impossible to count those who never even tried because they feared what faced them.

Even if a firm has higher unit costs, it may nevertheless be more efficient. Superior firms create more value out of the resources they use. They offer products that consumers value more highly relative to what it costs to supply them. Total results are what count for consumers and sellers, not whether some engineer or economist postulates that two or more different firms should have equal costs for the same production plans.

IS EFFICIENCY AN ENTRY BARRIER?[26]

Although classical economists were much concerned about entry barriers, they were worried about the ones that governments create. Their theory was that those barriers reduce consumers' welfare. Their experience, and ours, suggests that it is difficult to pull down such barriers as government erects. Although many government barriers are artificial in the sense that they do not enhance qualities that consumers favor, it is more clinical to call them political barriers rather than artificial ones. For they are demanded and supplied in political markets, in which such arrangements are as natural as can be, and there are now so many of them that they are coming to seem normal as well.

We should distinguish political entry barriers from the kinds of efficiency advantages that benefit consumers. It is strange to call cost and quality advantages "barriers to entry" if they are just what consumers want. Such qualities and advantages *improve* efficiency, as the preceding discussion of learning, technical efficiency, and better business decisions showed.

Analysis and communication should improve if we just stop calling such advantages entry barriers at all. First, such advantages often translate into immediate consumer benefits, and always tend to benefit consumers over the long haul. Second, to the benefit of consumers, such advantages would—and ought to—exclude less efficient firms in unconcentrated as well as concentrated industries. There, none would claim that consumers have been hurt because entry of less efficient firms has been "barred." It is dangerous, as well as inconsistent, to apply one definition of consumer benefits to unconcentrated industries and quite another to those that are concentrated. Double standards lead to policy and propaganda confusions between competition and monopoly: what is beneficial competition gets misdiagnosed as hurtful and monopolistic.

CAPITAL REQUIREMENTS

Absolutely Large Capital Requirements

Although *capital requirements* is a popular notion in the industrial organization literature, it is seldom defined precisely. For present purposes, it is enough to say that the relevant capital requirement is the minimum investment needed to produce some good efficiently. No one interested in maximizing economic welfare should object to the efficient production of goods that consumers want, or to the amount of capital minimally necessary to do it.

One issue is whether absolutely large capital requirements bar entry. Another issue is whether and how one could acquire or maintain monopoly by *artificially* increasing the amount of capital that competitors require. It is sometimes said that vertical integration, advertising, requirements contracts, cumulative volume discounts, and other practices impede entry in one of those ways or the other. Later chapters evaluate those factors in detail.

The question at issue now is whether the *absolute* cost of facilities—not the *relative* size of efficient firms—is a barrier to entry. In particular, as is well known, the cost of building even the minimum optimal size (MOS) plant or firm is absolutely large for many industries. The larger this absolute cost, the story goes, the harder it is to enter the industry. Large capital requirements are therefore said to be a barrier to entry: they make noncompetitive structures and policies more likely to occur and longer lasting when they do occur. As Joe Bain put it in a classic irrelevancy, in many industries the costs of even the smallest efficient plant "will not be forthcoming from savings out of salary or from the winnings in a poker game."

In fact, of course, most such investments are made with savings from *many* natural persons, firms, and syndicates, not from single individuals acting alone. That is what securities issues, borrowing and lending, and open capital markets are all about. And—it should be noted—there are lots of absolutely large firms that routinely raise large capital, which they use to expand facilities in their own industries and to diversify into industries that are new to them. Even if there were something to the theory that large investments are hard for *new* firms to make, that should not intimidate the large number of successful large firms already in existence.

The risk to each of many investors need not rise with the absolute total size of an investment project. Furthermore, other things equal—risk and quality of management, for example—large security issues actually cost less per dollar of capital raised than smaller issues do.

Nevertheless, let us adopt for now heroic assumptions favoring Bain's hypothesis. Assume that we have determined the cost-minimizing combination of ownership shares and bonds needed to raise capital for every size of investment project, and that the average cost of capital *does* rise with the dollar cost of an MOS firm. Even so, this would not bar entry in any artificial sense that shelters monopoly. If a firm or industry earns economic profits, it is earning more than the minimum needed to retain all its resources in the long run. That minimum necessary return includes any investment-size premium, risk premium, or any other premium applicable to that firm or industry.

No doubt it would be difficult to calculate precisely what the normal, minimum, competitive rate of return is, for either a firm or an industry. But Bain and those who followed his lead were apparently able either to calculate it; or, at least, to recognize when the elusive competitive return is being exceeded. Fine. Let's proceed under the weak assumption that such a competitive rate of return exists in principle.

Suppose, for example, that the normal "standard" or "average" competitive return on capital is 15 percent per annum, to which adjustments must be made for specific cases.[27] Suppose we analyze an industry that is a little riskier than average, which requires adding a risk premium of 2 percentage points. On top of that, the minimum capital required for a firm to operate efficiently in this industry is unusually large, which somehow requires a large additional premium of 8 percentage points. One could argue that there are more than two premia that should be considered; or that risk, MOS, and capital cost are not easily separable. But that is not the point. It is the *total* normal return that matters, and it is irrelevant whether one premium or many must be added to get it. What matters is that we have included whatever it is that is relevant, including whatever worried Bain. Assume that we include everything that matters.

For the industry in question, then, the total competitive rate of return would be 15 + 2 + 8 = 25 percent per year. The question, remember, is whether the 8 percentage point premium for large capital investment excludes entry and competition. If higher returns than 25 percent per annum are being earned, because of monopoly for example, entry is attractive—by the definition of competitive returns. More is being earned than is necessary to attract, hold, and use all factors necessary for efficient operation in that industry, including risk bearing, large capital, and everything else. And, if the rate of return is more than compensatory, it is better to earn it on large investments rather than small ones, even if the amount of capital required had somehow been inflated artificially. The conclusion seems to be that a premium for large capital requirements will not deter entry or bolster monopoly.

Theories like Bain's imply another peculiarity. Suppose that larger capital investments really do impose above-average costs of capital. Critics of industrial concentration assert that the larger firms are typically much larger than efficiency requires, and that much smaller firms can be equally efficient. If so, and if Bain were correct, a smaller entrant that is otherwise equally efficient would be absolutely *more* efficient than larger firms because it will use less capital and have a lower average cost of capital. Exclusionary effects of large capital requirements would show up only if entrants were somehow artificially compelled to use more capital per unit of output than the resident large firms do.

This is one side of the story. Is there another? One argument is that firms already established in an industry—what we might call resident firms—have much lower capital costs than entrants. By some attributions their costs might even look to be near zero. Resident firms' original investments may already have been depreciated or written off; or their capital goods may have been bought long ago, when things in general cost much less and interest rates were lower. But for locating monopoly, or measuring monopoly profits, or for deciding whether more firms "should" enter, historic and accounting book-costs are simply irrelevant. They will not have incorporated opportunity costs and will not have capitalized competitive rents, if any. For any of those tasks, current replacement and opportunity costs are relevant, at the margin. If the calculated profits that Bain was excited about were based on low historic or book-costs, those profits were measured incorrectly. They were grossly overstated.

The second potential objection is that resident firms may have financed some or most of their investments out of their own earnings; whereas a new firm will have to finance in the open market, in which capital is assertedly more expensive. At least part of this discrepancy is mirage; the rest, if there is any, is an efficiency rent that ought to have been capitalized. At each step of the way, inside investments made with internally generated funds should meet or beat returns on opportunities forgone in the external capital market, taking into account risk, information, and transaction costs. Inside funds have significant opportunity costs; they are not really free. And, if—because of transactions and information costs, for example—internal financing really is more efficient, that is an efficiency worth praising. It is surely not an artificial barrier.

Another objection is that the real capital costs of seasoned firms may (not must) be lower than those for untried managements or completely new firms. That is entirely possible, of course, because there is less information to go on when firms have no track record and when the perceived risks of investing in them are greater. But what is artificial, pernicious, or even remediable about that? Any "remedy" would force investors to finance everyone who asks, and to finance them all at the same terms. This would call for capital rationing, inefficient allocation, and a destruction of investors' rights and freedoms. Investors would be compelled to lend to people they do not know, or trust, or believe in.

Finally, some complain that capital markets are either imperfect or perverse. No market is perfect. Capital markets have financed firms that go broke, firms that do middling-well, and firms that have succeeded spectacularly. But money capital is among the most homogeneous and mobile of resources, and those who deal in it are both knowledgeable and attracted to wealth. Investors on both sides of that market have the best information and best reason to put capital where risk-adjusted gains are highest. A theory of perverse capital markets implies that outsiders will be able to find a lot of discrepancies that would make them and insiders rich. Taking advantage of such discrepancies tends to remove them. They are not likely to persist.

Of course large capital investments may be positively correlated with *accounting* profits that have not been adjusted for risk. Expensive, durable, and specialized investment goods are subject to great risk. Furthermore, large investments may be a proxy for complex tasks and complex firms that are difficult for just any Tom, Dick, or Jane to create and manage successfully. There may simply not be enough of the right kinds of managerial teams to support swarms of efficient, complex firms in every industry. Those who are good enough to do it earn quasi-rents for the firms that employ them. Finally, large investments may be especially subject to evaluation lags, measurement errors, and so on.

Sunk Costs

Recently, Baumol and Willig argued that it is sunk costs, rather than fixed costs, that can bar entry. Fixed costs can be avoided by going out of business. Sunk costs, on the other hand "are those costs that (in some short or intermediate run) cannot be eliminated, even by total cessation of production. As such, once committed, sunk costs are no longer a portion of the opportunity costs of production."[28] This is supposed to cut both ways. The bad news for such a firm is that it hurts to get stuck with large sunk costs when business falls off. The good news for resident monopolies, however, is that firms now in the industry have an edge because they have already incurred their sunk costs. Newcomers have a cost disadvantage even if they are equally "efficient," for "The need to sink costs can be a barrier to entry. . . . the incremental cost, as seen by a potential entrant, includes the full amount of the sunk costs, which is a bygone to the incumbent."[29]

The argument seems to be that a resident monopoly can charge prices that would cover *total* costs, even a newcomer's fixed, variable, and sunk costs, without inducing entry. A newcomer *would* enter if it expected the monopoly's prices to persist in the long run. But it fears that they will not and thinks that it would be in deep trouble in a price-cutting contest with the resident firms, whose costs were already sunk. *Everybody* would indeed be in deep trouble if prices after entry do not cover whatever costs are relevant at that stage. By that time, however, the newcomer's costs also would have been sunk, and newcomer and oldtimer would have equally low costs, and presumably equal losses, if losses there be.

This is not an *absolute* capital-requirements theory. It depends upon the size of efficient firms *relative* to the market, and on whether predatory pricing (or threats of it) pays, topics that are discussed in Chapter 9.

SUMMARY

Before asserting that "barriers to entry" or other sinister forces explain the number and identify of firms in an industry, it seems sensible to ask whether nonsinister costs and demands explain them. On the whole, it appears, costs and demands can explain a lot.

Although opinions differ, there seems to be little reason to reject out of hand the hypothesis that costs and demand play a reasonable or even a benign role in determining the firm-structure of industry.

QUESTIONS

1. Are technological economies inherently more desirable or necessarily more important than economies in finance, design, marketing, and management? Discuss and explain.

2. What, if any, theory and empirical evidence is there to support the engineers' two-thirds rule, according to which costs per unit of capacity rise at the rate of the cube root of capacity squared?

3. Define *barrier to entry* in a way relevant to consumer welfare. Give and defend an example.

4. Show how costs and demands determine the number and sizes of firms in atomistic competition when (1) all firms have identical costs; (2) costs differ among firms.

5. Explain constant, decreasing, and increasing returns-to-scale.

6. *Efficiency* is more than a question of econometricians' or engineers' cost curves. What else is there?

7. Draw a diagram to illustrate the following case: the demand for some product is so small relative to the most efficient size of firm that there is room for only one firm, "too small" a firm at that.

   In what sense does this "bar" entry? Explain whether the result is "efficient" or "inefficient."

8. Much the same industries have been concentrated (or unconcentrated) in most countries. What could explain that?

9. Does risk limit the size of plants and firms? Explain.

10. Are fixed and sunk costs identical? Explain.

NOTES

1. As Demsetz shows, however, there may be many potential firms seeking to *become* part of the market. See Harold Demsetz, "Why Regulate Public Utilities?" *Journal of Law & Economics*, 11 (April 1968), pp. 55–65.

2. Nicholas Georgescu-Roegen, "The Economics of Production," *American Economic Review*, 60 (May 1970), pp. 1–2.

3. Milton Friedman, *Price Theory: A Provisional Text* (Chicago: Aldine Publishing Company, 1962), pp. 96, 140.

4. Brazil, the last or one of the last to produce VW's Beetles, apparently stopped producing them in 1986 and introduced the Fox, a new model.

5. Armen A. Alchian, "Costs and Output," in *The Allocation of Economic Resources: Essays in Honor of Bernard F. Haley*, eds. M. Abramovitz and others (Palo Alto, Calif.: Stanford

University Press, 1959); A. A. Alchian, "Reliability of Progress Curves in Airframe Production," *Econometrica*, 31, no. 4 (October 1963), pp. 679–93; A. A. Alchian and William R. Allen, *Exchange and Production Theory in Use* (Belmont, Calif.: Wadsworth Publishing Co., Inc., 1969), pp. 287–312; A. A. Alchian, "Cost," *International Encyclopedia of the Social Sciences*, vol. 3 (New York: Macmillan, Inc. and The Free Press, 1968), pp. 404–14; John S. McGee, "Economies of Size in Auto Body Manufacture," *Journal of Law & Economics*, 16 (October 1973), pp. 239–73; Walter Y. Oi, "The Neoclassical Foundations of Progress Functions," *Economic Journal*, 77 (September 1967), pp. 579–94; Jack Hirshleifer, "The Firm's Cost Function: A Successful Reconstruction?" *The Journal of Business*, 35 (July 1962), pp. 235–55.

6. John S. McGee, *In Defense of Industrial Concentration* (New York: Praeger Publishers, 1971); McGee, "Economies of Size in Auto Body Manufacture"; McGee, "Efficiency and Economies of Size," in *Industrial Concentration: The New Learning* eds. H. J. Goldschmid, H. M. Mann, and J. F. Weston (Boston: Little, Brown & Company, 1974), pp. 55–97.

7. For discussions of what theorists say the firm is and what limits its extent, see R. H. Coase, "The Nature of the Firm," *Economica*, New Series, vol. 4 (November 1937), pp. 386–405, reprinted in G. J. Stigler and K. E. Boulding, eds., *Readings in Price Theory* (Homewood, Ill.: Richard D. Irwin, Inc., 1952), pp. 331–51; and Armen A. Alchian and Harold Demsetz, "Production, Information Costs, and Economic Organization," *American Economic Review*, 62 (December 1972), pp. 777–95.

8. A splendid introduction is E. A. G. Robinson, *The Structure of Competitive Industry* (Chicago: University of Chicago Press, 1959).

9. Adam Smith, *An Inquiry into the Nature and Causes of the Wealth of Nations* (New York: Modern Library, 1937), pp. 3–21.

10. Ibid., pp. 4–5.

11. For example, see John Haldi and David Whitcomb, "Economies of Scale in Industrial Plants," *Journal of Political Economy*, 75 (August 1967), pp. 379–85; and Frederick T. Moore, "Economies of Scale: Some Statistical Evidence," *Quarterly Journal of Economics*, 73 (May 1959), pp. 232–45.

12. McGee, "Economies of Size in Auto Body Manufacture."

13. Joan Robinson, *The Economics of Imperfect Competition* (London: Macmillan and Co., Limited, 1933), pp. 38–39. When Demsetz sought a simple example of scale economies he chose die-stamped license plates. Harold Demsetz, "Why Regulate Utilities?" *Journal of Law & Economics*, 11 (April 1968), pp. 55, 57–58.

14. For example, in producing ships during WWI and WWII; and aircraft during WWII.

15. There is a large and varied literature on learning and "progress" functions. Spence's work emphasizes its effects on industrial structure and competition. See, for example, A. Michael Spence, "The Learning Curve and Competition," *The Bell Journal of Economics*, 12, no. 1 (Spring 1981), pp. 49–70.

16. The following derives from McGee, *In Defense of Industrial Concentration*, Chapter 3.

17. For example, if for a given serial volume, combinations of shorter runs yield lower costs than one longer run, the longer run will not be used, and is irrelevant.

18. The absolute value of arc elasticity is $\Delta Q/Q \, / \, \Delta P/P$. If price is arbitrarily held to average cost, in our example, $\Delta P/P = .2909$. For *each* firm, minimum cost occurs at an increased production rate, $\Delta q/q = .1818$. And $.1818/.2909 = .625$. If the elasticity of total demand is precisely $-.625$, $\Delta Q/Q \, / \, .2909 = -.625$, and $\Delta Q/Q = .1818$. The maximum number of

efficient size firms is now the original number *times* $\Delta Q/Q$ / $\Delta q/q$ = .1818/ .1818 = 1. For a given price (i.e., cost) effect, $\Delta P/P$, the absolute value of the elasticity of demand will be greater as $\Delta Q/Q$ is greater, and the ratio $\Delta Q/Q$ / $\Delta q/q$ will be larger other things the same). If elasticity is -1.25, $\Delta Q/Q$ / $-.2909$ = -1.25 and $\Delta Q/Q$ = .3636. Therefore, the number of efficient sized firms would be the original number *times* $\Delta Q/Q$ / $\Delta q/q$ = .3636/.1818 = 2.

19. One way of putting it is that, in Table 7-1, for example, average cost with respect to the first three terms, i.e. $(.5X^3 - 6X^2 + 70X)$ / MX, reaches a (different) minimum at the same rate of output for different values of M, the length of production period.

20. See McGee, *In Defense of Industrial Concentration*, pp. 42–47; and Spence, "The Learning Curve and Competition."

21. Spence, "The Learning Curve and Competition," p. 53.

22. It is a complicated problem. This incomplete model does not show why *that*, rather than some other, number enters. Nor can it show how the output of each firm, or the market price, vary through time. For, among other things, the values of those variables depend upon the duration and intensity of industry demand; upon anticipated output share of an unspecified number of firms through time; and upon the relationship (if any) of these factors to price. By assumption, the discount rate is zero.

23. Spence, "The Learning Curve and Competition," p. 68.

24. For example, see Joe S. Bain, "Economies of Scale, Concentration, and the Condition of Entry in Twenty Manufacturing Industries," *American Economic Review*, 64 (1954), pp. 15–39, at 39; reprinted in R. B. Heflebower and G. W. Stocking, eds., *Readings in Industrial Organization* (Homewood, Ill.: Richard D . Irwin, Inc., 1958), pp. 46–68.

25. See Chapter 9 and Chapter 13 for full discussions.

26. See Chapter 9 for a fuller discussion.

27. Chapter 14 analyzes a sample of 61 industry categories for which the average return on assets was 15 percent per annum.

28. William J. Baumol and Robert D. Willig, "Fixed Costs, Sunk Costs, Entry Barriers, and Sustainability of Monopoly," *Quarterly Journal of Economics*, 96 (August 1981), pp. 405–31, at p. 406.

29. Ibid., p. 418.

8 PATENTS

INTRODUCTION

Patents can affect the kind and rate of invention and innovation overall[1]; change the size, structure, and performance of old industries; and give new industries different structures and performance than they would otherwise have. Patents are therefore a proper topic for industrial organization economics.

This chapter presents an economic rationale for a patent system. Although the object is to create property rights in inventions and new ways of doing things, it is more accurate to say that patentees have a preferred position in *claiming* such property rights.[2] To explain the general mechanics of patent use, the chapter presents a simple but powerful analysis that can also explain what specific patents do. Theory is applied to important real cases in which patent abuses allegedly strangled competition, with a discussion of policy problems that patent abuses pose.[3]

Those who want to learn to solve their own real problems can pick up some useful tools and methods in the Appendix. But to understand the rest of this chapter it is not necessary even to look at that material, let alone to master it.

AN ECONOMIC RATIONALE FOR PATENTS

The Venetian Republic, which befriended scientists (including Galileo), established patents in the fifteenth century.[4] From its beginning, the U.S. Constitution also called for a patent system.[5] Now, as then, however, some argue that governments should not grant patents because they create and preserve monopoly.[6] Whether the charge is correct is a question of theory and fact. Even if did create a lot of monopoly, however, the patent system would look better than some other government policies that restrict competition without offering any efficiency and welfare compensations. Whether we want to encourage invention or offer justice to inventors, it looks more reasonable to create property rights in new ideas than, by default, to submit them to rules of capture such as governed buffalo hunting and crude oil production in the old days.[7]

One major study found that small firms and individual inventors remain a powerful inventive force.[8] That many inventors are self-employed individuals does not mean that prospects for profits are irrelevant to how much inventing they do. Although such inventors typically sell (assign) their patents to firms, some of them very large, does not mean that a patent system works against their interests. It is plausible that people of small means benefit from having property rights in what they produce. Law gives them a better chance to collect for their inventions. According to logic and history, we should expect the long-term output of inventions to rise as the expected return to inventive effort rises.[9] Not all inventors are compulsive tinkerers who work equally hard whether they are paid or not. At least some of them are spurred on by a chance to obtain great wealth. Furthermore, innovators—who put new ideas into practical commercial use—*are* demonstrably responsive to money incentives.[10] Without property, there may be insufficient inducement to provide proper amounts of valuable services.

People with inventive talent will be more inclined to cultivate and use it if they are permitted to keep the fruits. If anyone can use a new technique without paying for it, the inventor will have trouble selling what he has produced. He might have to rely on himself, using such talents as he has in applying his discovery, and try to preserve his secrets. But if an inventor can effectively exclude others from using his discovery, he has real ownership and a better chance to sell it. None of this says how much and what kind of invention is best; how it can be got at least cost; or whether a 17-year patent grant is, all things considered, more beneficial than one given for a year, or forever.[11]

It might be argued that a patent system cannot induce too much activity of sorts that lead to patented inventions, since no patentee can charge for his patent more than it is worth, and most will get a good deal less.[12] Indeed, according to Kenneth Arrow, a Nobel laureate, private property and markets give us too little invention because it is a very risky business.[13] That is presumably because inventors and investors dislike risk, or because they make mistakes, problems for which there is no cheap remedy. Even government statisticians and decision makers have been known to make mistakes. In comparing how private markets and government programs handle invention, it may be fairer simply to set aside the question of mistakes until we can decide which process makes more of them.

Whether inventors are risk-averse is an open question. Many of them have not been intimidated by risk, and some act as though they like it. They may in fact risk more than a professional gambler would say is prudent, given the returns reasonably to be expected. By some standards, that would lead to *overinvestment* in invention. And, by raising the expected private returns from an invention, patents encourage any such tendency to plunge.[14]

An old argument to the same effect is that a patent system induces would-be inventors to enter a race to the pole, winner-take-all. The first to arrive claims a whole new territory and everything it can earn. If that is the kind of competition that patents produce, the story goes, it does not maximize the present worth of resources devoted to invention and research. Resources would be dissipated in premature and duplicative inventive activity. Altogether, the race might cost more than it is worth.[15] This story may not accurately portray patent competition, and it surely does not compare real patent systems with alternatives that are actually achievable.

The analogy with a race to the pole is incomplete. Inventors and innovators are not racing to secure a single well-defined monopoly grant. They are searching for valuable ways to accomplish a broad variety of results. They are competing on all value and cost dimensions that interest consumers. They are not merely competing to buy monopoly profits bestowed by a uniquely defined government grant.

Besides asking whether a patent system is "optimal" in the face of uncertainty and risk, we should ask whether it will hurt consumers in other ways. It might. The last section in the chapter shows how some patentees have tried to use trivial or invalid patents to sanctify collusive pricing. And it is easy, on paper, to create hypothetical cases in which the introduction of new things benefits some consumers while hurting others even more. Then, too, under real patent systems some kinds of discoveries are patentable while others are not. Judged by standards of perfection, that kind of discrimination may generate too much of some kinds of search, and too little of others. But no real institution, including patents, can be perfect.

It is not clear that the rivalry to invent and innovate creates significant hurtful externalities; that the contestants pay less for resources than they ought; or that anything practical could be done to improve matters. And, it is clear, a patent system is not all bad: without it, some discoveries *will* come late, if they come at all.

Although it is often said that patents and competition are incompatible, that raises important questions of fact. First, to what extent do patents bestow monopoly power along with property rights? Second, are the benefits from property rights larger than harms created by increased monopoly? We turn now to the motives and powers of patentees.

ECONOMICS OF PATENT USE

Although some of them are altruistic, it is safer to assume that inventors maximize their wealth, and that firms using the patents also do so.[16] These assumptions generate testable hypotheses that are often confirmed.

Whether a patent is valid is a legal question that only litigation can settle definitively.[17] Whether a patent bestows monopoly power is an economic question involving the number and quality of patented and unpatented substitutes it faces. Further, a patent may be valueless even though it is legally valid and bestows a monopoly: it may cover something that costs more than it is worth. Even though the preponderance of patents are invalid, or valueless, or both, we begin by analyzing valid patents that are valuable. Examples include the basic patents that covered Bell telephones, Alcoa's alumina-reduction processes, and Xerox copying machines. The kinds of patents analyzed here are therefore the kinds that patentees pray for rather than the kinds they usually get.

Even if they do create monopolies, patents do not necessarily increase industrial *concentration*. For one thing, we do not know what concentration would have been without a patent, or even whether such a product would have emerged without it. And a patentee may license large number of firms to use his patents. Chapter 7 shows that costs and demands explain much, if not all, industrial structure. Patents, too, operate on industry structure by affecting costs and demands. Some patents seem to give the trappings of monopoly power—a downward-sloping demand and so on. But such power normally comes from winning a *competition* between what the patent covers and other ways of doing things. In any case, as we will see, such power as a patent bestows tends to be exerted through whatever industrial structure is needed to minimize total costs, including costs of dealing with licensees. Patents will lead to greater concentration than production costs alone would require if it is too costly to get an unconcentrated industry to pay what it is supposed to for using the patent. These propositions will be examined in what follows.

A New Product

A patent may create a new product and a new industry to produce it. The new product cannot be made legally without using the new patent. The long-run demand for the new product is substantially less than infinitely elastic over a range of prices. Assume the patentee knows the long-run demand for the product; the minimum long-run payments needed to nurture a producing industry of various sizes; and the short- and long-run cost curves of potential producing firms. If large firms incur high costs in producing the new good, the patentee will be encouraged to license a larger number of smaller firms.

Figure 8-1 illustrates the problem. The long run supply function, LRS, shows the minimum long-run costs that manufacturing firms must cover to make the product. As drawn, these costs are constant. *DD* shows the demand for the product made under the patent, and shows for each output rate the maximum price that can be charged per unit of the product. In this simple case assume that the patentee cannot charge different royalty rates to different licensees. What royalty rate should the patentee charge?

The problem can be solved with Alfred Marshall's derived-demand analysis. If for any reason Q_2 output were produced, it would fetch a price of P_2 per unit. Since precisely P_2 *production* costs per unit must be incurred, the royalty rate would have to be zero to achieve that much output. Consequently, the demand curve for the patent, measured in product units, passes through Q_2. The maximum per-unit royalty that can be maintained at any output rate is the difference between the product demand price and production costs at that rate. The (derived) demand for the *patent* (in product equivalents) is dp-dp; and MR is the corresponding marginal revenue to the patentee. Note that the patentee has an interest in producing the product most efficiently, for lower costs increase the amount it can take as royalties. Assume that the marginal cost incurred by the patentee in licensing, policing and so on, is PC-PC.

The patentee has a peculiar advantage: the patent is an indispensable factor of pro-

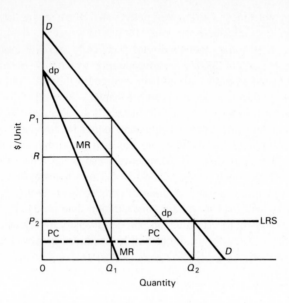

Figure 8-1 Patent Licensing for a
Competitive Producing Industry

Source: Adapted from John S. McGee,
"Patent Exploitation: Some Economic
and Legal Problems," *Journal of Law &
Economics*, The University of Chicago
Press, 9 (Oct. 1966), pp. 135–62.

duction, and licensees can be made to pay for it as though it is used in fixed proportions.[18]
By choosing an appropriate royalty per unit of finished product, the patentee can determine the size of the whole producing industry and, therefore, the price that consumers pay. In Figure 8-1 it charges a royalty of R per unit of product. Starting from the other costs of production, that royalty raises the licensing industry's supply function to P_1. The production rate will be Q_1, and the product will fetch a price of P_1. The industry is then effectively monopolized, even though the structure and earnings of the producing segment satisfy usual competitive criteria. But there is nothing evil or anti-economic in all this. The inventor has provided a new product and consumer satisfaction even for the seventeen years during which his patent controls. The only complaint seems to be that nonzero royalties make the industry smaller than it would be if royalties were zero, as can be seen in Figure 8-1 by noting what happens at the end of the seventeenth year, when the patent expires. The royalty rate falls to zero; the supply function becomes LRS; output expands to Q_2; and price falls to P_2. Thereafter consumers reap all benefits from the invention, the patentee none.

    The same apparatus can be used to analyze other problems involving new products. For example, how could a patentee decide whether to license outsiders or to produce the whole output itself? So far, we assumed that large producing companies would be inefficient, and that the patentee achieves lowest production costs by licensing many small producers. It then maximizes money income through a judicious choice of royalty rate. This is most easily seen when there are zero costs of enforcing royalty contracts with licensees. But if the cost of checking up on multiple licensees is greater than the efficiency lost by having only one producing company, the patentee has an incentive to license only one firm, or to produce the total desired output itself. And, though the structure (and, depending upon the patentee's bookkeeping, earnings) of the producing industry would now fail competitive tests, consumers as well as patentee would be better off for at least the term of patent grant. For, with lower costs, output would be higher and price lower. When the patent expires, the patentee or its sole licensee would have a de facto monopoly that would take time to erode. This apparent disadvantage of single-firm production could, in theory, be compared with the magnitude of earlier benefits.

Unlike the situation shown in Figure 8-1, a competitively organized manufacturing industry might have an upward-sloping supply curve, which could encourage the patentee to vertically integrate into manufacturing.[19] As shown in Chapter 2, supply curves can slope upwards for various reasons, including that firms own different qualities of factors. Suppose that costs of potential licensees differ greatly. Charging uniform royalties leaves the more efficient licensees with rents—a residue of revenues over cost. If the patentee could extract these rents, it could increase its profits while lowering price to consumers in the bargain. If the patentee's long-run marginal cost of manufacture were identical with (or even somewhat higher than) that of numerous licensees, it might manufacture for its own account rather than license.[20] If its own manufacturing cost is lower than the sum of license-enforcement (policing) cost and licensees' manufacturing costs, this would increase output and lower price of product based on the patent.[21]

One motive for vertical integration is to facilitate price discrimination.[22] Substantial *dis*economies of large scale in manufacturing plus different price elasticities of demand amongst markets pose a dilemma. Charging uniform royalties to multiple licensees will not yield the desired results; and discriminatory royalties[23] alone will not work unless the different markets can be separated. For customers will tend to shift from high-royalty licensees to low-royalty licensees (with the latter encouraging the process), reducing the patentee's earnings. In principle, licensees could be restricted to make only certain products or to sell only for specific end uses.[24] But policing licensees may raise total costs above those incurred when the patentee produces and sells directly for itself.[25]

Note now the problems that arise when size economies dictate that only one firm manufacture the product. This would encourage but does not compel a patentee to produce the whole output itself. Figure 8-2 shows manufacturing cost MC and product demand PD applicable should the patentee create a monopoly manufacturer through exclusive license.

If—contrary to assumption—competition in manufacturing were feasible at the same costs, cpd would be the derived demand for the patent, and CMRP the accompanying marginal revenue. To simplify, assume that marginal costs of patent policing and administration are zero. It might then seem sensible to charge the prospective patentee a unit royalty of R_1, hoping for an output of Q_1, and price of P_1, essentially as occurred in the other examples involving many competing licensees. Because the monopolist-licensee does not have a competitive supply function, however, no such simple patent demand can be derived; and the *licensee* faces a negatively sloped product marginal revenue, MR. If a royalty of R_1 is charged, the licensee's marginal cost, including royalty, is P_1. If left alone, the licensee will sell Q_2 output at a price of P_2, which does not maximize the patentee's royalty income.

There are various ways out. One of them is for the patentee itself to become the manufacturing monopolist, which is less attractive if its own manufacturing costs would

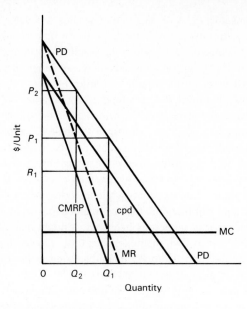

Figure 8-2 Patent Licensing for a Monopoly Producing Industry

Source: Adapted from John S. McGee, "Patent Exploitation: Some Economic and Legal Problems," *Journal of Law & Economics*, The University of Chicago Press, 9 (Oct. 1966), pp. 135–62.

be significantly higher than an outsider's.[26] Another possibility is to license a single firm with the proviso that a maximum price of P_1 be charged (or a quantity of Q_1 be sold). Some patentees with one or a few licensees have actually specified minimum production quantities or maximum prices, changing them when economic conditions change.

There are other ways to skin the cat. Even when size economies dictate that a single firm do the manufacturing, any of a number of different firms might be able to do that job. Only one need be chosen. Under such conditions, the patentee could simply sell its patent outright to the highest bidder. If there were several potential manufacturers, with the most efficient not much more efficient than several others, an auction could extract most of the rents that the patent generates. Similarly, the patentee could auction off a short- or long-term license to the highest bidder. Either scheme awards rights to the manufacturer who will make the most for the patentee. With perfect knowledge, this would be the lowest cost producer. If the patentee specifies price or output to the successful licensee it may be because it knows more about manufacturing costs and demand than the manufacturer does.

A Cost-reducing Patent for an Old Product

A second major type of patent reduces the costs of producing an old, that is preexisting, product.[27] We will assume that the *manufacturing* industry is competitive both before and after the innovation. Figure 8-3 illustrates the problem. *DD* is the product demand curve facing the competitive manufacturing industry. LRS would be the long-run supply, and P_1 the price, of the product if the patent were not used. LRS(P) shows what the long-run product supply would be *if* the patent could be employed at a zero royalty rate. Marginal

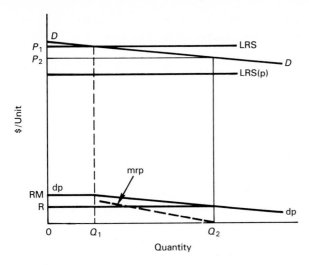

Figure 8-3 A Cost-Saving Patent

Source: Adapted from John S. McGee, "Patent Exploitation: Some Economic and Legal Problems," *Journal of Law & Economics*, The University of Chicago Press, 9 (Oct. 1966), pp. 135–62.

patent revenue is mrp; marginal patent cost is zero. The derived patent demand, dp, has a horizontal section at RM, maximum royalty. The maximum unit royalty, RM, is a little less than the unit cost savings accomplished by using the patent. No one will pay more, since it would still be possible to use unpatented techniques. Although it should be apparent that the patentee will not reduce the output and raise the price of the finished product, courts sometimes miss the point.[28] Indeed, as in Figure 8-3, unit royalties are usually much less than the cost savings that patents permit: maximum royalties are RM; the actual royalty is 0R per unit of product.[29] That royalties for cost saving patents are usually *much* lower than the cost savings they permit suggests that long-run product demand elasticities are higher than textbook illustrators imply, or that the patents themselves usually face considerable total competition. Even in the least favorable cases, prices under the new patent will be somewhat lower than before and will be much lower after the patent expires.

Competing Patents

We have dealt so far with instances in which only a single patent can accomplish a desired result. That is relatively rare. If each of many patentees has a valid patent that covers the same new product or permits the same cost reduction for one old product, none can charge much more than the bare costs of patent licensing and administration.[30] Nevertheless, if all such patents could be brought under one control, monopoly prices could be charged for a useful though all-too-common idea. Starting from this kind of parable, it is easy to argue that unified control of competing patents is hurtful and should be avoided. In addition to the common complaint that unnecessary monopoly is bad, other indictments come to mind. If he moves quickly and quietly, a promoter who invents only the idea of merging the patents could pay practically nothing to each patentee. Inventors might get even less than they had spent on their discovery. Thus, it might be argued, a central objective of the patent system—to reward inventors—would have been frustrated; a kind of noninventor rewarded; and the public required to pay.

Another possible problem is patent "suppression." As an example, take John M. Browning, the great American gun inventor. Browning took out at least 128 patents, almost all of them for repeating sporting and military firearms of various types.[31] Browning sold many of his patents outright for lump sums. At least once he sold one buyer a package of several patents, each one covering a firearm design closely competitive with the others. Out of one bundle of, say, four patented designs, only one would be put into serial production.[32] It could be asserted, and we will assume, that the other patents were "suppressed." Nevertheless, an assumption is not a definition; and we need to examine what suppression means. Even if all four designs appeal equally to consumers, costs of manufacturing them may differ.[33] Alternatively, consumer preferences can make one design more profitable than the others. In either case, a firm might buy all four patents, but use only one. The others would, then, be suppressed.

In each instance it is the inferior patents that are suppressed.[34] Even so, it could be argued that none should be suppressed. This argument presumably rests upon the higher price that suppression permits for the surviving patent (and product), and upon an allegedly low "social" opportunity cost of using inventions already made. Even though they are inferior, the other patents might pay if a monopoly price were charged for the superior good. Unless there is collusion, separately held inferior patents would reduce the price of the superior one; and, in the limit, produce competitive outcomes. There is an analogy in cartel economics: high-cost firms that are shut down when an industry is competitive have to be reckoned with if a cartel is formed. When the cartel raises prices, it may pay outsiders to reopen high-cost plants, a phenomenon that limits cartel power.

Problems in Determining Patent Policy

Various policy proposals have been made with respect to patents. Unfortunately, it is not clear what the best policy is. Take the problem of combining several patents from different patentees. Coordinated exploitation of complements can be good for inventors, manufacturers, and consumers. Furthermore, waiting for litigation to determine who owns what can be very expensive. But courts have had a hard time telling whether patents are complementary or competitive.[35]

It is sometimes said that fewer but "more important" patents should be granted. This might solve the problem of combining competing patents merely by sharply reducing the number of patents that exist to be combined. The proposal may have merit, perhaps by reducing costs of search, uncertainty, threat and litigation. On the other hand, someone in the patent office would have to decide what is important. This would give great administrative discretion and inevitably cause mistakes, if not worse, in judging what will become most important. Whether patents are worthless or valuable is best decided in the open market. Furthermore, granting fewer and broader patents tends to increase the present power of each one, as the history of aluminum and telephone patents may illustrate. And if issuing narrower patents creates the danger of ''small'' improvements that stretch patent coverage over time, it would at the same time ease the subversion of each one. For present purposes it is enough to note an extreme hypothetical case, in which the patent office literally grants a patent for *every* application. By facing squarely the same problems that arise in judging mergers of firms, and restrictive sale covenants, sensible rules might be devised for evaluating purchases (or licenses under) competing patents of *different* patentees.

Now take the problem of suppression. In addition to the difficulty of enforcing rules against it, there are more fundamental troubles. As the discussion of John Browning showed, rules against suppression affect how much an inventor will be able to earn. It is not possible to reduce returns to a given stock of capital, including patents and knowledge, without affecting how it will grow for the future. And, it is clear, an inventor may get more for his package of patents by selling them all to one firm rather than selling one each to several firms. This is not only because there may be economies of large-scale, multiple-design production; but because it is difficult to predict which patent will be best. It can also happen because the patents compete. A monopoly is more valuable than a license to compete.[36] Thus, it may appear desirable to compel patentees to get all patents into use, perhaps through forfeiture for nonuse or compelling sale or license of competing patents to competing firms on terms that permit each to produce. However, it should be recognized that, even if there were no cost savings from complementary products, or uncertainty about which patents are really good, forced use would reduce the return to any inventor who has several competing ideas. It may not be desirable to do that.[37]

Still another sort of patent suppression is perennially cited as an example of capitalist exploitation. A monopoly will, the story goes, use a purely cost-saving invention only if it increases the present value of expected profits, as when average total costs with the new process are lower than average variable costs with the old. But it may buy (or develop) some that it does not use, if for no other reason than that someone else will.[38] Outsiders starting from scratch would use the new process if the average total costs it permits are the lowest obtainable and lower than expected prices. It is sometimes overlooked that much the same distinction applies between present and prospective producers even in a competitive industry. Of course final outputs and prices would depend upon whether the process itself were exploited by a monopolist, that is, under a powerful patent.

The objections to a monopoly's suppressing cost-saving innovations are that, if the patent were licensed royalty-free to outsiders or small fringe producers in a monopolized industry, the monopoly could be eroded; or that the rate of innovation could thereby be speeded up, since such price-takers will adopt the process if it permits new average total costs that are lower than expected *prices*. All that sounds delightful, indeed; but what would it do to the patentee? Under such a policy, the patentee will get less for his invention than if all parties (including the monopolist) were, in effect, permitted to bid for it. For in maximizing profits from its invention, a patentee induces monopoly-level prices and outputs in the goods market. If need be, to obtain such a monopoly one should be willing to bid almost up to the full value of monopoly profits realizable. It *is* true that intelligent, self-coerced consumer organizations, if created at low cost, or the state acting in their behalf, could outbid a monopolist to get the patent, produce net benefits, yet pay off the inventor. But reform literature says little about that.

Thus, much, if not all, the criticism of patent suppression comes from using a zero-profit competitive standard for inventions already made, a standard that the patent laws were designed to displace. But patent reform can affect inventors as well as manufacturer-monopolists. The resultant of both effects of any proposed change in patent law should presumably be appraised before embracing it.

Other policy issues include whether royalty rates should be regulated, and how long patents should run. Pankaj Tandon accepts that patents have actually encouraged research and development; but he argues that compulsory patent licensing (at optimal royalty rates) and an optimal length of patent life are necessary to maximize net social benefits, defined as the sum of consumer and producer surplus.[39] The ideal patent life, he says, is infinite. The ideal royalty rate would, of course, have to be imposed coercively. Note that the ideal royalty would have to be determined before it could be imposed, a formidable task even in theory. Tandon shows how it could be done, theoretically, by a benign state using perfect information. To get the positive incentive effect of high expected returns from research and development (R&D), Tandon would extend patent life to infinity. This reduces what he sees as a dead-weight loss due to nonzero patent royalties, by lowering the royalty rate needed to obtain a given return to R&D. This trade-off is possible because, following Hotelling, the asserted dead-weight loss "is proportionate to the *square* of the royalty rate."[40] Following Hotelling, the deadweight loss—relative to pure competition—is:

$$(1) \qquad 1/2(\Delta P \Delta Q).$$

The *relative* monopoly price distortion $= \Delta P/P$. For convenience,

$$(2) \qquad t = \Delta P/P$$

$$(3) \qquad P(\Delta P/P) = \Delta P = Pt.$$

Call the elasticity of demand, E. Then:

$$(4) \qquad |E| = (\Delta Q/Q)/t.$$

and

$$(5) \qquad |E| \, Qt = \Delta Q.$$

Substitute (3) and (5) into (1):

$$\text{d.w.l.} = 1/2 \, (\Delta P \Delta Q)$$

$$1/2 \, [(Pt)(|E| \, Qt)] = 1/2 \, Pt^2 |E| Q.$$

How all this could be done in practice is not clear, though Tandon must think it would be easier to accomplish than the alternative he dismisses. The alternative "would be to pay each inventor a lump sum equal in value to the present value of the potential revenue stream, and then to make the invention free for anyone to use. Aside from the difficulty of assessing ex ante the value of an invention, this would place an impossible strain on the treasury.'' The part about straining the treasury may be right; but it is odd that Tandon relies on the ''difficulty'' of assessing the value of an invention. For his own scheme requires more information than that one would.

CASE STUDIES

Earlier sections of this chapter discussed the rationale for a patent system, and presented tools for analyzing what patents do. More needs to be said now about abuses of the unusual rights that patents bestow. This section discusses real examples of alleged patent abuses.[41] One of them is using patents to cloak cartel activities that, in the absence of patents, would clearly be unlawful. Several patentees may collusively monopolize a product using patents that are valid, invalid, or contested. Even if none of the patents were valid, for example, it might nevertheless pay to pretend that one or more is. A second abuse is merging, cross-licensing, exchanging, or pooling two or more patents to carve up markets and monopolize a broad industry comprising many products.

Before starting, it is necessary to state two important reservations. First, court decisions often do not clearly tell us what was really going on. This is partly because patent use tends to be complex, and partly because court decisions are sometimes confusing or just plain wrong. This explains why *allegedly collusive* may continue to be an accurate characterization even after defendants have been found guilty.

Second, although we want to prevent patent abuses, we do not want to constrain patentees too tightly. It hurts consumers if patent conflicts hamstring industry, or if patents are exploited inefficiently. It is not good so tightly to constrain patent mergers and cross-licenses that owners of overlapping or interfering patents can only sue one another interminably while their patents remain unpracticed and useless. The *Line Material* case seems to be an example.[42] There, one commercially feasible patented invention relied upon patented technical features of another impractical invention. Neither was any good without the other. Nevertheless, on antitrust grounds the Supreme Court struck down cross-licensing contracts that would have resolved the impasse.

Allegedly Collusive Patent Use

Standard Sanitary. This case involves a little of everything, which is grounds for suspicion in itself.[43] Besides patents, we find exclusive dealing, zone pricing, deferred rebates, vertical price fixing, and agreements to exclude second-quality merchandise from domestic trade.

Standard Sanitary owned a patent for enameling iron utensils, and produced about 50 percent of the sanitary enameled ironware—bathtubs, sinks, and so on. Rivals owned at least two other competing patents, and unpatented techniques also existed. Edwin L. Wayman, secretary of the industry trade association, obtained options on Standard's and two other (allegedly infringing) patents; and licensed other firms to use them. Standard and the licensees accounted for 85 percent of the business. Terms of these licenses and related agreements were a central issue in the case.

Wayman and five representatives of the licensee manufacturers jointly determined mandatory selling prices for goods manufactured under the patents. This strongly suggests that a simple price-fixing cartel was screening its activities with hollow patents. The owner of valid and valuable patents could get maximum profits through royalties that he set unilaterally, and would not want to determine prices jointly with licensees. Another ground for suspicion is that net royalties were very small, suggesting that the real money was coming from increased product prices. Paid on the basis of number of active furnaces, "royalties" were really performance bonds or deferred rebates, 80 percent of which were returned if licensees adhered to price and related agreements. Unless, as is possible, all furnaces had equal capacity and either ran at full capacity or were shut down, the number of furnaces is not a precise output measure. Further, cartels often suppressed second-quality goods to prevent sales of first-quality merchandise at second-quality prices. Finally, if, as the court asserts, both the Dithridge and Lindsay patents were infringements, it is odd that Standard did not curb them. In fact, Wayman bought options on them. And if these were competing but not infringing patents, exploiting them jointly might have created unnecessary monopoly power.

This was a cartel and the Supreme Court was right to proscribe it. Apparently none of the patents was strong. In the absence of a cartel, competition could have been substantial. Even so, the Supreme Court decision itself causes trouble. Its theory that evil is done when monopoly effects are transmitted from the manufacturing level through distribution is an incorrect and dangerous standard. *Any* strong patent tends to give its owner "control" over a derivative industry from start to finish.

Gypsum.[44]   U.S. Gypsum (USG) and others were charged with violating Sections 1 and 2 of the Sherman Act, "by conspiring to fix prices on patented gypsum board and unpatented gypsum products . . . ," namely gypsum plasterboard, gypsum lath, gypsum wallboard, and gypsum plaster. The government also charged that five of USG's patents "were invalid and void."

Before 1912, the core of gypsum board was exposed on all four edges. In that year, USG was assigned the Utzman patent, with process and product claims for closed-edge board. This product was said to be superior, yet cheaper to produce. In a 1921 infringement suit, a circuit court of appeals upheld the Utzman patent and found that it had been infringed. Then, in 1929, the Supreme Court said, USG used patent license agreements to control "the price and terms of sale of virtually all gypsum board."

But control over prices would end when the Utzman patent expired. To fill that gap when the Utzman patent did expire, USG acquired patent rights for adding soap foam to gypsum slurry, creating bubbles and producing a lighter and cheaper gypsum board. Contemporary documents indicate that this patent was not very valuable as a patent. Nevertheless, everyone recognized that it could be combined with a starch patent to fix prices industry-wide for an additional 17 years.

USG's price bulletins incorporated a basing-point system, and a system of "uniform billing weights'' to avoid freight differences arising from actual weight differences in the product. That patented board prices rose after 1929 is also suspicious. It would be odd for a cost-saving patent to have that effect any time. And, since the nation was sliding into the deepest and longest depression in history, it is worse than merely odd. The construction industry almost died.

The Supreme Court found defendants guilty of Sherman law violations, reversing the lower court.

Thermal Cracking Patents.[45]   Crude oils are complex mixtures, different parts of which evaporate at different temperatures. Before thermal cracking was invented, saleable petroleum products were removed from crude oil by stills similar in principle to those used to distill alcoholic liquors. Distillation simply *separates* different parts of the crude oil without transforming molecular structures. Gasoline boils out at low temperatures; kerosene, then fuel oils, boil out at progressively higher temperatures. This was the technology before cracking was invented.

Distillation could not alter the proportions of fuels that crude oil contained. When the demand for gasoline grew much faster than that for kerosene and fuel oils, the only ways to get more gasoline were to discover new crudes with more gasoline in them, or to distill more of the same crude oils, dumping for whatever it would fetch such additional fuel oil as had to be produced along with the gasoline. Thermal cracking changed all this. It put alchemy into the oil business, on a large scale at that.[46] By cooking fuel oil under pressure, crackers changed molecular structures, increasing gasoline production from the crude oil you had to start. Crackers converted fuel oil into gasoline and a little fuel oil to boot. Perhaps changing lead into gold would have been more remarkable.[47] For such processes to be worth anything, however, they must increase total product values by more than they increase costs. Crackers only work in one direction: they can not transform gasoline into fuel oil. Crackers work off the difference in price between gasoline and fuel oil and would have been worthless if gasoline had sold for less than fuel oil.

Employees of the Standard Oil Co. (Indiana) invented the Burton cracking process, which was patented in 1913. Even early versions doubled gasoline yields and reduced gasoline costs by about 28 percent. By 1924, the Burton process had earned Standard about $150 million, more than $26 million in royalties alone.[48]

In 1920 and 1921, about ten other patented cracking processes were introduced.[49] Some of these, and perhaps a few others as well, worked and were potentially valuable. They were also close substitutes. Which if any of these patents would be found valid if tested in the courts, and whether they would be forced to compete with one another were questions involving many millions of dollars.

One of the new processes was based on various patents of Mr. Jesse A. Dubbs and his son, Carbon Petroleum Dubbs. Some of the Dubbs designs and patents related to a patent application made in 1909, four years before Burton's. Dubbs's process was superior to Burton's.[50] Not only that: as early as 1915 Dubbs started attacking the Burton patents as infringing his own. And, as time went by, legal validity of all the major thermal cracking patents was put at risk.

Even while the lawsuit ground on, at least three patent pools were formed. In 1921, the Texas and Indiana companies pooled their patents; and, in 1923, the Gasoline Products and Texas companies harmonized theirs. The companies involved claimed that they had pooled patents solely to avoid litigation and other costs. Alternative ways of avoiding such costs are less suspicious. They include dedicating all the patents to the public; and licensing and sublicensing royalty-free all around. The grounds for suspicion are that, if two or more of the competing patents were upheld in the courts, it would pay to exploit them cooperatively rather than competitively.

Those who thought that the suit would quickly invalidate the Dubbs patents were mistaken. The case lasted 15 years and cost $3 million to $4 million dollars before it was settled. In January 1931 the Shell, California, Indiana, Texas, and New Jersey companies bought UOP, the company that then owned the Dubbs patents.[51] The Gasoline Products Company, owner of the Cross patents, also joined into an agreement not to sue the principals or their licensees for patent infringement. The government attacked these arrangements, among others, as violating the Sherman Antitrust Act.

In 1934, in the Great Depression, UOP reduced royalties to ten cents per barrel; and, in 1938—with thermal patents aging and the new, superior catalytic cracking processes spreading—to five cents. By 1944, when thermal cracking was in decline, and catalytic cracking was taking over the field, the rate fell to three cents.[52] External competition from a quite different process ultimately was a more powerful lever than competition among thermal patents had been.

The government claimed that defendants had unlawfully suppressed competition among their patents and that their royalties were oppressive. The U.S. Supreme Court found them innocent, in part, apparently, because it wrongly concluded that the relevant "industry" was neither cracking patents nor cracked gasoline, but all gasoline. The relevant market for this case should have been cracking patents, the demand for which is *derived* from the substantial demand for cracked gasoline, given the prices of crude oil and the costs of distillation processes. The Appendix explains this in detail.

The Supreme Court asked whether a 26 percent market share gave cracked gasoline a monopoly position, and concluded it did not. The Court would presumably have been more hostile if the cracked gasoline share had been much larger, which is exactly backwards. The question should have been whether defendants had conspired in the *patent* market, raising royalties, as a result of which less cracked gasoline was produced. There was a market for patents as well as for the product, and the Court looked at the wrong market.

The real question is whether the price of gasoline was as low as noncollusive patent exploitation permits. Given a stable demand for all gasoline, its price is determined by the total supply of gasoline, cracked plus straight-run. Significant changes in the supply of cracked gasoline change the price of all gasoline. And changes in the royalty rate change the supply of cracked gasoline. A large number of competing patentees would obtain essentially zero royalties and the price of all gasoline would be significantly lower. The Appendix shows how profitable and restrictive a cracking-patent cartel could be even if the share of cracked gasoline were much smaller than 26 percent of the total gasoline market.

This does not prove that the defendants in the *Cracking Patents* case conspired to fix royalty rates. It shows that it could pay in similar circumstances, even when patents govern only a minority share of some larger total "market." The Court did not think that was possible, even if there had been collusion.

In January 1931, the Court found for defendants. A group of major refiners then bought UOP. These two events consolidated the principal thermal cracking patents. By this time, some of the basic patents had expired. Nevertheless, it would be a while before catalytic cracking buried the old thermal processes.[53]

Massing Patents to Carve Up and Divide Markets

Hartford Empire.[54]   Defendants in this complicated section 1 and 2 Sherman Act case were nine corporations and 61 individuals. The printed transcript of record exceeds 16,500 pages.[55] In 1909, "persons interested in Corning" had formed the Empire Machine Company to develop and hold patents. Hartford-Fairmont Co. had been formed in 1912 to bring together two companies interested in glass manufacture and engineers interested in patents for automatic glass-making machinery. At that point, Corning was principally in the noncontainer "pressed and blown" glass fields.

Owens-Illinois was a large glass manufacturer whose Mr. Owens had developed the suction-type machine, the first fully automatic bottle blowing machine. The Owens Company was mainly interested in the narrow-neck container field and it gave exclusive licenses for limited fields.

The gob feeder machine, a substitute for the Owens process, appeared. It could efficiently produce a wider variety of containers, and had other advantages. Owens, as well as others—including Hartford-Fairmont—took out patents on gob feeders and licensed for their use.

Because of Corning's Empire Company, Corning and Hartford recognized that they could collide over gob feeder patents. Among other things, Corning might decide to go into the container field itself. In 1916, Corning (through Empire) got an exclusive license to use Hartford patents in the pressed and blown field; and Hartford got an exclusive license to use Empire patents in the container field. This division of fields looks anticompetitive on its face.

In 1922, Corning and Hartford created Hartford-Empire to take over their assets relating to glass machinery. Thus, though the patent problems of Corning vis-à-vis Hartford had been resolved, after 1916 Owens and Hartford were fighting in court over gob feeders. In 1924 they, too, came to terms. Among other things, Owens retained its patented suction forming machines. Owens got a nonexclusive, nondivisible, and nonassignable license under present (and future) Hartford patents for manufacturing glassware; but Owens agreed it would neither sell nor license gob feeders, and would not enter the pressed and blown field reserved to Corning under the earlier agreements. Owens and Hartford were to share equally in Hartford's divisible income in excess of $6 million per year.

Acting jointly, by 1926 Hartford and Owens got "controlling patents" on gob feeders. Since Corning and Hartford had already more or less merged their patent interests, all three had been brought together within about 14 years.

Hazel-Atlas ranked second after Owens in making glass containers and was using its own feeder patents. After the courts split in deciding patent litigation between Hartford and Hazel, they settled; in 1934 Hartford and Owens moved over to make room for Hazel's royalty share. Owens retained its suction process; Corning retained its pressed and blown field. According to the Supreme Court, "The result of this combination was that resistance to Hartford's licensing campaign disappeared and practically the entire industry took licenses from Hartford."

Thatcher Manufacturing eventually got what amounted to exclusive rights under the Hartford milk bottle patents. Although this might have reflected enormous size economies in milk bottle production, James Brown concluded that Hartford simply made a mistake: it later took away Thatcher's monopoly. Ball Brothers (fruit jars) had used its own as well as Owens's suction machines. In 1933 it took a license from Hartford. Hazel, Ball, and Owens then divided most of the fruit jar field by agreement.

In many cases Hartford limited the permissible glassware output of licensees, which raises questions: why couldn't they achieve the same result through royalty rates alone? Anyway, why not permit low-cost licensees to produce it all? This question comes up in many patent cases, including *Line Material*. According to the Court, Hartford, Owens, and others proceeded also to tie up patents on certain "adjunct" machines: "it became impossible to use Hartford feeders with any other forming machine than one licensed by Hartford or used by its consent, and as respects stackers and lehrs, Hartford achieved a similar dominant status." Among other things this, like the *Shoe Machinery* case, raises questions about tie-ins and requirements contracts.[56] According to the Supreme Court, "In 1935 certain new agreements were made," principally concerning Corning, Hartford, and Hazel.

Members of the Glass Container Association of America, formed in 1919, accounted for 82 percent of U.S. glass container production in 1933, and some 92 percent thereafter. The lower court found that the association had assigned production quotas. Does the existence of the association and the role it was alleged to have played suggest that the patents were invalid? That key patents were expiring, permitting outsiders to operate, though perhaps at a cost disadvantage? Perhaps fields not protected by patents were the association's chief concern. The Temporary National Economic Committee had found that certain gob feeder patents were pending, and hence inoperative, from 1914 to 1937.

An impressive number of patents figure in this case. By 1938, Hartford held some 600; Corning, upwards of 100; Owens, 60; and Lynch, 12. These patents were allegedly pooled so that, according to the Supreme Court, "94% of the glass containers manufactured in this country on feeders and formers were made on machinery licensed under the pooled patents."

After the 1938 TNEC study, and commencement of this suit, the agreements changed substantially. In 1939 the association also changed its statistical reports and other procedures. Nevertheless, the Supreme Court said, "Hartford retained dominance of the gob feeder field. Owens, although its basic patent had expired, continued, by virtue of improvement patents, to dominate the suction field. Owens, Lynch, and Hartford were the leaders, if not altogether dominant in the forming machine field.''

The government sought to dissolve Hartford and compel royalty-free patent licensing. By then, the Supreme Court said, Hartford had reduced royalties to a " 'standard' level to all its licensees." According to the Court, the government did "not assert, or attempt to prove, that these royalties were not reasonable in amount," whatever "reasonable" might mean and however it could be proved.

According to the Supreme Court, certain "restrictive" features were dropped: ". . . no licensee was restricted either as to kind or quantity of glassware it might manufacture by use of the patented machines, and no patent owner was restricted by formal agreement as to the use or licensing of its patents." Shortly before trial Hartford sold three patents to Corning for a substantial sum. "Two of the assigned patents have expired and Corning professes its willingness to dedicate the third to the public." Hartford continued to lease its machinery.

In rewriting the lower court's remedial decree, the Supreme Court refused to compel royalty-free licensing: "if, as we must assume on this record, a defendant owns valid patents, it is difficult to say that, however much in the past such defendant has abused the rights thereby conferred, it must now dedicate them to the public." This was the first case in which an antitrust decree—here reversed—compelled royalty-free patent licensing. Royalties on the relevant machines were, instead, to be "fair and reasonable." Although it is unclear how anybody could define "fair and reasonable," courts tried to do it in two subsequent *Hartford-Empire* proceedings. The Glass Container Association was ordered dissolved.

SUMMARY

One rationale for a patent system is to increase economic welfare by creating property rights in new products and techniques, increasing expected returns and encouraging investments in invention and innovation. Although some patents have created and preserved highly profitable monopolies, most of them do not create monopoly or much of anything else.

The argument that a patent system contributes to economic welfare rests on several assumptions. First, important inventions would not have been made in the absence of a patent system, or would have been made significantly later. Second, patents do not misallocate resources by inducing *too much* invention and innovation on net balance. Third, abuses, including those discussed in the previous section, do not swamp the other benefits.

Economic analysis and industrial histories show how patentees can increase the power of individual patents in various ways, some of which help consumers and some of which hurt. Consumers benefit when complementary patents are combined or otherwise harmonized. Consumers may also benefit when long and expensive patent litigation and impasse are settled by agreement. Unfortunately, however, agreements can also hurt consumers, and it is sometimes hard to tell in a specific instance whether benefits outweigh the hurts.

Economic analysis shows what factors courts should consider when they appraise patent use, and suggests how to fit them together.

It is tempting to increase competition by demolishing the strong patents on which some monopoly rests. From time to time, our antitrust authorities and courts succumb to the temptation. But demolishing patents today reduces the expected value of inventions yet to be made, undermining the basic reason for having patents in the first place. That medicine has such drastic side effects that it should not be prescribed routinely by whatever antitrust enforcers happen to be in office at the time. Not, at least, before we can have a full fundamental review of the patent system and the constitutional base on which it stands.

QUESTIONS

1. "The optimal patent policy for small, backward nations is to have no patents at all and steal inventions brazenly from countries that are technologically advanced." Discuss.

2. Explain and critically evaluate the basic economic rationale for patent systems.

3. Suppose that all inventors are compulsive tinkerers who are not interested in money. Where does that leave the basic rationale for a patent system? How about innovative firms that put inventions to commercial use but do not themselves invent?

4. Tandon's theory is that patents should be forever, not 17 years. Why? Discuss.

5. Since a patent bestows an exclusive right, it surely must bestow monopoly power. Discuss.

6. Since patents bestow monopoly power in and of themselves, there is no sense worrying further about mergers or pools of patents. Discuss.

7. Under some circumstances, a patent enriches the patentee but leaves (other) consumers little or no better off. What circumstances? By conventional economic welfare standards, how does this case look?

8. What problems does a patentee face if there are large economies of size in putting the patent into production? How can those problems be solved?

9. John Moses Browning sold "packages" of several patents at a time to a single firearms manufacturer. Why didn't he sell each patent to a different firm?

10. Since it is in principle possible to create strong monopolies by combining two or more patents, it is tempting to outlaw the practice. But there may be bad side effects of doing so. What are they? Can you think of ways to solve this problem?

11. What does *patent suppression* mean?

12. Mr. Justice Brandeis said that patents on processes producing only 26 percent of the nation's gasoline did not bestow monopoly power. Explain and comment. Would your conclusion change if the 26 percent share did not involve patents?

13. Do the *Standard Sanitary* and *Gypsum* cases look suspicious? Why?

14. What did patents have to do with dividing up glass-container markets? Were many patents involved?

APPENDIX TO CHAPTER 8

INTRODUCTION

This appendix takes up where a 1966 article left off.[57] Posner and Easterbrook misunderstood parts of that article, including the basic refining technology.[58] For example, they ask: "If cracking was a less expensive method of producing gasoline, why didn't it [completely] sweep the market?" The answer they give to their own strange question is incorrect.

The first stage of petroleum refining is distillation and practically all crude oil is distilled. The raw materials that crackers use are fuel oils that—along with straight-run gasoline—were produced by distilling crude. In that sense, cracking and distillation are complementary processes. Distillation produces gasoline directly from crude. Crackers do not produce gasoline directly from crude, but use as inputs certain products of distillation. Crackers could not produce any gasoline without distillation products, let alone produce all the gasoline on their own. They could not "sweep the market."

As we will see, cracking *is*, in a sense, a "less expensive method of producing gasoline"; but not in the way that Posner and Easterbrook envision. The large quantity of gasoline we buy would be substantially more expensive if there were no crackers. All gasoline would have to be made by distilling crude oil, and a great deal more crude oil would have to be distilled.

The purpose of the following discussion is, first, to clarify these and other matters; second, to present new models that can also be used on other problems than patents.

THE BASIC MODEL

Pre-Cracking Technology

Assume that there is only one quality of crude oil and only two petroleum products. Crude oil costs a constant $1.65 a barrel. Distilling costs a constant $0.10 a barrel of crude run. Buying a barrel of crude and distilling it therefore costs $1.75. Distilling a barrel of crude yields 0.25 barrel of gasoline and 0.75 barrel of fuel oil.

Marginal revenue from distillation is the total revenue added by running another barrel of crude. In long-run competitive equilibrium, total cost equals total revenue and—in the long run and short run—marginal cost equals marginal revenue. Call the price of gasoline P_G and the price of fuel oil P_F. The long-run equilibrium condition for distillation is:

(1) $$[P_G(0.25)] + [P_F(0.75)] = \$1.65 + \$0.10 = \$1.75.$$

In this model, equilibrium is established solely through *product* price changes, brought about by changing the quantities of crude run and products sold.[59] The demand function for gasoline is:

(2) $P_G = 11.5788 - .037894\ Q_G.$

The demand for fuel oil is:

(3) $P_F = 10.4740 - .01579\ Q_F.$

These demands show how product prices are determined by the quantity of finished products produced. In each case, the demand price is the average revenue from a whole barrel of the finished product. To find equilibrium for the distillation industry, we need also to know how *product* prices and quantities are related to quantities of crude oil run to stills. As equation (1) showed, the average gasoline revenue got from distilling one barrel of crude is $P_G(0.25)$, and $P_F(0.75)$ is the average fuel oil revenue from distillation. Into these revenue expressions, substitute the equations defining P_G and P_F—equations (2), (3). This substitution yields an expression for the (total) average revenue derived from crude runs:

(4)   AR = [11.5788 − (.0094735 Run)] [0.25]

                    + [10.4740 − (.0118425 Run)] [0.75]

              = (2.8947 − .002368375 Run) + (7.8555 − .008881875)

         AR = 10.7502 − .011250250 Run.

In distillation industry equilibrium, price equals average revenue and average revenue equals average cost:

AR(Run) = AC(Run),

where AC is a constant $1.75 per barrel of crude run, including the market price of crude and the cost of distillation services. That is,

(5)   10.7502 − .011250250 Run = $1.75, and, therefore

                              Run = 800.

Physical quantities in the model are measured in thousands of barrels per day. For the product demands and distillation costs and yields given, the industry runs 800 thousand barrels of crude per day. Distilling each barrel of crude yields 0.25 barrel of gasoline and 0.75 barrel of fuel oil. Equilibrium product market quantities are therefore 200 thousand barrels of gasoline per day and 600 thousand barrels of fuel oil. P_G = $4.00/bbl; P_F = $1/bbl.

This was the situation before cracking was invented.

Cracking

Now introduce cracking. Crackers can convert a barrel of fuel oil into 0.25 barrel of gasoline plus 0.80 barrel of fuel oil. The *net* cracker yield of fuel oil (NY_F) is fuel oil produced less fuel oil fed, namely, *minus* .2 barrel for each barrel fed. The net yield of gasoline

(NY$_G$) is 0.25 barrel produced less zero barrel fed, namely *plus* 0.25 barrel. In long-run competitive equilibrium, average revenue and average cost from cracking must be equal. Calculating on the basis of yields, this equilibrium condition comes to:

$$(6) \qquad [(P_G)(NY_G)] + [(P_F)(NY_F)] = 0.20 + R,$$

where R is the royalty rate charged per barrel of fuel oil fed to crackers—called *feed* here. The lower R is, the more cracking will be done. With more cracking, more gasoline is produced out of the same amount of crude oil and the price of gasoline is lower. As more fuel oil is cracked, the price of fuel oil rises. These product price changes reduce the margin between light- and heavy-product prices, the margin that crackers live on. When the revenue added by cracking equals the long-run marginal cost of cracking, the cracking services industry is in full equilibrium.

Equation (1) showed the competitive equilibrium condition for distillation.[60] Equation (6) shows the equilibrium condition for cracking. Cracking and distillation prices, inputs, and outputs must all be compatible with one another in equilibrium. The distillation equation shows the relationship between product prices and distillation costs that competition forces in the absence of cracking. The cracking equation shows how product prices and cracking costs must be related.

If revenues from distillation exceed the costs of distillation and crude oil, distillation capacity will expand until product prices fall enough, or crude prices rise enough, to make distillation revenues equal to distillation costs. And, even in the short run, the price of gasoline cannot exceed the price of fuel oil by more than the marginal cost of cracking fuel oil into gasoline. And, in the long run, adjustments in cracking capacity will keep the spread between gasoline and fuel oil prices equal to cracking costs, and cracking revenues equal to cracking costs.

As a result, competition produces ineluctable relationships within and between refining processes. If it weren't for that, any product prices would be sustainable so long as they cleared the product markets and forced distillation costs and revenues to equality. Cracking imposes an additional discipline. Because these processes are interrelated, even the *spread* between product prices is also strictly determined.

From equations (1) and (6) we derive the distillation and the cracking equations for P_G (or P_F):

From distillation:

$$(7) \qquad P_G = 7.00 - 3.00\,P_F$$

From cracking:

$$(8) \qquad P_G = 0.80 + 4R + 0.8\,P_F.$$

Solving those equations simultaneously, we get:

$$(9) \qquad P_F = 1.6316 - 1.0526\,R$$

$$(10) \qquad P_G = 2.1052 + 3.1578\,R.$$

R, remember, is the royalty charged for cracking a barrel of fuel oil. For any royalty rate, from equations (9) and (10) we can calculate long-run equilibrium product prices. For any product prices, from equations (2) and (3) we can calculate the quantities demanded. At a royalty rate of $0.60 per barrel cracked, for example, gasoline would fetch $4.00 and fuel oil $1.00—precisely the situation before cracking had been invented. That is, at a royalty rate of $0.60, the usefulness of the patent is negated completely and no cracking will be done. The patentee is not likely to want that.

A Single-Firm Cracking-Patent Monopoly. Suppose a single patentee controls thermal cracking. It will license at rate R, which maximizes net royalty income. How is R determined? According to equation (10),

$$P_G = 2.1052 + 3.1578\,R.$$

And, from the gasoline demand function, equation (2), we derive

$$Q_G = 305.55761 - 26.3894\,P_G.$$

Therefore,

$$Q_G = 305.55761 - [26.3894\,(2.1052 + 3.1578\,R)]$$

(11) $$Q_G = 250 - 83\,1/3\,R.$$

Define Feed to be the daily barrels of fuel oil fed to crackers. Then Feed equals the amount of cracking needed to produce the total quantity of gasoline demanded—Q_G—*minus* gasoline produced by distilling 800 thousand bbls/day of crude. In the example, cracking produces 0.25 barrel of gasoline for each barrel of fuel oil cracked. That is,

(12) $$\text{Feed} = (Q_G - 200)\,/\,.25 = [(250 - 83\,1/3\,R) - 200]\,/\,.25$$

$$= 200 - 333\,1/3\,R.$$

The total revenue from the patent—TR_P—is the royalty charged per barrel of feed *times* the number of barrels of feed:

(13) $$\text{TR}_P = \text{Feed}(R) = 200\,R - 333\,1/3\,R^2.$$

Assume that the total costs of patent administration, licensing, and so on are

$$\text{TC}_P = .01\ \text{Feed}.$$

From equation (12) we have it that Feed is a function of R. Therefore,

(14) $$\text{TC}_P = 0.01\,(200 - 333\,1/3\,R)$$
$$= 2 - 3\,1/3\,R.$$

Total profits to the patentee are P_P:

$$P_P = \text{TR}_P - \text{TC}_P = [200R - 333\,1/3\,R^2] - [2 - 3\,1/3\,R]$$

$$P_P = 203\,1/3\,R - 333\,1/3\,R^2 - 2.$$

To solve for R, maximize profits with respect to R:

$$\delta P_P/\delta R = 203\ 1/3 - 666\ 2/3\ R = 0$$

$$R^* = .305.$$

This kind of analysis underlies the graphical treatment in McGee's 1966 article.[61] The profit-maximizing royalty rate is $0.305 per barrel of fuel oil cracked. From equation (12) we get

$$\text{Feed} = 200 - 333\ 1/3\ R = 98\ 1/3$$

that is, 98,333.33 barrels per day. With this rate of feed, crackers produce 24.5833 thousand barrels per day (mbd) of gasoline and, net, *minus* 19 2/3 mbd of fuel oil. In addition, of course, distillation produces 200 mbd of gasoline and 600 mbd of fuel oil. Total products are, then:

$$Q_G = 200 + 24.5833 = 224.5833$$

$$Q_F = 600 - 19.6666 = 580.3333.$$

Equations (9) and (10) show product prices as functions of R. According to

(15) $\qquad\qquad\qquad R^* = 0.305.$

$$P_F = 1.6316 - 1.0526\ R = 1.310557$$
$$P_G = 2.1052 + 3.1578\ R = 3.068329.$$

From inverses of the product demand functions—equations (2) and (3)—we have it that

$$Q_F = 663.3312223 - 63.33122229\ P_F = 580.332.$$

$$Q_G = 305.55761 - 26.3894\ P_G = 224.5862.$$

Ignoring rounding errors, the system is consistent. It cross-checks and balances.

These solutions, remember, assume that a single patentee has a monopoly of thermal cracking. An interesting analysis is to compare the single-firm solutions with those for (1) pure competition and (2) Cournot oligopoly. From equation (12) we derive the inverse:

(16) $\qquad$ 333 1/3 $R = 200 -$ Feed

$$R = (200 - \text{Feed})\ /\ 333\ 1/3 = 0.60 - .003\ \text{Feed}.$$

Equation (16) is the demand for the patent, in terms of fuel oil feed rates. If pure competition in patent exploitation were possible the royalty rate would equal the cost of patent administration.

$TC_P = 0.01$ Feed, from which we derive (14). In long-run equilibrium, Average cost $=$ MC:

(17) $\qquad\qquad\qquad$ AC $=$ MC $=$ $0.01 per barrel; and

$\qquad\qquad\qquad\qquad R = $ MC $=$ $0.01 per barrel of feed.

In competitive equilibrium, therefore, R = \$0.01 and

$$\text{Feed} = 196\ 2/3$$

$$P_G = 2.136778$$

$$P_F = 1.621074.$$

These results make generally good sense. Competition among patentees cuts royalties drastically and increases the amount of cracking. Gasoline prices fall; fuel oil prices rise.

Four Cournot Patentees.   Suppose, by contrast, that there are four identical patentees acting like Cournot oligopolists. Feed will be 4/5 of the competitive amount, that is, 0.8 (196 2/3) = 157 1/3. Following equation (16) we find the royalty rate:

$$R = 0.60 - .003\ \text{Feed}.$$

$$R = 0.60 - [0.003\ (157\ 1/3)] = 0.128.$$

With that royalty rate,

$$P_G = 2.5094$$

$$P_F = 1.4969.$$

Historical data on thermal cracking royalties are not satisfactory. Data showing the basic UOP (Dubbs) royalty rate—15 cents per barrel of charge—do not change from 1922 through 1933, whether UOP was "fighting" the other major patent holders or—after 1931—was owned by them.[62] The royalty rate for Jersey's (Tube and Tank) process was reportedly 10 or 12 cents per barrel of charge in 1922, reduced like the other processes, in 1934, 1938, and in the 1940s,[63] by which time catalytic cracking was emerging.

Summary.   Note the royalty rates generated in this relatively simple model. The hypothetical single-firm patent monopoly gets 30.5 cents per barrel of feedstock charged. Four Cournot oligopoly patentees charge 12.8, which is very close to actual royalties charged during some periods. If it had been feasible, pure competition among many rival patentees would, in this model, have brought royalties down to 1 cent per barrel.

In descending order of importance, the principal criteria for these models were theoretic soundness, clarity, and a reasonable degree of realism. But good data for that period are hard to come by, and the model does not use full-blown empirical estimates of demand, yield, and cost parameters. It might be wrong, therefore, to take the models literally before doing additional research.

A SIX-EQUATION MODEL

Before proceeding to the most general and complex models, let's study an intermediate, six-equation version of the model with which we started. It paves the way for more complicated models to follow. We start with demand equations for the two products. The products are unrelated in demand. Their quantities are measured in thousands of barrels per day.

$$P_G = 11.5788 - .037894\, Q_G$$

$$P_F = 10.4740 - .01579\, Q_F.$$

All crude oil is distilled, at marginal cost— C(Dist). In this version, the marginal cost is a constant 10 cents per barrel.

From each barrel of crude oil, distillation yields .25 barrel of gasoline and .75 barrel of fuel oil. Refiners will pay no more for a barrel of crude oil than it contributes, gross, to total revenues, minus the marginal cost of distilling it. The amount of distillation services applied is Q(Dist), measured in units of thousands of barrels of crude run to stills per day.

The cracking process feeds fuel oil and produces gasoline and fuel oil. For each barrel of fuel oil fed, crackers produce .25 barrel of gasoline and .80 barrel of fuel oil. The net cracking yield of gasoline is, thus, .25 barrel of gasoline. The net cracking yield of fuel oil is negative:

$$.8 - 1. = -.2 \text{ barrel of fuel oil.}$$

If cracking-patent royalties were zero, the (remaining) marginal cost of cracking would be C(Crack). In this simplest model, C(Crack) is a constant .20 per barrel.

Casual inspection does not clearly reveal where the equations came from or how they were derived. Equations (1) and (2) rearrange equations for the prices of (i) gasoline and (ii) fuel oil. Equation (3) comes from the expression for the quantity of crude oil run to stills. And Q(Crude) $= Q$(Dist). Equation (4) comes from the marginal cost of distillation. Equation (5) solves for the profit-maximizing quantity of fuel oil fed to crackers. The sixth equation comes from R, the royalty-rate relationship.

From the price of gasoline, P_G, we derive:

(1) $$P_G + 0P_F + .0094735\, Q(\text{Crude}) + .0094735\, Q(\text{Feed})$$
$$+ 0C(\text{Dist}) + 0R = 11.5788$$

From the price of fuel oil, we derive:

(2) $$0P_G + P_F + .0118425\, Q(\text{Crude}) - .003158\, Q(\text{Feed})$$
$$+ 0C\,(\text{Dist}) + 0R = 10.4740$$

The quantity of crude oil distilled is determined by the demand for and supply of crude, from which we have:

(3) $$125P_G + 375P_F - Q(\text{Crude}) + 0Q(\text{Feed})$$
$$- 500\, C(\text{Dist}) + 0R = 25$$

In this version, the marginal cost of distillation is a constant .10 per barrel, which gives us:

(4) $$0P_G + 0P_F + 0Q(\text{Crude}) + 0Q(\text{Feed}) + C(\text{Dist}) + 0R = .10$$

We define R in terms of the derived demand for the patent. The demand price for the patent is the value of net product yields minus the constant .20 per barrel marginal cost of cracking. This gives us:

(5) $.25P_G - .2P_F + 0Q(\text{Crude}) + 0Q(\text{Feed})$

$$+ 0C \text{ (Dist)} - R = .20$$

The single-firm cracking patent monopoly determines the profit-maximizing rate at which crackers will be used, $Q(\text{Feed})$.

$$\text{dP(Patent)} = .25\,P_G - .2\,P_F - C(\text{Crack})$$

$$= .25\,P_G - .2\,P_F - .20$$

$$\text{TR(Patent)} = \text{dP(Patent)}\,[Q(\text{Feed})]$$

$$= .25\,P_G\,[Q(\text{Feed})] - .2\,P_F\,[Q(\text{Feed})] - .2\,[Q(\text{Feed})]$$

$$\text{MR(Patent)} = .25\,P_G - .2\,P_F - .002999975\,Q(\text{Feed}) - .2$$

$$\text{MC(Patent)} = .01$$

$$\text{MR} = \text{MC:}$$

$$Q(\text{Feed}) = 83.33402778\,P_G - 66.66722223\,P_F - 70.00058334$$

From this we get equation (6):

(6) $83.33402778\,P_G - 66.6672223\,P_F + 0(\text{Crude})$

$$- Q(\text{Feed}) + 0C(\text{Dist}) + 0R = 70.00058334$$

Given appropriate parameter values, this approach yields the same solutions as the simplest model with which we started:

$$P_G = 3.06842$$

$$P_F = 1.31053$$

$$Q(\text{Crude}) = 800.001$$

$$C(\text{Dist}) = .10$$

$$R = .305$$

$$Q(\text{Feed}) = 98.33410$$

MODELS WITH INCREASING COSTS

Turn now to more complex and general models. All use the same product demand functions and refining yields as before. The simplest model assumed constant marginal costs of crude oil, distillation, and cracking. Here we incorporate upward-sloping supply functions for crude oil, cracking, and distillation. Among other things, this permits us to have one or more of these functions upward-sloping. It is often helpful, for example, to have supply functions upward-sloping in the short run and constant in the long run.

All crude oil is distilled, at an upward-sloping marginal cost, $C(\text{Dist})$:

$$C(\text{Dist}) = .05 + .0000625 \ Q(\text{Crude}).$$

$$C(\text{Crack}) = .10 + .0005 \ Q(\text{Feed}).$$

Note that Feed and Crack measurement units are identical and their quantities are equal. The total market supply of crude oil is given by the equation for its supply price:

$$sP(\text{Crude}) = .05 + .002 \ Q(\text{Crude}).$$

Crude oil is measured in thousands of barrels per day.

Distinguish three cases. In the first, there is a single-firm cracking-patent monopoly. In the second case, a number of patentees compete so fervently that the royalty rate is forced down to the bare marginal cost of running a competitive patent business. In the third case all patents have expired and royalties (and patent administration costs) are zero.

Single-Firm Patent Monopoly

Suppose, as for a time was true, that a single firm owns the thermal cracking patent(s). By altering its royalty rate, a monopoly patentee can significantly affect product prices. To find R^*, the royalty rate that maximizes its profits, the patentee recognizes that R affects products prices, which—in turn—affect the demand for cracking.

The first five equations are, in general, like those used in competitive models. The first equation comes from those that determine the price of gasoline. The demand price for gasoline, remember, is

$$P_G = 11.5788 - .037894 \ Q_G.$$

In general form,

$$Q_G = .25 \ Q(\text{Crude}) + .25 \ Q(\text{Feed}).$$

Therefore,

$$P_G = 11.5788 - .037894 \ [.25 \ Q(\text{Crude}) + .25 \ Q(\text{Feed})].$$

From which we obtain:

(1) $P_G + 0P_F + .0094735 \ Q(\text{Crude}) + .0094735 \ Q(\text{Feed})$

$$+ \ 0C(\text{Dist}) + 0R = 11.5788.$$

The second equation—the price for fuel oil—is derived analogously.

$$P_F = 10.4740 - .01579 \ Q_F, \text{ and}$$

$$Q_F = .75 \ Q(\text{Crude}) - .20 \ Q(\text{Feed}).$$

Therefore,

$$P_F = 10.4740 - .01579 [.75 \, Q(\text{Crude}) - .20 \, Q(\text{Feed})]; \text{ and}$$

$$P_F + .011843 \, Q(\text{Crude}) - .003158 \, Q(\text{Feed}) = 10.4740.$$

From that we derive equation (2):

(2) $\quad 0P_G + P_F \, .0118425 \, Q(\text{Crude}) - .003158 \, Q(\text{Feed}) + 0C(\text{Dist})$

$\quad\quad + 0R = 10.4740.$

The next problem is to determine the quantity of crude oil distilled. The demand price for a barrel of crude oil, dP(Crude) is the value of products distilled from it, minus the marginal cost of distillation. All crude is distilled, and we make the quantity of distillation equal to the quantity of the crude.

$$dP(\text{Crude}) = P_G \, (.25) + P_F \, (.75) - C(\text{Dist}).$$

$$sP(\text{Crude}) = .05 + .002 \, Q(\text{Crude})$$

$$dP = sP, \text{ and}$$

$$.002 \, Q(\text{Crude}) = .25 \, P_G + .75 \, P_F - C(\text{Dist}) + 0Q(\text{Feed}) + 0R - .05.$$

$$Q(\text{Crude}) = 125 \, P_G + 375 \, P_F - 500 \, C(\text{Dist}) + 0Q(\text{Feed}) + 0R - 25.$$

Rearranging, we get:

(3) $\quad 125 \, P_G + 375 \, P_F - Q(\text{Crude}) + 0Q(\text{Feed}) - 500 \, C(\text{Dist}) + 0R = 25$

We now have to determine the cost of distillation services. In this model, $Q(\text{Dist}) = Q(\text{Crude})$. Therefore,

$$C(\text{Dist}) = .05 + .0000625 \, Q(\text{Crude}), \text{ from which we get:}$$

(4) $\quad 0P_G + 0P_F - .0000625 \, Q(\text{Crude}) + 0Q(\text{Feed}) + C(\text{Dist}) + 0R = .05$

We measure the amount of cracking done in thousand-barrel units of fuel oil fed to the crackers daily—$Q(\text{Feed})$. $Q(\text{Feed})$ is determined by the demand for and marginal cost of cracking services. The demand price for cracking equals the yield of gasoline times its price, plus the net yield of fuel oil times its price. The net yield of fuel oil, remember, is negative:

$$dP(\text{Crack}) = .25 \, P_G - .2 \, P_F.$$

The supply price of cracking equals its marginal cost plus the royalty rate per barrel of fuel oil fed:

$$sP(\text{Crack}) = .10 + .0005 \, Q(\text{Feed}) + R.$$

To determine $Q(\text{Feed})$, we bring the demand and supply of cracking services to equality:

$$.25 \, P_G - .2 \, P_F = .10 + .0005 \, Q(\text{Feed}) + R$$

$$.0005 \ Q(\text{Feed}) = .25 \ P_G - .2 \ P_F - .10 - R$$
$$Q(\text{Feed}) = 500 \ P_G - 400 \ P_F - 200 - 2{,}000 \ R.$$

From this, we derive the fifth equation:

$$(5) -500 \ P_G + 400 \ P_F + 0Q(\text{Crude}) + Q(\text{Feed}) + 0C(\text{Dist}) + 2{,}000 \ R = -200$$

The sixth equation determines R^*, the royalty rate that maximizes patentee's profit.

As in other fixed-proportions derived-demand models, the demand price (average revenue) for the patent is the total additional revenue got from cracking a barrel of feed, minus the marginal cost of cracking:

$$d\text{P} = .25 \ P_G - .20 \ P_F - [.10 + .0005 \ Q(\text{Feed})].$$

The patentee's total royalty revenue equals the price for using the patent per barrel of feed times the number of barrels fed:

$$.25 \ P_G \ Q(\text{Feed}) - .20 \ P_F \ Q(\text{Feed}) - .10 \ Q(\text{Feed}) - .0005 \ Q(\text{Feed})^2.$$

By differentiating that expression with respect to Q (Feed), we obtain marginal revenue:[64]

$$\text{MR} = .25 \ P_G + .25 \ [\delta P_G/\delta Q(\text{Feed})] - .2 \ P_F$$
$$- .2 \ [\delta P_F/\delta Q(\text{Feed})] - .10 - .0010 \ Q(\text{Feed}).$$
$$\text{MR} = .25 \ P_G - .002368375 \ Q(\text{Feed}) - .2 \ P_F$$
$$- .0006316 \ Q(\text{Feed}) - .10 - .001 \ Q(\text{Feed}).$$

Assume that patentee's total cost of patent administration is $.01 \ Q(\text{Feed})$. Its marginal cost is therefore $.01$. MC = MR:

$$.25 \ P_G - .20 \ P_F - .003999975 \ Q(\text{Feed}) - .10 - .01.$$

To maximize profits, the patentee has to induce refiners to feed crackers at the rate Q^*:

$$Q^*(\text{Feed}) = 62.50039063 \ P_G - 50.0003125 \ P_F - 27.50017188.$$

Substitute that equation for $Q^*(\text{Feed})$ into the following equation. It is derived from equation (5), which, when there is atomistic competition, is used to solve for $Q(\text{Feed})$:

$$-500 \ P_G + 400 \ P_F + Q(\text{Feed}) + 2{,}000 \ R + 200 = 0.$$

This substitution yields R^*:

$$-500 \ P_G + 400 \ P_F + \{62.50039063 \ P_G - 50.0003125 \ P_F - 27.50017188\}$$
$$+ 2{,}000 \ R^* = 0.$$
$$2000 \ R^* = 437.4996094 \ P_G - 349.9996875 \ P_F - 172.4998281.$$
$$R^* = .218749805 \ P_G - .174999844 \ P_F - .0860.$$

This gives us the sixth equation:

(6) $.218749805\, P_G - .174999844\, P_F + 0Q(\text{Crude}) + 0Q(\text{Feed}) + 0C(\text{Dist})$
$$- R^* = .0860.$$

Given the parameters assumed here, the patent-monopoly equilibrium solutions are:

$$P_G = 3.06887;\ P_F = 1.31038;\ Q(\text{Crude}) = 800.001;\ Q(\text{Feed}) = 98.2865;$$
$$C(\text{Dist}) = .10;\ R^* = .356.$$

Competition Among Cracking-Process Patentees _____

In this second case, several different firms own cracking patents and compete fervently in licensing them. As a result, R equals the bare marginal cost of licensing and administering patent use. The sixth equation of this system determines this marginal cost and—therefore—R. Assume that cost is a constant $.01 per barrel.

   This case could also be handled with five equations, by adding R to the C(Crack) function.

(1) $P_G + 0P_F + .0094735\, Q(\text{Crude}) + .0094735\, Q(\text{Feed})$
$$+ 0C(\text{Dist}) + 0R = 11.5788$$

(2) $0P_G + P_F + .0118425\, Q(\text{Crude}) - .003158\, Q(\text{Feed})$
$$+ 0C(\text{Dist}) + 0R = 10.4740$$

(3) $125\, P_G + 375\, P_F - Q(\text{Crude}) + 0Q(\text{Feed}) - 500\, C(\text{Dist}) + 0R = 25$

(4) $0P_G + 0P_F - .0000625\, Q(\text{Crude}) + 0Q(\text{Feed}) + C(\text{Dist}) + 0R = .05$

(5) $-500\, P_G + 400\, P_F + 0Q(\text{Crude}) + Q(\text{Feed}) + Q(\text{Dist}) + 2{,}000\, R = -200$

(6) $0P_G + 0P_F + 0Q(\text{Crude}) + 0Q(\text{Feed}) + 0C(\text{Dist}) - R = -.01$

For the parameters assumed,

$$P_G = 2.13234$$
$$P_F = 1.62256$$
$$Q(\text{Crude}) = 800.002$$
$$Q(\text{Feed}) = 197.144$$
$$C(\text{Dist}) = .10$$
$$R = .01$$

In the third case, below, we will see zero patent costs and royalties. Here, with $R = $.01/\text{bbl}$, rather than zero, gasoline price is a little higher; fuel oil is a little cheaper; and 2,857 fewer barrels of fuel oil are cracked per day. That is, with slightly higher royalties, cracking is a less effective substitute for crude oil in increasing gasoline output above distillation-only levels.

The crucial divide between cracking-no-cracking occurs at the royalty rate of $.70 per barrel of fuel oil fed. This is higher than the $.60 figure from the simplest model because here the marginal cost of cracking is assumed to *fall* at less cracking is done. When $R = .70$, the following equilibrium values follow:[65]

$$P_G = \$4.00$$

$$P_F = \$1.00$$

$$Q(\text{Crude}) = 800.00000$$

$$Q(\text{Feed}) = 0.00007$$

$$C(\text{Dist}) = 0.10$$

Competition After All Cracking Patents Have Expired _____

Here, all patents have expired and $R = 0$. For this case, use a five-equation system:

(1) $\quad\quad\quad P_G + 0P_F + .0094735\ Q(\text{Crude}) + .0094735\ Q(\text{Feed})$
$\quad\quad\quad\quad\quad\quad + 0C(\text{Dist}) = 11.5788$

(2) $\quad\quad\quad 0P_G + P_F + .0118425\ Q(\text{Crude}) - .003158\ Q(\text{Feed})$
$\quad\quad\quad\quad\quad\quad + 0C(\text{Dist}) = 10.4740$

(3) $\quad\quad 125\ P_G + 375\ P_F - Q(\text{Crude}) + 0Q(\text{Feed}) - 500\ C(\text{Dist}) = 25$

(4) $\quad\quad 0P_G + 0P_F - .0000625\ Q(\text{Crude}) + 0Q(\text{Feed}) + C(\text{Dist}) = .05$

(5) $\quad\quad -500\ P_G + 400\ P_F + 0Q(\text{Crude}) + Q(\text{Feed}) + 0C(\text{Dist}) = -200$

As before, Equations (1) and (2) solve for the prices of gasoline and fuel oil. Equation (3) solves for the quantity of crude oil run to stills. Equation (4) gives us the marginal cost of distillation, $C(\text{Dist})$. Equation (5) solves for the quantity of fuel oil fed to crackers, $Q(\text{Feed})$.

For the parameters assumed, some solution values are:

$$P_G = 2.10527$$

$$P_F = 1.63158$$

$$Q(\text{Crude}) = 800.00200$$

$$Q(\text{Feed}) = 200.001$$

$$C(\text{Dist}) = .10$$

Models of these sorts can be used to show the (sometimes unexpected) results of changing parameter values. Suppose the demand for gasoline increases significantly, becoming

$$P_G = 11.5788 - .019\ Q_G$$

$$= 11.5788 - .019\ [.25\ Q(\text{Crude})] - .019\ [.25\ Q(\text{Feed})]$$

$$= 11.5788 - .00475\ Q(\text{Crude}) - .00475\ Q(\text{Feed}).$$

As a result, we obtain the following new equation, which we substitute for the old equation (1):

(1)′ $P_G + 0P_F + .00475\ Q(\text{Crude}) + .00475\ Q(\text{Feed})$
          $+ 0C(\text{Dist}) = 11.5788.$

Solving the new system, we get:

$$P_G = 3.30201$$

$$P_F = 1.65773$$

$$Q(\text{Crude}) = 954.570$$

$$Q(\text{Feed}) = 787.912$$

$$C(\text{Dist}) = .10966$$

NOTES

1. That question is pursued in Chapter 15.

2. *Claiming* is the right word. Cynics who are familiar with patent law sometimes say that a patent is merely a license to sue.

3. For more detailed analyses see J. S. McGee, "Patent Exploitation: Some Economic and Legal Problems," *Journal of Law & Economics*, 9 (October 1966), pp. 135–62; Kenneth Arrow, "Economic Welfare and the Allocation of Resources for Invention," in *The Rate and Direction of Inventive Activity: Economic and Social Factors* (Princeton, N.J.: Princeton University Press, 1962), pp. 609–25; Pankaj Tandon, "Optimal Patents with Compulsory Licensing," *Journal of Political Economy*, 90 (June 1982), pp. 470–86, and sources cited there.

4. Fritz Machlup, *An Economic Review of the Patent System, Study No. 15*, U.S. Congress, Senate, Subcommittee on Patents, Trademarks, and Copyrights, 85th Cong. 2nd sess. (Washington, D.C.: 1958).

5. *Constitution of the United States*, Article I, section 8; James Madison, "The Federalist No. 43, in *The Federalist* (New York: Modern Library, [n.d.]), pp. 278–79.

6. Those to whom the government grants patents are called *patentees*. The government, which grants the patents, is *patentor*.

7. Chapter 17 discusses these cases.

8. John Jewkes, David Sawers, and Richard Stillerman, *The Sources of Invention* (New York: St. Martin's Press, Inc., 1959).

9. Jacob Schmookler, "Technological Change and the Law of Industrial Growth," in W. Alderson and others, eds., *Patents and Progress* (Homewood, Ill.: Richard D. Irwin, Inc., 1965); and "Technological Change and Economic Theory," *American Economic Review*, 55 (May 1965), pp. 333–41, at pp. 333, 335.

10. See Chapter 15.

11. Aaron Director discussed perpetual grants years ago. See also Pankaj Tandon, "Optimal Patents with Compulsory Licensing."

12. Compare Arrow, "Economic Welfare and Invention," and McGee, "Patent Exploitation."

13. Arrow suggests government intervention to increase inventive activities, on the theory that ". . . highly risky business activities, including invention . . . should be undertaken if the expected return exceeds the market rate of return, no matter what the variance is." Arrow, "Economic Welfare and Invention," p. 613.

14. It should be added, however, that those who do plunge pay the full market value of the resources they buy.

15. Compare William J. Fellner, "The Influence of Market Structure on Technological Progress," *Quarterly Journal of Economics*, 65 (November 1951), pp. 560–67; I. Horowitz, "Firm Size and Research Activity," *Southern Economic Journal*, 28 (January 1962), pp. 298–301; "Research Inclinations of a Cournot Oligopolist," *Review of Economic Studies*, 30 (June 1963), pp. 128–30; F. M. Scherer, "Research and Development Resource Allocation Under Rivalry," *Quarterly Journal of Economics*, 81 (August 1967), pp. 359–94; Yoram Barzel, "Optimal Timing of Innovations," *Review of Economics and Statistics*, 50 (March 1968), pp. 348–55; W. L. Baldwin and G. L. Childs, "The Fast Second and Rivalry in Research and Development," *Southern Economic Journal*, 36 (July 1969), pp. 18–24; Morton Kamien and Nancy Schwartz, "Potential Rivalry, Monopoly Profits, and the Pace of Inventive Activity," *Review of Economic Studies*, 45 (October 1978), pp. 547–57; "Timing of Innovations Under Rivalry," *Econometrica*, 40 (January 1972), pp. 43–60; "On the Degree of Rivalry for Maximum Innovative Activity," *Quarterly Journal of Economics*, 90 (May 1976), pp. 245–60.

16. Charging zero royalties may satisfy an altruistic patentee who wants to help only those who benefit from his or her invention. A profit-maximizing altruist, on the other hand, has more to give away and can distribute it to whomever he or she chooses.

17. This correctly suggests that many patents granted by the Patent Office would turn out to be invalid if tested in the courts. Patent adversaries often settle out of court for this as well as other reasons.

18. Variable proportions are more common. For example, though a union can fix the wage level, employers usually can substitute capital for labor. Thus three major factors limit the power of the usual monopolist of a production factor: entry; factor subsitution in production; and the competition of other final goods that are partial substitutes for that produced by the industry in question. The patentee may be able at least to reduce the first and avoid the second.

19. A firm is said to be vertically integrated when it performs for itself functions that have been or could be performed by its customers or suppliers. See Chapter 12.

20. There are ambiguities: the patentee might have to pay the capitalized rental value for the scarce or superior factors needed to do the job himself or herself, and then would be as badly off as if he or she licensed. This seems less likely if a new-product patent creates a new manufacturing industry from scratch and if the scarce factor has poor alternative uses. With good information the patentee could then strip out prospective rents through discriminatory contracts with licensees. Perhaps perfect lump-sum discrimination (if feasible) plus royalties, would be necessary to do as well if the patentee licenses.

21. See Chapter 12.

22. For detailed analyses of Alcoa, a famous example, see Martin K. Perry, "Price Discrimination and Forward Integration," *Bell Journal of Economics and Management Science*, 9 (Spring 1978), pp. 209–17; and "Forward Integration by Alcoa: 1888–1930," *Journal of Industrial Economics*, 29 (September 1980), pp. 37–53.

23. Highest for low-elasticity markets; lowest for high-elasticity markets.

24. Note the case of milk bottles, discussed later on in this chapter in connection with the *Hartford-Empire* case.

25. Policing direct sales is not costless, either. Customers have to be kept honest, since they tend to "misclassify" themselves, and one's own employees also bear watching. But costs of keeping low-royalty licensees honest would be avoided.

    Suppose that a patent permits different sizes or types of goods to be produced at similar costs, and that demand elasticities differ amongst them. For example, the cost of producing larger sizes of bottles is likely to be a smaller proportion of the price of the final (filled) product. In such cases, discriminatory royalties may be needed to maximize the patentee's income, while efficient production may encourage licensing each producer for all markets.

    It may be hard to keep everyone honest even if demand elasticities do not differ among the products. For cost differences among licensees, or among the plants of the same licensees, ideally call for royalty discrimination. Even for single-plant licenses, licensees have an incentive to conspire against the patentee. They may overreport production from high-cost, low-royalty plants, and so on. Whenever conditions encourage licensees to underreport, the patentee may either avoid licensing altogether or monitor production from each plant. It may pay to limit quantities produced from high-cost, low-royalty plants.

26. It is apparent that P_1 would be the best price to be charged by a firm merging patentee and manufacturer, or by a patentee whose manufacturing costs are MC and as low as anybody's.

27. Some real patents affect both product quality and costs. A combination of the two cases, arbitrarily separated here, can be used to analyze such cases.

28. For example, see Mr. Justice Brandeis's opinion in *Standard Oil* v. *U.S.*, 283 U.S. 163 (1931).

29. Actual royalties might (almost) reach this ceiling if, for example, patent marginal revenue were negative for outputs greater than that reached before the invention—Q_1 in Figure 8-3. This occurs when derived patent demand elasticities are less than one, sign ignored. Thus, the lower patent demand elasticities are, the less output will expand. For any given output, patent elasticities tend to be lower as the *product* demand elasticity is lower; as, for a given product demand, costs of inputs other than the patent are greater; and as substitutes for the patent are poorer.

30. Even though a license would be cheap, why would anyone bother to take one out? Because the patents are *valid*, he may be sued if he does not.

31. They covered "more than eighty separate and distinct firearms. . . ." John Browning and Curt Gentry, *John M. Browning, American Gunmaker* (Garden City, N.Y.: Doubleday & Co., Inc., 1964), p. vii. For example, Browning patents covered the Winchester model 1894, perhaps the most popular sporting rifle in history and one that is still produced in large numbers; the BAR (Browning Automatic Rifle) famous in two world wars; the U.S. Army's .45 Automatic Colt Pistol; and various other machine guns and the like, all of which achieved enormous total production.

32. Winchester bought 44 Browning gun designs, of which 10 were manufactured. Browning and Gentry, *Browning, American Gunmaker*, pp. 124–26, 131–33, 242, 264. It is a question of fact, in all such cases, how many separate designs there are. Overlapping patent claims or specifications, or complementary or overlapping design features may collapse many into one. In Browning's case, there were several separate designs.

33. Even if each appealed most strongly to a different group, this would not guarantee their concurrent production by one firm that held all patents. For costs, the strength of substitution, and own-price elasticities enter the question.

34. It should be noted that if there were only one market and if royalties were zero, as when patents expire or if no design were ever patented, competition would also tend to force out all but the single "best" design. If there were four separate consumer markets, all four might coexist even under competition; but this seems likely to result in multiple patent exploitation under monopoly as well.

35. These difficulties of recognition and assessment can be seen, for example, in *Standard Oil Co.* v. *United States*, 283 U.S. 163 (1931), and *United States* v. *Line Material Co.*, 333 U.S. 287 (1948).

36. If the costs and demands are the same whether one or all patents are used, and if there are not significant scale economies, the patentee might choose to license all patents, and to license many producers. No patent would then be suppressed, but by choosing the appropriate royalty the same (monopoly) results would occur as though there were only one patent. Nevertheless, royalties and product prices would still be lower if each patent were owned and exploited independently by a different person.

37. Why doesn't the inventor suppress all but one patent himself, as he can legally do in the United States? If a buyer is to pay as much for the one superior patent as for all he would require at least a binding promise from the patentee that the remaining ones will not be used.

38. Even if the old process is governed by a basic patent to which the new is only a subsidiary improvement, there may be trouble dealing with the owner of a complement that one day will be valuable.

39. Pankaj Tandon, "Optimal Patents with Compulsory Licensing," p. 473.

40. Ibid., p. 475.

41. This chapter omits patent cases that involve tying contracts, which are discussed further in Chapter 9.

42. *U.S.* v. *Line Material Co., et al.*, 68 S. Ct. 550 (1948).

43. *Standard Sanitary Manufacturing Company* v. *United States*, 226 U.S. 20 (1912).

44. *U.S.* v. *U.S. Gypsum Co.*, 333 U.S. 364 (1948).

45. *Standard Oil Co.* v. *U.S.*, 283 U.S. 163 (1931).

46. For helpful background, see John L. Enos, *Petroleum Progress and Profits* (Cambridge,

Mass.: The MIT Press, 1962); Kendall Beaton, *Enterprise in Oil: A History of Shell in the United States* (New York: Appleton-Century-Crofts, 1957); David McKnight, Jr., *A Study of Patents on Petroleum Cracking, with Special Reference to Their Present Status* (Austin, Texas: Bureau of Industrial Chemistry, University of Texas, Pub. No. 3831, August 15, 1938).

47. Readers should work out the theory for an economics of (imaginary) lead-into-gold alchemy.

48. Enos, *Petroleum Progress and Profits*, p. 309.

49. Ibid., p. 60. Some were impractical.

50. Ibid., pp. 60–69.

51. Ibid., p. 89. Each subscribing company got a paid-up license under UOP patents. Beaton, *Enterprise in Oil*, p. 257.

52. Enos, *Petroleum Progress and Profits*, pp. 91, 214, 286, 311. Beaton, *Enterprise in Oil*, p. 258, says UOP's royalty rate fell to ten cents in 1932, rather than in 1934.

53. For later developments, see McGee, "Patent Exploitation," p. 159.

54. *Hartford Empire* v. *U.S.*, 323 U.S. 386 (1945).

55. A useful guide is James A. Brown, *Antitrust and Competition in the Glass Container Industry* (unpublished Ph.D thesis, Duke University, 1966). Also see *Attorney General's Committee Report* (1955).

56. See Chapter 9.

57. McGee, "Patent Exploitation."

58. R. A. Posner and F. H. Easterbrook, *Antitrust: Cases, Economic Notes and Other Materials*, 2d ed. (St. Paul, Minn.: West Publishing Co., 1981), pp. 274–76.

59. This is because of the assumptions that the supply of crude oil is perfectly elastic and the marginal cost of distillation is constant. In more general models, changes in crude oil prices and distillation costs also influence the equilibrium. Such a model is developed later in this Appendix.

60. $[P_G(0.25)] + [P_F(0.75)] = 1.75$.

61. McGee, "Patent Exploitation," Figures IV-A, IV-B.

62. Enos, *Petroleum Progress and Profits*, p. 311. Royalty discounts (1924 or 1926) for very large users are discussed by Enos at p. 90; and in Beaton, *Enterprise in Oil*, p. 253. Enos's royalty data for Standard (Indiana) end with 1924. The original type of Burton units stopped operating in 1917; the improved Burton-Clark units stopped in 1931. Enos, p. 56.

63. Enos, *Petroleum Progress and Profits*, pp. 111, 245, 304, 126–28. Compare p. 322, which gives a royalty of 12 cents in 1922.

64. For each barrel change in rate of cracker feed, the price of gasoline changes by the net gasoline yield per barrel of feed *times* the slope of the gasoline demand function, $-.0094735$. Each one-barrel change in cracker feed changes the price of fuel oil by .003158.

65. Unless we force the computer to recognize technological realities, it will sometimes try to run crackers backwards! When $R = .71$, for example, there is negative cracking—which might cause an explosion in the real world. One way we can keep the model closer to reality is by constraining Q(Feed) to be zero or positive.

9 | MONOPOLIZING PRACTICES

INTRODUCTION

Although practices alleged to increase or maintain monopoly make a long list, it is debatable how well they really work. It is sometimes unclear even how a practice functions mechanically, let alone what effects it has. Lawyers commonly include such mysteries in their "characterization problem" category, which usually means that they are not sure what was going on in a specific case.

This chapter analyzes five leading candidates for inclusion on the all-time hit parade of monopolizing practices. (Chapter 16 later discusses the theory and empirical evidence about advertising). First, the present chapter briefly reviews collusion; Chapter 6 discussed it in detail. The next topic is mergers, appropriate policies with respect to which are hotly debated. Predatory pricing is the next subject, with theory and some fascinating new empirical findings. The next section analyzes limit pricing, which though it earns profits for firms already in an industry, nevertheless supposedly can repel equally efficient potential entrants. In analyzing all-or-none and compound pricing, the final section sheds new light on requirements contracts and tie-in sales.

Some of the practices discussed in this chapter are said to "bar entry," an indictment that has also been made even against the efficiencies discussed in Chapter 7. Barrier to entry is a label. It is a serious mistake to characterize efficiency differences among firms as entry barriers. Inherent, natural requirements for efficiency are not artificial barriers. It is not useful to say that weak, slow, and ill-coordinated people are barred from professional sports; or that people with small talents and little training are barred from occupations that require a lot of that. And it is at least misleading to say that a competitive price "bars" those with higher costs from competing in an industry.

Consumers will do better if we apply the term *barrier to entry* only to *artificial* conditions that prevent equally efficient producers from competing. In this context, "artificial" means requiring inputs or ways of doing things that consumers do not value. Government franchises and other limitations on entry are classic examples. Although some libertarians as well as interventionists would include patents, that is debatable, as Chapter 8 noted.

A useful vision of barriers is one in which willing suppliers and willing demanders are separated by an artificial obstruction that keeps them from trading. Unfortunately, the diagnosis that there are barriers to entry has been so overused that it has become little more than a name for ignorance. It is an undefined label used, for example, to attribute an anti-economic cause to industrial concentration that somebody asserts is higher than is necessary or desirable; or to explain why some industries are more profitable than others. It is worth noting before we start that efficiency and competitive prices will always "exclude" firms that can not offer consumers as good a deal. That is just what markets are supposed to do.

COLLUSION

Though Chapter 6 discussed collusion and cartels in detail, we need a brief restatement to put them into perspective as monopolizing practices that are well documented and well understood.

Collusion is a very old practice. Hammurabi, Aristotle, Adam Smith, and many other early observers commented on it. According to Adam Smith, "People of the same trade seldom meet together, even for merriment and diversion, but the conversation ends in a conspiracy against the public, or in some contrivance to raise prices."[1]

A cartel will attract entrants unless, unlike most, it devises some way to obstruct entry. Whether entrants join the cartel or operate outside of it, entry will eventually increase the number of firms and reduce concentration. This is troublesome, since we are forever hearing that those are sure signs that a trade is competitive. They are signs that entry is not barred and that a trade may be getting *more* competitive—rather different things.

MERGERS

Whether mergers benefit consumers or hurt them depends upon costs and demand. Many believe that mergers are hard to justify on efficiency grounds and fear they will make firms much larger than efficiency requires, create monopoly, and reduce net consumer benefits. They prefer that firms grow internally to achieve such size economies as there are, and that mergers be limited by law. The theory discussed in Chapter 13 shows that mergers need not produce monopoly power and may benefit consumers.[2] Unfortunately, there is much disagreement about what mergers actually do in general and in specific cases.

Under some conditions, theory and history suggest, firms can acquire very large market shares, and possibly monopoly, by merging with competitors, and they may buy out entrants as they appear. The traditional view was that cartels, government regulations, and mergers are the *supreme* monopolizing techniques, and that many past mergers in effect institutionalized cartels, making them more complete and durable. Trying to explain why law should treat mergers and cartels differently is harder than it sounds.[3] It is not completely satisfactory to say that cartels never improve efficiency, whereas mergers can.

There have been at least three big merger waves in the U.S.: 1895 to 1904; the 1920s; and one that began about 1965 and ended about 1971.[4] These merger waves differ in overall magnitude, and in the types and sizes of firms that went into and emerged from the mergers. Mergers in the first wave typically involved relatively large numbers of large firms and created absolutely large firms, many of which also had large market shares. Some of them, including U.S. Steel and American Can, were large enough that people called them monopolies, or dominant firms at the least. Some claim that the Forchheimer model discussed in Chapter 5 describes their postmerger behavior.

Mergers in the second wave typically involved fewer and smaller firms, producing firms with smaller market shares than those in the first wave. Stigler characterized the first wave as mergers for monopoly and the second as mergers for oligopoly.[5] Many of these mergers were vertical and some simply increased the geographic areas over which regulated utility monopolies operated, arguably without increasing market shares anywhere. The third wave has been characterized as conglomerate, because these mergers typically produced more diversified firms without significantly increasing market shares in individual markets or products. But it also included a number of mergers between oil companies operating in different parts of the country or at different vertical levels of the industry—crude oil production, refining, marketing.

Evaluating the economic effects of a merger is difficult, especially before it has been consummated. The antitrust laws do not prohibit mergers per se; but a genuine rule of reason would involve trade-off analyses of the sort discussed in Chapter 13. It is not easy to describe what our merger law is at any moment. Most times since 1950, antitrust authorities have discouraged horizontal acquisitions by firms with substantial market shares, unless they take over firms that are otherwise likely to fail.[6]

One way in which merger law can be tightened or loosened over time is to change the definitions of substantial market share and substantial concentration. Many believe that our merger law has sometimes been too restrictive, preventing some efficiency-enhancing mergers and delaying or preventing economic improvement.[7] Although some critics of antitrust policy complain that it has prevented too many good mergers, most critics probably believe that antitrust has more serious deficiencies than that.

Although it is hard to be sure about the economic effects of mergers, it is easier to say something about their structural effects: for a time, at least, mergers tend to increase concentration and reduce the number of firms.

PREDATORY PRICING[8]

Theory

Lawyers and economists are resourceful and imaginative. Over the years, they have hypothesized all manner of predatory practices, including predatory pricing; "premature" (and therefore predatory) introduction of superior products; predatory introduction of superior production processes; and so on. Some of the more recent cases, *IBM* and *Kodak*, for example,[9] involve predatory innovation; but here we will concentrate on predatory pricing, the kind of predation with which antitrust policy was originally concerned.

Before diving into the details, it is well to note a fundamental fact. All the practices that have been denounced as predatory—lowering prices, improving products and production processes, for example—are *competitive* practices that hurt competitors but benefit consumers. If there is a legitimate reason to curb such practices it must be that they can be excessive in *degree*. They are surely not objectionable in and of themselves. This means, at the very least, that a defensible policy against such practices must carefully differentiate between helpful and hurtful *degrees* of competitive practices. That is not easy to do, and imperils competition if it fails.[10]

The theory of predatory pricing is that it will pay a firm to achieve or retain monopoly by cutting prices below normal nonpredatory levels. In this theory, the predator considers the costs of below-normal prices an investment that will produce a larger discounted stream of monopoly profits in the future. On this theory, predatory pricing is privately rational but socially wasteful behavior. From the consumers' point of view, pathological, excessive price cutting would end by killing competition itself.

We start by noting what "losing money" really means. Accountants say that a loss occurs whenever costs exceed revenues, which conjures up visions of income statements littered with red numbers. All that is fine for accountants. For rational economic decisions, however, the costs and revenues of any program must be defined with respect to the best *alternative* costs and revenues that are achievable. It is opportunity costs and revenues that really matter: profit forgone is also a loss.[11] Suppose, for example, that there are two alternatives. One will yield a present-value profit of $1 million. The other will yield a present-value profit of $2 million. Choosing the first alternative would actually lose $1 million, no matter what an accountant says after you do it.

In business, wealth maximization is a survivorship property as well as merely a preference. Investors can alter their portfolios, selling shares in firms that look less good and buying shares in firms that look better. Firms can also be bought and sold outright, and managements can be changed.

Striving for wealth reduces the chance that one business will prey on another merely to satisfy an executive's taste for sport, sadism, or masochism. Such tastes can be satisfied more efficiently in specialized markets that cater to them, and can be more fully satisfied the more wealth one has. Fun is fun and sport is sport. Business is business. In short, the dominant objective of business is to benefit itself rather than to hurt someone else. In discussing predatory competition, it is wise to distinguish pathology from normalcy. Normal competition helps consumers, but can be hard on competitors, especially those that are less efficient. Quite normal competition grinds down, kills off, and gobbles up less efficient competitors, dispersing their assets to other firms and other fields. It is a mistake, therefore, to diagnose competition as predatory just because firms have been bruised, or even ruined utterly. And, it is clear, lower prices benefit consumers.

In the absence of law, some kinds of predatory practices may pay. This would be true of arson, mayhem, and assassination, for example, to the extent they cost less than the losses they impose on others. Evil examples of high loss-to-cost leverage include theft and extortion. They transfer wealth, but shrink total wealth in the process. Removing this kind of mechanical advantage is a fundamental reason for creating government and law in the first place.

But the kinds of predation that economists worry about are very different. They are *more* costly to predator than to prey (remember that a profit forgone is also a loss). When that is true, extortion won't work. Victims will not pay more to avoid a hurt than the hurt would cost them. And the hurt is smaller than it costs the predator to cause it.

But what about predatory pricing as an investment to increase future monopoly profits? Even though the predator's loss exceeds the victim's loss, can't the predator's future gains exceed its own near-term loss? Assume that the predatory firm is larger than the prey and that both have equally low minimum costs. Suppose that the predator cuts price below average total cost and that in the same circumstances a nonpredator would not. This costs the predator more than the prey, since it sells more output at losing prices. It will also cost the predator an increasing amount of money: cutting price requires you to increase total output to clear the market, and the prey will reduce output at the lower price. It may even shut down completely. To hold the artificially low price, the predator must increase its total output, more so as the prey reduces its output.

Some argue that eventually the prey's plant will wear out and not be replaced, which they admit will take time and losses to accomplish. The plant would not be replaced if such low prices were expected to persist. But they won't persist. The theory of rational predation says that you cut prices now to raise them later even more, and that the discounted stream of profits is expected to be positive. If the victim knows this is a predatory campaign, it *knows* the low prices cannot persist. It will pay victims to stick it out.

Suppose, instead, that the predator cuts price below average *variable* cost to get the job done fast, and that the victim shuts down. This leaves the predator with an even larger share of the losses, and—what is worse—leaves the victim's plant intact. It can be brought back into production once the price is raised, as raised it will be.

Nevertheless, some say that the firm with the longer purse can somehow win. But liquid reserves are costly. And if the victim is covering average variable cost, as it is when shut down, it suffers no liquidity drain. Or, at all events, shutdown or not, it suffers proportionately smaller liquidity drain than the predator. A predator must have disproportionately larger financial reserves, and disproportionate reserves are disproportionately costly.

Although it seems unlikely, suppose a victim mistakenly gives up and closes his plant down permanently. The predator would like to buy the plant, cheap, because otherwise it will rise again to plague him when he advances prices, which is the plan. Present law is unlikely to permit a substantial firm to buy its competitors' plants, especially in circumstances that look like this. Contrary to some opinion, therefore, present merger law is probably less favorable to predation than it had been in the bad old days, when mergers could be completed wholesale.

Predatory price cutting does not look any more effective for disciplining competitors than it is for killing them outright. Why should it threaten those who are thinking about entering the industry? Predation costs the disciplinarian more than it costs the victims. And if predation works inefficiently on *existing* competitors, why should entrants believe it will work against them once they enter and become active competitors? Business threats are not credible unless it would pay to carry them out.

Finally, if future contracts can be made, or if commodities can be stored, a predator's life will be especially hard. In the first case, a victim can contract ahead to supply goods for less than the predator hopes to charge in the future. In the second, customers (and victims!) can stock up on cheap goods during the price war.

Experimental economics uses computer models to simulate market processes. Even with assumptions that favor successful predation—the large firm has lower costs, for example—Isaac and Smith didn't turn up predatory behavior in 10 experiments. And they found that the remedies often suggested to prevent predatory conduct increased prices and reduced efficiency.[12]

Empirical Evidence

Most of the discussion to this point has been about theory. What about the factual record? Various authors have studied the histories of a number of firms alleged to have used predatory pricing. With one important exception, these largely impressionistic studies found little to suggest that predation has been a serious impediment to competition or a well-traveled road to monopoly. The impressive exception is fascinating quantitative research that Malcolm Burns did on the old American Tobacco Company, a famous monopoly that James Buchanan ("Buck") Duke created by mergers at the turn of the century, then lost in an adverse 1911 antitrust decision.[13] Burns published three papers on American Tobacco. In order of dates of publication, they are referred to here as Burns (I), Burns (II), and Burns (III).[14]

According to Eliot Jones[15]—who, incidentally, believed that predatory pricing *can* work—Duke built his first monopoly in 1890, in the cigarette business, by forming the American Tobacco Company, a consolidation of the five principal cigarette manufacturers. Before this, American had 40 percent of the U.S. cigarette market; the consolidation gave it 95 percent. Jones said that predatory pricing did not figure in the cigarette consolidation. As he put it, "Competition among them, it is true, had been quite vigorous. . . . But there is little reason to believe that this competition had been ruinous to the parties concerned. . . . certainly the leading concern found the profits enormous."[16] Profits from cigarettes allegedly subsidized American's subsequent adventures in plug, snuff and fine-cut tobacco, and cigars.

Burns (III) gives several reasons for not analyzing Duke's cigarette acquisitions statistically: only a few firms were involved; they were multiproduct firms, which complicates earnings estimation; and, in any case, there were no suitable data for any cigarette firm alleged to have been the target of predatory pricing.[17] Jones claimed that machine manufacture was transforming the cigarette industry, and that this helped Duke monopolize it. The contrast with cigars is sharp: handmade cigars continued to prosper, which, Jones says, frustrated attempts to monopolize that field. Even so, American continued to acquire cigarette companies:

> In addition to the endeavor to maintain its position by monopolizing the machinery for the manufacture of cigarettes, the cigarette trust employed another policy—a policy which it continued throughout its whole career. This was the acquisition, at high prices if necessary, of its most vigorous competitors. Cigarette companies in considerable numbers were acquired after 1890, as a means of retaining the monopolistic position originally attained.[18]

American moved to monopolize plug (chewing) tobacco once it had monopolized cigarettes. After buying the National Tobacco Works and its popular plug brands in 1891, American tried unsuccessfully to consolidate other plug manufacturers in 1893 or 1894, when it did 5 or 6 percent of the plug business. Price competition heated up around 1894; Burns says the "war" began around January 1895. A "fighting brand" was a product that the trusts allegedly priced low to hurt competitors. American's fighting brand was, poetically enough, Battle Ax, a significant part of its product line. Apparently American suffered *accounting* losses of $3.3 million to $4.1 million in the plug wars, 1895 to 1899. If its alternative was to enjoy *monopoly* profits starting then, these short-run losses were really larger than accounting suggests. On the other hand, the price war might have cut down on future entry, thereby preserving long-term monopoly profits.

Burns (I) presents a wonderful case study illustrating one problem that McGee claimed predators face: well-financed opportunists may profit by financing or buying out firms that are targets of predatory campaigns.[19] A predator would then have to pay more than if the prey could have been cut off from external financing, then pulled down. According to Burns (I), Thomas F. Ryan and other financiers allied themselves with Liggett & Myers (L&M), the largest independent plug manufacturer and a target of American's predatory campaign. This team of opportunists bought an option to buy L&M and after a short time netted $5.887 million by selling it to American.

Burns (I) wondered how well the original L&M shareholders fared. They seem to have done all right:

> It is impossible to establish conclusively that Liggett & Myers shared in the trusts' expected monopoly profits through an enhanced acquisition price, because the merger terms that the company initially rejected are unknown. The available data indicate, however, that its stockholders did receive modest but still significant capital gains.[20]

Burns says that Drummond Tobacco sold out for a "quite generous" price, and the price paid for L&M looks even better than that, judged by the simpler technique with which Burns (I) estimated values of firms.[21] Even so, of course, actual or threatened predation may have worked better in other instances, as Burns claims.

As one of five major econometric procedures used in his third article, Burns pulled the 25 *plug* manufacturers out of the total sample and evaluated them separately. He concluded that "the long and costly plug war evidently failed to yield any direct savings from the 10 victims purchased at its conclusion."[22] Even if "direct" savings were nil, a fearful reputation for predatory conduct and merciless underpayment might nevertheless pay off by lowering *future* acquisition prices.

This leaves acquisitions that American made later, during and following "active competition" in the fine-cut tobacco segment of the industry. Only two firms in Burns's sample made large quantities of fine-cut tobacco after 1898. In any case, Burns claims substantial *percentage* markdowns and attributes them to the reputation for nastiness that American earned in the plug wars.

Taken together, Burns and Jones give us a lot of numbers to compare and it is not certain how to compare them fairly. One comparison suggests there may have been no "savings" at all. Burns estimates that the fine-cut tobacco war itself may have knocked down acquisition prices by a *net* of $.87 million. But if that is correct, American seems to have "saved" much less than the $3.3 million to $4.1 million loss it had suffered in the preceding plug wars. Assume that these plug-war losses bought American a bad enough reputation to reduce the costs of later acquisitions by precisely as much as Burns says. If so, the reputation seems to have cost too much. If we take these numbers literally, American ended up in the hole, $2.43 million to $3.23 million, net. This ignores that American may have driven hard bargains in buying competitors that are *not* included in Burns's sample.

This brings us to some details of Burns's data and econometric procedures. Although Burns's work is ingenious and sophisticated, he concedes that the data on earnings and risk are badly measured. As a result, he "cleansed" the earnings figures of acquired competitors, partly by "excluding any figure for a targeted competitor that appeared extremely low."[23] On top of that, "Annual earnings were reported by only 15 [out of 43] competitors [acquired] and vary from one to eight observations per firm in the years immediately preceding acquisition. Fragmentary estimates of unit profit margins for independent manufacturers are also available between 1890 and 1906."[24]

Data for the trust, however, are "remarkably complete," and to some extent Burns used *trust* data to estimate *competitors'* earnings, margins, and return on investment.[25] And he used *those* to determine what the "values" of acquired competitors ought to have been. But if their costs were higher than American's, this procedure would overstate the acquired firms' "true" or normally competitive value. The margins of firms that American did *not* buy were lower than American's, which suggests that their costs were higher.[26] Since Burns had "typically" to estimate the margins of competitors that American *did* acquire, it is natural to wonder whether he overestimated their profitability and normal value. He may not have: Burns argues that American bought its most successful (and presumably most efficient) competitors.

It is easy for a critic to go wrong interpreting work as rich and complex as Burns's. Burns (II) argues that there were large economies of size for both firms and plants in cigarettes and in the plug, smoking, fine-cut, and snuff lines. By 1899, American seems to have acquired all the leading plug manufacturers[27]; most leading smoking tobacco manufacturers by 1899, all by 1902[28]; all leading snuff manufacturers by 1900[29]; two of three leading fine-cut producers by 1898, the third by 1902.[30] Product-for-product, some of these early acquisitions operated larger plants than American had. In fine-cut and snuff, several had larger total outputs than American did before it bought them.

But the acquisition prices of firms in Burns's sample declined dramatically over time.[31] After March 1900, by which time American had apparently bought most of its large competitors, these prices are lowest of all. Competitors bought later were markedly cheaper and may have been substantially smaller. Did they have also have high costs, low profits, and low normal values as compared with American? If so, using American's margins and profits tends to overstate acquired competitors' earnings and "true values," and to exaggerate the amounts that American should have paid for them in the absence of predatory threat or reputation.

Second, Burns valued American's *losses* at current levels, not at post–price war monopoly levels. And shouldn't the *future* earnings of American and those attributed to firms acquired, be "offset" for risk, as the past earnings were?

It is hard to develop a reputation for something if you keep it secret. As contemporary accounts suggest, Burns believes that some of American's price cutting was secret and that some was brazen. He considers various possibilities: did American's competitors have an "erroneous perception"[32] about price wars, or rational expectations about them; was price cutting secret,[33] or was it for reputation building.[34]

Whatever can be claimed for Burns's data and econometric procedures, how could predation or threats of predation efficiently reduce acquisition costs *if* each predatory campaign were more expensive to predator than to prey? Theory outlined earlier suggests that predatory price cutting will be a losing strategy unless competitors irrationally panic and rout under threat and pressure. Wouldn't each predatory campaign reduce the capital value of predator more than that of prey, and not be a credible threat to a rational competitor?

Burns's fascinating study applies sophisticated econometric techniques to the best data he could find, sparse and flawed though they are. He concludes that these data are consistent with American Tobacco's having used predatory pricing, or the reputation and threat of it, to reduce prices it paid for some of the competitors it bought. Burns may be right, of course, for any of various reasons. Perhaps its competitors were unsophisticated, misinformed, or worse; or maybe American itself added up the pluses and minuses wrong and went to war when it shouldn't. Or maybe capital markets were hopelessly out of joint. And so on. In any case, even if Burns is right, the least toxic antitrust medicine might simply be to prevent firms from accomplishing monopoly positions through industry-wide acquisitions.

Suppose that Burns is wrong, or that merger policy itself is sufficient to deter predation by denying its fruits. If predatory pricing is not, and is not likely to be, a significant clog on the competitive process, why would people still carry on about it? First, many people need to believe in bad-acts theories of business, which partly explains why clichés in fiction and radical ideology are so durable.

Second, economists who believe that there is more industrial concentration than there ought to be need to explain why it persists. They have lost many of the old explanations and are trying to hold on to the rest. Research has demonstrated that efficiency explanations of industrial structure cannot be dismissed. Massive mergers have long been outlawed and can no longer be used to explain present industry structures. Empirical and theoretical support for traditional monopolizing practices and entry barriers has been undermined drastically. What is left, besides efficiency? At that point, radical reformers find it attractive to speculate that large firms stay large and prosperous by acting ugly.

Third, less efficient competitors do not like competition at all and are always interested in ways to soften it. One way is to reduce price competition, by legally restricting those who would use it. Treble-damage suits that are based on predatory theories are one way to paralyze active competitors. Fourth, regulators and politicians would have less to do if people believe that things work reasonably well when left alone. Theories like predatory pricing assert that regulation is needed to save competition from itself. This increases the demand for rules and laws, and for those who make and use them. Because predatory theories are an excuse for lawsuits, some lawyers like them a lot. Reducing the grounds for antitrust suits reduces the demand for lawyers and for the consultants who help them. It can be argued that consumers are not the most powerful constituency favoring antitrust.

Although we will not go into the practice here, predatory *purchase* pricing has also been alleged—in the 1946 *American Tobacco* case, for example. The correct analysis of that practice closely parallels that applied to predatory *selling* prices. Allegations of predation do not stop with prices. Some have alleged predatory innovation, advertising, product quality, and so on. In these cases, too, the appropriate analysis closely parallels that developed for predatory pricing.

LIMIT-PRICING THEORIES

Possibly for the same kinds of reasons just discussed in connection with predatory pricing, there is a substantial demand for theories to explain how firms can stay large and prosperous while, at the same time, equally efficient competitors do not enter. Limit-pricing theories claim to offer such an explanation. Although he may not have originated such theories, Joe Bain made them famous. But Nobel Laureate Franco Modigliani has the clearest version and that is the one we start with here.[35]

Figure 9-1 shows how that version works. All such theories begin with an industry demand curve, a long-run average cost that is accessible to all firms, and decision rules (behavioral postulates) for the firms involved. Suppose, as Figure 9-1 shows, that the industry demand is DD, and that a potential entrant's (and the resident monopoly's) long-run average cost curve is LRAC. If a potential entrant can be made to believe that the firm now in the industry will not change its output rate when he enters, the entrant would have as its own only that part of industry demand that lies *below* the monopoly's preentry price. Entry would then force price down below the preentry level, by an amount that depends upon the slope of industry demand, and how much output the entrant offers. Assume that entrants have the same long-run cost function as the monopoly, LRAC in Figure 9-1. The potential entrant thinks like a Cournot duopolist and assumes that the monopoly's output

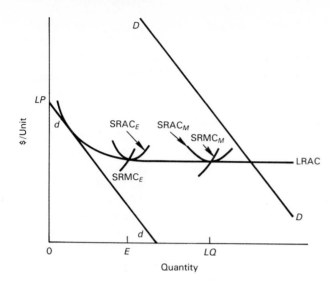

$/Unit

Quantity

Figure 9-1 The Basic Limit-Pricing Model

Source: Adapted from Franco Modigliani, "New Developments on the Oligopoly Front," *Journal of Political Economy*, The University of Chicago Press, 66 (June 1958), pp 215–32.

would remain constant even after entry. This means that the relevant demand (*dd*) facing a new firm has the same *slope* as that of the whole industry demand. But in this theory the monopoly does *not* follow Cournot rules.

The theory is asymmetric. In effect, the monopoly calculates its limit price by sliding the industry demand curve downward in a parallel fashion till it becomes tangent with the LRAC curve. A price trivially below the price-axis intercept of such an extended tangent line is, according to the theory, a limit price (LP). For then, *if* the monopoly holds its output rate (LQ) dead steady, any amount supplied by the entrant would drive price below the entrant's break-even point. The monopoly has left the entrant no output for which the postentry price will cover his average cost. If entry does occur, however, the monopoly will also lose wealth. How much it loses depends upon cost, demand, and the scale of entry.

Limit-pricing monopoly is different from closed monopoly. Price is lower and output is larger than if entry were legally blocked. This theory has the monopolist charging somewhat less now and in the future to avoid having to charge much less in the future. This limit price is supposed to repel entrants even though it yields supercompetitive returns. The nearest the entrant could come to breaking even would be at a scale smaller than that at which LRAC reaches a minimum value. Entry at larger scales would be even worse. For example, if he entered at even the smallest scale required to minimize average cost, the postentry price would then be even lower.

Such theories are used to argue that a monopoly can prosper at the same time that it is able to exclude equally efficient competitors. Unfortunately for both the theories and the monopoly, this kind of limit pricing simply does not work. It is unappealing both as theory and common sense. Neither is it consistent with empirical evidence, which includes a lot of entry.

What is wrong with the logic? First, if entrants can contract directly with consumers or with middlemen, limit pricing would not work. According to the limit-pricing theory, consumers are paying and can expect to continue paying prices substantially above the average costs that new firms can achieve. Entrants could underbid the monopolist and leave consumers better off.

Second, limit pricing rests upon an implicit threat: the monopoly will not reduce its own output if entry should occur. This threat is not credible because it would not pay to carry it out. Suppose an entrant decides that it will come in at the smallest scale at which it can achieve minimum average cost. Figure 9-1 shows that *if* the monopolist holds output constant in the face of entry, the entrant would lose money. But the monopoly would lose even more. The ex-monopoly has more attractive alternatives than this if entry does occur. The entrant should therefore assume that the monopoly will not act like that. More attractive alternatives include so-called dominant-firm pricing, Cournot-style duopoly pricing, a cartel, and—perhaps—even marginal cost competitive pricing. Because our theory says that perfect competition is ideal, economists tend to be biased against everything but atomistic competition. Confronted by the alternatives just listed, however, many economists would prefer all of them (except, possibly, the cartel) over single-firm monopoly. Unless government supports it, even a cartel might not be so bad. Lacking such support, cartels tend to be fragile and impermanent. Cheating or entry eventually weaken or destroy them and lower price.

But economists tend to prefer marginal-cost pricing, which in many cases is more sensible for an ex-monopolist than holding output constant would be. If marginal cost pricing does break out, price would be determined by industry demand and the horizontal summation of marginal cost for all firms in the industry. The value of marginal costs would be brought to equality for all active firms. Whatever the number of firms might be, such *results* are competitive in the textbook sense, and like atomistic competition, may not please the competitors themselves. If demand does not grow after marginal-cost competition takes over, prices can even fall below average total cost, forcing rates of return below the normal long-run competitive level. For there could be too much capacity, even by long-run competitive standards.

Third, those who want to believe in limit pricing should reconsider what they believe about oligopoly. Some oligopoly theories assert that sellers try to maximize *group* profits.[36] The theory of limit pricing causes trouble for such theories. If limit pricing repels entrants it is because they expect to encounter die-hard resistance that is *not* compatible with group profit maximization. This may be one reason why limit-pricing theorists do not draw postentry *marginal* cost and *marginal* revenue functions.

Finally, limit-pricing theory is even less plausible when applied to oligopoly than it is in the case of single-firm monopoly. Single-firm monopolies are rare and are not really what limit-price theorists claim to be concerned with. They claim to be worried about the performance of concentrated industries, that is, oligopoly. But it is extremely unlikely that noncolluding oligopolists could form the disciplined solid front necessary to make even the bluff on which limit pricing depends. For, once entry occurs, each of several firms has an incentive to cut its own output, leaving the others to stand and die.

But there is more wrong with limit-pricing theories than economic logic. Such theories founder on the empirical evidence.[37] First, if long-run average costs are flat beyond the minimum efficient size, the theory predicts that there will be single-firm monopoly everywhere. If limit pricing works, the first member of every industry could have practiced it from the beginning and kept everyone else out forever. The limit price is determined by the *slope* of industry demand, no matter how big the market is. It would be hard to explain how actual industrial structures evolved if limit pricing had been in effect.

Although Oliver Williamson proposed more complex limit-pricing models, they are subject to the same criticisms.[38] By varying it suitably, Figure 9-2 could be used to illustrate all of Williamson's basic cases. As before, *DD* is the total market demand, and LRAC is accessible to both the monopoly and entrants. Figure 9-2 shows what Williamson says will happen if law permits a monopoly to expand output after entry. It assumes both that the monopoly is willing to expand output and that potential entrants believe it would do so. Suppose, as Figure 9-2 assumes, that law permits the monopoly to expand output so long as it prices no lower than short-run marginal cost, *and* that the monopoly would expand up to this legal limit.[39] For each price (and corresponding value of marginal cost) an entrant would have to make do with whatever market demand the monopoly does not satisfy.

According to Williamson's logic, a law requiring only that price be at least as high as marginal cost makes entrants' residual demand flatter than in Modigliani's theory. For Williamson's monopoly would be allowed to expand output after entry. The monopoly could choose a scale of plant such that this (flatter) residual demand would be tangent to an entrant's LRAC curve. According to Williamson, the monopoly's "optimal" scale is one that produces this tangency, though he does not prove it. Following that kind of logic, no one will enter if he knows what he is doing. Nor is that all. Given its marginal cost and

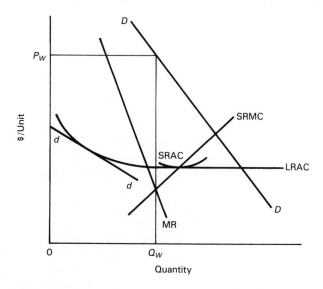

Figure 9-2 Limit Pricing with Excess Capacity

Source: Adapted from Oliver E. Williamson, "Predatory Pricing: A Strategic and Welfare Analysis," 87 *Yale Law Journal* pp. 284–340 (December 1977).

marginal revenue, the monopoly could now charge a preentry price of P_W. This is higher than Modigliani's limit price, though lower than a legally protected closed-monopoly price. According to this theory, the monopoly could charge a higher price before entry because it is willing to increase output substantially if entry should occur. The monopoly's ability to flood the market comes from the idle capacity it built for this purpose. But that saddles it with higher costs, perhaps forever.

It is not clear how Williamson thinks a monopoly would behave if there were *no* law against predatory pricing. Nor is it clear whether his theory says limit pricing *will* exclude entry; or, that it would simply wipe out rivals whenever they do appear. If his logic and economics were correct, any of the limit-pricing models that Williamson considers could exclude entry altogether. Barring mistakes, no oligopolist would have to go down with his ship, for no entrants would show up to sink him. There would be no predatory histories to litigate, for there would not have been any entry. If would-be entrants believed in limit pricing it would not even be necessary to make explicit threats. The threats implicit in the models would be enough to do the trick.

That industrial histories show a good deal of entry looks inconsistent with the theory, unless there were lots of mistakes. And, mistaken or not, a good deal of that entry somehow worked out, which also does not support the theory that the implicit threats would work if carried out. Such evidence, as well as economics and logic, suggest that something is wrong with the theory. Even if law permitted them, such threats—implicit or explicit—are not credible. In each case, the strategic behavior postulated would be more costly to monopoly than to entrant. Indeed, as Williamson's own diagrams show, an entrant of efficient size would completely wreck any monopoly that behaved that way. And, if its older plants wear out first, the monopoly would be first to die.

Laws against ugly behavior in which people do not engage are merely redundant. If they discourage innocuous or beneficial behavior, they are worse than that. Predatory pricing looks less dangerous than the rules with which Williamson would combat it. Williamson's rules would penalize competitive business practices that are completely innocent of any predatory purpose or predatory effect.[40]

In spite of what Williamson says, rules like his would come to be applied to workably competitive, and even to price-taker industries. Whenever firms have different costs, there would be big trouble, for prices that are compensatory to some firms are lethal to others. Williamson seems to believe that limit and strategic pricing have significantly retarded deconcentration and competition. This leaves little role for superior efficiency, and it conflicts with both logic and history. Such theories are not likely to be confined to allegedly predatory incidents. They would indict superior leading firms who "threaten" merely by being there. Any firm that retains a large market share could be charged with limit pricing.

Logic and history make trouble for limit-pricing theories. Laws based on limit-pricing theories would make trouble for us all. Normal and beneficial competition produces results that could be denounced because they superficially look like limit pricing. An important case is superior firms that continue to lead their industries, because they produce the same or better products more efficiently. Less competent present and would-be competitors are "excluded" only in the sense that they cannot do as good a job, which is poor reason to denounce those who can. Law should not encourage competitors to complain whenever more successful firms are unwilling to move over and leave a warm bed for them.

Some results that might be attributed to strategic limit pricing can occur even when several equally efficient firms engage in price-taker competition. Unless it expects discounted postentry prices to exceed discounted total costs, a firm will not enter even a thoroughly competitive industry that is completely innocent of "strategic" behavior. If efficient firm size is not negligible and demand is not growing, entry will reduce price even in an industry of price takers. Firms of nonnegligible size add capacity and output in lumps, not in tiny grains. This can cause firms to stay out, even when the present preentry price somewhat exceeds average total cost.

When size economies produce firms that are not tiny relative to total demand, even the most intense competition achievable need not result in precise equality among price, marginal cost, and average total cost. Suppose that, although there are only a few firms in an industry, each takes the market price as given and acts like a pure competitor. If efficient firms are large relative to demand, persistent profits are possible, simply because of this lumpiness in firm size. This can be seen in Figure 9-3, which shows market demand DD, the cost curves of a single firm, and the supply and demand equilibrium resulting from four (S_4) and from five (S_5) such identical firms. S_4 is the horizontal summation of the four firms' short-run marginal costs for the relevant range. Price equals marginal cost. The so-called optimum size of firms is $0S$. At a price that covers minimum average total cost, the market will support no more than four efficient firms. Five would break the market utterly, and all of them would lose money if they continue to behave as

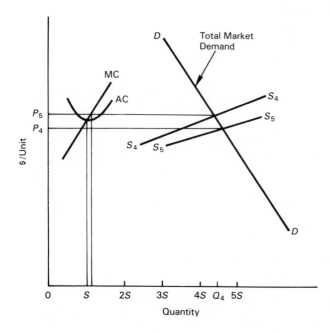

Figure 9-3 Competitive Equilibrium with Profits: Four "Lumpy" Firms

price takers. If would-be entrants do not misjudge this situation, a fifth firm will not enter. Price will therefore exceed average cost, and firms presently in the industry will enjoy profits. Because one additional firm of efficient size would ruin all, it does not enter, even though no one is in any way trying to keep anybody out.

Of course, mistakes occur in the real world. Costs and demands may unexpectedly shift, or fail to shift as expected. If a fifth firm does enter, price will fall and losses ensue. If the firms have different costs, price can fall to or below average variable cost for some. Shutdowns and failures may also occur. Yet no one has been preying on anybody, and no one has been trying to exclude entry.

ALL-OR-NONE PRICING AND COMPOUND PRICING

Introduction

The sellers analyzed in this section have significant monopoly power. As always, such power requires that substitutability for what the monopoly offers be significantly incomplete overall.[41] Concentrating, first, on how people *use* powers they start with, we simply *assume* where their monopoly came from. Our sellers are single-firm patent monopolies; but the analysis developed here also applies to other situations.

Many firms sell at a fixed price per unit and permit buyers to take as many units as they please. This section analyzes all-or-none pricing and compound pricing, which are much more complex practices. Here is an example of an all-or-none offer: "to get *any* of this good, you must take 1,000 units of it per month and pay $100,000 for the package."[42] DeBeer's Ltd., the diamond cartel, reputedly sells one-of-a-kind assortments of uncut diamonds in something like the same spirit.

Compound pricing makes the price (or availability) of some goods conditional on the purchase (or nonpurchase) of other goods.[43] Requirements contracts and tie-ins are two important examples. A requirements contract obligates you to buy the good from only one seller. A tying contract lets you buy the good only if you buy another good as well.

All-or-none pricing is sometimes denounced as exploitative because it takes away much or most of the surplus that buyers would otherwise enjoy.[44] Compound pricing has been denounced for "monopolizing" or exerting "leverage," on the theory that it enlarges partial monopolies that sellers already have, or creates new monopolies of something else. Leverage theory entered U.S. antitrust law explicitly via the Clayton Act of 1914, which outlaws any lease or sale, price or discount, made "on the condition . . . that the lessee or purchaser . . . shall not use or deal in the goods . . . of a competitor . . . where the effect . . . may be to substantially lessen competition or tend to create a monopoly."[45]

Fixed Proportions

From 1917 until the 1950s at least, the prevailing view was that compound pricing schemes are effective monopolizing techniques.[46] In the early 1950s, if not before, Professor Aaron Director of the University of Chicago was teaching that the prevailing view was mistaken. Director's colleagues and students applied his theories and developed some of their own.[47]

Director and Ward S. Bowman, Jr. discussed memorable cases in which sellers apparently used tie-ins to "meter" the use of patented machines and to charge users accordingly.[48] Some companies leased or sold their machines on the condition that users also buy from them all of certain *complementary* goods used with the machines, as we will now see.

Go back to the 1890s, when high-button shoes were fashionable. Each such shoe used a number of buttons, and a patented machine to staple them on saved labor and found a good market.[49] Each cycle of the machine used one staple to attach one button to a shoe. Staples, buttons, and machine cycles were all used in fixed proportions, one-to-one in this simplest of cases. In principle, you could have measured fastened-button output equally accurately by counting machine cycles with a meter; or by counting staples used or buttons attached.

Figure 9-4 presents a stylized version of this case. D is a shoe manufacturer's derived net demand for machine service-units, after paying competitive prices for labor and materials used with the machine. AP is the value of *average* product added by the machine and is its all-or-none demand function.[50] Output is buttons fastened per month. MC is the machine monopoly's average and marginal cost of supplying a machine to the shoe manufacturer. If it charged a monthly rental of $0PRQ_2$, the monopoly would just break even. Under simple monopoly pricing, the shoe manufacturer would pay the machine firm $0S$ per button fastened, or $0STQ_1$ per month. In principle, at least, the machine could yield

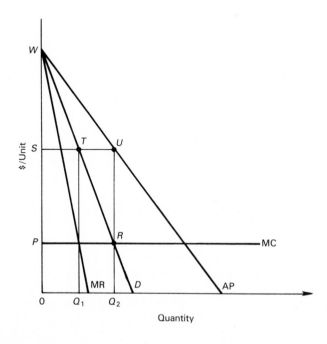

Figure 9-4 Pricing a Button-Fastening Machine

highest profits under all-or-none pricing, which could take various forms. The monopoly might require the manufacturer to fasten $0Q_2$ buttons per month (the ''competitive'' output) and to pay a total of $0SUQ_2$ per month to keep the machine. That would extract the total dollar value under the demand function, which is *all* the value that the machine adds to the shoe manufacturer's output.[51] Or it could charge $0PRQ_2$ monthly rental plus RU per button fastened.

Or it could, and apparently did, charge a monthly rental of $0PRQ_2$, on the condition that users buy only staples supplied by the monopoly at a surcharge of RU each above their competitive market value. Such a scheme would have been ingenious even if all shoe manufacturers had been alike. It looks even better because they were not identical. The machine was worth more to shoe manufacturers who used it more, and under this scheme they paid more to use it. And as Figure 9-4 shows, profits, staple use, and fastened-button output are all higher than they would have been under simple monopoly pricing of the machine. It is evident that the tie-in does not monopolize staples, the tied good.

Given the special features of this case, a tie-in achieves all-or-none pricing via metering. A tamperproof billing meter would produce identical results, and, it should be noted, the machine manufacturer would not have monopolized meters if it had used them in this way. Apart from whatever differences there might be in the costs of using them, *all* these pricing schemes are equivalent.

A firm pricing in this way is not using its original monopoly power to leverage its way into a second monopoly. It is still exploiting the same demand for the same services. It has simply made more money from the same monopoly it started with. Professor Director doubted that tie-ins are used to extend monopoly, because—as in Figure 9-4—all-or-none pricing extracts all the value and uses up all the power that inheres in a monopoly good. Once that much has been extracted, there is no more value—or power—to use in monopolizing anything else. This assumes, of course, both that all-or-none pricing is feasible and that it is more profitable than any other feasible alternative. These are crucial assumptions.

If no other scheme can get more out of one good than all-or-none pricing can, monopolies should favor all-or-none above all other types of contracts. Director therefore concluded that tie-ins had not been used to get second monopolies, but for other purposes altogether.

Besides metering, what else could tie-ins be used for? Under fixed proportions, monopolizing through tie-ins won't work. When consumers or producers use goods in fixed proportions, it is the *total* cost of the combination that matters, not their individual prices, which within limits can be arbitrary. Take an $85 pair of shoes. If the manufacturer ''ties'' the left and right shoes, it matters not whether the left is separately priced at $5 and the right at $80; or vice versa. Any pair of prices that totals the same comes to the same so far as buyers are concerned.

Figure 9-5 summarizes the logic. D is the demand for a product that incorporates two components, 1 and 2, in fixed proportions, one-to-one.[52] MC_1 and MC_2 are the marginal costs of components 1 and 2. ΣMC is the sum of component marginal costs. Fixity of proportions gives a monopoly of *either* component the same powers and profits as a monopoly of both, as Figure 9-5 shows. In either case, the profit-maximizing price of the

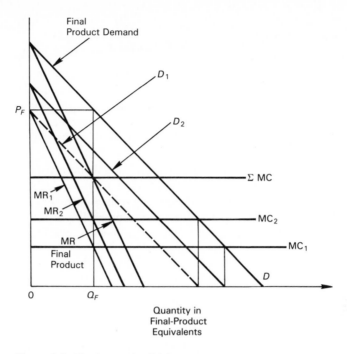

Figure 9-5   Fixed-proportion Pricing

combination is P_F and output is Q_F. A monopoly of component 1 gains nothing by tying the other component and raising its price. An increase in the price of component 2 lowers by the same amount the profit-maximizing price for component 1. The profit-maximizing price of the combination remains at P_F, no matter what.

Firms that tie under fixed proportions therefore appear to be doing something other than monopolizing the tied good. What on earth could it be? Bowman's categories of explanations seem to be exhaustive.[53] In addition to metering, he noted several others, including evading government price regulations or cheating on private price-fixing agreements; minimizing costs; and assuring the qualities of goods that buyers want.

During World War I, the U.S. government and some large firms used threats and persuasion to hold prices below competitive market-clearing levels. As its steel supplier and the government wanted, Gratz, a steel wholesaler, sold steel cotton-bale ties for less than their market-clearing price, but required buyers also to buy six yards of (unregulated) jute bagging with every set of six bale ties. Director and Bowman said this simply evaded the artificial price ceiling set for bale ties and raised them to market-clearing levels, which by most standards is an efficient thing to do. The Federal Trade Commission's claim that Gratz was trying to monopolize jute bagging is debatable if not ludicrous.[54]

During World War II, price controls in the U.S. were widespread, direct, and detailed. Though prices of many products were controlled by law, some were not. Whiskey was price-controlled; rum and wine were not. Some liquor suppliers tied wine and rum to whiskey, effectively raising the price of whiskey. Tie-ins have also been used to undercut cartel prices and manufacturers' suggested retail prices, by knocking down prices of other products cleverly included in a package, or by giving "excessive" trade-ins.

New shoes are commonly sold in pairs, with laces, and in a box. New cars are sold with engines, wheels and tires, seats, paint, and a variety of other components. This is not because their manufacturers are monopolizing laces, or paint and all the rest. Such packages may realize economies from producing a limited number of models; limit costly bargaining on each feature and component; or reduce the costs of assuring the convenience, safety, and quality of the whole package.

Similarly, both buyers and sellers can benefit from requirements and exclusive-dealing contracts that reduce risk and costs, as many no doubt do.

The revolution that Director's amazing insights started ultimately prevailed almost everywhere.[55] The most popular view today is probably that compound pricing is not an effective monopolizing tool; but is either innocuous or beneficial, increasing efficiency and technological progress for example.

But the powerful and simple analysis from which those views come rests on a special assumption: fixed proportions. What happens when proportions are variable?[56]

Variable Proportions

In most economic decisions and processes goods are used in variable proportions, the analysis of which is inevitably more complicated. When proportions of production inputs are variable, a manufacturer can partially or completely substitute some inputs for others, using them in different proportions. Consumers substitute in much the same way when we choose and use consumer goods.

In the fixed-proportions illustrations that Director and Bowman made famous, the tied input effectively measured *and* charged for output, to which machine use was geared one-to-one. The price of the metering tied good was raised enough above the competitive level to mop up all the surplus, a large sum of money. And the tying contract required relatively little information to do all this. For example, knowing how much the machine saved a shoe manufacturer per button fastened was a large part of that solution.[57]

It seems clear that a seller with perfect information and zero contract-enforcement costs would want to use all-or-none pricing even with variable-proportions production. Although this would earn higher profits than compound pricing, it would not exert leverage, and that would be that. But simple schemes do not seem to accomplish all-or-none pricing when proportions are variable; and the costs of using different schemes need to be considered.

When proportions are variable, all-or-none requires a lot of information, including customers' costs and output. And nothing so obvious as fixed-proportions staples is available to provide it. Counting output directly, as with a meter, could do that job; but using tie-ins to do the metering supposedly makes any other meters unnecessary. If you can measure outputs directly and cheaply, you do not need tie-ins to do it. Tie-ins that don't measure properly are not very good for all-or-none pricing.

Suppose a monopoly wants to price a good all-or-none, even though it is used in variable proportions. There is usually more than one way to produce something, especially in the long run. When proportions are variable, buyers substitute away from goods that become relatively expensive. Earlier discussion of Figure 9-4 noted several (equivalent) versions of the textbook all-or-none solution. Take a closer look at one of them. Suppose the monopoly compels buyers to take the same quantity as they would if the monopoly good were priced competitively, at marginal cost. It then charges for that quantity the lump sum that extracts as much of the producer surplus as is possible.

That sounds better than it actually works, when proportions are variable. Imposing a large lump-sum charge for a specific quantity is not a reliable way to price factors of production all-or-none. Firms starting from scratch or adjusting in the long run will change their size, shape, and methods drastically in response to such a contract. The lump-sum contract creates a large new ''fixed cost,'' which they must pay if they produce at all. They will have to use the quantity of the monopoly good required by contract, but—in the long run—will ''dilute'' that quantity by substituting large quantities of factors that the monopoly does not control. McGee (1987) found that some such all-or-none approximations were poor approximations, indeed. They yielded smaller profits than did tie-in sales, even when contracting and enforcement costs were identical for both schemes.

In principle, one way to solve this pricing problem is to dictate the quantities of *all* factors that buyers use, an awe-inspiring task unless you have complete knowledge and costless enforcement. Another more realistic solution is to impose a surcharge *per unit of output*, just like a tax or patent royalty. That can approximate all-or-none results reasonably closely; but it is a far cry from monitoring output with staples used in a fixed proportion to output, which required little information and may not have cost much to apply.

In fact, information is not free and neither is contract enforcement. And some contracts are likely to cost more than others. We must therefore consider additional possibilities. Take a simple one: suppose all-or-none pricing is infeasible or too costly, while compound pricing is both feasible and more profitable than simple monopoly pricing. Some form of compound pricing will then be used. With what effects?

We assume that, at a higher cost, the same good can be produced even if one or more preferred ingredients is completely unavailable. Cost advantage creates but also limits the power to use all-or-none and compound schemes. Compound pricing, like all-or-none, rests upon a studied willingness to sell a buyer nothing at all. Both schemes offer buyers two options: accept this offer or do without my goods altogether. Differences in contract details distinguish compound pricing from all-or-none. Given the prices of other goods, no monopoly can extract more than the costs it could impose by withholding its goods altogether. A worthwhile compound pricing scheme must satisfy certain conditions. Buyers must be willing altogether to do without goods excluded by the contract rather than losing the monopoly good for which the contract is offered. But a *buyer* will not accept the deal unless it makes him better off than he would be with none of the good at all. Second, the scheme adopted must profit the *seller* more than alternatives do. Under some circumstances, requirements and tying contracts can satisfy those conditions. The problem is to compare what compound and other pricing practices do.[58]

Requirements Contracts.   Here the seller offers to sell his good(s) only to those who do not buy certain substitute goods from other sellers. Before the *Motion Picture Patents* case of 1917, patent monopolies could legally do that. Computer simulations show that a profitable requirements contract can completely exclude a relatively close substitute that would be viable under either competition or simple monopoly pricing. The requirements contract greatly increases demand for and profitability of the monopoly good. Given the production and market parameters McGee assumed, the requirements contract on one good earned 43 percent higher profits than simple monopoly pricing could. It also significantly reduced consumer surplus and the total of profits and consumer surplus. Happily, there are limits to how far any monopoly can push the original monopoly power it has. A contract attempting to exclude *two* substitute goods failed.

If such requirements contracts do not exert leverage, many will say they come close enough. By some standards, schemes like this look "predatory," since they can bury competing goods and firms. It is true, however, that in one sense the surviving good must be superior: buyers will go without the excluded good altogether rather than going without the contract good altogether. On the other hand, normal competitive and simple monopoly pricing permit buyers to use some of all goods, making piecemeal substitutions among them as they please.

Although to this point the discussion *assumes* that the requirements contracts did not reduce risks or costs, they may do so. That raises important questions with respect to policy, which will be discussed after we deal with tie-ins.

A Tie-in Contract.   Here, a firm with a monopoly of one good sells only to those who also buy from it a partially substitutable good that was, or could be, produced and sold competitively. The monopoly either buys the tied good in the open market or makes it for itself. In either case, it sells the two goods together, recognizing their interdependence as any multiple-product monopoly would.[59] The best guess is that the firm will raise the price of both the tying and tied goods. In McGee's computer simulations, profits are only a little lower than a firm could have earned if it had started with patent monopolies of *both* products, and *twice* as profitable as simple monopoly pricing of the original (tying) good with which the firm started. Tie-ins reduced consumer surplus and the sum of producer and consumer surpluses.

Policy.   Contrary to some opinion, compound pricing is not necessarily innocuous or benign. It can produce price, output, profit, and welfare results that are practically indistinguishable from those got when a firm increases its monopoly power through agreements or mergers with competitors.

A firm prospers when arson, embargo, or plague shuts down its competitors; or when government subsidizes complementary goods. Mergers and agreements have been used to increase the number of related goods under one control and to coordinate their prices. Compound pricing is yet another way to affect the terms on which related goods are sold. When all-or-none pricing is too costly for sellers to use, they will use something else. This analysis shows how tie-ins and requirements contracts can extend control to other goods and extract more profits than simple pricing can.[60]

None of this denies that, if information and enforcement costs were zero, all-or-none pricing would be the most profitable of the pricing schemes analyzed here. But all-or-none schemes are often infeasible or too costly, partly because they need to measure final-good output (or value). If it is efficient to measure output with mechanical or electronic meters, it would be redundant to use tie-ins as meters. But meters cost something and may be vulnerable to tampering, and a tied complement can meter well when used in fixed proportions. However, tie-ins are presumptively illegal for patented goods and suspect in the company of what courts call ''market power.'' By itself, input pricing does not closely approximate all-or-none pricing when input proportions are variable. Even a variable-proportions input could be priced all-or-none by using *direct* measurements of final output; but that is difficult and costly. It may also be illegal.[61]

In sum, it is doubtful that all-or-none pricing is generally feasible, let alone the most profitable alternative. And it is unlikely that all compound pricing schemes are merely paler approximations of all-or-none pricing. *All* the compound schemes analyzed here can be much more profitable and hurtful to consumers than simple monopoly pricing is. By traditional welfare standards, compound pricing is not just like all-or-none pricing, only less so.

This new analysis has an important policy implication: it is less clear now what the best policy is. Many think that exclusionary contracts should be permitted whenever they may reduce costs or risks, or enhance qualities that customers want. It can also be argued, as the great Oliver Wendell Holmes did, that permitting such contracts would leave property rights in a tidier and more consistent condition, without extracting more than the goods are inherently worth. Holmes, like Director, correctly said that the worst a seller does to you is denying his goods altogether, then argued that property rights should permit him to do that.[62] Requirements contracts used in that way can raise returns from multiple-product monopoly, encouraging multiple-patent exploitation and, perhaps, invention and innovation as well.

But this is not the end of the matter: there are strong economic objections to that kind of contract.[63] If all-or-none pricing were always the most profitable pricing practice, it is what monopolies would always use. And, if we can agree that all-or-none pricing exerts no leverage, there would *be* no leverage. But all-or-none is not by a long shot the only kind of monopoly pricing there is.

My right to deny you my goods is one thing. The right additionally to deny you someone else's is something else. It permits me to weaken property rights in the goods that are excluded. More important than that, perhaps, is that such contracts can reduce consumer surplus, and national income and wealth. In the conditions assumed, requirements contracts look predatory. They can completely exclude a competitive good without benefitting consumers in the process. And if requirements contracts are the most profitable alternative available, pushing the competitor out does not sacrifice any monopoly profits.

It seems reasonable to require apparently monopolizing compound-pricing schemes to offer some defense or extenuation. Showing that compound pricing *can* hurt consumers does not prove that it usually does; or even that it does so in a specific case. Real-world sellers may have less (or more) market power than the hypothetical firms analyzed here. And tie-ins, exclusive dealing, and requirements contracts may reduce costs and increase quality.

In practice, therefore, it will be hard to tell which of these schemes help and which ones hurt. Indeed, it is sometimes hard to tell even what *type* of pricing real firms actually practice. Some earlier diagnoses may have been mistaken. Some tie-in requirements contracts diagnosed as metering-type approximations to all-or-none pricing may have been something else. It is not clear what some of these arrangements really did.[64] One reason may be that we have trouble seeing what we believe to be impossible.

SUMMARY

The consumers' case against collusion and cartels is relatively strong, and efficient policies against them are feasible. An anticollusion program is the strong center of antitrust theory and policy.

The case against mergers is much weaker. Mergers can *create* large market shares and, possibly, substantial monopoly power. But the best guess is that a monopoly so created will decline unless it innovates and prices and operates efficiently, or has cornered some nonexpansible resource. Although mergers can create monopoly, the monopoly will not endure unaided. And, among other advantages claimed for them are that mergers can speedily bury bad managements, combine old and new ways of doing things faster, and more quickly realize economies of large size.

Chapter 13 suggests how we might improve merger analysis in principle. But accurately forecasting whether a specific merger will help or hurt consumers demands a lot from frail mortals. As a result, the policy alternatives are unsatisfying. For some time the rhetoric of U.S. merger policy and court decisions has sounded technical and precise, citing, as it has, Herfindahl concentration coefficients, estimates of how "easy" or "hard" entry is, and other arcane constructs, which Chapter 11 will discuss in detail.

In mid-1984, for example, the Antitrust Division of the Department of Justice (DJ) issued yet another set of guidelines to tell the public about its current merger policies. The guidelines defined three classes of industrial concentration. First, "unconcentrated" markets have Herfindahl indexes of less than 1,000, the equivalent of an industry with ten equal-sized firms, or, roughly—so DJ said its research suggested—one in which the four largest firms do half the business. The second class includes "moderately concentrated" industries, with as few as six equal-sized firms or four firms doing up to 70 percent of the business. The third class is "highly concentrated," and includes industries more concentrated than that. According to these guidelines, DJ would not challenge mergers that left markets in the unconcentrated class. DJ would probably challenge mergers that raised concentration in a moderately concentrated industry by 100 Herfindahl index points or more, and would challenge mergers that raised concentration in highly concentrated industries by more than 50 Herfindahl index points.[65]

The substance of merger policy is much less precise than all that arithmetic sounds, as it must be. In practice, for example, concentration figures depend upon how and by whom they are constructed. And, whatever the numbers may be, merger policy has provided enough exceptions and qualifications to justify "yes," "no," or "maybe" decisions.

It is cautious, and may sound reasonable, to propose only slight shifts toward one edge of our present merger policy or the other. But even the center of merger policy is hard to pin down, and its edges get defined in the Supreme Court, if at all. At the extremes of theoretical policies, some would permit all mergers; others would permit none. Some would permit all mergers, but later dissolve firms declared to have kept monopoly too long, without redeeming social benefits. This may place too much weight on dissolution and other anti-"monopoly" policies, whose history is checkered—as Chapter 20 suggests.

From one extreme to another, opinions differ greatly about predatory pricing and what to do about it. This chapter argues that rational firms are unlikely to try for or achieve monopoly power via predatory pricing. For some time, this view has been popular, perhaps the majority view, amongst industrial organization economists. The argument assumes that predatory pricing is too costly to use on rational competitors and that viable business executives are rational. Recent court decisions, particularly *Matsushita Electric*, show that this view of the economics has greatly influenced the law.[66]

From his impressive econometric research, Malcolm Burns concludes that this view must change, and he is not alone.[67] He says that American Tobacco successfully used predatory pricing to create its monopoly, and that it paid off. It is not clear whether, if this is so, it was because American's competitors were irrational, or whether people have learned better since. In any case, though he used sophisticated econometric techniques and the best data that exist, the data do not seem to be very good. Good or not, some of these numbers suggest that American's pricing strategy, if that's what it was, did not pay after all. If it did not pay, we might face the distressing possibility that American made a mistake, too. This would not be unsettling unless such mistakes and irrationality are common. Economic theories that rely on irrationality and mistakes are hard to use and so far have not contributed much to the science.

In any case, what policy makes sense? It is undeniable that lower prices help consumers and that it is not easy to determine whether price competition is predatory. Some think it is impossible to determine which price cuts hurt consumers because they are predatory and which price cuts help consumers because they are not predatory. Some think that courts endanger competition when they even try to make the distinction.[68] One obvious possibility, with its own costs and risks, is to remain hostile towards massive industry-wide mergers. That would deny the kinds of monopoly fruits that Burns says American Tobacco bought cheap.

Economic theory and industrial history suggest that limit pricing, a passive cousin of predatory pricing, menaces competition little or not at all, which is just as well. Rules sufficient to stop it, if it exists, would chill the quest for industrial superiority and encourage live-and-let-live noncompetitiveness.

All-or-none pricing would not create monopoly or magnify the monopoly power with which a firm starts. It would take more consumer surplus than simple monopoly pricing would, and in the case of patents would help consumers, if at all, by encouraging some new products and processes that we would not otherwise enjoy.

Compound pricing, including requirements contracts and tying contracts, is not the same as all-or-none pricing. Tie-ins under fixed proportions do not seem to hurt consumers and antitrust can justifiably ignore them. Tie-ins and variable proportions are a potentially dangerous combination that deserves our suspicion. When applied to goods used in variable proportions, requirements contracts and tying arrangements can hurt consumers and worthy competitors as well. But effectuating good policy towards compound pricing is not so easy. Requirements contracts can reduce cost and risks, to the benefit of all concerned. They can also reduce consumer surplus and competition.

QUESTIONS

1. "A rapid increase in the number of firms is as likely to mean that an industry has been monopolized as that it is highly competitive." Explain and comment.
2. The economy is not static; times and technology change, as do many other things. Explain how an industry would achieve the following efficiencies when mergers are permitted and when they are not:
   a. displace bad managements with good
   b. adjust to a technological change that doubles the most efficient size of firm.
3. "Although we still do not know why so many important mergers took place around the turn of the century, note that typewriters were invented around 1876, telephones about 1886." Comment and explain.
4. Under what conditions is extortion likely to succeed?
5. Since lower prices benefit them, why should consumers worry about predatory price cutting?
6. What does *predatory price cutting* mean? Outline and defend a policy to prevent it.
7. List and explain some factors that help a predatory price cutter to obtain a monopoly, and some factors that hurt its chances.
8. "Limit pricing is a passive cousin of predatory price cutting." Explain and comment.
9. Market shares of many of the large firms created by merger between 1895 and 1904 declined significantly within a few years. What, if anything, does this say about the theory of limit pricing? Explain.
10. "Limit pricing would be harder for an oligopoly or cartel to practice than for a single-firm oligopoly." Comment and explain.
11. Carefully outline the button-fastening machine story told in the text. Did the machine owner get a second monopoly, in staples for example? If not, what was it doing?
12. The Federal Trade Commission claimed Gratz tried to monopolize jute bagging by tying 6 yards of it to every 6 cotton-bale ties. Evaluate their claim.
13. Tying rum to whiskey during World War II arguably avoided or reduced a liquor "shortage." Explain.
14. How could a requirements contract reduce costs or risks?
15. Explain how requirements contracts could hurt consumers. What information would you need to decide whether a specific requirements contract helps or hurts them?

NOTES

1. Adam Smith, *The Wealth of Nations* (New York: Modern Library, 1937), Chapter X, Part II, p. 128.

2. They may decrease costs and prices, decrease costs but raise prices, or raise prices without reducing costs. Most economists seem to think that cartels are injurious and that the net effects of mergers are mixed and difficult to measure.

3. For example, see the exchange between Harold Demsetz and Louis Schwartz (a lawyer). Demsetz argued that antitrust laws should concentrate on "explicit contracts to collude." Schwartz asked Demsetz whether he was "calling a horizontal merger an explicit contract to collude." Demsetz replied "I guess I am not, no." H. J. Goldschmid, H. M. Mann, and J. F. Weston eds., *Industrial Concentration: The New Learning* (Boston: Little, Brown & Company, 1974), p. 236.

4. Some experts date these waves differently than others. One can date the waves from trough to trough, peak to peak, or mark periods in which merger activity is greater than trend values. See Yale Brozen, *Concentration, Mergers, and Public Policy* (New York: Macmillan, Inc., 1982); Jesse Markham, "Survey of the Evidence and Findings on Mergers," in *Business Concentration and Price Policy*, ed. G. J. Stigler (Princeton, N.J.: Princeton University Press, 1955), pp. 141–82; Ralph Nelson, *Merger Movements in American Industry 1895–1956* (Princeton, N.J.: Princeton University Press, 1959); and Peter O. Steiner, *Mergers* (Ann Arbor, Mich.: University of Michigan Press, 1975).

5. George J. Stigler, "Monopoly and Oligopoly by Merger," *The Organization of Industry* (Homewood, Ill.: Richard D. Irwin, Inc., 1968), Chapter 8, pp. 95–112.

6. See U.S. Department of Justice, Antitrust Division, *U.S. Department of Justice Merger Guidelines*, June 14, 1984, pp. 1–31; 1984 Commerce Clearing House *Trade Regulation Reporter*, § 4490. For a review of how such guidelines have evolved, from a predecessor of official Department of Justice (DJ) guides (1955) through the DJ guides of 1968, 1982, and 1984, see Thomas M. Jorde, "Restoring Predictability to Merger Guideline Analysis," *Contemporary Policy Issues*, 4 (July 1986), pp. 1–21; and James Langenfeld, "Impact of Antitrust Guidelines on Business," ibid., pp. 22–29.

7. The strongest statement of this view is Yale Brozen, *Concentration, Mergers, and Public Policy* (1982).

    See the discussion later in this chapter about preventing mergers that may result in predatory or below-cost pricing.

8. There is a large literature on this subject. For example, see John S. McGee, "Predatory Price Cutting: The Standard Oil (N.J.) Case," *Journal of Law & Economics*, 1 (October 1958), pp. 137–69; McGee, "Predatory Pricing Revisited," *Journal of Law & Economics*, 23 (October 1980), pp. 289–330; Frank H. Easterbrook, "Predatory Strategies and Counterstrategies," 48 *Chicago Law Review* 263 (1981); Harold Demsetz, "Barriers to Entry," *The American Economic Review*, 72 (March 1982), pp. 47–57; B. S. Yamey, "Predatory Price Cutting: Notes and Comments," *Journal of Law & Economics*, 15 (April 1972), pp. 129–42; Phillip Areeda and Donald F. Turner, "Predatory Pricing and Related Practices Under Section 2 of the Sherman Act," 88 *Harvard Law Review* (February 1975), pp. 679–733; Areeda and Turner, "Scherer on Predatory Pricing: A Reply," 89 *Harvard Law Review* (1976), pp. 891–900; Areeda and Turner, *Antitrust Law: An Analysis of Antitrust Principles and Their*

Application (Boston: Little, Brown & Company, 1978), vol. III, pp. 150–94; Areeda and Turner, "Williamson on Predatory Pricing," 87 *Yale Law Journal* (June 1978), pp. 1337–52; R. H. Bork and W. S. Bowman, Jr., "The Goals of Antitrust," 65 *Columbia Law Review* 363 (1965); Bork and Bowman, "The Crisis in Antitrust," *Fortune*, 68 (December 1963), p. 138; Lester G. Telser, "Cutthroat Competition and the Long Purse," *Journal of Law & Economics*, 9 (October 1966), pp. 259–77; George J. Stigler, "Imperfections in the Capital Market," *Journal of Political Economy*, 75 (June 1967), pp. 287–92, reprinted in Stigler's *The Organization of Industry* (Homewood, Ill.: Richard D. Irwin, Inc., 1968), pp. 113–22; Richard Zerbe, "The American Sugar Refining Company, 1887–1914: The Story of Monopoly," *Journal of Law & Economics*, 12 (October 1969), pp. 339–75; Kenneth G. Elzinga, "Predatory Pricing: The Case of the Gunpowder Trust," *Journal of Law & Economics*, 13 (April 1970), pp. 223–40; Roland H. Koller II, "The Myth of Predatory Pricing: An Empirical Study," in *The Competitive Economy: Selected Readings*, ed. Yale Brozen (Morristown, N.J.: General Learning Press, 1975), pp. 418–28; Richard A. Posner, *Antitrust Law: An Economic Perspective* (Chicago: The University of Chicago Press, 1976), pp. 184–96; Posner, "The Chicago School of Antitrust Analysis," 127 *Univ. of Pa. Law. Rev.* (1979), pp. 925–48, at pp. 939–44; F. M. Scherer, "Predatory Pricing and the Sherman Act: A Comment," 89 *Harvard Law Review* (March 1976), pp. 869–90; Scherer, "Some Last Words on Predatory Pricing," 89 *Harvard Law Review* (March 1976), pp. 901–3; Oliver E. Williamson, "Predatory Pricing: A Strategic and Welfare Analysis," 87 *Yale Law Journal* (December 1977), pp. 284–340; Williamson, "A Preliminary Response," 87 *Yale Law Journal* (1978), p. 1353; Robert H. Bork, *The Antitrust Paradox: A Policy at War with Itself* (New York: Basic Books, Inc., Publishers, 1978); Randall Mariger, "Predatory Price Cutting: The Standard Oil of New Jersey Case Revisited," *Explorations in Economic History*, 15 (October 1978), pp. 341–67; William J. Baumol, "Quasi-Permanence of Price Reductions: A Policy for Prevention of Predatory Pricing," 89 *Yale Law Journal* 1 (November 1979), pp. 1–26; and Paul L. Joskow and Alvin K. Klevorick, "A Framework for Analyzing Predatory Pricing Policy," 89 *Yale Law Journal* (December 1979), pp. 213–70.

9. See Chapter 20.

10. There have doubtless been instances in which firms have *reduced* competition by preventing mergers that might hurt them. A Supreme Court decision in early December 1986 may limit this tactic in the future. Stephen Wermiel, "Justices Restrict Antitrust Suits by Competitors," *The Wall Street Journal*, 10 December 1986, pp. 2, 24. Monfort of Colorado, Inc., a meat packer, in 1983 got an injunction that kept Cargill Inc. (Excel Corp.) from buying the Spencer Beef division of Land O' Lakes, Inc., on grounds that the successor company might use predatory or below-cost prices to reduce competition. The Supreme Court reversed, which presumably restricts, although it may not eliminate, granting such injunctions in the future.

    Perhaps the wisest policy is to wait until what is arguably a predatory campaign has actually occurred, rather than anticipating what may or may not happen. Indeed, it is arguable that the best course for consumers is to make *all* price cutting legal under the antitrust laws.

11. R. H. Coase, "The Problem of Social Cost," *Journal of Law & Economics*, 3 (October 1960), pp. 1–44.

12. R. Mark Isaac and Vernon L. Smith, "In Search of Predatory Pricing," *Journal of Political Economy*, 93 (April 1985), pp. 320–45. See also D. Coursey, R. M. Isaac, and V. L. Smith,

"Natural Monopoly and Contested Markets: Some Experimental Results," *Journal of Political Economy*, 27 (April 1984), pp. 91–114.

13. *U.S. v. American Tobacco Co.*, 221 U.S. 106 (1911).

14. Malcolm R. Burns, "Outside Intervention in Monopolistic Price Warfare: The Case of the 'Plug War' and the Union Tobacco Company," *Business History Review*, 56, no. 1 (Spring 1982), pp. 33–53; Burns, "Economies of Scale in Tobacco Manufacture, 1897–1910," *Journal of Economic History*, 43 (June 1983), pp. 461–74; and Burns, "Predatory Pricing and the Acquisition Cost of Competitors," *Journal of Political Economy*, 94 (April 1986), pp. 266–96.

15. Eliot Jones, *The Trust Problem in the United States* (New York: Macmillan, Inc., 1921).

16. Ibid., p. 124.

17. Burns, "Predatory Pricing," p. 268, note.

18. Jones, *The Trust Problem*, pp. 125–26.

19. Burns quotes an assertion that McGee made in 1958: "Even if there is widespread bankruptcy, wise men will see the value to the monopolist of bringing the facilities under his control, and find it profitable to purchase them at some price below what the monopolist can be expected to pay if he must. Since the monopolist is presumably interested in profits, and has a notion of the effect of discount factors on future income, he cannot afford to wait forever. Properties that a would-be monopolist needs to control can be an attractive investment." John S. McGee, "Predatory Price Cutting: The Standard Oil (N.J.) Case," *Journal of Law & Economics*, 1 (October 1958), p. 141.

20. Burns, "Outside Intervention," p. 50.

21. Ibid., p. 52.

22. Burns, "Predatory Pricing," p. 289.

23. Ibid., p. 292.

24. Ibid., p. 291, note.

25. Ibid., pp. 274, 291, 293.

26. Ibid., p. 293.

27. Burns, "Economies of Scale," Table 1, p. 467.

28. Ibid., Table 3, p. 469.

29. Ibid., Table 5, p. 471.

30. Ibid., Table 7, p. 472.

31. Burns, "Predatory Pricing," Table 1, p. 279.

32. Ibid., p. 271.

33. Ibid., p. 271.

34. Ibid., pp. 275, 289.

35. Franco Modigliani, "New Developments on the Oligopoly Front," *Journal of Political Economy*, 66 (June 1958), pp. 215–32. See also Donald Dewey, *The Theory of Imperfect Competition: A Radical Reconstruction* (New York: Columbia University Press, 1969).

36. Theories of Chamberlin and Fellner, discussed in Chapter 5, are examples.

37. Compare Dean A. Worcester, Jr., "Why 'Dominant Firms' Decline," *Journal of Political Economy*, 65 (August 1957), pp. 338–47; Worcester, *Monopoly, Big Business, and Welfare*

in the Postwar United States (Seattle: University of Washington Press, 1967); Dale K. Osborne, "The Role of Entry in Oligopoly Theory," *Journal of Political Economy*, 72 (August 1964), pp. 395–402; Stigler, *The Organization of Industry*, pp. 67–70; B. Peter Pashigian, "Limit Price and the Market Share of the Leading Firm," *Journal of Industrial Economics*, 16 (July 1968), pp. 165–77; John T. Wenders, "Entry and Monopoly Pricing," *Journal of Political Economy*, 75 (October 1967), pp. 755–60.

38. Williamson, "Predatory Pricing: A Strategic and Welfare Analysis."

39. Figure 9-2 draws but does not formally "derive" what Williamson calls the *optimal scale*. To draw this kind of diagram, first choose for the potential entrant a residual demand that meets Williamson's criterion: a tangency of demand with long-run average cost. Next, draw average and marginal plant costs that are consistent with the tangent residual demand drawn in the first step.

40. This is surely true of rules he would apply to dominant-firm pricing, as pointed out in McGee, "Predatory Pricing Revisited."

41. For further discussion of this point, see Chapter 10 and Chapter 11 of this book.

42. Clear explanations of all-or-none pricing for *consumer* goods include David Friedman, *Price Theory* (Cincinnati: South-Western Publishing Co., 1986), pp. 79–82, 93–95; Jack Hirshleifer, *Price Theory and Applications*, 3rd ed. (Englewood Cliffs, N.J.: Prentice-Hall, Inc., 1984), pp. 260–61; George J. Stigler, *The Theory of Price*, 3rd ed. (New York: Macmillan, Inc., 1966), pp. 78–81; Milton Friedman, *Price Theory* (Chicago: Aldine Publishing Co., 1976), pp. 15–16.

43. For a more complete treatment of these practices, see John S. McGee, "Compound Pricing," *Economic Inquiry*, 25 (April 1987), pp. 315–39.

44. For example, see Posner, *Antitrust Law*, pp. 176–81.

45. 15 United States Code Annotated Section 14.

46. See, for example, *Motion Picture Patents Co.* v. *Universal Film Mfg. Co.*, 243 U.S. 502 (1917); *FTC* v. *Gratz*, 253 U.S. 421 (1920), especially Mr. Justice Brandeis's dissent; *Standard Fashion Co.* v. *Magrane-Houston Co.* 258 U.S. 346 (1922); *IBM* v. *U.S.*, 298 U.S. 131 (1936); *Standard Oil Co. of California* v. *U.S.*, 69 S. Ct. 1051 (1949); *Times Picayune Pub. Co.* v. *U.S.*, 345 U.S. 594 (1953); Carl Kaysen and Donald F. Turner, *Antitrust Policy: An Economic and Legal Analysis* (Cambridge, Mass.: Harvard University Press, 1959), p. 157.

47. Aaron Director and Edward H. Levi, "Law and the Future: Trade Regulation," 51 *Northwestern Univ. Law Review* 286 (1956); Ward S. Bowman, Jr., "Tying Arrangements and the Leverage Problem," 67 *Yale Law Journal* (November 1957), pp. 19–36; Meyer L. Burstein, "A Theory of Full-Line Forcing," 55 *Northwestern Univ. Law Review* 62 (March–April 1960); Bowman, *Patent and Antitrust Law* (Chicago: University of Chicago Press, 1973); Bork, *The Antitrust Paradox: A Policy at War with Itself.*

48. Ward S. Bowman, "Tying Arrangements."

49. *Heaton-Peninsular Button-Fastener Co.* v. *Eureka Specialty Co.*, 77 Fed. 288 (1896).

50. See Friedman, *Price Theory*, Figure 2.2, p. 15.

51. A monthly charge equal to area $OWRQ_2$ would extract total producer surplus from the machine. $OSUQ_2$ has that same area. SWT and TUR are congruent triangles, which have equal areas.

52. *What* the proportion is does not fundamentally affect the analysis so long as it is fixed. When the proportion is not one-to-one, the quantity scales of the components and the combination differ. A simple way to deal with that is to measure all of them in final-product equivalents. If four tires are used to make one car, four tires are a final-product-equivalent unit.

53. Bowman, "Tying Arrangements."

54. *FTC* v. *Gratz*, 253 U.S. 421 (1920): here, in the end, Gratz finally won its case.

55. See Posner, *Antitrust Law*, Chapter 8, and sources cited there. For a small sample of recent opinions, see papers presented at Antitrust and Economic Efficiency, a conference sponsored by the Hoover Institution in 1984: Benjamin Klein and Lester Saft, "The Law and Economics of Franchise Tying Contracts," *Journal of Law & Economics* 28 (May 1985), pp. 345–61; Keith Leffler, "Toward a Reasonable Rule of Reason: Comments," *Journal of Law & Economics* 18 (May 1985), pp. 381–86; Richard Markovits, "The Functions, Allocative Efficiency, and Legality of Tie-Ins: A Comment," *Journal of Law & Economics* 28 (May 1985), pp. 387–404.

56. There is an analogous question about vertical integration. See Chapter 12; and John S. McGee and Lowell Bassett. "Vertical Integration Revisited," *Journal of Law & Economics*, 19 (April 1976), pp. 17–38.

57. Chapter 8 discusses how to set patent royalties for maximum profits.

58. The comparisons are complicated. Computer simulations are one way to make them. See McGee, "Compound Pricing."

59. John R. Hicks, "Annual Survey of Economic Theory," *Econometrica*, 3 (January 1935), pp. 1–20; R. G. D. Allen, *Mathematical Analysis for Economists* (London: Macmillan and Company, Limited, 1938), pp. 350–62; Martin J. Bailey, "Price and Output Determination by a Firm Selling Related Products," *American Economic Review*, 44 (March 1954), pp. 82–93.

60. Compare Roger D. Blair and David L. Kaserman, *Antitrust Economics* (Homewood, Ill.: Richard D. Irwin, Inc., 1985), pp. 403–4; Posner, *Antitrust Law*, p. 173; and Lester G. Telser, "Theory of Monopoly of Complementary Goods," *Journal of Business*, 52, no. 2 (1979), pp. 211–30. No method gets "two profits" from one good. But some methods get larger profits from it than others can, and with startlingly different results. Blair and Kaserman are simply wrong about what compound pricing can do with goods used in variable proportions.

61. See Posner, *Antitrust Law*, p. 201.

62. See Holmes's wonderful, though problematic, dissent in *Motion Picture Patents Co.* v. *Universal Film Mfg. Co.*, 243 U.S. 502 (1917), pp. 519–20.

63. Carl R. Cutter pointed them out to the author.

64. Examples include *Bell* v. *Cherokee Aviation*, 660 F.2d 1123 (1981); F. J. Cummings and W. E. Ruther, "The Northern Pacific Case," *Journal of Law & Economics*, 22 (October 1979), pp. 329–50; *Kentucky Fried Chicken* v. *Diversified Packaging Corp.*, 549 F.2d 368 (1977); F. C. Meltzer and S. H. Mancke, "Tying Arrangements as Insurance," *Industrial Organization Review*, 3, no. 2 (1975), pp. 98–103; John Peterman, "The International Salt Case," *Journal of Law & Economics*, 22 (October 1979), pp. 351–64.

65. U.S. Department of Justice, Antitrust Division, *Merger Guidelines* (June 14, 1984), pp. 1–31, at pp. 14–15, 1984 Commerce Clearing House *Trade Regulation Reporter*, §4490.

Also see Thomas M. Jorde, "Restoring Predictability to Merger Guideline Analysis," *Contemporary Policy Issues*, 4 (July 1986), pp. 1–21; and James Langenfeld, "Impact of Antitrust Guidelines on Business," ibid., pp. 22–29.

66. *Matsushita Electric Industrial Co.* v. *Zenith Radio Corp.*, 106 S. Ct. 1348 (1986).

67. Roger D. Blair and David L. Kaserman, *Antitrust Economics* (1985), p. 124.

68. For example, see Demsetz, "Barriers to Entry."

10 THE THEORY OF PRODUCTS AND MONOPOLY

INTRODUCTION

This chapter presents the concepts we need to appraise empirical measurements of concentration (the subject of the next chapter) and monopoly power (the subject of several chapters to come).

This chapter first defines products and product demand. Next it discusses monopoly, then describes and analyzes important predisposing conditions for monopoly. Some of these are necessary conditions for monopoly itself; others make monopoly more likely by making it especially profitable. Factors that limit the powers that monopolies have are discussed, and finally, the contrasts between open and closed monopolies.

THE NATURE OF A PRODUCT AND THE DEMAND FOR IT

We can go a long way with the basic economics of goods, demands, and industries. But these fundamental notions are not quite enough to make or evaluate empirical studies of concentration and monopoly. What more do we need and where can we find it? Two different schools or branches of economic theory are obvious places to begin.

We can attribute the first body of theory to Alfred Marshall, the great English neoclassical economist. George Stigler, a Nobel laureate, brought first-class Marshallian economics into industrial organization.[1] The second theoretical approach can be traced to Leon Walras, a mathematical economist of the last century. His intellectual descendants include E. H. Chamberlin, Robert Triffin, and Robert Bishop, famous economists trained at Harvard.

Marshall

In Marshallian analysis, *good* and *industry* are useful classifications that let us pull out and analyze one commodity at a time, ignoring until further notice a host of other things in which we have no immediate interest. Typically this analysis concentrates on commodities with well-known common names that are defined by the consensus of ordinary usage, until a need for more detailed specifications arises. In this system, *good* is an elastic notion to be altered as needed for the theoretical analysis or policy problem at hand.

In principle, classification systems do not alter the underlying realities; they merely organize them. How we organize things can, it is true, influence what we see and how we view it.

As we will see, the theory and empirical tests that economists commonly use to analyze concentration and monopoly are closely related to a couple of standard measurements: *own-elasticity*, one of Marshall's innovations, and *cross-elasticity* of demand. Own-elasticity of demand measures how the demand for a good responds to a small change in its *own* price. The cross-elasticity of demand for a good measures how its demand changes in response to a small change in the price of *another* good. Take two hypothetical goods, X and Y. The own-elasticity of demand for good X is defined as:

$$(\delta qX/\delta pX)(pX/qX);$$

and the cross-elasticity of demand for good X, in terms of the price of good Y is:

$$(\delta qX/\delta pY)(pY/qX),$$

where, in both cases, the q's designate quantities demanded each time period. For *substitute* goods, the cross-elasticity is positive: changing the price of one good moves demands for its substitutes in the same direction. Reducing the price of corn syrup reduces the demand for sugar. For *complements*, cross-elasticity is negative: changing the price of one good moves demands for its complements in the opposite direction. Reducing the price of automobiles increases the demand for gasoline. Cross-elasticities are zero for *unrelated* goods. Changes in the price of one good have no effect on the demands for other goods unrelated to it.

This is fine as far as it goes; but, to keep things straight, we need to know exactly how good X and its demand function are being defined. In defining and measuring demand functions, what factors are being held constant? Factors typically held constant include real income; prices and characteristics of related (substitute and complementary) goods; consumers' tastes; and time.

Suppose we have all the information we want about a large number of real commodities. These data are relevant to at least two types of industrial organization questions. First, how distinctive or unique is one of these commodities, say, men's leather shoes? Distinctive enough that a single-firm men's leather shoe industry, or one that is cartelized, would be significantly monopolistic for a significantly long time? Second, which commodities (footwear and nonfootwear commodities, for example) *should* reasonably be lumped together, recognizing both their similarity to one another, and their collective distinctiveness as compared with other commodities *not* lumped in with them?

Take an example of the first type of problem. Is men's leather shoe production so concentrated that we should fear monopoly results? We can start by analyzing *demand* substitutability for men's leather shoes. If it faced a large number of relatively poor substitutes, or one or a few good ones, even a single-firm "monopoly" of men's leather shoes could have little or no monopoly *power*. At the other extreme, what if the own-price elasticity of demand for men's leather shoes were approximately zero over a "significant" period of time. That would end questions about substitutes in *demand*: there are none. A single-firm monopoly of men's leather shoes might have some monopoly power.

That does not mean that there *is* a monopoly of men's leather shoes, but that there *could* be one, depending upon other conditions. Whether there is depends also upon substitutability in *production*. Suppose that independent manufacturers of, say, women's or children's shoes or other kinds of commodities altogether, would quickly switch into the business if the price of men's leather shoes should rise a little. A monopolistic increase in the price of men's shoes would induce entry from producers of other goods related in production. It would matter if this kind of entry is faster than creating wholly new firms to enter the men's leather shoe business. Uniqueness in demand is not enough to create a durable monopoly.

In general, however, own-price elasticity of demand for one narrowly defined common commodity is unlikely to be zero if it is measured over any significant time period. Other things equal, how inelastic does its demand have to be for a single-firm monopoly of the commodity to have "significant" monopoly effects? For how long? Unfortunately, these important questions do not have simple, precise answers.

What about broader categories of similar goods? Take a specific example of aggregating a narrow species of goods into a larger genus. Suppose we decide to lump men's leather shoes in with other goods, rather than analyzing them separately. Suppose we classify each of the other commodities into different boxes, according to how they are related to men's leather shoes: substitutes, complements, and unrelated commodities. When all the goods have been sorted, which, if any of them, should go with men's leather shoes into a meaningful composite, perhaps "footwear?" Do sandals go in? Leather house slippers? Professional boxing shoes? Skateboards? And so on. If ordinary goods are to be lumped together, it is reasonable to include in each class of goods only those that respond more to the price changes of others classed with them than to the price changes of goods outside the group.

To define a commodity in terms of substitution in demand, we could, in principle, put into a box the name of a candidate that has a highly (perhaps infinitely) elastic demand. We could then keep adding substitutes until the group has a markedly lower composite own-elasticity of demand. It does not help much to call something a good if its own-elasticity of demand is infinite: relative to other commodities, it has no distinctiveness.

But just how much is *markedly lower*; or *highly elastic*? Over what time period should we measure the elasticities on which such a classification system rests? According to traditional Marshallian methodology, answers to such questions depend upon the nature of the problem, and the patience, instincts, and tastes of the analyst. We must therefore face two things squarely. First, the differences that matter here are differences of degree. Second, there is no natural or physical principle that determines where we segment the continuum. Who does the work can significantly influence where the partitions get placed. In later chapters, we will see how the subjectivity of such procedures plagues empirical work and policy applications. Shoes may sound like a relatively easy commodity to analyze, yet the U.S. Supreme Court made a mess of it.[2]

Whether a demand curve derived in this way is influenced by the structure or behavior of the industry making the product is an open question. For convenience, economists typically assume that there is no such relationship. For example, we typically use the same demand function to compare what would happen if the same good were sold, first, by an atomistic industry, then alternatively by a single-firm monopoly. Convenient though it is, that procedure is questionable. Later discussion shows that product changes can affect industry structure, and vice versa; and that changes in industry structure can affect the quality of and demand for products over time.

It is consistent with Marshallian methodology to treat as an industry whatever group of firms produces commodity X. This analysis then recognizes relationships between good X and other commodities in two principal ways. First, by assuming that the price of related goods remains constant, the industry demand function for good X itself recognizes their interrelationships. Own-elasticity measures the total substitutability of other goods for good X. Second, *changes* in the prices of related goods *shift* the demand for good X, and changes in the price of good X shift the demands for other related goods. Whether it is legitimate and useful to use this kind of partial equilibrium analysis one good at a time depends upon how large these shifts will be in fact. If, to analyze one good, we always have to use a general equilibrium analysis, involving many goods and many shifts, we are lost. The approach described next runs that risk.

Chamberlin, Triffin, and Bishop

This approach abandons industries as Marshall used them. As Triffin saw it, "In the general pure theory of value, the group and the industry are useless concepts."[3] The emphasis shifts to individual firms and individual products, and to a web of interfirm and interproduct relationships. The Marshallian good or commodity drifts in a sea of cross-elasticities. Bishop navigated and tried to chart this water using technical relationships between own- and cross-elasticities of demand. Everything is a matter of degree. And, as he points out, different economists interpret these relationships very differently.

Bishop's scheme starts from how distinctive the product of each firm is.[4] Under certain simplifying assumptions, the *own* price elasticity of demand for one firm's product simply equals its cross-elasticity of demand with respect to each of several (identically close) substitutes *times* the number of substitutes.

The essence of the matter is total substitutability, as can easily be seen. The *sign* of cross-elasticities is positive for substitutes: lowering the price of one substitute lowers the demand for another. The *sign* of a good's own-elasticity is negative: increasing its price lowers the quantity of it demanded. If the cross-elasticity between a monopoly good and one substitute is 0.1, a 1 percent increase in the price of the monopoly good would lose to the other good only about 0.1 percent of the demand it now enjoys, and so on. If there were 100 of even such remote substitutes as those, though, the monopoly good would lose 10 percent of its demand.

A product is relatively distinctive if there is no good substitute for it *and* no significant number even of remote substitutes. How distinctive a firm's or industry's output is thus depends on the degree of *total* substitutability of all other goods and services. A product is not unique if it faces a large number of (even) remote substitutes. Total substitutability is measured by own-elasticity of demand. If that number is low over long periods, the good is relatively distinctive.

So far, so good; except for two things. First, from the outside looking in, it is hard to diagnose monopoly using only own-elasticities of industry demand. The test is ambiguous. Although it is true that a profit-maximizing monopoly sets prices so that the absolute value of its own elasticity exceeds 1, that can also happen under competition. Some competitive industries might therefore get counted as monopolies. Second, empirical estimates of demand elasticity are hard to come by and econometric procedures commonly used to make them inspire limited confidence. If we knew the firm's marginal cost, we could indirectly estimate own-elasticity of demand by assuming that it is maximizing profits. Chapter 14 goes a little further into that subject.

Substitution in Supply

For any monopoly problem, we have to consider another factor: *supply* substitutability among industries (or firms). That is, how much (and how fast) can other industries switch into the production of stuff produced by this one? If other industries can do so when the price of this good rises modestly, low *demand* elasticity is not enough to give monopoly power. A significant price advance cannot hold in the face of large increases in the supply of substitutes.

As abstruse as all this may seem, it is crucial to regulation and other policies toward competition and monopoly. If the basic problem of defining commodity and industry is intractable, policy will blunder, fumble, and flounder.

MONOPOLY

Monopoly literally means one seller; but one seller of what? Because few if any goods face *no* substitutes, that question can only be answered in degree, as we saw is true when defining *any* good. *How much* and *for how long* are inevitably involved. There is no sharp dividing line or cut-off point. For now, it will do to assert that a necessary condition for monopoly is that the total demand function for a good is significantly downward sloping for a significant period of time. That is, all other goods taken together offer only limited substitutability. A single-firm monopoly of such a good could substantially advance its price relative to the others and, if there were little or no entry, could hold it for a significant time without completely losing its customers. Entry is crucial: how long does it take; how much of it will there be at each of various prices?

It is sometimes said that a monopoly faces no competition, in the limited senses both that it has a significantly different demand function of its own; and that it takes as given whatever sellers in other industries do.[5] That is, it has no competitors within its own industry and takes for granted what other industries do. None of these assertions is highly satisfying, let alone definitive. These fundamental definitional problems have caused much trouble in regulatory and antitrust cases.

By the end of the nineteen thirties, it was common to hear either that monopoly is itself a type of market imperfection or that it requires market imperfections. But, looking back, the theory seems to have been rather muddled. Joan Robinson's classic, after all, had claimed to create an economics of *imperfect* competition,[6] the distinguishing feature of which was that firms faced downward-sloping demand functions, while perfect competition required perfectly elastic demands for each firm.[7] One question was whether oligopoly and "monopolistic competition" were imperfect or intermediate cases lying between single-firm monopoly and perfect competition.

Many seem to have believed in *two* theories of atomistic competition, in both of which each firm's demand function was perfectly elastic. If the market were free of "frictions," the competition was perfect. If not, it was "pure." In this conception, *market* imperfection seemed to have more to do with mistakes, frictions, and lags than it had to do with monopoly.

E. H. Chamberlin used three categories of competition: pure and perfect atomism, in both of which firm demands were perfectly elastic, and monopolistic competition, his own contribution, in which numerous firms faced downward-sloping demand functions owing to differences in their relatively closely related products.[8] It was not clear whether pure competition could occur even when markets were imperfect, or whether monopoly could occur even when markets were perfect. For example, Chamberlin says that oligopoly could *occur* in perfect markets; but would act like a monopoly if it did. That he did not claim the same thing even for atomism was probably an error.[9]

In Chamberlin's view, the perfection of a market was determined by the quality and cost of information, and the speed and costs of adjustments—in short, by the absence of frictions. Although it is possible to talk separately about market perfection and monopoly, and we often do so, many economists today think they are closely related. As we saw in chapters 2 and 3, monopoly misallocation and government inefficiency would disappear if information were perfect and adjustments were costless and instantaneous.

PREDISPOSING CONDITIONS FOR MONOPOLY

Long ago Professor Aaron Director noted that many of the same industries appear to have been monopolized in different countries at various times. This suggested to him that certain conditions are especially attractive to monopolizers, or that they predispose an industry to monopoly. It should be possible to indicate factors that make it easier to get a monopoly or to increase the exploitative power and profits of monopoly once it is accomplished. Some of these factors are especially relevant to single-firm monopoly; some to cartels. Some apply to both. What are the factors that favor monopolization?

Low Demand Elasticity

For monopolizing a product, it helps if its demand elasticity is low at the competitive price, ideally zero, and if it increases little at higher prices. That gives a monopoly more power to raise price without losing too many customers. Now that we are dreaming of ideal conditions, it would also help if demand elasticity *decreases* as time passes, or at least increases little or not at all. Either phenomenon would be unusual. Price elasticity of demand tends to increase over time. For one thing, entry of new goods and new firms takes time. For another, it takes consumers time to make adjustments and to switch even to those substitutes that are already present in the market. A rise in the price of gasoline, for example, affects gasoline consumption relatively little at first. Then consumers replace spark plugs and points, inflate tires hard, tune engines and adjust carburetors, and make other relatively small adjustments. Next, people start driving less, car-pool more, and cram more errands into each trip. Later still, car manufacturers redesign their vehicles, reducing weight and increasing fuel economy, and consumers buy them. All this takes time; but as the clock runs, consumer adjustments become more complete.

Low Supply Elasticity of Substitutes

It helps a monopolizer if the price elasticity of supply of substitutes is low, ideally zero, and increases little or not at all over time. The larger the supply elasticity of substitutes, the less power the monopoly has. And the faster supply elasticities of substitutes increase, the faster monopoly will lose its grip.

Let's work through an example, step by step. Monopolization of an industry is inhibited by how much the supplies of substitutes will increase in response. As a competitive industry is converted into a monopoly, its price rises. So does the demand for substitutes; but what about their supply response? If there is none, the monopoly's long-run demand is less elastic, and it can profitably raise price more. If the supply response of substitutes is large, monopoly price increases are much more severely limited. This is a variation of the proposition that the net demand for a monopoly's own good falls as the number and quality of substitutes grows.

Low Monopolization Costs

It costs something to achieve monopoly (or anything else). To favor monopoly, these costs should of course be low, ideally zero, and they must at all events be less than the increase in gross profits expected from monopolization. Monopolization costs are fairly evident in the case of merging many firms, or forming cartels with many members. More subtle, perhaps, are costs of lobbying or bribing legislatures and parliaments, and preparing public relations campaigns to anaesthetize consumers before bleeding them. An industry may, for example, get prohibitive quotas or tariffs on imported substitutes, partly by lobbying congress directly and partly by convincing consumers that imports hurt the nation and are unpatriotic.

Cartels usually spend some money to reduce cheating by their members. It helps if these policing costs are low, and there is some reason to believe that it costs less to police a few firms than many.

Under certain circumstances government will pay at least some of these costs of monopolization, though there is a danger that government would then assume some of the monopoly gains along with its costs. An important question is what kind of political system and institutions are most congenial to monopoly. Government enforcement is likely to be more effective than nonviolent private enforcement can be, and government-promoted cartels are likely to be stronger as a consequence.[10] Nevertheless, politicians and antitrust policy have historically been particularly hostile to purely private schemes, that is, to the *weaker* ones![11]

Of course, Congress, the Department of Justice, and the Federal Trade Commission are all government institutions and might be expected to favor other government institutions over private ones. Furthermore, government institutions all bask in the fiction that what they do is, by definition, well intentioned. In the circumstances, then, it is surprising that governments are as divided about antimonopoly policy as they are. Localities, states, and different arms of the federal government have often been in conflict.

Slow Entry

It helps monopoly if entry to its industry is slow. This is an acutely important special case of the second aid to monopoly that was just discussed: low supply elasticity of substitutes. And products like your own are the closest substitutes there can be. Entry menaces any monopolizing scheme. In the limit, of which there are apparently few cases, the monopolization of some scarce resource may serve to strangle entry altogether. Entrants hurt a monopoly even when they can be brought into a cartel or bought up and plowed under. It is not just the entry and maintenance of "independents" that is to be feared; it is the arrival of additional productive capacity, even if firms formally allied with you are the ones who bring it into play.

In general, it is dangerous to monopolize a field in which efficient firms are small relative to the market. In that case, first, an entrant knows that its entry alone will not have catastrophic price effects. Second, in the case of cartels, numerous firms increase the need for policing at the same time as they increase the costs of policing. Other things equal, it would help if the market can support only one efficient firm; that is, if the industry is a natural monopoly. A major part of monopolizing would then be to find the most profitable route by which to reach this *natural* destination.

Perhaps the simplest theories about entry into monopolistic markets are the dominant-firm models (see Chapter 4). Other entry theories involve predatory pricing and limit pricing, both of which were discussed in Chapter 9. And, surely, even the theories of pure competition can tell us a lot about entry.

No News Is Good News

It is to be hoped, if not expected, that news of an industry's high monopoly profits will spread slowly, ideally not at all. This could slow entry; and it might help on the legal, political, regulatory, and public relations fronts as well.

Segregated Product Markets

The total demand for a product can often be divided into two or more separate markets that have different demand elasticities. In the limit, it might even be possible to insulate each customer from the rest. All this encourages price discrimination, increasing revenue from each rate of output.[12]

Specialized Inputs

An industry may buy an input the supply of which is upward sloping. Examples include aluminum, steel, oil, and some chemicals industries. By acting as a monopsony, a monopoly of such an industry could increase its profits. It may even be able to divide and deal separately with different markets in which the factor is sold, discriminating monopsonistically in the prices it pays. This reduces the total cost of buying a given amount of the factor, also increasing profit.[13]

A Valuable Product Made at Low Cost

Merely achieving a monopoly is not enough, even if it could be made to last a long time. The object is to achieve a highly profitable monopoly, which calls for demand prices that are high relative to costs. Another way of saying this is that manufacturing and marketing costs, in addition to those strictly monopolizing costs of organizing and policing, should be low, ideally zero. Though it sounds reasonable that the good should have large demand, it helps reduce policing and—possibly—entry problems if efficient firm sizes increase correspondingly. A good that is popular, habit forming, and relatively cheap to make also sounds appealing. Opiates, liquors, tobacco, salt, and pepper come to mind.

Low-Cost Ways to Impose Large Costs on Competitors

A monopoly is fortunate if it can cheaply impose large costs upon entrants or cartel defectors. To work, the costs imposed should also exceed profits to be got from entering or defecting.[14] Legend has it that the Mafia uses such leverage, in part at least because those in illegal trades cannot rely upon law to enforce their contracts or otherwise protect them.

Standardized Products

A standardized product can reduce the cost of cartel policing, because cheating is easier to detect. As nice as product standardization sounds, it is not an overriding objective in itself. Reducing product variety can cost potential profits. Consumers have different tastes and do not like being crammed into the same kinds of shoes, cars, and houses. They will pay more for goods that fit their tastes better. Standardized products can also make it harder to price discriminate, reducing profits as a result.

This list of ten factors is no doubt too short, in the sense that other conditions can probably be found. In some respects, at least, this list is also too long: few real-world monopolies have scored very high on all these counts; and the factors enumerated could be compressed into fewer and broader categories.

THE LIMITS OF MONOPOLY POWER

Take the case of a single-firm monopoly, the only producer of a product for which there are few poor substitutes and no very good one. It faces a demand curve that, for a considerable time, is much less than infinitely elastic over a significant price interval.

Since what people do depends partly upon what they want, we must face the issue of whether firms maximize profits. For profit maximization is both a goal and a constraint on behavior.

Several theories seem to deny that monopolies profit-maximize in general or minimize costs in particular. As Nobel laureate Sir John Hicks put it in 1935,

> It seems not at all unlikely that people in monopolistic positions will very often be people with sharply rising subjective costs; if this is so, they are likely to exploit their advantage much more by not bothering to get very near the position of maximum profit, than by straining themselves to get very close to it. The best of all monopoly profits is a quiet life.[15]

Hicks's theory seems to be that monopolies are more likely to be run by people who value certainty and ease especially highly relative to money. But living the quiet life of a professor in an English university may not have made Hicks an expert on the motivations of tycoons.

A theory by Alchian and Kessel is rather different.[16] They start with the proposition that all monopoly exists by sufferance of the state: government has the force to regulate or eliminate any monopoly. If, as they say, there is a limit to the profits that government will tolerate, a monopoly that exceeds that limit risks ruin. Take the case of a monopoly that has the economic power to earn significantly higher profits than government will tolerate. It would be prohibitively costly for that monopoly to increase money profits beyond government tolerance. If Alchian and Kessel are right, government is not allergic to a monopoly's extracting nonpecuniary returns in lieu of the money profits it must forgo. As a result, they predict, strong monopolies will satisfy strong personal tastes that are too expensive to indulge in competitive industries. Examples include luxurious offices; uncommonly attractive staffs; and age, sex, and racial discrimination.

Much has been written about nonmaximizing theories of management behavior, and what they imply for real behavior and performance. Only the barest introduction to that large literature is possible here;[17] but a few points need to be made. Everybody knows that owners of firms and other properties do not have exactly the same interests as their employees, including hired managers and executives. Both groups want money and other things; and each group is devoted to its own interests, which in some part conflict with the other's. It costs something to keep employees making money for owners instead of feathering their own nests and enjoying themselves. Information is imperfect and costly, and hired team management and production can never produce ideal results. What it can do is to maximize profits within the limits of information and monitoring costs. Such costs are unavoidable unless everyone does everything for himself, an absurd idea that would forgo tremendous economies obtainable from large-scale team management and production.

A defensible working hypothesis, therefore, is that firms do maximize profits in the only sense that matters. If it costs more than a dollar to increase gross profits by one dollar, profits *are* being maximized. In any case, assuming that firms maximize profits generates testable hypotheses, many of which can be confirmed. What nonmaximizing theories can do for us is less clear. In Joan Robinson's words, ''If individuals act in an erratic way only statistical methods will serve to discover the laws of economics, and if individuals act in a predictable way, but from a large number of complicated motives, the economist must resign his task to the psychologist.''[18]

If a monopoly firm seeks maximum profits, what can it do and what can it not do? No monopoly can raise price without limit. It can determine and change the price of its product by choosing its rate of output. Unless it is regulated in perverse ways, a profit-maximizing monopoly will try to minimize costs. It will choose prices to maximize the present value of its future profits. If the firm does not maximize profits, its assets will sell at a discount in the market and—if information is good—an outside enterpriser will buy the firm, making from the monopoly what it is really worth.

If entry is blocked by law, and perhaps even if it is not, the firm will charge more and produce less than equally efficient competition would permit. If entry is not blocked, but the monopoly has a cost advantage, it can charge a price that exceeds its own costs. Whether it can also charge a price that exceeds the costs of potential competitors is an interesting question already discussed in Chapters 7 and 9, and discussed further in Chapter 13, where the so-called welfare trade-offs are analyzed in detail.

The original owner of a successful monopoly can enjoy higher returns on capital than competition would permit. If there is competition in the purchase of firms, however, second owners of the monopoly will earn only the competitive rate of return on what they had to pay to acquire it.

A monopoly benefits by selling customers what they like, but charges more than it costs to provide it. The monopoly will not unnecessarily coerce or alienate customers. Its clerks are not more likely to eat garlic, step on customers' feet, or otherwise be unpleasant. Even inattention, let alone insult and boorishness, imposes costs upon consumers. Rather than imposing on consumers pain-costs (for which it is not paid), a monopoly would do better to extract the money equivalent in the form of money. Even a sadistic or swinish monopolist, if there are any, is well advised to maximize money profits, and to buy what he wants personally with the greater wealth this will provide him.

As noted above, a monopoly is often able to charge (or pay) different prices for the same product—that is, discriminate. Significant price discrimination could not persist in price-taker competition. Rightly or wrongly, therefore, many economists believe that persistent price discrimination is a symptom of monopoly, and that—when it occurs in an unconcentrated industrial structure—it is also a symptom of collusion. Whether price discrimination is in some sense desirable is another matter. There are conditions, for example, in which discrimination increases output, partly removing the curse of monopoly. A special case is one in which some output will be produced when discrimination is permitted, while none will be produced if it is not. Small towns that have one doctor, one icehouse, or one theater are homely examples.

OPEN AND CLOSED MONOPOLY

It is useful to distinguish two different sorts of monopoly. First, a monopoly can be established and protected by law. This is sometimes called closed monopoly, for entry is simply prohibited. It seems to be the original concept of monopoly, and it makes sense: the existence and durability of such monopoly has a clear and reasonable explanation. No one has to imagine how it might have got there and why it endures. The second kind of monopoly is not established or protected by law, and is sometimes called open monopoly. The formation and preservation of such a monopoly has to be explained in other ways than state intervention.

Though it might hurt consumers, open monopoly offers an opportunity to anyone who can put his own resources into niches where profitable monopolies reside. If we believe that monopolies are long-run phenomena, we should ask how they endure. Economic literature nominates several leading candidates, including government closure; a tight control over some severely limited resource; superior efficiency; predatory and other "bad practices"; and poor and costly information.

SUMMARY

Even the sole seller of some commodity may have little or no monopoly power. Monopoly power comes from controlling a distinctive good for which total substitution from other goods is significantly incomplete. This means that no very close substitutes and relatively few poorer ones are being sold by firms not collaborating with the monopoly.

Monopoly requires that two kinds of substitution be relatively incomplete: substitution in demand, and substitution in production. The first depends upon consumer tastes and the characteristics of the goods. The second is determined by the ease and speed with which suppliers can switch over to produce goods brought under monopoly control.

Own- and cross-elasticities of demand and supply are a useful way to conceptualize such problems; but the precision they seem to offer is largely illusory. A fine, bright dividing line between competition and monopoly is hard to define and harder to see, if one exists at all. Monopoly is a question of degree.

Which industries tend to monopoly does not seem to be determined by accident. That specific demand and cost conditions encourage monopoly is consistent with similarities in the patterns of monopolization observable among different countries.

Faced with favorable conditions or not, no monopoly has unlimited powers. Greed itself is one limit to what monopolies (and the rest of us) do. Another is that substitutes tend to grow stronger over time as consumers adjust to the terms that monopoly imposes, and as other producers shift their resources to capture some of the profits that monopoly creates.

Closed monopoly is protected by government; open monopoly is not. Perfect information and zero contract and adjustment costs could presumably prevent, destroy, or reform either type. In that sense, at least, monopoly is an imperfection.

QUESTIONS

1. Define and explain *own-elasticity of demand*. What does it have to do with monopoly?

2. Define and explain *cross-elasticity of demand*. What does it have to do with substitutes? Complements? Unrelated goods? Monopoly?

3. Given certain assumptions, the own-elasticity of total demand for a good is the sum of the cross-elasticities of substitutes for it. Explain.

4. How can we decide whether goods are unique, distinctive, or commonplace?

5. "Low demand elasticity is not enough to give even a sole supplier monopoly power. Supply elasticities also enter the question." Explain.

6. Compare monopoly profits for two industries, in one of which demand elasticities are low at the competitive price and in the other they are significantly higher. (Hint: Assume that the same horizontal cost function applies to both industries, and that cost is the same under competition and single-firm monopoly. Show the competitive equilibrium solution for a relatively steep linear demand function. Draw a much flatter linear demand function that runs through that same price-quantity equilibrium point. Those two *competitive* solutions are now identical. Then derive a marginal revenue for each demand function, and show how single-firm monopoly solutions differ for the two markets.) Explain.

7. What does *profit maximization* really mean? How can you tell whether firms maximize profits?

8. Suppose that monopolies do not maximize profits. Suppose, given equal costs, that they charge *lower* prices than profit-maximizing firms would. Would this kind of monopoly also cause welfare losses?

9. Do you expect a monopoly to treat customers inattentively or callously, as compared with competitive firms? Why?

10. Do you expect monopolies to be less innovative and progressive technologically than competitive firms? Why? Rewrite your answer after you finish this book.

11. Draw simple demand and cost functions for a hypothetical closed monopoly that is highly profitable. That monopoly now sells out for the highest competitive bid. What rate of return do you think the new owners or purchasers will earn?

NOTES

1. For a powerful statement of differences between Marshallian and Chamberlinian market analysis, see George J. Stigler, Lecture 2, in *Five Lectures on Economic Problems* (London: Longman Greens, 1949).

2. *Brown Shoe Co.* v. *United States*, 370 U.S. 294 (1962).

3. Robert Triffin, *Monopolistic Competition and General Equilibrium Theory* (Cambridge, Mass.: Harvard University Press, 1940), p. 89.

4. Robert Bishop, "Elasticities, Cross-Elasticities, and Market Relationships," *American Economic Review*, 62, no. 5 (December 1952), pp. 779–803; and "Reply," *American Economic Review*, 45 (June 1955), pp. 382–86.

5. See Mancur Olson and David McFarland, "The Restoration of Pure Monopoly and the Concept of the Industry," *Quarterly Journal of Economics*, 76 (November 1962), pp. 613–31.

6. Joan Robinson, *The Economics of Imperfect Competition* (London: Macmillan and Co., Limited, 1946).

7. Ibid., p. 18.

8. Edward H. Chamberlin, *The Theory of Monopolistic Competition* (Cambridge, Mass.: Harvard University Press, 1946), Chapter 5.

9. By contrast, Stigler's conclusion is explicit, clean, and consistent. *If* collusion were free and information perfect, firms would collude no matter how numerous they were. George J. Stigler, "A Theory of Oligopoly," *The Organization of Industry* (Homewood, Ill.: Richard D. Irwin, Inc., 1968), pp. 39–40.

10. See *Parker* v. *Brown*, 317 U.S. 341 (1943), and the examples discussed in Chapter 17 and Chapter 18.

11. This may be changing. In 1985, the Supreme Court decided that antitrust immunity can not be bestowed merely by an industry's self-regulation. It requires some unspecified degree of state participation and a "regulatory structure," as when, in the Court's words, "the State as sovereign clearly intends to displace competition in a particular field with a regulatory structure." *Southern Motor Carriers Rate Conference, Inc.* v. *U.S.*, 105 S. Ct. 1721 (1985).

12. For a classical analysis of price discrimination, see Robinson, *Economics of Imperfect Competition*, Chapter 15.

13. See Chapter 6.

14. Examples include cartels requiring members to deposit liquid assets to be forfeited if they breach an agreement; and deferred rebates of the kind found in the *Mogul Steamship* case. *Mogul Steamship Co.* v. *McGregor, Gow & Co.* (1892), App. Cas. 25. See John S. McGee, "Ocean Freight Rate Conferences and the American Merchant Marine," 27 *University of Chicago Law Review*, 2 (Winter 1960), pp. 191–314.

15. J. R. Hicks, "Annual Survey of Economic Theory: The Theory of Monopoly," *Econometrica*, 3 (January 1935), pp. 1–20; reprinted in G. Stigler and K. Boulding, eds.,

Readings in Price Theory (Homewood, Ill.: Richard D. Irwin, Inc., 1952), pp. 361–83, at p. 369.

16. Armen A. Alchian and Reuben A. Kessel, "Competition, Monopoly, and the Pursuit of Pecuniary Gain," in National Bureau of Economic Research, *Aspects of Labor Economics* (Princeton, N.J.: Princeton University Press, 1962), pp. 157–75.

17. Harvey Leibenstein, "Allocative Efficiency v. 'X-Efficiency,' " *American Economic Review*, 56 (June 1966), pp. 392–415; George J. Stigler, "The Xistence of X-Efficiency," *American Economic Review*, 68 (March 1976), pp. 213–16; Michael Jensen and William Meckling, "Theory of the Firm: Managerial Behavior, Agency Costs, and Ownership Structure," *Journal of Financial Economics*, 3 (1978), pp. 305–60; and Kenneth W. Clarkson, "Managerial Behavior in Non-Proprietary Organizations," in *The Economics of Non-Proprietary Organizations*, eds. K. Clarkson and D. L. Martin (Greenwich, Conn.: JAI Press, 1980).

18. Joan Robinson, *The Economics of Imperfect Competition*, p. 6.

MEASURING CONCENTRATION AND MONOPOLY

INTRODUCTION

This chapter shows how economists typically measure industrial concentration and monopoly power, and analyzes whether profits or price-cost margins can reliably locate where a monopoly problem exists, or indicate how much a monopoly reduces our economic welfare. The information provided in this chapter will be a big help when we come to appraise the empirical evidence presented in chapters 14 to 16.

The next section describes product and industry statistics collected in the U.S. by the Bureau of the Census (Census) and, for a few years, by the Federal Trade Commission (FTC), and shows how these data can be used to calculate various concentration ratios and indexes. To reduce their mass for easier review, the following section boils down some of the major theories about how industrial concentration and performance are related. The final section critically analyzes the use of profitability and price-cost indexes as measures of monopoly power.

MEASURING CONCENTRATION

Reasons for Measuring Concentration

Concentration ratios and other measures of industrial structures became popular in industrial organization economics for disparate reasons. At one pole are scientific motives. Economists knew that the physical sciences had made great progress by measuring things and testing hypotheses empirically.

Chapter 4 showed that the first economic theories about market structures came on the scene more than one hundred fifty years ago, long before there were many data to measure structure. Much later, theoretical works of Chamberlin (1933), Robinson (1933) and Lerner (1934) hypothesized that market structure affects market performance.[1] And in 1932 Berle and Means asserted that real market structures were changing fast: "The principles of duopoly have become more important than those of free competition."[2] The National Resources Committee's *Structure of the American Economy* (1939) seems to be the earliest published compilation of concentration ratios for the panoply of Census industries. Later statistical (or quasi-statistical) works confirmed that atomistic industry structures are not ubiquitous. Although this was not a novel revelation—classical and neoclassical economists knew that long before—here were lots of *numbers*, some of which looked frightening.

And, even though they lacked convincing evidence that some relevant kind of concentration was increasing rapidly, it is not surprising that economists should wonder whether differences in market structure make any difference. Once data became available in wholesale lots, economists made the most of them.

Some other reasons for the interest in figures on industrial concentration are less scientific. Although many economists, including famous and fine ones, had always been interested in public policy problems, the 1930s offered especially good growing conditions for all stripes and colors of critics and reformers. Many said that the economic system had broken down, owing to monetary collapse, or monopoly and price rigidity, or both. G. C. Means claimed that professional corporate managers had concentrated so much power into relatively few hands that the worth and legitimacy of private property were not what they used to be; and that the price rigidity that resulted had caused or prolonged the depression.[3] No longer, critics said, did the economy work as traditional economics said it should. Many believed that competition had given way to monopoly, oligopoly, and imperfect competition, all of which were closely related to something called concentration.

In the 1930s, it seems, relatively few claimed that the economy was doing just fine. Consider two of the policy alternatives that were being discussed. At one end were those who would scrap the private-property market system in favor of a state-controlled economy. Toward the other end were those who wanted "merely" to change the structure of banking and other industries.

Extremists wanted to tear down the property and market system altogether, and were happy to include economic concentration among their reasons for doing so. Some defenders of private property and individual freedom, including Henry Simons, wanted both 100 percent reserve banking and legal limits on industrial concentration.[4]

Aggregate Concentration

In the 1930s, Berle and Means popularized what is now called aggregate concentration or macroconcentration. It measures the relative size of absolutely large firms, economy-wide and irrespective of industry, and has nothing obvious to do with competition in markets for individual products or in individual industries as economists understand them. For the

TABLE 11–1 Percentage of manufacturing value added originating in the 100 largest firms

Year	Percent
1947	23
1958	30
1963	33
1967	33
1972	33
1977	33
1982	33

whole U.S., aggregate concentration measures such things as the percentage of value added originating in or the total corporate assets owned by the largest 100, 200, or some other number of firms. Manufacturing value added is one of the five measures of aggregate concentration that Weiss used in a 1983 article on this subject.[5] Table 11-1 shows percentages of total value added by the 100 largest manufacturing firms during a 35-year period, 1947 to 1982.

It is questionable whether aggregate concentration is useful to predict or explain much of anything, and probably most economists in the mainstream today are skeptical about it.[6] Though many economists doubt that this index means much one way or another for monopoly studies, it has changed little in twenty years or more.

Manufacturing Products and Industries

By contrast with the doubtful case for measuring aggregate concentration, there is a good deal of systematic theory about concentration in markets and industries—so-called microconcentration.[7] To study that subject empirically, however, we need to define markets and industries and devise ways to measure differences in the business structures we find in them.[8] There are several ways to do both things.

Most empirical work on concentration is about the manufacturing sector of the U.S. economy. In the 1982 census, manufacturing accounted for about 21 percent of Gross Domestic Product, more than any other single sector, though its share has been declining steadily.[9] Since 1899, manufacturing has been defined to exclude ''hand industries,'' and includes plants or factories (''establishments'') that use power-driven machinery or equipment. Very small establishments are not covered, a more serious problem in some industries than others. Retail bakeries, cotton gins, and the building of structures or fixed equipment are excluded from manufacturing. Logging, printing, and dairies are included.

Manufacturing censuses have been made at varying intervals, and with increasing detail. Starting with 1967, censuses have been made every five years (in years ending in 2 and 7). Considerable time elapses before the data are processed and published. Broad summaries of data from the 1982 census, for example, began to be published in 1986.[10] There have also been annual sample surveys for most years since 1949.

Data gathered in these censuses are classified following definitions set down in the Standard Industrial Classification (SIC), devised by the Bureau of the Budget and used by many government agencies to collect and organize general-purpose data. It is interesting that those who administer tariffs developed a different classification system.

The Census classification scheme is mechanically similar to the Dewey Decimal library-book system: the fewer the digits a category has, the broader it is. The broadest categories in the Census system are 20 two-digit Major Industry Groups (20 through 39), as listed in Table 11-2. These groups differ greatly in size. In 1982, the value added by group 35, nonelectrical machinery, was $102.3 billion. Value added by group 31, leather and leather products, was $4.8 billion, less than one-twentieth as large.[11]

Included in each two-digit Major Industry Group are one or more four-digit manufacturing industries (in 1982 there were a total of 450). To make principles more concrete, examine group 25 more closely. Furniture and Fixtures includes the six four-digit *household*-furniture industries enumerated in Table 11-3, plus two four-digit *office*-furniture industries, one for steel furniture and one for wood.For example, industry 2511 includes "wood furniture commonly used in dwellings," "wood kitchen cabinets produced on a factory basis," and "camp furniture."

Each four-digit industry includes one or more five-digit "product classes." These are the primary product classes used to define each industry. (In 1982 there were 1,500 of them altogether.) Concentration ratios for product classes were first prepared in 1954. Industry 2511, "Wood Furniture," for example, includes six five-digit product classes, as shown in Table 11-4. One of them is 25112, "Wood Living Room, Library, Family Room, and Den Furniture;" another is "Infants' and Children's Wood Furniture." Here, wood furniture has been differentiated and split according to the part of a house in which it is most likely to be used, and the age of people for whom it is designed. It seems reasonable that firms producing furniture classified into one of these definitions should be able to

TABLE 11–2 Two-digit major industry groups

20.	Food and Kindred Products
21.	Tobacco Manufactures
22.	Textile Mill Products
23.	Apparel and Other Fabricated Textile Products
24.	Lumber and Wood Products, Except Furniture
25.	Furniture and Fixtures
26.	Paper and Allied Products
27.	Printing and Publishing
28.	Chemicals and Allied Products
29.	Petroleum and Coal Products
30.	Rubber and Misc. Plastics Products
31.	Leather and Leather Products
32.	Stone, Clay, and Glass Products
33.	Primary Metal Industries
34.	Fabricated Metal Products
35.	Machinery (Except Electrical)
36.	Electrical and Electronic Equipment
37.	Transportation Equipment
38.	Instruments and Related Products
39.	Miscellaneous Manufactures

TABLE 11–3   Four-digit industries

2511	Wood Household Furniture, Excluding Upholstered
2512	Upholstered Household Furniture
2514	Metal Household Furniture
2515	Mattresses and Bedsprings (Including Folding and Dual Purpose Beds)
2517	Wood TV and Radio Cabinets
2519	Household Furniture, n.e.c.

produce other classes of furniture if the price were right. It also seems plausible that consumers will be willing to switch among some of these classes if their relative prices change much.

Suppose, as is typical, that an establishment produces several different "product classes." It ships more of product class 25113 than any other, though perhaps not by much. In that case all of the establishment's output will be classified into industry 2511, Wood Household Furniture, even though it may also make a good deal of office furniture, or other products that are not furniture at all.

Each product class includes one or more seven-digit products. (In 1982 there were about 11,000 of them altogether.) Product class 25113, just referred to, includes six seven-digit products, listed in Table 11-5. The perils of ignoring substitution are even more apparent here.

This review of the furniture classifications demonstrates one thing at least: neither substitution in demand nor substitution in supply has been decisive in defining these products and industries.[12] It is clear that Census classifications differ significantly from the economic concepts of products, industries, and markets. The principles of Census classification have been to group together things that are (1) technologically similar (for example, Electrical Measuring Instruments and Test Equipment); or (2) similar in function (House Slippers); or (3) made with similar inputs (Miscellaneous Fabricated Wire Products); or (4) produced with similar processes (Electroplating and Polishing).[13]

Each industry is defined to include certain primary product classes and products; and, for the most part, all of each product is defined to be primary to one industry. In both the economic sense and, to much lesser degree, the SIC sense, however, some products are primary to more than one industry.

In some cases, what economists would consider identical products are separately designated and classified. For example, industry 3315 is ferrous wire produced by firms that *buy* rods and bars and draw them into wire. Industry 3312 includes wire drawn from

TABLE 11–4   Wood household furniture "product classes"

25112	Wood Living Room, Library, Family Room and Den Furniture
25113	Wood Dining Room and Kitchen Furniture (Except Cabinets)
25115	Wood Bedroom Furniture
25116	Infants' and Children's Wood Furniture
25117	Wood Outdoor Furniture and Unassembled Wood Furniture
25110	Unspecified Kinds of Wood Household Furn.

TABLE 11–5   Wood household furniture "products"

2511311	Dining Tables, 30-in. × 40-in. and Larger
2511331	Dining Chairs
2511351	Buffets and Servers, Dining Room
2511371	China and Corner Cabinets, Dining Room
2511398	Other Dining and Kitchen Furn. (incl. Breakfast Sets, Jr. Dining, Chairs, Stools, Tables Not Sold as a Set)
2511300	Unspecified Kinds of Wood D.R. and Kitchen Furniture (Except Cabinets)

rods and bars that were made in the same establishment. But in both cases we are dealing with ferrous wire. Other products primary to more than one industry are prepared meats, which are common to both 2011, Meat Packing Plants, and to 2013, Prepared Meat Products; knit apparel; laminated glass; fertilizer; and lubricating oils. Census treats beet and cane sugar as different products and different industries.[14]

So much for the scheme of classification. What is put into it? The reporting unit is the "establishment," which for manufacturing means a plant, mill, or factory that has one physical location and one payroll. Establishments included in the census must turn in a variety of data, including values of products shipped, (sometimes) value added, employment, and power consumption. Minimum employment and other cut-off standards for inclusion in the census have varied over time.

However heterogeneous they may be, the total value of *all* products shipped from each establishment is classified into only one industry. Usually, each product is primary to only one industry, the notion being that each industry should be defined by a list of products that are "primary" to it. Assume, as is usually true, that an establishment produces several products. That product with the *largest* dollar value (not necessarily as much as 50 percent) determines the industry into which all of that establishment's shipments will be classified. Census has used a "resistance factor" to keep establishments from shifting from one industry to another between censuses unless the changes are large.[15] Even so, the shifts have been substantial. In general, the larger establishments shifted most.

Because an establishment typically produces more than one product, some products get counted into an industry's totals even though they are not primary to that industry and therefore do not formally belong to that industry's definition. And some products that actually are primary to one industry will get counted in another industry's totals. Although prepared from 1958 census data, Table 11-6 is still an excellent illustration of what this problem involves. For computing the *industry* concentration ratio for industry 3452, the denominator was 880. For computing *product* concentration ratios, the denominator was 860. The specialization ratio omits miscellaneous receipts and is approximately the proportion of total industry shipments made up of primary products, that is, 755/827 = .91. The coverage ratio is the proportion of total shipments of primary products made by establishments that are classified in the industry itself, that is, 755/860 = .88.

The coverage and specialization ratios in this example are approximately typical for 1958. One objective of the classification system has been to keep specialization ratios above 80 percent, and coverage ratios above 70 percent, if possible.[16] There are famous

TABLE 11–6 Coverage and specialization (millions of dollars)

	Shipments by Establishments Classified in Industry 3452 (Bolts, Nuts, Washers, Etc.)	Shipments by Establishments Classified in Other Industries Than 3452	Total Shipments All Sources
1. Industry 3452:			
Primary Products	755	105	860
Product Class.:			
34521—Bolts, Nuts, and Other Standard Fasteners	574	96	670
34522—Special Industrial Fasteners	171	8	179
34520—Industrial Fasteners	10	1	11
SUBTOTAL	(755)		
2. Other Secondary Products (Not Included in 3452)	72		
3. Miscellaneous Receipts (Contract Work, Repair Work, Sales of Scrap, Resale, Etc.)	54		
TOTAL SHIPMENT	880		

Source: Example from 1958 Census (1962 Senate Report).

instances in which that objective was not reached. For example, Conklin and Goldstein noted that, in an earlier census,

> . . . only 54 per cent of the total production of suspenders and garters is accounted for by establishments in the suspenders and garters industry, the remaining 46 per cent being made as secondary products by establishments in other industries. . . . And although the beehive coke oven industry produces nothing but coke products, its coke production represents only 9 per cent of the total coke output.[17]

In census year 1982, the coverage ratio for industry 3452, discussed earlier, had risen to .95; specialization, to .93. In other words, only 5 percent of the products defined as primary to industry 3452 were produced by establishments classified into other industries. Recent censuses may have increased coverage ratios on average. But there were relatively low coverage ratios for four-digit industries such as flour and other grain mill products (.70); cotton weaving mills (.54); men's and boys' underwear (.37); lubricating oils and greases (.46); steel wire (.44); cold finishing of steel shapes (.32); steel pipe and tube (.47); primary, and secondary, nonferrous metals (.50, .31); and so on.

Measuring Industry Concentration

Market shares of the largest firms have been calculated both for industries and commodities, at the seven-digit, five-digit, and four-digit (product-group) level of detail. When computed on a commodity basis, denominators of the concentration ratios include the values of all (primary) products irrespective of the ''industry'' in which they were made.

Concentration ratios are the most popular measure of industrial structure. They are typically used to show what percentage of a Census industry's shipments the largest four firms account for.[18] Concentration ratios measure structure at only one point in a size-distribution. Figure 11-1 shows that industries having the same four-firm concentration ratio (CR_4) can have very different structures otherwise. Some structural theories, including Cournot's, say that they would behave differently.

Concentration ratios can be computed and used the other way around: how many firms account for some specific share of the industry output? For example, suppose we think that a cartel must have at least 80 percent of industry output to produce a significantly monopolistic effect. Suppose we also believe that no more than four firms can collude effectively, given the restrictions imposed by hostile antitrust law. Then, presumably, we would like to know which industries have four-firm CRs greater than 80 percent.

H—the Herfindahl (or Hirschman) index has become a popular measure of industrial concentration.[19] For years, people calculated the index as the sum of the squares of individual firms' market shares *expressed as decimal fractions*. So calculated, the index could take on values from 0 to 1. Later, presumably to expand the scale for fine-tuning, as

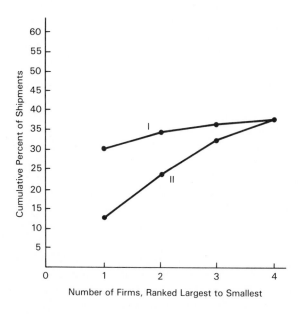

Figure 11-1 Two Concentration Curves with the Same CR_4

with the spread-band on a shortwave radio receiver, the Federal Trade Commission (FTC) and others summed the squares of shares expressed as percentages: .15 became 15. In this new version of the H index, values can range from 0 to 10,000. This puts 10,000 times as many measuring lines on the tuning dial, without at all increasing the precision of the data used.

To compute a "full" Herfindahl index, we need shares for all firms in the industry. A "truncated" Herfindahl ignores smaller firms and uses only the shares of the largest, say, 50 firms. Since small firms add little to the index, a truncated index can closely approximate the full index without requiring nearly so many data and computations. Ralph Nelson, for example, computed a concentration ratio for each industry using shares of the largest 50 firms, and the 1982 Census of Manufactures, for the first time, publishes 50-firm indexes for many four-digit industries.[20]

The original definition of H gave a single-firm monopoly an index value of 1.0; and an industry of five equal-sized firms an index of .2. Since the reciprocal of 1 is $1/1 = 1$; and the reciprocal of .2 is $1/.2 = 5$, the reciprocal of the original version of H has been used as a number-of-firms equivalent.[21]

In the new version, the share of a firm having 20 percent of a market is written as 20, which is then squared and added to squared shares of the other firms. H for an industry of five equal sized firms is 5 times $20^2 = 2,000$. The new-version Herfindahl index is 10,000 times as big as the old. To get the number-equivalent from the *new* version, divide the new index value by 10,000, then take the reciprocal of that number.

What, if anything, is wrong with these industry classifications and concentration measures depends upon what we use them for. In particular, there are big problems if we use them to analyze monopoly and competition. Though it is debatable whether even *ideal* concentration measures could adequately deal with those issues, *these* measures are a long way from ideal. Product definitions are often too narrow, judged by both supply and demand substitutability. Some industries may be too broad. There are also the problems of coverage and specialization referred to earlier.

Another problem arises because exports go into the shipment data while imports do not. As a result, if some large firms are relatively large exporters, their relative position in the domestic industry is overstated arithmetically.[22] For the many U.S. industries that face significant import competition (tin, steel, newsprint, whiskey, cameras, radios, stereos, TVs, cars, watches, computers, tools, etc.), market shares and concentration ratios computed from Census data use too small a denominator and are therefore overstated.

When, as is often the case, we want to compare concentration over time, (as from one Census to another), a subtle bias intrudes. Some of the industry definitions change— especially for those industries that are growing a lot or otherwise experiencing great change. Usually, therefore, economists who make such comparisons use only industries whose definitions have not changed much between the dates being compared. In general, those are the industries that have been shaken least by market forces. The definitions of only 146 out of 439 industries remained the same between 1947 and 1972. It appears that average concentration increased for this group of 146 over the 25 years. More than one-half of the industries that were in the most concentrated one-fourth of all industries in 1972 did not even exist as independent industry classifications in 1947. Comparing the

439 categories for which a CR exists for both 1947 and 1972, CR fell on average. This is consistent with other evidence supporting the hypothesis that concentration behaves differently accordingly as industries change much or little.[23]

Analyses that correlate or otherwise show relationships between profit rates and concentration ratios are very popular. It is common, for example, to determine statistically whether and to what degree differences in industry concentration "explain" differences in industry profitability. This drags in another problem in addition to the conceptual and measurement problems that beset the profits figures themselves. First, profit data apply to firms, not establishments.[24] But the census industry and concentration data are based on establishments. Second, profit data are available from the Internal Revenue Service, but at the two-digit and three-digit level of detail. This means either that the profit data must be converted into a four-digit framework, or that the concentration data must be converted into a two- or three-digit framework. If the leading four companies in the industries being combined are not identical (and they rarely are), this procedure "will invariably produce a figure that exaggerates the true 3- or 2-digit concentration figures."[25]

In computing an industry concentration ratio, Census defines a company to be a legal entity owning one or more establishments classified into that industry. But a real company typically operates in, and is therefore counted in, several industry classifications. A company is counted as operating in an industry if it owns one or more establishments that are classified into that industry. The company's size (and ultimately rank) in a Census industry is measured by the value of all products shipped by its establishments in that industry. Neither the top plants nor the top companies are necessarily the same from year to year.

Furthermore, there are no coverage or specialization ratios for *companies*. The value of shipments by the larger companies may be overstated or understated. Indeed, there is no assurance even that the "largest-four" actually do "account for the largest shipments of primary products classified in an industry category."[26] For the company figures cannot be adjusted for plant diversification. Different degrees of vertical integration also matter. A vertically integrated firm reports transfers like nonintegrated firms do. Its shipments can get counted two or more times. Vertically integrated firms are overweighted (except, possibly, with the more refined value-added measures).

Although it is ridiculous to demand perfect data before doing any empirical work, the Census data deficiencies detailed here are serious. They greatly reduce, if they do not destroy, the value of these data for analyzing monopoly and competition. As the Census itself put it years ago, the data classifications were

> . . . developed over a period of years to serve the general purposes of the census and other governmental statistics . . . the classifications were not designed to establish categories necessarily denoting coherent or relevant markets in the true competitive sense, or to provide a basis for measuring monopoly power.[27]

Despite this disclaimer by the agency that collects the data and computes the concentration ratios, economists have used these numbers to do just what Census warned against. Indeed, they have used them for little else.

E. H. Chamberlin's *Theory of Monopolistic Competition* went about as far as one could in claiming that even firms in the same retail trade offer products so distinct that each has significant monopoly power. Even so, Chamberlin criticized the artificiality of Census categories. As he put it,

> "Industry" or "commodity" boundaries are a snare and a delusion—in the highest degree arbitrarily drawn, establishing at once wholly false implications both as to competition of substitutes within their limits, which supposedly stops at their borders, and as to the possibility of ruling on the presence or absence of oligopolistic forces by the simple device of counting the number of producers included.[28]

To remedy some of the conceptual and data deficiencies discussed here, the FTC collected so-called Line-of-Business data starting with the year 1974, and for a few years after. Unfortunately, these data have special deficiencies of their own. The object was to collect and analyze accounting data and shipments for each of some 275 lines of business. According to Weiss, "An LB generally corresponds to one or a few related four-digit products as defined by the census. The Line of Business survey also collected the value of shipments for each five-digit product of a surveyed firm."[29] One objective was to attribute costs, revenues, and "profits" to specific products. To do that, they had to allocate joint and common costs, which can only be done arbitrarily. Although a number of studies used them, these data are no longer being collected.[30] In 1985, George J. Benston published an important article about them.[31]

Having dealt with some of the basic classifications and data, we turn now to various measures of concentration that have been confected from them. (We will return to the "profit" data at a later point.)

Sometimes concentration measures for individual industries are weighted, then averaged, to estimate overall concentration. The kinds of weights chosen can affect the averages significantly. Furthermore, it is well to recognize that weighted-average concentration is determined by concentration as measured in each industry and by the relative importance (weight) of individual industries. Measured over time, average concentration can rise even though concentration in every single industry is going down (because industries of above-average concentration are growing faster); and conversely. The same phenomenon occurs in comparing overall growth rates for the U.S. and the Soviet Union.

Table 11-7 traces average four-firm concentration for Census industries, weighted by value added, for the period 1947 to 1972.[32] Weighted-average concentration ratios

TABLE 11–7   Weighted-average four-firm concentration ratios

Year	Average CR_4
1947	35.3
1954	36.9
1958	37.0
1963	38.9
1966	39.0
1972	39.2

have not yet been published for the 1982 Census, but the unweighted average is about 38.[33]

Table 11-8 shows 1982 concentration ratios (CR_4) for 38 four-digit industries and 50-firm Herfindahl indexes (H50) for 37 of them. This sample is neither random nor scientific. For example, its average CR_4 is about 46, about 8 percentage points higher than

TABLE 11–8 Concentration in selected four-digit industries: 1982 census

Industry	CR_4	H50	HNE
Meat Packing	29	325	31
Canned Fruit and Vegetables	21	214	47
Frozen Fruit and Vegetables	27	306	33
Cereal Breakfast Foods	86	NA	NA
Malt Beverages	77	2,089	5
Dist. Liquor (Except Brandy)	46	741	14
Weaving Mills, Cotton	41	645	16
Narrow Fabric Mills	20	209	48
Tire Cord and Fabric	81	2,584	4
Women's and Misses Dresses	6	24	417
Wood Household Furniture	16	106	94
Folding Paperboard Boxes	22	212	47
Set-Up Paperboard Boxes	15	132	76
Book Publishing	17	190	53
Greeting Card Publishing	84	2,840	4
Pharmaceuticals	26	318	31
Soap and Detergent	60	1,306	8
Toilet Preparations	34	469	21
Petroleum Refining	28	380	26
Tires and Tubes	66	1,591	6
Men's Footwear (Except Athletic)	28	378	26
Women's Footwear (Except Athletic)	38	492	20
Flat Glass	85	2,032	5
Glass Containers	50	966	10
Cement, Hydraulic	31	469	21
Vitreous Plumbing Fixtures	63	1,360	7
Gypsum Products	76	1,993	5
Blast Furnace and Steel Mills	42	650	15
Primary Aluminum	64	1,704	6
Metal Cans	50	790	13
Bolts, Nuts, Rivets, Washers	13	102	98
Turbines & Turbine Generator Sets	84	2,602	4
Oil Field Machinery	27	315	32
Elec. Computing Equipment	43	793	13
Household Refrigerators and Freezers	94	2,745	4
Radio and TV Sets	49	751	13
Semi-Conductors and Related Devices	40	597	17
Burial Caskets	52	1,247	8

Source: U.S. Bureau of the Census, *1982 Census of Manufactures, Concentration Ratios in Manufacturing* (Washington, D.C.: April 1986).

the average for all industries in 1982. HNE is the Herfindahl number-equivalent, got by taking the reciprocal of H divided by 10,000: HNE $= 1 / (H / 10,000)$.

There are even more measures of industrial concentration than have been mentioned here. Is there any reason to prefer one over the others? Perhaps a choice should depend upon more than esthetic considerations. It sounds rational to choose the measure that best explains or predicts something that matters. We can significantly change the level of measured concentration merely by how we measure firm size.[34] Using after-tax income, for example, usually gives the highest weighted average; sales, the lowest. We can also significantly change the level of measured concentration by classifying industries as national, regional, or local.[35]

H is appealing partly because it throws out less information; but that wouldn't matter if what it keeps does not matter. For a long time, economists used whatever indexes were easiest to get and rationalized the choice by saying that one was about as good as another, since they were all reasonably highly correlated. Stigler noted that the correlation of three-firm and four-firm ratios was spurious: the correlation between CR_3 and the share of the fourth-largest firm is not very good. Stigler was the first systematically to link the measurement of concentration to a theory of concentration. According to Stigler's oligopoly theory, the relevant explanatory variables include the number of sellers *and* the number of buyers. For either, he argues, the Herfindahl index—with its implication of number-equivalence—seems a reasonable choice.[36]

THEORIES ABOUT CONCENTRATION AND PERFORMANCE

Many economists claim that industrial concentration and performance are clearly related in theory. If that is so, we should be able to find some empirical relationship between them. To do it, we need measures both of concentration and performance.

In some classical theories of oligopoly, the number of firms, rather than a concentration ratio, occupies center stage. But concentration and the number of firms are related. In Cournot, for example, for given costs and demand, the absolute level of price, the height of price relative to marginal costs, and dead-weight loss all increase as the *number* of firms falls. And since firms are assumed to be identical, these measures of bad effects would also be related to at least some measures of concentration (to CR_4, when there are four or more firms; to the number of firms accounting for 80 percent; or to H, for example).

In Bertrand and Edgeworth, performance improves as we go from one firm to two, then remains constant.

For collusion theories, including Stigler's, the relevant index is sometimes asserted to be something like H, or the number of firms accounting for 70 percent or 80 percent of sales. Performance is supposed to improve rapidly as concentration falls from a high starting level. For example, performance improves dramatically as we go from one firm to two. Put in another way, only when concentration is very high do such theories posit much difference from competitive results.

Demsetz and Day seem to say that, if we have institutions that permit access to markets, the only numbers that are relevant are the costs of transactions and enough (perhaps two) noncolluding firms seeking, or interested in, access. And these numbers have little or nothing to do with concentration as it is commonly measured in industrial organization.

Note that *aggregate* concentration is not represented by any sort of systematic economic theory, or—even—any clear theory about politics.

Thus may we summarize some of the main theories from which economists inferred that the study of concentration might prove useful. But, in McGee's words,

> . . . there is still no coherent and consistent theory of oligopoly. There are many conflicting theories of oligopoly, and predicted behavior depends crucially upon the types of assumptions made * * * Depending upon which theory one chooses, increasing the number of firms may *increase* prices (even above the single firm monopoly level), may lower prices, or may leave prices unchanged.[37]

And, as Harold Demsetz bluntly put it, "We have no theory that allows us to deduce from the observable degree of concentration in a particular market whether or not price and output are competitive."[38]

MEASURING MONOPOLY EFFECTS

Profits: Some Conceptual and Measurement Problems

It is dangerous to use profits to locate monopoly, to assess its severity, or to demonstrate that concentration is a proxy for any welfare loss properly attributable to monopoly. Some of the problems are conceptual; some are mechanical or statistical.

First, there is a considerable gap between economic profit and the accounting "profits" that are the raw stuff with which such studies commence.[39] One obvious difference is that economic profit is *net* of the opportunity costs of capital and other factors owned by the firm; simple accounting profit is not. To make sensible monopoly diagnoses, accounting profits must, at the very least, somehow be adjusted by deducting a normal rate of return in comparable alternative employments. "Comparable employments" suggests that something ought to be done about risk; but it is extremely difficult to do. The amount of adjustment needed varies amongst industries and firms. Riskier undertakings need higher accounting profits to be equally attractive as less risky ones. *Expected* riskiness, the risk perceived going in, is what we really want to know, and it is not clear how to estimate it. For it may not be related to the recorded history of fluctuations, failures, and so on. It is risky to walk across Niagara Falls on a wire no matter whether anyone engaged in that business has ever fallen.[40] Accounting profits do not accurately correct for price level changes. The average age, durability, and kinds of assets differ among firms and industries. Price level changes therefore affect their true profitability differently.

In addition, "profit" data are collected on a company-wide basis, whereas monopoly is a *product* question, not a company-wide question. If a company is diversified, concentration measured for *product* classes is being compared with company "profitability" measured over all the stuff it produces. Below-cost sales of government-financed plant and equipment have not been made uniformly amongst industries.[41] Firm and industry profits are sensitive to the time period over which they are averaged.[42]

But even after suitable profit adjustments are made, other problems remain. For monopoly is neither a necessary nor sufficient condition for either economic or accounting profits. Large inframarginal rents have been earned in atomistic industries. And, even in atomistic and other thoroughly competitive industries, getting back to full long-run equilibrium can take a long time. Monopoly is not a sufficient condition for profits, either. Even well-managed monopoly may lose money or barely cover costs. The valuation of assets is also crucial. Even if two single-firm monopolies face identical demand curves and have identical marginal cost functions, differences in fixed costs cause profit rates to differ. In Figure 11-2, AC_1 is the average cost function of a single-firm monopolist. Profits are zero. If average cost were AC_2, profits would be *Pcab*, per unit time.

Similarly, two single-firm monopolies with identical cost functions can earn different profit rates because they face different demand functions. Not all monopolies are profitable; not all atomistic industries are not. Thus it is dangerous to identify or rank monopolies by accounting profit rates. Even when the data are refined, the symptoms are ambiguous.

In any case, the whole diagnostic procedure is wrong-minded, which can be more serious than whether the laboratory tests are done right. The economic objection to monopoly has nothing to do with profits, anyway. A necessary (but not sufficient) condition for traditional monopoly resource misallocation is that price significantly and persistently exceeds *marginal cost*; and, it is sometimes asserted, the amount of loss from monopoly is related to the amount of that discrepancy.[43] Even when there really is a welfare loss, this measure confuses a *cause* with the measure of effects, which is a serious confusion. The

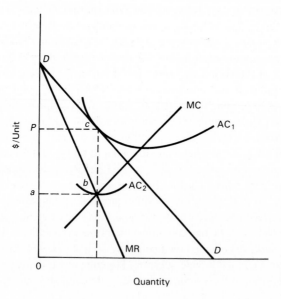

Figure 11-2 Profits Depend on Fixed Costs

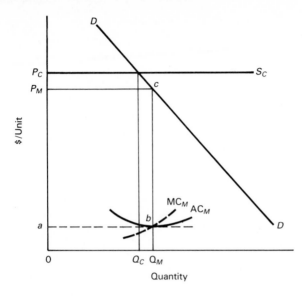

Figure 11-3 Monopoly Price May Be Lower Than Competitive Price

proximate cause of an accident may be that a bus hit a tree; but this does not measure the loss from the accident: the bus may be empty or full; the alternative may have been to hit a train, or to go over a cliff, and so on.

What is more, price-marginal cost discrepancies are *not* sufficient conditions for welfare loss. Far from it: they are consistent with net welfare *gains*. Much depends upon how costs and product qualities affect and are affected by industrial structure or regulation. Figure 11-3 shows what can happen if costs and concentration are related. *DD* is an industry demand curve. If the industry were forced to become atomistic, S_C would be the supply function, and P_C the price. MC_M and AC_M are the marginal and average cost functions. P_M is the resulting price, Q_M the quantity sold per unit time. Under atomism, and with price P_C, there are zero profits. With what passes for monopoly, profits are enormous: *Pmabc*. Yet, as Figure 11-3 shows, consumers and producers are better off with monopoly than with atomism. In such a case, it would be strange to argue for atomism because concentration produces high profits. But this is precisely what believers in structural theories of economic performance often argue.[44]

Indexes of Monopoly Power

Even in principle, monopoly-power indexes—such as Lerner's $(P - MC) / P$—cannot reliably measure the severity of monopoly effects. Several illustrations show why. Each comparison involves two profit-maximizing single-firm monopolies that have identical marginal costs but different demand functions.

In Figure 11-4, monopoly 1 faces demand D_1; monopoly 2 faces D_2. At each price, the elasticity of D_1 is equal to that of D_2. Both firms have the same marginal cost. Both charge the same price. Both have the same Lerner monopoly index: $(P_1 - MC_1) / P_1 =$

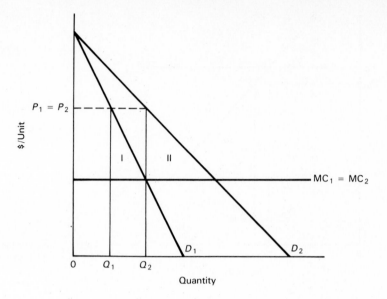

Figure 11-4   Different Dead-Weight Loss, Same Lerner Index

$(P_2 - MC_2) / P_2$. But monopoly 2 is much more serious, if both last the same amount of time: its dead-weight loss (as measured by area II) is double that of area I. It is true in this case that an absolutely larger profit (assuming equal risk), but not the profit *rate* (if assets are proportional with output rate), is associated with the larger allocation loss. Any satisfaction this affords is premature. Note Figure 11-5.

Monopolists 1 and 2 set the same price (D_1 and D_2 have the same elasticity and marginal revenue for $P_1 = P_2$). Their Lerner indexes are identical. Even their absolute profits are identical (if risks are). But their dead-weight loss differs: it will equal area I for monopoly 1, and areas I and II for monopoly 2.

If that is not enough, note Figure 11-6. Monopolies 1 and 2 charge the same price, earn the same absolute profit (at equal risk), and have the same Lerner index. Their dead-weight effects again differ; but their ranking has shifted: the dead-weight effect for monopoly 2 is now only area I; that for monopoly 1 is area I and area II.

Figure 11-7(a) shows the relevant functions for one single-firm monopoly; 11-7(b) shows them for another. Quantities demanded in 11-7(b) fall to zero at twice the price at which those in 11-7(a) fall to zero; and, at each output rate, the value of marginal cost for 11-7(b) is twice as high as for 11-7(a). At zero price, the quantity of B demanded is twice that of A. At their respective wealth-maximizing outputs, therefore, $P_B = 2P_A$, and $MC_B = 2MC_A$. Thus the Lerner index of monopoly power is the same for both industries. If investments are proportional to outputs, the rate of return is much higher in B, which makes the profit index seem a better diagnostic tool than the Lerner index in this case. We will return to this question shortly. Unfortunately, however, the dead-weight losses (as measured by areas A and B) are *not* equal. The Lerner index misleads again.

Figures 11-4 through 11-7 have shown how two different industries with *equal*

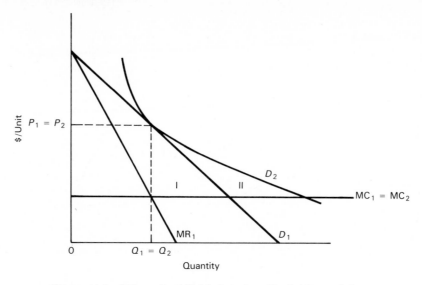

Figure 11-5 Different Dead-Weight Loss from Identical Lerner Indexes

Lerner indexes can generate very different economic welfare. All but the last of the comparisons (Figure 11-7) also show how equal profit rates are compatible with greatly unequal monopoly effects. Figure 11-2 shows one way in which identical monopoly effects are compatible with greatly different profit rates, depending upon asset valuation. Figure

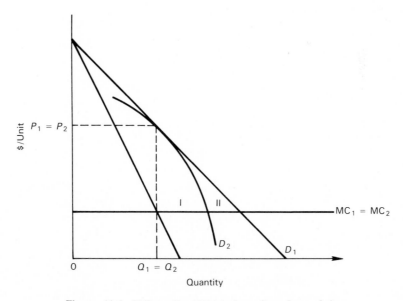

Figure 11-6 Different Dead-Weight Loss, Same Lerner Index

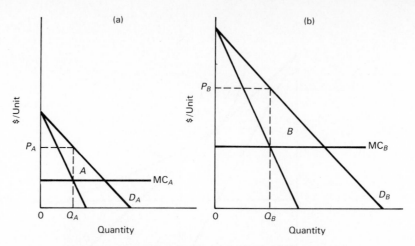

Figure 11-7   Different Dead-Weight Losses, Same Lerner Index

11-3 shows a case in which, because concentration is more efficient, high profits and a high Lerner index are clearly better than a zero profit rate and a zero Lerner index.

Figure 11-8 reveals other troublesome problems. In 11-8(a) a single-firm monopoly produces at literally zero costs. Very low investment and marginal cost will yield much the same results. 11-8(b) shows cost and revenue functions for another single-firm monopoly. The Lerner index for monopoly A equals 1, the highest possible. With literally zero investment, it has the highest conceivable profit rate. Suitably low nonzero invest-

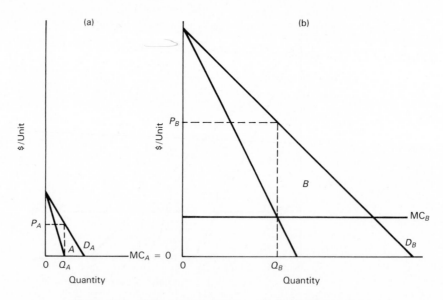

Figure 11-8   Higher Dead-Weight Loss with a Lower Lerner Index

ments can make the rate of return as high as one pleases. Monopoly *B* has a lower Lerner index, and a profit rate that can be much lower than *A*, depending upon the investment levels assumed. Yet monopoly *B* has a much worse monopoly effect.

All of this leaves the Lerner index in tatters, and profit tests gravely wounded.[45] We can now complete the job on profits.

Monopoly welfare loss is related to the product of monopolistic output reduction and price enhancement, profitable or not. Profits, on the other hand, arise because total revenues exceed *total* costs. They reflect a discrepancy between average cost and price. Even in the context of the misleading price-cost index approach just analyzed, profits would be a useful clue to the *existence* of monopoly if and only if marginal cost and average cost are equal. Since there is no reason to suppose that they are always equal, the profit rate is not a dependable substitute for the monopoly index. And, as we will now see, the profit test has no relevance of its own.

For example, note Figure 11-9. The diagram shows three very different situations. In each case, price is $0P$, output $0Q$. Profits, both in total and as a ratio to sales, are equal in all three cases. Only the firms' cost functions differ. Yet it would clearly be wrong to use the profit rate as either a test for the *existence* of monopoly or as an index for ranking the severity of monopoly effects. In the first case, with marginal cost MC_1, and average cost AC_1, there are profits but no monopoly. In the second, with marginal cost MC_2 equal to average cost AC_2, there are the same profits as before, but price exceeds marginal cost. Similarly, but more so, in the third case. Even if based on good data, either of the profit tests would indicate that these situations are equally monopolistic. They surely are not. Whether it would be sensible to "remedy" any of them is a different question; and Figure 11-9 cannot answer it. Chapter 13, Welfare Trade-offs, develops a framework for answering it.

Furthermore, even if the profit rate *were* a reliable symptom of monopoly, it is not reliable for establishing public policy priorities. Even if we ignore the disquieting theory of second best, and are sure that we have found monopoly via profit tests, monopoly profits and monopoly resource misallocation are just completely different things. Two di-

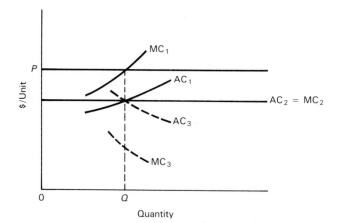

Figure 11-9 Profit Tests Fail to Distinguish Zero-Monopoly and Different Degrees of Monopoly

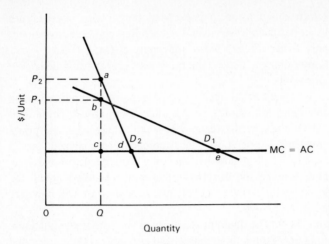

Figure 11-10   The Profit Test
Reverses the True Monopoly-
Power Rank

agrams further illustrate the distinction. In Figure 11-10, D_1 is the demand facing one
industry, D_2 that facing another. Long-run marginal cost, MC, is assumed to be constant
and equal for both industries. Assume that each industry is concentrated, and that there is
no collusion. P_1 and P_2 are the prices charged in the first and second industries. Output
rates, Q, are equal in the two industries. Profits are substantially higher in industry 2.

But the classical dead-weight loss is larger in industry 1: the area of *bce* is greater
than that of *acd*. No matter how well it is performed, the profit test reverses the true
ranking for Figure 11-10. In Figure 11-11, *profits* are equal for two concentrated industries operating on two different demand curves (D_1, D_2). Their MCs and prices are identical. Dead-weight losses are not. For Figure 11-11, the profit test does not discriminate

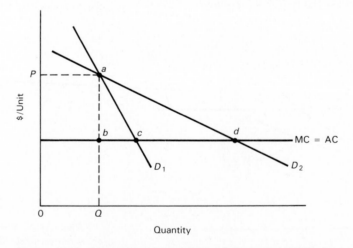

Figure 11-11   Identical Profit Rates Yielding Different Dead-Weight Loss

when it should; for Figure 11-10, it discriminates perversely. What worse can be said of any standard?

For all these reasons, neither profitability nor the index of monopoly power reliably gauges the "monopoly problem," specifically or in general.

Nor is this all. Most statistical studies have relied upon Census Bureau "industry" classifications.[46] The adequacy of these classifications for economic analysis varies greatly, among other reasons because the degree of substitution in demand and in supply is not the primary rationale underlying the separate "industry" (or, even, "product") classifications.[47] Another conceptually related problem arises when "industry" profits and concentration are being related statistically. The whole output of individual manufacturing establishments is assigned to only one industry, no matter how varied that output may be. This last problem is attributable to intraestablishment and interestablishment diversification. Finally, financial data from which profits are derived are collected from companies, on a company basis. Company data are consolidated. The revenues and costs of a company are generally allocated to the *single* industry most important to it.

Some of these data deficiencies can be remedied. Unfortunately, corrections have to be ad hoc, since there are no objective criteria for making them. Chapters 14, 15, and 16 say more about empirical studies purporting to explain profitability in terms of concentration and other factors.

SUMMARY

The Census Bureau collects product and industry statistics for a variety of reasons that have nothing to do with analyzing the "monopoly problem," and substitution in demand or production are not, it is clear, the principal criterion by which Census definitions are made. Some products and industries are misleadingly broad by economic standards, others are misleadingly narrow.

The basic reporting unit is the "establishment," *all* of whose output, no matter how varied it may be, is assigned to *one* "industry." Which industry an establishment is assigned to depends upon which single one of its products is most important. This system of classification has some drawbacks. In the retailing sector of the economy, for example, department stores sell a lot of shoes; but they are not classified into shoe retailing because their shoe business is typically smaller than several other individual lines. *That* kind of problem caused big trouble in the *Brown Shoe* case, among others.[48]

More generally, Census classification tends to overstate concentration in industries with low "coverage" ratios. In that case, much of a good's output really comes from other industries, and is not counted in the denominator of concentration ratios as presented. A similar problem arises with respect to imports, which are not counted. In some important cases, autos, computers, and steel, to name just three, this grossly overstates the market shares of U.S. producers.

"Aggregate" concentration lacks a theory to associate it with monopoly resource misallocation, and it is not clear whether it has any other economic significance. One claim is that it influences politics and societal values in some way. In any case, it appears that aggregate concentration in the U.S. has been stable for many years.

A more fundamental problem even than establishment classification and product definitions are conceptual deficiencies in popular measures of monopoly power and monopoly effects. Profits and price-cost margins give unreliable and sometimes perverse results when used to indicate the existence and power of monopoly or to measure the effect of monopoly on economic welfare.

QUESTIONS

1. Review the official titles of the wood household furniture "industry," "product classes," and "products" that are listed in tables 11-2 through 11-4. What specific questions about substitution in demand and production do those definitions raise?

2. One reason that Census collects data separately for the beet and cane sugar industries may be that sugar companies want the data collected separately. In principle, how would you decide whether there is really only one sugar industry, or two, from an economic standpoint?

3. The following are (percentage) market shares of all six firms in a hypothetical Census industry: 30, 25, 15, 12, 10, 8. Use them to calculate a four-firm concentration ratio; an old-style Herfindahl index; and a new-style Herfindahl index. What is the numbers-equivalent of (either) of the Herfindahl index values? Prove your answer.

4. Suppose a Census industry has a 40 percent coverage ratio, a specialization ratio of 100 percent, and a concentration ratio of 80 percent. What do you propose as a first approximation to a "corrected" concentration ratio if there are zero imports? If imports are equal to domestic production? What would enter into a second approximation?

5. Explain the Lerner index of monopoly and comment on some situations in which it leads to debatable diagnoses.

6. What conceptual and practical problems arise in using accounting profits to find monopoly, or to evaluate welfare losses owing to monopoly?

7. Suppose you read that, over time, the concentration ratio in every industry rose while weighted-average concentration fell. Is that possible? Explain.

NOTES

1. Edward H. Chamberlin, *The Theory of Monopolistic Competition* (Cambridge, Mass.: Harvard University Press, 1933); Joan Robinson, *The Economics of Imperfect Competition* (London: Macmillan and Co., Limited, 1946); Abba P. Lerner, "The Concept of Monopoly and the Measurement of Monopoly Power," *Review of Economic Studies*, 1, no. 3 (June 1934), pp. 157–75.

2. Adolph A. Berle and Gardiner C. Means, *The Modern Corporation and Private Property* (New York: Macmillan, Inc., 1932), p. 45.

3. G. C. Means, *Industrial Prices and Their Relative Inflexibility*, 74th Cong., 1st sess., U.S. Senate, Document 13 (1935). There is some question how much price rigidity there actually has been, and what causes it. Are some prices less flexible because of industry concentration, because changing or storing output is cheaper than changing prices, or because of other demand and cost factors? Compare G. J. Stigler and J. Kindahl, *The Behavior of Industrial Prices* (New York: Columbia University Press, 1970); and Dennis W. Carlton, "The Rigidity of Prices," *American Economic Review*, 76 (September 1986), pp. 457–65.

4. Henry C. Simons, *Economic Policy for a Free Society* (Chicago: University of Chicago Press, 1948).

5. Leonard W. Weiss, "The Extent and Effects of Aggregate Concentration," *Journal of Law & Economics*, 26 (June 1983), pp. 429–55, at p. 432.

6. Weiss, "The Extent and Effects of Aggregate Concentration," pp. 429–55; John S. McGee, "Professor Weiss on Concentration," *Journal of Law & Economics*, 26 (June 1983), pp. 457–65.

7. Economists have been clearer about the concept of a market than about how to define markets empirically: "A market, according to the masters, is the area within which the price of a commodity tends to uniformity, allowance being made for transportation costs." G. J. Stigler, *The Theory of Price*, 3rd ed. (New York: Macmillan, Inc., 1966), p. 85. See also Stigler, "The Economists and the Problem of Monopoly," *American Economic Review* 72 (May 1982), pp. 1–11.

8. An instructive empirical study is George J. Stigler and Robert A. Sherwin, "The Extent of the Market," *The Journal of Law & Economics*, 28 (October 1985), pp. 555–85.

9. Government accounted for 12.1 percent; agriculture, forestry, and fisheries for 2.8 percent.

10. U.S. Bureau of the Census, *1982 Census of Manufactures, General Summary, Pt. 1* (Washington, D.C.: March 1986).

11. Value added measures net additions to output value, rather than gross sales. For the 1982 Census, it is defined as follows:

   VA = [value of shipments (incl. resales and misc. receipts)] + [ending inventories of finished goods & work in progress] − [beginning inventories] − [materials, supplies, fuel, electricity, cost of resales, cost of contract work].

   1982 Census of Manufactures, General Summary, Pt. 1, pp. xxiii–xxiv.

12. See George J. Stigler, "Introduction," in *Business Concentration and Price Policy*, ed., G. J. Stigler (Princeton, N.J.: Princeton University Press, 1955), pp. 3–14, still the best statement in print; Maxwell R. Conklin and Harold T. Goldstein, "Census Principles of Industry and Product Classification, Manufacturing Industries," ibid., pp. 15–36, and "Comments," pp. 36–55; and Gideon Rosenbluth, "Measures of Concentration," ibid., pp. 57–95.

13. McKie stresses similarity of function as a criterion; Conklin and Goldstein stress similarity of production processes. James W. McKie, "Industry Classification and Sector Measures of Industrial Production," *Bureau of the Census Working Paper No. 20* (Washington, D.C.: U.S. Department of Commerce, 1965); Maxwell R. Conklin and Harold T. Goldstein, "Census Principles," ibid., pp. 15–36; Harold T. Goldstein, "Historical Comparability of Census Manufacturing Industries," *Bureau of the Census Working Paper No. 9* (Washington, D.C.: U.S. Department of Commerce, 1959).

14. Census has apparently made some progress in curing such anomalies. See *1982 Census of Manufactures, Concentration Ratios in Manufacturing* (Washington, D.C.: Bureau of the Census, April 1986), Table 7, pp. 7 and 177–80.

15. The latest version of the resistance formula is described in *1982 Census of Manufactures, General Summary, Pt. 1*, p. xiii, which also notes that "A resistance formula of the ASM [Annual Survey of Manufactures] type was first used in the 1963 census of manufactures."

16. McKie, "Industry Classification," pp.3–4,

17. Conklin and Goldstein, "Census Principles," p. 20.

18. Concentration ratios have been computed for Census industries, product classes, commodity groups, and so on. Measures of size have included value of shipments, employment, and assets. In the U.S. concentration ratios are often shown for the four, eight, and twenty largest firms, but never for fewer than four. In the United Kingdom, published concentration ratios are usually for the largest three firms, and never for fewer. Gideon Rosenbluth, "Measures of Concentration," in *Business Concentration and Price Policy*, ed. G. J. Stigler (Princeton, N.J.: Princeton University Press, 1955), pp. 57–94, at pages 66, 70–75. Also see M. A. Utton, *Industrial Concentration* (Harmondsworth, England: Penguin Books, Inc., 1970), p. 81. But compare Michael Waterson, *Economic Theory of the Industry* (Cambridge: Cambridge University Press, 1984), pp. 169, 193.

19. Hirschman seems to have invented what most people now call the "Herfindahl" index; but he used it in a study of international trade. Albert O. Hirschman, *National Power and Structure of Foreign Trade* (Berkeley and Los Angeles, Calif.: University of California Press, 1945). Herfindahl introduced the index to industrial organization. Orris C. Herfindahl, *Concentration in the Steel Industry* (unpublished Columbia University Ph.D. dissertation, 1950).

20. Ralph L. Nelson, *Concentration in the Manufacturing Industries in the United States* (New Haven, Conn.: Yale University Press, 1963); *1982 Census of Manufactures, Concentration Ratios in Manufacturing*, April 1986.

21. For a claim that these number equivalents do not correlate with price-cost margins, see Richard A. Miller, "Numbers Equivalents, Relative Entropy, and Concentration Ratios: A Comparison Using Market Performance," *Southern Economic Journal*, 39 (July 1972), pp. 107–12. On the other hand, price-cost margins themselves have been so heavily criticized as a performance measure that a lack of correlation with them may be no cause for alarm. See S. J. Liebowitz, "What do Price-Cost Margins Show?" *Journal of Law & Economics*, 25 (October 1982), pp. 231–46.

22. Betty Bock, "Concentration Patterns in Manufacturing," *An Anthology of Studies on Industrial Concentration by the Conference Board: 1958–1972* (New York: The Conference Board, 1973), Section II, p. 34.

23. Ibid., pp. 106, 108, and 112.

24. For recent claims that accounting figures are irrelevant to firms, too, see Franklin M. Fisher and John J. McGowan, "On the Misuse of Accounting Rates of Return to Infer Monopoly Profits," *American Economic Review*, 73 (March 1983), pp. 82–97; and F. M. Fisher, J. J. McGowan, and Joen E. Greenwood, *Folded, Spindled, and Mutilated: Economic Analysis and U.S. v. IBM* (Cambridge, Mass.: MIT Press, 1983), Chapter 7.

25. Bock, "Dialogue on Concentration, Oligopoly, and Profit," *An Anthology: 1958–1972*, Section IX, p. 22.

26. Ibid., p. 14.

27. *Concentration Ratios in Manufacturing Industry: 1963*, a Report prepared by Bureau of the Census for Subcommittee on Antitrust and Monopoly of the Committee on the Judiciary, U.S. Senate, Part 1 (Washington, D.C.: U.S. Government Printing Office, 1966), p. viii.

28. E. H. Chamberlin, "Product Heterogeneity and Public Policy," *American Economic Review*, 40 (May 1950), pp. 85–92, at pp. 86–87.

29. Weiss, "The Extent and Effects of Aggregate Concentration," p. 440.

30. For a description and analysis of the data, see McGee, "Professor Weiss on Concentration."

31. George J. Benston, "The Validity of Profits-Structure with Particular Reference to the FTC's Line of Business Data," *American Economic Review*, 75 (March 1985), pp. 37–67.
   Debate about these data continued in 1987. F. M. Scherer, et al., "The Validity of Studies with Line of Business Data: Comment," *American Economic Review*, 77 (March 1987), pp. 205–17; George J. Benston, "The Validity of Studies with Line of Business Data: Reply," *ibid.*, pp. 218–27.

32. Many studies purport to show how industrial concentration has changed over time. For example, see G. Warren Nutter, *The Extent of Enterprise Monopoly in the United States: 1899–1939* (Chicago: University of Chicago Press, 1951); H. A. Einhorn, "Competition in American Industry, 1939–1958," *Journal of Political Economy*, 74 (October 1966), pp. 506–11; D. R. Kamerschen, "An Empirical Test of Oligopoly Theories," *Journal of Political Economy*, 76 (July/August 1968), pp. 615–34.

33. *1982 Census of Manufactures, Concentration Ratios.*

34. Willard F. Mueller, "Statement, Economic Concentration—Overall and Conglomerate Aspects," Senate Subcommittee on Antitrust and Monopoly, *Hearings* (July 1964), pp. 109–29.

35. David Schwartzman and Joan Bodoff, "Concentration in Regional and Local Industries," *Southern Economic Journal*, 37 (January 1971), pp. 343–48.

36. See also Robert W. Kilpatrick, "The Choice Among Alternative Measures of Industrial Concentration," *Review of Economics and Statistics*, 49 (May 1967), pp. 258–60.

37. J. S. McGee, *In Defense of Industrial Concentration* (New York: Praeger Publishers, 1971), p. 74.

38. Harold Demsetz, "Why Regulate Utilities?" *Journal of Law & Economics*, 11 (April 1968), pp. 55–65.

39. Yale Brozen, "Significance of Profit Data for Antitrust Policy," *The Antitrust Bulletin*, 14 (Spring 1969), pp. 119–39; Report of the Attorney General's National Committee to Study the Antitrust Laws, March 31, 1955, at pp. 322–24; Donald F. Turner, Testimony on Dual Distribution, *Hearings Before the Senate Subcommittee on Antitrust and Monopoly*, 89th Cong., 2nd sess., pt. 2 (Washington, D.C.: U.S. Government Printing Office, March 31, 1966), pp. 273–75, 279–88; William T. Hogan, S.J.,"Difficulties in the Determination of Unit Costs of Production," 37 *University of Detroit Law Journal* (October 1959), pp.121–42. Rather different arguments against using accounting profits appear in Fisher, McGowan, and Greenwood, *Folded, Spindled, and Mutilated*, Chapter 7; and Fisher and McGowan, "Misuse of Accounting Rates of Return."

40. See I. N. Fisher and G. R. Hall, "Risk and Corporate Rates of Return," *Quarterly Journal of Economics*, 83, no. 1 (February 1969), pp. 79–92; James Bothwell and Theodore E. Keeler, "Profits, Market Structure, and Portfolio Risk," in *Essays on Industrial Organization in Honor of Joe S. Bain*, eds. Robert T. Masson and P. D. Qualls (Cambridge, Mass.:

Ballinger Publishing Co., 1976); Roger Sherman, *The Economics of Industry* (Boston: Little, Brown & Co., 1974), pp. 89–119.

41. Robert J. Gordon, "$45 Billion of U.S. Private Investment Has Been Mislaid," *American Economic Review*, 59 (June 1969), pp. 221–38.

42. Yale Brozen, "The Antitrust Task Force Deconcentration Recommendation," *Journal of Law & Economics*, 13 (October 1970), pp. 279–92.

43. A now classic article may be responsible: Abba P. Lerner, "The Concept of Monopoly and the Measurement of Monopoly Power," *Review of Economic Studies*, 1, no. 3 (June 1934), pp. 157–75. As Lerner put it, "The loss involved in monopoly can be seen in the divergence between price and this marginal cost." Ibid., p. 165.

   Some deficiencies of such indexes have long been recognized. See, for example, Tibor Scitovsky, "Economic Theory and the Measurement of Concentration," in *Business Concentration and Price Policy*, ed. G. J. Stigler (Princeton, N.J.: Princeton University Press, 1955), pp. 101–13. Compare also John P. Miller, "Measures of Monopoly Power and Concentration," ibid., pp. 119–39, at pp. 123–29; and Joe S. Bain, "Comment," ibid., pp. 139–40.

   Criticisms raised in this chapter, however, are different from those.

44. Because, in Figure 11-3, concentration clearly lowers cost, some will argue that *regulated* monopoly is better still. Marginal-cost, or average-cost, pricing would further improve the consumers' position. But Figure 11-3 simply cannot support that argument without help: consumer surplus *would* unambiguously be increased only if the costs of regulation were zero, which they are not. Since Figure 11-3 does not specify the costs of regulation, we cannot be sure that the benefits of regulation would be greater than the costs.

45. Nevertheless, the so-called price-cost margins, a doubtful empirical stand-in for the Lerner Index, were surprisingly popular for a time. For a discussion of the link between Lerner indexes and price-cost margins, see Thomas R. Saving, "Concentration Ratios and the Degree of Monopoly," *International Economic Review*, 11 (February 1970), pp. 139–46. For a devastating criticism of price-cost margins, see S. J. Liebowitz, "What Do Census Price-Cost Margins Measure?" *Journal of Law & Economics*, 25 (October 1982), pp. 231–46.

46. For 1973–1977, the FTC gathered annual Line of Business Data. They pose their own problems. See John S. McGee, "Professor Weiss on Concentration," *Journal of Law & Economics*, 26 (June 1983), pp. 462–63; George J. Benston, "The Validity of Profits-Structure with Particular Reference to the FTC's Line of Business Data," *American Economic Review*, 75 (March 1985), pp. 37–67. On April 11, 1984, the Federal Trade Commission voted 4 to 1 to stop collecting line of business data. *FTC News*, 12 April 1984.

47. Edward H. Chamberlin, "Product Heterogeneity and Public Policy," *American Economic Review*, 40 (May 1950), pp. 86–87; "Measuring the Degree of Monopoly and Competition," in *Monopoly and Competition and Their Regulation*, ed. E. H. Chamberlin (New York: St. Martin's Press, Inc., 1954), pp. 255–67; John P. Miller, "Measures of Monopoly Power and Concentration: Their Economic Significance," *Business Concentration and Price Policy*, ed. G. J. Stigler (Princeton, N.J.: Princeton University Press, 1955), pp. 119–39; Edward Mason, "Market Power and Business Conduct: Some Comments," *American Economic Review*, 46 (May 1956), pp. 471–81, especially p. 480; Stigler, "Introduction" to *Business Concentration and Price Policy*, pp. 3–14; Maxwell R. Conklin and Harold T. Goldstein, "Census Principles," ibid., pp. 15–36, and "Comments," pp. 36–55; Gideon Rosenbluth, "Measures of Concentration," ibid., pp. 57–95; U.S. Department of Commerce, Bureau of the Census, *Concentration Ratios in Manufacturing Industry, 1958* (Washington, D.C.: Bureau of the Census, 1962), pp. 1–6; U.S. Department of Commerce, Bureau of the Census, *Concentration Ratios in Manufacturing Industry, 1963, Part 1* (Washington, D.C.: 1966), pp. v–viii, xi–xvii; *The Significance of Concentration Ratios*, No. 1 (Washington, D.C.: Chamber of Commerce of the U.S., June 1957), 8pp.; *The Statistical Bases of Concentration Ratios*, No. 2 (Washington, D.C.: Chamber of Commerce of the U.S., June 1957), 26 pp.; Eugene Singer, ''The Structure of Industrial Concentration Indexes,'' *The Antitrust Bulletin*, 10, nos. 1 and 2 (January–April 1965), pp. 75, 101–4.

48. *Brown Shoe* v. *United States*, 370 U.S. 294 (1962).

12 | ECONOMICS OF VERTICAL INTEGRATION[1]

INTRODUCTION

We all think we know vertical integration when we see it. Firms that operate oil wells, pipelines, refineries, and service stations, for example, are said to be vertically integrated, since they work at more than one level of a series of levels leading from raw materials down to the final consumer. But the production processes in which any firm is engaged are further divisible and, in principle at least, could be undertaken by separate firms. *All* firms are therefore vertically integrated.[2]

Firms in industries of every structure and type produce for their own account goods and services that could be bought or hired from other firms. These same firms also buy or hire goods and services from other firms, and sell goods and services to firms and households. Like everything else, buying and selling in external markets cost resources. There are costs of searching out buyers and sellers, transacting, contracting, enforcing, and so on. Transfers within a firm also cost resources, including those required to establish and police incentive systems for good performance, to coordinate, and to plan.

Firms routinely decide whether to ''make or buy.''[3] When a firm does for itself, we can call it vertical integration; but what is really involved are the same economic factors that explain the existence, size, shape, and functions of *any* firm; or exchange itself.[4]

Although vertical integration is ubiquitous, much law is hostile to it. Courts and antitrust agencies are suspicious of vertical integration partly *because* it can lower costs.[5] Another reason for hostility is the belief that integration can harm competition or resource allocation.[6] With integration, as with other business structure and conduct, economists and courts tend to emphasize rare pathology more than normal and beneficial forms and day-to-day behavior. Many overlook that vertical integration is ubiquitous and can be beneficial.

Academic and legal controversy about vertical integration has been going on for a long time.

This chapter has several objectives: briefly to sketch the evolution of modern theories about vertical integration; to present additional rationales for vertical integration; to interpret, criticize, and improve the theoretical analysis; to delineate areas of agreement and disagreement among economists; and to indicate ways in which public policy can go wrong. When we are done, we will have a framework into which the facts of specific industries or specific incidents can be arranged and with which general economic or legal arguments can be evaluated.[7]

The next section outlines a simple and powerful theory of vertical integration under fixed-proportions conditions. The sections that follow present and evaluate the traditional criticisms of vertical integration; and then discuss efficiencies that vertical integration can generate. The last section discusses the effects of vertical integration given variable-proportions production, a realistic but enormously complicating assumption.

FIXED PROPORTIONS IN PRODUCTION

Before 1954, economic reasoning about vertical integration tended to be loose and unsystematic, and what the courts said about it did not seem to be based upon any coherent economic theory at all. By 1954 a number of court cases had placed vertical integration at risk: it would be hard to defend if accompanied by even a hint of "power" or "abuse." Robert Bork's classic 1954 article identified and analyzed antitrust law with respect to vertical integration, tracing hostility to it to earlier origins than had previously been suspected; and overturned economic theories and arguments then commonly advanced against it.[8] This rigorous new analysis immediately began undermining the old views and ultimately pulled them down.

The new analysis assumed fixed proportions in production, which means that the *proportions* of outputs from the different levels of an industry remain constant for all relevant prices and outputs—as in Marshall's famous derived-demand analysis of knives, blades, and handles.[9] If a knife must be made from one blade and one handle, the ratio of blades to handles remains unchanged, no matter how much the price of blades changes relative to handles. Similarly, proportions are fixed if a ton of steel *must* incorporate 1.3 tons of ore. That is what fixed proportions means here, whether it refers to factors of production, or components. Fixed-proportions models have been used earlier in this book, notably in chapters 8 and 9.

Figure 12-1 reviews the basic fixed-proportions model. D_S is the final demand for finished steel, the production of which requires two levels, *ore* and (steel) *plants*, which are used in fixed proportions. Output has been measured in finished-steel units. Marshall's derived-demand analysis, used earlier in chapters 8 and 9, derives the demand for each of these levels as follows. The net derived demand for ore, labelled D_O, is the final demand

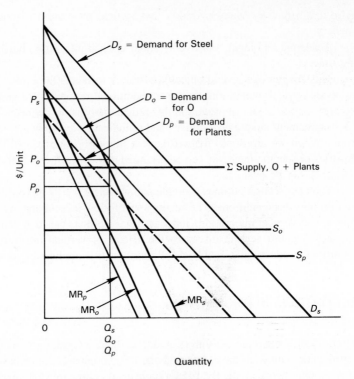

Figure 12-1 A Fixed-Proportions Steel Industry

for steel *minus* the costs of the other input, plants. The net demand for plants, D_P, in turn, is the final demand for steel *minus* the costs of ore.[10]

A nonintegrated monopoly of ore would charge P_O for it. Plants would fetch the competitive price, S_P. The final price of steel, the sum of P_O and P_P, would be P_S. Quantities would be Q_S, Q_O, and Q_P. A nonintegrated monopoly of plants would charge P_P for each unit of plant services. Ore would be competitively priced at S_O. The final price of finished steel would be P_S, the same as it would be with a monopoly of ore.

An integrated monopoly of *both* ore and plants would charge P_S, the same as a monopoly of either ore or plants would charge. In short, under these conditions, vertically integrated monopoly produces the same results as a nonintegrated monopoly of either of the levels.

Under fixed proportions, control of any level controls all: halving the output of ore halves the output of steel. In the absence of cost savings, fixed proportions for a two-level industry implies that final outputs and prices are the same whether there is monopoly at the first level and competition at the second; competition at the first and monopoly at the second; or one integrated monopoly that controls both levels. If there are fixed proportions, traditional objections to vertical integration simply collapse, though the traditional issue of horizontal monopoly remains. Cost savings then emerge as the central explanation of integration.

Costs and revenues explain everything that a business does. Firms may integrate vertically to lower costs, raise revenues, or reduce uncertainty.[11]

TRADITIONAL ARGUMENTS AGAINST VERTICAL INTEGRATION

Profits will rise if a seller increases its revenues for a given level of costs. Traditional treatments emphasize three ways in which vertical integration can raise revenues: facilitating price discrimination; avoiding price controls; and increasing monopoly power and price. Courts and popular opinion do not favor any of them.

Price Discrimination

Under certain circumstances, vertical integration can facilitate price discrimination. For example, Alcoa wanted to sell aluminum for several new uses, including power-transmission cable and engine pistons. For the first use, aluminum had to be priced low to compete with copper cable. For the second, it could carry a higher price. But if Alcoa tried to sell aluminum ingot at two different prices to independent fabricators, the two-price structure would probably collapse. Unless they can be tightly constrained by strong contracts enforced at great expense, cable makers would buy ingot cheap, and resell it to piston makers, from whom Alcoa could not then extract the higher price. But by fabricating cable itself, Alcoa could preserve a two-price structure, expand the usage of aluminum by serving both markets, and profit. It apparently did the same thing in selling aluminum sheets to rail car manufacturers.

Many economists do not regard this kind of pricing as bad. Some economists, and many judges, on the other hand, do. This is partly because they do not like discrimination; but partly, perhaps, because they did not understand what was really going on. In *Alcoa*, for example, judge Learned Hand thought ingots had been priced high and sheets priced low, to squeeze independent fabricators out of the business, monopolizing that level of the industry.

Evading Price Controls

Vertical integration can also increase revenues by minimizing the effects of price controls. If, for example, a legal ceiling were placed on iron ore but not on products, integrated firms could evade the ceiling. One type of integration or tie-in can also evade price *floors*. Aaron Director hypothesized that land-grant railroads were undercutting ICC rate minima when they leased lands to "tied" shippers for less than the open-market value of the land. If Director was right, the court was mistaken in concluding that the railroad had used a coercive tie-in contract to monopolize rail transport or ranching, or both. But the court might not have been any more sympathetic if they *had* believed the railroads were merely evading and eroding artificially high ICC rates.[12] In *A&P-ACCO* for example, the court disliked practices undermining the shelter that Robinson-Patman had built for traditional brokers.

Monopolizing

Vertical integration has been denounced for increasing monopoly power and price. How can it do it? Various ways have been asserted, including reducing the number or size of markets, squeezing margins, subsidizing some levels at the expense of others, and increasing capital requirements to bar entry.

Vertical integration reduces the number of market transactions and, in the limit, may even reduce the number of external markets. The theory that this is bad seems to assume that the number or size of markets should be kept above some critical but unspecified level. In *Socony-Vacuum*,[13] markets and prices were regarded as the central nervous system of the economy, in which more ganglia are preferable to less. The smallness of the "spot" gasoline market, in which nonintegrated refiners and marketers traded, was central to the government's case. The court believed that small markets are easily manipulated and do not produce true prices. That theory asserts that integration threatens competition by making open markets fewer, smaller, and easier to manipulate. But more fundamental questions, surely, are whether existing markets *are* open and freely interconnected, and whether new ones can be created as demand and cost conditions call for them.

But interfirm transactions are not costless. Costs can often be lowered by reducing the number and volume of interfirm transactions. Maintaining or increasing the number of markets artificially would be an expensive mistake. If it is cheaper to make rather than buy, there is some presumption that integration is desirable.[14]

Foreclosure.   And old claim is that integration, whether by merger or otherwise, lessens competition or promotes monopoly by foreclosing nonintegrated firms. Foreclosure seldom means that an integrated firm actually got a monopoly. Usually it means merely that nonintegrated firms have been injured or inconvenienced, which may eventually lead to monopoly. The comfort of competitors is not a good way to judge how well markets and competition are working. The object of the market process is to benefit consumers. Unfortunately, *Brown Shoe*, *Clorox*, and other cases suggest that efficiencies produced through integration can be used to *disqualify* the integration.

We often hear that vertical integration is cumulative. The FTC has argued that one vertical integration leads to others, so that the same degree of concentration prevailing at one level will tend to be reproduced at the other. Assume that integration is spreading in some industry. Why is it? With what effects?

In the first place, the term *vertical integration* must include all cases in which there are *intrafirm* transfers of goods or services that could be or have been exchanged *between* separate firms. There is a great deal of vertical integration that seems neither to attract attention nor cause alarm; and the degree of integration in any industry varies over time as an evolutionary response to economic change.

Suppose that two sequential economic activities are performed by two industries, one of which sells to the other. No firm has previously operated in both industries. Suppose people recognize that firms can now reduce the cost of one or both of these functions by combining them under one management. We should expect entry by integrated firms, or mergers between previously independent supplier and customer firms, or both. When size economies differ between levels, the number of firms merged from each level will differ. When the first mergers occur, some will say the business of customers (or suppliers) has been foreclosed, although a lot of business is still transacted in the open market. Nevertheless, to the extent that integration reduces costs, integrated firms will increase both their profits and market shares. Profits and shares of nonintegrated firms will fall. Those who figure out what's going on and can copy it will also integrate. Those who don't will suffer. Consumers gain. It would be anomalous if antitrust law prevents *that* kind of foreclosure, whether it occurs via mergers or *de novo* integration. The FTC historically complained that the profitability of firms that do integrate, and the declining profitability of those that do not, will set off a wave of such integrations—which indeed it should. The larger the economies that can be achieved, the more decisive the incentive to integrate. If that be foreclosure, consumers and the FTC should welcome it.

Note the foreclosure and waste that occur when law discourages integration by merger. If vertical mergers are prevented, some firms will have to integrate by bringing new resources into the industry, increasing redundancy. How rapidly and completely integration occurs then depends both upon how deeply the nonintegrated firms cut their prices and upon the efficiency and legality of requirements contracts and other arrangements substituting for integration. To the extent that vertical integration by merger is not permitted, firms not investing newly in integration would be foreclosed from the markets *and* from the prosperity enjoyed by those who do. And to *that* extent there will be a wasteful duplication of facilities that mergers could have avoided.

Now, if there had been no cost savings to motivate the integration in the first place, it is not clear how foreclosure in any sense could occur. In that case, vertical mergers, or internally generated integration, would not increase the efficiency of firms engaging in them. The business of firms merged might be lost to those who previously supplied them. But so long as some firms do not integrate, there will be corresponding firms to supply or buy from. For, since—by assumption—no one's absolute or relative efficiency will have been altered by all of this integration, for a given demand curve—on which integration in and of itself will have no effect—the total volume of business will be unchanged. Everybody's share, integrated or not, should be unchanged. And if every firm vertically integrates by merger, obviously no one would be foreclosed from anything.

Anticompetitive squeezes. Law cases complain about at least three kinds of squeeze: price, supply, and quality. We will take them in turn, after a brief introduction. The beauty of the term *squeeze* is that it conjures up physical analogies without really explaining anything. The term creates visions of force being exerted against objects that are unable to extricate themselves: the vise, the tongs, the fist closing in a crushing movement. It seems reasonable to assume that a price squeeze requires control over price at two levels, at least, for a substantial period.

Not only are these physical analogies misleading and prejudicial. They are also difficult to defend against. Every industry has periods in which there are superficial evidences of a squeeze, no matter how competitive the industry or how innocuous the events. Furthermore, a proper defense also requires digging into the general meaning and specific applicability of the whole notion of squeeze itself.

Why would anyone want to use squeezes? A rational monopolist wants to do everything as cheaply as possible and will use outside intermediaries to the extent that they can do what he wants more cheaply than he can do it himself. If there is any such thing as a purposeful squeeze, it sacrifices short-run profits to stamp out competition in the long run. That is a type of predatory conduct, which was analyzed in Chapter 9.

This brings us to the so-called supply squeeze. The government has sometimes said that the limiting case of a supply squeeze is simply refusing to sell to competitors; that is, a refusal to deal. Why would a monopolist want to do that? Any supplier wants to minimize the cost of producing the output he wants, and will use outsiders to the extent necessary to do it.

But distortions do arise from time to time, because of government price regulation for example. This sometimes encourages vertical integration. It may also make it necessary to cut off customers whom it would otherwise be desirable to serve. Suppose, for example, that the government places ceiling prices on inputs or components. The monopolist finds that the inputs are now worth more to himself than he is permitted legally to charge somebody else for them. Under these circumstances he will reduce sales to outsiders.[15] Similar effects can occur without integration. If price and other regulations do not fall evenly everywhere, competitive manufacturers will sell their limited output where it brings the highest prices. This may mean cutting off old customers. But it has nothing to do with monopolizing anything. Indeed, many economists will say that the results complained of are in the public interest. Even when it is being manipulated by the government, the price system rations resources, moving them to places in which they are worth more from those in which they contribute less.

We now come to the so-called quality squeeze. A&P, then the largest retail grocery chain, owned ACCO, a produce buyer and broker for A&P and other firms that competed with A&P.[16] The government convinced the courts that ACCO chose the best fruits and vegetables for A&P and left the inferior stuff for its competitors. Why that would pay is not obvious. Good stuff is worth more than bad. Bad goods must be discounted to sell. Since buyers differ, it often pays to offer different qualities at appropriately different prices.

Antique sources claim another sort of squeeze. Without much evidence, McLean and Haigh note the old story that John D. Rockefeller managed to get a railroad to raise rates against some competing refiners, as a consequence of which they were willing to enter into the Standard Oil camp.[17] As they tell it, it is not clear whether or to what extent vertical integration has anything to do with the story. Similarly, in the nineteenth century, a ring of rice merchants (called BAPS) had a tight monopoly on the rice trade out of Rangoon. A ring of British shipowners, so the story goes, could not monopolize the general cargo trade in and out of Rangoon so long as BAPS controlled enough cargo that it could charter tramp ships: tramps calling for Rangoon rice brought general cargo into Rangoon and beat down the rates. Accordingly, we are told, the shipowners offered low rates to ship BAPS's rice, with the proviso that BAPS stop chartering tramp ships on its own. This assertedly gave the shipping ring a tighter hold on general cargo and rates.[18]

In either case, tight bilateral monopoly, rather than vertical integration, seems to be involved. If there is an acceptable theory showing how vertical integration itself aided monopolization, it must apply to unusual conditions. What is needed is *tight* control at both levels. So tight, in fact, that traditional Sherman Law principles could be applied without relying on vertical integration theories at all. Furthermore, a rare bottleneck or critical mass seems to be required. The existence of rival suppliers would make it even less likely that any of these squeezes could work mechanically, whatever the rationality of undertaking them in the first place.

Subsidies within Integrated Firms.   Over the years, many have claimed that profit from one level of an integrated firm is used to subsidize other levels. (See *Reading Rail-road* and *A&P-ACCO*, for example.) Although Adelman and Bork have criticized these arguments in detail, we should briefly review a few fundamental points. First, some of these arguments merely state the obvious: a wealthy firm (or person) can hurt competitors if it is willing to throw away money to do it. Vertical integration has nothing to do with it. Second, courts have been confused by bookkeeping conventions that are completely fictional. Although it can matter for taxes and the like, how accountants apportion profits and losses among departments or divisions does not affect the fundamental economic analysis. Third, courts have objected to firms' reducing costs by performing for themselves functions also performed by nonintegrated specialists. That is, they oppose the efficiencies of vertical integration. Fourth, firms do not do things for themselves *free*. They incur real cost to do them and profits, if any, do not reduce costs. Furthermore, goods and services have market values *outside* the firm, and these opportunity costs must not be ignored.

Vertical Integration as a Barrier to Entry.   It is sometimes said that vertical integration discourages entry. How? Assume that the integration being denounced does not increase efficiency. The usual argument is that, to compete with an integrated firm, an entrant must also be integrated to avoid squeezes and other nastiness, and that this increases the capital required, barring entry. The argument is illogical and unrealistic. First, it would not be necessary for any firm to enter on both levels, since efficiency would not require vertical integration. Consumers are well served when enough *different* firms enter on each level, and that is what we should expect to happen.

In the second place, it is not clear how higher capital requirements would bar entry even if efficiency did require an entrant to enter at both levels. In such a case, whether because of competitive disequilibrium or monopoly, there are profits over and above returns needed to attract capital into the trade. Why, then, won't entry occur? Chapter 7 discussed this issue in detail.

We can now pause to see where we are. If vertical integration improves efficiency, consumers should welcome it. In the process, any producers who lag will tend to be foreclosed, as they should be. If vertical integration does not produce significant economies, there is no reason either to oppose or applaud it, and no one is foreclosed from anything, induced to start a bandwagon effect, or barred from entry.

Transmission of Monopoly Power.   Another claim is that integration transmits monopoly power. However much horizontal power there was before, it is not integration that transmits it. Nor does integration magnify monopoly profits, at least under conditions of fixed proportions. All available monopoly profits can be extracted at either level. All of whatever monopoly power exists will be exerted or transmitted from either level without vertical integration. Integration has no further transmission effect.

The last section of this chapter inquires whether vertical integration is a more effective monopolizing technique under variable-proportions conditions.

EFFICIENCIES CLAIMED FOR VERTICAL INTEGRATION

We have so far discussed how integration can raise a firm's revenues, an effect to which law tends to be hostile. Contrary to popular claims, however, increasing revenue is not always a bad thing, as the discussion at the end of this section shows.

We turn first, however, to ways in which vertical integration either lowers costs or results from lower costs. Reducing costs should appeal greatly to consumers and those who claim to protect them.

Anything that reduces the costs of a given result increases the possibility for profit. Because it saves resources required to do a job, it is also likely to help consumers. Vertical integration often has these results. And, when firms have different cost functions for activities that figure in their business, they will attain integration to different degrees and attain different sizes for the same reason.

Technological Imperatives

As Bork notes, courts have treated vertical integration more favorably when it is typical of a whole industry, has an apparent technological explanation, and is not accompanied by "abuses." Steel is the favorite example: everyone cites it, and most writers cite nothing else. Vertically integrated steel companies avoid the cost of reheating metal between stages and are able to use, rather than waste, byproducts such as furnace gases.

Technical factors like these have also been found in other industries. D. H. Wallace noted several examples in the aluminum industry.[19] Perhaps the closest parallel with heat loss in steel is the case of electrical energy:

> In addition to savings from adjusting [alumina] reduction to a base load of energy, ownership of power sometimes eliminates the necessity of converting from alternating to direct current. Purchased power usually arrives in the form of alternating current which must go through converters before use in the reduction cells. If the hydro-electric plant is owned, and the reduction works situated close by, direct current generators may be employed which feed the energy directly into the cells. Transforming from high voltages to low is also avoided if the

two plants are adjacent. Most of the aluminum companies have secured savings of this sort at some locations. However, these gains are not always possible.

Because the other examples Wallace gives are less obviously "technological," they will be discussed below.

Technological explanations of vertical integration are not wholly satisfying, for several reasons. First, it is *proximity* of related plants that seems to be crucial; but plants don't *have* to be commonly owned merely to be close together. Under some conditions, plants should no doubt be located close together to save resources. The real problem may be that when such close and dedicated plants are separately owned, each becomes hostage to the other. Discussion below shows what this implies. Second, there was vertical integration in the aluminum industry even when these plants were not close together and when metal *was* reheated. Third, although there probably always were gross savings from not reheating iron and steel, typical steel firms were not always vertically integrated. The very existence of unintegrated pig-iron firms, and a whole "merchant-iron" market, show this, as, indeed, does the history of major firms going into the formation of U.S. Steel. It seems that the size of savings from the proximity of plants differs from industry to industry and from time to time; that gross savings from the proximity of plants may be offset by costs of materials, transportation, distribution, and so on; and that more than physical proximity is needed to explain vertical integration by common *ownership*.

Although physical proximity is not wholly irrelevant, modern analysis suggests that we should look for other savings, for example in the costs of transactions, contract, coordination, incentives, inventories, policing, and risk. Given certain additional conditions, the fortunes of adjoining facilities are utterly interdependent. If adjoining dedicated facilities are separately owned, neither firm will relish being hostage to the other. Each firm must rely heavily upon the other. A strike against one management—under a labor contract *it* negotiated—cripples the other. One management can try to extort better terms from the other by threatening to shut down or slow down. Expansion of one facility requires expansion of the other, and so on. When the facilities are specialized, expensive, and long lived, their crucial interdependency argues either for vertical integration by ownership, or through a long-term contract. Contracts would either have to incorporate decision and coordination rules for every conceivable important contingency, which is manifestly impossible; create a third firm or body to run the two in coordination; or otherwise approximate the results of out-and-out integration. The form chosen should accomplish the overall task most efficiently.

None of that simplifies life or economic analysis. Anyone can see that something is saved when the same metal is not heated three times. The kinds of cost savings relevant to modern theories, however, are difficult either to demonstrate or measure.

Assuring the Quality of Inputs

"Small" variations in the quality of inputs can be extremely important—disastrous at the limit. The question is whether the right qualities are got more cheaply by purchasing in the market or by producing for oneself.

There is an enormous range of possibilities. The sugar content of a ton of beets is sensitive to climate, the seeds used, and the methods and timing of cultivation. The sugar content of beets affects their value and the efficiency with which a refinery operates.[20] This has led to contracts between factories and growers that are so detailed and tight as to approximate vertical integration.[21] One alternative arrangement would be for refineries to sample and analyze each of thousands of loads of beets, and to pay for them following a complex price schedule. But in view of what beets are worth, it would simply be too costly.

A more general problem occurs in many industries. In modern industry, even one bad part can produce an enormous loss. There may be no satisfactory way to sue an independently owned firm and to collect enough to offset the loss.

Donald Wallace used input quality to explain some vertical integration in the aluminum industry. Because the quality of bauxite, alumina, carbon electrodes, and furnace linings is crucial to the quality and cost of aluminum, "an aluminum firm can hardly afford to entrust" their quality "to the disinterested efficiency of an independent concern." That may be right; but modern analysis might deemphasize technical relationships, and ask whether the costs of obtaining appropriate input qualities is lower when the firm produces and tests quality for itself.

The question becomes whether, to assure the appropriate quality, the total costs of quality control and inspection, incentives, correction, and policing are lower under vertical integration.

Assuring the Right Quantities of Inputs at the Right Time

Demands and tastes change, and products and component specifications have to be altered. Inventories, specifications, and outputs have to be adjusted. Some refining firms, for example, alter their gasoline blends seasonally, several times each year, and have different blends for different regions. And, in general, it is costly for various levels of an industry to get badly out of step. Whether firms use outside markets or in-house supplies, they must consider the costs of signals and adjustments that are required to keep the levels coordinated. The theory and practice of production scheduling and inventory control may suggest whether and when integration lowers costs.[22]

Reducing Costs Imposed by Governments

Turnover taxes and certain kinds of sales taxes are the most obvious examples. Even income taxes can encourage do-it-yourself techniques. At least some of the monopoly-avoidance cases can also be discussed in this section. In fixing transport charges and other prices, or controlling output—as in crude oil—governments have often encouraged integration. Similarly, legal hostility to long-term contracts, resale-price maintenance, franchises, requirements or loyalty contracts, and the like, tends to make vertical integration more attractive.

Lowering Costs: Bypassing Monopoly

Steel producers stood to lose if someone else monopolizes iron ore; railroads stood to lose if someone monopolizes the anthracite coal fields; oil refiners were concerned when states undertook to control crude oil output. In such cases, vertical integration lowers overall costs and increases consumer benefits. Basic questions are whether, first, there is really significant monopoly power; and, second, whether things would be worse without the vertical integration. If there is going to be "exploitative monopoly" at some level, whether because of regulation or economies of size, vertical integration reduces the resource misallocation.

Integrated firms do not exploit themselves. They do not sell to themselves at monopoly prices. This is better than the situation in which rank strangers own the two levels and try to exploit each other. Similarly, if the government monopolizes public utilities or truck transportation, for example, it will often pay to integrate backwards to sidestep the monopoly toll.

Lowering Costs When There Is Monopsony

When an input is supplied competitively under conditions of increasing supply price, it may pay a buyer to integrate into the input market. Assume that a scarce input, say, iron ore, is found under lands that are also suitable for grazing or farming, and that for the latter uses price of such lands is constant, no matter at what prospective rate iron ore might be produced.[23] Assume that the long-run supply price of iron ore, including rent (values above what could have been earned in, say, farming), increases with larger demand (and its rate of output). As a consequence, rents will be earned from such lands as output of the steel industry increases (see Figure 12-2). Whether a steel firm is an atomis-

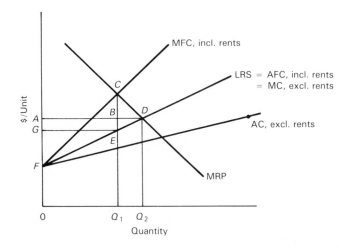

Figure 12-2 Monopsony Lowering Price by Extracting Input Rents

Source: John S. McGee and Lowell Bassett, "Vertical Integration Revisited," *Journal of Law & Economics*, The University of Chicago Press, 19 (April 1976), pp. 17–38.

tic competitor in steel (but a local monopsonist in buying ore), or has steel completely monopolized, the marginal factor cost (MFC) of ore is the relevant cost by which the steel firm determines its rate of purchases. For the given marginal revenue product curve (MRP), the steel firm will buy $0Q_1$ ore per unit time at price 0G. Rents to ore producers are GEF per unit time, the capitalized value of which constitutes the price at which the ore firms can be bought if they believe that their output rate will continue to be $0Q_1$.[24] They are worth more than this as part of an integrated ore and steel firm. If the steel firm buys them, the relevant marginal factor cost (excluding rents) becomes that part of the LRS defined for output rates greater than Q_1, and additional profits are captured as the outputs of ore and steel are increased to Q_2. It is hard to see how this can hurt consumers: owners of ore-bearing land would be as well paid as if output had continued to be only $0Q_1$—at which point it *would* have remained without integration—and consumers get more steel. Although the steel producer is better off, in the extreme case he would be willing to pay virtually all of the increased profits to landowners. These results follow for "standard" theoretical assumptions about the *steel* industry: single-firm monopoly, joint-profit-maximizing cartels, atomistic competition, Cournot oligopoly, and so on. If law and other conditions permit, the steel firm might achieve the same effects as integration, through long-term ore purchasing contracts and purchase-price discrimination for example. Many economists, and law, would probably treat such arrangements as quasi-integration and be equally hostile toward them.[25]

It might be argued that we would be even better off than that if we could substitute competitive conditions in both steel and ore for the monopoly and monopsony with which this example started. Each steel firm would then face a perfectly elastic supply of ore. But if there is a problem, it is horizontal monopoly (ore purchasing in this case), which, though it has nothing to do with vertical integration, may not be worth curing in any case. This analysis assumes that real resource costs are *not* changed by vertical integration. If, however, integration reduces those costs, too, that is yet another argument for it. The directions of effects produced are the same under constant and rising factor supply price, though magnitudes may differ. Integration that does this is to the good, under single-firm monopoly, Cournot oligopoly, joint-profit-maximizing cartels, atomism, and so on.

Lowering Costs of Marketing, Distribution, and Sales Promotion _____

Integration may reduce the costs of getting products into consumers' hands. The question is whether costs of functions that consumers want are lowered overall.[26] Suppose, for example, that an unintegrated auto body manufacturer advertises and otherwise contacts and communicates with *both* automobile manufacturers and automobile consumers. Automobile manufacturers also advertise and otherwise contact and communicate with consumers. It may be cheaper for an integrated firm simultaneously to advertise both *body* and total *car* and otherwise communicate with consumers, avoiding costly duplication of efforts.

In principle, contracting the appropriate degree of coordination between unintegrated levels could produce the same result as integration. But this may be infeasible or too expensive in the real world.

Inferences About Integration and Efficiency _____

What, if anything, can we infer about the efficiencies of integration when law is hostile to it? Assume that an incipient vertical merger movement is stopped cold by hostile law, as may have happened in shoe manufacture plus retailing, and in cement manufacture plus concrete mixing.[27] If, after the legal assault has won, no further vertical integration is accomplished by internal growth does this suggest that vertical integration has no legitimate economic rationale or results? For cement, Mueller concluded, the absence of subsequent integration by internal growth "suggests that there were no compelling real economies of integrated operations underlying the vertical mergers in this industry."[28] Whether Mueller is right about cement is a question of fact. In general, however, his standard is defective. First, governmental opposition to integration by merger tells the industry that it is being closely watched. And, since there is legal opposition to vertical integration whether it is accomplished by merger or not, the industry may get cold feet.

Second, internal growth is a slippery concept. If a cement manufacturing firm buys or merges with a concrete-mixing firm, most would call that acquisition or merger. If, instead, it buys or rents gravel pits, trucks, and offices, most would call that internal growth. In both cases, the firm goes into the market for inputs and assets and buys or rents them, presumably adopting the lowest cost route for expansion. In both cases, the firm grows. In the first case, the number of firms in concrete mixing does not grow—though output may; in the second, the number of firms grows. There is no way for an outsider to decide in advance which route is better, since there may be a trade-off between price and cost effects.

Take a hypothetical example in which the assumed cost effects are small enough to be plausible but not so small as to be trivial. Suppose that a cement manufacturing firm (with 20 percent of that business) knows that by buying enough outside firms to do all of its own concrete mixing it can reduce by 4 percent the average and marginal costs of bringing mixed concrete to those who buy it. Assume further that cement manufacturing has constant marginal cost.

If government permits the acquisitions, and only one cement manufacturer integrates in that way, price effects on concrete will be small. Only about 20 percent of the concrete is thereby produced and sold more efficiently, and—in terms of the final price—costs are lowered by "only" 4 percent. The price effect on concrete is smaller than the cost effect. The integrating firm's profits (and output) will rise. Firms *not* integrating will lose market share, and their profits will fall. These effects occur under atomistic competition, joint-profit-maximizing cartels, and so on, to consumers' benefit. Similarly, if *all* cement manufacturers integrate by merger and reduce costs by 4 percent, in the short run prices will fall (by less than 4 percent), the industry will prosper, and consumers will be better off.[29] With open entry, price (and profit) will decline further, until full equilibrium is reached.

The situation would be very different if government does *not* permit integration by merger. Wouldn't cement manufacturers still integrate by building mixing organizations and facilities *de novo*? Perhaps; but perhaps not as soon. Suppose the same 4 percent cost saving can be got through internal growth, assuming that integration is completely balanced.[30] That is, one must match cement capacity with mixing capacity. Even if only one cement manufacturer adds new mixing capacity, the final market price and mixing margin fall. Suppose the appropriate capacity addition is about 20 percent. If the relevant demand elasticity is -1, price would fall by about 20 percent; 10 percent for an elasticity of -2; and 5 percent for an elasticity of -4.[31] For even the least of these price effects, it would not pay any such cement manufacturer to integrate by internal growth: costs will fall only 4 percent, an unattractive trade.

If several or *all* cement manufacturing firms could reap the same cost advantages through integration, similar analysis applies. Prohibiting vertical mergers hurts cement manufacturers, the independent cement-mixing industry, and buyers of concrete. Cement-producing and cement-mixing firms are worth more integrated than separately owned. Merger contracts could share the present value of 4 percent annual cost savings. There are no savings to share when vertical mergers are prohibited. For vertical integration through internal growth either will not occur; or, if it does, would leave the now redundant unintegrated independent mixers to perish out in the cold. If cement manufacturers were not permitted to buy or hire *anything* from the present nonintegrated mixers, there would be a sizeable waste. Resources tied up in the mixing field would be almost doubled if cement manufacturers have to create another whole mixing industry to achieve the cost savings.

It will not do to dismiss all this waste as a short-run phenomenon. The question is whether the waste can be avoided. Some clearly meritorious vertical integration that would take place if mergers are permitted will be deferred or not take place if they are not.

Another theoretic anomaly sheds light on the practical problem. In theory, a single-firm cement monopoly would—if mergers are prohibited—find it pays to create a whole new mixing industry from scratch, leaving the old one wholly cut off and redundant. Unless integration through merger is prohibited, this absurdity would not occur if, for the relevant output rate, total variable costs of the old industry are lower than total costs of the new. Contracts between the old mixing industry and the monopolist could in principle be arranged to benefit both. Unfortunately, contracts that could avoid the waste might also be denounced, this time as covert or *contractual* integration.

This reveals an apparent paradox: Mueller warns us not to use polar models of pure competition or monopoly to analyze the effects of vertical integration.[32] Yet his own inference—that vertical integration does not reduce costs if firms are not willing to build new rather than buy old mixing capacity—holds, it if holds at all, *only* for the polar models whose use he decries. If there were single-firm monopoly or atomistic competition, for example, his inference seems sounder, although it might still be cheaper and faster to buy rather than build.

Integration Because of Superior Efficiency

The cost explanations of vertical integration considered so far tend to be mechanistic and inherent. They also illustrate only a one-direction causality: vertical integration lowers costs. On the other hand, a firm may integrate *because* it has lower costs, rather than the other way around. Understanding the make-or-buy decision is crucial to understanding the size, structure, and output-mix of firms.

Firms compare the *prices* of what they buy with what it would *cost* to supply themselves. If price is higher than cost, they have an incentive to integrate. It is easy to overlook superior efficiency as a reason for such price-cost divergences. Adelman is a rare exception. He claims, for example, that A&P's manufacturing facilities were uncommonly efficient and profitable.[33]

Differences in Opinions and Individual Circumstances: Mergers

Simple differences of opinions are responsible for many purchases and sales. Some conglomerate, some horizontal, and some vertical integration has been accomplished through merger. Some of these mergers occurred because they matched highly individual circumstances like tax loss–carryover situations, or vastly different appraisals of the future.

Such explanations overlap others, including superior efficiency. If one firm appraises the future better, it *is* more efficient. If one firm has profits against which to write off losses, it *has been* more efficient. If one firm has talent and facilities with which to make more of an opportunity, it *is* more efficient.

McLean and Haigh note instances in which integration occurred because different oil firms faced different circumstances.

R&D and Related Matters

People do less of things from which they do not expect to benefit. It is worthwhile to do things under some legal constraints but not under others. For example, a basic rationale for patents is that, in the absence of property rights, the revenues that some discoverers or innovators can expect to receive will not cover cost and risk, or—at least—that the return to research and discovery will be lower.

This is one reason why some firms do their own (''are vertically integrated'' into) research and development (R&D), engineering, and design.[34] Many important discoveries and improvements are not patentable, and some that are cannot be efficiently employed under such protection as patents afford. Piracy of trade secrets and premature disclosure of novelty reduce revenue. For equal costs, revenues from novelty may be higher when firms perform such functions for themselves. Take the case of a novel product, process, or ingredient that is valuable but not patentable. If sold separately in an outside market, some of such items will be analyzed and copied, and the innovator will lose the fruits of his efforts. When incorporated into a finished product, they may not be so quickly or effectively copied. Even *deferring* emulation will raise expected revenues, and make investment in discovery more attractive. That is simply not a bad thing. It can be argued that these are cases in which integration increases revenue because the costs of alternative arrangements—including contracting and policing outsiders—are too high. But the revenue side should not be overlooked.

Superior Products: Integration, Franchising, and Price Maintenance ____

Some effects of vertical integration may be achieved short of ownership. Oil companies, for example, *dis*integrated vertically because of anti-chainstore taxation and the costs of Social Security and other laws. Yet even stations that are run (under lease-back arrangements or requirements contracts) by "independent" operators stand in a contractually integrated relationship. It can also be argued that purely vertical price fixing or resale price maintenance is similar to vertical integration.

Law has sometimes treated different *forms* of vertical control very differently. For example, GE and Westinghouse fixed retail prices of their light bulbs by claiming that dealers took the bulbs on consignment and did not own them. They were simply agents, subject to laws of agency. That formality got more favorable treatment than open vertical price fixing by manufacturers did.[35] Yet the economic effects may not differ. We are told that—in the absence of statutory permission—vertical price fixing is prohibited per se, just as is horizontal price fixing of the cartel type.

When law imposes different rules for different business forms that have the same motives and effects, the forms tend to change. Justice's Douglas, Hughes, and Brandeis noted this tendency in some of their opinions.

The law and economics of vertical integration and resale price maintenance need to be reconciled, as well as put right. There would be a rational objection to vertical integration if it increases horizontal monopoly without compensations to consumers. Horizontal monopoly can and ought to be attacked as a horizontal problem, if attacked at all.

The economics of vertical integration suggests that resale price maintenance gets worse legal treatment than it deserves.[36] The vertically integrated firm chooses the mix of qualities and services that consumers prefer and charges the profit-maximizing price. A vertically integrated firm commonly tells its retail stores how much to charge. It will not let that division act like a monopsonist, or otherwise let it take too much for providing distribution services.

Why, then, should we keep an unintegrated firm from doing the same thing, in this case by specifying the price (and gross margin) that independent retailers can get? The only obvious reason is that vertical price determination might somehow increase monopoly. A cartel of dealers or wholesalers, for example, would no doubt welcome legally enforceable contracts to maintain the monopoly prices they set. And a cartel of manufacturers could use resale price maintenance both to remove excuses for price cutting and to make it less profitable. Bowman and Telser believed that's what was going on in the old *GE Light Bulb* case.

But what are the affirmative arguments for resale price maintenance? They are that it provides the locations, qualities, and services that consumers prefer. Without resale price maintenance, price-cutting dealers will freeload on those who offer services, ultimately leaving competition only on the price dimension. According to another argument, higher margins make dealers especially anxious to keep handling the price-protected lines, which encourages them to do what the manufacturer wants. This includes shunning counterfeits, and promoting and respecting the brand-name capital in which the manufacturer has invested so much. Or, without guaranteed margins, fewer and less convenient outlets will be provided, leaving consumers worse off.

If law were neutral, sellers could choose either vertical integration or resale price maintenance to provide just what consumers want. They would choose the more efficient way. Earlier discussion rejected Willard Mueller's test for whether there are cost savings from vertical integration. There is an analogy in the case of resale price maintenance. That manufacturers do not integrate vertically when resale price maintenance is unlawful does not prove that resale price maintenance would have been a bad thing.

Consumers are willing to pay more to get what they prefer. One way to get more revenue and improve economic well being is to supply what consumers want. Vertical integration, quasi-integration through franchise and other contracts, and resale price maintenance are some of the ways in which this can be done. Integration becomes more attractive when law is relatively hostile to the other ways.

Few products are sold and used in pure and simple form in which the mix and quality of characteristics are fixed. Electrical and gas utilities, for example, have found it desirable to integrate into the service (and/or sale) of heating, cooking, and lighting appliances. Apart from periods of governmentally induced crisis and shortage, we can easily find places where gasoline and oil are sold. Service stations have bold signs, often with brand names that are shorthand proclamations of high quality products plus rest rooms, directions, windshield and headlamp cleaning, and tire checking, that are offered there. The number and kind of automobiles bought, and how much people are willing to pay for them, depend among other things upon whether consumers think they must service and repair them at home or can easily find someone else to do it. Singer sewing machines were sold through outlets that offered sewing lessons. Most products are bought (and consumed) with other complementary goods, and their worth to consumers can sometimes be increased significantly by assuring that the right combination of service and price is provided. This may call for some form of vertical integration, quasi-integration, resale price maintenance, or franchising.

A large part of the anti–price maintenance literature is now suspect. It slighted the whole problem of transactions, contracting, and policing costs. It judged actual business practices against what would ideally happen in a world in which such costs do not exist.

Additionally, industrial histories reveal instances in which revenues, and general economic benefits, were increased through integration, simply because outsiders could not be convinced that something new could even be done, or that it would be worthwhile. The Aluminum Company of America (Alcoa) integrated forward from producing raw ingots into manufacturing products, thereby opening up and proving new uses for aluminum. Similarly, when the automobile industry started, gasoline superseded kerosene— much of which had been sold on regular routes, house-to-house, like milk and ice. With the ascendancy of automobiles and the decline of household kerosene demand, oil companies integrated forward quickly to create a new industry: service stations.

Western Electric and the old Bell system claimed that vertical integration had improved efficiency in various ways, including discovery, innovation, and coordination.[37]

Preserve Revenue by Preventing Monopoly at Another Level _____

Finally, some vertical integration undoubtedly occurred to prevent someone else from monopolizing another level of the industry. One reason is to avoid giving up revenue to another firm.

VARIABLE PROPORTIONS _____

Theories that assumed fixed proportions made enormous headway in analyzing vertical integration. After 1954, fixed-proportions models appeared more frequently in economic literature.[38] According to Bork's 1969 paper, "a vertical acquisition can never create or increase a restriction of output."[39] Similarly, according to Mueller, "It can be demonstrated theoretically that a monopolist does not have a profit incentive for integrating into a competitive industry unless doing so results in economies of combined operations."[40]

It was not clear for some time whether variable proportions would change all this. Although theory gets much more complicated when components or inputs are used in variable proportions, that is surely a more realistic assumption. Economics is largely about substitution, and most goods can be produced in a variety of ways.[41] If the price of iron ore rises, it is plausible that more iron will be extracted from a given tonnage of ore, that somewhat more steel scrap will be used to charge the furnaces, and that other kinds of substitution will occur. Except for patents, variable proportions is usually a more realistic assumption.[42]

John Vernon and Daniel Graham studied the question. Their short note precipitated several longer articles, none of which is wholly satisfactory.[43]

A Single-Period Model _____

The first step is to develop a simple one-period economic model to see whether additional profits are available to a monopoly that integrates backwards or forwards. Until further notice, assume that entry by other firms is equally "difficult" regardless of which level the monopoly is on. (This assumption is relaxed later in the discussion.) Assume it is not possible for the monopoly to discriminate perfectly; or to price "all-or-none"; or to set multiple-part tariffs that approximate those results.[44] In other words, the monopoly can only price simply, setting unit price and letting buyers choose quantities.

Let Z be a good that is produced using two (or more) factors (or components) as inputs, and assume that the technological relationship between inputs and output remains unchanged whether the industry is competitive or monopolized. This assumption asserts that the integration under analysis does not save resources.[45] All inputs, and the product, are produced at constant average costs.

There is only one maximum monopoly profit to be gained, as determined by the demand for the product and the lowest costs of manufacturing it. A monopolist of the inputs produces them at the same costs as competitive industries could. A monopoly of the product market, buying inputs at competitive prices, can achieve the maximum overall profit. Backward integration from a product market monopoly to the input markets cannot increase overall profit, since the maximum profit is already being taken.

By contrast, note what would happen if the product, Z, were produced competitively, while a monopoly gets control of one input. The other input is produced competitively. The monopolized input is dearer relative to the input that is produced competitively. The producers of Z will use relatively (as well as absolutely) less of the dearer, monopolized input for two separate reasons. First, the monopolized input has become absolutely more expensive, which raises the cost functions of final good manufacturers. For a given product demand, therefore, output must be reduced. Second, the monopolized input has become *relatively* dearer as compared with the other input. If these inputs are partially substitutable one for the other—that is, if there is *variable* proportions in production—producers of Z will change their technique of production by using less of the monopolized input and more of the other(s). Given variable proportions, producers adjust to a rise in input price(s) both by reducing their output *and* by changing the mix of their inputs so as to use relatively less of the dearer input(s). Although this is the best they can do under the circumstances, their input mix has been "distorted": in principle there are cheaper ways of producing, given the real resource costs incurred to produce the inputs.

In Figure 12-3, competitive industry Z uses a monopoly-priced input Y and a competitively priced input X to produce Q_o output at point 1.[46] The slope of M/M equals the ratio of these input prices. Measured in units of X, profits from the monopolized input Y are what industry Z spends on X and Y *minus* the real costs of producing the inputs, namely M *minus* I. An integrated monopoly of Z that buys both inputs competitively

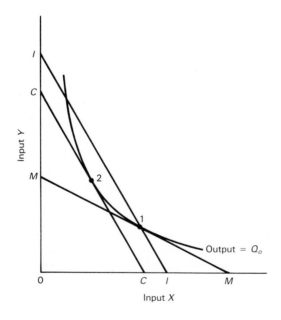

Figure 12-3 One Efficiency Gain from Vertical Integration: Proper Input Proportions.

Source: Adapted from J. M. Vernon and D. A. Graham, "Profitability & Monopolization by Vertical Integration," *Journal of Political Economy*, The University of Chicago Press, 79 (July/August 1971) pp. 924–25.

would use the input mix shown at point 2, because the price and marginal cost ratio of Y to X is C/C (and I/I). A Z monopoly, or an integrated Z and Y monopoly, could achieve that same Q_o output (and sell it at the same price) at point 2, increasing profit by at least I minus C, the value of inputs that efficient production saves.

If there had been *fixed* proportions in production, there would have been no production inefficiency and no such dead-weight loss. The lowest real-cost techniques would always be employed, and a monopoly over any input could control the whole industry and extract the maximum profit.[47] With variable proportions, however, a monopoly over the final product will be more profitable than a monopoly over anything less than all of the inputs.

Although they use similar analytic frameworks, the works by Vernon and Graham, Schmalansee, Hay, and Westfield differ significantly in emphasis, detail, and interpretation. Recall the history of vertical integration theories sketched earlier. Earlier work assumed fixed proportions and asserted that a monopoly of some input has—to oversimplify—no incentive to integrate forward, unless there are cost savings.[48] The motivation and principal effect of more recent papers is to weaken that conclusion, which depended heavily upon the fixed proportions model.

Assume that two significantly substitutable inputs, X and Y, are used to produce good Z, and are used for nothing else. Abstract from any additional functions and factors that are involved, at level Z, in making the product out of X and Y. A sole supplier of input X integrates forward, somehow directly monopolizing the manufacture of the product, Z. His profits rise, owing—recent writers say—to vertical integration, which is not quite right. It is unexplained historical accident that placed the original monopoly on X: In the very beginning, why didn't the firm simply monopolize the product market Z and concern itself no more with monopolizing either X or Y? Alternatively, given the historical accident of a monopoly over X, why doesn't the monopolist merge or agree with producers of Y to monopolize Y and X, rather than integrating forward? As we will see, conclusions and interpretations are influenced by the starting point of the analysis, and by which of various alternatives are compared.

In the basic model, there are two potential sources of increased profits. The first is changing input combinations to minimize real costs. The second is increasing monopoly power by controlling more substitutes. Among other things, this raises the question of whether in a specific case the cost-reducing effect dominates the price-raising effect.

In the model at hand, a single-firm monopoly of one input faces significant substitution from competing suppliers of the other. If it cost nothing to establish durable monopoly, it would pay someone to monopolize *both* inputs. This serves the common desire to control substitutes and raise price. In addition, there is the traditional desire to minimize cost. A single firm that monopolizes both inputs accomplishes both ends. So, alternatively, would an unintegrated single-firm monopoly of the final product alone. Apart from avoiding monopolization by someone else, neither alternative type of monopoly would gain from vertical integration per se. Nor—as compared with these unintegrated monopolies at either level—would consumers lose from a balanced, vertically integrated monopoly.

If the price-raising effect dominates the cost-reducing effect, the real culprit is increased horizontal monopoly, not vertical integration. Schmalansee, Hay, and Westfield are not sure whether vertical integration would raise or lower the final product price. Because of the point from which they begin and the alternatives they consider, it is easy to see why. If an existing monopoly of only one input integrates forward and somehow monopolizes a previously competitive product industry, there is both a cost-reducing and a monopoly-increasing effect. Will final price rise or fall? The crucial question is: as compared with what? Schmalansee, Hay, and Westfield overlook some relevant comparisons.

The following analysis can help. Five alternative arrangements should be compared: (1) competition in all input markets and in the final product; (2) monopoly over one input, and competition everywhere else; (3) monopoly over all inputs, competition in the final product; (4) monopoly over the final product and competition everywhere else; (5) one partially integrated monopoly controlling one input and the final product.

Schmalansee and Hay compare (5) with (2). But, on the basis of the production relations assumed, for each output total real costs would be identical for the first, third, fourth, and fifth alternatives. In all these cases, costs will be lower than in the second case. Final price will be identical for the third, fourth, and fifth. In all these cases, price will be higher than in the first case.

Thus, *every* result that Schmalansee and Hay attribute to integration also occurs for at least two *nonintegrated* alternative arrangements, which means that integration is neither the unique nor the crucial ingredient. For the kind of cost relations assumed, final price will be higher for the second category than the first. For Schmalansee and Hay, one troublesome question seems to be in what direction will it differ from the rest.

From the profit standpoint, the trouble with monopolizing only one input (the second alternative) is that substitution (i.e., input demand elasticity) is greater than it might be. A price rise for the one factor induces firms to minimize (a necessarily higher) cost by partially shifting away from the monopolized factor. Unless such a partial monopoly is worthwhile, it would never be exercised. Rents can only be wrenched from an excess of revenues over costs. If costs rise more than revenues, it will not work. Other things the same, it will be more worthwhile the smaller the degree of substitution. If the degree of substitution is small, there is less incentive to broaden the monopoly—and the smaller is the distortion from ''improper'' production mix. Suppressing factor substitution means that the elasticity of demand for the input package is linked, step by step, with the final demand for the product. The final product price under condition (5) may be either lower or higher than under condition (2): the price-enhancing tendency of a broader monopoly is at least partly, perhaps wholly, offset by the efficiency-enhancing tendency of integration. *Costs* will be lower for (5).

Thus even if the final product price rises when factor competition is suppressed, that price will be the same as under either complete monopoly integration, or unintegrated single-firm product monopoly. It is fundamentally a question of comparing the results of equivalent degrees of horizontal monopoly, not about something called vertical integration. Furthermore Schmalansee and Hay agree that, as with all monopoly problems, efficiency aspects must be considered along with price. There is no objection to that. But, it should be noted, for equivalent degrees of monopoly, integration in this case is no more and no less *production*-efficient than unintegrated monopoly of all factors, or product monopoly, or competition.

Chapter 9 briefly discussed the compound pricing models that McGee published in 1987. Those same models shed light on variable-proportions vertical integration. Assume that the same five-input production recipes used in his article, and referred to in Chapter 9, also apply here.[49] We can use McGee's published results to give us perspective and a sense of scale. A competitive downstream industry buying all five inputs competitively would charge $6.64 per unit for the consumer good it makes from them. A single-firm monopoly of input number 1 would price it at $51.75, much higher than the competitive level, $21. As a result, average and marginal costs—and final price—of the competitive manufacturing industry would rise from $6.64 to $8.04.

By contrast, an unintegrated single-firm monopoly of the *final consumer good* that buys all factors competitively would have much greater monopoly power than a monopoly of only one factor of production. It would also produce at lower costs, with the most efficient mix of inputs. For the cost and demand conditions assumed, efficiency gains do not counterbalance the enormous increase in monopoly power, and final price of the consumer good would rise to $23.32. Furthermore, losses in consumer surplus would be larger than the gains in production efficiency. Even pricing input number 1 all-or-none would yield smaller profits than a completely integrated monopoly of *all* these inputs would earn.[50]

But all this mischief comes from grossly increased *horizontal* monopoly power, not vertical integration. A nonintegrated monopoly of all the *inputs* would be precisely as bad as a nonintegrated retail monopoly that buys all these inputs in competitive markets.

Finally, we must note that the empirical implications of theories are not irrelevant. The papers of Vernon and Graham, Schmalansee, Hay, and Westfield are all devoted to explaining *forward* integration, for which there are already many theoretical and practical explanations. Their theories neither apply to, predict, nor explain *backward* integration, of which there are many real examples.

The Effect of Time

So far, we have discussed single-period vertical integration and single-period monopoly profits. This section extends the analysis to take account of time. A monopolist seeks to maximize the present value of profits, that is, the discounted profit stream over time. Are additional profits available from forward or backward integration? The present value depends upon how large profits are each period, how long profits last, and when they occur. The size of a constant discount rate does not affect the comparisons made.

We have previously seen that profitability per period can be greater for a broader monopoly than for a narrower monopoly. There remains the question whether vertical integration can affect how long a monopoly endures.

It has long been asserted that a vertically integrated monopoly can combat nonintegrated entrants with price squeezes and other nasty tricks. As a result, entrants need to integrate in self-defense. This, the story goes, raises capital requirements for entry and prolongs or increases the static monopoly effect.[51] But the resident firm, integrated itself, also has to carry whatever costs integration entails. Chapter 7 discusses capital requirements as a barrier to entry and finds them problematic at best.[52]

The present value of monopoly profits, or of resource misallocation, is a function of the result per period and the duration of the result.[53] In principle, there are two ways of linking vertical integration to the duration of monopoly. First, we could ask whether and how vertical integration increases resource scarcity; engenders more favorable legal treatment; lowers cost; or drastically raises optimal firm size relative to the market. Second, we could simply *assume* that monopoly will last longer in one industry than the other, and inquire whether such a condition would have different effects if the two industries were then integrated. We will take this second approach.

To simplify, assume that there is no monopsony and that integration does not alter costs.[54] Under these heroic assumptions, how, then, would integration affect the longevity of monopoly? As before, let Z be the output produced using two or more inputs, and assume that the industry production function remains unchanged whether the industry is competitive or monopolized. If Z is manufactured using fixed proportions among the inputs, all of the available profits at one time period can be captured by a monopoly of any single input or by a monopoly of the final good, Z.

What happens depends upon information, law, and the distribution of skills. If he were certain which monopoly will last longest, under fixed proportions a monopolizer might be tempted to choose that level and ignore the rest.[55] But that risks a bilateral monopoly created if someone else monopolizes the other level. Bilateral monopoly has unhappy implications for profits, production efficiency, and final prices to consumers. Permitting vertical integration would not increase either the breadth or duration of monopoly, and would favor production efficiency and consumer satisfaction. If a monopolist integrates beyond the most durable monopoly, it would do so to avoid the costs of someone else's monopolizing the other level(s).

Uncertainty about which level will support the most durable monopoly encourages vertical integration as a hedge. But, when the dusts settle, vertical integration will not be found to have increased the duration of monopoly: if the monopolist had chosen the right level, unintegrated monopoly would endure as long as integrated monopoly. Mistaken choice *would* reduce the duration of unintegrated monopoly: a simple vertical disintegration that left intact the monopoly power inherent in each level would not. In addition, such a disintegration would produce the disadvantages of bilateral monopoly, referred to earlier. If law permits monopoly at each stage, integration is preferable and should not be discouraged.

Turn now to variable proportions. Purely for illustration, return to the simple parable about iron ore and steel. *Ore* is shorthand for input markets, and assume that steel is the final product market. Assume that some ore is indispensable to the production of steel, and that only a one-price policy is feasible: there is no possibility of all-or-none (perfectly discriminatory) pricing. Whether vertical integration can be said to increase the present value of profits then depends upon what constraints we assume (including law and the distribution of information and talent); and, of course, upon what alternatives we compare it with.

As noted earlier, the one-period profit from the product market monopoly is greater than the profit that could be captured in any one of the input markets. However, it is possible that entry into some input market may be slower than entry into the product market. Assume that there is certainty, and that the one firm permitted or competent to monopolize either level is not permitted to integrate vertically. In that case, the firm would monopolize the product market first, since it yields larger profits per period. When that monopoly erodes, the firm would move into and monopolize such inputs as it could. Profits would not be as high in the second phase as in the first, and costs would be higher because the factor mix becomes distorted.

If, on the other hand, two or more firms *can* monopolize independently and efficiently, *and* if vertical integration is permitted, the first choice is less appealing. There is then a strong incentive to integrate.

If another firm monopolizes ore, this creates bilateral monopoly, the avoidance of which is good reason for the steel monopoly to integrate from the beginning. Integration for this reason seems preferable to bilateral monopoly during the whole period that the steel monopoly endures: it minimizes production costs without increasing the monopoly effect. With bilateral monopoly, erosion of the steel monopoly would still leave the ore monopolist in charge. Input distortion then raises costs, an effect that would have to be weighed against reduced monopoly. Complete vertical integration from the start would avoid bilateral monopoly complications, permit maximum production efficiency, increase profits in every period, and—thus—increase present value.[56]

We must be careful in interpreting these results. It looks as though vertical integration made the least durable monopoly (steel) as durable as the most durable monopoly (ore). A good deal more than vertical integration is needed to produce that result. First, it requires a tight and durable monopoly over ore, which deserves an explanation, and possibly can offer some defense. Second, in the absence of all-embracing, perfectly efficient contracting, the monopoly would have to refuse to sell ore to anyone who would enter the steel industry.[57] In short, such results require exceedingly tight assumptions: no one can produce steel without ore, all ore is owned by the single-firm steel monopoly, and the steel firm will not sell ore.

Hermetically sealed hypothetical examples like these should not be used to oppose real-world vertical integration. First, our parable deals with an ironclad single-firm monopoly that, by assumption, is not defensible on efficiency grounds (including size economies, superior management, efficiencies arising out of integration itself, copyrights, and patents).[58] Except possibly for monopoly created by law, there are few such cases,[59] and famous antitrust cases about vertical integration—like *Brown Shoe* and the *Concrete* cases—are not even remote approximations. Even in our parables, monopoly is a question of horizontal power that should be analyzed and appraised directly. Second, the argument simply *assumes* that integration occurs because *input* monopolies are more durable than those that can be established in products markets. If this is not the case, however, product monopoly could take all, and integration has nothing to do with how durable monopoly is.

SUMMARY

Assuming fixed proportions greatly simplifies the economics of vertical integration. Under that assumption, there seems to be no economic case against vertical integration, except possibly that it facilitates price discrimination.

Although the variable-proportions assumption is more realistic, it greatly complicates the analysis, and, in the end, strengthens the case against vertical integration little or not at all. In analyzing the price effects that follow vertical integration, we must weigh two opposing forces. First, vertical integration reduces cost, by achieving the most efficient input mix if nothing else. Second, vertical integration may also increase monopoly power, just as would a merger of the input industries themselves—even without integration. Although it is true that integration under this assumption could sometimes be *followed* by higher final prices, it is not integration that causes it. *Every* such result attributed to integration also occurs for at least two *nonintegrated* alternative arrangements, which means that integration is neither the unique nor the crucial ingredient.

Broadening a monopoly may increase profits; but we must be careful about what we attribute to vertical integration itself. Among other things, vertical integration has efficiency-raising aspects. In the case of monopsony in the face of a scarce resource, vertical integration itself tends to reduce the misallocation of resources. Integration that avoids or breaks monopoly on another level benefits consumers. No matter what the state of competition at, say, the manufacturing level, it is desirable to avoid unnecessary monopoly in distribution (and vice versa.) For example, breaking down bilateral monopoly by vertical integration or otherwise is economically beneficial.

In sum, when vertical integration lowers real costs, breaks monopoly, or avoids monopoly, it is desirable to realize these good effects without legal delay.

Economic analysis makes one wonder why there is so much opposition to vertical integration. The real problem, if one exists, is horizontal monopoly power. It is, however, prudent to recognize that, as Bork wrote in 1954,

> A comparison of the law and economics of vertical integration makes it clear that the two bear little resemblance. If the law in this area is to be concerned with the kind of competition with which economists are familiar, the concept of vertical integration will have to be abandoned as an analytical tool. The idea of horizontal integration is sufficient to the tasks of the Sherman Law, and presents, in the guise of market definition, problems enough for judicial ingenuity.[60]

QUESTIONS

1. What *is* vertical integration?
2. GE and Westinghouse apparently conspired to fix the price of light bulbs at the manufacturing level. They may have conspired to fix prices at the retail level as well, using price maintenance contracts. Would that have been redundant; or could it have strengthened their conspiracy? Explain.

3. Explain and comment on squeezes as a monopolizing practice.

4. Suppose a monopoly at one level integrates into another level. Does this mean that entrants would have to come in at both levels (to avoid squeezes), which increases capital requirements and bars entry?

5. Why would Alcoa want to discriminate in selling aluminum at different prices accordingly as it was used in electric cable, sheets for streamlined trains, pots and pans, engine parts? How would vertical integration into producing these items help Alcoa discriminate?

6. How, if at all, does resale price maintenance (RPM) differ from vertical integration? What cases can be made for and against RPM?

7. Does vertical integration transmit monopoly power from one level to another? Explain.

8. How could vertical integration lower costs?

9. How could vertical integration take place because a firm *has* lower costs?

10. Picture and explain the basic, fixed-proportions model of a two-level industry. Show whether vertical integration produces different prices and quantities than would a nonintegrated monopoly at either level.

NOTES

1. See J. S. McGee and Lowell Bassett, "Vertical Integration Revisited," *Journal of Law and Economics*, 19 (April 1976), p. 17.

2. According to a leading authority, there is vertical integration whenever a firm "transmits from one of its departments to another a good or service which could, without major adaptation, be sold in the market." Morris A. Adelman, "Integration and Antitrust Policy," 63 *Harvard Law Review* 27 (1949). For ways used to measure vertical integration, see Adelman, "Concept and Statistical Measurement of Vertical Integration," in *Business Concentration and Price Policy*, ed. George J. Stigler (Princeton, N.J.: Princeton University Press, 1955), pp. 281–322; and Irston R. Barnes, "Comment," ibid., pp. 322–30.

   The most profound theoretical guide to what firms are and why they do what they do is R. H. Coase, "The Nature of the Firm," *Economica* 4, (n.s. 1937), pp. 386–405, reprinted in George J. Stigler and Kenneth Boulding, eds., *Readings in Price Theory* (Homewood, Ill.: Richard D. Irwin, Inc., 1952), pp. 331–51. A more recent study is Sanford J. Grossman and Oliver D. Hart, "The Costs and Benefits of Ownership: A Theory of Vertical and Lateral Integration," *Journal of Political Economy*, 94 (August 1986), pp. 691–719.

3. An interesting study of a real industry is Scott F. Masten, "The Organization of Production: Evidence from the Aerospace Industry," *Journal of Law & Economics*, 27 (October 1984), pp. 403–17.

4. "There is doubt, indeed, that we want a theory of vertical integration except as part of a theory of the functions of a firm." George J. Stigler, *The Organization of Industry* (Homewood, Ill.: Richard D. Irwin, Inc., 1968), p. 138. For parts of an emerging "theory of the functions of a firm," consult Coase, "The Nature of the Firm"; O. E. Williamson, "The Vertical Integration of Production: Market Failure Considerations," *American Economic Review*, 61 (May 1971), pp. 112–23; R. N. McKean, "Discussion," ibid., pp. 124–25; and A. A. Alchian and H. Demsetz, "Production, Information Costs, and Economic Organization," *American Economic Review* (December 1972), pp. 777–95.

Vertical integration is often observed in industries in which there is not even a hint of harmful monopoly power. When integration occurs in more concentrated industries it is therefore questionable to assert that its only purpose or result is "monopoly power." A condition common to everything is unable to explain differences between things.

5. See *Brown Shoe*, for example. *Brown Shoe Co.* v. *United States*, 370 U.S. 294 (1962).

6. See, for example, F. M. Scherer, *Industrial Market Structure and Economic Performance* (Chicago: Rand McNally College Publishing Company, 1970), pp. 69–70.

7. Two recent FTC studies are Thomas R. Overstreet, Jr., *Resale Price Maintenance: Economic Theories and Empirical Evidence* (Washington, D.C.: Bureau of Economics Staff Report to the Federal Trade Commission, November 1983); and Edward C. Gallick, *Exclusive Dealing and Vertical Integration: The Efficiency of Contracts in the Tuna Industry* (Washington, D.C.: Bureau of Economics Staff Report to the Federal Trade Commission, August 1984).

8. Robert H. Bork, "Vertical Integration and the Sherman Act: The Legal History of an Economic Misconception," 22 *University of Chicago Law Review* (Autumn 1954), pp. 157–201. Bork was not alone in arguing that popular arguments against vertical integration were wrong: M. A. Adelman, Aaron Director, J. J. Spengler, and others had each analyzed at least part of the problem. For example, see Adelman, "Integration and Antitrust Policy;" J. J. Spengler, "Vertical Integration and Antitrust Policy," *Journal of Political Economy*, 58 (August 1950), pp. 347–52. Vertical integration was one subject of Aaron Director's socratic analysis, which contributed much to an oral tradition in and around the University of Chicago. For example, see the student note, "Vertical Forestalling under the Antitrust Laws," 19 *University of Chicago Law Review* (1952). For a review of even earlier analyses, see F. Machlup and M. Taber, "Bilateral Monopoly, Successive Monopoly, and Vertical Integration," *Economica*, 27 (May 1960), pp. 101–17.

9. Alfred Marshall, *Principles of Economics*, 8th Edition (New York: Macmillan, Inc., 1949), pp. 384, 852–53.

10. The analysis works for any number of levels, proceeding step by step. To derive the net demand for any component, subtract from the final demand the sum of costs of all the other components.

11. One study of the oil industry claims that integrated firms enjoyed more *stable* profits than nonintegrated firms. J. G. McLean and R. W. Haigh, *The Growth of Integrated Oil Companies* (Boston: Graduate School of Business Administration, Harvard University, 1954), pp. 663–64.

12. It is not clear *what* the railroad was doing. See W. E. Ruther, "The Northern Pacific Case," *Journal of Law & Economics*, 22 (October 1979), pp. 329–50.

13. *U.S.* v. *Socony Vacuum Oil Co.*, 310 U.S. 150 (1940).

14. Two modern classics are R. H. Coase, "The Nature of the Firm"; and George J. Stigler, "The Division of Labor is Limited by the Extent of the Market," in Stigler, *The Organization of Industry*, pp. 129–41.

15. Compare Jack E. Gelfand, "Vertical Integration in the Steel Industry," Temple University, *Economics and Business Bulletin*, December 1958, pp. 9–15.

16. For the full story, see Morris A. Adelman, *A&P: A Study in Price-Cost Behavior and Public Policy* (Cambridge, Mass.: Harvard University Press, 1959).

17. See note 11.

18. John S. McGee, "Ocean Freight-Rate Conferences and the American Merchant Marine," 27 *University of Chicago Law Review* 2 (Winter 1960), pp. 191–314.

19. D. H. Wallace, *Market Control in the Aluminum Industry* (Cambridge, Mass.: Harvard University Press, 1937), pp. 179–88.

20. See the appendix to Chapter 6 for a model of sugar-beet refining.

21. John S. McGee, "Government Intervention in the Spanish Sugar Industry," *Journal of Law & Economics*, 7 (October 1964), pp. 121–72.

22. Wallace found a related source of economies even when the same kind of inventories are not involved: gearing the base load of a power plant to the energy need of one large aluminum plant, as opposed to the peak loads for many buyers. Wallace, *Market Control in the Aluminum Industry*, pp. 183–84.

23. Joan Robinson, *The Economics of Imperfect Competition* (London: Macmillan and Co., Limited, 1946), pp. 133–42.

24. Starting from scratch, before steel and ore production actually commence, a potential steel producer could have bought the ore-bearing lands at still lower prices, *if* he had better information than landowners. By paying their value as farm lands, or a trifle more, he could have bought them all.

25. If increasing supply prices are due to technological externalities that are internal to the supplying *industry*, then marginal social cost is coincident with marginal factor cost for the buying monopsonist. In this case, unintegrated monopsony leads to the correct allocation of resources.

26. Morris Adelman's book on A&P is suggestive. M. Adelman, *A&P: A Study in Price-Cost Behavior and Public Policy* (Cambridge, Mass.: Harvard University Press, 1959), pp. 120–22, 124–25, 168–69, 171–72, 241, 248–96, 382–83, 392–94, 411–12.

27. Willard F. Mueller, "Public Policy Toward Vertical Mergers," in *Public Policy Toward Mergers*, eds. J. Fred Weston and Sam Peltzman (Pacific Palisades, Calif.: Goodyear Publishing Co., Inc., 1969), pp. 156–62.

28. Ibid., p. 162.

29. This assumes that the output that minimizes the firm's average cost is the same before and after integration. Other possibilities are discussed in Lowell R. Bassett and Thomas E. Borcherding, "The Relationship Between Firm Size and Factor Price," *Quarterly Journal of Economics*, 74 (August 1970), pp. 518–22.

30. This ignores important possibilities, including that cost savings, increased profits, and increased consumer benefits may be *deferred* substantially (deferred benefits are less attractive than immediate benefits); and that the costs of integrating may be lower if mergers are permitted.

31. "Relevant demand" depends upon what kind of pricing model is assumed. The demand facing a dominant firm, for example, subtracts from total market demand the quantity followers will market at each price. Since followers shrink with lower prices and expand with higher prices, the demand elasticity facing the dominant firm tends to be a good deal higher than that facing the industry as a whole. Presumably the dominant firm would choose an output rate at which the absolute value of its demand elasticity is greater than 1.

32. W. F. Mueller, "Public Policy Toward Vertical Mergers," in *Public Policy Towards Mergers*, eds. Weston and Peltzman, pp. 153–55, 162–64.

33. Adelman, *A&P*.

34. There are obviously other considerations as well, including lowered costs of contact, contract, and coordination.

35. *U.S.* v. *General Electric Co.*, 272 U.S. 476 (1926).

36. A recent study of the politics and economics of this practice is Howard P. Marvel and Stephen McCafferty, "The Political Economy of Resale Price Maintenance," *Journal of Political Economy*, 94 (October 1986), pp. 1074–95.

37. James R. Billingsley, Vice President Regulatory Matters, Western Electric Company, "Values of Vertical Integration in the Bell System," address given at the Sixth Annual Seminar on Economics of Public Utilities, Oshkosh, Wisc., March 8, 1973. Also see McKinsey & Company, Inc., *A Study of Western Electric's Performance* (New York: American Telephone & Telegraph Company, 1969); and *Engineering and Operations in the Bell System* (n.p.: Bell Telephone Laboratories, Incorporated, 1977).

38. For example, see Eugene M. Singer, *Antitrust Economics* (Englewood Cliffs, N.J.: Prentice-Hall, Inc., 1968), pp. 206–11, espec. p. 208; Douglas Needham, *Economic Analysis and Industrial Structure* (New York: Holt, Rinehart & Winston, 1969), p. 118; and F. M. Scherer, *Industrial Market Structure* (Chicago: Rand McNally and Company, 1970) pp. 243, 250.

39. R. H. Bork, "Vertical Integration and Competitive Process," in *Public Policy Toward Mergers*, eds. Weston and Peltzman, pp. 139–49, at p. 142.

40. W. F. Mueller, "Public Policy Toward Vertical Mergers," ibid., p.153.

41. "The production coefficients are in general variable: there is no unique quantity of land (or other input) necessary to produce a bushel of wheat. * * * The phenomenon of substitution is well-nigh ubiquitous. * * * Even if all production coefficients are variable—and this of course no one can know—there remains the question: how variable? If a technical coefficient ranges only between 1/11 and 1/12 (roughly the average technological coefficient of professors per student), it may be simpler for many questions to assume it is fixed." George J. Stigler, *The Theory of Price*, 3rd ed. (New York: Macmillan, Inc., 1966), pp. 114, 115, 118.

42. Bork wrote his 1954 article while a member of the Antitrust Project at the University of Chicago. During that time there were discussions about the usefulness of variable proportions models in analyzing vertical integration and other subjects. Compare Bork, "Vertical Integration and the Sherman Act," pages 171–73; 196–97; and Ward S. Bowman, Jr., "Tying Arrangements and the Leverage Problem," *Yale Law Journal*, 67 (November 1957), pp. 19–36.

43. J. M. Vernon and D. A. Graham, "Profitability of Monopolization by Vertical Integration," *Journal of Political Economy*, 79 (July/August1971), pp. 924–25. That note precipitated still other papers: Richard Schmalansee, "A Note on the Theory of Vertical Integration," *Journal of Political Economy*, 81 (March/April 1973), pp. 442–49 (citing Vernon and Graham); and George E. Hay, "An Economic Analysis of Vertical Integration," *Industrial Organization Review*, 1 (1973), pp. 188–98 (citing Vernon and Graham, and Schmalansee); McGee and Bassett, "Vertical Integration Revisited"; F. M. Westfield, "Vertical Integration: Does Product Price Rise or Fall?" *American Economic Review*, 71 (June 1981), p. 334.

44. If costs were not related to industry structure, and income effects were nil, a perfectly discriminating single-firm monopoly could achieve the competitive output solution. And a monopoly of even one indispensable input could extract all available rents through all-or-none contracting. That monopolies never actually discriminate *perfectly* is commonly attributed to the quality and costs of information, law, contracting, and enforcement. An input monopolist at an early level would have to overcome enormous informational and contractual complexities to accomplish all-or-none pricing. See Chapter 9.

45. Because this implies that a monopoly uses exactly the same resources as everyone else, it cannot explain why it is able to monopolize. In fact, monopoly commonly employs one or more *different* resources, a state license or franchise, for example. The assumption that monopoly enjoys neither economies of size nor superior efficiencies leaves its existence and persistence unexplained.

46. Vernon and Graham, "Profitability of Monopolization by Vertical Integration."

47. Of course, if—contrary to the present assumption—an input monopoly *could* specify both price and quantity (in an all-or-none contract) and at least one unit of this input is required to produce the final product, it could, in effect, specify fixed proportions and thus extract all the profit even though technical substitution is possible among the inputs in the production process.

48. It can be argued in its defense that the fixed-proportions assumption holds monopoly power constant over all the alternative industry arrangements to be compared, and thus reveals the effects of integration pure and simple. Nevertheless, purely by assumption fixed proportions maximizes the amount of "monopoly" that any input supplier has, and denies the significance of price-induced distortions in production techniques.

49. For details, see John S. McGee, "Compound Pricing," *Economic Inquiry*, (April 1987), pp. 315–39.

50. For an analysis of the *path* of price movements (at all levels) as vertical integration proceeds, see Herman C. Quirmbach, "The Path of Price Changes in Vertical Integration," *Journal of Political Economy*, 94 (October 1986), pp. 1110–19.

51. It is wrong to assume either that capital requirements will be raised by vertical integration or that raising them *would* raise entry barriers. There would be no increase in capital requirements and—by assumption—no cost disadvantage if different, unintegrated firms enter at each level and trade with each other. If integration does lower costs, of course, that is enough to explain and justify it.

52. Also see Bork, "Vertical Integration and the Sherman Act," p. 195; G. J. Stigler, *Organization of Industry*, pp. 113–22; J. S. McGee, "Comment," *American Economic Review*, 57 (May 1967), pp. 269–71; McGee, *In Defense of Industrial Concentration*, pp. 45, 49–52.

53. Profits and resource misallocation are very different things. See Chapter 11.

54. Integration often reduces costs, increases output, and generates welcome efficiencies. As a result, ignoring these possibilities, as we do here purely to simplify, seriously biases discussion of policy alternatives.

55. Apart from state interventions, there is no satisfactory general explanation of why one monopoly endures longer than another. Instead, there are proximate explanations that are themselves unexplained: natural scarcities of skills, resources, or information; differences in laws; differences in efficiency; differences in exogenous forces like changes in taste, income, and technology; and differences in optimal firm sizes relative to demands. It is not even clear how many of these explanations are different.

56. It should be noted, however, that—except for state-supported monopoly—the existence of two or more competent firms raises the issue of whether *any* monopoly can be formed, or persist.

57. It is difficult to define *refusal to deal* operationally. It should include *de facto* refusals to deal, such as "offers" to sell ore at prices that when added to outsiders' costs of producing steel are higher than the monopolist's profit-maximizing steel price. But a definition that broad can hurt beneficial arrangements: If an integrated firm is more efficient, even if its ore prices were

in fact competitive, they will look prohibitively high to less-efficient prospective steel producers.

58. For discussions of the efficiency rationale for patents, see Chapter 8; J. S. McGee, "Patent Exploitation: Some Economic and Legal Problems," *Journal of Law & Economics*, 9 (October 1966), pp. 135–62; and Scherer, *Industrial Market Structure and Economic Performance*, pp. 379–99.

59. They are rare or nonexistent in Sherman Law monopoly and monopolizing cases. *Standard Oil* (1911) and *American Tobacco* (1911), for example, do not appear to rest on vertical integration, but on product supply. Perhaps *Alcoa* is the closest approximation; but Alcoa's "power," probably rested on ore and ingots, not on pots, pans, and other final goods.

60. Bork, "Vertical Integration and the Sherman Act," p. 201.

WELFARE TRADE-OFFS

INTRODUCTION

In contrasting the performance of concentrated and unconcentrated industries, economists usually assume that both kinds of industrial structures have the same costs. This chapter drops that peculiar and unrealistic assumption. As we will see, the ways in which industrial structure relates to cost and other efficiencies are crucial. It is impossible to evaluate industry concentration without explicitly taking such relationships into account.

The first section presents static models showing different ways in which costs and industrial structure can be related. This section also shows how to apply traditional economic welfare standards to different cases. Taking those models as a point of departure, the next section extends the theory, informally tracing out dynamic as well as static implications that are important for informed policy making.

THE BASIC MODELS

Efficiency has both static and dynamic aspects. Economists' standard two-dimensional diagrams,[1] which compare monopoly and competitive prices and outputs, are barely adequate to treat static differences. They generally fail to settle dynamic questions.[2] First, the static cost question.

When we discuss public policies with respect to the structure of industries, we are of course talking about the desirability of having government change existing structures. We should recognize that forced changes in the number of firms are likely to alter costs. Suppose that concentration arises because of economies of mass production, or superior products, or different efficiencies in different firms. If those kinds of forces caused concentration in the first place, forcibly increasing the number of firms will raise costs or otherwise reduce net benefits.

Our first task, therefore, is explicitly to show ways in which costs and concentration may be related. Our second task is to show how a given level of concentration affects the relationship of price to cost. We can then show how concentration and economic welfare are related. We need some theory to demonstrate precisely what can happen. Theories that are indefinite about the effects we are looking for are not much help. We need to know how costs affect concentration and how concentration affects performance—costs considered.

This section concentrates on Cournot's very definite theory about industrial structure. In Cournot's world, larger numbers of sellers reduce the spread between marginal cost and price. Even so, artificially raising the number of sellers can actually raise costs and reduce economic welfare. Indeed, it can raise costs so much that prices rise absolutely. Few would applaud that result. An important question is whether, even if forcing an increase in the number of firms reduces price *relative* to marginal cost, an increase in cost partly or wholly offsets that effect. In general, we should always evaluate cost changes along with any increase in ''competitiveness'' that a change in the number of firms produces.

In Cournot's model there is a clear relationship between the number of firms and the *difference* between price and marginal cost. That, however, would not be enough to justify increasing the number of firms via government action. Because a rational policy with respect to industrial structure must also consider the effects on costs and demands. If Cournot is right, relatively few firms give us approximately atomistic results even when large firms are no more efficient than small ones. Starting from an industry of only one firm, small increases in the number of sellers produce large price and output effects. For a given number of sellers, price will more nearly approach the competitive norm as the elasticity of industry demand is higher; and the oligopoly industry in question may face a highly elastic industry demand, especially in the long run.

To get rid of needless complications, the following analyses do not use downward- or upward-sloping long-run average cost functions to show relationships between costs and the size of firms. Instead, they use different *levels* of constant-cost functions to show cost differences for different industrial structures. Relevant comparisons are then easier to make and understand. This simplification ignores some formal properties of increasing-returns to scale, but necessary substance remains—especially since many efficiencies do not arise from economies of scale anyway.[3]

If larger firms have lower costs, a concentrated industry can give better results than less concentrated structures, even if it behaves as Cournot said. There are four major possibilities.

Oligopoly Lowers Costs without Affecting Price

In Figure 13-1, let *DD* be the industry demand for a homogeneous product. $LRMC_O$ is the minimum long-run marginal and average cost achievable. Assume that it can be achieved only when the industry is oligopolistic. Assume that this oligopoly manages to get price

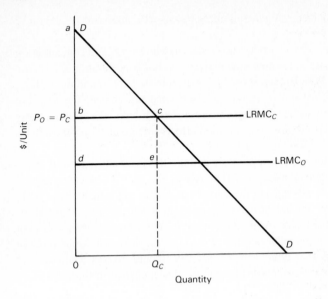

Figure 13-1 Oligopoly Lowers Costs without Affecting Price

above marginal and average cost, as Cournot's theory says, for example. Substantially lower concentration would lead to higher costs. For example, let $LRMC_C$ be the long-run marginal and average cost under a proposed industrial deconcentration scheme that brings price and marginal cost to practical equality. Let P_C be the resulting price. Let's call it "competitive." Even when, as here, oligopoly cost is lower, its price may conceivably be the same as, lower than, or higher than the competitive price. Consider these possibilities in turn.

If the oligopoly price is equal to P_C, consumer surplus is *abc* for either oligopoly or competition.[4] There are zero profits under competition, but *bcde* profits under oligopoly. These profits precisely measure the value of resources saved through greater efficiency. Consumers of this product are equally well off, and producers are better off: The sum of profits and consumer surplus is greater under oligopoly than under competition. And the resources saved here help consumers elsewhere. It is hard to understand why we should attack such a situation unless what we really want to do is simply to punish successful producers.[5]

Oligopoly Lowers Cost and Price

Figure 13-2 illustrates the possibility that costs and prices may both be lower under oligopoly than under competition. Competitive price is P_C; oligopoly price is P_O. Under competition, consumer surplus is *abc*, and there are no profits. Under oligopoly, consumers are even better off, and there are also profits of *defg*. These profits *understate* the value of resources saved through greater efficiency. Since both consumers and producers are better off under oligopoly, it would be even harder to justify forced deconcentration.

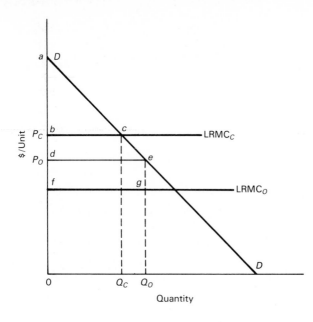

Figure 13-2 Oligopoly Lowers
Cost and Price

Oligopoly Lowers Cost, Raises Price _____

Figure 13-3 illustrates the possibility that prices may be higher under oligopoly, even though costs are lower. Oliver Williamson popularized this mixed or trade-off case.[6] Cournot's theory neatly complements this kind of analysis, since Cournot oligopoly does not maximize joint profits, but produces much larger output than would single-firm monopoly. Thus there is no requirement, or even reason, for oligopolists to maximize group profits or to operate in the elastic range of industry demand. As a result, it would not be surprising, in a Cournot world, if oligopoly turned out to be allocatively superior to pure competition. In a Bertrand-Edgeworth world, this is even more likely, with as few as two firms. But it is surely possible even in Fellner's world, where several firms act almost like one.

Some oppose measuring welfare as the sum of consumer and producer surplus, because that ignores the income redistribution effect and assumes that oligopolists are as deserving as consumers. This argument would be more impressive if someone had demonstrated that sellers are less deserving, and in what proportion.

By *assumption*, the sense of which will be considered later, price under competition is P_C; under oligopoly it is P_O. Consumer surplus is larger under competition, by an amount *bcdef*; but profits are higher under oligopoly by *bcgh*. Under oligopoly, the area *bcde* cancels: it is lost by consumers but gained by producers. Hence, whether the sum of profits and consumer surplus is higher under oligopoly depends upon whether *degh*, the "net" profit increase due to efficiency, is greater than *cef*, the dead-weight misallocation loss. In such a case, finding the trade-off between efficiency and concentration is neces-

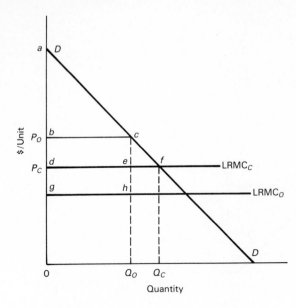

Figure 13-3 Oligopoly Lowers Cost But Raises Price

Source: Adapted from Oliver E. Williamson, "Economies as an Antitrust Defense," *American Economic Review*, 58 (March 1968), figure 1, p. 21.

sary to evaluate the case for industrial deconcentration. This is so even though price is *assumed* to be higher under oligopoly.

For closed monopoly—in which entry is impossible—this type of trade-off may confront us, waiving dynamic considerations. But closed monopoly and closed oligopoly are rare. When entry is possible, one theory says, oligopoly price will not be greater than the competitive price. If it were, entry would occur. According to this theory, if P_C is an atomistically competitive price, no single entrant would affect price significantly, and entry will occur.[7]

If there is single-firm monopoly rather than oligopoly, however, another theory must be considered. According to this theory, a type of limit pricing, a single-firm monopoly with a significant cost advantage could charge the full monopoly price, higher than P_C, even when entry is open. If anyone less efficient enters, the monopoly could set price below entrants' cost, but above its own, and watch them wither. According to this theory, no one will enter when the monopoly has a significant cost advantage. All know what will happen if they do. There is no objection to assuming that entrants know what will happen. But what about middlemen and consumers? If everybody sees the big picture, why can't entrants contract to charge lower average prices than the monopoly would provide? What is more, single-firm monopoly is very rare. Oligopolists would have to be well coordinated to make this sad scenario work. It is doubtful that noncolluding oligopolists could raise price above P_C. To do that requires that they also have enough coordination and discipline to pull off the kind of price cut the theory calls for in the face of entry.

But it does not pay monopolists to do everything they are physically capable of doing, and it would not pay them to do that if entry actually occurs.

A variant of this cost-*advantage* entry-barrier theory is the Baumol-Willig sunk-cost theory, which was discussed in Chapter 7. It argues that sunk costs, rather than fixed costs, can bar entry. Sunk costs "are those costs that (in some short or intermediate run) cannot be eliminated, even by total cessation of production. As such, once committed, sunk costs are no longer a portion of the opportunity costs of production."[8] Sunk costs are thus supposed to cut both ways. It is sad to get stuck with sunk costs when things go bad; yet firms now in the industry have an edge because they have already incurred their sunk costs. "The need to sink costs can be a barrier to entry. . . . the incremental cost, as seen by a potential entrant, includes the full amount of the sunk costs, which is a bygone to the incumbent."[9]

Even in pessimistic versions, this case is not predatory in the strictest sense: only less efficient competitors could be kept out. In any case, it may simply cost too much to deconcentrate a concentrated industry of this sort.

In short, Williamson's trade-off theory may underestimate the power of entry.

Oligopoly Price Is Higher, Costs the Same

We come now to the most famous and influential trade-off case of all. Indeed, it is the oligopoly version of the most common textbook version of monopoly, analyzed earlier in Chapter 2. Figure 13-4 illustrates it. In this case, atomistic competition and oligopoly have identical costs and offer the same product. Yet somehow the oligopoly manages to raise price to P_O. As a result, consumers lose *bced* in surplus, which the oligopoly gets as profits. But consumers also lose *cef* in surplus, which nobody gains. That is the dead-weight loss. Unless entry is closed by law, however, it is not obvious that this case is of any practical importance. Although it might occur, it is unlikely to persist. Entrants suffer

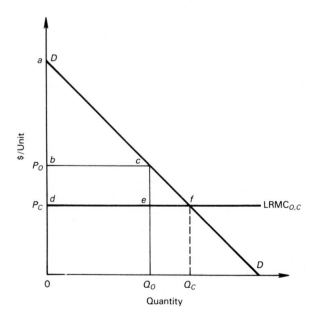

Figure 13-4 Oligopoly Cost Is Unchanged, But Price Is Higher

no cost disadvantage, and this kind of oligopoly would presumably evolve into competition.

It is arguable, therefore, that neither Williamson's case nor this one is likely to persist unless an oligopoly is preserved by law. If true, this would leave us with the first two possibilities, and with Bork's and Bowman's major policy conclusions.[10]

As Chapters 3, 4, 5, and 7 showed, much of economic theory is ambiguous about how concentration, costs, and price are interrelated. Even theories predicting that concentration raises price above cost are not enough to sanctify antitrust assaults or government regulation. The level of costs and the values of products simply must be considered. Indeed, if public policy is to make sense, still other static problems ought to be acknowledged. One of them is the theory of second best, which cautions about effects that an antimonopoly program may have on other industries as well.

Also involved are complex dynamic problems, including the effects that industry structure has on cost-saving innovations and product improvements. That these are related to industrial structure and government regulation seems plausible, though there is much debate about what that relationship is, as chapters 14 and 15 will show.

SIZE AND EFFICIENCY: EXTENDING THE THEORY

Costs Aren't Everything

The models just presented concentrated on relationships between firm sizes and cost. So did the theories, statistical cost estimates, and engineering studies discussed in Chapter 7. But there is more to efficiency than *cost*. For example, a cheap way to put a pound of flesh on a human frame, or to sustain a given level of physical activity, is to eat grains directly. A more expensive way is to feed the grains to livestock and eat the meat they produce. The indirect and more expensive method results in technical conversion losses, which might carelessly be called "inefficiencies." But there is more to life and economics than technical or engineering standards. Many people like meat, fish, and fowl. For a given technical effect, they have to pay more for them and are glad to do so. In any question of economic "efficiency," consumers' satisfactions are at least as important as costs. Classical liberals and their modern counterparts believe that ignoring what consumers want is tyranny or leads to it.

An important ideal and policy goal of many economists is to have in every industry as many "optimum-sized" firms as the market can support. And, since many believe that long-run average firm costs decline up to a certain size, then turn constant, a popular version of this goal is to have the largest possible number of the *smallest* firms that could be "efficient." That is, they would fill up each industry with firms of "minimum optimum size."

The roots of these notions are close to the surface and easy to trace. In typical textbook models of atomistic competition, droves of small firms produce one identical product, and are usually assumed to have identical cost functions as well. In such a simple model, the total cost of producing a homogeneous product at a given annual rate is minimized when each firm produces at the minimum point of its long-run average cost curve, when—in other words—each is of the "optimum size." Furthermore, some theories about the effects of concentration assert that competition increases with the number of firms. Thus—the story goes—the "right" number of firms produces the "competitive" results at the "right" cost.

It is a fact that even the purely technical economies of size have not yet been exhausted in some real-world industries, and there are also economies of size in other business functions besides manufacturing. Industrial deconcentration schemes that raise costs can obviously hurt consumers. But there is an even more fundamental problem. It is wrong to suppose that cost-minimizing is the only kind of efficiency that counts. For, even if a firm grows far past the output rates and volumes required for lowest average cost, this does not mean that it should be broken up or induced to shrink.

Experience abundantly demonstrates that in a specific case it is not easy to quantify the relevant cost curves, and that most outsiders have little idea of what is really going on. But, in addition to the difficulties and mistakes involved in discovering what costs are, the basic problem is that the naive view misconceives what an economy should be minimizing and what it should be maximizing. Consumers are not indifferent to product characteristics and there is no reason why they should be.

Suppose that, for a fixed period of production, firms' unit costs are minimized at an annual output rate of say, one million, then rise for larger outputs. If we sought artificially to minimize the industry's unit costs, each firm would have to be that size. But surely it is not desirable to minimize the costs of stuff that consumers do not want, since the object of economic efficiency is to maximize individuals' satisfaction. At any point, consumers are not equally attracted to all of the products of all producers, and consumers' preferences change over time. Suppose that the costs of women's shoes could be minimized by forcing producers to offer only one model, in one color and a narrow range of sizes. Those for whom the shoes are too large will have to fill them up with innersoles or wear more stockings. Or suppose that the unit costs of men's boots can be minimized by forcing all producers to make only one size and one model: black (which hides leather flaws), in sizes 9, 10, and 11, all D-width. A commissar's pride in the "minimum costs" thereby achieved would be small comfort to those whom the shoes and boots do not fit or do not otherwise please. And it is far from certain whether enough of such footwear could be sold to cover costs, minimum or not. That partly depends upon whether the law is rigorously enforced and imports are prohibited.

It makes no sense to minimize costs of stuff consumers do not want, or to permit consumers to buy the goods they want only if they are produced at "minimum costs." Suppose that there is a producer who sells many fewer than one million units per year. Unit costs could be reduced if only its customers could be induced to buy more. To minimize costs, do we say that the producer must make and sell none? That it must make and sell more? How would we achieve either result? We could compel some consumers who prefer something else to buy what the smaller producer offers. This would lower its unit costs; but it would reduce consumers' satisfaction.

Note the obverse. If a firm is currently selling substantially more than one million units a year, the naive view is that it is too large to minimize unit costs. By assumption, if it could somehow be reduced to one million units, unit costs could be reduced. How could that result be accomplished? The firm could be forced to turn the additional business away by rationing, by raising prices, or by purposefully making its product less attractive. These remedies will induce some of its customers to do without or to switch to competitors whose products they do not like as much. If administered relentlessly, such medicines can reduce the firm to cost-minimizing size, or less. But none of these cures makes much sense if we want to maximize individuals' satisfaction. Left alone, consumers and the firms that seek to serve them will weigh the available trade-offs among cost, price, and quality. Consumers are perfectly content to pay at least the additional costs required to get additional output of what they want. They like it better than the alternatives.

Similar analysis governs cases in which unit costs reach a minimum value, then remain constant for larger outputs. Cost minimization in the naive, limited sense is not a dominant objective.

Gains from Trade

The economics of trade offers some perspective on this.[11] Recall the situation of Robinson Crusoe before Mr. Friday arrives. Crusoe possesses his own personal skills and knowledge, some tools and other resources from the outside world, and some local resources. Like everyone else, he also has a variety of wants. His resources are scarce relative to his wants. Scarcity compels choice. Like all the rest of us, he must choose amongst competing uses of his skills, time, and other resources. He uses what he has to best advantage, given his tastes. He allocates resources so as to minimize the cost of all results. He maximizes his net benefits given the real alternatives. Crusoe is both production-efficient and utility-efficient. He is production-efficient because the cost of what he does will be as low as possible; and utility-efficient because, with the resources he has, he will maximize his satisfactions by choosing the right kinds and amounts of goods to produce. Though they are generated by only a single person who is both producer and consumer, these results meet the same criteria as have evolved in the theory of atomistic competition.

Nevertheless, Crusoe is liable to be rather badly off as compared with consumers in larger economies that have lots of oligopoly and even some monopoly. To improve their lot, individuals have historically abandoned self-sufficiency in favor of trade, often with monopolistic trading partners. People do not trade unless it makes them better off. Benefits from trade arise under several conditions, including differences in individuals' tastes, skills, and endowments. If there are economies of large-scale production, specialization also pays on that account, and trade emerges.

In a complex economy, there are many producers, traders, and consumers. And, within the limits of differing tastes, and the varied competence of business teams and different bundles of production factors, there is continuous pressure on costs and on prices. Nevertheless, since tastes and competence differ, there will never be enough of the right kind of resources to drive all prices to the level of costs for all producers. In any real world it is inevitable that the demand for different things, relative to the array of competencies of firms and factors to produce them, will not everywhere produce the same relationship of price to cost.

There are very substantial gains from specialization and trade, because of, not in spite of, the profits either or both traders earn. Indeed, as Alchian and Allen put it, "profit is part of the product." The only costs relevant to traders and consumers are the costs of doing things themselves and the various prices offered in the marketplace. Enormous profit is perfectly consistent with the very best that is achievable, given all the real alternatives. If markets are open in the sense that present and potential producers are free to offer the products and terms they wish, and consumers are free to accept what they regard as the best offers going, there is a rebuttable presumption that benefits from trade will be as high as realistically can be. Freedom to trade and the desire to do the best one can are powerful forces. Firms occupy a piece of the market by providing, on good terms, what consumers want.

Government and Closed Markets

At this point, it will help to review and reformulate the role of government, which was discussed in Chapter 2. Within limits, the real trading alternatives can be influenced by state action. Although precisely what a state is and how it behaves are not completely settled, one distinguishing feature is that the state asserts a monopoly of the legal supply of coercion and violence. State rules can exclude from the marketplace specific traders or particular kinds and sizes of traders, and have often attempted to limit the number of traders or the quantities and qualities they are permitted to offer.

It is impossible to spell out every kind of action the state can take. Nevertheless, both the history and logic of state licensure, franchising and regulation, and the sale of privilege, are rich enough to deserve our attention. Under cost, demand, and constitutional conditions that are evidently not rare, accomplishing and keeping monopoly through state action has been very attractive to some teachers, farmers, doctors, lawyers, unions, business people, and many others. The precise outcomes, of course, depend not only upon product demands and costs. The details of the governmental apparatus and mechanisms for determining who has what power also matter. However, for present purposes, they are not crucial. We need not stop now to ask how much is paid to whom, and in what coin.

Suppose someone effectively monopolizes an industry under a state franchise that permits him to choose output and price, and otherwise to manage the business as he likes. Under these circumstances, we should expect that the business will come to produce each output as cheaply as can be managed, although it is possible to write into the franchise some constraints that significantly alter the sense in which that is true. Suppose that the monopoly is production-efficient in the usual sense. As always, consumers adjust as best they can.

Economists of liberal persuasion historically opposed such arrangements for several reasons. One is that such a franchise would not be valuable, and therefore would not be sought, unless it excludes from the market some resources, traders, and offers that would otherwise appear. It contrives an artificial scarcity and keeps outsiders from remedying it. As a consequence, the argument goes, consumers are hurt by more than the franchise earns, and this is perverse.

If all of that is so, some reason for granting the franchise, or for operating it in such a way, must be found. Possibilities are that the hurts are diffused over many consumers, whereas the gains are relatively concentrated; and that it is too costly for consumers effectively to confederate. If it were costless for consumers to organize, they could obtain a better result all around, either by preventing the franchise, by buying and operating it themselves, or inducing the present owner to produce and price appropriately.

Such costs of confederating and transacting, rather than the fact that there is a single seller, may be the heart of the matter. If there were only one consumer, she would bear all of the loss and would not have the cost of identifying and coalescing with other customers to do something about it. Instead, she could independently negotiate with the franchise monopoly to produce the ''right'' amount of the good in question; buy out the monopoly; or, alternatively, bargain with the state to prevent the franchise at the start or to rescind it. It is true that the franchise, or its prospect, will cost the consumer; but under zero-cost negotiation it will not then cost her more than the monopoly gains. There will have been a straightforward transfer of wealth. Those who love the consumer more than they love whoever benefits from the franchise, can, of course, still choose to oppose the franchise.[12]

Under at least some circumstances, therefore, franchise monopolies—and the closed markets they imply—cause mischief. Following the same line, in the presence of these kinds of state exclusions, we should not presume that we will obtain overall efficiency in the traditional sense. Accordingly, there is less reason to suppose that the size and structure of an industry under state franchise monopoly is to be explained by traditional notions of superior efficiency. For example, under state monopoly, there will be people on the outside who are competent and willing to offer as good or better terms; but the artificial requirement of the franchise (not the evaluation of consumers) keeps them outside, looking in.[13] It is artificial in that crucial sense.

Open Markets

When markets are open, sellers earn a place by offering consumers a better deal. To obtain a closed market, a seller offers what an authority considers to be a better deal. Government authorities often can get a better deal for themselves by closing markets and excluding traders and trades, as history shows. Many economists of the liberal persuasion have also decried the immediate and prospective tyrannies such arrangements generate, not to mention corruption and dispiriting sales of privilege.

In contrast, examine the case of a new open market, occupied at first by only one seller, but free of state closures. People are likely to call the first seller a monopolist. New sellers, if their costs are lower than the monopolist's prices, come into the market or bid to do so. On net balance, each such challenger benefits consumers, and hurts the monopoly, more than it benefits itself. But apart from offering the best terms, it is not clear how the monopolist can keep them out. For several reasons, it cannot effectively bribe the newcomers to go away.[14] One reason is that no one can be sure whom and how many would have to be bribed, only partly because a threat is known to be genuine only when it is effectuated. Another is that some promises, including most promises not to enter, are unenforceable in our system of law.

For all of these reasons, in the absence of artificial strictures there is a strong presumption that the existing structure of industry is the efficient structure. Open markets are an environment within which powerful and appraising evolutionary forces are at work. The kind of competition often overlooked is that between different ways of doing things, including technologies and techniques, and the organization of firms; different products; and different services. There is competition, selection, and choice within firms as well as between firms; there is competition within and amongst fields, and both inside and outside competition to displace inferior performers from their places in the field. Never have consumers had so many real options, most of which have made their way on the basis of how efficiently they serve consumers' wants.

Hundreds of huge firms, and millions of large and small ones, are continuously searching for profitable fields. The prices consumers pay are not only bids to present suppliers; they are also bids to anyone who thinks he can do better for the consumers. Market research, compilations of potential customers, and informal discussions with buyers are daily tests of whether it would pay for new or old suppliers to bid for consumers' custom by offering better terms. The capital markets churn away, funneling capital from low-return to high-return areas. Firms daily choose whether to make or buy—and large firms often have large customers. Firms in any particular field are constantly appraising the prices and prospective costs that are in effect in other fields. If prices significantly exceed the costs of a prospective entrant, he enters. If different product qualities yield a higher difference between revenues than between costs—that is, if they would produce higher net benefits—different products will be offered. If different techniques or forms of organization show promise, someone is likely to try them.

The market is an enormous information network that signals when opportunities exist, and moves resources to take advantage of them.[15] In the process, consumer benefits tend truly to be maximized, within the real-world constraints of the amount and qualities of resources, information, and the competence of different business teams.

If any firm should be larger than efficiency requires, and charge higher prices than the costs of its present and prospective competitors, the competitors and the market will shrink the larger firm. If any firm should innovate better techniques, or offer a superior product at the same costs as its competitors, the market will respond and the firm will grow. If any firm offers the same product as its competitors at lower costs, that firm will prosper and grow. If any firm is so large as to be inefficient, there will be internal and external challenges to put things right; if they are not righted, the firm's present and prospective competitors will outstrip it.

One can ask, of course, how long it takes all these tendencies to work themselves out. Perhaps a better question is whether some alternative system does the job faster and better.

The Reform of Market Forces

As Stigler pointed out, evolutionary processes produce survivors that are well adapted to their total environment.[16] This raises three very different kinds of questions. First, some critics seem to think the kinds and sizes of firms that survive are not in fact well adapted to the environment we have. Such criticisms range from charges of gross internal inefficiency to complaints that customers are badly catered to. In general, such deficiencies imply that it would pay someone to correct them. Apparently the critics believe they know enough about efficiency, costs, and revenues in specific industries to conclude that results are bad. The critics must also believe they alone know how bad things are, which is strange: they have been telling the rest of us about it for a long time. Unless government shelters it, such "bad" performance cannot persist if others learn about it. A state of information sufficient to discern the bad performance should therefore be sufficient to guarantee that the bad performance will not persist. Millions of firms and people who know what they are doing are constantly looking for places in which they can improve the current economic adjustments. Anyone who believes he has found one can bet against the market. If he is right, he deserves to become rich.

A second issue is whether something is correctably wrong with the legal, business, and industrial environment itself, and whether and in what sense it pays to correct it. It goes without saying that, by some standard, no real environment is perfect. Suppose that certain successful survivors got where they are through, say, fraud, arson, mayhem, or theft, and that—by economic standards—it clearly pays to reduce the amount of such activities. One way to do it is to make such activities more expensive in a variety of ways. Punishment is one way; but in tolerable societies punishment is imposed because of bad things that specific people can be proved to have done.

It is easy to get agreement about things like mayhem and theft. But it is dangerous to carry this kind of environmental reform too far, too fast. A great many governmental policies were allegedly developed to help consumers by improving the business and professional environment. Many of them—including franchising, licensure, allocations, and other market closures—frustrate consumers and competitors, and they concentrate enormous power in the state. In every field there are those who would benefit from slowing the pace, by either excluding or taxing the efficient.

There is a good case for discouraging cartels—although it is well to recognize that not everyone agrees either about what a cartel is, or whether we should evaluate the benefits and costs of individual cartels, case by case. Similarly, many oppose massive mergers that would mop up an entire industry and all of the better resources used to perform in it.

Going beyond those first steps, we are in increasingly dangerous territory. One risk we run is to confuse changes in general rules of the game with imposing penalties against beneficially superior performers. This brings us to the next problem. It is the impropriety of striking directly at the characteristics of successful survivors—such as their size and profitability—rather than at bad things they can be shown to have done. This is an especially hazardous confusion in dealing with things like industrial structure, for logic and fact suggest that, in open markets, beneficially superior performers do tend to rise to the top. Law that strikes at the characteristics of the best discourages the good performance that is associated with those very characteristics. It can be argued that law has, in several respects, already taken conduct rules too far—the Robinson-Patman Act is an example. Nevertheless, we can appropriately continue to look out for specific kinds of identifiable conduct that have anti-economic consequences. Chapter 9 discussed monopolizing practices, for example. That approach seems better by far than penalizing characteristics typically associated with good performance.

There are even more serious threats that pure economic theory tends to neglect. Some policy proposals that are based on economic analysis have in recent years threatened the system of law and politics that has served us well. Substituting a principle of guilt by characteristic for that of guilt by deed is, if history can be believed, liable to produce generally unhappy consequences. Furthermore, there is the issue of concentrated economic and political power, with which extremist reformers of industrial structures claim they will help us. On the contrary, they may bury us. They would compel firms to justify their size and existence to government agencies on the basis of what some engineers or economists assert is efficient.

Apart from the economics, this creates serious difficulties. First, in open markets, successful large firms have already justified themselves to millions of consumers and to potential competitors who have decided against competing for consumer dollars. Unless an efficiency tribunal ratifies market results, it substitutes its decisions for those of millions of free individuals. If that does not increase the concentration of economic and political power, nothing does. This would be dangerous even if it produced better economic results. Many economists believe, however, that open-market forces adjust more flexibly and accurately, and better balance costs and tastes than state agencies do. Their theory has several layers. First, we might as well recognize the facts about self-interest. People do not become unselfish just because they hold a government office or job. There is some reason to believe that exercising self-interest from a government job produces different results than exercising it in open markets. Economists, lawyers, and politicians—like everyone else—try to do as well as they can. A thoroughgoing policy of industrial deconcentration would hurt us as consumers. But some of us could make it up in what we sell: laws of this kind increase the demand for services of lawyers and economists, not to mention those who would actually manage and work in the government agencies. Imagine the position of a politician under a constitution that permits very little policy other than letting markets run. For this reason, when economists pontificate about policy improvement, they can always find a sympathetic audience pursuing its own self-interest. Second, some fear that bureaucrats tend to get out of touch with consumers' preferences. If they do, we may get decisions that are based on badly measured and out-of-date estimates of demands and costs.

Third, a policy of forced industrial deconcentration is curiously discordant with the basic spirit of antitrust law itself, as well as with the liberal tradition in general. When a legal decision or administrative rule breaks up a firm, it denies market access to a group of people and bundle of resources. If private parties did that, they would be denounced for monopolizing. Indeed, the total result is likely to be much worse than monopolizing as defined in antitrust law. Denying a firm access to a specific geographic market segment would be illegal and (presumably) bad enough. But the same business teams could still serve the rest. Deconcentration destroys that organization without correspondingly increasing the capability of others to serve.

Even now, there is some support for policies to dissolve firms claimed to be larger than necessary to be "efficient." In the United States there has so far been little support for forcing smaller firms to merge into the putative efficient size. On the other hand, out of admiration for the accomplishments of large-scale American enterprise, many in foreign lands favor state programs for "rationalization," which usually means pushing or pulling smaller firms into amalgamations.

Either policy has important drawbacks. In the first place, the number, kinds, and costs of firms that will even enter an industry expected to suffer such involuntary reforms will change. For they now face a tax on firm sizes other than those acclaimed as optimal by some government authority and the engineers and economists it listens to. This will influence the number, kinds, and amounts of products as well as firms; and consumers' preferences will not be permitted to determine the outcome.

Another crucial problem is incentive. The shock of surgical reform—whether by grafting on or cutting off—will shift the costs and drives not only of those directly affected by the operation, but also of others in the industry as well. Trauma influences those who see it as well as those who feel it. Unless a law that forces dissolutions guarantees that it will be used just once in any industry—a promise that is not enforceable—it will reduce the incentive to excel. Performance may therefore be very poor indeed, no matter how the superior teams are dispersed after dissolution.

For several reasons, we cannot generally specify precisely how much forced deconcentration will reduce efficiency. It is tempting to guess that cutting a firm with an 80 percent market share into four equal-sized bits will produce the same costs and performance as are observed in the firm that now serves 20 percent of the market. In some cases this might conceivably be true, as for example when economies of pure size are the whole story. But one should ask why the 80-percent firm was able to design and sell enough more units to achieve the economies, and what will happen to the teams that made this result possible. The 20-percent firm may in fact be better at what it does, and more efficient for the size it is, than any single fragment that would survive when the leading firm is atomized. In that case, costs are lower for the 20-percent firm than they would be for the surviving new fragments. On the other hand, if the essential teams that initially produced the superior results were somehow transferred to one surviving entity, its performance would be better—and the performance of the other three fragments, worse—than that of the original 20-percent firm. It could also be expected to grow to a very considerable market share as time moves on.

Apart from governmental interferences, the only certain way a firm can hold or improve its position is by offering what consumers consider to be equal or greater value per dollar. If firms have different competence to offer desired products at reasonable cost, some firms will be bigger and do better than others. This seems to be both fair and efficient. It provides an incentive to excel, which serves both consumers and those who achieve the superior performance.

Besides underestimating the difficulties of measuring costs and values, proposals to influence firm sizes via government policies tend to ignore differences in the qualities and talents of different people and different firms. As a result, they blunt the important incentives to serve and succeed as best one can. Assertions that efficiency cannot "justify" business size lack a secure basis in good theory and solid facts.

Most empirical estimates of the overall dead-weight loss due to monopoly are not relevant to the trade-off theories discussed here.[17] For such estimates typically *assume*, without demonstrating, that the costs of monopoly and competition are the same, then attribute above-average profits to monopoly, which has already been *assumed* to have no efficiency justification.[18] Even so, most such studies conclude that the total dead-weight monopoly welfare loss is small, and some of them conclude that it is nonexistent. The trouble is that what passes in these studies for monopolies are probably the most beneficial structures; relative to other structures, they produce welfare *gains*, not welfare losses. Chapter 14 discusses those studies in detail.

The vision of market-oriented economists is that, in the absence of state intervention, we emerge with the closest achievable approximation to optimal industrial structures in the long run. Still the best statement of this point of view is that of Robert H. Bork, then a distinguished law professor and now a federal Circuit Court of Appeals judge:

> In judging whether it is worthwhile to break up a concentrated industry structure it is necessary to estimate whether more will be gained through the predicted end to noncompetitive pricing or lost through the destruction of industrial efficiency. When the structure has been created by recent merger or by predatory business practice, neither of which necessarily demonstrates efficiency, a policy of dissolution is intelligible. . . . When firms grow to sizes that create concentration or when such a structure is created by merger and persists for many years, there is a very strong prima facie case that the firms' sizes are related to efficiency. By efficiency I mean "competitive effectiveness" within the bounds of the law, and competitive effectiveness means service to consumers. If the leading firms in an concentrated industry are restricting their output in order to obtain prices above the competitive level, their efficiencies must be sufficiently superior to that of all actual and potential rivals to offset that behavior. Were this not so, rivals would be enabled to expand their market shares because of the abnormally high prices and would thus deconcentrate the industry. Market rivalry thus automatically weighs the respective influences of efficiency and output restriction and arrives at the firm sizes and market structures that serve consumers best.[19]

To answer the trade-off question definitively, we would have to estimate and compare costs under greater and lesser concentration. Only relatively recently has the question even been asked that way. More recently, still, some empirical evidence has emerged. As Chapter 14 will show, some of these studies suggest that the industrial structures observed tend to be cost- and quality-justified.

Chapter 11 explained and criticized measures of industrial concentration that have been used to study monopoly problems empirically. The next chapter discusses some implications of what may by now be hundreds of empirical studies made during the last thirty-seven years.[20]

SUMMARY

Economic efficiency and consumer welfare involve more than minimizing costs. Product *values* matter as well. Consumers want maximum benefits, net of costs.

Careful study of the four welfare trade-off cases discussed in this chapter suggests that some possibilities are more plausible than others. Unless markets are closed by government, there is a strong but rebuttable presumption that the industrial structures we get in the long run are the closest achievable approximations to "optimal." Those who would alter industrial structures should therefore bear the burden of proof.

QUESTIONS

1. Present and evaluate Williamson's trade-off case in detail.
2. Of the four trade-off models presented, which of them do you think are most common in the real world? Why?
3. Williamson doubted that the profits received by owners of oligopolies should be counted equally, dollar-for-dollar, with the benefits consumers receive. That is, why not treat each stockholder as some fraction of a whole person? Discuss.
4. What, if any, incentive problems arise if government proceeds against firms on the basis of their characteristics, against *highly profitable* firms, for example?
5. Some theories suggest that the single-firm monopoly price can exceed the average costs of potential entrants if the monopoly has lower costs than entrants. Explain and discuss. Would the same be true of noncolluding oligopolists? Explain.
6. Can firms that are larger (or smaller) than the cost-minimizing optimal size nevertheless serve consumers best?
7. In what circumstances would a survival-of-the-fittest economic system serve consumers badly? Discuss.
8. We frequently hear that firms are unnecessarily large, leading to an excessive concentration of economic power. How could that situation be cured, and by whom? Where would the power then lie, and would that power be less concentrated than it now is? Discuss.
9. Chapter 2 introduced the subject of government franchises, favors, and restrictions. This chapter continued the discussion. What leads governments to do such things, many of which do not look scratch-start efficient?
10. Does the story of Robinson Crusoe contribute anything to the theory of gains-from-trade? What if you must trade with highly profitable oligopolies? Explain.

NOTES

1. For example, Chapter 7 noted that *volumes* as well as *rates* of production affect costs.
2. The third section of this chapter, and Chapter 15, allude to dynamic effects.
3. See Chapter 7.
4. Given appropriate assumptions, consumer surplus is equal to the area under the demand curve and above the current price. G. J. Stigler, *The Theory of Price* (New York: Macmillan, Inc., 1966), p. 80.
5. If it is, someone ought explicitly to evaluate the costs and spectator enjoyment relevant to the punishment.

6. Oliver E. Williamson, "Economies as an Antitrust Defense," *American Economic Review* 58 (March 1968), pp. 18–36; "Correction and Reply," *American Economic Review*, 58 (December 1968), pp. 1372–76; "Allocative Efficiency and the Limits of Antitrust," *American Economic Review*, 59 (May 1969), pp. 105–18.

7. Compare the limit-pricing theory, discussed in Chapter 9.

8. William J. Baumol and Robert D. Willig, "Fixed Costs, Sunk Costs, Entry Barriers, and Sustainability of Monopoly," *Quarterly Journal of Economics*, 96 (August 1981), pp. 405–31, at p. 406.

9. Ibid., p. 418.

10. Robert H. Bork and Ward S. Bowman, "The Crisis in Antitrust," *Columbia Law Review*, 65 (March 1965), pp. 363–76; R. H. Bork, "The Goals of Antitrust Policy," *American Economic Review*, 57 (May 1967), pp. 242–53.

11. See A. A. Alchian and W. R. Allen, *Exchange and Production Theory in Use* (Belmont, Calif.: Wadsworth Publishing Co., Inc., 1969), or their counterpart volume, *University Economics* (Belmont, Calif.: Wadsworth Publishing Co., Inc., 2nd ed. 1967; 3rd ed., 1971). Of special interest are the chapters "Basis of Exchange" and "Production, Exchange, Specialization and Efficiency."

12. Some economists believe that this line of argument is dangerously incomplete. If there is a good prospect for valuable monopoly franchises, substantial resources will be "wasted" on acquiring them. See Gordon Tullock, "The Welfare Costs of Tariffs, Monopolies, and Theft," *Western Economic Journal*, 5 (June 1967), pp. 224–32; and Richard A. Posner, "The Social Cost of Monopoly and Regulation," *Journal of Political Economy*, 83 (August 1975), pp. 807–27.

    It is now fashionable, if not informative, to call such efforts *rent seeking*. But most if not all we do is rent seeking.

13. As always, we must be cautious in designing empirical tests. It is difficult for us to admit that we are responsible for our own failures. No matter how open and competitive markets may be, there will be discontents blaming their failures on "the system," "market," "government," "Big Business," or someone else. And some laws encourage such claims.

14. As cartel histories show, a seller can benefit if others reduce output and raise prices. The "independent" will then sell more goods and make more money per unit of investment than those who carry the load of reducing output. See Chapter 4 and Chapter 6.

15. Much economic analysis ignores the indispensable role that markets play in producing information. As a partial corrective, see F. A. Hayek, "The Use of Knowledge in Society," *American Economic Review* 35 (September 1945), pp. 519–30.

16. George J. Stigler, "The Economies of Scale," *Journal of Law & Economics*, 1 (October 1958), pp. 54–71.

17. The next chapter discusses such studies.

18. See, for example, Arnold C. Harberger, "Monopoly and Resource Allocation," *American Economic Review*, 44 (May 1954), pp. 77–87; Dean A. Worcester, Jr., "New Estimates of the Welfare Loss to Monopoly, U.S. 1956–1969," *Southern Economic Review*, 40 (October 1973), pp. 234–45; "Comment," *American Economic Review*, 65 (December 1975), pp. 1015–23; David Schwartzman, "The Effect of Monopoly on Price," *Journal of Political Economy*, 67 (August 1959), pp. 352–62, and "A Correction," *Journal of Political Economy*, 69 (October 1961), p. 494; Joan Bodoff, "Monopoly and Price Revisited," in *The*

Competitive Economy, Selected Readings, ed. Yale Brozen (Morristown, N.J.: Learning Press: 1975), pp. 175–85; John S. Chipman and James C. Moore, "Compensating Variation, Consumer's Surplus, and Welfare," *American Economic Review*, 70 (December 1980), pp. 933–49; and D. R. Kamerschen, "An Estimation of the Welfare Losses for Monopoly in the American Economy," *Western Economic Journal*, 4 (Summer 1966), pp. 221–36; and Micha Gisser, "Price Leadership and Welfare Losses in U.S. Manufacturing," *American Economic Review*, 76 (September 1986), pp. 756–67.

These and other studies are discussed in Chapter 14.

19. In Phil Neal and others, "Report of the White House Task Force on Antitrust Policy," *Antitrust Law and Economics Review*, 2 (Winter 1968–1969), p. 11.

20. For numerous citations to and clear analyses of many of these studies, see Yale Brozen, *Concentration, Mergers, and Public Policy* (New York: Macmillan, Inc., 1982).

14

EMPIRICAL EVIDENCE ABOUT THE EFFECTS OF INDUSTRY CONCENTRATION

INTRODUCTION

Earlier chapters discussed what economic welfare means,[1] presented theories about how industrial concentration might affect it,[2] and showed how the measures of industrial concentration and profits commonly used for empirical work can cause trouble.[3]

The economic objection to monopoly is not that it makes monopolists rich but that it reduces total welfare, making the rest of us poorer. Profits are an unreliable symptom of monopoly and a poor measure of economic losses that monopoly might cause. Even in theory, Lerner's price-cost margin is subject to the same criticism, and popular approximations of it are arguably neither prices, costs, nor margins.

Interesting though the oligopoly and dominant-firm theories are, it would be nice to know what industrial concentration *actually* does. That is not so easy to find out. Partly because it is hard to do experiments in economics, it has become popular to use statistical procedures instead. Because our data usually contain errors and a lot of other things besides the relationships we are trying to find, the trick is to unscramble a statistical omelette. Some empirical work in economics looks as though the analyst kept tickling or shaking the data until they coughed up what he was looking for.

In informal conversation, one fine economist who does a lot of empirical work put it that the signal-to-noise ratio is usually low in economics. His metaphor is apt. Doing empirical research in industrial organization is sometimes like trying to receive a broadcast from a weak shortwave radio station transmitting on one of the tropical bands. There is often so much noise that gaps and ambiguities remain no matter how good our equipment is or how well we use it.

Modern economists do not use naive, obsolete equipment. Their statistical techniques rank with the best used in any discipline. The problems are nevertheless so difficult that sophisticated statistical tools are often not enough, given the kinds of data we have. And economists tend to push the data and tools harder and stretch their conclusions further than is justified.[4] As Edward Leamer put it,

> A fragile inference is not worth taking seriously. All scientific disciplines routinely subject their inferences to studies of fragility. Why should economics be different? * * * We must insist that all empirical studies offer convincing evidence of inferential sturdiness. We need to be shown that minor changes in the list of variables do not alter fundamentally the conclusions, nor does a slight reweighting of observations, nor corrections for dependence among observations, *etcetera, etcetera.*[5]

The first section of this chapter explains some statistical methods typically used in industrial organization. This helps us understand empirical studies discussed later in this chapter and in chapters 15 and 16. The next section discusses the early work by Joe Bain that started a wave of empirical studies in industrial organization. The following section discusses evidence that concentration raises prices. After that there is an evaluation of the large volume of statistical studies that, by 1970, may have convinced most economists that the structure-performance paradigm is scientific fact. The next section appraises revisionist theories and empirical studies coming on the scene by about 1968. Their collision with the old-line structuralist orthodoxy may have changed industrial organization permanently. The following section discusses economy-wide estimates of the welfare losses that monopoly might cause.

AN INTRODUCTION TO STATISTICAL METHODS

Obviously, no brief introduction such as this can substitute for full-blown courses in statistics. But even a brief review can cover what we need to translate multiple-variable regression equations, which, fortunately, are not so profound or impenetrable as they sound.[6] We will go through an example that illustrates the basic methodology and illuminates some of the problems that arise in using it. Make no mistake: this is an illustration, nothing more. Using it as a scientific discovery is hazardous to truth; using it as the basis for policy would be hazardous to the nation's health.[7]

This example uses FTC line-of-business (LB) data for 1977, the last year for which they were gathered. They were not published until 1985.[8] FTC published no concentration ratios with these data. Our 1977 four-firm concentration data for four-digit industries come from a 1986 Bureau of the Census publication that reports data for 1982 and for earlier years.[9]

As usual, Census provided no profit data to correspond with the concentration ratios and other numbers that it published for 1977. Chapter 11 noted that economists typically use three-digit Internal Revenue Service (IRS) profits data together with concentration and other data from the Census. Chapter 11 discussed and criticized both of these kinds of data for analyzing monopoly problems, but there are two excuses for using them in an example. First, with these data we do not have to decant three-digit IRS financial data into a four-digit census-industry pot, or broaden four-digit industries into three-digit classes. But, until someone publishes concentration data derived from the line-of-business data themselves, we still have the problem of using concentration and financial data from different sources. The second, a common and rather lame excuse for using whatever data are at hand, is that these data are readily available. As a result, anyone who wants to can easily check this example, or make up his own, using the same data sources.

FTC published several kinds of 1977 data that could be used for illustration. They offer two different measures of profits: operating income/assets (π/K); and operating income/sales (π/S). FTC published both as percentages: the ratio .154 becomes 15.4. There are two measures of selling costs. Advertising is measured by media advertising/sales (Adv/S). Total selling-cost intensity is total selling expenses/sales (Sell/S). Both are measured in percentages: the ratio .043 becomes 4.3. Research and development that the firm does on its own and for its own account is divided by sales, and named CoRD/S here. *Total* R&D divided by sales we call TotRD/S. Both R&D measures are expressed in percentages: the ratio .079 becomes 7.9. The value of capital assets employed is measured as assets divided by sales, which we call Ast/S, and express as a percentage: the ratio .333 becomes 33.3.

To measure industrial structures, our example uses four-firm concentration ratios (CR_4) published by the Census Bureau for the year 1977. We express CR_4 in percentages: .33 becomes 33.

The original structure-performance paradigm, remember, asserted that industry structure determines or significantly affects industry performance.[10] Most statistical work uses profits or price-cost margins as measures of performance, and concentration ratios or Herfindahl indexes as measures of structure. Later versions of this paradigm incorporate additional variables asserted to affect performance. In either case, the theories are put in the same basic form for statistical estimation.

Most such studies try statistically to explain variations in the profitability of different industries or lines of business, measured in our example by π/K. This is our *independent variable*, the variable to be explained. Take the simplest version of the paradigm first. It uses CR_4 as the sole explanation of π/K. We call unexplained variations ϵ, the *disturbance* or *error* term, a name for our ignorance as well as for random variations and errors in measurement. Using the technique called ordinary least squares (OLS), we determine the value of constants in the linear estimating equation that minimizes the sum of squared differences between the equation and the values of the dependent variable we use as data. Call these constants Betas, β_0, β_1, β_2, and so on. The simplest structure-performance paradigm becomes, then:

$$\pi/K = \beta_0 + \beta_1(CR_4) + \epsilon$$

Out of the 259 Industry Categories in the FTC sample, we use a nonrandom sample of 61. This purposefully raises the question of sample bias, a source of trouble in Bain's early work, as Brozen noted, and in much later work as well. Average concentration, for example, is substantially higher in our sample ($CR_4 = 47$) than in Census industries for the same year ($CR_4 = 38$). One might argue that the bias, if any, arose innocently: the sample includes only those industries satisfying "reasonable" criteria. For each industry included, FTC published all 7 of the variables discussed earlier, and Census published a four-firm concentration ratio for a "related" four-digit industry.[11]

Biased or not, this sample yields the following linear estimating equation, commonly called a regression equation:

$$\pi/K = 11.337 + .077847 \; CR_4$$

$$(1.6562)$$

This says, literally, that a one-percentage-point increase in the concentration ratio is on average accompanied by (almost) an eight-hundredth percentage point increase in profits/ assets. That is a pretty small effect. On top of that, the equation yields a coefficient of determination (R^2) of .044, (only .028 when adjusted for degrees of freedom). Non-statisticians may decide that this analysis gives them little to write home about: the equation "explains" only about 2.8 percent of the total variation in π/K.[12]

The number in parentheses under the coefficient of CR_4 is the t-ratio, got by dividing the estimated value of the coefficient by its standard error, a measure of the scatter around it. Statisticians have greater confidence in coefficients that have relatively large t-ratios, for the scatter around them is relatively small.

Given the number of observations we have (61) and the variables we estimate in this equation (2, including the constant), conventional tests lead statisticians to say that the estimated coefficient on CR_4 is not "statistically significant." That is, there is a significant chance that the true value of this coefficient is zero. The probability of finding this large a t-value is about 10.3 percent even when concentration and profits are not related at all. We can have only 89.7 percent confidence that the true coefficient is not zero and, therefore, that CR_4 has any explanatory power at all. Here is a rough test for significance at the 95 percent level: a coefficient is significantly different from zero if, ignoring sign, its t-value exceeds 2.0.

Let's see what happens when we try to explain π/K by increasing the number of explanatory variables. This time, use concentration and advertising:

$$\pi/K = 10.978 + .058501 \; CR_4 + .58718 \; Adv/S$$

$$(1.2328) \qquad\qquad (1.7695)$$

In this version, advertising seems to have more power to explain profits than concentration does. Furthermore, taking advertising into account seems both to weaken and decrease the reliability of any contribution that concentration may have made. Indeed, neither concentration nor advertising is statistically significant at the 95 percent level. Adjusted R^2 is now .0621; the equation "explains" 6.2 percent of the total sample variation in π/K. Some will think this is not very much to cheer about. There is no doubt, of course, that we can draw other samples displaying substantially higher (or lower) R^2s.

For this same sample, now use still more explanatory variables: concentration, advertising, company R&D, and assets/sales:

$$\pi/K = 17.998 + .098278\ CR_4 + .44109\ \text{Adv}/S - .82562\ \text{CoRd}/S - .10909\ \text{Ast}/S$$

$$(2.1982) \qquad (1.4239) \qquad (-1.3223) \qquad (-3.7399)$$

Adjusted R^2 has improved substantially, to .2469. The equation "explains" 24.7 percent of the sample variation in π/K, a claim that may not sound very impressive either. But many R^2s that are lower than this have been published in economic journals, especially before it became popular to do weighted regressions, using such procedures as Generalized Least Squares (GLS). Anyhow, though you would never know it from watching what some economists do, maximizing R^2s is not supposed to be the object of regression analysis.[13]

In this equation, CR_4 seemingly explains a little more than it did in the earlier regressions, and is now statistically significant at the 95 percent level. Industries with high capital intensiveness, as measured by Ast/S, tend to have lower profits, and that coefficient is statistically significant. Industries with higher company R&D tend to have *lower* profits; but that coefficient is not statistically different from zero. Advertising looks relatively weaker than it did before, and is not statistically significant. Company R&D is not statistically significant, either.

Analysts almost always offer explanations for the numbers they expose to public view. Does a positive, though weak, relationship between profits and concentration come from collusion, superior efficiency of larger firms, or both; or from something else altogether? Advertising, as Chapter 16 will note, might increase profits because it differentiates products and increases monopoly power, distorts profit figures (owing to tax laws and accounting conventions), helps superior firms introduce new and better products, or because it does something else.

Though Company R&D may seem to be negatively related to profits, it is not statistically significant.[14] Perhaps, the analyst might say, a mirage has been produced by the accounting and tax treatment of R&D. Or perhaps R&D does pay off, but only after a lag, so that we should use advertising for one year and profits for a later year. Or something else may be involved.

Assets/sales purports to measure capital intensiveness, about which industrial organization economists have been ambivalent historically.[15] As Chapter 7 showed, Bain and other economists have claimed that high capital requirements bar entry, preserve monopoly, and keep profits high. In this example, however, capital intensiveness is *negatively* related to profitability.

Those interested in science and scientific method will be interested in the kinds of explanations that are offered when such relationships pop up. When a *positive* relationship between capital intensiveness and profits showed up, the old view was that this is because large capital requirements bar entry and shelter monopoly. When a *negative* relationship shows up for capital (or R&D), we now hear, instead, that large firms are inefficient and use too much capital (or R&D). In either case, concentrated industries and the large firms that are in them get criticized. They lose points no matter how the statistical relationships turn out. That sounds unfair as well as unscientific.

So much for our example, which even if it does nothing else can help us decipher typical regression equations that industrial organization economists publish.

STATISTICAL ANALYSIS BEGINS: JOE BAIN _____

Joe Bain's 1951 article seems to be the first quantitative study of the relationship between industry concentration and profitability.[16] This article started the procession of empirical studies that goes on yet. It should be noted, to his credit, that Bain's inferences were much more cautious than those drawn by many who followed him.

Rightly or wrongly, many economists inferred two major conclusions from Bain's work. First, the more concentrated industries earn monopoly profits. Second, industrial concentration is higher than can be justified by superior performance or economies of size. It is, instead, preserved by "barriers to entry," "product differentiation," or other baleful influences. Chapter 7 discussed relationships between firm size and efficiency and Chapter 9 discussed barriers to entry. Chapter 7 argues that we should use *economies of size* to mean efficiencies achievable merely by being large, and *efficiencies of performance* to explain why some firms prosper and grow even when there are no economies to be realized from large size alone.

For a long time Bain's findings remained unchallenged. Then, in 1963, George Stigler concluded that such relationship as there was between profits and concentration was weak and unstable over time.[17] In 1971, Yale Brozen studied Bain's work in detail and found it wanting in ways common to later work as well.[18] Brozen criticized both the sample of industries that Bain chose and the way he analyzed it. We will discuss peculiarities of Bain's sample after reviewing his major conclusion and how he reached it. For his 1951 article, Bain analyzed a sample of 42 three- and four-digit Census industries, of the sort described in Chapter 11. He used *eight-firm* concentration ratios to split his sample into concentrated and unconcentrated halves. Industries with eight-firm concentration ratios greater than 70 percent averaged 11.8 percent profits per annum. Those with eight-firm concentration ratios lower than 70 percent averaged a 7.5 percent return. Brozen found, however, that if we measure industry concentration by the *four-firm* ratio, the difference in profit rate between the more concentrated and less concentrated halves of the sample falls from 4.4 percent to 3.3 percent, a reduction of about a fourth. And, according to Brozen, "If averages of group averages, which Bain suggests is the appropriate procedure . . . are used, the difference between the more and less concentrated (four firm) halves of his sample shrinks by nearly 50 percent (from 4.4 percent to 2.4 percent)."

There are other problems with Bain's sample and what he did with it. Bain's 1951 article studied the period 1936 to 1940. The 1935 Census of Manufactures had covered 340 industries, for only 149 of which both concentration and profit data were available. Bain had to decide which firms to use in calculating profits for each industry. He included only listed firms covered by the Securities and Exchange Commission (SEC), that is, the largest corporations. This threw out more than half of the 149 industries for which there were some data for both concentration and profits and, on other grounds, Bain winnowed out all but 76 of the rest. For an industry to be included in his sample, Bain required that profit data be available for *more* than two firms. That requirement got rid of another 34 industries, a group, Bain candidly conceded, in which profits and concentration were *inversely* related!

In short, Bain ended up using 42 industries out of 149 Census industries for which industry concentration and profits for one or more firms were available. Brozen, on the other hand, analyzed FTC data for 1939 and 1940, practically the same as Bain's period. These data cover 78 and 75 industries, respectively. Brozen found that the earnings of the concentrated and unconcentrated groups of industries were virtually identical. Industries with eight-firm concentration ratios greater than 70 percent earned only about .07 percentage points more than the unconcentrated group, a statistically insignificant difference.

For the book he published in 1956, Bain chose twenty industries to analyze rates of return in 1936 to 1940 and in 1947 to 1951.[19] In this study, Bain designated industries as having very high, substantial, or moderate to low "barriers to entry." F. M. Scherer noted that "one problem, of course, is the subjective character of the entry barrier classifications."[20] That something *was* wrong is suggested by what happened to industries that were supposed to be very difficult to enter. In Scherer's words, "Many of the very high barrier industries have experienced substantial new entry—e.g., in automobiles, from importers; in fountain pens and typewriters, through technological innovation; in nickel . . . ; in sulphur . . . ; and in distilled liquor."[21] Eighteen of these twenty industries had also been in the sample Bain used for his 1951 article. His choice of the eighteen was biased: in 1936 to 1940, earnings of its concentrated and unconcentrated halves differed by 6.2 percentage points, an almost 50 percent greater difference than even his biased 42-industry sample had displayed. Brozen illustrated how small and biased samples mislead, by arbitrarily selecting another sample of twenty industries, in which the concentrated half had *lower* earnings.

Bain's samples were biased by his choice of industries and his choice of firms to represent industry profitability. For his *Barriers* book, Bain computed industry profits for the four (or fewer) largest firms in each industry. The average number of firms for which the SEC had profit data was eight per industry. In typewriters, the firms that SEC and Bain used were the same. As Brozen showed, Bain used only industries for which SEC reported profits for more than *two* firms. For the industries that Bain chose to use in 1951, however, Brozen used *all* the firms for which SEC reported profits. On average, the leading four firms in *concentrated* industries were more profitable than the rest; on average, the leading firms in the *unconcentrated* industries earned lower returns than did the rest. All of which biased Bain's results. By raising returns for the concentrated group and lowering them for the unconcentrated group, it increased the apparent difference between them.

Merely by recalculating Bain's 1956 study using the criteria used for his 1951 study, Brozen shrank the profit difference between concentrated and unconcentrated groups about one-third. In addition, Brozen showed that quite contrary inferences could be drawn from Bain's own samples taken at face value. First, Bain's sample apparently shows industries out of long-run equilibrium, to the extent that it shows anything:

> The average rate of return in the unconcentrated industries used in Bain's sample moved up from 2.1 percentage points below the 1936–1940 average for his total sample to only 0.5 percentage points below the 1953–1957 average for the total sample. The average rate of return in the concentrated industries in Bain's sample moved down from 2.2 percentage points above the total sample average to 0.6 percentage points above the total sample average.[22]

Second, says Brozen, Bain's biased sampling not only picked up short-run disequilibrium rather than monopoly situations. It may also have picked up a specific kind of disequilibrium. As noted earlier, Brozen had discovered that larger firms earned more than smaller ones in seven out of nine concentrated industries. That was the case in only two out of seven of the unconcentrated industries. Brozen concludes that concentrated industries got concentrated because they generated, or were subject to, efficiencies favoring larger firms. The smaller firms had not yet adjusted by dropping out or growing up, and in the interim were earning less. The contrary may have been happening in the unconcentrated group of industries. Something to which smaller firms were better able to adjust had occurred; the larger firms had not yet shrunk or dropped out. Smaller firms earned more because they had adjusted better.

In each concentrated industry in which leading firms were more profitable, Brozen found, four-firm concentration did rise between 1935 and 1947. Concentration declined in the three concentrated industries in which leading firms earned less than smaller firms. Conversely, in the five unconcentrated industries in which the leading firms earned less than smaller firms, concentration declined.

According to Brozen, data on profits and concentration support the theory that market forces concentrate industries where efficiency calls for greater concentration, and deconcentrates where efficiency calls for less concentration.[23] Michael Mann tried to confirm Bain's results by using a 30-industry sample and Brozen responded. Mann admitted that he had used ''instinctive judgment'' to make his classification and define his variables. Brozen cited two serious flaws. First, the results are very sensitive to which industries are included. To illustrate the point, Brozen added two industries (3561–pumps and compressors and 3471–lighting fixtures) to Mann's less-concentrated industries. The difference in profitability between the two groups then vanished. Second, by lengthening the period, as he had done with Bain's work, Brozen found that earnings of the more profitable group fell towards the average rate; earnings of the less concentrated group rose toward the average.[24] Such earnings differences as Mann had found did not persist.[25]

DIRECT PRICE COMPARISONS

The theoretical welfare trade-offs analyzed in Chapter 13 directly compared prices and costs under different industry structures. It is not so easy to do that empirically. The first problem is to compare prices and costs of the *same* product sold in markets in which structure differs. The second problem is how to hold constant costs, demands, risks, and everything else *but* structure. The quality of such empirical studies depends importantly upon how well those problems have been solved, and there has been much debate about that.

Formal Quantitative Studies

Chapter 5 reviewed Stigler's oligopoly theory in detail. When he developed his theory, Stigler also tested it with data on newspaper and radio advertising rates. The brief statistical investigations he made purport to show how price differed among markets comprising different numbers of firms, given whatever other conditions existed in those markets. He concluded that newspaper advertising rates were about 10.5 percent higher in towns having one evening newspaper than in those having two; and that on average, a 10 percent increase in the number of AM radio stations is accompanied by only a .7 percent reduction in spot commercial rates. In Stigler's theory, remember, "the number of buyers, the proportion of new buyers and the relative sizes of firms are as important as the number of rivals."[26]

Reuben Kessel's complex regression analyses use data for several thousand tax-exempt bond issues floated between 1959 and 1967. They led him to conclude that

> . . . the prices received by issuers of tax-exempts increase as the number of bids increases. . . . [and] selling prices increase as [the number of] bids increase. Hence, as the number of bids increases, the difference between buying and selling prices of underwriters decreases and the selling prices of underwriters increase. For the issuers of tax-exempts, these effects are additive; both operate to reduce the costs of borrowing.[27]

After reviewing studies of personal bank services, and gasoline and groceries at retail, Scherer concluded:

> Although one can, as always, quarrel with the particular samples, controls, and methods employed in these studies, their overall thrust is unambiguous. Prices do tend to be higher when markets are highly concentrated than when they are not.[28]

Informal (Casual) Empiricism

In addition to the more formal statistical studies that attempt to measure the effects of industrial concentration, there are a number of important, though informal, empirical observations. There can be absolutely no doubt that many concentrated industries—those with few firms, or those in which a few large firms account for most sales—have behaved competitively, in any useful sense that the term *competitive* may have. Important demonstrations of this can be found in histories of individual industries, which show how they evolved and performed over time. Indeed, important demonstrations can be found in the histories of cartels themselves, including the famous Addyston Pipe cartel, which is discussed briefly in Chapter 6. What the *Addyston* case suggests is no fluke. After analyzing all conspiracy cases that the Department of Justice brought under the Sherman law, Richard Posner said:

> . . . the vast majority of cases involve 20 or fewer conspirators and almost two-thirds involve 10 or fewer; and where large numbers are involved, invariably a trade association is instrumental in effectuating the conspiracy. The prevalence of small-number express collusion cases (twice only has the Department ever challenged "conscious parallelism," or tacit collusion, as such) casts some doubt on the practical importance of tacit collusion. and small-numbers cases may be under-represented in a sample that consists of Department of Justice proceedings. The Department's price-fixing cases . . . are frequently based on tips and testimony of defecting conspirators or disgruntled employees, and the larger the number of con-

spirators the greater the likelihood of evidence of this sort turning up and leading to prosecution. On the other hand, buyers are an important source of information too, so that the number of conspirators is plainly not the only variable in detectability.[29]

Later work by Hay and Kelley confirms these findings.[30] Among other things, such histories demonstrate that oligopoly or concentration alone were not able to achieve monopoly prices, outputs, and profits. Indeed, they suggest that explicit collusion, not oligopolistic mutual interdependence, was necessary to get other than competitive outcomes. Even if, contrary to fact, concentration were incompatible with competition, that is not enough to make a case against concentration. For atomistic competition, the standard of excellence, may itself turn out to be either unobtainable or more costly. Chapters 3, 7, and 13 discussed those problems.

Agenda for Future Research

Opportunities to compare prices generated by different industrial structures have not been exhausted. It may be possible to point the artillery in a different direction, aiming at explanations of *prices* rather than profits or price-cost margins. This is admittedly very difficult when products vary at each point and change over time. But the payoff might be big, not only in evaluating concentration but in diagnosing and evaluating cartels (and other business and contract forms) as well. There are two obvious data sources to mine. First, it is still unclear what price effects great mergers have, including those consummated at the turn of the century in the U.S. And it appears that little has been done with data from other countries. Second, it may yet be possible to do this job using old (and new) industry studies.

MORE STATISTICAL SUPPORT FOR THE STRUCTURALIST PARADIGM

After Bain, empirical work on structure and performance became distinctly more formal and complex. Later studies depart from Bain's methodology by putting continuous variables (including concentration) into multiple regression equations, rather than comparing the average profits of concentrated and unconcentrated industry groups.[31] Most of this work, however, continued to use some measure of profits as the variable to be explained. Though little will be said about it here, there is another literature based on so-called price-cost margins, one criticism of which is that it depends on numbers that are neither prices nor costs.[32]

Most of the post-Bain statistical studies used similar data and statistical methodology. They continued to attack the same problem: how can one improve the power of structural variables to explain interindustry differences in profitability? They used an increasing number of variables, including such things as concentration ratios (or individual firm sizes), advertising, and accounting values of capital employed in industrial establishments.[33] And they brought in more powerful statistical artillery to batter down the walls.

Earlier studies, starting with Joe Bain's, showed positive, though rather weak, positive correlations between industry concentration and average industry profits. More important than the statistical relationships those studies claimed, however, is what people thought the findings meant. Most seem to have thought they showed noncollusive oligopolies behaving like monopolies; or concentrated industries conspiring effectively; or some of each. In either case, the story went, concentration breeds monopoly performance. We will call this the ''structuralist'' point of view.

In 1974, probably a majority of economists believed in the structuralist paradigm. In 1974, for example, Professor Leonard Weiss, a structuralist, reviewed in detail 81 published statistical studies about how structure and performance are related, and mentioned a number of others. With the exception of notable studies by Stigler and Brozen, most of the rest claimed a positive, statistically significant relationship between concentration and profitability.[34] Experience in Great Britain appears to have been a little different: ''possibly a majority of U.K. studies find concentration not to be a significant determinant of profitability.''[35]

Authors of some of the studies that Weiss reviewed in 1974 had judged entry conditions subjectively, deciding, for example, whether entry barriers were low, moderate, or high.[36] Some others used continuous variables claimed to be proxies for such barriers. Examples are the book value of capital invested in the larger establishments (absolute capital requirements), advertising intensity, and plant size (economies of size).[37] A number of studies corrected for regional industries, whose concentration ratios were said to be too low; and import-affected industries, whose concentration ratios were said to be too high; and so on. There has been much debate about how all these adjustments and interpretations influence the results, and, indeed, about what the results really are.

People interested in formulating national policies with respect to mergers and concentration tend to be interested in whether there is a critical level beyond which higher concentration starts hurting competition and consumers. There is little evidence with which to answer the question. Bain had looked, and Stigler had noted that ''there is no relationship between profitability and concentration if H [the Herfindahl index of concentration] is less than 0.250 or the share of the four largest firms is less than about 80 percent.''[38]

The quest for a critical level of concentration has so far proved unsuccessful, even if we grant that concentration operates as the structuralists claim.[39]

PARADIGM LOST?

A large and growing difference between old-line structural orthodoxy and the newer views was the reason for holding the conference at which Weiss presented his review of 81 concentration-profit studies in 1974.[40] Although positive correlations between the size and market share of *individual firms* and their profitability had shown up in empirical studies for many years, especially in the fields of corporate history and finance, it took a long time for industrial organization economists to realize what the findings might mean for them.[41]

Economic theory asserts that, within atomistically competitive industries and cartels alike, more efficient firms become larger and more profitable. Unless they are more efficient, dominant firms or cartels of larger firms should have *lower* profit rates than smaller outside firms that compete against them. Neither collusion nor noncollusive oligopoly should be expected to make larger firms *more* profitable than smaller ones, unless they are more efficient. Chapters 7 and 13 of this present book reviewed those propositions in detail. In three of the four hypothetical cases analyzed in Chapter 13, lower costs account for some or all of the greater profits earned by concentrated industries.

It may seem strange that industrial organization so long ignored superior efficiency as a possible explanation of differences in profitability: the competition, cartel, dominant-firm, and Cournot models—all of the precise models in fact—predict that lower-cost firms will have larger market shares and higher profits.

There seem to have been several reasons for the delay. First, some economists who believed in the efficiency hypothesis wanted nothing to do with the kinds of data that were available to test it. Earlier chapters of this book, for example, argued that the measures of concentration and profits are not very good, and, indeed, that they are not even very relevant to the monopoly problem.

Second, the belief system of those doing most of the empirical work seems to have diverted their attention from efficiency explanations. For one thing, the structuralist paradigm at best ignored efficiency explanations of concentration. Another was the conventional wisdom that (1) economies of scale are the only kind of size economies that matter; and (2) that scale economies typically peter out at relatively small firm sizes, after which greater size *cannot* be justified by efficiency.

Although it is a large antelope with extraordinary lyre-shaped horns, the kudu is elusive and alert. Its grey coat and form blend perfectly into the African bush, through which it moves as quietly as smoke. It is hard enough to see kudus when you believe they exist. Demsetz was right: "believing is seeing."[42]

Economists in the first group would make no progress testing the efficiency hypothesis empirically if they were content merely to complain about how bad the data are, that concentration and profits might not really be related, and that profits are not relevant anyway. And economists in the second group would make no progress testing the efficiency hypothesis until they took it seriously.

One way to begin was simply to *assume* that the data are good enough to merit serious statistical study. Even so, two important problems remained. First, are concentration and profits significantly and positively correlated? That is, do industries with high concentration tend to have higher profits? Second, if so, is this because concentration raises prices or because larger firms have lower costs or both?

Opinions about concentration and performance had begun to change a good while before Weiss presented his review in 1974. It is difficult to date such changes precisely and, because innovators deserve (and expect) recognition, it is dangerous to try. The following well-intentioned though incomplete account takes the risk.[43]

In 1965 and 1967, Bork and Bowman published early statements of the new views,[44] and Chapter 13 quoted from a powerful statement that Robert H. Bork made in 1969. In it, Bork claimed, on theoretical grounds, that deconcentrating industrial structures by law would hurt consumers, since it would dissolve the most efficient firms and raise costs. Competition would already have eroded large market shares not justified by superior efficiency.

In 1971 McGee and Brozen published works that Scherer says are the "antecedents" of Demsetz's important 1973 study, discussed later.[45] At book length, McGee argued (on theoretical and casual empirical grounds) that persistent high profits are more likely to come from superior efficiency than monopolistic price raising, and that existing industrial structures are likely to be the most efficient structures. First, history of several real industries suggested why concentrated industries tend to have higher average profits than unconcentrated industries: larger firms in concentrated industries tend to earn higher profits than small ones, and—by definition—the profits of larger firms are weighted more heavily in calculating average profits of concentrated industries. Second, monopoly is not the only reason why large firms can have higher profits. Others are that their costs are lower, that consumers prefer their products, or both. That is, because superior efficiency produces higher profits.

The *empirical* approach to industrial organization changed drastically once economists recognized and began explicitly to test efficiency claims that earlier theoretic work had made. In his 1973 study, Harold Demsetz indirectly tested efficiency explanations of concentrated industrial structures by analyzing the pattern of 1963 earnings *within* 95 three-digit industries.[46] He sorted firms in each industry into four different asset-size classes, and computed accounting rates of returns for each class. In each of several regressions, he took as his independent variable *differences* in profitability between the largest firms and one size-class of smaller firms in the same industries. The independent (explanatory) variable was the four-firm concentration ratio for each industry. In Demsetz's notation, R_4 is the rate of return earned by firms in the largest size-class, and R_1 is the rate of return for firms in the smallest size-class. (R_2 and R_3 are earnings of firms in the two intermediate size-classes.) $C(63)$ is the four-firm concentration ratio for each industry in 1963.

The strongest results show up in profit differences between the largest and smallest firms:

$$R_4 - R_1 = -1.4 + .21C(63) \qquad [R^2 = .09]$$

$$(.07)$$

Note that the number in parentheses is *not* a *t*-ratio, unlike the example given in the first section of this chapter. It is the standard error—the scatter around the coefficient. Dividing the coefficient value (.21) by the standard error (.07) gives the *t*-ratio, approximately 3 in this case—a relatively satisfying number. Concentration was significant at the 99 percent level. Regressions using $R_3 - R_1$, and $R_2 - R_1$ were significant at the 95 percent confidence level.

The rate of return for the smallest firms did not increase with concentration, and in general the same was true for the other two classes of smaller firms. And, with increases in concentration, the differences in earnings between small and large firms increased.

On the basis of his theory and empirical findings, Demsetz suggested that leading firms are larger and more profitable because they are more efficient, and that deconcentrating concentrated industries would probably reduce efficiency.[47]

In 1977, Sam Peltzman *directly* tested the efficiency explanation of concentration in a complex statistical tour de force.[48] To measure the costs and benefits of concentration, he estimated three relationships empirically from data for 165 four-digit manufacturing industries, 1947 to 1967. The first relationship is the price of the good, as a function of an index of factors that shift demand; an index of factors shifting costs; and a measure of industry structure (CR_4). Second is cost, as a function of outside factors determining the cost index (a factor-price index), plus market structure (CR_4). The third relationship summarizes the *total* effect that a change in industry concentration had on price during the periods considered: the change in cost accompanying a change in concentration *times* the change in price accompanying that change in cost; *plus* the change in price as a direct consequence of a change in concentration.

One of Peltzman's conclusions is that "Briefly, more concentration raises profitability not because prices rise, but because they fall less than costs."[49] He concluded that higher profits could arise out of either superior efficiency or monopolistic price raising, or both; but that superior efficiency is in fact largely responsible. Furthermore, his empirical estimates suggest that a policy of industrial de-deconcentration would do much more harm than good. In his words,

> Most practitioners have chosen to interpret the profitability-concentration relationship as evidence for collusion. A minority has emphasized the concentration-efficiency nexus. The emphasis here is consistent with an eclectic view, but one in which efficiency effects predominate. . . . any extensive deconcentration program would risk imposing losses which are many times greater than the typical estimates of the benefits such a policy might have been thought to produce.[50]

In 1980, Scherer said Peltzman went too far. As he put it,

> Several empirical studies have used whole-company data to examine the relationship between profitability, weighted average industry concentration, and weighted average individual market shares. All but Shepherd's effort, which used a peculiarly specified industry structure measure, revealed statistically significant profit increases with *both* higher industry concentration *and* higher firm market shares or an interaction of the two variables. The implication is that both monopoly price raising and scale economy or other effects related to firm size coexist.[51]

Clarke, Davies, and Waterson—British economists using U.K. data—also concluded that the picture is not as clear as Peltzman claimed. Although they emerged saying "that the within-industry empirical methodology is of limited value," the data suggested to them "that, in general, both efficiency and market power effects are at work."[52]

But efficiency explanations tend to be supported when regressions include both industry concentration and the market share of individual firms among variables used to explain profitability. When both variables are included, industry concentration tends to lose its explanatory power. *Within* concentrated industries, larger firms tend to have higher profit rates, which is consistent with Bork and Bowman, Brozen, Demsetz, McGee, and Peltzman.

In 1983, for example, David J. Ravenscraft published results from ambitious, multivariable regression analyses using both FTC line-of-business and Census industry data for 1975.[53] He found that, other things equal, profits are positively related to the reporting entities' market shares, and not significantly related to four-firm concentration of the industry of which they are part. Ravenscraft concluded that his analysis supports the theory that differential profits are due to competitive efficiency rather than to collusion.

Later work done with these Line of Business data tend to confirm Ravenscraft's 1983 study, and may have undermined orthodox structuralism even further. In 1987, for example, F. M. Scherer et al. said these studies show:

> . . . that individual market share effects are . . . much more powerful than the traditionally emphasized concentration effects in explaining profitability. With most specifications, concentration coefficients turn out to be *negative* [but] The positive and significant market share relationships alone cannot discriminate between monopoly power and efficiency or cost advantage hypotheses.[54]

Though there continues to be debate about what should take its place, the orthodox structure-performance paradigm has declined markedly.

ECONOMY-WIDE MEASURES OF MONOPOLY OR MONOPOLY EFFECTS _____

How Much of the U.S. Economy Is Monopolistic? _____

Consider three major studies estimating the extent of monopoly in the United States: one by George Stigler; one by Warren Nutter; and one by Nutter and H. A. Einhorn.[55]

Using structural and other criteria to classify each economic activity, Stigler estimated the percentage of U.S. national income produced in each of four categories in 1939: competitive (55.2 percent); cartels compelled by government (2.5 percent); private monopoly (24.4 percent); and not allocable, that is, government, religion, private education, and nonprofit (17.9 percent). Disregarding the unallocable category, his estimates were: competitive (67.3 percent); compulsory cartels (3.1 percent) and monopoly (29.7 percent).

By assuming that in other years each activity retained the same monopolistic or competitive status that it had in 1939, Stigler constructed two time series. One shows for each of several years the percentage of the *total* U.S. labor force employed in activities classified as monopolized in 1939; the other shows for each year the percentage of the *manufacturing* labor force employed in industries classified as monopolized in 1939. By the first measure, monopoly in the U.S. rose from about 10 percent in 1870 to 13 percent in 1890, 17.5 percent in 1910, to 20 percent in 1920 and 1930. It declined to about 19 percent in 1940. By the second measure, monopoly manufacturing employed 27 percent in 1899 and, with the growth of the (allegedly monopolistic) auto industry, reached 34.5 percent in 1919, from which peak it declined to around 31.8 percent in 1939.

As Stigler put it, "It is my present judgment that competition declined moderately from the Civil War to the end of the 19th Century, and thereafter increased moderately."

Nutter's study is a larger and more thorough work—it was his Ph.D. dissertation and involved an awesome archaeological expedition into old documents and data. The basic objective was to test widespread assertions that concentration in the U.S. had increased alarmingly over time. He explicitly ignored labor monopoly, a significant amount of which has arisen because of government policy, unions, and licensure.

One problem is what to do with regulated industries: some, such as trucking, were unconcentrated but regulated. Regulation might have made them perform more like monopoly than like competitive industries. Others, such as public utilities and railroads, were concentrated but regulated. Regulation might have made them perform more like competitive than like monopoly industries. Nutter handled this problem by giving us alternative estimates. A second problem arises because Nutter classified only monopoly activities explicitly, leaving everything else competitive by definition. Since there is less information (concentration data, for example) about earlier periods, ignorance alone would lead you to conclude that there were fewer monopolies in early periods, more in later ¯periods, and that there had been a trend toward monopoly over time. The information bias itself therefore tends to produce an illusory increase in monopoly over time. To solve that problem, Nutter gives us another choice of estimates. One uses the best available evidence for both periods. That produces the kind of bias just noted. Another estimate uses for the later period data comparable to those that had to be used for the earlier period.

Although Nutter was careful to give us several different comparisons, one is enough for present purposes. It includes agriculture, mining, construction, manufacturing, trade, finance, transport and communications, and public utilities (including radio and services). Using comparable data sources for both years, Nutter estimated that 17.4 percent of U.S. national income was produced by monopolistic industries in 1899 and 12.9 percent in 1937, a substantial decline. Using the best data for 1937, and suffering the bias referred to, gives 21.2 percent for that year, suggesting that there had been a substantial increase in monopoly.

In 1969, Einhorn updated Nutter's study to 1958. His equal-information estimate was 15.8 percent for 1958. His information-biased estimate is 20.2 percent for that year.

Though such estimates can never be precise, they suggest that concentration and monopoly have not increased dramatically over the long term. Indeed, relying so heavily on structural tests as they do, and ignoring imports, they are likely to overstate the amount of monopoly and monopoly effects.

Estimates of the Economy-Wide Monopoly Dead-Weight Loss _____

Many claim that formal statistical studies such as previous sections discussed can reveal which industries are monopolized, how profitable they are, and perhaps the specific factors that are responsible. But, as chapters 11 and 13 show, monopoly profits and dead-weight losses due to monopoly are very different things.

What kind of evidence and methodology have been used to estimate the total monopoly dead-weight loss for the whole economy? How big is it? With few exceptions, the empirical estimates *assume*, without demonstrating, that the costs of monopoly and competition are identical, then attribute above-average profits to monopoly, which is *assumed* to have no possible efficiency justification.[56] That is, they assume the situation pictured in Figure 2-7 in Chapter 2, and Figure 13-4 in Chapter 13. This is only one of several possibilities, of course, and not even the most likely one, as both economic theory and recent empirical studies of profitability and concentration suggest.

Chapter 13 discussed the other possibilities in detail. For example, profits might precisely measure the value of resources saved because large firms and concentrated industries are the more efficient organizations. Profits might even underestimate such resource savings and consumer benefits. Price-cost ratios that look high may actually come from prices that are *lower* than alternative structures would produce. There may be, in short, an efficiency explanation and defense for the price and the concentrated industry structure that produced it.

With the exception of Schwartzman and Bodoff, writers on dead-weight losses seem to have overlooked those other possibilities. Schwartzman and Bodoff analyze price-cost ratios of different structures of the *same* industries, by comparing different places or times.[57] Theirs is not the complete answer to the problem, however, even apart from whether price-cost ratios measure what they are supposed to. A higher ratio, for example, is consistent with lower prices, and with equal prices and lower costs. A ratio is a ratio, nothing more.

In any case, however, Harberger's treatment is a stunning example of applied price theory, since it estimates the area of a triangle given only one point.[58] Using U.S. manufacturing industry profit data for the stable period 1924 to 1928, Harberger estimates welfare-loss triangles of the sort shown in Figure 13-4 in Chapter 13. He concludes that the loss due to monopoly in manufacturing was on the order of only one-tenth of one percent of our national income. Critics noted that, since profits are a small part of national income, any profit-based measure of welfare loss is bound to be relatively small. Notwithstanding that criticism, however, there is a good chance that Harberger's is an overestimate: Figure 13-4 does not picture the most probable situation, let alone the only possible one. Profits are only part of the total benefit that an efficient industry organization brings.

Stigler criticized Harberger's assuming industry demand functions with price elasticity equal to -1, on the grounds that profit-maximizing monopolies operate with higher price elasticities than that.[59] This criticism is misplaced. Even cartelized industries do not usually achieve the same results as a single-firm monopoly would. Elasticities facing firms are higher than elasticities facing industries, and Harberger was quite properly analyzing industries.

In any case, many such estimates have been made since. Worcester and Schwartzman, like Harberger, conclude that the monopoly effect is small.[60] In a study published in 1986, Micha Gisser follows Worcester (1975) in using a dominant-firm theory to arrive at one of his estimates: the monopoly loss in 1977 was about one-eighth of one percent of U.S. gross national product. In his words, ''. . . estimates . . . derived from an industry model characterized by price leadership lend strong support to Harberger's findings of thirty years ago.''[61]

In an unusual, elegant, and powerful demonstration, Alberts, like Bodoff, concludes that the monopoly dead-weight loss is nonexistent.[62]

Some analysts have claimed higher losses than Harberger showed, partly by assuming that concentrated industries do not minimize costs or maximize profits; that resources get squandered in attempts to achieve monopoly; and that demand elasticities are very high.[63] But all such arguments are profoundly suspect. For one thing, as Chapters 10 and 13 suggest, we have to be careful about what profit maximization means in the real world. That is, all profit maximization is constrained by the costs of reducing costs and raising revenues. Profits *are* maximized when it costs more than a dollar to increase revenues or reduce costs one dollar. We should, as well, question the ability of inefficient monopolies to exclude firms that have not been weakened by dry rot. And, finally, even if such tales of incompetence and sloth were true, *people* would be benefitting from whatever inflation in costs there might be. Not all of the cost inflation, if any there be, would therefore be a net loss. You would have to add in with profits and consumer surplus such gains as the underachievers and malingerers got.

Just as we have seen in other fields of industrial organization, empirical studies of overall dead-weight losses superficially appear to offer something for everyone. Those who believe that such losses are large enough to deserve remedy can find studies to support their concern. And there are studies to support those who believe the loss is small or nonexistent. None of these studies, however, faces a fundamental issue: what if the greater profits come from greater efficiency? One serious criticism is that what passes for monopolies in these studies are probably the most beneficial structures; that is, relative to other structures, they produce welfare *gains*, not losses.

SUMMARY

Where all this leaves us is difficult to put briefly; but several things do stand out.

The old orthodox structuralist view had been that industry concentration increases profits because it leads to collusion or to oligopoly, which allegedly comes to the same thing. If that were true, however, larger firms in concentrated as well as unconcentrated industries would not have larger market shares and profit rates *unless* they are more efficient. And if larger firms *are* more efficient, theories that concentration equals monopoly are in trouble from two sides. First, *competition* itself would generate just the kind of relationship observed between profits and size. This suggests that concentrated industries may be competitive after all. Second, dissolving or punishing large firms in concentrated industries is liable to do more harm than good, whether the industries are competitive or not: reducing concentration would raise costs. That forced deconcentration could reduce prices at all, or enough to compensate, is problematic. Attacking the most efficient firms in industry is scarcely to be recommended.

The relationship between profits and concentration weakens, sometimes disappears, and often turns negative when the regression equations include certain other explanatory variables. This tends to happen, for example, when the market share of individual firms, or industry advertising intensity, is included as a separate explanatory variable.[64] Industry concentration apparently has less to do with the profitability of individual firms or size classes of firms than their market shares do. Since that is consistent with a competitive process in which firms get large because they are efficient, or are efficient because they are large, it undermines the old wisdom that started with Bain.

Although the controversy is far from settled, many economists have changed their minds about what the cross-industry statistical studies show. Many now believe that, on average and over manufacturing as a whole, concentrated industries tend to be more profitable partly because firms with larger shares have lower costs and partly because, for one reason or another, their prices have remained above *their own* costs—at least for a while.[65]

According to economic theory, that is surely possible; but we should be careful about what *price raising* means. Firms with lower costs are larger and more profitable in standard noncollusive models including those for dominant-firm industries and Cournot oligopoly. That price exceeds the costs of low-cost firms encourages efficiency and is just, among other things. But there has been no price raising in any sense that consumers should lament or want to change. And, as shown in chapters 11 and 13, even an unregulated single-firm monopoly might be so efficient that its price-cost ratio is high while, at the same time, it charges a lower price than a less concentrated industry would. Or its resource-saving efficiency might outweigh the effects of an absolutely higher price, if price had somehow been raised.

What about collusion? Suppose an industry contains firms of various sizes. If smaller firms are coconspirators with larger firms that have lower costs, these high-cost small firms should have lower profits in a well-run cartel. Smaller firms *outside* a conspiracy among larger firms should have higher rates of profits than conspirators that have no efficiency advantages; lower profit rates if the conspirators have substantial efficiency advantages; and—improbably—exactly equal profits if their cost disadvantage were precisely counterbalanced by their price-taker output expansionism.[66]

Being consistent is as hard for economists as for anybody else. In the days when virtually all statistical studies claimed that concentration and profits are positively related, believers in the concentration-equals-monopoly doctrine said the concentration and profits data were plenty good enough to reveal the truth. Some nonbelievers claimed that the concentration and profits data were not good; others declared that profits and monopoly dead-weight loss are quite different things in any case; some made both points.

Statistical studies have severely tested the consistency and objectivity of both camps. Once the concentration-equals-monopoly theory started to decline, old believers in it started saying that the data are not so good after all. When industry concentration collapsed as an explainer of profitability in their regressions, Comanor and Wilson, for example, recovered quickly: ". . . the concentration ratio measures only one dimension of market structure, and is therefore an inadequate indicator of market power, which depends on additional structural variables as well as on established behavior patterns.''[67] Recently Schmalansee wrote that the old structural variables and theories look so bad because of inflation, badly measured industrial structures and profits, and cyclical and long-term disequilibrium.[68] The disbelievers have also come under stress. Longtime critics of both the data and the structuralist paradigm are now being tempted to claim that the data are better than we used to think.

It is well to note, however, that recent studies by Demsetz, Peltzman, and Ravenscraft are *conceptually* different from the old ones, though they use some of the same data. The newer studies partly allow for the effect of firm size and patterns of costs and profits *within* industries, which is at least relevant in principle. The older studies mostly relied on interindustry, cross-sectional studies, the conceptual deficiencies of which we will now review.

It is one thing, as an academic exercise, statistically to relate measures of profits, an ambiguous and badly measured symptom, to concentration data derived from flawed statistical categories. It is quite another to base policy prescriptions upon what tumbles out. It is usually not clear whether profits have actually been disentangled and measured; whether, if they have been, they are due to monopoly or something else; whether concentration has been measured meaningfully; and, if so, whether it is related to monopoly, to something else, or to nothing else in particular.

The old cross-sectional studies purported to show, on average and amongst *different* industries, a statistical relationship between profits and concentration. Even if the data were wonderful and the procedures dead right, it is not clear how relevant they would be: the *policy* question is whether reducing concentration *within* one or more industries would improve performance within them. The implicit assumption was that the relationship *amongst* industries also applied to changes *within* industries. That was a remarkable assumption.

By making two logical leaps, some analysts then offered policy prescriptions that would apply to *specific* industries. The first leap was to equate profit rates with monopoly and to judge the severity of the latter from the size of the former. The second was to assume that concentration caused the profits and constitutes the monopoly. As a result, we were told, reducing concentration could get rid of them both; or fines and decrees could improve performance, if dissolution can't be got. From average, interindustry relationships between doubtful measures a short road to economic reform was paved.

For years, though, a few economists had claimed that, in the absence of state intervention, the optimal industrial structure is likely to be the one that actually emerges in the long run. To answer the trade-off question directly and definitively, we would need to estimate and compare costs under greater and lesser concentration. Only relatively recently has the question even been asked that way. More recently, still, as shown above, empirical evidence has emerged. Such evidence as we now have is consistent with the theory that industrial structures tend to be cost- and quality-justified.

Starting from that point of view, it would not be surprising to conclude that the economy-wide loss from *open* (rather than closed) monopolies in the United States is relatively small, and may be zero.

QUESTIONS

1. Explain the structure-performance paradigm. Specify a simple version of it that we can test statistically or informally.

2. ''Why have industrial organization economists spent so much time explaining interindustry profit differences when profits have little or nothing to do with the harm that monopoly does?'' Explain and comment.

3. What basically, did Bain do? Did he measure price effects, or dead-weight losses from monopoly? What, if anything, was problematic about his samples?

4. What did Brozen mean by *disequilibrium*? How does it enter into his analysis?

5. According to Brozen, what happens to concentration over time when the profits of larger firms in an industry are higher than those of small firms? Lower? What could cause that?

6. According to Brozen, over time what happens to the profit rates of extremely profitable firms in an industry? To the profit rates of industries whose profits are far above average? On average, what happens to the concentration of extremely concentrated industries? What could cause these phenomena?

7. What is a statistically significant regression coefficient? Does it establish causality?

8. What does R^2 mean? Does it reveal the extent to which an estimating equation demonstrates causality?

9. What, if anything, about the structure-performance paradigm can we infer from characteristics of conspiracy cases brought under U.S. antitrust laws?

10. On theoretical grounds, the welfare trade-off analysis of Chapter 13 suggests that two cases are most probable. First, concentration lowers cost without lowering price. Second, concentration lowers price *and* cost, but lowers cost more than price. After reviewing those cases in Chapter 13—if you need to—predict what patterns of firm size and profits, and concentration, you expect to find empirically. How could you test whether those predictions are right?

11. What patterns of firm size and profits, and concentration do Demsetz, Peltzman, and Ravenscraft claim to find? Explain.

12. Outline the relationships among costs, market shares, and concentration predicted by the theories of (a) atomistic competition; (b) Cournot oligopoly; (c) perfect cartel; (d) the dominant firm.

13. Most of those who criticized Harberger's (relatively low) estimate of economy-wide loss from monopoly say it is too low. McGee says it is probably too high. Explain and comment.

14. Some critics of Harberger said he underestimates the dead-weight loss because he does not recognize that large firms are inefficient. Draw a welfare trade-off diagram illustrating this case, in which costs are higher than they ought to be. How could this happen? What does inefficient mean? How could that situation persist? How could you test empirically for its existence or persistence?

NOTES

1. Chapters 2 and 3.
2. Chapters 2, 3, 4, 5, 13.

3. Chapters 10 and 11.

4. Edward E. Leamer, "Let's Take the Con out of Econometrics," *American Economic Review*, 73 (March 1983), pp. 31–43; M. McAleer, A. R. Pagan, and P. A. Volker, "What Will Take the Con out of Econometrics?" *American Economic Review*, 75 (June 1985), 293–307; and Edward E. Leamer, "Sensitivity Analyses Would Help," *American Economic Review*, 75 (June 1985), pp. 308–13.

5. Leamer, "Sensitivity Analyses Would Help," p. 308. For other cautions and admonitions about econometrics, see Peter Kennedy, *A Guide to Econometrics*, 2nd ed. (Cambridge, Mass.: MIT Press, 1985), pp. 40–42, 1–2, 6, 113–15, and Chapter 15: Forecasting.

6. For comprehensible explanations, see Potluri Rao and Roger LeRoy Miller, *Applied Econometrics*, (Belmont, Calif.: Wadsworth Publishing Co., Inc., 1971); and Kennedy, *A Guide to Econometrics*.

7. The author is profoundly suspicious of the data from which he constructed the example, and, indeed, of the approaches it represents. He makes absolutely no claims for its scientific validity. A sufficient excuse for presenting the example is that these are the sorts of data and methods used in most of the recent research.

8. *Annual Line of Business Report, 1977*, Statistical Report of the Bureau of Economics to the Federal Trade Commission (Washington, D.C.: April 1985).

9. U.S. Bureau of the Census, *1982 Census of Manufactures, Concentration Ratios in Manufacturing* (Washington, D.C.: April 1986).

10. See Chapter 1.

11. FTC, *Statistical Report: Annual Line of Business Report 1977*, Appendix E, Industry Category List for FTC Form LB, 1977, pp. 309–20.

12. Indeed, the adjusted R^2, adjusted for degrees of freedom, is only .0282. By that standard, the equation explains 2.8 percent of the total variation.

   In this sample of 61 industry categories, the average return on assets was about 15 percent. The highest (cereal breakfast foods) was 39.4 percent; the lowest (beet sugar) was −1.9 percent. CR_4 ranged from 8 (metal doors, sash, frames, and molding) to 89 (cereal breakfast foods), and averaged 47.

13. As Peter Kennedy put it, "Using techniques that adopt specifications on the basis of searches for high R^2 or high t values is called data-mining, fishing, grubbing, or number-crunching. This methodology is described eloquently by Coase: 'if you torture the data long enough, Nature will confess.' In reference to this unjustified (but unfortunately typical) means of specifying relationships, Leamer . . . is moved to comment: 'There are two things you are better off not watching in the making: sausages and econometric estimates.'" Kennedy, *A Guide to Econometrics*, p. 76.

14. In this sample, media advertising/sales varies from zero to 13.8 percent, averaging 2.17 percent.

15. In this sample, assets/sales ranges from 22.7 to 235.9, averaging 68.73.

16. Joe S. Bain, "Relation of Profit Rate to Industry Concentration: American Manufacturing, 1936–1940," *Quarterly Journal of Economics*, 65 (August 1951), p. 293.

17. George J. Stigler, *Capital and Rates of Return in Manufacturing Industries* (Princeton, N.J.: Princeton University Press, 1963). For a different view, see Robert W. Kilpatrick, "Stigler on the Relationship Between Industry Profit Rates and Market Concentration," *Journal of Political Economy*, 76 (May/June 1968), pp. 479–88.

18. Yale Brozen, "Bain's Concentration and Rates of Return Revisited," *Journal of Law & Economics*, 14 (October 1971), pp. 351–69.

19. Joe S. Bain, *Barriers to New Competition* (Cambridge, Mass.: Harvard University Press, 1956).

20. F. M. Scherer, *Industrial Market Structure and Economic Performance*, 2nd ed. (Chicago: Rand McNally College Publishing Company, 1980), p. 277.

21. Ibid., p. 277, note.

22. Yale Brozen, "Bain's Concentration," pp. 352–53. Also see his "The Antitrust Task Force Deconcentration Recommendation," *Journal of Law & Economics*, 13 (October 1970), pp. 279–92.

23. Yale Brozen, "Antitrust Task Force," p. 263. See also J. T. Wenders, "Deconcentration Reconsidered," *Journal of Law & Economics*, 14 (October 1971), pp. 485–88; Brozen, "Deconcentration Reconsidered: Comment," ibid., pp. 489–91; P. W. MacAvoy, J. W. Mackie, and L. E. Preston, "High and Stable Concentration Levels, Profitability, and Public Policy: A Response," ibid., pp. 493–99; Brozen, "The Persistence of 'High Rates of Return' in High-Stable Concentration Industries," ibid., pp. 501–12.

24. Brozen, "Antitrust Task Force," pp. 290–92; H. M. Mann, "Seller Concentration, Barriers to Entry, and Rates of Return in Thirty Industries, 1950–1960," *Review of Economics and Statistics*, 48 (August 1966), pp. 296–307.

25. For a claim that higher profits *do* persist, see Dennis Mueller, "The Persistence of Profits Above the Norm," *Economica*, 44 (November 1977), pp. 369–80.

26. George J. Stigler, "A Theory of Oligopoly," reprinted (with an addendum) in Stigler, *The Organization of Industry* (Homewood, Ill.: Richard D. Irwin, Inc., 1968), pp. 39–63, at p. 57. Stigler also studied 1939 steel prices, concluding that list prices were cut more on products with lower Herfindahl concentration indexes in 1938. Ibid., pp. 59–60.

27. Reuben Kessel, "A Study of the Effects of Competition in the Tax-exempt Bond Market," *Journal of Political Economy*, 79 (July/August 1971), pp. 706–38, at p. 723.

28. Scherer, *Industrial Market Structure and Economic Performance* (1980), p. 288. Scherer cites Frederick W. Bell and Neil B. Murphy, "Impact of Market Structure on the Price of a Commercial Banking Service," *Review of Economics and Statistics*, 51 (May 1969), pp. 210–13; R. C. Aspinwall, "Market Structure and Commercial Bank Mortgage Interest Rates," *Southern Economic Journal*, 36 (April 1970), pp. 376–84; Arnold A. Heggestad and John J. Mingo, "Prices, Non-Prices, and Concentration in Commercial Banking," *Journal of Money, Credit and Banking*, 8 (February 1976), pp. 107–17; Heggestad and Mingo, "The Competitive Condition of U.S. Banking Markets and the Impact of Structural Reform," *Journal of Finance*, 32 (June 1977), pp. 649–61; Howard P. Marvel, "Competition and Price Levels in the Retail Gasoline Market," *Review of Economics and Statistics*, 60 (May 1978), pp. 252–58; Bruce W. Marion and others, *The Profit and Price Performance of Leading Food Chains, 1970–74*, a study for the Joint Economic Committee of the U.S. Congress (Washington, D.C.: Government Printing Office, April 1977); and [for debates about the Marion-Mueller study] Joint Economic Committee, Hearings: *Prices and Profits of Leading Retail Food Chains, 1970–74*, 95th Cong., 1st sess., 1977.

   A later study is F. E. Geithman, H. P. Marvel, and L. W. Weiss, "Concentration, Price, and Critical Concentration Ratios," *Review of Economics and Statistics*, 63 (August 1981), pp. 346–53.

29. Richard A. Posner, "A Statistical Study of Antitrust Enforcement," *Journal of Law & Economics*, 13 (October 1970), pp. 365–420, at 399, 402.

30. George A. Hay and Daniel Kelley, "An Empirical Study of Price Fixing Conspiracies," *Journal of Law & Economics*, 17 (April 1974), pp. 13–38, at 20–21.

31. For citations to work done before 1974, see Leonard Weiss, "The Concentration-Profits Relationship and Antitrust," in *Industrial Concentration: The New Learning*, eds. Harvey J. Goldschmid, H. M. Mann, and J. F. Weston (Boston: Little, Brown & Company, 1974), pp. 184–231.

Work of this kind includes William S. Comanor and Thomas A. Wilson, "Advertising, Market Structure, and Performance," *Review of Economics and Statistics*, 49 (November 1967), pp. 423–40 (which de-emphasizes concentration as an explanatory variable); M. Hall and L. W. Weiss, "Firm Size and Profitability," *Review of Economics and Statistics*, 49 (August 1967), pp. 319–31; R. A. Miller, "Market Structure and Industrial Performance: Relation of Profit Rates to Concentration, Advertising Intensity, and Diversity," *Journal of Industrial Economics*, 17 (April 1969), pp. 104–18; FTC, *Economic Report on the Influence of Market Share on the Profit Performance of Food Manufacturing Industries* (Washington, D.C., 1969); B. T. Gale, "Market Share and Rate of Return," *Review of Economics and Statistics*, 54 (November 1972), pp. 412–23; William G. Shepherd, "The Elements of Market Structure," *Review of Economics and Statistics,* 54 (February 1972), pp. 25–35; Shepherd, *The Treatment of Market Power* (New York: Columbia University Press, 1975); Timothy G. Sullivan, "A Note on Market Power and Returns to Stockholders," *Review of Economics and Statistics*, 59 (February 1977), pp. 108–13; Stavros B. Thomadakis, "A Value-Based Test of Profitability and Market Structure," *Review of Economics and Statistics*, 59 (May 1977), pp. 179–85; J. C. H. Jones, L. Laudadio, and M. Percy, "Profitability and Market Structure: A Cross-Section Comparison of Canadian and American Manufacturing Industry," *Journal of Industrial Economics*, 25 (March 1977), pp. 195–211; and Stephen Martin, *Market, Firm, and Economic Performance* (New York: New York University Press, 1983).

David J. Ravenscraft, "Structure-Profit Relationships at the Line of Business and Industry Level," *Review of Economics and Statistics*, 65 (February 1983), pp. 22–31 is so different that it is discussed in the next subsection of this chapter.

32. For detailed criticism, see S. J. Liebowitz, "What Do Census Price-Cost Margins Measure?" *Journal of Law & Economics*, 25 (October 1982), pp. 231–46. Price-cost margin studies include Norman Collins and Lee Preston, "Price-Cost Margins and Industry Structure," *Review of Economics and Statistics*, 51 (August 1969), pp. 271–86; Howard P. Marvel, "Competition and Price Levels in the Retail Gasoline Market," *Review of Economics and Statistics*, 60 (May 1978), pp. 252–58, and John Kwoka, "The Effect of Market Share Distribution on Industry Performance," *Review of Economics and Statistics*, 61 (February 1979), pp. 101–9.

33. Statistical studies of this kind became increasingly popular even in courts of law. For an explanation of the techniques used, written by a distinguished statistician-economist, see Franklin M. Fisher, "The Use of Multiple Regression Analysis in Legal Proceedings," *Columbia Law Review* (May 1980), pp. 702–36.

34. Weiss, "The Concentration-Profits Relationship and Antitrust," in *Industrial Concentration: The New Learning*, eds. Goldschmid, Mann, and Weston, pp. 184–231.

A major exception was Stigler, *Capital and Rates of Return in Manufacturing Industries*. For a different view of Stigler's data, see Robert W. Kilpatrick, "Stigler on the Relationship Between Industry Profit Rates and Market Concentration,'' *Journal of Political Economy*, 76 (May/June 1968), pp. 479–88.

    See also Stigler, "A Note on Profitability, Competition, and Concentration," Chapter 13 in his *The Organization of Industry* (Homewood, Ill.: Richard D. Irwin, Inc., 1968), pp. 142–46. According to Stigler, most empirical studies suggest that the profits of Census or IRS industries are positively but weakly related to industry concentration ratios. And, in earlier studies, at least, the statistical relationship seemed to improve with sloppier industry definitions: "The disquieting feature is the fact that profitability is better correlated with crude industry measures (food) than with more sharply defined industries (canned fruits and vegetables)." Ibid., pp. 145–46.

35. Michael Waterson, *Economic Theory of the Industry* (Cambridge, England: Cambridge University Press, 1984), p. 200.

36. One example is Michael H. Mann, "The Interaction of Barriers and Concentration: A Reply," *Journal of Industrial Economics*, 19 (July 1971), pp. 291–93.

37. Notable examples (that also de-emphasize concentration!) are William S. Comanor and Thomas A. Wilson, "Advertising, Market Structure, and Performance," *Review of Economics and Statistics*, 49 (November 1967), pp. 423–40; and William G. Shepherd, "Elements of Market Structure," *Review of Economics and Statistics*, 54 (February 1972), pp. 25–37, especially at p. 35.

38. Stigler, "Theory of Oligopoly," in *The Organization of Industry*, p. 59.

39. As Leonard Weiss put it, ". . . I just can't answer the question and I don't think anybody can. . . . though I produced reams and reams of printout and struggled and struggled, I was never able to come to a convincing solution, and I don't think I have seen a convincing solution. There are some studies that seem to show critical concentration ratios—a four-firm of 50 or an eight-firm of 70; Bains's original study seemed to show that. There are others where it is almost impossible to determine such a break. * * * I don't even know if that critical line exists. As far as the statistical evidence goes, I am afraid the answer has to be we don't know." "Dialogue," in *Industrial Concentration: The New Learning*, eds. Goldschmid, Mann, and Weston, p. 243.

40. Harvey J. Goldschmid, "Director's Preface," *Industrial Concentration: The New Learning*, pp. vii–viii.

41. A relatively early example is W. L. Crum, *Corporate Size and Earning Power* (Cambridge, Mass.: Harvard University Press, 1939). But David R. Kamerschen, "The Influence of Ownership and Control on Profit Rates," *American Economic Review*, 58 (June 1968), pp. 432–46 concludes that "Another variable which was statistically important, but which is theoretically unappealing, is the level of sales revenue." Ibid., p. 446. Also see N. Collins and L. Preston, "Price-Cost Margins and Industry Structure," *Review of Economics and Statistics*, 51 (August 1969), pp. 271–86; M. Hall and L. Weiss, "Firm Size and Profitability," *Review of Economics and Statistics*, 49 (August 1967), pp. 319–31; P. Asch and M. Marcus, "Returns to Scale in Advertising," *Antitrust Bulletin*, 15 (Spring 1970), pp. 33–42; John M. Blair, *Economic Concentration* (New York: Harcourt Brace Jovanovich, Inc., 1972), pp. 177–185; S. I. Ornstein, "Concentration and Profits," *Journal of Business* (1972), pp. 519–41; and Shepherd, "The Elements of Market Structure," pp. 25–37.

42. Harold Demsetz, "Two Systems of Belief About Monopoly," in *Industrial Concentration: The New Learning*, eds. Goldschmid, Mann, and Weston, p. 164.

43. A recent book gives a similar list of major contributors to what it calls the "New Learning"

and the "Chicago School" of industrial organization. This source lists them in alphabetical order: Bork, Bowman, Demsetz, McGee, Ornstein, Peltzman, Posner, Stigler, and Telser. William L. Baldwin, *Market Power, Competition, and Antitrust Policy* (Homewood, Ill.: Richard D. Irwin, Inc. 1987), p. 303.

44. Robert H. Bork and Ward S. Bowman, "The Crisis in Antitrust," *Columbia Univ. Law Review*, 65 (March 1965), pp. 363–76; and Robert H. Bork, "The Goals of Antitrust Policy," *American Economic Review*, 57 (May 1967), pp. 242–53.

45. Scherer cites as "antecedents" Yale Brozen, "Concentration and Structural and Market Disequilibria," *Antitrust Bulletin*, 16 (Summer 1971), pp. 241–48; "and (especially)" John S. McGee, *In Defense of Industrial Concentration* (New York: Praeger Publishers, 1971), especially pp. 41–52, 75–79.

46. Harold Demsetz, "Industry Structure, Market Rivalry, and Public Policy," *Journal of Law & Economics*, 16 (April 1973), pp. 1–9; Demsetz, "The Market Concentration Doctrine: An Examination of Evidence and a Discussion of Policy" (Washington, D.C.: American Enterprise Institute for Public Policy Research, August 1973), pp. 1–30; and Demsetz, "Two Systems of Belief About Monopoly," in *Industrial Concentration: The New Learning*, eds. Goldschmid, Mann, and Weston, pp. 164–84.

47. Also see D. K. Round, "Industrial Structure, Market Rivalry and Public Policy: Some Australian Evidence," *Journal of Law & Economics*, 18 (April 1975), pp. 273–81; and D. N. Winn and D. A. Leabo, "Rates of Return, Concentration, and Growth—Question of Disequilibrium," *Journal of Law & Economics*, 17 (April 1974), pp. 97–115.

48. Sam Peltzman, "The Gains and Losses from Industrial Concentration," *Journal of Law & Economics*, 20 (October 1977), pp. 229–63. At pages 232 and 245, he cites the line of argument found in McGee (1971) and Demsetz (1973).

    Also see Steven Lustgarten, "Gains and Losses from Concentration: A Comment," *Journal of Law & Economics*, 22 (April 1979), p. 183. For a criticism of Peltzman, see F. M. Scherer, "The Causes and Consequences of Rising Industrial Concentration: A Comment," ibid., pp. 191–208; and Peltzman, "A Reply," ibid., 209–11.

49. Peltzman, "The Gains and Losses," p. 257.

50. Ibid., pp. 262–63.

51. Scherer, *Industrial Market Structure* (1980), p. 283 cites: James A. Dalton and David W. Penn, *The Quality of Data as a Factor in Analyses of Structure-Performance Relationships* (FTC Staff Report, Washington, D.C.: Government Printing Office, 1971); Blake Imel and Peter Helmberger, "Estimation of Structure-Profit Relationships with Application to the Food Processing Sector," *American Economic Review*, 61 (September 1971), pp. 614–27; John M. Vernon and Marjorie B. McElroy, "Comment," *American Economic Review*, 63 (September 1973), pp. 763–69; Shepherd, "The Elements of Market Structure"; Bradley T. Gayle, "Market Share and Rate of Return," *Review of Economics and Statistics*, 54 (November 1972), pp. 412–25; and James A. Dalton and Stanford L. Levin, "Market Power: Concentration and Market Share," *Industrial Organization Review*, 5 (1977), pp. 27–35.

52. Roger Clarke, Stephen Davies, and Michael Waterson, "The Profitability-Concentration Relation: Market Power or Efficiency?" *Journal of Industrial Economics*, 32 (June 1984), pp. 435–50, at p. 448.

53. David J. Ravenscraft, "Structure-Profit Relationships at the Line of Business and Industry Level," *Review of Economics and Statistics*, 65 (February 1983), pp. 22–31.

349

54. F. M. Scherer et al., "The Validity of Studies with Line of Business Data: Comment," *American Economic Review*, 77 (March 1987), p. 206.

55. George J. Stigler, "Competition in the United States," in his *Five Lectures on Economic Problems* (London: Longmans, Green, 1949), pp. 46–65; G. Warren Nutter, *The Extent of Enterprise Monopoly in the United States: 1899–1939* (Chicago: University of Chicago Press, 1951); G. W. Nutter and H. A. Einhorn, *Enterprise Monopoly in the United States: 1899–1958* (New York: Columbia University Press, 1969).

56. Arnold C. Harberger, "Monopoly and Resource Allocation," *American Economic Review*, 54 (May 1954), pp. 77–87; Dean A. Worcester, Jr., "Innovations in the Calculation of Welfare Loss to Monopoly," *Western Economic Journal*, 7 (September 1969), pp. 234–43; Worcester, "New Estimates of the Welfare Loss to Monopoly, U.S. 1956–1969," *Southern Economic Review*, 40 (October 1973), pp. 234–45; Worcester, "On Monopoly Welfare Losses: Comment," *American Economic Review*, 65 (December 1975), pp. 1015–23; David Schwartzman, "The Effect of Monopoly on Price," *Journal of Political Economy*, 67 (August 1959), pp. 352–62; Schwartzman, "The Burden of Monopoly," *Journal of Political Economy*, 68 (December 1960), pp. 627–30; "The Effect of Monopoly: A Correction," *Journal of Political Economy*, 69 (October 1961), p. 494; Joan Bodoff, "Monopoly and Price Revisited," in *The Competitive Economy: Selected Readings*, ed. Yale Brozen (Morristown, N.J.: General Learning Press, 1975), pp. 175–85.

57. David Schwartzman, "The Effect of Monopoly on Price," pp. 352–62; Joan Bodoff, "Monopoly and Price Revisited," pp. 175–85.

58. Arnold C. Harberger, "Monopoly and Resource Allocation" (May 1954), pp. 77–87. Also see Harberger, "Three Basic Postulates for Applied Welfare Economics: An Interpretive Essay," *Journal of Economic Literature*, 9 (September 1971), pp. 785–97; and Robert D. Willig, "Consumer's Surplus Without Apology," *American Economic Review*, 66 (September 1976), pp. 589–97.

59. George J. Stigler, "The Statistics of Monopoly and Merger," *Journal of Political Economy*, 64 (February 1956), pp. 33–40, at p. 34.

60. Worcester, "New Estimates of the Welfare Loss to Monopoly," pp. 234–45; Schwartzman, "The Burden of Monopoly," pp. 627–30; and for disagreements among Worcester, Bergson, and Carson, see *American Economic Review*, 65 (December 1975), pp. 1008–31.

61. Micha Gisser, "Price Leadership and Welfare Losses in U.S. Manufacturing," *American Economic Review*, 76 (September 1986), pp. 756–67, at p. 766.

62. William W. Alberts, "Do Oligopolists Earn 'Noncompetitive' Rates of Return?" *American Economic Review*, 74 (September 1984), pp. 624–32.

63. See Gordon Tullock, "The Welfare Costs of Tariffs, Monopolies, and Theft," *Western Economic Journal*, 5 (June 1967), pp. 224–32; D. R. Kamerschen, "An Estimation of the Welfare Losses for Monopoly in the American Economy," *Western Economic Journal*, 4 (Summer 1966), pp. 221–36; Abram Bergson, "On Monopoly Welfare Losses," *American Economic Review*, 63 (December 1973), pp. 853–70; Bergson, "A Note on Consumer's Surplus," *Journal of Economic Literature*, 13 (March 1975), pp. 38–44. For criticisms of Bergson's methods, see R. Carson, "On Monopoly Welfare Losses: Comment," *American Economic Review*, 65 (December 1975), pp. 1008–14; and Worcester, "Comment," ibid., pp. 1015–23.
   Most such studies use industry data. An exception is Keith Dowling and Dennis

Muller, "The Social Costs of Monopoly Power," *Economic Journal*, 88 (December 1978), pp. 727–48. Their estimates of dead-weight losses in the U.S. and U.K. are relatively high.

64. Scherer et al., "Line of Business Data Studies," *American Economic Review*, 77 (March 1987), p. 208.

65. Ibid., pp. 205–17.

66. A relatively recent article on cost-reducing plus price-raising effects is R. Clarke, S. Davies, and M. Waterson, "The Profitability-Concentration Relation: Market Power or Efficiency?" *Journal of Industrial Economics*, 32 (June 1984), pp. 435–51.

67. William S. Comanor and Thomas A. Wilson, "Advertising, Market Structure, and Performance," *Review of Economics and Statistics*, 49 (November 1967), 423–40, at p. 424.

68. Richard Schmalansee, "Do Markets Matter Much?" *American Economic Review*, 75 (June 1985), pp. 341–351.

15

CONCENTRATION, INVENTION, AND INNOVATION: EMPIRICAL EVIDENCE

INTRODUCTION

Technology is the total present knowledge about how to do and make things—a quintessential book of recipes and ingredients. Invention adds new entries to that book. Innovation borrows information from the book and puts it to new uses. Taken together, technology, invention, and innovation appear to have been extremely important.[1]

Years ago, economists discovered that growth in the quantity of capital explains only a relatively small part of the increase in output per worker that has occurred over long periods. They gave a name to the unexplained source of all this unexplained increase in productivity: technological improvement. One can object to *defining* all of this unexplained statistical residual as technological improvement, on the grounds that it includes effects of factors that many do not regard as quite so technological. For that residual includes size economies that demand growth makes accessible; cost reductions from improved business methods, and from exploiting new deposits of minerals; and so on. In any case, however, even by narrow definitions technological progress has mattered.

We need no training in economics to believe that innovations can create new industries and transform the structure and performance of old ones: we see it happening every day. Even if they get no patents, those who introduce new products or ways of doing things may come to supply all or most of their markets and seem to have monopoly power—at least for a while. A patent system may reinforce those effects.

In the competitive struggle, firms that do not invent or innovate tend to be outstripped by those that do, lose ground, and may even disappear completely. As we have already noted in Chapter 3, Joseph Schumpeter claimed that this "new" type of competition is more powerful and beneficial than the atomistic competition pictured in textbooks, "as much more effective . . . as a bombardment is in comparison with forcing a door."[2]

Because invention and innovation can alter industrial structure, the present structure of industry is a result of past inventions and innovations, among other things. Whether causality also runs the other way is less obvious. Does industry structure affect invention or innovation? A single-firm monopoly seems to have more to gain from a cost-saving innovation than would each of a swarm of small firms. And if piracy of ideas were more likely in an industry of many firms, firms in unconcentrated industries should be less inclined to research, invent, and innovate. Economies of size in invention and innovation would also encourage progressiveness in larger firms and concentrated industries.

On the other hand, however, a monopoly would not introduce a new process until using it could bring total average cost below the marginal cost got by using the old ways. If they could ever have come up with it in the first place, competitive newcomers might introduce a new process earlier, as soon as it offered costs lower than price.

Even this brief introduction suggests several interesting and vexing questions about invention and innovation. There are a number of opposing theories.[3] This chapter discusses the theory relevant to processes of invention and innovation and summarizes empirical studies purporting to show how industry structure is related to invention and innovation.[4] The next section outlines the basic theory, and the following one explains what the empirical problem is. The last section briefly surveys the empirical findings themselves.

THEORY

Chapter 13 compares economic welfare produced by unconcentrated and concentrated industrial structures, which some believe is the same as comparing competition and monopoly. Suppose that concentrated industries really are more profitable. As chapters 13 and 14 note, this could happen because concentration raises prices or lowers costs or both. One question would then be whether the price-raising effects of concentration, if there are any, are outweighed by resource savings. The answer, as chapters 13 and 14 show, can be yes. This is basically because absolutely lower costs apply to all the output, whereas any reduction in the total of producer and consumer surplus is a result of any monopolistic *reduction* in output.

The welfare comparisons made in Chapter 13 were static, and did not show what happens as time runs; but they are a starting point for analyzing the dynamic effects, which are what count in reality. As Scherer put it,

> . . . in the long run, it is dynamic performance that counts. . . . an output handicap amounting to 10 percent of gross national product owing to static inefficiency is surmounted in just five years if the output growth rate can be raised through more rapid technological progress from 3 to 5 percent per annum, or in 20 years if the growth rate can be increased from 3 to 3.5 percent.[5]

Schumpeter's point was that the dynamic struggle for leadership has lowered real costs and benefited consumers greatly, despite what may have looked like substantial static concentration and monopoly power at each step of the way.

Much has been published on the relationships, if any, that exist between industry structure and invention and innovation.[6] The most influential standards of economic efficiency and welfare derive from static economic theory, which takes technology, tastes, and the panoply of consumption goods to be given and constant. Yet it is clear that well-being can be increased by new techniques and products, as well as by using the right amounts of those we already have.

Earlier discussion noted that industrial structure may affect invention and innovation; and that invention and innovation may affect industrial structure. As noted in Chapter 3, innovations may concentrate previously unconcentrated industries; may reduce concentration; or may have no net effect.[7] That empirical work in industrial organization has so much emphasized causal relationships that operate in the opposite direction may be a major oversight.[8] For convenience, however, we will start there, too, deferring the second effect until later.

Change is not sacred and trying to maximize it makes little sense. A more reasonable conceptual objective is to maximize consumer and producer surplus through time. We do not want to apply too many resources to invention and innovation, and we do not want to invest them prematurely. Those resources could be used for consumption and alternative investments.

To start off, arbitrarily divide profit-making activities into three functional parts: invention, innovation, all other activities. As with other functions, there is in principle no reason to require every firm to do *any* invention for itself, let alone to do all of that in which it comes to have an interest. It is dangerous to conclude that a firm is progressive or unprogressive because it spends much or little on inventive activity altogether, or in its own shops and laboratories.[9] Since firms differ, we should expect some of them to do best with small laboratories, others with large ones, and some with none at all. Some may be fast to invent and slow to practice; others may be slow to invent but fast to practice. Some others may be slow at both but good at perfecting products or techniques created by somebody else. It is not obvious that one approach does more for consumers than another; or, indeed, that either is better for consumers than doing *old* things really well. It is astonishing, therefore, that so much of the literature seems to assume that large-scale, rapid invention and innovation are inherently superior things.

THE EMPIRICAL PROBLEM

What does the empirical work on invention and innovation measure? It estimates three different things. First, the quantity of resources used in certain activities (expenditures on research and development, or the numbers of engineers and scientists employed, for example.) Second, the number of patents received. Third, the weighted or unweighted number of inventions made.

One problem with such numbers is that they may not measure inventive *output* very well. This is an obvious problem for those studies that measure output by the amount of resources used in R&D and other inventive activities. For one thing, inputs are not outputs and for most purposes it is not desirable to use as many inputs as we possibly can. If we want to evaluate the progressiveness of firms, it would be nice to have good direct measures of output rather than relying on input measures, partly because the input figures themselves are questionable. The problem is not completely solved by asserting a positive correlation between inputs and outputs over firms of all sizes. One problem is correlating inputs with another measure that is also deficient. Another is that averages are not enough. Departures from the averages are the essence of what we should be after.

Take a couple of extreme examples. Suppose that *within* each industry large and small firms use the same amount of inventive resources per unit of firm size; but that larger firms always get higher real inventive output for each level of inventive inputs. If, by choice or necessity, we use inputs as a measure of inventive output, we would conclude that large and small firms are equally productive. Or suppose that smaller firms always use fewer inputs relative to their size than larger firms do, simply because they are able to use those inputs more efficiently. Using inputs as a measure of output makes the smaller firms look *less* productive and less efficient.

Although it looks as though some kind of *output* is what we want, what kind is it?[10] In empirical work, two measures of inventive output have been popular: the number of patents, and the number of "important" inventions. The number of patents is not an ideal output measure: some inventions are not patented; not all patents are equally important. Trying to weight innovations and inventions by their importance is fraught with conceptual and measurement problems—and susceptible to biased manipulation.[11]

Ideally, the goal is to maximize the discounted sum of profit and consumer surplus. Even a perfectly accurate *ranking* of different innovations is likely to mislead about total and marginal benefits. Furthermore, the rankings themselves tend to be highly subjective.

There is no easy way out: measuring economic benefits requires a lot of data or a lot of assumptions. Chapter 8, about patents, developed a fixed-proportions model that can also be used here. For a cost-saving innovation, for example, we need two cost functions—one with and one without the innovation—and part of a demand function. That such appraisals are extremely difficult points up one advantage of having open markets to do the appraisals for us. But there is something to be gained by trying to do the analyses and to do them right. It forces us to think through, and reveal, what we are assuming and what goal we seek.[12]

Neither profitability nor output is an ideal proxy for what we want. It is not a mistake to include profit in a benefit measure; but it is a mistake to include nothing else. And benefits are the product of output and other things. Some cases of large outputs may produce smaller benefits than others in which output effects are small.

EMPIRICAL STUDIES _____

Two main approaches have been used in empirical studies of industrial structure, invention, and innovation. First, how different is the performance of firms within the same industry? Second, how does performance differ among industries?

Differences within Industries

James Worley's is an early study on this subject. He used 1955 and 1956 data for a sample of 198 "very large firms," which he classified into eight broad (two-digit) industry groups. For each industry, he regressed firms' R&D employment on their total employment. In only two industry groups was it reasonably clear that larger firms employed a larger proportion of R&D personnel, and in some they seemed to employ a smaller proportion. From this Worley concluded "that the evidence calls for a more convincing case for bigness than has so far been marshaled."[13]

Evidence like this hardly supports any conclusion. No one wants to maximize R&D employment. Sorting diversified firms among a few broad categories is dangerous. A sample limited to the largest firms—which are the ones that employ R&D people—ignores a crucial part of the relationship between size and R&D.[14]

Hamberg's study, and Comanor's, confirmed Worley's statistical findings.[15] Mansfield's works show how far small samples and problematic data can be pushed.[16] He used a sample of 30-odd large firms in five broadly defined industries. Mansfield concluded that large firms in the chemical industry spent relatively more on R&D. In three industries, large firms spent less relative to sales. In steel, they *may* have spent less.[17] To estimate what these expenditures produced, Mansfield regressed the number of industries' inventions—weighted by a guess at their importance—on R&D expenditures and firm size (sales). Noting the "crudeness of these results," Mansfield nevertheless reached several tentative conclusions. First, the number of significant inventions that a firm makes is significantly related to how much it spends on R&D. Second, ". . . contrary to popular belief, the inventive output per dollar of R&D expenditure in most of these cases [two out of three!] seems to be lower in the largest of these [very large!] firms than in large and medium-sized firms." Third, "except for chemicals, the results do not indicate any marked advantage of the largest-scale research activities over large and medium-sized ones."[18]

Mansfield was one of the first to study how profitable R&D investments are. To do it, he developed an "exploratory" econometric model that is, as he put it, "by no means a practical tool."[19] According to his estimates, investment in R&D was profitable, averaging 40 percent to 60 percent per year in petroleum, for example. He found "no evidence that such frequently used variables as the industry's ratio of R&D expenditures to sales, its rate of growth, or its concentration ratio exert an important influence on its rate of technological change."[20]

In 1963, Mansfield published a remarkable paper on innovation, defined as the first application of inventions in four industries. In three out of the four industries, the largest four firms looked relatively innovative, by Mansfield's standards.[21]

Although he made relatively little of them, Mansfield's findings about how fast innovative firms grow are potentially important. Although innovative firms in steel and in petroleum refining had not been growing faster than comparable firms just before innovating, they quickly outstripped rivals after they did. This is what we would expect. Firms doing research, invention, and innovation believe it pays. If they succeed, they grow faster than their competitors. At any point, their absolute and relative size and profitability reflect their success in those fields, as well as in the other business functions.

Henry Grabowski concluded that until about 1966 the four leading U.S. pharmaceutical companies made about the same proportion of new drug introductions as their market share of prescription drugs. In the next five-year period, however, the largest firms' share of new drug introductions was almost twice as large as their share of drug sales.[22]

Perhaps the most popular view is that, save for exceptional cases such as the chemical and auto industries, invention and innovation increase more than proportionately with firm size up to some point, then level out or decline.

There may or may not be a relationship between the present size of a firm and its future success as researcher, inventor, and innovator—or anything else. If there is none, neither concentration nor deconcentration will occur as a consequence of success in those activities. If, on the other hand, smaller firms do better than large ones, the industry will deconcentrate. If large firms do better, the industry will concentrate. In short, there is a relationship between past successes and the present size of firms, and between future successes and the future sizes of firms.

If—as some critics suggest—large firms perform these activities too little or too late they will pay for it in lower profits and lower growth. If this is right, public policy might contribute more by keeping entry and exit open, than by taxing concentration or otherwise altering industrial structures.

Progressiveness and Inventiveness Among Industries

So far we have discussed studies of how much different sizes of firms *within* an industry tend to spend on R&D, to invent, and to innovate. A fundamentally different question is how different industries perform. Much of the empirical work seeks to explain why R&D employment (or expenditures), inventions, patents, and innovations vary among industries.[23]

These kinds of studies are subject to the same conceptual and measurement problems that we have encountered before, plus more. They, too, use concentration as an index of monopoly. Some additional problems arise from badly measured outputs, which are the variable to be explained; from interindustry differences in technologies and technological opportunities, which are difficult to conceptualize and measure; and from problematic conceptions of economic objectives. These problems can be seen in famous early studies, as well as the most recent ones.

To find a relationship between innovation and industry concentration, Oliver Williamson pooled Mansfield's small samples of firms in steel, petroleum, and bituminous coal.[24] Using four-firm concentration ratios as the measure of monopoly, he found that, "according to the linear model, the four largest firms in an industry appear to contribute less than their proportionate share of innovations when the concentration ratio exceeds 50 percent, . . . and more than their proportionate share when the concentration ratio is less than 50 percent."[25]

F. M. Scherer used the same basic procedure on patent and R&D data for samples of 448, 352, and 152 leading industrial firms.[26] Among other things, he recognized that some industries simply have more favorable *opportunities* for invention and innovation than others do, something that should be recognized and held constant in comparing what they manage to accomplish. As a matter of fact, he said, such differences are important: "interindustry differences unrelated to mere sales volume account for a major proportion of the variance in corporate patenting." In any case, "patent outputs increase less than proportionately with increases in sales among corporations large enough to appear on Fortune's 1955 list."[27] In his later work, Scherer modified these conclusions somewhat, finding a "modest correlation" between concentration and the employment of scientists, holding technological opportunity constant. But this positive correlation seemed to play out at concentration ratios larger than 50 or 55 percent.[28]

For what it is worth, Greer and Rhoades concluded that, for a mixture of industries and periods, *increases* in industry productivity were positively related with industry concentration, holding other variables constant.[29] This is consistent with Peltzman's and Brozen's views.[30]

Interindustry studies suffer from serious conceptual flaws. First, it seems strange to suppose that the value of patents or innovations should be more similar in different industries than within the same industry. Second, even if they measured interindustry "progressiveness" without error, these studies cannot support some of the public policy proposals their authors made. How, for example, could antitrust policy be used to alter total progressiveness? Can anyone imagine how it could alter average concentration *across* industries? By shrinking more concentrated industries or expanding unconcentrated industries? It could, at some cost, deconcentrate *individual* industries, but interindustry studies do not show what would happen to progressiveness within an industry if the industry were deconcentrated—or concentrated—through public policy. At most, these studies show how firm size and concentration and progressiveness are related in one industry as compared with other very different industries.

A parable of beasts suggests what the problem is. Suppose we find a clear positive relationship between the average adult weight and gestation period of different species, and confirm a negative relationship between the average body weight of a species and its birthrate. It would, even so, be wrong to assume that we could increase the elephant birthrate either by sawing off elephants' legs, putting adult elephants on a rigorous diet, or crossing mice with elephants. What is wrong is that the policies proposed are inconsistent with the theory and facts of life, and are based on statistical relationships that are irrelevant for the problem at hand.[31]

Although Scherer and Williamson brought up the notion of maximizing progressiveness by altering industrial concentration, interindustry studies are no help if the object is to maximize the net *values* of progressiveness. Go back to the animal parable. It is not clear why anyone would want to maximize the total number of animal births, irrespective of species. Different animals have different values, at least to Man. It is not clear that we should even want to try converting low-birthrate elephants into high-birthrate shrews, since they have different functions and uses.

SUMMARY

There are serious problems with the kinds of studies discussed in this chapter. The first is with what they measure. This chapter argues that, even in principle, only studies measuring variations within industries have much relevancy for public policy. Second, however relevant the studies may be, there is considerable ambiguity about what they show. As Jesse Markham put it,

> Clearly, any answers to how inventive and innovative efforts are affected by firm size hangs on an extraordinarily slender reed that may alternatively bend upward or droop downward, depending on the species of statistical zephyrs blowing at the time. Similarly, we are equally unsure about the precise relationship between market power and inventive and innovative effort.[32]

Third, the policy implications would be confusing even if these studies were clear. Those who believe that markets work reasonably well should expect the market itself both to reveal and adjust to advantages or disadvantages of size, progressiveness, and so on. If studies of technological change reveal anything, it is that things do not stay the same. There is nothing immutable about the best type or size of firm or structure of industry. Those who believe that markets work slowly and imprecisely should consider whether the alternatives they have in mind are clearly better. There is little or no evidence that governments adapt to or anticipate change better than market systems do. Antitrust policy is one example. After calculating how long it takes to try major antitrust cases, Posner concluded that "it seems unlikely that administrative methods of deconcentration will work significantly more rapidly than the market."[33]

As Mansfield, Minasian, and others have argued, investments in R&D and innovations respond to the profit motive. We should be suspicious of schemes that drastically change the incentives of firms that are now leaders in their fields or aspire to be leaders in the future.

QUESTIONS

1. Define *technology*, *invention*, and *innovation*. What is the statistical measure commonly used to indicate how important technological progress has been in aggregate? Is that measure likely to include anything else besides technological progress? Explain.
2. Chapter 3 discussed the case of diesel-electric locomotives. Use that case study to evaluate Schumpeter's theory that competition from new products and ways of doing things is often more important than competition among firms offering the same products.
3. Suppose that monopoly imposes a static dead-weight loss of 5 percent of national income, but raises output 2.5 percent per year because it innovates faster. Where would that leave us at the end of two years? Three years?
4. Is it possible to have too rapid or too much technological progress? Discuss and explain.

5. ''Most of the empirical work asks whether industry concentration affects invention or innovation, rather than asking whether invention and innovation affect concentration.'' From a policy standpoint, what difference, if any, does that make?

6. In what sense does a single-firm monopoly have more to gain from innovating? Is there any tendency, on the other hand, for a single-firm monopoly to innovate more slowly?

7. ''If some firms innovate better than others, we should expect them on that account to grow faster than others. In the limit, concentration may come to be substantial. But, if market forces work reasonably well, we should expect industry structures to reflect only net advantages of size economies, innovations, and so on. The structure we get tends to be the best structure, all things considered.'' Explain, discuss, and evaluate.

8. Firms that grew large because of successful invention and innovation are sometimes attacked as monopolies and threatened with dissolution or regulation. Take the case of such a firm that achieves monopoly because of past innovations but will, with certainty, never innovate again. Why *not* break it up? Discuss.

9. One problem with empirical work is how to measure inventive and innovative *output*. What kinds of measures have been used? What difference does it make?

10. Show in a diagram how, in theory, one could measure the importance of a cost-saving innovation. (Hint: review the fixed-proportions model used to analyze cost-saving inventions in Chapter 8.)

NOTES

1. Major studies include Edward Denison, *Accounting for United States Economic Growth, 1929–1969* (Washington, D.C.: Brookings Institution, 1974), especially pp. 131–37; John W. Kendrick, *Productivity Trends in the United States* (Princeton, N.J.: Princeton University Press, 1961); Kendrick, ed., *Input, Output, and Productivity Change* (Princeton, N.J.: Princeton University Press, 1961); Zvi Griliches, ed., *R&D, Patents, and Productivity* (Chicago: University of Chicago Press, 1984); Morton I. Kamien and Nancy L. Schwartz, *Market Structure and Innovation* (New York: Cambridge University Press, 1982); Albert N. Link, *Research and Development Activity in U.S. Manufacturing* (New York: Praeger Publishers, 1981); Edwin Mansfield, *The Economics of Technological Change* (New York: John Wiley & Sons, Inc., 1968); Mansfield, *Industrial Research and Technological Innovation* (New York: W.W. Norton & Co., Inc., 1968); Robert Solow, ''Technological Change and the Aggregate Production Function,'' *Review of Economics and Statistics*, 39 (August 1957), pp. 312–20.

2. Joseph A. Schumpeter, *Capitalism, Socialism, and Democracy*, 2nd ed. (New York: Harper & Row Publishers, Inc., 1947), pp. 84–85.

3. Although in other respects their theories differ greatly, both Schumpeter and Galbraith asserted that large firms and concentrated industries are the main source of invention and innovation. Schumpeter, *Capitalism, Socialism, and Democracy*; John Kenneth Galbraith, *American Capitalism: The Concept of Countervailing Power* (Boston: Houghton Mifflin Company, 1956).

4. For a survey of and citations to studies published before 1970, see Morton I. Kamien and

Nancy L. Schwartz, "Market Structure and Innovation: A Survey," *Journal of Economic Literature*, 13 (March 1975), pp. 1–37.

5. F. M. Scherer, *Industrial Market Structure and Economic Performance* (Chicago: Rand McNally College Publishing Company, 1980), p. 407.

6. A recent survey of work on this and related topics is Griliches, ed., *R&D, Patents, and Productivity*. A survey article is Kamien and Schwartz, "Market Structure and Innovation." See also John S. McGee, *In Defense of Industrial Concentration* (New York: Praeger Publishers, 1971).

7. For an opinionated but interesting discussion of the impact of specific technological changes on concentration, see John M. Blair, *Economic Concentration: Structure, Behavior, and Public Policy* (New York: Harcourt Brace Jovanovich, Inc., 1972), chapters 5, 6.

8. Although Mansfield recognized that effects go in both directions, most of his work is about how structure affects change. But see his "Size of Firm, Market Structure, and Innovation," *Journal of Political Economy*, 71 (December 1963), pp. 556–76. Scherer, too, emphasized that directional effect, and went further in emphasizing the effect of *rivalry* upon change. F. M. Scherer, "Market Structure and the Employment of Scientists and Engineers," *American Economic Review*, 57 (June 1967), pp. 524–30; Scherer, "Firm Size, Market Structure, Opportunity, and the Output of Patented Inventions," *American Economic Review*, 55 (December 1965), pp. 1097–1112; and Scherer, "Research and Development Resource Allocation Under Rivalry," *Quarterly Journal of Economics*, 81 (August 1967), pp. 359–94.

   Hamberg also (briefly) recognized that causality might run either way; but studied effects of structure on R&D employment. D. Hamberg, "Size of Firm, Oligopoly, and Research: The Evidence," *Canadian Journal of Economics and Political Science*, 30 (February 1964), p. 66, note 7.

   Note Griliches's warning: Zvi Griliches, "Comment," in Richard R. Nelson, ed., *The Rate and Direction of Inventive Activity* (Princeton, N.J.: Princeton University Press, 1962), p. 353.

9. Ronald H. Coase, "The Nature of the Firm," in K. E. Boulding and G. J. Stigler, eds., *Readings in Price Theory* (Homewood, Ill.: Richard D. Irwin, Inc, 1952), p. 331–51.

10. Simon Kuznets, "Inventive Activity: Problems of Definition and Measurement," in *The Rate and Direction of Inventive Activity*, Richard R. Nelson, ed., pp. 19–43; Barkev S. Sanders, "Some Difficulties in Measuring Inventive Activity," ibid., pp. 53–77.

11. Jacob Schmookler, *Invention and Economic Growth* (Cambridge, Mass.: Harvard University Press, 1966); B. Branch, "Research and Development and its Relation to Sales Growth," *Journal of Economics and Business*, 25 (Winter 1973), pp. 107–11.

12. For a pioneering effort, measuring the effects of an agricultural innovation, see Zvi Griliches, "Research Costs and Social Returns: Hybrid Corn and Related Innovations," *Journal of Political Economy*, 66 (October 1958), pp. 419–43.

13. James S. Worley, "Industrial Research and the New Competition," *Journal of Political Economy*, 69 (April 1961), pp. 183–86. See also his "The Changing Direction of Research and Development Among Firms," in *The Rate and Direction of Inventive Activity*, ed. Richard R. Nelson, pp. 233–51.

14. R&D expenditures have been highly concentrated. Six industries spent more than four-fifths of the total in 1977, and larger firms spent most of that. U.S. National Science Foundation, *Research and Development in Industry Funds, Scientists, and Engineers* (Washington, D.C.: 1979).

15. D. Hamberg, "Size of Firm, Oligopoly, and Research: The Evidence," pp. 62–75; William S. Comanor, "Market Structure, Product Differentiation, and Industrial Research," *Quarterly Journal of Economics*, 81 (November 1967), pp. 639–57.

16. Mansfield, *Industrial Research*; Mansfield, *The Economics of Technological Change*, and sources cited therein.

17. Mansfield, *Industrial Research*, pp. 43, 63–64.

18. Ibid., pp. 41–42.

19. Ibid., p. 65. Also see Jora Minasian, "The Economics of Research and Development," in *The Rate and Direction of Inventive Activity*, pp. 93–141; and "Research and Development, Production Functions, and Rates of Return," *American Economic Review*, 59 (May 1969), pp. 80–85.

20. Mansfield, *Industrial Research*, p. 78.

21. Mansfield, "Size of Firm, Market Structure, and Innovation," *Journal of Political Economy*, 71 (December 1963), pp. 556–76; and Mansfield, *Industrial Research*, pp. 83–108.

22. Henry G. Grabowski, *Drug Regulation and Innovation* (Washington, D.C.: American Enterprise Institute, 1976).

23. Examples are Oliver E. Williamson, "Innovation and Market Structure," *Journal of Political Economy*, 73 (February 1965), pp. 67–73; F. M. Scherer, "Firm Size, Market Structure, Opportunity, and the Output of Patented Inventions," *American Economic Review*, 55 (December 1965), pp. 1097–1125; Scherer, "Market Structure and the Employment of Engineers," *American Economic Review*, 57 (June 1967), pp. 524–30; and Comanor, "Market Structure," pp. 639–57.

24. Williamson, "Innovation and Market Structure."

25. Ibid., p. 70.

26. Scherer, "Firm Size."

27. Ibid., pp. 1102–3, 1106.

28. Scherer, "Market Structure and the Employment of Engineers," p. 530. See also Comanor, "Market Structure."

29. Douglas F. Greer and Stephen A. Rhoades, "Concentration and Productivity Changes in the Long and Short Run," *Southern Economic Journal*, 43 (October 1976), pp. 1031–44.

30. Sam Peltzman, "The Gains and Losses from Industrial Concentration," *Journal of Law & Economics*, 20 (October 1977), pp. 229–63; and Yale Brozen, *Concentration, Mergers, and Public Policy* (New York: Macmillan, Inc., 1982).

31. J. B. S. Haldane, "On Being the Right Size," reprinted in *The World of Mathematics*, vol. II (New York: Simon & Schuster, Inc., 1965), pp. 952–57.

32. Jesse Markham, "Market Structure, Business Conduct, and Innovation," *American Economic Review*, 55 (May 1965), pp. 323–32, at p. 330.

33. Richard A. Posner, "A Statistical Study of Antitrust Enforcement," *Journal of Law & Economics*, 13 (October 1970), pp. 365–420, at p. 417, note.

16 | ADVERTISING

INTRODUCTION

Advertising makes many people uneasy. A complete explanation of this disquietude, if one were possible, would be longer than this chapter ought to be. It would also be subtler: in seeking clarity and brevity, the following exposition may oversimplify and exaggerate some of the arguments that people make—though not by much.

Part of the distaste for advertising is due to snobbery and elitism, traits that are, ironically, rather common. It is hard to be elite while admiring what the masses do. Many academics and others in the intellectual trades look down on popular products and the kinds of advertising that are typically used to promote them. Mass advertising appeals to the lowest common denominator, they say, and weakens culture and civilization by debasing language, mind, and taste.

On the other hand, of course, there would be no advertising if *everyone* recoiled from it. Many consumers respond positively to advertising, and do not see it as a menace at all. As Demsetz put it,

> The source of our interest in advertising is in the concern shown by intellectuals, not the general public. . . . The intellectual . . . looks at this life and finds things not quite to his liking. People do not behave as he would like them to. They purchase swimming pools, Cadillacs, and tickets to football games. Since many of us are in the business of selling a different life style, it is quite natural . . . to view commercial advertising . . . as an obstacle to our effort to persuade others to adopt the good life as the reformist intellectual sees it.[1]

True though that may be, it is unlikely to satisfy the critics, who claim that advertising is expensive and—at best—squanders talents that could have refined our palates and enriched our lives: Madison Avenue uses up brigades of writers and artists in cola wars, carnival pitches for useless wrinkle creams, and skits showing that indistinguishable beers are decisively different after all. An additional pain to intellectuals and artists is that advertising pays so much better than the finer arts.

Economic theory offers other criticisms that sound more scientific and value-free. As Brozen points out, textbook perfect competition is for many economists the true god and if perfect competitors existed they would not advertise.[2] When they encounter advertising in a real market, economists recognize that information and competition are not *perfect*. They then infer that, by textbook standards, performance is not all it ought (ideally) to be. For example, it is conceivable that advertising by *imperfect* competitors could generate so much smoke that simple shopping becomes a costly hit or miss affair. Consumers grope their way through the marketplace half-blinded, often ending up with poor stuff bought at high prices—or so the story goes.

And, as if *competitive* smoke and confusion would not be bad enough, advertising might also create and preserve *monopoly* power, raising the prices of everything that advertisers find it profitable to offer, including quality goods as well as trash. If advertising can make a product seem unique, increasing demand and making it less elastic, it can raise the spread between price and costs, increasing profits and hurting consumers. So long as an aura of uniqueness can be made to last, competition can be staved off.

Although such criticisms are popular, some think they are wrong or overwrought, as we will see. The next section outlines two major groups of theories about advertising. The section after that reviews some empirical studies that purport to tell us what advertising actually does.

THEORIES ABOUT ADVERTISING

Advertising Improves Information, Enlarges Markets, and Eases Entry

Advertising occurs in a world in which information is neither perfect nor free. Whatever their esthetic contribution may be, restaurant and motel road signs are welcome sights to tired and hungry travellers. Shop signs and show windows tell consumers something useful about the immediate market environment, and telephone directories tell us where, in a broader market, various products can be bought. That kind of information is especially valuable to new sellers and new buyers. Local TV, radio, and newspaper ads also tell us about special deals on products we are already familiar with. And, by telling buyers about new products, new firms, and new terms, advertising aids entry and increases competition.[3]

Ignorance, like transport costs and tariffs, can Balkanize markets and keep them separate. It seems plausible, therefore, that information can help erode local monopoly positions, and, conversely, that monopoly power can be increased by taxing or prohibiting some kinds of information. In theory, at least, advertising can make markets function more perfectly. On the other hand, everybody can recall ads that seemed uninformative or misleading. Some believe that this is a serious and common problem rather than a relatively trivial exception.

Advertising Misleads, Breeds Monopoly, and Hurts Consumers

These theories take several forms. Advertising misleads or brainwashes consumers into believing that advertised products are better than they are, increasing demand for them and reducing their demand elasticity. Or, after enticing buyers, advertising traps and holds them fast. Now inert, addled, or addicted, consumers are immune to other sellers' blandishments, including lower prices. In this theory, advertising works like flypaper or an addictive drug, blunting competition and permitting prices to be raised above costs. By creating brand loyalty and impeding entry, advertising perpetuates monopolistic mischiefs.[4]

   None of this is as straightforward as it sounds, partly because image advertising may not be able to do the job without help. For one thing, it is doubtful that advertising keeps consumers buying things they don't like. Advertising may be able to attract a consumer once, which might be enough to make money on things a consumer buys infrequently—lightning rods, root canals, and engine rebuilds, for example.[5] For one-time attraction to work in favor of bad goods generally, however, word-of-mouth needs to be put out of service. Or perhaps many brands *are* pretty much the same, and consumers stop trying competing goods once advertising attracts them to something that they like reasonably well. In that case, consumers would be reasonably well served no matter which brand they chose.

   Basically, the monopolizing theory seems to be that, although advertising can attract enough customers to *create* monopoly, would-be competitors can't then use advertising or other means to wrest customers away from monopolies so created. Why does advertising pull only one way? And what is the nature of the challenger's disadvantage? Perhaps some firms choose better advertising agencies than others, which sounds like superior skill or efficiency or good luck, which may not last forever. Or perhaps it is size economies in or owing to advertising that compel monopoly. Or perhaps the large capital required to advertise bars entry. Chapter 7 discussed economies of size and capital requirements.

   And, if advertising is not accompanied by greater real value, why can't a nonadvertiser or a simple price-advertiser conquer all?

   In a variant of these theories, the villain becomes oligopoly waste rather than profit-maximizing exploitation. Some think that, however it evolves, oligopoly eliminates price competition yet permits or encourages wasteful competition in advertising, resulting in meretricious "product differentiation." Or perhaps promotional expenditures by individual firms cancel each other—like the attempts of sports spectators to get a better view, first by standing; then by standing on tiptoe; then by sitting on one another's shoulders. In the end, after much exertion, no one is better off than at the start. According to this notion, advertising adds wastefully to costs and to the prices that consumers pay and may not even profit those who advertise.

If, as some theories assert, however, oligopoly really implies collusion, oligopolists should stop competing in advertising. Instead, they would do only so much advertising as maximizes group profits. Taming competition in advertising may be easier than preventing price competition: a good deal of advertising data are readily available, and cooperating advertisers could also pay an outside agent to monitor their expenditures even more closely.

EMPIRICAL EVIDENCE

It is well to recognize that the empirical literature about advertising is large, contentious, and inconclusive about some important matters. But progress has been made.[6]

Is Advertising Informative or Manipulative?

Although economic theory is somewhat ambiguous on this point, common sense and observation suggest that truthful advertising can increase competition and efficiency because it informs. Consumers benefit from knowing what products exist, what they do, what they cost, and where to get them.[7] Those who fear that advertising will eventually gobble up our national income are overly apprehensive. In 1970, the total of $19.55 billion spent on advertising in the U.S. came to 2.41 percent of the national income, and in 1984 came to 2.97 percent.[8]

For years, newspaper advertising has accounted for around 30 percent of the total and much of the newspaper advertising is obviously informative. Probably the least informational ads are carried by radio, TV, and magazines—about a third of the total. Even so, this includes spot, local, and other ads that *are* informational. In 1970, about 42 percent of all advertising was local; in 1984, about 43 percent.[9]

Telser may have been the first to argue that the number and characteristics of customers, and the costs of sellers' contacting them by different means, better explain the level of advertising than do industry concentration and monopoly. He noted significant differences among cases such as glass eyeballs, autos, chess sets, funeral vaults, cigarettes, hairspray, and toothpaste.

More recent studies have attempted to determine whether advertising of specific classes of products is informative or manipulative. Leffler, for example, studied advertising of prescription drugs.[10]

Does Advertising Monopolize?

Advertising and Natural Monopoly.   Massive economies of size in buying or using advertising might lead to monopoly. It is true that advertising in tiny doses does not pay and that there are quantity discounts in buying advertising. Within limits, advertising that covers larger markets, or that is repeated in the same market, can lower the cost of advertising per message delivered and per sale made. The real question is how large those effects are and whether they increase firm size so much that competition weakens or dies.

In 1958, Stigler found that consumer goods industries advertised more intensively than producer goods industries and that there was no significant relationship between advertising and the optimal size of firm.[11] In a 1962 study of cigarette advertising,[12] Telser concluded that cigarette advertising had historically been more like an investment tool used competitively than a weapon used to monopolize. The ad hoc variable that best explained variations in advertising over time was the introduction of new products and new brands. And, like other tools, advertisements wear out: advertising good will decayed at the rate of about 15 to 20 percent per year. The rate of return to advertising varied among firms; but it was not stratospheric for any of them. In the period 1913 to 1929, cigarette firms carried advertising well into the region of decreasing returns, as competitors would. Kristian Palda's prize-winning study of the Lydia Pinkham Co. confirmed that advertising is an investment, complete with lags and lingering effects.[13] The Federal Trade Commission claimed that Procter & Gamble, a seasoned and successful mass advertiser, should not be permitted to buy a bleach company, among other things because advertising economies of the combined companies would run competing bleach companies into the ground.[14] After careful study, however, John Peterman concluded that the FTC's theory and facts were simply wrong.[15]

Advertising and Concentration.   Several studies have found a weak, positive relationship between advertising intensity and industry concentration. But such results are sensitive to sample size and the breadth of industry definitions. Furthermore, positive correlations have shown up for producer goods as well as for consumer goods, which causes trouble for image theories of advertising. Producer goods are bought by informed professionals who, because they are interested in measurable qualities and productivity, are not swayed by images of the sort that advertising supposedly can create out of air and impress upon consumers' simpler minds.[16]

Telser's 1964 article is an early and influential study about how advertising and concentration are related.[17] Using data for three-digit industries, Telser regressed advertising intensity (the ratio of advertising expenditures to sales) on four-firm concentration ratios. For 1947, 1954, and 1958 the relationship is positive, but very weak.[18] And such correlation as there was *fell* when Telser included industries that he had left out of his sample.[19] Results were no more impressive for correlations between *changes* in advertising and *changes* in concentration. Correlations between 1947 and 1958, and 1954 and 1958, were actually negative. Telser reasoned that, if advertising can insulate against competition, heavily advertised goods should have more stable market shares. He estimated the brand-share stability of products in three heavily advertised product categories, here ranked from highest to lowest advertising intensity: perfumes, drugs, soaps. Contrary to what the theory predicts, the brand shares of food products, which were less intensively advertised, were markedly more stable than those of toiletries, which were advertised much more intensively. Furthermore, toiletry brands have a shorter life expectancy than brands of food products.[20] In 1967, Mann, Henning, and Meehan claimed that Telser had been wrong.[21] Telser countered that their claim rested on a small and biased sample of 14 industries. They had excluded "several industries for which advertising intensities are very high such as cleansers and toiletries and several with moderately high advertising intensities such as cigars and pharmaceuticals." When Telser expanded their sample from 14 to 26 industries, he found an *inverse* relationship between advertising intensity and concentration! As he put it,

> . . . the correlation between the concentration ratio and the advertising intensity is unimpressive. It is certainly true that a judicious choice of industries from these 26 can raise the R^2 from an anemic 0.01 to a healthy 0.6. All this really proves is that there is a considerable variation in the sampled relation between concentration and advertising intensity.[22]

Advertising may be a source of monopoly; but it is also an instrument of entry and competition: "The net effect reveals itself by the absence of a dependable relation between the advertising intensity and the concentration ratio."[23] There is much disagreement about all of this.[24] Schmalansee's theory is that advertising does not *necessarily* prevent entry: asymmetries in consumer tastes are ultimately the villain. Barring those, newcomers can compete by offering equally good products and equally good advertising.[25]

In 1974, Brozen argued that advertising does not lock in customers and bar new entry. On the contrary, he said, advertising increases the rate of entry and destabilizes market shares. He cited studies of liquor, beer, cigarettes, and pharmaceuticals to make his point.[26] In 1956, Bain had said that only one industry—liquor—had "very high entry barriers" *solely* because of advertising and selling costs.[27] And liquor distillers did advertise heavily. Yet in 1967 James Ferguson found that entry into the liquor industry had been remarkably high, in terms of both new firms and new plants. Of 76 liquor plants operating in 1965, 22 had entered in 1944 or later. And, of the 35 liquor companies, 12 were new entrants. The more popular brands advertised less per case, which—according to Greer (1971)—was also true for beer. According to Brozen, the share of the largest four liquor companies fell from 75 percent in 1947 to 54 percent in 1967. Indeed the share of the top 20 was declining at the same time that they were increasing their share of industry advertising.

Tennant found that before it was dissolved in 1911, American Tobacco, with an 83 percent market share, had advertised much less than did the successor companies created by the dissolution.[28] Outside companies (independents), which were small before and after dissolution, changed their advertising little. And citing a 1977 study by Telser and associates, Brozen concluded that increasing the intensity with which ethical pharmaceuticals are promoted increased entry.

In summary, Brozen said,

> . . . if advertising served only to differentiate products and create loyalty, . . . we would not see the large disparities in advertising intensities among brands and product categories that are observed. The disparities are systematically related to customer turnover, . . . rate of innovation, growth of market, profitability of product, cost of search, price and age of product, number of prospective customers, and standardization. If advertising plays a role in creating

customer loyalty, decreasing firm demand elasticity, and differentiating product, it is a small role and not yet unambiguously detected in any empirical study.[29]

Furthermore, even if—contrary to fact—the statistical relationship between advertising and concentration were robust, it would not demonstrate that either advertising or concentration is bad. Suppose, for example, that there are benign or innocuous reasons why large firms advertise more. Data for concentrated industries would then tend to show more advertising: large firms produce a larger share of output in concentrated industries. Reasoning that large firms are more likely to be large advertisers, Brozen says that one might expect a positive relationship on that ground alone. Among other things, Brozen expects larger firms to serve larger geographic markets. If that is true, their advertising can reach more customers and the customers it reaches are less likely to move out of areas they do serve. As a result, large firms serving large areas "are . . . in a better position to make advertising claims and to have them verified by purchasers"; and are likely to introduce more new products and to introduce them more frequently. In fact, the market shares of individual firms and industry concentration are not closely related to advertising in many industries, including whiskey and beer.[30]

Many studies have found a weak positive correlation between industry advertising intensity and concentration. The most likely explanation, Brozen says, is that large firms can raise capital more cheaply than smaller ones, and that—though it is capital-intensive—advertising is sometimes the most efficient way to sell. For various industries, Brozen correlated four-firm concentration ratios, advertising, the book value of depreciable assets, and the ratio of payrolls to the value of shipments. From those statistics, he infers that,

> Firms do not deliberately choose a capital intensive technology to raise a barrier to entry. If they did, they could be undersold by others using a less capital intensive technology. Capital intensive technologies are chosen when they are the low-cost method of production . . . Where a large investment in advertising is required industries tend to be more concentrated for the same reason as when capital intensive technology is required for economical production. Large firms can raise capital at lower cost and offer lower prices to buyers.[31]

Advertising and Prices. People for years have said that advertised goods must be of higher quality. Otherwise, it would make no sense to spend money promoting them.[32] Variants of this theory, some more complex and pretentious than others, picture advertisers as guaranteeing superior quality by offering themselves as hostages to consumers. Unless enough consumers buy, are satisfied, and buy again, those who use advertising will lose the large sums they invested in it.[33] Few empirical studies have been made to test such theories.

It is not easy to be sure how advertising affects prices, partly because the quality of advertised and unadvertised products may differ. In 1964, Telser noted studies showing that, on average, prices of advertised goods were higher. But he also noted that their average quality may be higher and more consistent.[34]

Lee Benham, on the other hand, showed that prescription eyeglasses cost about half as much in states that did not restrict eyeglass advertising as in those that prohibited it altogether. Prices were not quite that much lower in states that permitted only ads that did not quote specific prices.[35] Advertising seemed to make a larger market out of smaller ones, enabling low-price sellers to inform and attract more customers, lowering costs and prices in the process. Similarly, Robert Steiner found that television advertising lowered the markup and price of toys.[36] By contrast, advertised prescription drugs tend to cost much more than their unadvertised chemical equivalents.

Advertising and Profits. The earliest empirical study of empirical relationships between advertising and profits may be an article that Comanor and Wilson (C&W) published in 1967, mostly about the period 1954 to 1957.[37] As is usual in industrial organization, their analysis is cross-sectional, across industries. Each industry is taken as one observation: the performance of firms *within* each industry is not being compared. If we use Census data for *industries*, it is true, little else can be done: data reported for each industry lump together and average the performance of firms classified into it. Among other things, this leads to conceptual problems discussed in Chapters 14 and 15.

C&W used multiple-regression analysis to explain differences in profitability among 41 three-digit industries producing consumer goods. As shown in Chapter 14, this procedure shows how differences in profit rates for industries in that sample correspond with variations in each of several other explanatory variables taken separately, and with variations in all of the explanatory variables taken together. The estimate of covariation for each variable separately is called its regression coefficient. The estimate of total covariation is the multiple-correlation coefficient, R. R-squared, the coefficient of total determination, shows what proportion of the total variation in, say, profits is "explained" by the covariation with all the explanatory variables taken together.

It pays to translate the names that authors give to variables they use. By profitability, which is what they want to explain, C&W mean after-tax profits divided by book equity. C&W use different combinations of several variables, of which we will examine five here. First is advertising intensity, measured as the advertising expenditures of larger firms divided by their sales. Second is what they treat as absolute capital requirements, but which is really the average book value of those largest establishments producing at least 50 percent of the industry's output. Third is industry growth, measured as the ratio of 1957 to 1947 shipments. The fourth variable identifies the three (out of 41) industries that C&W say served regional rather than national markets. Fifth is the four-firm industry concentration ratio.

Multiple-regression analysis is popular in economics and other fields in which laboratory experiments are rare. But it is unusual for regression analyses in industrial organization to develop R^2s as high as C&W got after they adjusted for large unexplained differences in the profits of different industries.[38] Even after excluding the motor vehicles industry, for example, C&W's regressions on four variables—advertising/sales, book capital in large plants, demand growth, and regional market—seemed to explain 62 percent of the interindustry variation in after-tax profits on book equity. Their study attracted attention because it claimed a statistically significant positive relationship between industry profits and advertising intensity. As they put it, "Industries with high advertising outlays earn, on average, a profit rate which exceeds that of other industries by nearly four percentage points. This differential represents a 50 percent increase in profit rates." Over the long run, however, one of their negative findings proved to be more important. Once they had brought in advertising to help explain industry profitability, industry concentration lost its explanatory power altogether, or turned to being a (statistically insignificant) *negative* influence!

In an article that Comanor published in another journal that same month, he refers to "the presumed relationship between concentration and market power."[39] C&W, however, try to explain that concentration variables do not help partly because they are *not* good proxies for monopoly power. As they saw it, " . . . the concentration ratio measures only one dimension of market structure, and is therefore an inadequate indicator of market power, which depends on additional structural variables as well as on established behavior patterns."[40]

What about public policy implications, if any? In principle, at least, government taxation and antitrust actions could change the degree of industrial concentration. The usual reason given for reducing industrial concentration is to reduce "monopoly power," wherever higher than average profits indicate that some is present. Following that tack, a structuralist might be expected to applaud industry concentration if it leads systematically to lower profits. But that is not how C&W saw things. They asserted that higher profits to industries that advertise heavily occur because advertising creates entry barriers, with the "resulting achievement of market power." As they saw it: "Current polices which tend to emphasize the role played by concentration may need to be supplemented by those concerned directly with the nature and extent of product differentiation. Policies dealing with these matters would be an important component in any general policy designed to promote competition."[41]

It is not very clear what this means. It is doubtful that consumers would be well served by policies whose diagnostic principle and operating guide are to locate profits and reduce them once found. Are we to prohibit all or certain kinds of advertising? Would taxing it do? How much? Nor do regressions such as C&W's tell us what to do about the other factors they say also increase profits. Are we willing (or able) to break up individual industrial plants, or to reduce the growth rate of industrial output and magically transform regional industries into national industries?[42]

Although they emphasize advertising, C&W found that quite different factors accounted for almost 80 percent of the interindustry variation in four-firm *concentration*: the historic accounting cost and relative size of the larger establishments; and the regional-industry dummy variable. That sounds consistent with the hypothesis that concentration is determined by economies of size and the size of markets—factors discussed in Chapter 7.

Although C&W struggled mightily to harmonize all this, they appear to have failed. Lacking evidence that advertising increases concentration and that concentration reduces competition, they also failed to show how advertising reduces competition in some other way. They assert that advertising bars entry; but apparently that does not show up via concentration. Just how *does* advertising work to increase "market power"?

There are other problems, too. Although they recognize that advertising is a risky investment, C&W do nothing to adjust profits for this and other kinds of risk differences among industries. (Chapters 10, 13 and 14 discuss this problem in more detail.) Nor do they distinguish between Census *establishments* and plants in the economic sense. Many firms have multiple establishments that are specialized parts of a complex whole, not merely duplicates. They do not have multiple plants in the economic sense.

And C&W made at least a conceptual error in dealing with the advertising expenditures themselves. Although they are like capital investments in machinery and plant, expenditures such as advertising, training, and research and development (R&D) are typically written off as expenses, and are not reported as capital investments. This omits intangible capital, including that from advertising, from the denominator of the "profits" ratio. This tends to overstate the profitability of firms and industries that do a lot of advertising and to bias cross-sectional estimates of any advertising-profits relationship.[43] How important this bias is depends, among other things, on the rates at which other asset values and the good will from advertising depreciate, facts that economists disagree about.

After capitalizing advertising over the same arbitrary period for all industries in his sample, Weiss concluded that Comanor and Wilson's basic finding held up: a positive correlation between advertising and profits remained.[44] When Ayanian studied six industries, he found that the depreciation rate of advertising investments varied significantly among industries, from 5 percent to 46 percent. When he took such variations into account, the correlation between advertising and profits evaporated. As a result, he claimed the correlation had been spurious.[45] In 1971, Peles found that advertising depreciated at significantly different rates in the three industries he studied.

Bloch concluded that C&W and Weiss should have used the advertising intensities of *firms*, not industries. Using FTC advertising and profit data for individual firms, and depreciating advertising, he concluded that profits and advertising were unrelated.[46] In 1975 Ayanian noted that mergers lead us into double counting: counting an acquired firm's past advertising adds to the value of that investment incorporated into its acquisition value.[47] In 1979, Demsetz found that the positive relationship between advertising and profits was equally strong for producer and consumer goods industries.[48] That undermines the popular theory that consumers, unlike producers, are irrational and dumb and fall prey to exploitative monopolists who do magic tricks with advertising. As Brozen put it, "no one argues that advertising cements the loyalties of professional purchasing agents buying producer goods."[49] Demsetz also studied the correlation between profits in one year with profits several years down the line. Apart from biases arising from the accounting treatment of advertising, he concluded, this relationship was at least as weak for industries that advertise a lot as for those that don't.

Building on Stigler's theory of information, Nagle constructed an alternative theory of brand loyalty; discussed relationships for the same goods at different times and in different places; and used Comanor and Wilson's own cross-sectional data to test notions that advertising clogs entry.[50] He concludes that:

> . . . final confirmation of advertising's competitive effect requires still further research. The limited evidence we have, however, indicates that advertising positively affects the competitiveness of an industry. The contrary position that advertising creates an entry barrier rests on

cross-sectional empirical studies that cannot support it. The cross-industry correlation between advertising and profit rates is as consistent with the hypothesis that advertising is a means of overcoming brand loyalty as it is with the hypothesis that advertising causes such loyalty.[51]

And that is not all. As Telser showed, the efficacy of advertising varies greatly among industries for reasons that are inherent and innocuous, including the nature of the products and whether mass markets are involved. Brozen has noted additional reasons why advertising and profitability are likely to be positively correlated, for a time at least. For some kinds of goods, mass advertising is necessary to attract enough volume to achieve efficiency in production and other business functions. And, it is now well known, introducing new products offers a chance for large gains, in the short run at least; but it also typically calls for advertising. If and to the extent that advertising significantly increases the capital intensity of efficient firms, it tends to increase their size, and large firms seem to have a cost advantage in raising large capital.

SUMMARY

Two theories about advertising are especially popular in industrial organization economics. They are as different as night and day. According to the first theory, advertising lowers the cost of bringing valuable information to buyers, eases the entry of new products and new firms, increases competition, and lowers price. There is substantial empirical evidence to support that theory.

According to the second theory, advertising pollutes language, mind, and taste; builds and preserves monopoly by creating fake value where none is real, making consumers inert, and raising costs of entry; and is nothing but offsetting waste under conditions of oligopoly rivalry. Many believe that the high profitability of some products, including skin emollients and other cosmetics, is preserved by using false claims to create false hopes; and, more generally, that advertising entrenches leading firms and repels newcomers who offer better products.

There continues to be disagreement about how advertising works and what role it plays in competition and efficiency. Advertising is often associated with relatively or absolutely large firms that serve mass markets efficiently. Their profits rest on efficiency but are correlated with advertising. On the other hand, many believe that advertising can somehow create enough, and durable enough, image and aura to unjustifiably reward those who succeed at it. According to this view, successful advertisers make too much money for too long. Armored against the offerings of nonadvertisers or less successful advertisers, they are able to raise price far above the total cost of the inputs they buy, including advertising itself.

Figuring out what advertising does is job enough. Advertising poses other vexing problems, too. Suppose, as seems plausible, that we believe some advertising helps consumers and some of it hurts. It would be nice to know which kind is which and how to predict the conditions under which each result will occur. Even if we can find out, however, it would be hard to formulate appropriate policies.

In protecting free speech, the Constitution permits many claims that are self-serving and misleading, and some that are purposefully false. And it is quite impossible to remove all the consumer ignorance and psychological quirks that advertising is supposed to exploit. Enforcing laws against false claims and image making could cause trouble for more things than diet plans and soap. Among others, teachers, schools, and politicians would be in for it, too.

QUESTIONS

1. Briefly state what the two major groups of theories say advertising does.
2. Does it bother you that some people with strong brand preferences can't distinguish their favorites from other brands in blindfold tests?
3. Many people say they would like to prohibit false or misleading advertising. Are college and university catalogs false or misleading? More or less so than Sears Roebuck catalogs? Textbooks? Political speeches and platforms? Press conferences held by politicians, and by government employees?
4. Why do you suppose doctors, dentists, and lawyers, among other professionals, have often opposed advertising bitterly? How could advertising of eyeglasses or professional services possibly lower prices?
5. How does advertising fit into the theory of perfect competition?
6. If advertising attracts customers, why can't it be used to attract a monopoly's customers and erode its powers?
7. Is there any reason to believe that advertising can make entry easier for new firms? For new products?
8. Suppose your firm's advertising raises price above average cost. That is, you now receive a price that more than covers your costs, including advertising. Why can't a nonadvertising competitor profitably sell at less than your price but more than your costs?
9. Briefly outline the theory that significant advertising of a good is a reliable signal that the good has superior quality.
10. When the government prevented cigarette companies from advertising on TV, their profits soared. In 1911, the government dissolved the American Tobacco Co. into several competing firms, after which cigarette advertising soared and profits fell. Explain and comment.
11. Briefly state the argument that tax and accounting treatment of advertising expenditures tends to distort statistical relationships between advertising and profits.

NOTES

1. Harold Demsetz, "Commentary," in *Issues in Advertising: The Economics of Persuasion*, ed. David G. Tuerck (Washington, D.C.: American Enterprise Institute, 1978), pp. 267–68.

2. See Yale Brozen, *Concentration, Mergers, and Public Policy* (New York: Macmillan, Inc., 1982), Chapter 9.

3. George J. Stigler, *The Organization of Industry* (Homewood, Ill.: Richard D. Irwin, Inc., 1968), pp. 179–80, 182, 184.

4. That popular theory is examined and displaced in Thomas T. Nagle, "Do Advertising-Profitability Studies Really Show That Advertising Creates a Barrier to Entry?" *Journal of Law & Economics*, 24 (October 1981), pp. 333–49. But see Michael Spence, "Notes on Advertising, Economies of Scale, and Entry Barriers," *Quarterly Journal of Economics*, 95 (November 1980), pp. 493–507.

5. Michael Darby and Edi Karni, "Free Competition and the Optimal Amount of Fraud," *Journal of Law & Economics*, 16 (April 1973), pp. 67–88.

6. For example, see Yale Brozen, *Concentration, Mergers, and Public Policy*; Stanley I. Ornstein, *Industrial Concentration and Advertising Intensity* (Washington, D.C.: American Enterprise Institute, 1977); Dean A. Worcester, Jr. (with Ronald Nesse), *Welfare Gains from Advertising: The Problem of Regulation* (Washington, D.C.: American Enterprise Institute, 1978); James M. Ferguson, *Advertising and Competition: Theory, Measurement, Fact* (Cambridge, Mass.: Ballinger Publishing Co., 1975); Julian Simon, *Issues in the Economics of Advertising* (Urbana, Ill.: University of Illinois Press: 1970); A. D. Strickland and L. W. Weiss, "Advertising, Concentration, and Price-Cost Margins," *Journal of Political Economy*, 84 (October 1976), pp. 1109–21; William Comanor and Thomas Wilson, "The Effect of Advertising on Competition: A Survey," *Journal of Economic Literature*, 17 (June 1979), pp. 453–76; Comanor and Wilson, "Advertising, Market Structure, and Performance," *Review of Economics and Statistics*, 49 (November 1967), pp. 423–40; Comanor and Wilson, *Advertising and Market Power* (Cambridge, Mass.: Harvard University Press, 1974); and Nagle, "Do Advertising-Profitability Studies Really Show That Advertising Creates a Barrier to Entry?"

7. Lester G. Telser, "How Much Does It Pay Whom to Advertise?" *American Economic Review*, 51 (May 1961), pp. 194–205; Telser, "Advertising and Cigarettes," *Journal of Political Economy*, 70 (October 1962), pp. 471–79; Telser, "Advertising and Competition," *Journal of Political Economy*, 62 (December 1964), pp. 537–62; Telser, "Some Aspects of the Economics of Advertising," *Journal of Business*, 41 (April 1968), pp. 166–73; and Telser, "Another Look at Advertising and Concentration," *Journal of Industrial Economics*, 18 (November 1969), pp. 85–94; George J. Stigler, "The Economics of Information," *Journal of Political Economy*, 69 (1961), pp. 213–25, reprinted in *The Organization of Industry*, pp. 179–80, 182, 184; Phillip Nelson, "Information and Consumer Behavior," *Journal of Political Economy*, 78 (March/April 1970), pp. 311–29; and Nelson, "Advertising as Information," *Journal of Political Economy*, 82 (July/August 1974), pp. 729–54.

8. U.S. Bureau of the Census, *Statistical Abstract of the United States: 1986* (Washington, D.C.: U.S. Government Printing Office, December 1985), pp. 428, 431–35.

9. Ibid., p. 552.

10. Keith Leffler, "Persuasion or Information? The Economics of Prescription Drug Advertising," *Journal of Law & Economics*, 14 (April 1981), pp. 45-74.

11. George J. Stigler, "The Economies of Scale," *Journal of Law & Economics*, 1 (October 1958), pp. 54–71, reprinted, with addenda, in *The Organization of Industry*, pp. 71–94, especially pp. 81, 84. See also Stigler, "The Economics of Information," *Journal of Political Economy*, 69 (June 1961), pp. 213–25.

12. Telser, "Advertising and Cigarettes" (1962).

13. Kristian Palda, *The Measurement of Cumulative Advertising Effects* (Englewood Cliffs, N.J.: Prentice-Hall, Inc., 1964).

14. *FTC* v. *Procter & Gamble*, 386 U.S. 568 (1967).

15. John Peterman, "The Clorox Case and the Television Rate Structures," *Journal of Law & Economics*, 11 (October 1968), pp. 321–422. See also David Blank, "Television Advertising: The Great Discount Illusion, or Tonypandy Revisited," *Journal of Business*, 41 (January 1968), pp. 10–38.

16. Yale Brozen, *Concentration, Mergers, and Public Policy*, Chapter 9, p. 268. Brozen tabulates some data from Ornstein's 1977 study.

17. Telser, "Advertising and Competition."

18. The coefficient of determination, R^2, was around .03; and a 1 percent increase in advertising intensity was associated with only a .08 percent increase in concentration.

19. Nonalcoholic beverages, motor vehicles, motor vehicle parts and accessories.

20. Neither does more recent work show advertising as an assurance of brand loyalty. See, for example, J. F. Engel, D. Kollat, and R. Blackwell, eds., *Consumer Behavior: Selected Readings*, 2nd. ed. (Hillsdale, Ill.: Dryden Press, 1973), Chapter 23; and Jean-Jacques Lambin, *Advertising, Competition, and Market Conduct in Oligopoly Over Time* (Amsterdam: North-Holland Press, 1976).

21. H. M. Mann, J. A. Henning, and J. W. Meehan, Jr., "Advertising and Concentration: An Empirical Investigation," *Journal of Industrial Economics*, 16 (November 1967), pp. 34–45.

22. Telser, "Another Look at Advertising and Concentration," p. 93.

23. *Ibid.*, p. 94. Also see Morton Schnabel, "A Note on Advertising and Industrial Concentration," *Journal of Political Economy*, 78 (September/October 1970), pp. 1191–94; Stanley Ornstein, "The Advertising-Concentration Controversy," *Southern Economic Journal*, 43 (July 1976), pp. 892–902; and Ornstein, *Industrial Concentration and Advertising Intensity* (Washington, D.C.: American Enterprise Institute, 1977).

24. Compare, for example, Douglas Greer, "Advertising and Market Concentration," *Southern Economic Journal*, 38 (July 1971), pp. 19–32; William Shepherd, "The Elements of Market Structure," *Review of Economics and Statistics*, 54 (February 1972), pp. 25–37; Roger Sherman and Robert Tollison, "Advertising and Profitability," *Review of Economics and Statistics*, 53 (November 1971), pp. 397–407; Willard Mueller and Larry Hamm, "Trends in Industrial Market Concentration, 1947 to 1970," *Review of Economics and Statistics*, 56 (November 1974), pp. 511–20; Neil Wright, "Product Differentiation, Concentration, and Changes in Concentration," *Review of Economics and Statistics*, 60 (November 1978), pp. 628–31.

25. Richard Schmalensee, "Brand Loyalty and Barriers to Entry," *Southern Economic Journal*, 40 (April 1974), pp. 579–88. But see his "Entry Deterrence in the Ready-To-Eat Breakfast Cereal Industry," *Bell Journal*, 9 (Autumn 1979), pp. 305–27. For a criticism, see Comanor and Wilson, "The Effect of Advertising on Competition: A Survey," pp. 455–56.

26. Yale Brozen, "Entry Barriers: Advertising and Product Differentiation," in *Industrial Concentration: the New Learning*, eds. H. J. Goldschmid, H. M. Mann, and J. F. Weston (Boston: Little, Brown & Company, 1974), pp. 115–37.

27. Joe S. Bain, *Barriers to New Competition: Their Character and Consequences in Manufacturing Industries* (Cambridge, Mass.: Harvard University Press, 1956).

28. Richard Tennant, *The American Cigarette Industry* (New Haven, Conn.: Yale University Press, 1950).

29. Brozen, "Entry Barriers," p. 132.

30. Brozen, *Concentration, Mergers, and Public Policy*, p. 269.

31. Ibid., p. 270.

32. Phillip Nelson, "Advertising as Information," *Journal of Political Economy*, 81 (July/August 1974), pp. 729–54; and Richard E. Kihlstrom and Michael H. Riordan, "Advertising as a Signal," *Journal of Political Economy*, 92 (June 1984), pp. 427–50.

33. Though they used the assertion to argue another point, Comanor and Wilson in 1967 noted that "this investment in market penetration will involve a particularly risky use of funds since it does not generally create tangible assets which can be resold in the event of failure. The required rate of return on such capital will therefore be high." William Comanor and Thomas Wilson, "Advertising, Market Structure, and Performance" (November 1967), pp. 423–40, at p. 426.

34. Telser, "Advertising and Competition," pp. 537–62, at p. 542. Also see U.S. Federal Trade Commission, *Chain Stores: Quality of Canned Fruits and Vegetables* (Washington, D.C.: U.S. Government Printing Office, 1933). For more recent data on *price* differences, see U.S. National Commission on Food Marketing, *Special Studies in Food Marketing, No. 10* (Washington, D.C.: U.S. Government Printing Office, 1966).

35. Lee Benham, "The Effect of Advertising on the Price of Eyeglasses, *Journal of Law & Economics*, 15 (October 1972), pp. 337–52; and Lee Benham and Alexandra Benham, "Regulating Through the Professions: A Perspective on Information Control," *Journal of Law & Economics*, 18 (October 1975), pp. 421–47.

36. Robert Steiner, "Does Advertising Lower Consumer Prices?" *Journal of Marketing*, 37 (October 1973), pp. 19–26.

37. W. S. Comanor and T. A. Wilson, "Advertising, Market Structure, and Performance," pp. 423–40. See also their "Advertising and the Advantages of Size," *American Economic Review*, 59 (May 1969), pp. 87–98, and *Advertising and Market Power*.

38. Their smaller industries tended to have large unexplained residuals, possibly—they speculate—because small industries have small firms and the variance in profit rates is larger for small firms.

39. William S. Comanor, "Market Structure, Product Differentiation, and Industrial Research," *Quarterly Journal of Economics*, 81 (November 1967), pp. 639–57, at p. 657.

40. Comanor and Wilson, "Advertising, Market Structure, and Performance," p. 424.

41. Ibid., pp. 437–38.

42. Comanor and Wilson later suggested imposing higher postal rates for junk mail, taxing advertising more heavily, and limiting and purifying advertising through more stringent government regulation. Comanor and Wilson, *Advertising and Market Power* (Cambridge, Mass.: Harvard University Press, 1974), pp. 252–53.

43. Robert Ayanian, "The Profit Rates and Economic Performance of Drug Firms," in *Drug Development and Marketing*, ed. Robert E. Helm (Washington, D.C.: American Enterprise Institute, 1975); Harry Bloch, "Advertising and Profitability: A Reappraisal," *Journal of Political Economy*, 82 (March/April 1974), pp. 267–86; Kenneth W. Clarkson, *Intangible Capital and Rates of Return: Effects of Research and Promotion on Profitability* (Washington, D.C.: American Enterprise Institute, 1977).

44. Leonard Weiss, "Advertising, Profits, and Corporate Taxes," *Review of Economics and Statistics*, 51 (November 1969), pp. 426–30. See also J. J. Siegfried and L. Weiss, "Advertising, Profits, and Corporate Taxes Revisited," *Review of Economics and Statistics*, 56 (May 1974), pp. 195–200.

45. Robert Ayanian, "Advertising and Rate of Return," *Journal of Law and Economics*, 18 (October 1975), pp. 479–506.

46. Bloch, "Advertising and Profitability: A Reappraisal," pp. 267–86.

47. Ayanian, "Advertising and Rate of Return."

48. Harold Demsetz, "Accounting for Advertising as a Barrier to Entry," *Journal of Business* 52 (July 1979), p. 345.

49. Yale Brozen, *Concentration, Mergers, and Public Policy*, p. 259.

50. Nagle, "Do Advertising-Profitability Studies Really Show that Advertising Creates a Barrier to Entry?" pp. 333–49.

51. Ibid., p. 349.

17 REGULATING EXTERNALITIES

INTRODUCTION

In the past, economists were quick to recommend regulation whenever markets did not operate as the theory of perfect competition suggested they should. It is easy to see why. We easily convinced ourselves that reality is not as nice as the outcomes shown in models of perfection. Real-world processes do not work perfectly and competition is never pure. In the real world, results are often untidy; a market may be working towards one long-run equilibrium when conditions change and it begins to move toward another. On paper, at least, it was easy to show that perfect regulatory schemes can produce better results than those we actually get in the absence of regulation. The basic trouble with this was that we were comparing the actual with the ideal. One reason we did it was that we had forgotten that real regulation can be a good deal worse than ideal regulation.

Today, however, informed by theories about regulations and regulators, and massive recent research showing how real regulation works, we are more skeptical about what regulation can accomplish. This research suggests that much regulation does not do what proponents said it would do, or costs too much.

One central article of classical faith—and of the laissez faire philosophy taken as a whole—was that every proposed extension of state activity and authority should be examined under a presumption of error, for several reasons. One is that a law may not actually do what is honestly intended by it. Another is that it will do what is really intended; but that the intention is wrong or too costly. Finally, the state tends to grow so powerful that it jeopardizes freedom.

The next section reviews modern theories about regulations and regulators. These theories have drastically changed how we think about regulatory processes and prospects. The section after that deals with spillovers involving radio interference, airport noise, bees, lighthouses, and land use and zoning. The following section presents three case studies of natural resources subject to serious external effects: buffalo, fish, and crude oil.

THEORIES OF REGULATION AND REGULATORS ⎯⎯⎯⎯⎯⎯⎯⎯⎯⎯⎯⎯⎯

Theorizing about the effects of regulation is not a new development. Alfred Marshall's writings and *The Wealth of Nations* are examples from earlier days. Giants in the history of economics assessed English laws, including trade barriers.

A 1962 article by Stigler and Friedland marked a modern turning point by admonishing us to stop reading laws, debates, and court opinions to ascertain the effects of state action.[1] Textbooks of the day stressed motives of a statute, as discerned in its title and language, and did little to separate announced purpose from real net effects. Stigler and Friedland said that we should test directly for effects, an admonition that can also be found in classical economics. The Stigler-Friedland article uses modern quantitative methods, which was unusual in the regulatory literature even at that late date.

Remarkably, too, Stigler and Friedland concluded that public utility regulation in the U.S. had not really done anything, although it had used up resources in accomplishing nothing. It is true that they found a curious dispersion of rates under regulation; but they made little of it. They explained the finding of noneffect by arguing both that there really had been little or nothing for such regulation to do in the first place, and that regulators can not simultaneously control all relevant price and nonprice dimensions of products and transactions. The latter explanation accords with a conviction that business and markets adjust flexibly.

Following Stigler and Friedland, others did one case study after another. Most of them did not show noneffect, but rather effects that many would call inefficient, wasteful, or bad. On the whole these studies confirmed the classical opinion that much regulation is unnecessary or mistaken, as well as bolstering Stigler's theory that industries often seek and "buy" regulation that governments supply.

This brings us to three articles presenting theories of regulation that began taking over in the 1970s. Stigler sought an economic theory of regulation "to explain who will receive the benefits of or burdens of regulation, what form regulation will take, and the effects of regulation upon the allocation of resources."[2] His "central thesis . . . is that, as a rule, regulation is acquired by the industry and is designed and operated primarily for its benefit." He adduces evidence in support of the thesis and reaches a discomfiting conclusion: "Until the basic logic of political life is developed, reformers will be ill-equipped to use the state for their reforms, and victims of the pervasive use of the state's support of special groups will be helpless to protect themselves."[3]

Claiming that Stigler's theory could not explain everything, Richard Posner tried to discriminate amongst and to appraise a variety of regulatory theories that had achieved wide circulation.[4] The two prevailing theories were, first, that regulation prevents monopoly exploitation and produces approximately competitive results; and, second, that regulation helps the regulated. To those theories, Posner added that regulation redistributes goods and income, just as taxation and subsidies do.

Posner's second article notes that there is not yet a single unified theory of regulation, but rather a substantial number and variety of theories, which can be classified into two broad categories.[5] First, the public-interest theories; and second, the capture theories. The public-interest theory is that regulation seeks to do good. The capture theory sees regulatory agencies being captured by those they are supposed to control. Posner claimed that neither theory holds up very well when tested against history.

Posner claimed that Stigler's theory is "incredible" at its limit: how does one explain "institutions that enabled genuine public interest considerations to influence the formation of policy?"[6] These include the U.S. Constitution (and, one could argue, law itself). It is not safe to assume that public-interest claims are always shams. We might as well recognize that the effects of economic regulation are very "difficult to trace." This makes it hard to figure out who gains and loses, let alone how much.

Sam Peltzman also contributed a theory of the demand for and supply of government regulations. It comes down to determining the size and makeup of political coalitions.[7]

The questions that Stigler, Posner, and Peltzman raise about regulation are important. Yet they also pose extremely challenging theoretical puzzles. If the results of government intervention and growth really are poor, why do voters permit, let alone encourage, government to keep on growing?

There are various possibilities. First, maybe the specific or overall results of government expansion are not bad, but are wonderful after all, and we are getting what is good for us. Or, at least, once government programs somehow get into place, it costs more to get rid of them than the losses they cause. This is the scratch-start inefficiency argument presented in Chapter 2.

The second explanation relies on ignorance. Maybe the results are bad; but most voters are ignorant of the effects, and perhaps it is too costly to teach them better. Or perhaps political fraud is effective, and politicians and others can profit by systematically misleading the electorate. And there's no denying that it is very difficult and time consuming for outsiders to predict in detail the costs and benefits of specific laws, government policies, and regulations. It also costs something and takes time to inform the electorate about all this. In the interim, of course, those who benefit got a policy that helps them, and the rest of us have been stuck with larger wastes and inefficiencies that—for some reason—turn out to be practically irreversible. Costs of information, coalitions, and transactions are too high relative to the loss.

Unless the electorate really understands and adheres to basic economic principles, the story goes, we can never explain, and therefore cannot prevent, wave after wave of complex governmental mischiefs. Some who like this explanation urge improved information and education. Stigler notes, however, that the U.S. is relatively well educated, and that increased formal education may not have turned the tide. Others emphasize putting limits on what the state will be permitted to do.

A third explanation is that many of these governmental policies and activities actually are bad overall, and everyone knows they are bad, but they are practically irresistible. This is so because they help some group a lot and hurt each of the rest of us only a little. So little, in fact, that it does not pay us to form an effective political opposition.

Some who believe in this explanation urge constitutional and budgetary limitations on how much and what kinds of things governments will be permitted to do; or urge changing the ways legislatures work.

There are other possibilities as well. An important task, therefore, is to find an explanation. Stigler's research agenda is to find out what government regulations and programs purport to do; their probable effects; who gains and loses from them, and how much.

If we say that government regulates whenever it significantly alters prices, quantities, qualities, or profits, there is a lot of regulation.[8] It is interesting to examine a few of the many reasons historically given for regulating economic activities. To control hurtful "externalities" or spillover effects, for example, governments regulate pollution, financial firms and markets, and the exploitation of common-property resources such as crude oil and migratory fish.[9]

To protect the consumer's health and purse, governments have regulated foods and drugs, licensed health-care professionals, and specified how to advertise, price, and sell "complex" goods and services ranging from used cars to new stocks and bonds. Whether consumers benefited from all this is debatable.[10]

To protect consumers against real or imagined *monopoly* exploitation, governments have regulated prices, profits, and quality of service. It is fair to say that some of these regulations created and preserved monopoly instead of reducing it. Some other "anti-monopoly" regulations were imposed when there was little or no monopoly threat at all.

As Coase summed it up,

> It is now generally accepted by students of the subject that most (perhaps almost all) government regulation is anti-competitive and harmful in its effects * * * there have been many studies of regulated industries which make it abundantly clear that producers are able to secure arrangements with government regulation that they were not able to secure through the delimitation of property rights.[11]

Beneficial or not, regulation in the U.S. and elsewhere has expanded greatly. The number of regulatory agencies has grown. So have their employment and budgets. And industries that are directly regulated in significant ways have accounted for a growing share of the national income.[12] But there is some evidence that this growth will not proceed indefinitely, without limit. In the Carter and Reagan administrations, for example, some deregulation actually occurred.

There is no doubt that many government regulations affect or are affected by the structure and performance of industry, which are the central topics of industrial organization economics. By that standard, there is good reason to include government regulation in studies of industrial organization.

To keep this book within tolerable limits, however, it will discuss examples of only three classes of regulations. This chapter discusses problems with external effects—so-called spillovers—and regulations that are supposed to deal with them. The next chapter discusses regulations that are supposed to control monopoloid industries, including public utilities; and—at the other pole—agricultural price and output regulations designed to transfer income from taxpayers to farmers, who work in unconcentrated industries. We will have to abstract and simplify drastically to do even that much: direct regulation is a whole field of study in itself.

SPILLOVERS

Radio and TV

Spillover effects—externalities—are a common rationale for government ownership and regulation. Chapter 3, for example, discussed classic parables from the old literature about externalities: factories emitting smokes and fumes; spark-emitting locomotives; and pollutions of various kinds.

In 1959, Ronald H. Coase published his "The Federal Communications Commission."[13] In it, he analyzed an important and misunderstood example of externalities: radio stations' jamming one another's programs. In the early days of radio, stations did not have well-specified property rights to specific broadcast frequencies. Their messages sometimes interfered with and cancelled one another, resulting, some said, in a "sea of noise." The ostensible reason for government regulation of radio was that unrestricted entry into broadcasting had led to wastes, confusion, and chaos.[14] One solution would have been to create and sell property rights in specific frequencies, letting it go at that. That was not to be. Rather than auctioning off rights to different parts of the radio spectrum, which it claimed to own, the federal government issued free licenses for limited periods, and regulated what licensee stations could do.

The kind of regulation we got is odd in several respects, as Coase points out. In addition, misdiagnosing the cause of problems in radio has caused trouble about more important things than radio. First, those who urged government ownership and regulation, rather than outright sale, did so partly because the radio spectrum is a scarce resource. Since all goods are scarce, that argument seems to justify government ownership and control of everything. On the contrary: many economists believe that scarcity argues for private property rights and market pricing, rather than arbitrary government pricing and allocations. Although markets for radio frequencies, or anything else, do not work well when property rights are ill defined, government can help create and defend property rights.

Second, the available radio spectrum is not as constant as it sounds. It is determined by several factors, including technology. Technological improvements have made it possible to carry more messages within a given spectrum, and have expanded the spectrum itself.

Third, the way in which frequencies have actually been assigned—or leased—has produced some strange results: though nominally temporary, in practice occupancy rights to the radio and TV spectrum have usually been permanent and unpriced, with the government asserting ownership. And the government limited the number of frequencies and licensees more drastically than technology and economics permit.

The government has imposed substantial control over the types and content of programs, and it might be able to impose even more. Some have worried about the implications for censorship and freedom. For better or worse, however, selling the spectrum outright need not keep the government from regulating broadcast content and quality. To the extent that government control of broadcast content is constitutional, it could be exerted over outright owners as well as lessees.

Although they enjoy those regulations that protect them from competition, broadcasting companies may not like some of the others. Regulations of program content, advertising, and the amount of time that must be spent on local news and educational TV may be examples, though it is hard for outsiders to be sure. Then too, the allocation of different parts of the broadcast spectrum—between governmental and private users, for example—looks "inefficient" in the usual sense of that word.

Because government gave away the frequencies rather than auctioning them off, and because it limited the number of broadcasters in each market, the first owners of broadcasting stations got very valuable franchises.[15] Years ago, when dollars were worth more, J. Harvey Levin reckoned that a license to broadcast TV programs was worth more than $2 million per station, on average. More recent sales of radio and TV stations reveal much higher prices.[16]

Competitive auctions of spectrum rights theoretically could have eliminated that windfall, and, after Coase wrote, people started thinking about how such a scheme would work in practice.[17] Auctioning off the frequencies would have made it possible to scrap or shrink a substantial regulatory effort. For various reasons, and to the relief of most TV licensees, the FCC traditionally limited and interfered with competition from community antenna (CATV) and pay TV systems.

Fourth, although most of us missed the point, Coase also explained the kinds of arrangements broadcast companies could make if they owned their frequencies outright. In addition to buying and selling frequencies, they could contract with one another to apportion hours of operation, determine the power at which programs are broadcast, and so on. These contracts could eliminate wasteful interferences and otherwise permit the net value of the broadcast spectrum to be maximized.

Such a scheme might work very well in radio and TV, where numbers on the same frequencies can be small. There are industries, however, in which transactions costs are so high that simple negotiations among the parties are not a practical remedy. Some sort of regulation or liability rule seems to be desirable. It is one thing if nobody realizes that a substance or activity will, with substantial delay, do great harm. The result is rather like a fault-free accident. It is quite another thing when people who cause the harm know it will occur and seek to cover it up. That is fraud at best. The earlier discussion of an economic rationale for law noted that it is appropriate to punish harmful activities severely when the joint conditional probability of detection *and* a guilty verdict is low. To maximize net outputs, it seems reasonable to impose liability on those who know what is going on and can most cheaply put things right.

Prohibiting activities outright removes all (nonpolitical) possibilities to negotiate and contract. The traditionally dominant principles that Professor Pigou gave us are generally shaky and sometimes downright wrong. Usually, simple taxes on spillovers cannot be expected to do the job. A tax solution to airport noise problems, for example, seems to require taxing those who benefit from reduced noise as well as those who make the noise.[18]

It is striking how many readers remember Coase's rule for zero transactions costs, but forget his analyses of problems that arise when those costs are large.

Baxter and Altree: Airport Noise[19]

Pigou mistakenly assumed that government inaction, rather than explicit government policy, caused the harms from spark-emitting railroad locomotives. It may also seem natural to suppose that the nuisance of aircraft noise occurs because government failed to get involved. According to Baxter and Altree (B&A), however, that assumption is also wrong: government involvement is part of the problem. Statutes and regulations, plus city, state, and federal airport ownership actually impede the economic solution by removing or restricting liability for damages caused. In principle, at least, that could all be changed. Assuming that it could be changed, what ought to be done?

B&A see three major alternatives: the expanded firm, the assessment district, and time-limited easements. They prefer the third, which is the only one discussed here. It comprises several steps and features. First, on the basis of noise measured on the ground, they would calculate noise contour lines, outside of which noise is negligible. For O'Hare Airport in Chicago, for example, measurement would generate several long, narrow fingers. These noise contour lines would be remeasured and redrawn periodically.

Second, using funds from landing fees levied on air carriers, each airport would buy two to three year easements from owners of property within the noise lines. The price of these easements would equal the reduction in appraised open-market rental value due to airport activities. Owners of the properties would pay the costs of appraisals. B&A claim that sales values wouldn't do: purchasers would be willing to buy the properties for discounted rental values *plus* damages expected to be collected.

B&A claim that this scheme would give the incentives needed to achieve an optimal solution. Airlines would use the right mix of aircraft characteristics, including noisiness, and change them appropriately as technology changes. At the same time, property owners on the ground would design and plan for efficiency. They would, according to B&A, do just the right amounts of sound screening and soundproofing.

As B&A recognize, their plan faces serious practical difficulties, including its need for homogeneous—i.e., federal—law, and abrogation of present landing-fee schedules.

Bees and Lighthouses

Sidgwick's imaginary lighthouse and the imaginary bees of Meade and Bator are classic textbook examples of imperfections, inefficiencies, and market failures that occur when factors are unpriced. According to the textbooks, there will be too few bees and lighthouses, because it is impossible to collect for the benefits they produce. Fortunately, the textbooks suffer both from theoretic flaws and misapprehension of the facts.

Coase, for example, found that private companies in Great Britain had built lighthouses for profit, agreeing with the state about charges to be levied on ships in port.[20] Some critics said this history does not refute the public-good story, since it involved a combination of state and private efforts. On the other hand, of course, the state is always involved in creating and enforcing property rights.

Textbook versions of honeybee economics are even worse than those about lighthouses.[21] Beekeeping is not in fact a good example of so-called market failure, unpriced factors of production, and inefficient resource allocation. By creating a fable, rather than looking at the facts, it was Meade and Bator who created an externality. In fact, farmers and orchardists pay to have bees pollinate their crops. Services of the bees are priced and sold.

Even a genuine externality, however, is not in itself sufficient to justify state intervention, regulations, and rules. For the relevant costs and uncertainties may be as great for government as for private markets.

Land-Use Zoning

Most people seem to believe that zoning is necessary to avoid chaos and waste in modern cities. That belief has come under academic attack in the last fifteen or twenty years. For example, Houston, Texas is a major city that has no zoning law. It is not a festering slum, and it is not a starving ward of places that do enjoy the benefits of zoning laws.[22]

Empirical studies of Pittsburgh, which does have zoning, also shake popular beliefs.[23] Judging from land use and real estate values there, several conclusions seem sustainable. First, tastes and conditions vary within major cities. What is a nuisance to some people is an amenity to others. What imposes a net diseconomy in one zoning district does not seem to impose a net diseconomy in other districts. Second, present zoning restrictions seem to be unnecessarily detailed to maximize the value of residential properties. Third, spillover effects are surprisingly local, within narrowly defined neighborhoods. Major effects seem to occur within two or three hundred *feet*. This suggests that negotiations and contracts need not involve hopelessly large areas and numbers of people. Small coalitions of neighbors may be able to avoid wasteful damage by contract and purchase.

According to Rueter, however, two arguments for zoning do remain. Restricting development may lower the costs of providing streets, sewers, and water. Zoning may also reduce the costs of developing large parcels, by reducing "free-rider" and transactions costs problems.

NATURAL RESOURCES: BUFFALOES, FISH, AND OIL

Introduction

Years ago, a bright and witty graduate student gave a seminar report on "Conservation," with especial emphasis upon helium gas. He asserted a criterion for quickly deciding whether a book on conservation would be worth reading or not. The bad ones, he said, featured illustrations of buffaloes or American Indians, some as frontispieces. The others did not. That rule may or may not work; but the official seal of the U.S. Department of Interior features a buffalo.

Fish, bison, oil, broadcasting, and land use are cases in which unregulated exploitation allegedly produces economic mischief—although sometimes it is not clear against what feasible alternative the mischief has been measured. It must be remembered that—whether we are talking about conservation or the economic problem in general—the object of the game is to maximize net present values. From an economic standpoint complete nonuse is not usually the preferred solution.

For centuries, the African elephant has been killed for ivory; until recently it was legally hunted for sport, and it is illegally hunted even now. Indeed, it is said that members of African governments have participated directly in the wholesale slaughter of elephants for ivory—in violation of laws already on their books. Royal guards in Europe were for long outfitted in bearskin hats. The American buffalo was virtually exterminated to satisfy the market for lap robes; the American elk (wapiti) to furnish teeth to decorate watch fobs worn by members of a fraternal order. Then there are migratory waterfowl, and the passenger pigeons, killed in the millions by market hunters to serve at tables in home and restaurant. The rhino has been trapped, poisoned, and shot for horns that fetch a substantial price in the Orient. Tigers, leopards, jaguars, and other cats are poisoned, snared, and shot for their valuable pelts. Some species of fish and whales are said to be overexploited and in danger of extinction.

Only rarely do critics of all this note the difference between these cases and domestic animal husbandry. Few worry that beef cattle will become extinct through overkilling. The bison, by contrast, weigh heavily upon our conscience. Among other things, it will be instructive to find how these cases are similar and how they differ. Each of the sad histories just mentioned played out under a fatal handicap: there were no effective property rights in *live* creatures. On top of that, it is asserted that certain biological and technical characteristics made things even worse. It does not appear, however, that the technical problems would produce mischief except for the property-rights problem. Yet it has been traditional to emphasize technical problems and greed in discussing these pathological cases. Few go to the root of the problem, which is badly defined property rights.

Cases like fish and buffalo can be used variously. For example, critics of open markets and individuals' maximizing conduct have used them as horror-story support for a more general claim: "competition" and "greed" produce "market failure" and "waste." Some have extended that argument to all "natural resources," vaguely defined; and a few to claim that the state should regulate or own virtually everything. And producers themselves sometimes claim that their industries will suffer a fate similar to the buffalo's unless they get the kinds of regulations they want.

Although relatively few Western economists oppose private property and competition under all conditions, it is popular to say that unbridled competition in exploiting "natural resources" produces poor economic results. Still others believe that destructive competition is pathological and rare; or remediable by establishing property rights rather than regulations. An unbiased approach is to study these cases as examples of specific and peculiar pathologies that may conceivably merit some kind of cure. We should note at the outset that markets cannot be expected to work very well when property rights are ill defined with respect to exclusivity, transferability, and permanence. Each of these dimensions merits further discussion.

In following sections of this chapter we will examine some cases of natural resources, briefly analyzing the legal and other institutional forms devised as remedies. It is noteworthy that private cures achieved by merger or contract arguably increase the concentration of control and would probably violate the antitrust laws unless they were cloaked in state regulations. For future reference, note that the crude oil program discussed later was an indispensable, though offstage, character in *Socony Vacuum* (1940), a famous antitrust case cited in Chapter 19.

The technological problems claimed to plague these industries turn out to be externalities or spillovers. That is, the costs and benefits perceived by each firm do not include everything that ought to be included. Some real costs are external to what each producer does: he does not pay all the costs. Similarly, he does not derive all the benefits of some other courses of action. As a result, each—and therefore all—of the producers produces too much too fast, and at costs that are in one way or another higher than they ought to be.

Although they may in practice overlap, it is useful to distinguish three sources of external effects. The first two are said to occur with animals and fish. A third, arguably also a form of crowding, occurs in crude petroleum. The first two are well known and called stock externalities, and crowding externalities; the third can be called rate-of-production externalities. Stock externalities are said to exist when the cost functions of each producer, and the total costs of all of them together, rise as the total amount (stock) of the resource being exploited declines. That is,

$$\delta Cost\ /\ \delta Stock < 0$$

For example, each cast of a net and each fishing voyage can catch more fish at the same cost when there are a lot of fish than when there are few. The same kind of thing happens in hunting some wild animals or birds. But that is not all, which is one of the main points. So far, we have merely described a simple fact of life, not an externality. The externality arises because each of many producers concludes that his own efforts have little or no effect on the total stock being exploited, and no one is in a position to take the total effect into account. That sounds plausible whenever the number of producers is large, each producer is small, and the stock is very large. But the sum of many small kills need not be small. The total effect that all producers have on the stock can be substantial.

Crowding externalities occur when two or more firms interfere with one another, reducing output for a given total effort and cost. Simple examples are fishing boats' fouling one another's lines or nets; and hunters' ruining one another's stalks and drives. In such a case:

$$\delta Cost\ /\ \delta Number\ of\ producers > 0$$

Yet, arguably, no individual producer has an incentive to leave the hunting or fishing ground. A single owner of the resource would try to avoid any such interference among its employees.

There can be crowding externalities in crude oil production as well. And, although in some respects the crude oil rate-of-production externality also looks like a form of crowding, or stock externality, it is sufficiently distinct and important to be treated separately, as we will see later in this chapter.

Buffalo[24]

The simplest fishery models are not very graceful in explaining biological extinction due to commercial pressures.[25]

Although the following discussion emphasizes buffalo running as strict and unsubsidized business, U.S. government policy may also have had some effect. Some influential U.S. Army officers correctly referred to the buffalo as the Indians' Commissary. They believed that the Plains Indians, with whom they were at war, could best be wiped out or forced into submission by exterminating the buffalo. Correctly or not, some say that U.S. Army posts subsidized buffalo hunters by giving them provisions and cartridges.[26]

When the white man came to what is now the U.S., perhaps 50 million to 100 million bison lived here. By 1889 there were about 85 wild buffalo left, plus 256 in captivity and 200 in Yellowstone.[27] In the 1700s, bison had been widely distributed: in the east, they occurred from Pennsylvania south to Georgia; westward through Indiana, Illinois, Minnesota, and Idaho; and southward from Idaho, through New Mexico and Texas. These great herds retreated from succeeding waves of human settlement.

The American bison, as its numbers and geographic extent suggest, was well adapted to its habitat. It was tough enough to make long seasonal migrations to find food. Its coat protected it from appalling winds, rains, cold, and snows. Animal predators were no match for healthy adult buffalo, though they could take the very young, the old, and the sick.

Human predators were something else. Buffalo were gregarious, easily tracked and easily seen. Even towards the end, they seem not to have become extremely wary, but stood stolidly or milled quietly about while shot after shot was fired.

On top of being easy game, the buffalo was worth a good deal when killed. Winter hides made warm sleeping and sleigh robes. Buffalo leather, tough and long lasting, ultimately provided many of the drive belts used to power machinery in U.S. factories. The meat was edible and nutritious, and there was a lot of it on an adult buffalo. At equal prices, it is true, most preferred good beef as a steady diet, and some Indians preferred mule or horse meat. Although it had adapted wonderfully to natural conditions and offered real value to human predators, as a widespread herd animal the buffalo would ultimately have lost out in competition with cattle and other crops, no matter what anyone could have done. Agriculture as we know it now was incompatible with vast herds of wild bison. But what happened was so spectacular, fast, and so often lamented, that it deserves further discussion.

As suggested earlier, the absence of property rights in live buffalo would have proved fatal even in the absence of some other complications. Some of the Indian Nations had acted as though they did have property rights in live buffalo, or—at all events—killed them at a rate that did not threaten the herds' survival. White settlers and soldiers destroyed whatever property rights in buffalo the Plains Indians had enjoyed, and did not replace them with any workable alternative scheme.

No one effectively owned live buffalo. The law of capture, which came to apply, means that whoever kills a buffalo owns it. If you could hold onto them, you owned all the dead animals in your possession. Complete ownership would have been difficult to establish in any case, partly because some herds migrated long distances; and—for a long time—each main herd occupied a lot of ground even when it was not migrating.

It appears that entry into buffalo hunting was not artificially restricted. It may even have been encouraged as a part of military and civil policy. Producing units, and perhaps the firms that owned them, were small. According to Tober, a typical hunting team of the 1870s and 1880s—outfitted by a merchant—contained about five people: a principal shooter, two skinners, a cook, and a stretcher (to care for the hides). The mix of skills and total number of people may have varied with the density of buffalo and other factors. When things went well, a skilled shooter could take 40 to 100 buffalo in a single ''stand'' before moving. That adds up to a lot of buffalo to be skinned before the hides began to deteriorate and lose value. The number of riflemen, skinners, wagons, and so on (capacity) used by a firm was presumably limited by coordination and control costs and was surely limited by the number of buffalo likely to be sighted and shot. If each party operated alone, a large one would be harder for hostile Indians to overrun, though perhaps easier for Indians to find. Several small parties might operate within signalling distance of one another, coming together in case of trouble.[28] The number of operating units and firms must have been large. Tober says, for example, that perhaps two-thirds of the 1873 population of Dodge City (4,000) were buffalo hunters. What the markets for hide buyers and outfitters were like is an open question. Assume that we can legitimately use an atomistic market model to explain what happened.

No single buffalo hunting firm could have substantially reduced, let alone exterminated, the buffalo herds. There is evidence that, in the beginning, hunters believed buffalo were inexhaustible. Later, even when many believed that the herds were doomed, none believed that his own role was significant. No single buffalo hunting firm had any interest in contributing to a conservation program or restraining its own kill rate. The fishery models deal with sustainable yields, a visionary and largely irrelevant ideal in cases like bison.[29] Since no one owned them, no one could manage live buffalo herds as domestic animals are managed. It would not pay to count as part of the cost of animals killed today their contribution to future herd values when they are allowed to reproduce and mature. Buffalo hunters simply disregarded additions to future herd value that a specific buffalo would make if it were spared, and they were rational to do so.[30] There was little or no future value that any single hunter could expect to get if he spared any buffalo that came under his rifle sights. That animal, or the whole herd, might wander away, or someone else would shoot the beast.

By contrast, the value of taking a buffalo now was substantial. In 1870, the hunters themselves realized prices of about $2 for bull hides, $1.75 for cow and calf hides, and $.25 for tongues. Later on, even meat fetched a price, and by 1886 buffalo robes had become so scarce that they brought $25 to $30 each.

Most of a hunting party's costs were fixed costs once it went on campaign. The long run was not great in calendar time, and most resources used in the trade had alternative uses and could readily move out of this trade to another once a campaign was finished; and vice versa.

A factory-loaded .45-120-550 Sharps cartridge cost about $0.25, most of which value is attributable to the reuseable brass cartridge case. Hunters commonly reused each cartridge case repeatedly, by reloading it in the field with new powder and primers, and hand-cast bullets. Up to the capacity of skinners, stretchers, and wagons, a firm's short-run money cost of producing one dead buffalo might have been as low as the value of primer, powder, and lead used. It would not be surprising if a typical hunting firm's cost looked like those shown in Figure 17-1, though the absolute capacity limitation, which makes MC climb vertically at capacity, and other details shown there do not critically affect the results.

If there is no vertical section in MC, or if we ignore it for simplicity, we get a market system like that shown in Figure 17-2. It shows one firm's cost functions and an overall short-run market equilibrium.

These cost functions are drawn on the assumption that there are no stock externalities, crowding externalities, or other such externalities, at least up the last few bison. To analyze cases in which there are stock externalities, we can define the cost functions to include population-size effects. If, for example, there are stock effects of the usual kind, firm and market costs will rise as population declines, and vice versa.

Transport costs of the hunting firm are another complication. Supply wagons grow lighter on the trip out, which to some extent compensates for a growing load of skins. Once committed to a trip, however, transport equipment may have no alternative value while in the hunting field. Their costs are fixed.

So long as price exceeds marginal cost, it pays to kill all the marketable buffalo you can, up to the limits of wagon and skinner capacity. In the long run, the firm, or industry, or both can increase or reduce capacity.

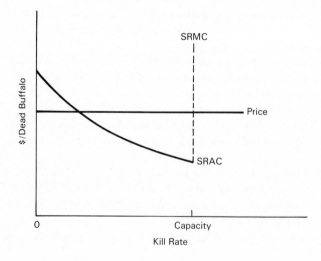

Figure 17-1 A Buffalo Hunter's Cost Curves and Demand

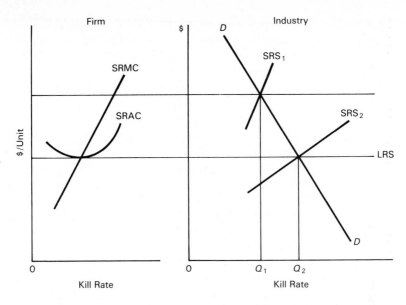

Figure 17-2 Equilibrium Processes in the Buffalo-Hunting Industry

The total industry kill rate during any period depends upon various biological and economic factors: the size and geographic distribution of herds; costs of each firm, which depend upon technology and prices, qualities of firearms, equipment, information, labor, and management; and the number of firms engaged in the trade.

In achieving short- or long-run *economic* equilibrium, several things are happening together. First, the profit-maximizing output is clearing the market on price. That output may be smaller, equal to, or larger than the sustainable yield (SY) from the starting population value. If it is larger than SY, the population shrinks. Suppose, as sounds plausible for highly visible animals that associate in herds, that population externalities or stock externalities do not raise the firm's cost functions until right up to the last few bison. That is, almost up to the very end, the cost functions of a firm do not rise as total population falls. The hope for stable biological equilibrium short of extinction then lies with reaching an *economic* equilibrium that is consistent with population values larger than the extinction limit. That is, if the industry starts with supernormal profits, it will expand, and population and sustainable yield be damned.

Figure 17-2 assumes that the industry starts with a short-run equilibrium Q_1 that is *greater* than SY for the starting population, and that this continues to be so. SRS will start shifting out and down from SRS_1 toward SRS_2, as new firms enter. Price and profits fall, but aggregate output rises. Assume that, at every step in moving toward SRS_2, population is falling. There is no reason to suppose that the kill rate exceeded sustainable yield at the very beginning. Things started out more favorably for the herds. In either case, however, there is no danger of extinction if falling prices close off entry and stabilize output so that the long-run economic equilibrium kill rate, Q_2, is also a sustainable yield. That is more likely to happen if demand is not increasing; if average costs start out close to maximum demand prices; if demand is inelastic with respect to price.

Suppose, on the other hand, that the industry starts with a Q_1 that is smaller than the SY from the starting population, which was probably the case. That sounds better for the bison. Remember, though, that the industry began very profitably. As a result, it expanded. Unless price declines close off such an expansion before rates of output exceed SY, population starts dropping.

Up to this point, the assumption has been that the long-run supply of buffalo kills was perfectly elastic. It may not have been. Suppose, for example, that one or more factors of production become more expensive as the industry expands, less costly as it contracts. Such effects would have to be considered, along with the effects of stock externalities, if there are any. At a crucial stage, towards the end, costs of the few firms remaining may actually have been lower than they were before, in spite of a drastically reduced animal population.

One last alternative possibility remains. Suppose that, as seems plausible for some fish and conceivable even for bison, costs start rising as the animal population starts dropping. That would be better for the bison; but it may not be good enough. Everything depends upon whether rising costs and falling prices contract the industry or close off expansion before outputs become larger than the herds can stand. With a stable total market demand for buffalo, price falls as industry output expands. In the abstract, rising prices for bison products look bad for the herds. That depends somewhat on what causes them to rise. In such a model, an increase in costs raises price by less than the cost increase. Significant stock externalities, if any, would raise costs. External diseconomies, if any, would thus favor survival of the herds, but are not enough if the kill rate continues to exceed SY.

In any case, the demand for buffalo did not stay put. It increased. Furthermore, other threats appeared. Around 1871, improvements in tanning technology made it profitable to produce buffalo leather, in addition to the thick winter robes that had been the major product. This raised the value of summer hides and other low-quality hides, making it profitable to hunt year round. Refrigerator cars and smokehouses eventually made even buffalo meat saleable. Transport costs fell. The animals' natural habitat also was being eroded. Railroad expansion cut the herds in two, east to west. Barbed wire came in about 1870, and afterwards what had been open range was progressively cut up and fenced off.

There are crucial differences between the simplest fisheries model and the bison story. In the typical fisheries model, as we will see, the production function is *defined* as sustainable forever. It is therefore a long-run function, by definition. For bison, the so-called short-run situations proved determinative, which is likely in such cases without property rights *or* regulations.

As everybody knows, the bison was practically wiped out. Was this history "optimal" or "efficient"? In a crucial but unsatisfying sense, of course, it surely was: no one devised a better way to do things. And, of course, there is no reason to believe that bison ought to have been preserved in their old numbers. Ask how different farming and ranching in the Great Plains would be today if there were still several million wild bison roaming about. There is little reason to suppose that large numbers of domesticated, fenced bison would have survived in competition with domesticated cattle, sheep, and goats. There is no reason to believe that consumers today are worse off with what they got in exchange for the bison, even if bison had become completely extinct. Plains Indians' culture, on the other hand, was destroyed.

It is not hard to devise theoretical systems that look more reasonable than what actually happened. If they had been achievable at net cost savings, such systems would have altered the rates of production and the path of costs and prices through time. Marginal net revenues would have been equalized, period to period. If they were superior, why weren't such systems used? One possibility is that people either did not understand or could not have predicted what happened; or did not perceive the alternatives. Maybe; maybe not. On the other hand, the alternatives may have been too costly to achieve relative to the alleged benefits they theoretically offer.

As a purely theoretical matter, how could the hunting trade have been organized differently? The first and crucial problem would have been to create effective property rights in live animals. Effective property implies that nonowners can be kept from hunting buffalo, for the most part, at least. This would have been a remarkable accomplishment for a vast area in which cavalry, civil law, and armed settlers were very thin on the ground.

Suppose, however, that the state could have created effective property rights at costs less than the additional net economic values theoretically available. How could these rights have been used to achieve a better result?

One possible technique, if there were identifiable herds that maintained a separate existence, would have been for the state to sell at auction ownership rights in each herd to one firm. Such a firm would have every interest in treating the herd like any other crop, or livestock, and it is not obvious that society would be harmed. If the economic size of hunting firms requires more than one of them to a herd, the holder of the herd franchise could parcel out hunting rights for so many buffalo per year to the appropriate (that is, efficient) number of hunting firms. After about 1867, there were four main western herd groups, with some overlap.

If there are enough herds, this is consistent even with atomistic competition. Indeed, even if there are not, the social proceeds from bidding by would-be monopolists would extract the rents. Alternatively, as Demsetz suggests for a quite different problem, the state may have taken bids such that the firm offering lowest prices of buffalo products wins.

Another possibility would be continued state ownership, with production quotas sold to private firms at such a price per head as to bring apparent MC into equality with the best guess of "real" MC. There are obvious problems, even dangers, inherent in such a policy. What are they? They include problems of price setting by people who have little incentive to do it right; graft and fraud; "politics"; and so on. It also seems unlikely that such a scheme could change as flexibly and efficiently as private firms, in response to changing cost and demand conditions.

Another possibility, of course, is to prohibit hunting altogether. Even if it had been feasible to enforce prohibition, that would probably have preserved too many buffalo too long, even in terms of the usefulness of buffalo considered alone.[31] It would also interfere with the development of ranching and farming.

Fish

We deal here with commercial fishing, not sport angling. Before the white man came to North America, there may have been reasonably well defined family or tribal property rights in wild creatures including fish; human populations were small relative to the stocks of the resources being exploited; and the technology—though efficient—was primitive. Migratory fish were taken close in, as they returned to their home streams. In some places, including parts of the Pacific coast, fish were so plentiful and easily caught that the Indians prospered mightily, with much leisure time left over for carving, dance, architecture, story telling, and war.

When the white man came, valuable fish were abundant. The newcomers forced the Indians and their system of property rights aside. That white settlers substituted no effective system of property rights in live fish caused few problems at first. Later, however, conservationists and commercial fishermen began to decry what seemed to be happening. Many laws and regulations were passed. Theories about efficient fishery management were propounded. It is not clear whether the regulations or economic theories come first. Early economic theories include those propounded by Scott Gordon (1954), Anthony Scott (1957), and Ralph Turvey (1957). Later works include those by Lee Anderson (1977)[32]; Vernon Smith (1968, 1969)[33]; and J. R. Gould (1972).[34] Some of these theories are complicated and mathematical. Lee Anderson's book is a very helpful synthesis that uses geometry rather than symbolic logic.

Those who believe that business executives easily agree to raise prices should ask why they have so much trouble agreeing to exploit natural resources rationally, something that would also improve their lot. Agreements of any kind will be difficult to make whenever no one has well-defined property rights over the resources about which agreements are to be made, though the dominant conservation theories show little concern about that. Indeed, things are even worse. The theories assume that governments can work miracles by making rules, and largely ignore the possibility of making and selling property rights.

The principal fishing theories use a peculiar methodology. They start from a stylized logistic (or sigmoid) law of biological growth.[35] Figure 17-3 shows such a case. The assumption is that fish will follow that population law if humans leave them alone. Most theories do not bother much with questions such as what "time" it is when humans do start fishing, or exactly how we find out what stage the fishery is in.

Such laws may not apply to wild populations very well. They evolved from laboratory studies of fruit flies breeding in jars, and some field workers think that's where they ought to stay. Some game biologists and wardens in the field claim that periodic collapse, rather than stable upper asymptotes, are a crucial part of wild population dynamics. In any case, anchovy, sardine, and other fisheries have for centuries experienced massive and mysterious long-wave fluctuations. Some say they follow sudden warming in the oceans, due to a phenomenon called El Niño.

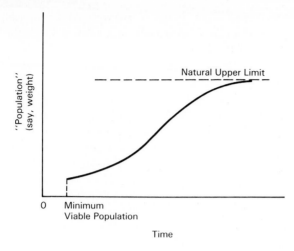

Figure 17-3 Natural Growth Processes in an Unexploited Fishery

However that may be, the next step in the economic theories was to derive a sustainable yield from such a growth law. At each instant there is some specific size of population, which has a specific rate of growth if left alone. By ignoring potentially important questions about the size distribution, age distribution, and sex distribution of that population, the simpler theories derive a sustainable yield (SY) for each population value. Figure 17-4 illustrates sustainable yield, as a function of population. SY is the first derivative of the growth function with respect to time; that is, the slope of the growth function as a function of population value. It is the natural rate of population increase per unit time, an amount that could be taken from the fishery each year, forever, without changing the population.

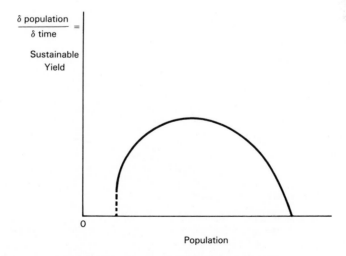

Figure 17-4 Sustainable Yields from a Fishery

In this literature, several assumptions are typical. There is atomistic competition within each fishery and among fisheries. The market price of fish is unaffected by the fishery's output. There are stock externalities, but—in the simplest theories—no crowding or other types of externalities. Live fish are common property, which is a euphemism for no property rights in live fish. That is, the law of capture is in effect: ownership is established by capture. Fishing catch is a function of the fishery population and the amount of fishing effort. To make life simple, assume that effort is supplied at a constant marginal and average cost per unit. Equal fishing effort catches few fish when the fishery population is small and many fish when it is large. Figure 17-5 shows this case, in which TR is the total sustainable revenue derivable from a fishery at a constant fish price, and TC is total fishing cost.

Entry is open to all. Each of many fishing firms maximizes its profit, given the price of fish and costs as it perceives them. Given the biological laws assumed, each sustainable yield and total revenue can be got at two widely different sizes of populations, with significantly different total fishing effort. Little effort (and little total cost) is required to get it if the population is large, as at point B. Much effort (and much cost) is required to get it if the population is small, as at point C. But there is no way that free entry and law of capture can achieve the correct—higher—fish population by reducing total fishing effort. For that would produce positive profits. If profits should ever appear, entry would follow, increasing fishing effort and reducing population, dissipating the profits by building up costs. These problems do not occur when owners raise the same species in ponds or pens, as they increasingly do in the southern U.S., Asia, and Norway, for example.

According to this analysis, unregulated, open-entry fishery exploitation produces the wrong quantity of fish, and produces it at excessive costs. It dissipates the net value (rent) of the fishery by attracting too many boats and fishermen, who overfish. True mar-

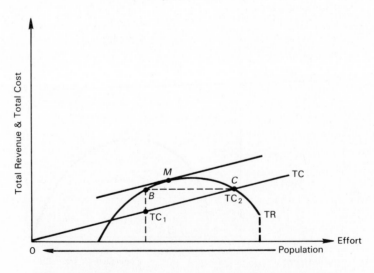

Figure 17-5 Open-Entry vs. Single-Owner Equilibrium for the Fishery

ginal cost is not equated with true marginal benefit, since no one is in command of the fishery to calculate the total cost and revenue effects of different levels of fishing activity. Net benefits from the fishery are not maximized. Neither is net economy-wide output.

To cure these disorders, governments have tried to achieve ''optimal''exploitation of the fishery through regulations, including taxes and limitations on entry, equipment, and catch. Much of the literature on fishery economics seems peculiar. What it considers ideal exploitation (and ideal regulation) is just what an unregulated single owner of the fishery would do. A single owner of the fishery would not dissipate its rents. It would maximize profits by equalizing marginal costs and marginal revenues; not by increasing total costs so as to eat up total revenue. That is, a sole owner would produce efficiently, as at point *M* in Figure 17-5, where marginal revenue and marginal cost are equal. One might think, therefore, that the object would be to achieve single-owner exploitation. Not at all. Instead, fishery regulators have used coercive regulations in trying to approximate what a sole owner would do voluntarily and as a matter of course to maximize its wealth.

It introduces what is, so to say, a red herring to claim that private property is not feasible when fish migrate long distances, through two or more state or national legal jurisdictions. It is true that some fish migrate over vast distances and that it would be too costly to mark and establish totally effective property rights in individual fish that can be caught on the high seas. It is also true that property rights limited to only those fish caught within one part of a fishery are not as good as property rights to all fish in the whole fishery. But that is no less true of the government regulations we now have. Governments now license, tax, and regulate fishing within those limited parts of the fisheries over which they have jurisdiction. If they can do that, they can surely accomplish a lesser task: create and enforce private property rights within the same parts of the fishery that they now regulate.

If a state, treaty organization, or any other entity can control, police, and exclude effectively enough to permit it to control entry, to regulate, or to tax, it has enough power to create at least partial property rights and to sell the resource. After all, the fundamental condition for creating property rights is the ability to exclude nonowners. If that condition can be met, property is feasible. Effective property rights require no more power to exclude than the government needs if it is effectively to tax *or* to exclude entrants under present regulations. And it would cost less in resources. No longer would the government have to regulate the minutest details of how and when fishermen catch fish. It is not obvious why it would have to determine the legal catch, either. But it could do so, at the cost of reducing the value of property rights in the fishery, and the maximum bids received for those rights.

Assume for now that the best way to create property rights is to sell the fishery at auction. The amount bid would depend upon what, if anything, the state agreed to do about policing and enforcing property rights, among other things. Indeed, a sale mechanism permits optimal policing by the low-cost policing agency. Compulsory merger or unitization would accomplish similar results.

Low income is a classic problem for fishermen the world over, and some have defended the present regulatory system as a good way to solve it. It has not worked. If the fishery management literature is correct, unit operation would lower costs and increase total rent. Selling a fishery at auction, for example, would provide funds that could be used to buy out present fishing firms, to police property rights, and for other useful purposes. The successful bidder could reemploy such fishermen as it needed.

Although the fishery management ideal has seemed to be what a sole-owner would accomplish, actual government regulation has not even come close to what a sole owner would do. In addition to its direct costs, regulation has created inefficiencies of its own. Entry limitations made it worthwhile for individual firms to devote resources to getting the quota, resulting in the sorts of rent dissipation exposed in other connections by Gordon Tullock, Anne Krueger, and others. Restrictions on the number of boats or firms encouraged other means of adjustment, and raised costs. Bigger and faster boats raised costs and dissipated rents. Governmental limitations on fishing gear and techniques inevitably created production-cost inefficiencies. Short seasons, small catch limits, and technically inefficient fishing gear are examples. Short seasons increase the amount of fish that has to be frozen, reducing its value to consumers, and lowering its price; and raising costs in the bargain.

Legitimate analyses should compare the effects of no regulations at all, the regulations specifically proposed, and creating and selling property rights in the fishery. If we know who gained from the types of commercial fishing regulations we have now, we might better explain how we came to have them. At some point, government faced a choice of rules, including property rights. Why it chose regulation is not certain.

Crude Oil

The U.S. oil industry started in Pennsylvania in 1859—before the climactic buffalo kills began. Strange though it may sound, the early history of crude oil production in the U.S. is similar to that of buffalo hunting. Oil is a good deal more important case than buffalo. Buffalo would have become a pest; oil involves greater economic values, and it is still theoretically possible to do something about it.

Even people in the industry refer to oil "pools," a misnomer carried over from the old days. Crude oil does not occur as lakes or pools locked away in underground caverns. It is found in the small spaces of rocks such as sandstone and limestone, which are more or less porous. If its pores are highly interconnected and petroleum can be moved through it readily, a formation is said to be permeable. Porosity and permeability vary within and among reservoirs. Formations that are relatively impermeable or tight may need fracturing or chemical treatment to produce. Oldtimers used explosives (torpedoes). Most crude oil is lighter than water, and is usually under considerable natural pressure when found. These pressures arise from energies in the reservoir. Reservoirs differ greatly in the kinds and amounts of energy they contain. Gas may be dissolved in the oil itself or, separated, press upon the oil from top or flanks.

Sometimes huge subterranean bodies of water press upon the oil, as in the case of the East Texas field and some tremendous reservoirs in the Middle East. Lighter than water and under high pressure, oil will migrate through any cracks or holes at which resistance is lower. Much of the oil originally in place long since migrated and disappeared in just that way as the earth shifted and cracked over the millennia.

Any oil that we have discovered was trapped and held by one or more formations of impermeable material.[36] Indeed, most prospecting for oil relies on locating unusual geological formations—anomalies—that are capable of trapping petroleum if there had been any about. Not all geological anomalies contain oil. Unfortunately, too, the characteristics of petroleum-bearing formations—reservoirs—vary considerably and it takes time and money to figure out how big each one is and how it works even after it has been located. Nor is it obvious how much oil there is in total, or how it is distributed within the reservoir. Although knowledge about such things has improved over time, estimates still vary greatly.

In any case, suppose that a new reservoir is discovered by drilling a well. High reservoir energies start flushing the oil out of the rock pores, pushing it towards the well bore. If all relevant information could be got quickly, intelligently coordinated use of the reservoir energy could get more oil out of the reservoir and get it out more cheaply. The reservoir energies are there for the asking, whereas pumps and pumping cost money.

Much depends upon what kind of reservoir it is and at the beginning it is hard to be sure.[37] Reservoir energies, which can decrease lifting costs and increase the quantity of oil ultimately recovered, may be conserved or wasted, depending, among other things, upon how many wells are drilled, where they are drilled, and the rate of flow permitted from each and all wells.

Perhaps the best illustration is a gas cap reservoir, in which oil and gas are both trapped in a single formation shaped like an inverted saucer. Gas is lighter than oil, and all of it is in a domed cap at the top of the formation. The oil is below the gas. If, by lucky accident or good planning, only the lower, flanking parts of the formation were drilled into first, the gas cap would expand like a spring, pushing the oil down the flanks to the well-bores and up to the surface. If the rate of oil withdrawal were not too fast, the gas would push evenly on the whole gas-oil contact, preserving a stable and even front and moving the oil out in a steady wave. Variations in permeability within the reservoir would not then be as menacing. Relatively little oil would be bypassed, cut off, and left behind. The same advantages could be got in water-drive reservoirs, by withdrawing the oil slowly enough to permit the water front to advance evenly and steadily. This would preserve reservoir pressures, reduce costs, and increase the amount of oil ultimately recovered.

On the other hand, the first wells might have been drilled into the gas cap itself, or close to the original line along which gas and oil had been in contact. If such wells were allowed to flow, all gas or mostly gas would be produced, quickly dissipating the gas cap and the energy it could have supplied. Getting oil out then requires pumps, or injecting fluids or gas, the costs of which could, in principle, have been avoided or deferred. And less oil would be recovered in the end.

Similar but less obvious problems can occur with dissolved-gas and water-drive reservoirs. In the first case, overly rapid withdrawal rates will bring pressure down to the bubble point, causing gas to come out of solution and race to the well-bores, marooning oil in the process. Both by lowering pressure and raising oil viscosity, this raises ultimate costs and reduces oil recovery. Viscous oil is difficult to move and may be lost. One symptom of excessive withdrawal rates is a high gas-oil ratio: lots of gas is produced per barrel of oil. Significant bypassing and loss of oil may also occur in water-drive reservoirs. In that case, symptoms are a high water-oil ratio and rapid decline in bottom-hole pressure. This happened in the East Texas field.

All this suggests that—for some kinds of reservoirs, at least—the placement of wells and the total rate of oil, water, and gas withdrawal affect costs, the total amount of oil recovered, as well as the discounted present value of oil recovered. Some reservoirs are *not* rate sensitive, including some on pump from the start, and some past the "flush production" stage.

Furthermore, the total fixed costs committed to a reservoir affect the total oil recovered per dollar invested, and there are sensible limits to how far such investments should be pushed for any reservoir. Major investments include the costs of land clearance and preparation; roads; well drilling and completion; and a variety of complementary equipment, including tanks, gathering and long-distance pipelines, and so on. Some of these appurtenances are subject to substantial economies of size. Examples are pipelines and tanks, the total costs of which can be kept down by having fewer and bigger ones. It is not only rule-of-capture exploitation that drives up costs. Some regulations, for example, prohibit commingling oil from different leases—or even different producing horizons— requiring more and smaller tanks. Some costs are sensitive to depth and other characteristics of the reservoir itself. Drilling costs, for example, rise exponentially with depth. For many reservoirs, it is possible to exhaust all the rents by drilling too many wells. Others produce from enormously thick oil-bearing formations and can tolerate a lot of drilling.

Finally, drilling and producing rigs require a certain amount of space. Even as late as the 1920s and 1930s drilling was sometimes so dense that derrick bases almost touched. Signal Hill and Santa Fe Springs, in California and parts of the East Texas field, were examples. Early photographs suggest that Russian oil fields looked similar in the early days. This is curious, because the czar owned oil in Russia and could have leased land so as to maximize rents from the reservoirs.[38] In any case, crowding raises surface drilling and operating costs.

None of these physical and economic characteristics poses insuperable problems when property rights in a reservoir are well specified. It is always true, of course, that information is costly and imperfect, which makes actual results worse than they would have been if only information could have been perfect and free. It is also true that we now know more about oil reservoirs, and most other things, than people knew in 1859 or 1932. Hindsight is not fair, and may not be relevant. Nor is judging the real world by unattainable ideals.

Problems arose in the U.S. because of the combined effects of legal principles and the pattern of surface ownership. We inherited from England the antique principle that the owner of land owns whatever minerals lie beneath it. Much of the rest of the world operated under older and very different laws and rights: the state owns subsurface minerals. It is paradoxical that in 1934, when oil was discovered in the British Isles, England abandoned the very rule we had inherited from her and kept. It is conceivable, however, that we may have come to much the same result in the U.S., whichever rules we adopted. Note, for example, how we have handled fish and other resources that the state *does* claim to own.

It was one thing to assert that surface owners own whatever oil underlies their property. It is quite another to enforce such a law. For one thing, no one really knows how much oil is under a specific property. For another, oil production in this country commenced after much of the country had been settled and there were typically many surface owners of lands overlying each oil reservoir. In some cases, whole towns sat on top of oil reservoirs. Hundreds or thousands of surface owners were already in place when the oil was found. This meant that ownership units normally did not coincide even approximately with the reservoir limits.

Problems arose at once. Experience showed that increased output from a neighbor's wells reduced the rate of flow from one's own. Lawsuits blossomed. Landowners claimed that neighbors were causing oil to migrate from beneath their land, and were taking it. They sought damages and injunctions. A workable legal rule would have to be applicable without endless and paralyzing litigation. By reaching back into the law with respect to percolating waters and wandering wild beasts, the law found one way out.[39] It emerged with what has come to be known as the rule of capture, which roughly provides that whoever reduces the oil to possession owns it, regardless of whether it has migrated from beneath a neighbor's land.[40] This is the rule that applied to buffalo hunting. Such a rule is easily applied, which is a merit in law; but it has some unhappy consequences. To achieve favorable drainage, and prevent unfavorable migration, any landowner may benefit by vigorous drilling to the limits of his property line, and by rapid withdrawal. What each finds it desirable to do may be done by all in a frenzy of "offset drilling." That is, a landowner would drill wells just within his property lines, and his neighbors would do likewise, hoping at least to cancel (offset), and perhaps to override effects of the others' wells. As George Stocking showed in his 1925 classic,[41] the first wave of wells formed patterns like the old British hollow squares of infantry, each neatly bordering a property over the reservoir.

As a consequence, reservoirs tended to be overdrilled and exploited too rapidly—or at least that is often said. It is not so easily proved, because costs of alternative arrangements were not zero, and it may not even have been clear what the alternatives were. In any case, drilling and development were much more costly, and reservoir energies were used less effectively than if a single coordinated effort could have been undertaken free. Wells were forced onto the pump early in the game, after a prolific period of flush or natural production had passed.

The story of oil production in the U.S. raises interesting questions. For example, just how large *were* the losses under rule of capture? And, similarly, if the losses were as great as claimed, why couldn't voluntary arrangements—contracts, agreements, mergers—have straightened everything out without producing the kinds of regulatory side effects that will be criticized later? And just what is it that makes it infeasible to avoid an enormous amount of what looks like waste? Is there evidence that state prorationing has done more good than harm? Finally, how—if at all—could the state contribute to a saner solution?

Did the rule of capture increase production costs substantially? A lot of evidence suggests that it raised them enormously. Exactly how much, of course, depends upon what alternative we use as a standard and upon whether the costs of achieving it have been counted in. In principle, there are several alternatives to rule-of-capture exploitation, including merger of some or all ownership interests in the field; private agreements to limit output; private unit development or unit production, or both; various kinds of state regulations; and so on.

In spite of the very large gains they seemed to offer, voluntary arrangements, including mergers and unitization, apparently were not used much. "As early as 1916, the U.S. Bureau of Mines called for unitization of U.S. oil fields; yet, by 1947, Joe Bain found only 12 fully unitized fields out of some 3,000 U.S. fields sampled."[42] One problem was that merger and unitization require for each lease estimates that are costly to make and subject to large errors. Another was that law was hostile in various ways. Some private agreements were made covertly, in fear of state and federal antitrust laws. Then, too, as discussed later, some states imposed other kinds of prohibitive restrictions. Though perhaps they produced few *reservoir-wide* units, voluntary private agreements were and are common in California. They deserve more study.

It is often said, however, that the fatal problem was prohibitive costs of reaching agreement when the number of producers is large, as it often was. "By March 1931, the Herfindahl-Index numbers equivalent based on well ownership was 64.6. By early 1933, there were over 1,000 small firms and 10,000 wells on the East Texas field."[43] There may be several interrelated problems, rather than just one. Together, they inhibit voluntary arrangements. First, as Coase demonstrated, prospects for contracting are grim when not even the legal *principles* of ownership and use have been established. By the 1880s, if not before, courts had begun articulating the law of capture reasonably clearly.[44] Second, even when the law is clear about what it takes to establish ownership, it is hard to buy, sell, or agree when nobody knows how much the negotiating parties really own. Part of the problem, of course, is that oil is hidden underground. When a reservoir is being developed, estimates of total oil in place vary greatly and change fast. How much oil underlies an individual lease is more uncertain yet. This physical obscurity complicates outright purchases of oil in place, under several alternative property rules.

Third, which property rule is in effect also affects uncertainties about reserves, outputs, and costs. How we are permitted to obtain and use property can affect what we do. Under the law of capture, for example, output from each lease depends not only upon how much oil underlies it, but upon what law permits the operator to do. The oil reserves and output that a firm will bring to (or keep out of) a unit or merger depend not only upon how much oil lies within its surface property lines; but also upon how much it can drain from other properties. The operator of a small lease in a big field is naturally more interested in draining from others' leases than he is in how the reservoir as a whole is affected by total *field* output, to which his contribution is relatively slight. Anyhow, as has been said in the oil fields for years, an operator is in a stronger position to negotiate a larger share if he quickly drills up his lease and is already producing at a fast clip by the time people start talking about rational exploitation. And, unfortunately, much damage can already have been done before serious negotiations are started, given the law of capture.

Analogously with small firms that will not join cartels unless they are either coerced or given a larger share than their size suggests, small oil producers have an incentive to stand outside unit agreements or mergers of ownership interests in the field. If there are enough firms of this kind, only compulsion can make coordination work.

Fourth, unconcentrated ownership causes other problems besides the incentive effects just discussed. Coase showed that the sheer number of firms can raise transactions costs prohibitively even in the absence of spillover effects. That is another reason why it would be nice to choose good rules at the start.

It is the technical and ownership problems just discussed that led many disinterested conservationists and economists to propose what they claimed were better solutions. A leading candidate is operating each reservoir as a single technological unit. This is called unitization or unit operation. Following McDonald, the theoretic advantages can be put formally.[45]

In maximizing the present value of net benefits from oil reservoirs, several related dimensions must be considered. A basic one is allocating production rates over time. Related is the question of the right number of wells, a complicated problem discussed only generally here. To simplify and shorten the exposition, assume that there are only two relevant time periods: time 0—the present, and time T—the future. Designate marginal net revenue by MNR. In general, MNR is the change in net revenue that could be produced by shifting a barrel of production from one period to the other. B measures the change in total oil ultimately recovered from a reservoir by shifting production between periods. In some kinds of reservoirs, as we have seen, increasing the current production rate will lower ultimate recovery. Reducing the current rate will increase it. In his example, McDonald has $B = .048$. That is, deferring production of one barrel will increase total ultimate recovery by .048 barrels. The relevant discount rate is r.

From the standpoint of a sole owner of a reservoir, or unit manager, maximizing the present value of net revenues requires achieving the following equality:

$$MNR_0 = (1 + B_T) [MNR_T / (1 + r)^T]$$

Under the law of capture and uncoordinated atomistic exploitation, each operator has a very different problem than a sole owner would have. A new factor intrudes. If I don't produce a barrel now I will *not* recover all of it later. The problem is adverse drainage. Call it X. X is the fraction of a barrel that neighbors will drain in period T if I postpone producing one barrel now, in period 0. McDonald uses $X = .12$. This negative factor tends to pull down my future net revenues:

$$MNR_0 = (1 - X_T) (1 + B_T) [MNR_T / (1 + r)^T]$$

As a result, the right-hand side of the equation is smaller than it would be under unit operation. Reestablishing the equality also reduces value of MNR_0. More production is shifted to the present, driving up marginal cost.

Furthermore, if it were costless to achieve, unit operation would raise the expected profitability of exploratory prospects, increasing exploration. That abstracts from the effects that unitization might have on oil prices. It also abstracts from the larger effects that state regulations produced. A single firm in charge of a whole reservoir would operate it as efficiently as information and law permit. In the early days of the U.S. industry, however, that was not to be. Libecap and Wiggins show how—commencing in 1930—the *federal* government accomplished an uncommon amount of unitization on federal lands.[46] In that year, Congress amended the Mineral Leasing Act of 1920 by empowering the Bureau of Land Management to compel unitization. The amendment was a "response to competitive extraction on the North Dome Kettleman Hills field of California that was reducing federal royalty income."[47] Compulsory unitization on federal lands requires only a simple majority vote of the operators involved and typically starts early, at the *exploration* stage. Federal lands did not, however, produce much oil during the industry's formative period. Much more research could be done on this subject, including a comparative analysis of federal offshore leases.

By contrast with federal policies, state governments did little to establish or approximate property rights to oil in the reservoir, which would have permitted a more rational organization. For example, what would happen if the owner of a discovery well gets rights to unitize the reservoir, analogously to patent principles? Law in some states, notably Texas, was hostile to unit agreements and handicapped them. They had to be approved by the Railroad Commission (RC); and could not increase field output above the per-well output schedule applied state wide to nonunitized fields. As we will see, private conservation in California was attacked under the federal antitrust laws.

This does not mean that the states did nothing. Many conservation regulations had been imposed in various states, some of them early in the industry's history. For example, regulations required sealing well bores to prevent leakage into sources of drinking water; and outlawed drilling into and drowning coal mines, hurtfully disposing of wastes, recklessly venting or flaring gas, and the like. Some laws sought to limit damage to the reservoirs by encouraging wider well-spacing and denouncing "underground waste." In general, wider well-spacing laws came in after other state regulations had already encouraged overdrilling and dense well-spacing.

But the basic property rights problem remained. Reform policies ran into two principal problems. First, how could every landowner be given a chance to get his fair share of oil in the reservoir? This was the equity problem that has long interfered with unit coordination and development, especially in Texas. The second was how to lower costs and increase the net value of production by somehow approximating what a single owner of the reservoir would do to maximize its own wealth. This can be called the efficiency problem. As is often true, the equity and efficiency goals conflicted, as did policies proposed to reach them. By the 1930s, attempts to accomplish these goals also got tangled up with attempts to control the *price* of oil.

As had been true from the beginning, demand for oil products in the U.S. grew steadily and large. One oil field after another was discovered, some of them large. Their histories were usually like this: because of ignorance, uncertainty, hostile law, high costs of organizing large numbers of independent oil operators, or other reasons, very few reservoirs were developed as units. It was every man for himself. If there were many operators, and perhaps even if there were only a few, each developed his drilling pattern and production rate independently, without regard for any influence on aggregate efficiency.

What were the consequences of all this? First, investment costs for the reservoir were higher than if it had been developed as a unit. Second, because the ownership units and the reservoir—the technological unit—typically did not coincide, costs often rose as the rate of withdrawal from the reservoir rose, and much of the oil originally in place could not be recovered. Third, a series of competitive equilibria were established such that costs were equal to revenues at the margin, perhaps with substantial pockets of scarcity rents remaining. These equilibria were, of course, established by a growing number of participants in each new field, a growing number of wells, and a rising cost structure. Fourth, if the reservoir was very large, crude oil prices tended to fall as the field was exploited, to reach their nadir with the field's peak, then, more slowly, to rise as field output went into a protracted decline. A new discovery would start the process again.

In the 1920s a number of large oil fields were discovered and brought into rapid production. Oil prices fluctuated widely. Conservationists and others clamored that the actual results were far worse than could theoretically have been achieved under an ideal policy; for example, developing each reservoir as a single technological unit.

This is about where things stood until October 6, 1930, after the Great Depression had begun, and as oil demand fell. At that point, "Dad" Joiner discovered the East Texas oil field, a 5 to 6 billion barrel reservoir, the largest discovered anywhere up to that time, and the largest discovery in the U.S. until Prudhoe Bay (in Alaska).[48] The field covered a large area (it was more than 45 miles long), and was cheap to drill. The reservoir was only 3,400 feet below the surface. It was blessed with a powerful water-drive mechanism; it was cursed with a multitude of surface owners. A feverish exploitation followed, with 10 thousand wells completed in little more than a year and 20 thousand to 30 thousand wells all told. Production soared to more than 700,000 barrels per day before autumn 1931. The whole oil price structure eroded as this huge new wave of oil hit the markets. Different sources give different price histories. Some claim that prices at the East Texas field fell to 10 cents per barrel. One 50,000 barrel lot assertedly went for 2 ½ cents per barrel.

Some things are clear. Many well-located nonintegrated refining companies prospered. But oil operators and royalty owners were alarmed by the current and expected crude oil price levels, and they were not alone. The prosperity of land-grant universities, school districts, and other nonprofit institutions was threatened by low oil prices, the result of huge output increases in the face of an inelastic market demand. And some engineers and conservationists bemoaned the technical effects of field developments that were rapid, massive, and uncoordinated. They feared that the East Texas reservoir was being butchered and wasted: pressures were being dissipated wantonly and, in the end, too much oil would be left in the ground.

Various motives were, thus, behind the growing clamor to do something. In the beginning nothing seemed to work, and conservation orders were ignored or flouted. Lawsuits proliferated. In 1931, the governor of Texas read the riot act, put troops into the field and temporarily shut it down. The overall crude oil price structure then rose significantly, a phenomenon that no one concerned ever forgot. From the beginning of effective market demand prorationing (MDP) in Texas and Louisiana, there can be no doubt that the state conservation authorities were interested in and affected by the level and stability of crude oil prices.[49] With few exceptions they have denied any interest in influencing prices.

Oil conservation regulations are bewilderingly complex. Rules and practices vary among states and over time. Several helpful studies attempt to sort them out.[50] For brevity and generality, we will discuss a stylized version of what the Railroad Commission of Texas (RC) did.

Texas law was directed to prevent various kinds of waste. First, physical waste, which occurs, for example, when the ultimate physical recovery of oil from a reservoir is not maximized; or when oil is poured out onto the ground. Second, economic waste, a rubric that implicitly covers notions like fair and stable prices. By legal definition, economic waste occurs whenever oil production exceeds reasonable market demand. Far from requiring unit development and operation, Texas law discouraged it. Notions of equity were politicized and codified into operating rules, exemptions, and exceptions. Anyone who assumes that the mass of RC regulations was designed to or did approximate the outcomes of sole-owner operations is in for a shock.

Differences between sole-owner and regulated operation are numerous and important. Well-spacing is one. Output rate is another. Cost minimization is another. There is also this amusing, though admittedly minor, example. Lovejoy and Homan report that:

> In 1962, two large operators in the East Texas field proposed that about seven-eighths of the wells in that field be abandoned and the field produced at the same rate from the remaining wells. The Texas Railroad Commission turned down the proposal on the grounds that it would depress the local economy that was dependent on the payrolls in the field.[51]

The RC continually stressed the concept of the maximum efficient rate of production (MER), which, in loose talk, it implied was used both for individual reservoirs and aggregate state production.[52] As we have seen, the ultimate physical recovery from certain kinds of reservoirs is a function of the rate at which the reservoir produces. MER was claimed to be the highest rate of production that is consistent with maximum ultimate physical recovery. It was claimed to be a purely engineering or technological concept, which may have been meant to praise it. "Efficient" sounds good, and "maximum efficient" sounds even better. MER is an example of successful false advertising and image creation in the regulatory-political arena.

The merits of MER as a polestar are highly doubtful, since, as a purely physical concept, it ignores such economic variables as prices, interest rates, and costs. Future values must be discounted. When prices are stable over time and the interest rate is greater than zero, MER is smaller than the most efficient rate. In any case, it is clear that MER was used mainly as a political slogan and for public relations purposes. That is the polite way of putting it.[53] MERs, as RC used the term in public pronouncements, were estimated for only a few fields and were not updated. If calculated at all, MERs were effectively disregarded where they did exist. The basic problem was that several large fields had huge MERs that, if produced, would have depressed price and caused interfield equity problems.

MER computed for a field should be determined by how a specific reservoir behaves as a single technological unit. That, paradoxically, is how the subject is approached in California, which is *not* a MDP state! There, the notion is applied only to fields the ultimate recovery from which is sensitive to rate of extraction. Not so in Texas, where distinctions are not made between rate-sensitive and other reservoirs, and where the top-maximum total production that would ever be permitted for a reservoir (pool) is actually built up backwards from the number and characteristics of wells, not reservoirs.[54] It is the sum of legally permitted top-maximum production rates permitted to each well, a number got from the schedules and formulas that apply state wide. In Texas, individual reservoir conditions therefore have little or nothing to do with pool MER in any sense, and even less to do with the economically most efficient pool or aggregate state output rate.

RC rules had a great deal to do with equity: no matter how small, each landowner should get at least one well, and each should get a fair output share—enough to keep him whole. Well-spacing exceptions to achieve that became notorious. Members of the RC are elected by popular vote. Responsiveness is one measure of how well government works and the state government of Texas has been more responsive to the clamor of its numerous small oil lessors and operators than federal government has been. That, ironically, is one reason oil regulation by the state of Texas looks worse to outside experts than regulation by federal authorities. For one thing, basing production allowables on the number of wells, as Texas tended to do, encourages landowners and operators to drill too many wells. RC's early production orders for East Texas allowed 225 barrels per day per well. According to Libecap and Wiggins,

> . . . prorationing rules in East Texas contributed to the drilling of 23,000 unnecessary wells at a per well cost of $26,000. As the number of wells rose, quotas were reduced to maintain targeted field output levels. They fell from 225 barrels per well in September 1931 to 37 barrels by December 1932. . . . Texas . . . gave special quotas of 40 barrels to high-cost pumping wells, more than . . . to free-flowing wells in East Texas. Accordingly, firms placed pumping units on their wells at a cost of $3,500 per well to qualify for the larger allocation.[55]

This bias toward small holders took other forms, too, and persisted until the courts struck them down in 1961 and 1962.[56] And deeper, higher cost wells got larger allowables. Wells with the highest cost were totally exempt from output regulation.

That is not all. For years on end, RC held legally permissible production far below either a real engineering MER or the scheduled top maximum allowable. Their avowed rationale was to prevent economic waste. The mechanism they used was market demand prorationing (MDP). The RC followed two basic principles. First, in no case may a well or reservoir produce more oil than its "yardstick" or "schedule" top-maximum allowable. This, ostensibly, prevents physical waste. Second, each month the RC determined the reasonable market demand (RMD) for Texas oil. Total state production could not exceed reasonable market demand for the month. It is commonly said that reasonable market demand was the amount RC expected purchasers of Texas oil to buy at current prices. That may be so, although it seems to make crude oil price changes a result of estimating errors rather than something else. In fact, prices were remarkably stable over long periods. California has not used the reasonable market demand concept since World War II.

RC applied its principles in several steps. It exempted from production controls certain types and categories of wells. These exempt wells included marginal or "stripper" wells that, because of high costs and moribund reservoirs, produced at very low rates, often less than ten barrels a day. But there were thousands of such wells and their aggregate output was large. The first step was to shelter these wells by letting them run flat out, and deducting their total expected output from the state wide reasonable market demand figure RC had arrived at.

Reasonable Market Demand (RMD) *minus* exempt production was what remained for the restricted (prorated) reservoirs and wells. RC allocated this output on a well-by-well, state wide basis. Suppose, for example, that RC set total RMD at 3 million barrels per day, and expected exempt wells to produce 1 million barrels per day. Two million barrels per day remained for the prorated wells. Suppose that their top-maximum schedule allowable totaled 3 million. The actual allowable production of each prorated well in the whole state then became two-thirds of its nominal schedule allowable.

This procedure produced several important effects. First, for unitized as well as the other prorated wells, price was substantially greater than marginal costs. Second, marginal costs were not brought to equality among different classes of wells. Costs were not minimized. Third, idle capacity had been artificially created, maintained, and increased. A member of RC estimated that, in 1956—when the first Suez Crisis began—Texas could have produced at least one million additional barrels per day without exceeding schedule allowables or damaging the reservoirs.[57] In 1962 and 1963, RC held prorated wells to 28 percent of their schedule allowables. Those marginal wells that were exempted if they produced 19-½ barrels per day, were running flat out at those rates. At the same time, thousands of lower-cost prorated wells in the East Texas field were held to 5-⅓ barrels per day.[58] It is clear that, even after World War II—from 1948 to 1972—Texas production was artificially held far below economic capacity. Furthermore, high cost wells got a larger share than they would have got under unregulated competition, private monopoly, or unit operation. It is illegal to buy and transfer production quotas. The RC claims that transferring quotas would shut down some wells and leave oil in the ground.

Fourth, many claimed that crude oil conservation in Texas operated like a cartel. In some respects that is true, depending upon what kind of cartel one has in mind. One example is the continued exploration, drilling, and growth of crude oil reserves. When any cartel fixes a price above the competitive level, entry will occur unless effective barriers can be erected. Entry into new fields was not restricted, and new wells got (at least) an aliquot share. If demand does not increase faster than entry, idle capacity will grow under cartel conditions. Entry will go forward until one of various possibilities materializes. The cartel may lose its grip: outsiders bulk so large that the cartel is impotent to do more than establish a competitive price, and the end is at hand. The industry will now be too large by competitive standards, and a painful period of adjustment will have to be undergone, unless growth in demand comes to the rescue. If, instead, state or other regulations preserve the cartel price, entry will continue until costs are bid up, permitting only a normal return to anyone entering; or each firm will have such a reduced share of the trade as to yield only a normal return because of the high cost of part-time operation. Some rationalization should then be expected to occur, if firms are permitted to pool and reallocate outputs, or to merge. In neither case was the economy well served, even though capacity grew enormously. For years, as the general cartel model suggests, excess crude producing capacity grew in the United States. And crude oil prices behaved in a way that defies a competitive explanation.

Conservation regulations of the sort RC imposed are worse than the simple cartel hypothesis suggests. Private cartels have an incentive to minimize costs by producing in the lowest cost facilities. The least efficient may be shut down entirely. But in Texas marginal properties were favored and produced more than they would have under either common-property competition, unit exploitation, or a well-run private cartel. Thus, "conservation" policy sharply curtailed output from rich flowing wells while stripper wells went full tilt, as might be expected of elected officials governing an industry that includes many small producers. The Suez crisis (October 1956 to Spring 1957) furnishes a pointed example. Even though under heavy pressures from the federal government, RC refused to increase allowable production selectively, rather than across the board for the state as a whole. Buyers wanted crude at the Gulf of Mexico, where it also could have been produced at lowest cost. But the RC refused a "discriminatory" allowable increase there. Possible reasons include political implications and difficulties in transferring payments from those privileged by cost and location to the other producers who would have had to acquiesce in the scheme.

Note that this type of arrangement does not seem to maximize the benefits even of the oil producers themselves. For the quotas of high-cost wells cannot be sold and applied to the production of low cost producers. One virtue claimed for RC regulation was that it stabilized oil prices. Statistical analysis confirms that result, if not its virtue. Risk doubtless imposes costs. So does stopping, starting, and changing the rate of production. As a response to these problems, years ago D. Gale Johnson advocated forward-price guarantees for agricultural products.[59] One practical problem, of course, is that government agencies with the power to reduce the variance of prices have the more valuable power to change the level of prices. They generally use it, as they did in oil.

In any case, one defense of market demand prorationing was that it protected marginal wells, which numbered in the thousands and taken together served substantial total reserves. The notion was that wide price fluctuations would force marginal wells to be abandoned prematurely, losing large reserves in the process. This would happen, the story went, because temporary shutdowns would become permanent abandonments. Shut-down wells sometimes suffer increased corrosion and sometimes lose circulation and do not resume production. There is considerable doubt that the problem is serious even on a physical or engineering level.

Judged by (the more relevant) economic criteria, the problem of abandonment and loss is still less important, if it exists at all. The operator of a marginal oil property will abandon it only when its present operating worth (taking alternatives into account) falls to zero or below. He will take into account as best he can the future costs and benefits of any reserves that will be lost. If knowledge were perfect, he would not abandon because of temporarily low prices, but only when the reserves are simply not worth keeping, and society should not grieve. If there is general error or irrationality, of course, some reserves would be abandoned when they should not be, and some would be kept when they should be abandoned. But there is a market for oil properties, and differences of opinion are responsible for other things than horse races. If anything, mistakes are more likely to produce too little abandonment than too much.[60] In any event, it is difficult to legislate against error, if for no other reason than that legislators and regulators themselves are also subject to it.

If the problem is that some operators in a reservoir will shut down while others will not, that problem can be attacked directly, as in fact it is, rather than through an elaborate system of price maintenance.

Before choosing the rules of the game, it would help to appraise the costs and benefits of alternative arrangements. That is no easy job. The alternatives include:

Law-of-capture exploitation

Engineering MER production limits, set reservoir by reservoir

Reasonable market demand prorationing, as seen in Texas

Voluntary unitization

Compulsory unitization

On paper, at least, unit operation looks like a clear winner. Under unit development and operation, there is one managerial unit in charge. There is no adverse drainage. Tremendous monopoly power is not likely to be created: even the largest domestic field provides a relatively small part of the total crude supply. A prudent unit operator will seek to minimize costs, and will not overdrill or produce oil too fast. Although compulsion may be necessary to achieve much unitization, a case can be made for it. It can be argued that unit development imposes an unrealistically great burden on knowledge and prudence, and may impose a heavy burden of coercion. But those burdens are not less under meticulous state regulation of production on a well-by-well basis. There are about 200 thousand wells in the state of Texas alone.

Real MER limits, or voluntary MER goals—as used by the California system—seem clearly better than either the rule of capture or Texas's market demand proration system. The Texas system seems to be so bad that it is not clearly better than the anarchistic rule of capture.[61] Taking into account discount factors, how much—if at all—are net values increased by the Texas programs? To say that physical recovery was increased is only to begin the argument, not to end it. For crude oil controls in the United States include state-created monopoly elements, and encouraged redundant capacity for such output as they permitted. Restrictive import policies enhanced these resource-allocation effects.

The most favorable case for regulations that Texas imposed would be that they minimized costs, which does not seem to have been the case. But in theory, it is not hard to show how a monopoly that produces even at zero costs may charge higher prices, and distort resource allocation more, than competitors struggling under a substantial cost burden. It is also true that a low-cost monopoly may produce larger net benefits than a higher-cost competition. Most experts seem to believe that even the Texas system was better than unregulated anarchy in oil.

Most experts seem to believe that it is not enough to stop at *voluntary* unitization.

There may be too many explanations of why there has been so little voluntary unitization. First, it was too costly to obtain voluntary agreements soon enough to do much good. Second, states like Texas actually discouraged unitization, and there is some evidence that the federal antitrust laws were hostile to private arrangements that were much more limited than that. In 1950, for example, the U.S. Department of Justice brought an antitrust suit against the Conservation Committee of California Oil Producers.[62] That suit was eventually dropped, about 1958.

Better answers might be got by studying experience on the outer continental shelf (OCS), where the federal government claims to own all the oil reservoirs and where unitization should have been easy to accomplish. Alaska should also be studied, as should the outcomes on all state and federal lands.

In practice, it seems unlikely that state regulations, taxes, and restrictions on entry and methods of production, can flexibly adjust to different market prices, or to technological and other changes that single owners adjust to routinely.

The next chapter discusses public-utility-type regulation and price and output controls in U.S. agriculture.

SUMMARY

The economic objective in dealing with external effects is to maximize net benefits of interrelated activities, *not* to minimize harms. Someone once said that without smoke Pittsburgh would have remained a small and poor village.

Technical facts surrounding specific externalities often determine whether a spillover is trivial or important; but in the absence of property rights problems it is arguable that there would be no such problems at all. It may seem strange, then, that regulatory efforts to solve such problems produce very different results than we might expect single or cooperating private owners to try for.

Government can improve the efficiency with which resources such as buffalo, fish, and crude oil are exploited. Its most obvious contribution is to help create and maintain property rights in the resources.

There is no doubt, either, that government has typically gone far beyond that role, with questionable results. Important examples seem to be radio and TV, land use, fish, and crude oil.

QUESTIONS

1. Explain what a spillover or externality is. Give examples of positive as well as negative spillovers.
2. "Radio and TV involves spillovers, all right; but the web of regulations that we got far exceeds what is necessary to solve that problem, creates monopoly, and bestows huge windfall gains on licensees." Explain and comment.

3. Coase noted that the government could have sold rights to radio and TV frequencies by auctioning them off to the highest bidders. Is this inconsistent with how Chapter 2 of this book suggests that franchise rights in a city stadium "ought" to be sold? Discuss and explain.

4. Is there an argument for "taxing" those who hear the airport noise as well as those who make it?

5. Explain the law of capture. Why would anyone adopt such an apparently bizarre scheme?

6. Explain the kinds of stock externalities and crowding externalities that can arise in commercial fishing.

7. In general terms, explain the sorts of regulations that have been used to regulate commercial fishing. How do these regulations compare with what would happen in a single-owner fishery?

8. Explain the kinds of externalities that arose in crude oil exploration and production in the U.S.

9. Explain and evaluate the following cures for externalities in the oil industry:
   Voluntary or mandatory unit development
   Engineering MER production ceilings, voluntary or mandatory
   Texas-style reasonable market demand prorationing

NOTES

1. G. J. Stigler and Claire Friedland, "What Can Regulators Regulate?" *Journal of Law & Economics*, 5 (October 1962), pp. 1–16.

2. G. J. Stigler, "The Theory of Economic Regulation," *The Bell Journal of Economics and Management Science*, 2 (Spring 1971), pp. 3–21.

3. Ibid., p. 18.

4. Richard A. Posner, "Taxation by Regulation," *The Bell Journal*, 2 (Spring 1971), pp. 22–50.

5. Richard A. Posner, "Theories of Economic Regulation," *The Bell Journal of Economics and Management Science*, 5 (Autumn 1974), pp. 335–58.

6. Ibid., p. 350.

7. Sam Peltzman, "Toward a More General Theory of Regulation," *Journal of Law & Economics*, 19 (August 1976), pp. 211–44.

8. John S. McGee, "Pricing in Publicly-Controlled Industries: U.S.A.," in D. C. Hague, ed. *Price Formation in Various Economies* (London: MacMillan Company, 1964), pp. 68–81.

9. Ronald H. Coase, "The Federal Communications Commission," *Journal of Law & Economics*, 2 (October 1959), pp. 1–40; George J. Stigler, "The Regulation of the Securities Markets," *Journal of Business*, 37 (April 1964), reprinted in Stigler, *The Citizen and the State: Essays on Regulation* (Chicago: University of Chicago Press, 1975), pp. 78–100; Thomas Moore, "Stock Market Margin Requirements," *Journal of Political Economy*, 74 (April 1966); Irving Schweiger and John McGee, "Chicago Banking," *Journal of Business*, 34 (July 1961); Sam Peltzman, "Entry in Commercial Banking," *Journal of Law & Economics*, 8 (October 1965), pp. 11–50; A. D. Tussing, "The Case for Bank Failure," *Journal of Law*

& Economics, 10 (October 1967), pp. 129–47; Linda Edwards and Franklin Edwards, "Measuring the Effectiveness of Regulation: the Case of Bank Entry Regulation," *Journal of Law & Economics*, 17 (October 1974), pp. 445–57.

For discussions of buffalo, fish, and crude oil, other examples of spillovers, see following sections of this chapter.

10. For a recent sampling of studies about consumer-protection regulations, see the papers prepared for a recent conference: "Consumer Protection Regulation: A Conference Sponsored by the Center for the Study of the Economy and the State," *Journal of Law & Economics*, 24 (December 1981).

See also Roger W. Weiss, "The Case for Federal Meat Inspection Examined," *Journal of Law & Economics*, 7 (October 1964), pp. 107–20; Paul W. MacAvoy, ed., *Federal Milk Marketing Orders and Price Supports* (Washington, D.C.: American Enterprise Institute, 1977); R. A. Ippolito and R. T. Masson, "The Social Cost of Government Regulation of Milk," *Journal of Law & Economics*, 21 (April 1978), pp. 33–65; Sam Peltzman, "An Evaluation of Consumer Protection Legislation: 1962 Drug Amendments," *Journal of Political Economy*, 81 (September/October 1973), pp. 1049–91; H. Grabowski, J. Vernon, and L. Thomas, "Estimating the Effects of Regulation on Innovation: An International Comparative Analysis of the Pharmaceutical Industry," *Journal of Law & Economics*, 21 (April 1978), pp. 133–63; L. Schneider, B. Klein, and K. Murphy, "Governmental Regulation of Cigarette Health Information," *Journal of Law & Economics*, 24 (December 1981), pp. 575–612; Raymond Urban and Richard Mancke, "Federal Regulation of Whiskey Labeling: From the Repeal of Prohibition to the Present," *Journal of Law & Economics*, 15 (October 1972), pp. 411–26; Janet Smith, "An Analysis of State Regulations Governing Liquor Store Licenses," *Journal of Law & Economics*, 25 (October 1982), pp. 301–19; Keith Leffler, "Physician Licensure: Competition and Monopoly in American Medicine," *Journal of Law & Economics*, 21 (April 1978), pp. 165–86; Lawrence Shephard, "Licensing Restrictions and the Cost of Dental Care," *Journal of Law & Economics*, 21 (April 1978), pp. 187–201; Deborah Haas-Wilson, "The Effect of Commercial Practice Restrictions: The Case of Optometry," *Journal of Law & Economics*, 29 [with a good bibliography] (April 1986), pp. 165–86; Lee Benham and Alexandra Benham, "Regulating Through the Professions: A Perspective on Information Control," *Journal of Law & Economics*, 18 (October 1975), pp. 421–47; Lee Benham, "The Effect of Advertising on the Price of Eyeglasses," *Journal of Law & Economics*, 15 (October 1972), pp. 337–52; William Lynk, "Regulatory Control of the Membership of Corporate Boards of Directors: The Blue Shield Case," *Journal of Law & Economics*, 24 (April 1981), pp. 159–73; Paul W. MacAvoy, ed., *Federal-State Regulation of the Pricing and Marketing of Insurance* (Washington, D.C.: American Enterprise Institute, 1977); P. E. Sand, "How Effective Is Safety Legislation?" *Journal of Law & Economics*, 11 (April 1968), pp. 165–79; Sam Peltzman, "The Regulation of Automobile Safety," in *Auto Safety Regulations: The Cure or the Problem?* eds. Henry G. Manne and Roger L. Miller (Glenridge, N.J.: Thomas Horton, 1976); Kenneth Clarkson, Charles W. Kadlec, and Arthur Laffer, *The Impact of Government Regulations on Competition in the U.S. Automobile Industry* (Boston: H. C. Wainright, 1979); Sam Peltzman, "The Effects of FTC Advertising Regulation," *Journal of Law & Economics*, 24 (December 1981), pp. 403–55; John C. Weicher, "Product Quality and Value in the New Home Market: Implications for Consumer Protection Regulation," ibid., pp. 365–97; Sanford Grossman, "The Informational Role of Warranties and Private Disclosures About Product Quality," ibid., pp. 461–83; Michael Darby and Edi Karni, "Free Competition and the Optimal Amount of Fraud," *Journal of Law & Economics*, 16 (April 1973), pp. 67–88.

11. R. H. Coase, "The Choice of the Institutional Framework: A Comment," *Journal of Law & Economics*, 17 (October 1974), pp. 493, 495.

12. See Kenneth W. Clarkson and Roger L. Miller, *Industrial Organization: Theory, Evidence, and Public Policy* (New York: McGraw-Hill Book Company, 1982), p. 453 (citing Center for the Study of American Business, Washington University, St. Louis); Paul W. MacAvoy, *The Regulated Industries and the Economy* (New York: W. W. Norton & Co., Inc., 1979); and Budgets of the U.S. Government.

On the growth of government overall, see G. Warren Nutter, *Growth of Government in the West* (Washington, D.C.: American Enterprise Institute, 1978); Sam Peltzman, "The Growth of Government," *Journal of Law & Economics*, 23 (October 1980), pp. 209–87; and Jack Hirschleifer, *Price Theory and Applications*, 3rd ed. (Englewood Cliffs, N.J.: Prentice-Hall, Inc., 1984), pp. 529–31.

13. *Journal of Law & Economics*, 2 (October 1959), pp. 1–40. Coase also wrote a second article about radio: "The Inter-department Radio Advisory Committee," *Journal of Law & Economics*, 5 (October 1962), pp. 17–47.

14. The problem is somewhat similar to those in buffalo hunting, crude oil production, and commercial fishing (cases discussed later).

15. Some might phrase it differently: "Even though government gave away the frequencies." For it is theoretically possible that prospective licensees, competing for a limited number of licenses, would have competed away all of the expected franchise values—through graft, for example. This does not appear to have happened.

16. For example, see Constance Mitchell, "Taft Will Sell 5 TV Stations For $240 Million," *The Wall Street Journal*, 18 November 1986, p. 20.

17. For example, see Jora Minasian, "Property Rights in Radiation: An Alternative Approach to Radio Frequency Allocation," *Journal of Law & Economics*, 18 (April 1975), pp. 221–72.

18. Ronald H. Coase, "The Problem of Social Cost," *Journal of Law & Economics*, 3 (October 1960), pp. 41–42.

19. W. F. Baxter and L. R. Altree, "Legal Aspects of Airport Noise," *Journal of Law & Economics*, 15 (April 1972), pp. 1–113.

20. R. H. Coase, "The Lighthouse in Economics," *Journal of Law & Economics*, 17 (October 1974), pp. 357–76.

21. Stephen N. S. Cheung, "The Fable of the Bees: An Economic Investigation," *Journal of Law & Economics*, 16 (April 1973), pp. 11–33; David B. Johnson, "Meade, Bees, and Externalities," ibid., pp. 35–52; and J. R. Gould, "Meade on External Economies: Should the Beneficiaries Be Taxed?" ibid., pp. 53–66.

22. Bernard H. Siegan, "Non-Zoning in Houston," *Journal of Law & Economics*, 13 (April 1970), pp. 71–147.

23. John P. Crecine, Otto A. Davis, and John E. Jackson, "Urban Property Markets: Some Empirical Results and Their Implications for Municipal Zoning," *Journal of Law & Economics*, 10 (October 1967), pp. 79–99; and F. H. Rueter, "Externalities in Urban Property Markets: An Empirical Test of the Zoning Ordinance of Pittsburgh," *Journal of Law & Economics*, 16 (October 1973), pp. 313–49.

24. When they came to the new world, Europeans often gave inappropriate names to wild creatures rather than using either technically correct names or those the Indians used. What most of us call buffalo are actually bison. What most of us call mountain goats are a type of antelope, and so on.

25. Perhaps the most relevant fishery-type model for explaining the history of our bison is Anderson's "forward-bending revenue curve" case, especially when average cost cuts it from below. Lee G. Anderson, *The Economics of Fisheries Management* (Baltimore: The Johns Hopkins University Press, 1977), pp. 96–98.

26. This may be so, although cartridges used by the Army would not fit the rifles that most of the professional buffalo hunters used. Many professional hunters reloaded their own ammunition in the field. Powder, lead, and the right size of primers would, therefore, have been useful to them.

27. James Allen Tober, *The Allocation of Wildlife Resources in the U.S., 1850–1900* (unpublished Ph.D. thesis, Yale University: 1974), p. 187.

28. A remarkable fight at Adobe Walls, in north Texas, seems to be an example, though perhaps fortuitous rather than planned.

29. The simpler fishery models *define* the (long-run) production functions as sustainable forever. For bison, the short-run solutions proved determinative, without either property rights or regulations.

30. In the case of domestic stock, these value additions are of several sorts: weight gain, quality gain, reproductive increase in herd size, and live-yield of other goods (e.g., milk).

31. Laws against hunting, or selling animal products, also tend to discourage efficient, law-abiding firms from preserving and investing in the animal assets. They lose a revenue stream. See Steve Hanke, "How to Save Alligators," *Policy Analysis*, 1, no. 1 (Winter 1975), pp. 218–20. In Germany, Austria, and Scotland, among other places, big-game animals and game birds have long been managed privately as a crop.

32. Anderson, *The Economics of Fisheries Management*.

33. "Economics of Production From Natural Resources," *American Economic Review*, 58 (June 1968), pp. 409–31.

34. J. R. Gould, "Extinction of a Fishery by Commercial Exploitation," *Journal of Political Economy*, 80 (September/October 1972), pp. 1031–38.

35. Many statistics and biostatistics books define and discuss the famous Pearl-Reed logistic functions. According to one source, the logistic function was named by Verhulst, a Belgian mathematician, who in 1838 used it to express the law of population growth. F. E. Croxton and D. J. Cowden, *Applied General Statistics* (Englewood Cliffs, N.J.: Prentice-Hall, Inc., 1939), p. 456.

36. Such formations include anticlines, stratigraphic traps, fault blocks, and salt-domes.

37. This problem of information should be kept in mind, since some critics of oil field practice, with the advantage of hindsight, simply assume that perfect knowledge and latest technology were free from the start.

38. See Robert W. Tolf, *The Russian Rockefellers* (Stanford, Calif.: Hoover Institution Press, 1976), photographic section and text at pp. 43–49, 98–101, 120, 142–44, 147–48.

39. The Pennsylvania Supreme Court classified oil and gas, by analogy, to "ferae naturae." *Westmoreland and Cambria Nat. Gas. Co.* v. *DeWitt*, 130 Pa. 235 (1889).

40. "What then can the neighbor do? Nothing; only go and do likewise." *Barnard* v. *Monongahela Nat. Gas Co.*, 216 Pa. 362 (1907).

41. George W. Stocking, *The Oil Industry and the Competitive System: A Study in Waste* (Boston: Houghton Mifflin Company, 1925).

42. Gary Libecap and Steven Wiggins, "Contractual Responses to the Common Pool:

Prorationing of Crude Oil Production,'' *American Economic Review*, 74 (March 1984), pp. 87–98, at p. 94. They cite Joe Bain, *The Petroleum Industry of the Pacific Coast*, vol. III (Berkeley, Calif.: University of California Press, 1947), p. 29.

Also see Stephen Wiggins and Gary Libecap, ''Oil Field Unitization: Contractual Failure in the Presence of Imperfect Information,'' *American Economic Review*, 75 (June 1985), pp. 368–85, at p. 368, citing Bain; and Libecap and Wiggins, ''The Influence of Private Contractual Failure on Regulation: The Case of Oil Field Unitization,'' *Journal of Political Economy*, 93 (August 1985), pp. 690–714.

43. Libecap and Wiggins, ''Contractual Responses to the Common Pool,'' p. 94.

44. See the cases cited earlier (in this chapter), in notes 39 and 40.

45. Stephen L. McDonald, *Petroleum Conservation in the United States: An Economic Analysis* (Baltimore: The Johns Hopkins Press, 1971).

46. Libecap and Wiggins, ''Unitization.''

47. They cite *Oil and Gas Journal*, July 3, 1930.

48. The first major discoveries in Saudi Arabia occurred in 1934, but were not exploited until the second world war ended.

49. See, for example, W. F. Lovejoy and P. T. Homan, *Economic Aspects of Oil Conservation Regulation* (Baltimore: The Johns Hopkins Press, 1967). As they put it: ''In . . . public hearings . . . in . . . market-demand states, prices are rarely, if ever, mentioned * * * The severe restrictions of output in states like Texas, Kansas, and Oklahoma in the 1930s were designed to have an immediate effect in changing the level of prices. . . . the present system *supports* prices, but does not actively attempt to revise them.'' Pp. 238–39.

50. For example, Lovejoy and Homan, *Oil Conservation Regulation*; Stephen L. McDonald, *Petroleum Conservation*; James M. McKie and Stephen L. McDonald, ''Petroleum Conservation in Theory and Practice,'' *Quarterly Journal of Economics*, 76 (February 1962), pp. 101–10.

51. Lovejoy and Homan, *Oil Conservation Regulation*, p. 121.

52. It is not clear who invented MER as concept or term. Some credit the Petroleum Administration for War—or its predecessor—for at least codifying the notion, at the start of WWII.

53. See Lovejoy and Homan, *Oil Conservation Regulation*, pp. 215–17.

54. Lovejoy and Homan put it this way: ''The regulatory agencies . . . set up formulas to regulate production per well, regardless of the reservoir in which wells are located. Production per reservoir is simply the composite result of production under the per-well formula, as modified by field orders to take account of special circumstances . . . departures can be found, such as basing production on MER's. Even in unitized fields the per-well production yardsticks and proration formulas usually dictate the pool allowable . . .'' Ibid., p. 217.

55. Libecap and Wiggins, ''Contractual Responses to the Common Pool,'' p. 96. Also see *Railroad Commission of Texas* v. *Rowan and Nicholls*, 107 F.2d 70.

56. *Atlantic Refining Co.* v. *Railroad Commission*, 346 S.W.2d. 801 (1961); and *Halbouty* v. *Railroad Commission*, 357 S.W. 364 (1962).

57. *Texas State House Reporter, Oil Regulation Report*, September 19, 1956, p. 2.

58. *Oil Regulation Report*, April 17, 1958, p. 3.

59. D. Gale Johnson, *Forward Prices for Agriculture* (Chicago: University of Chicago Press, 1947); and Theodore W. Schultz, *Agriculture in an Unstable Economy* (New York: McGraw-Hill Book Company, 1945).

60. It is possible to make money by buying and restarting facilities that should not have been closed down. It is harder to make money by buying facilities and closing down operations that are operating even though they should already have been shut down. The options in that case seem to be to buy out a publicly traded company or to sell it short.

61. See Morris A. Adelman, ''Efficiency of Resource Use in Crude Petroleum,'' *Southern Economic Review*, 31 (October 1964), pp. 101–22.

62. *U.S.* v. *Standard Oil of California, et al.*, Civil Action No. 11584-C.

18 REGULATION AT BOTH POLES: PUBLIC UTILITIES AND AGRICULTURE

INTRODUCTION

This chapter outlines the kinds of regulation applied in the U.S. to two very different structures of industry. Most of the directly regulated public utilities are highly concentrated, at least in local consumer markets. Examples are electric and gas utilities, and companies offering local telephone services. It is common to hear that these industries are natural monopolies; that is, one efficient firm can satisfy the whole market. Natural monopolies or not, these firms are commonly regulated on the theory that they would otherwise exploit consumers.

At the other pole are the agricultural industries, which are, on the whole, the least concentrated industries we have. They have been highly regulated nevertheless.

The next section briefly outlines the economic alternatives and problems that arise with such public utilities as may be natural monopolies. The following section briefly evaluates some agricultural regulations in the U.S.

PUBLIC UTILITIES

Our present notions about public utilities are deeply rooted in the past. Products "affected with the public interest" historically included such things as inns, bridges, and ferry crossings; but concepts like this tend to stretch over more and more activities. This one came in time to include grain elevators, railroads, buses, trucks—and many other things. In each case, the argument was that consumers needed regulation to protect them when they buy products that are "necessary," somehow special, or that are provided by monopolies. Some other antimonopoly regulations were imposed when there was little or no monopoly threat at all.[1]

At various points, we have seen that economies of size or the superior performance of some firms can produce highly concentrated industrial structures. Chapter 13 showed how superior efficiency can lower costs while generating substantial profits, and noted that, in theory, a perfectly efficient government regulation could in principle establish prices equal to those same lowest costs. This would be the best of both worlds, on paper.

Ironically, however, this situation poses severe regulatory problems at the same time that it seems to offer strong reasons to regulate. Suppose that, at declining average and marginal costs, one single-product firm could satisfy the total demand facing some industry. This is the clearest case of natural monopoly: a single-firm monopoly achieves lowest-cost production. Two or more firms will incur higher costs in producing the same output.

Ideal direct price regulation, of a sort never actually seen, is theoretically capable of achieving ideal results even under these conditions. Regulation might achieve the lowest possible costs through monopoly production, then force the monopoly to price at marginal cost. We would, then, theoretically have the best of all possible worlds. But there are problems. First, regulation as we know it simply does not work that way. Even its objective seems typically to be some variety of average cost pricing. Second, even if regulation accomplished marginal cost pricing, we would sometimes face the problem of having to make up losses out of subsidies, with possibly serious effects upon the firm's efficiency as well as upon business incentives generally. Third, regulation is not costless in either the economic or political sense. Fourth, there would have to be continuing and difficult appraisal of whether total cost plus subsidy is really smaller than total benefit.

On the other hand, an unregulated single-firm monopoly might exploit consumers unmercifully, since entry cannot be relied upon. Perhaps entry will not occur, because entrants will recognize that two *competing* firms will not be able to survive in the long run. And even if entry did occur, consumers might still lose: the cost savings achievable by single-firm production would be lost.

Figure 18-1 shows these natural monopoly demand and cost conditions and the *unregulated* single-firm profit-maximizing solution. Price is P_M, output is Q_M, and profits per period are the area marked R. Although one could make up other stories, it is reasonable to believe that the monopoly would be production-efficient: it will produce at minimum achievable production costs. Even so, some theorists say that this solution is not utility-efficient because P_M exceeds the marginal cost of production.[2] And, of course, many will object to the monopoly's "excessive" profits, that is, to monopoly returns in and of themselves.

It is tempting to say that regulation could put all this right, and Figure 18-2 pictures one way it might do so in theory. P_R is the price and Q_R the output if regulators choose the price that is both equal to marginal cost and that clears the market.

However much theorists may praise this ideal solution, the problems with it go far beyond those of estimating marginal costs and demands. First, in this kind of case, marginal costs are far below average costs, and a marginal-cost price therefore imposes large

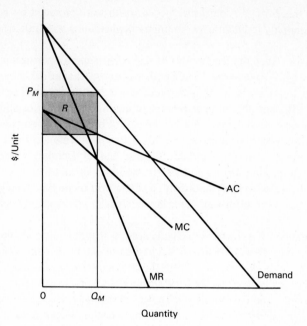

Figure 18-1 Unregulated Natural Monopoly

losses each period. If the capital is to be replaced, some source of additional revenue must be found. If all consumers were alike and if there were only one product, as is assumed here, a two-part tariff might work: for example, each user might pay a lump sum each month plus a marginal-cost price per unit.

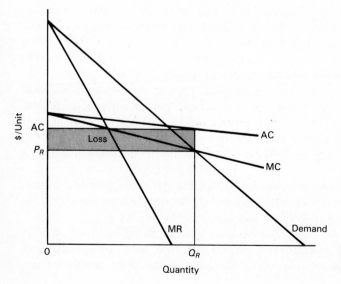

Figure 18-2 $P = MC$ Regulation of Natural Monopoly

Many theorists seem to believe that discriminatory tariffs, such as Ramsey-prices, may be the best compromise for multiple-product natural monopolies.[3] Their basic objective is to set prices that maximize consumer surplus, subject to the proviso that total revenues equal total costs. One version makes differences between prices and marginal costs inversely proportional to demand elasticities. This is zero-profit price discrimination.

In theory, at least, regulators with perfect information could set these or other types of ideal prices straightaway. In practice, they have often merely curried and worried the discriminatory tariffs that the regulated firms filed with them, hoping to produce in the end ''reasonable'' returns and political acceptance. In fact, of course, the regulatory process itself can grow costly, and any regulation based on costs and profits is likely to distort incentives to some degree. Regulation is not costless.

Another way to cover deficits is simply to float the enterprise on subsidies from the public treasury. This solution has been common, though much criticized in practice. Depending upon how it is done, it may approximate perfect marginal-cost pricing closely or hardly at all. In any case, there is an additional practical objection that Ronald Coase pointed out.[4] Any time users of a service do not have to pay its full costs as they go, we lose our hard-edged market test: how can we tell whether the service is even worth providing? Is the total benefit larger than the total cost including subsidy? Answering that question correctly has proved difficult both in regulating private firms and operating losing government enterprises such as Amtrak, the national rail passenger service whose ticket sales cover about one-third of the costs; and the Bay Area Rapid Transit System, in northern California.

Incentive problems also loom. A regulated enterprise that can count on subsidies to cover its costs has little incentive to hold costs down. Indeed, its managers have some incentives to raise costs. They may try to increase their own benefits until the costs of doing so reach limits of politically tolerable subsidies.

Figure 18-3 shows yet another regulatory possibility. It is to set a price that equals average cost, while clearing the market. Price would be $P = $ AC and output Q_R. That solution does not bring price to equality with marginal cost and it poses incentive problems of its own. One regulatory chore will be to decide whether the costs that are being covered are as low as can be, that is whether, in the regulatory jargon, they are ''reasonable.'' If regulators tend to accept whatever costs utilities submit, a utility has little incentive to keep costs as low as possible. When regulation does not permit a firm from profiting when it reduces costs, it has less incentive to do it. It may, however, be easier to estimate average costs than marginal costs, in one-product firms, at least. And if prices are regulated to produce a certain rate of return on capital included in the rate base, as is common in public utility regulation, there are circumstances in which it pays the firm to overinvest in assets the regulators accept in a rate base.[5]

A succession of nuclear-plant fiascos and bad efficiency ratings of U.S. power plants relative to foreign plants may explain an interesting recent development. At least a dozen states have adopted plant-efficiency standards for public utilities, penalizing those that do not meet the standards and rewarding those that do.[6]

Although there is considerable disagreement about how well regulation actually works, it is fair to say that many economists are not anxious to extend it, and many would

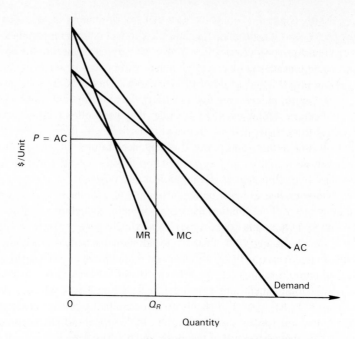

Figure 18-3 P = AC Regulation of Natural Monopoly

like to reduce the amount of government regulation that we already have. Harold Demsetz, for example, argues that we could approximate average-cost regulation without using regulatory commissions.[7] In his scheme, the bidder who offers to provide a service at the lowest price would get the utility franchise. Competition among prospective franchisees would produce essentially competitive prices and rates of return even when production of the service is a natural monopoly. Though this scheme might be simpler and less costly than commission regulation as we now know it, it still needs an agency to formulate the dimensions on which bidding will take place, to award the franchises, to enforce the contracts, and so on.

AGRICULTURE: REGULATED ATOMISM

Agriculture is not a homogeneous activity or industry. It is shorthand for a collection of interrelated farm and ranch activities. Most of the important agricultural products are produced by many sellers. Agriculture comprises the closest approximations to atomistic economic structures that the real world offers. From a traditional structuralist point of view, there is every reason to expect that atomistic competition exists and can be effective here, if anywhere; and it is not obvious why it should require much government regulation or support to work effectively.

After analyzing several characteristics sometimes used to justify government support, D. Gale Johnson, a famous agricultural economist, concluded that "No one or all of these considerations convince me that the present large scale program of price supports and other subsidies are any more warranted in agriculture than in almost any other part of the economy."[8] He saw a role for government spending on agricultural research and education, and, in theory, at least, in reducing the shocks and instabilities to which agriculture is subject. Unfortunately, however, ". . . most of the means to reduce instability are vulnerable to misuse in the American political scene."[9]

It is clear that agricultural programs in the U.S. have gone far beyond what economics can easily justify. Agriculture is a classic example of how regulation can redistribute income, in this case by taking from consumers to give to producers. Agricultural policies are strong evidence for Posner's claim that regulation is often used to redistribute income.[10]

The U.S. government started minor, superficial tinkering with agriculture in the early days of the republic; but significant regulation began in the 1930s, ostensibly to achieve equity and reduce poverty. Although equity is an imprecise ideal, it sometimes finds precise formulation. Agricultural policy is a good example. U.S. farmers were notably prosperous during the period 1910 to 1914, which is sometimes referred to as their Golden Age. The prices farmers received during those years were unusually high relative to the prices of things they bought. In fact, it would have been difficult to find any significant period that was more favorable to farmers. That apparently explains why the Agricultural Adjustment Act (AAA) of 1933 chose it as the benchmark establishing the ideal equitable relationship between farm and nonfarm prices.

Ideals are one thing. In practice, government did not guarantee support prices that would give farmers 100 percent of the purchasing-power (parity) they had from 1910 to 1914. They got lesser percentages, as established and changed periodically by law.[11] Those who want this kind of equity may lament that farmers got less than 100 percent parity prices. Complete parity, if possible, would have been even more heroically inefficient than what we got. After 1910 to 1914, productivity on farms increased much faster than in the economy as a whole. If productivity and costs had changed at the same rate on and off the farms, strict price parity would have tended to preserve the same mix of farm and nonfarm outputs as we got from 1910 to 1914. In the meantime, consumers' tastes and incomes had changed. They now prefer more meat and salad and less bread, for example. Given the productivity and cost changes that actually did occur, 100 percent parity would have produced a backward looking, grossly out of date product mix that did not respond to modern consumer preferences.

Every year since 1933, the U.S. government has placed price-support floors under at least some important agricultural products. Parity price supports have been applied most consistently to five "basic" farm commodities: cotton, corn, wheat, tobacco, and rice. Except for two years—1972 and 1973—those support prices were substantially higher than free-market levels. What kept the prices up? The most important mechanisms were acreage (or crop) limitations and huge government purchases—sometimes called *nonrecourse loans*. In effect, the government simply bought and stored everything that consumers would not buy at the inflated support prices. Even the physical storage of such surplus commodities became very expensive. Periodically, disheartening reports came out about major losses of stored crops, owing to spoilage, animal and insect pests, and fraud.

The federal government is showing signs that it wants to reform our agricultural programs.[12] In 1986 some agricultural programs changed in response to two facts. First, farmers continued to demand high agricultural prices and were politically strong enough to get them. Second, the U.S. could not sell agricultural products abroad at prices that would please its farmers. The solution adopted had been a favorite proposal found in elementary economics textbooks years ago. The government would continue to pay *farmers* prices that are markedly higher than competitive equilibrium levels, but would dump the products on foreign and domestic markets for whatever they would fetch. Under plausible economic assumptions, this kind of scheme can increase the explicit (tax and government budget) costs of programs to aid agriculture. Even so, the notion is that consumers, rather than firms in the storage and storage-building businesses and the vermin feasting on crops in government storage, should benefit from the low prices that open-market sales of such bountiful crops would bring.

In addition to programs for the basic commodities, there are special programs for sugar, milk, peanuts, raisins, prunes, citrus fruits, and other crops. More than forty Federal Marketing Orders regulate, indeed cartelize, agricultural products.[13] The milk programs are particularly complex and particularly shocking.[14] Perishables without price supports have benefited from having the U.S. government buy them here and give them away as foreign aid; and from school lunch subsidies, programs for making starch and livestock feed from surplus crops; and so on. In 1982, the U.S. Department of Agriculture spent at the rate of $45 billion per year, six percent of the federal budget, and more than $13,000 dollars for each farm worker in the country. As Clifton B. Luttrell summed it up,

> . . . the USDA has now moved into more exotic areas of activity such as rural recreation, farm labor housing, community facilities, etc. Its growth has followed the classic expansion pattern for bureaucracy. . . . The public at large . . . has lost $700 to $800 per family annually in recent years through higher food prices and taxes . . . to finance the programs. Furthermore, the lower-income farm workers and farm operators . . . have gained little.[15]

Governmental controls and regulations of agriculture have been persistent and massive. The reasons given for all this regulatory activity were to improve equity and reduce poverty. Yet government interventions into agriculture continued to increase long after many farmers achieved great prosperity, and the programs did little for the poorest farmers—who produce little that they can sell at the inflated prices. As President Reagan's Council of Economic Advisors put it in 1987,

> The farms with sales under $40,000 per year account for 72 percent of all farms, but only generate 10.3 percent of gross farm income. . . . These farms . . . receive only 9.5 percent of government payments. . . .

> Finally, a small number of farms (93,000, or only 4.1 percent of all farms) have gross sales of more than $250,000 and account for 48.8 percent of gross farm income. . . . Those with sales over $250,000 receive 32 percent of government payments, while those with sales over $500,000, representing 1.2 percent of all farms, receive 13.3 percent of such assistance.

. . . Compared with the past . . . poverty or low farm income is not as important a rationale for farm policy as it once was. Average net cash income per farm was $11,745 in 1960, or 58 percent of median family income, but, in 1985, stood at $19,256, 69 percent of median family income (all figures in 1985 dollars). In 1986, government payments were high enough to pay an equivalent of $42,000 to each U.S. commercial farm (those with sales above $100,000) while U.S. median family income was $27,735.[16]

High-flown political rhetoric notwithstanding, the government farm programs simply transferred enormous wealth from other taxpayers and consumers to farmers, ranchers, and government employees.

Free-market liberals criticize such programs for creating a huge bureaucracy; raising taxes, prices, and the real costs of farm output (by distorting the proportions of land and other inputs used); and delaying worthwhile long-run adjustments in the economy. If this assessment is correct, as every objective economic analysis suggests, the total welfare costs of U.S. agricultural programs, including costs to consumers, is much greater than the vast amounts government spent on them. If so, it would be useful to know how such policies are created and persist.

Even in ancient times, sages observed that people know their own business very well and understand what helps and hurts it. By bribery and otherwise, special interests often got government to help them, though others got hurt in the process. Some believed that good rulers, or democratic process, could prevent that, a belief that proved premature. For, among other things, it turned out that even in a democracy politicians can buy some citizens' votes with other citizens' wealth.

One theory was that policies will improve greatly once the people and their representatives learn the facts and how to use them. This (self-serving) theory was popular around universities long before agitators insisted that educators become reformers, or policy-relevant at the least. But how long should we wait before abandoning a theory? It is clear that there are now lots of literate people, college degrees, and people claiming to know the relevant facts and how they should be used. It is less obvious that policies, including our agricultural programs, have improved commensurately.

Perhaps part of the problem is that we have overestimated education and the common citizen: the theories and detailed facts needed to appraise public policies and regulations may be too difficult for ordinary people to sort out and understand. Some U.S. agricultural programs—milk and tobacco, for example—are undeniably complex. Although it is debatable how much the public could understand if they tried, most people still have no idea about the details and mechanics of agricultural and a lot of other programs. Politicians' lack of clarity and candor does not improve mass understanding. Misleading the voters may help to get such programs started. Terms such as *nonrecourse loans*, for example, were deceptive doubletalk.

Perhaps, though, the problem is not so much ignorance as it is intelligent indifference. In any case, how ignorant are we? Although ignorance and low IQs might explain how raids on consumers and the treasury began, they are less satisfying explanations of why such programs continue and why others get started. For a long time some critics have understood and publicized the details of agricultural programs. When the New Deal killed and buried pigs to raise the price of meat, newspapers had a field day. For years, editorials, cartoons, and barroom jokes told how farmers get paid for *not* growing cotton. Popular economics texts showed how agricultural price-support schemes work and whom they hurt. Most economists have opposed the programs for years. No politician could have the slightest doubt about what the programs do, and any voter who seriously wants to know more about them can find out. How, then, could we have got and continued to tolerate such programs?

Perhaps the best explanation is simplest. When constitutions permit large-scale interferences with market forces, political contests between consumers and special interests become important. Special interest legislation concentrates benefits narrowly. Individuals and groups that stand to gain a lot are willing to spend a lot to realize a large gain. Each of those who stands to lose little will spend little or nothing to avoid the loss. Under our constitution, therefore, consumers often lose the contest. Although the total dead-weight loss is large, each consumer loses a relatively small amount. So small that it may not pay the consumer even to inquire about the program. And, even if a consumer finds out about the program, it does not pay to do anything about it. It may not pay a political entrepreneur to help himself by helping consumers overthrow such programs, either. It is very costly to organize, articulate, and benefit from movements comprising millions of consumers, each of whom loses little.

Some may be encouraged to learn that most nations, not just the U.S., favor their farmers in various ways. After killing off several million peasants in the 1930s, for example, the Soviets have come to favor farm workers and bureaucrats substantially. And even Japan, currently a darling of many who praise "efficiency," persists in notoriously inefficient agricultural policies.[17] Japan's programs are said to cost each of its citizens around $600 a year. Western Europe spends as much as, perhaps more than, the U.S. does.[18]

SUMMARY

Though how many public utilities are actually natural monopolies is an open question, natural monopoly poses perplexing policy alternatives in theory. Doing nothing exposes consumers to monopoly exploitation. Regulation that covers costs but limits profits risks serious disincentive effects, subsidy abuses, and inefficiency.

Complex price-discrimination schemes such as Ramsey-pricing are ingenious, and interesting to economists. Ramsey-prices, for example, would maximize consumer welfare subject to the constraint that revenues (just) cover costs. That theoretically offers the best compromise between monopoly efficiency and consumer welfare, although the tendency for managers to exaggerate costs remains a real possibility.

Most countries subsidize agriculture in one way or another. U.S. agricultural policy confirms Posner's theory that much regulation redistributes income purposefully. Although it does not seem possible to defend such programs on welfare grounds, their persistent enormity is awe inspiring.

QUESTIONS

1. Picture the case of a natural monopoly arising from economies of size. Show the cost levels resulting from a government policy to have (and by law to preserve) two firms instead of one. Now show results for a four-firm policy.

2. Is it necessary to include in question 1 an expression such as "and by law preserve"? Discuss.

3. For the natural monopoly pictured in question 1, show the welfare effects of a policy of laissez faire.

4. For the natural monopoly pictured in question 1 carefully discuss the short- and long-run welfare implications of requiring the firm to price at marginal cost.

5. For the natural monopoly pictured in question 1 carefully discuss the short- and long-run welfare implications of requiring the firm to price at average cost.

6. Briefly state the constraints imposed on Ramsey-prices. Do these constraints avoid subsidies? Disincentive effects? Explain.

7. Suppose, as is surely true, that some agricultural "marketing" programs create and preserve compulsory cartels. How do such arrangements differ from purely private cartels? Discuss their welfare effects in general.

8. Using basic supply and demand, analyze the welfare effects of setting price of an agricultural commodity above the competitive level by having government buy and store the resulting surplus.

9. Use the same demand and costs used in question 8, but assume that government pays farmers the same amount per bushel of the commodity as it would pay to buy it under the scheme described in question 8, and lets price find its own level. Analyze the welfare implications.

10. Discuss the economic and political implications of dismantling government purchase and marketing programs and, instead, sending present farmers lifetime payments equal to what they receive from present programs.

NOTES

1. Paul W. MacAvoy, *Deregulation of Cable Television* (Washington, D.C.: American Enterprise Institute, 1977); John McGee, "Government Intervention in the Spanish Sugar Industry," *Journal of Law & Economics*, 7 (October 1964), pp. 121–72; Paul W. MacAvoy, *The Economic Effects of Regulation: The Trunk-Line Railroad Cartels and the Interstate Commerce Commission Before 1900* (Cambridge, Mass.: MIT Press, 1965); P. W. MacAvoy and James Sloss, *Regulation of Transport Innovation* (New York: Random House, Inc., 1967); D. W. Caves, L. R. Christensen, and J. A. Swanson, "Economic Performance in Regulated and Unregulated Environments: A Comparison of U.S. and Canadian Railroads," *Quarterly Journal of Economics*, 96 (November 1981), pp. 559–81; Robert Gerwig, "Natural Gas Production: A Study of the Costs of Regulation," *Journal of Law & Economics*, 5 (October 1962), pp. 69–92; Abba Lerner, "Conflicting Principles of Public Utility Pricing," *Journal of Law & Economics*, 7 (October 1964), pp. 61–70; John S. McGee, "Pricing in Publicly-

Controlled Industries,'' in *Price Formation in Various Economies*, ed. D. C. Hague (New York: St. Martin's Press, Inc., 1967); Paul W. MacAvoy, ''The Regulation Induced Shortage of Natural Gas,'' *Journal of Law & Economics*, 14 (April 1971), pp. 167–99; MacAvoy, *Price Formation in Natural Gas Fields* (New Haven, Conn.: Yale University Press, 1962); George Hilton, ''The Consistency of the Interstate Commerce Act,'' *Journal of Law & Economics*, 9 (October 1966), pp. 87–113; Robert W. Harbeson, ''Toward Better Resource Allocation in Transport,'' *Journal of Law & Economics*, 12 (October 1969), pp. 321–38; William Jordan, ''Producer Protection, Prior Market Structure, and the Effects of Government Regulation,'' *Journal of Law & Economics*, 25 (April 1972), pp. 151–76; Paul MacAvoy and John Snow, eds., *Regulation of Passenger Fares and Competition Among the Airlines* (Washington, D.C.: American Enterprise Institute, 1977); C. V. Olson and J. M. Trapani, ''Who Has Benefited from Regulation of the Airline Industry?'' *Journal of Law & Economics*, 24 (April 1981), pp. 75–93; W. Schwert, ''Using Financial Data to Measure Effects of Regulation,'' *Journal of Law & Economics*, 24 (April 1981), pp. 121–58; Thomas G. Moore, ''Airline Deregulation,'' *Journal of Law & Economics*, 29 (April 1985), pp. 1–28; Gabriel Kolko, *Railroads and Regulation* (Princeton, N.J.: Princeton University Press, 1970); Thomas Moore, *Freight Transportation Regulation: Surface Freight and the Interstate Commerce Commission* (Washington, D.C.: American Enterprise Institute, 1972); Paul MacAvoy and John Snow, eds., *Regulation of Entry and Pricing in Truck Transportation* (Washington, D.C.: American Enterprise Institute, 1977); Thomas Moore, ''The Beneficiaries of Trucking Regulation,'' *Journal of Law & Economics*, 21 (October 1978), pp. 327–43; Edmund Kitch, M. Isaacson, and D. Kasper, ''The Regulation of Taxicabs in Chicago,'' *Journal of Law & Economics*, 14 (October 1971), pp. 285–350; Edmund Kitch, ''The Yellow Cab Antitrust Case,'' *Journal of Law & Economics*, 15 (October 1972), pp. 327–36; Peter Swan, *On Buying a Job: The Regulation of Taxi Cabs in Canberra* (Turramurra, Australia: The Centre for Independent Studies, 1979); Ross Eckert and George Hilton, ''The Jitneys,'' *Journal of Law & Economics*, 15 (October 1972), pp. 293–325; Dennis Breen, ''The Monopoly Value of Household-Goods Carrier Operating Certificates,'' *Journal of Law & Economics*, 29 (April 1977), pp. 153–85.

2. See Chapter 2 for a discussion of this and other ideal properties of equilibrium in the theory of atomistic competition.

3. Ramsey-prices are named after a Cambridge University mathematician. Frank P. Ramsey, ''A Contribution to the Theory of Taxation,'' *The Economic Journal*, 37 (March 1927), pp. 27–61. For a tribute by a famous friend, see John Maynard Keynes, ''F. P. Ramsey,'' in *Essays in Biography* (New York: W. W. Norton & Co., Inc., 1963), pp. 239–54. Also see William J. Baumol and O. F. Bradford, ''Optimal Departures from Marginal Cost Pricing,'' *American Economic Review*, 60 (June 1970), pp. 265–83; and Stephen J. Brown and David S. Sibley, *The Theory of Public Utility Pricing* (New York: Cambridge University Press, 1986), pp. 39–43.

4. Ronald H. Coase, ''The Theory of Public Utility Pricing,'' in *The Economics of Regulation of Public Utilities*, a conference sponsored by Northwestern University, June 19–24, 1966, at pp. 96–106.

5. This tendency is now called the *Averch-Johnson effect*. How important it is in fact is another question. See H. Averch and L. L. Johnson, ''Behavior of the Firm Under Regulatory Constraint,'' *American Economic Review*, 52 (December 1962), pp. 1053–69.

6. Bill Paul, ''States Tighten Rules for Electric Utilities,'' *The Wall Street Journal*, 13 November 1986, p. 6.

7. Harold Demsetz, "Why Regulate Utilities?" *Journal of Law & Economics*, 11 (April 1968), pp. 55–65.

8. D. Gale Johnson, "Government and Agriculture: Is Agriculture a Special Case?" *The Journal of Law & Economics*, 1 (October 1958), pp. 122–36, at p. 136.

9. Ibid.

10. Richard A. Posner, "Taxation by Regulation," *The Bell Journal of Economics and Management Science*, 2 (Spring 1971), pp. 22–50.

11. Although the 1933 Act was the first to incorporate a specific price-parity formula, the 1938 AAA was the first to use the term *parity*. Geoffery Shepherd, "Appraisal of Alternative Concepts and Measures of Agricultural Parity Prices and Incomes," *Government Price Statistics*, Hearings Before the Subcommittee on Economic Statistics of the Joint Economic Committee, 1961, pp. 459–502.

12. *Economic Report of the President Transmitted to the Congress January 1987 Together with The Annual Report of the Council of Economic Advisors* (Washington, D.C.: U.S. Government Printing Office, 1987), pp. 147–78.

13. A recent study is Lawrence Shepard, "Cartelization of the California-Arizona Orange Industry, 1934–1981," *Journal of Law & Economics*, 29 (April 1986), pp. 83–123. Also see U.S. Department of Agriculture Marketing Service, *A Review of Federal Marketing Orders for Fruits, Vegetables, and Specialty Crops*, Agri. Econ. Rept. No. 477 (November 1981); P. Thor and E. Jesse, *Economic Effects of Terminating Federal Marketing Orders for California-Arizona Oranges*, USDA Econ. Research Serv. Tech. Bull. No. 1664 (1981); *USDA Guidelines for Fruit, Vegetable, and Specialty Crop Marketing Order* (25 January 1982); James Bovard, "Can Sunkist Wrap up the Lemon Industry?" *The Wall Street Journal*, 24 January 1985, p. 30.

14. J. H. Birnbaum, "Congress at a Cattle Crossing," *The Wall Street Journal*, 14 June 1983, p. 34; and Paul W. MacAvoy, ed., *Federal Milk Marketing Orders and Price Supports* (Washington, D.C.: American Enterprise Institute, 1977). A more recent article claims that state *retail* milk price fixing is consistent with politicians' maximizing the sum of milk producers' and milk marketers' votes. Ronald N. Johnson, "Retail Price Controls in the Dairy Industry: A Political Coalition Argument," *Journal of Law & Economics*, 28 (April 1985), pp. 55–75.

15. C. B. Luttrell, "Down on the Farm with Uncle Sam" (Los Angeles: International Institute for Economic Research, Original Paper 43, June 1983).

16. Annual Report of the Council of Economic Advisors (1987), p. 152.

17. For example, see Damon Darlin, "Powerful Bloc," *The Wall Street Journal*, 4 December 1986, pp. 1, 23.

18. Mitzi Ayala, "Farm Subsidies Yield Costly Harvest," *The Wall Street Journal* (4 June 1987), p. 22. For a comparison of U.S. and German farm supports, see Wendy L. Hall and Thomas L. Hall, "Rural Clouds," *The Wall Street Journal* (7 July 1987), pp. 1, 18.

<table>
<tr><td>

19

</td><td>

INTRODUCTION
TO ANTITRUST
POLICY

</td></tr>
</table>

INTRODUCTION

One rationale for antitrust law is that it can reduce direct governmental intervention to the minimum. It is supposed to do this by preventing excess concentration and by preserving competition, which will avoid problems that regulators would otherwise have to deal with. Perhaps antitrust law works out that way, although a closer look reveals that it too is regulation: it attempts to influence prices and outputs. And U.S. agriculture demonstrates that competitive structure and performance do not necessarily discourage government intervention and regulation.

Antitrust policy is supposed to improve market performance by reducing monopoly. The notion is that it will prevent monopolies from being created through mergers or agreements; dissolve or reform large firms alleged to have prevented competition actively (or perhaps that have merely been too successful); and discourage cartels by punishing those who participate in them.

It sounds reasonable to ask what the U.S. antitrust laws really do. Unfortunately, the question is very difficult to answer. Antitrust law is not a neatly wrapped bundle of spears that all point in one direction. First of all, there are several major federal antitrust statutes: the Sherman Law (1890); the Clayton Act (1914); the Federal Trade Commission Act (1914); the Robinson-Patman Act (1936); and the Celler Merger Act (1950). The Robinson-Patman and Celler Acts amended the Clayton Act profoundly and all the statutes have been amended in some degree over the years.

Second, the historical backgrounds of these statutes differ substantially, as do their objectives. Each statute has generated a stream of administrative rules and court decisions. Though many of these decisions are unclear, some are clearly inconsistent with competition and consumer welfare.

For these reasons, it is difficult to state briefly what "the" antitrust law means. It is even harder to tell what it has done. Most of what has been said about the effects of antitrust law is theoretical and speculative. There have been few attempts to *measure* the effects of antitrust law. Works by Stigler and Ross are exceptions.[1] And a paper published in 1985 concludes that ". . . our results do not support the contention that . . . Section 7 [of the Clayton Act, which restricts mergers] has served the public interest. While it is possible that the government's merger policy has deterred some anticompetitive mergers, . . . it has also protected rival producers from . . . increased competition due to efficient mergers."[2]

Although measuring what antitrust law has done may largely be beyond our tools and talents, economists have for years confidently taken opposing positions about it.[3] This book has only two chapters on antitrust law, scant introduction to a notoriously arcane subject. The first section of this chapter summarizes the antitrust statutes. The second section explains the concept of legislative intent and how it has been used. The third section analyzes some important price-fixing cases. The problem of whether firms are disseminating information or fixing prices is the subject of the fourth section. The fifth section discusses vertical integration and vertical price fixing. Price discrimination is the subject of the sixth.

SUMMARY OF THE ANTITRUST STATUTES

The Sherman Act[4]

The relevant sections read as follows:

> Sec. 1. Every contract, combination in the form of trust or otherwise, or conspiracy, in restraint of trade or commerce among the several States, or with foreign nations, is declared to be illegal.
>
> Every person who shall make any contract or engage in any combination or conspiracy hereby declared to be illegal shall be deemed guilty of a felony, and, on conviction thereof shall be punished by fine not exceeding one million dollars if a corporation, or, if any other person, one hundred thousand dollars, or by imprisonment not exceeding three years, or by both said punishments, in the discretion of the court.
>
> Sec. 2. Every person who shall monopolize, or attempt to monopolize, or combine or conspire with any other person or persons, to monopolize any part of the trade or commerce among the several States, or with foreign nations, shall be deemed guilty of a felony, and, on conviction thereof, shall be punished by fine not exceeding one million dollars if a corporation, or, if any other person, one hundred thousand dollars, or by imprisonment not exceeding three years, or by both said punishments, in the discretion of the court.

Antitrust law has at its disposal civil remedies as well as criminal penalties. Private parties, states, and the federal government can bring civil suits to obtain injunctions or damages. The U.S. can also seek dissolution, divestiture, and other remedies.

The Clayton Act[5]

One peculiarity of the Clayton Act is that it was intended to prevent monopoly problems in their incipiency. During debates on the Robinson-Patman Act—which amends Clayton—this intention was described as catching the weed in the seed before it comes to flower; and catching monopoly on the wing before it comes to roost. The notion that we should use law to prevent improbable prospective hurts has caused much trouble.

Sections 2(a) to 2(f) are fundamental amendments that Robinson-Patman made. Section 2(a) outlaws price discrimination in commerce,

> . . . where the effect of such discrimination may be substantially to lessen competition or tend to create a monopoly in any line of commerce, or to injure, destroy, or prevent competition with any person who either grants or knowingly receives the benefit of such discrimination, or with customers of either of them.

The words *injure, destroy, or prevent competition with any person* miniaturize and personalize the competitive process. This language is, and was meant to be, anti-competitive in spirit and effect, as later discussion shows.

Several provisos follow. First, price differentials are permissible if they make "only due allowance for differences in the cost of manufacture, sale, or delivery resulting from the differing methods or quantities in which such commodities are . . . sold or delivered." Second, even if such cost savings can be shown, however, the FTC may set limits on quantity discounts "where it finds that available purchasers in greater quantities are so few as to render differentials on account thereof unjustly discriminatory or promotive of monopoly in any line of commerce." Third, it is permissible to make price changes "from time to time" in the sale of perishable goods and seasonal and distress merchandise.

Section 2(b) is the meeting-competition proviso, the meaning of which has been heatedly debated. Under this statute, a prima facie case of price discrimination is made once a price difference is shown. Defendant has the burden of proof in rebutting that prima facie case. This section seems to say that a seller may rebut the prima facie case by showing that his differential was offered in "good faith to meet an equally low price of a competitor, or the services or facilities furnished by a competitor." For years that defense proved illusory, on the theory that it did not apply if competition was "injured," which was almost always.

Section 2(c) prohibits granting or receiving commissions, brokerage, or other payments "except for services rendered . . . either to the other party to such transaction or to an intermediary . . . acting . . . in behalf . . . or subject to . . . direct or indirect control, of any party to such transaction other than the person by whom such compensation is so granted or paid." Note that this section, and the one to follow, establish per se violations: no kind of competitive injury need be shown. This section penalizes integrated firms performing their own wholesaling and brokerage functions, and was meant to do so.

Section 2(d) requires payments a manufacturer or distributor makes for services or facilities that its customers furnish to be "available on proportionally equal terms to all other customers competing."

Under Section 2(e), it is unlawful for a seller to furnish services or facilities to one buyer unless it makes them available to competing buyers "on proportionally equal terms."

Section 2(f) makes it unlawful "knowingly to induce or receive a prohibited discriminatory price."

Full-line forcing, exclusive dealing, and tie-in sales are prohibited by Section 3 when they "may . . . substantially lessen competition or tend to create a monopoly in any line of commerce." This is part of the original Clayton Act of 1914. Chapter 9 discussed the economics of such practices.

Section 4 and its subsections deal with damage suits. Section 4 permits private treble-damage suits in federal district courts, for anyone "injured in his business or property by reason of anything forbidden in the antitrust laws." Section 4 (a) permits the federal government to sue for "actual" rather than triple damages. Section 4(c) permits states to sue for damages "on behalf of natural persons residing in such states . . . ," and 4(b) sets a four-year statute of limitation for actions under Sections 4, 4(a), and 4(c). This four-year limit is not cut and dried, however. "Fraudulent concealment," for example, starts a long count. And it is undeniably true that some antitrust decisions hinge on events from more distant pasts.

Government antitrust suits are sometimes only the beginning. Section 5(a) provides that final judgments or decrees in suits brought by the U.S. "shall be prima facie evidence against . . . defendant" in actions brought by other parties. Exposure to further treble-damage actions is, thus, one of the side effects of losing a suit brought by the government. Pleas of no contest are not prima facie evidence in other suits; nor are judgments or decrees "entered before any testimony has been taken." Section 5(b) spells out the statute of limitations for U.S. government suits.

By asserting "that the labor of a human being is not a commodity or article of commerce," Section 6 to some degree exempts from the antitrust laws "the existence and operation of labor, agricultural, or horticultural organizations, instituted for the purpose of mutual help, and not having capital stock or conducted for profit."

Section 7 is the antimerger provision. It prohibits mergers and acquisitions "in any line of commerce in any section of the country . . . ," where the effect "may be substantially to lessen competition, or to tend to create a monopoly." Exempt are "transactions duly consummated pursuant to authority given" by certain regulatory agencies: CAB, FCC, FPC, ICC, SEC, U.S. Maritime Commission, and the Secretary of Agriculture. Section 7(a) requires premerger notification and a 30-day waiting period when the acquiring and acquired companies are absolutely large (as measured by assets) and when the acquirer would get 15 percent or more of the voting securities or assets.

Among other things, business leaders have complained that they have no way of knowing whether the mergers they are contemplating are legal or illegal. In response, the Department of Justice issued *Merger Guidelines* in 1968, 1982, and 1984.[6] The Reagan administration permitted many mergers that previously might have come under fire.

The FTC Act

We will ignore this statute's prohibitions of false and misleading advertising, and some other peripheral matters, and concentrate on its core antitrust provisions.

Section 1 establishes a five-member Federal Trade Commission. Members are appointed by the president, for 7-year terms.

Section 5 created what has turned out to be a second Sherman Act: "Unfair methods of competition in commerce, and unfair or deceptive acts or practices in or affecting commerce, are hereby declared unlawful."

LEGISLATIVE INTENT

Neither lawyers, judges, economists, nor historians agree whether courts should try to interpret statutes in the light of what Congress intended them to do. One view is that legislative intent is a useful and legitimate concern *only* when the language of the statute is manifestly unclear. Some believe that legislative intent doesn't really exist, or is not discernible if it does. Others believe that legislative intent should not matter, even when it is clear.

Scholars, however, can use help from history when they try to understand things as complex yet vague as the antitrust statutes. And it may be just as well to check up on the courts, who often claim to be doing what Congress intended. Their claims may have changed the reach and cut of the law, both with respect to what Congress meant to begin with and with respect to earlier judicial precedents. What is more disturbing is that courts may thereby have arrogated the power to make sociological-economic and political-economic trade-offs, and be using that arrogated power without good reason or limit.

Another way to put this is that some anticonsumer interpretations of the antitrust laws have been cloaked in assertions about what Congress really intended. Peculiar versions of legislative intent have been used to shield peculiar theories of law, economics, and social policy. For example, *Alcoa*[7] and *Brown Shoe*[8] show how antitrust decisions give up efficiency to protect small, high-cost producers. The courts do not specify the terms of exchange or value weights that they use in making such trade-offs.

If nothing else, congressional intent may reveal tendencies for state power to grow beyond limits initially desired or even conceived.

The Sherman Act

Robert H. Bork argues—in spite of what has been said by some antitrust students and judges such as Learned Hand—that the Sherman Act was clearly intended to legislate a standard of consumer welfare; that is, a standard of efficient production and resource allocation.[9] According to Bork, *restraint of trade* clearly meant price increases that reduce output and total wealth. Furthermore, Congress wanted nonconspiratorial activity to be lawful—whatever structure of industry resulted—so long as it increased efficiency, lowered long-run price and excluded no one artificially or forcibly. *Monopoly* was not outlawed; *monopolizing* was. Senator Sherman and a majority of the Congress wanted to permit even single-firm monopoly if it arose from superior efficiency.

Finally, says Bork, there is no evidence that those who wrote or voted for the act wanted it to trade off economic efficiency to aid small enterprises; or to achieve unconcentrated industrial structures. And no one expected the Sherman Act to be an instrument of political or sociological reform.

At the very least, Bork's powerful argument suggests that we can protect consumers without having to repeal the Sherman Act. All we need is to return to what that law meant to begin with.

The Federal Trade Commission Act

The reach of the FTC Act has lengthened greatly since it was passed in 1914. Its Section 5, which denounces "unfair methods of competition," has grown into a "Baby Sherman Law." There is nothing babyish about its bite. Unfortunately, FTC increasingly applied the act to efficient but concentrated industrial *structures* and to business success as such, rather than to "unfair practices" in the sense historically intended.

The Clayton Act and the Robinson-Patman Act

The background and legislative history of the Robinson-Patman Act is something else.[10] This statute did not just go wrong as it grew up. It was conceived in error and born flawed.

Robinson-Patman is a populist anti–chain store bill passed during the Great Depression. Important modern forms of chain marketing in the U.S. go back to early examples such as A&P (1858). But the chains really became important in this country in the 1920s and 1930s. In the 1920s it became clear that the Clayton Act of 1914 could not prevent chains from buying and selling goods for less than single-unit stores, and the FTC brought no Section 2 Clayton Act cases between 1925 and 1933.

We can draw firm conclusions about congressional intent from the hearings and debates out of which Robinson-Patman emerged. First, H. B. Teegarden, attorney for the National American Wholesale Grocer's Association, wrote H.R. 8442, the basis of the Robinson-Patman Act. That association naturally opposed chain stores, which did their own wholesaling and did not patronize old-style wholesalers. Chain store growth came at the expense of retailers that old-line wholesalers did serve.

Second, many congressmen, including those sponsoring Robinson-Patman, were more interested in preserving certain economic classes—"the yeomanry of business" —than they were in preserving either efficiency or competition. Third, although the major push came from anti-chain interests, particularly those in the grocery, drug, wholesaling, and brokerage industries, Congress clearly intended the statute to be broadly applicable.

Congress *intended* to protect competitors and was less interested in protecting competition as a process. It did not want all the efficiencies that were attainable in manufacturing and distribution to be passed down to consumers. This shows most clearly in the act's quantity-limit rule; but it also appears in the *absolute* prohibition of brokerage "discrimination" and merchandising-service discrimination. In neither case does FTC have to show *any* kind of competitive injury.

SOME IMPORTANT PRICE-FIXING CASES

The Addyston Pipe Case (1898)[11]

This is one of the best-reasoned and most interesting of all antitrust cases. It also gave us the famous per se rule against price fixing, and a consumer-welfare standard for antitrust legislation. Chapter 6 provides additional details about how the defendants' cartel worked.

The Sherman Act became law on July 2, 1890. That *Addyston* was an early Sherman Act case, but not the first, made circuit court of appeals Judge Taft's task awkward as well as important. Federal regulation is limited by the interstate commerce clause of the Constitution. And the *Knight* case (1895) had held that the Sherman Act did not apply to sugar manufacturing because *manufacturing* is not interstate or foreign *commerce*. As Chief Justice Fuller put it, "Commerce succeeds to manufacture and is not a part of it." If the Supreme Court held to that interpretation, the Sherman Act—along with a lot of other federal regulation—would have been a dead issue. In *Addyston*, Taft had to decide whether the law applied to cast-iron pipe foundries, which were engaged in manufacturing just as obviously as sugar refiners were.[12] *Addyston* is about a secret bidding-ring cartel selling cast-iron pressure pipe to water and gas companies. We know so much as we do about it because the conspirators were caught red-handed. A disgruntled stenographer, J. E. McClure, turned over many cartel documents to the government.

Taft thought the case presented two questions. First, was the association of the defendants a contract, combination, or conspiracy in restraint of trade, within the meaning of the Sherman Act? Second, was the trade thus restrained trade between the states? The law reaches only interstate commerce.

Defendants contended that the association would have been valid at common law, before the Sherman Act was passed; that the federal antitrust law was intended to reach only agreements that were void and unenforceable at common law; and that 30 percent of a market is not a monopoly.

In *Trans-Missouri*,[13] the court dealt with a quasi-public organization—a railroad. *Addyston* defendants claimed, therefore, that *Trans-Missouri* did not apply to them. Taft avoided evaluating that distinction. He concluded, however, that restraints of trade that were merely unenforceable at common law violate the Sherman Act, if they are in interstate commerce. Contracts in unreasonable restraint of trade had not been unlawful at common law, in the sense of being criminal or calling for damages, but were simply void, and not enforceable by the courts.

But the Sherman Act made such contracts unlawful and punishable, and created a right of civil action for damages or injunction. Taft concluded, as did a (British) court in the 1894 *Nordenfelt* case, that: ''Whatever is injurious to the interests of the public is void on the ground of public policy.'' That is consistent with a consumer-interest or consumer-welfare theory of antitrust.

Agreements that did nothing more than fix prices had no defense in the common law and were void: ''. . . where the sole object of both parties in making the contract . . . is merely to restrain competition, and enhance or maintain prices, it would seem that there was nothing to justify or excuse the restraint, that it would necessarily have a tendency to monopoly, and therefore would be void.''

This, too, is famous language from Taft's opinion:

> It is true that there are some cases in which the courts, mistaking, as we conceive, the proper limits of the relaxation of the rules for determining the unreasonableness of restraints of trade, have set sail on a sea of doubt, and have assumed the power to say, in respect to contracts which have no other purpose and no other consideration on either side than the mutual restraint of the parties, how much restraint of competition is in the public interest, and how much is not.

From his review of precedents Taft concluded that, however reasonable the prices they fixed, however ruinous competition amongst them would otherwise have been, the defendants' agreement was void at common law and actionable under the Sherman Law because it is in restraint of trade and tends to monopoly.

That the cast-iron pipe cartel was only a partial monopoly did not save it. The court perpetually enjoined defendants from maintaining the combination and from doing any business thereunder.

The court here struck down a price-fixing cartel, not a single-firm monopoly, against which the law would remain toothless for some time. Soon after this decision, four of the six defendants merged to form the American Pipe and Foundry Company. United Pipe and Foundry Company then acquired American Pipe and Foundry, plus the other two defendants in Addyston, and some additional companies. The ultimate effect was that 70 to 75 percent of *national* capacity was concentrated in one firm. By the 1920s, this share had eroded to about 40 percent.

It was not until 1948, 50 years after *Addyston*, that the Department of Justice filed suit against U.S. Pipe and Foundry and four other firms, charging restraint of trade and monopoly.

American Tobacco (1946)[14]

Alcoa (1945), which is discussed in the next chapter, and this case are companions in a sense. When the *Alcoa* decision came down, many claimed that it outlawed even monopolies that are innocent of ''bad acts,'' and would reform U.S. industrial structure and performance. The parallel claim for *American Tobacco* was that it outlawed even nonconspiratorial oligopoly, and would reform industrial pricing and structure in the U.S.

In short, some asserted that, taken together, *Alcoa* and *American Tobacco* created a new Sherman Law. These claims were exaggerated.

American Tobacco was one of the "successor" companies carved out of the old tobacco trust in 1911, by a Sherman Act dissolution proceeding. The 1946 case suggests that the Department of Justice was not content with the kind of competition its dissolution suit had created in 1911. For this 1946 case convicted American and other major U.S. cigarette producers of conspiring to fix prices in the purchase of leaf tobacco and the sale of cigarettes, and to "monopolize"—that is, to exclude competitors in the cigarette market.

Though these firms may have been colluding, the evidence against them was wholly circumstantial. Indeed, most of the evidence was consistent with either collusion or monopoly.

In June 1931, as the economy fell toward the bottom of the Great Depression, the largest manufacturers of cigarettes in the U.S. raised their prices from $6.40 to $6.85 per 1,000. Five manufacturers of economy-brand cigarettes quickly expanded from 0.28 percent to 22.78 percent of the U.S. market. The popularity of roll-your-own cigarettes also soared. In early 1933, the producers of regular brands cut their prices to $5.50, which covered their full average cost. By December 1933, the share of economy-brand cigarettes—selling at $4.75—had declined to between 9 percent and 11 percent, still 35 *times* their share in June 1931. In 1939, they still had 14 percent of the market and really faded only after the trial, by which time national income had recovered from the depression.

That was the essence of the "monopolizing" and exclusion aspect of this case. In effect, the Supreme Court held that, first, the June 1931 price *rise* had been monopolistic, unwarranted, and excessive; and, second, that the 1933 price *cuts* were unwarranted and excessive and had excluded competitors in violation of Section 2 of the Sherman Act.

This case shows what other cases confirm: you can get into trouble with the antitrust laws by raising prices, by cutting prices, and by holding prices constant. And there were other extraordinary curiosa.

The defendants actually tried in court were R. J. Reynolds (Camels), American Tobacco (Lucky Strike), and Liggett & Meyers (Chesterfield). Three other defendants were permitted to plead no contest, on the understanding that they would share any penalties meted out should those firms tried be found guilty.

Though it sounds incredible, these other three—Lorillard, the fourth of the successor companies from the old trust; Phillip Morris; and British American were all treated both as co-conspirators and as victims of the conspiracy. Casting them in the role of victims was bizarre. British American's subsidiary was Brown & Williamson, which sold both economy and regular brands (Wings, Avalon, Kool, and Raleigh). So did Phillip Morris (Paul Jones, Phillip Morris). In 1931, Brown & Williamson and Phillip Morris together had 0.5 percent of the U.S. market. In 1939, they had 17.6 percent; in 1955, 19.4 percent.

British American paid fines for offenses that included trying to put Brown & Williamson, its own subsidiary, out of business. Phillip Morris paid fines for, in effect, trying unsuccessfully to put itself out of business. It had become a major competitor during the period when the Big Three were allegedly driving independents to the wall.

American Tobacco (1946) is troublesome in several ways. Many "facts" do not seem to be true. The economics and logic are doubtful and the remedy trivial. In addition, this case shows what happens when conflicting economic theories substitute for facts in legal matters. Most economists believe that nonconspiratorial oligopoly behaves differently than a single firm or cartel would. Some economists believe that three or four large firms and five or six fringe firms are more than enough to produce competitive results unless they somehow manage to collude, which—according to this view—will be difficult to do. See the discussion of the Addyston Pipe cartel in Chapter 6, for example. On the other hand, many believe that oligopolies, including those as loose as the one pictured in American Tobacco, act like cartels even without collusion.

But one of the worst things about this case is that it struck down price cuts on the grounds that they can reduce profits and market shares of other firms. Defining *monopolizing* and exclusion in this way makes price cutting a criminal offense, or at least suspect. Consumers benefit from lower prices. The object of antitrust should be to benefit consumers, not to shield competitors.

GE-Westinghouse (1960)[15]

During the 1950s, and perhaps earlier, 30-odd U.S. manufacturers of electrical equipment conspired to fix prices. Annual sales of such equipment totaled about $2 billion. Following TVA complaints about identical sealed bids, rapidly rising prices, and a British manufacturer's underbidding by one-third the delivered price of an expensive turbine generator, in 1959 the Department of Justice commenced investigations.

There is absolutely no doubt that the firms colluded. They held many secret meetings and used spy-novel procedures to cover them up. A grand jury handed down criminal indictments in 1960; Allis-Chalmers, one of the defendants, pleaded guilty and turned state's evidence. Several corporate and individual defendants were found guilty of violating Section 1 of the Sherman Law and fined a total of more than $1 million. Some individuals received jail sentences. In some 2,000 cases, private utility companies and state and local governments also sued for damages and may have got as much as $150 to $200 million.

There is considerable doubt about how well the conspiracy worked. See Chapter 6 for further details. In any case, however, most economists would deny any excuse for schemes like this and applaud the Sherman Law for taxing them.

Maricopa County Medical Society (1982)[16]

One problem is that this case rests "on an incomplete summary judgment record," and it is impossible to tell what the effects of this arrangement would have been. Mr. Justice Powell's dissent objected strongly to applying the per se rule ritualistically:

It is settled law that once an arrangement has been labeled as "price fixing" it is to be con-demned *per se*. But it is equally well settled that this characterization is not to be applied as a talisman to every arrangement that involves a literal fixing of prices. Many lawful contracts, mergers, and partnerships fix prices. But our cases require a more discerning approach. The inquiry in an antitrust case is not simply one of "determining whether two or more potential competitors have literally 'fixed a price' " . . . Before characterizing an arrangement as a *per se* price fixing agreement meriting condemnation, a court should determine whether it is a "naked restraint of trade with no purpose except stifling of competition" . . . As part of this inquiry, a court must determine whether the pro-competitive economies that the arrangement makes possible are substantial and realizable in the absence of such an agreement.

There is no way now to tell *what* the Maricopa arrangement would have done for consumers, because outlawing it per se as price fixing made performance irrelevant as a matter of law. In bare essence, however, this seems to be what was involved. Maricopa Foundation was a nonprofit corporation of 1,750 doctors practicing various specialties. About 70 percent of the medical practitioners in Maricopa County, Arizona, were mem-bers.

To at least seven different medical and health insurance plans that it approved, Maricopa offered a schedule of maximum fees that Maricopa members could receive for various insured services, and members approved the schedules by vote. Maricopa doctors could charge less if they chose, and could charge anything they chose to uninsured pa-tients. Insured patients could use other physicians than Maricopa's, but would be reim-bursed for no more than Maricopa fees. The court's opinion says that 85 to 95 percent of physicians in Maricopa County billed "at or above" levels set in the Maricopa maximum insurance schedules, which suggests important questions. About 70 percent of all Maricopa County physicians apparently belonged to Maricopa. Suppose that Maricopa schedules applied to 60 percent of the medical insurance "market." Sixty percent of that market would be *at* the Maricopa fee levels, by definition. All the rest might be above. One real question, therefore, is whether the Maricopa schedules were equal to or lower than fees charged other insured patients and other noninsured patients. The Court's arith-metic tells us *nothing* about that.

Citing *Socony-Vacuum* (1940), *Kiefer-Stewart* (1951), and *Albrecht* v. *Herald* (1968), the Court held that maximum-price fixing, like other price fixing, is unlawful per se. One reason is the fear that out-and-out cartel minimum-price fixing might "masquer-ade" in the guise of maximum fee schedules.

The Court minimizes a crucial point. This kind of arrangement could reduce med-ical fees, and the transactions and contracting costs incurred in providing health services and insurance: "The most that can be said for having doctors fix the maximum prices is that doctors may be able to do it more efficiently than insurers." That benefit is not con-temptible.

What would the Sherman Law do if each health plan took bids from individual doc-tors or medical partnerships? Or unilaterally set maximum fees, let individual doctors ac-cept or reject them, and sent insured patients the names of 1700-odd doctors who had accepted the schedules?

As things stand now, we can't tell whether this was a clever cartel scheme to fix *minimum* fees by seeming to set ceilings; or was a legitimate way to reduce medical costs and charges. Those who believe in predatory pricing may wonder whether the scheme might be holding down fees to punish outside physicians. These and other questions pop up in *Ball Hospital* (1986).[17]

Shared Monopoly

A strange and troubling development was the creation of a bundle of loosely-formed theories labelled *shared monopoly*. According to Harvard Law School Professor Phillip Areeda, "There are markets where no single firm possesses sufficient power to be considered a monopoly but where the behavior and economic performance of several firms approaches that of a single-firm monopolist."[18] What this may mean is "oligopoly, plus more." "Signalling" of price-fixing desires and intentions came to be a popular ingredient in such complaints.

To an economist, one difficulty is how to specify and test this theory. Another is why a policy to protect competition needs more than *American Tobacco* (1946), which may already go too far. As late as December 1979, FTC had five Section 5 FTC Act cases underway, including *Exxon* and *Cereals*. Some of these cases involved signalling, and all were asserted by the FTC to involve shared monopolies. These cases were dropped and the shared monopoly theory sold off, partly perhaps because of changes wrought by the Reagan administration.

DISSEMINATING PRICE INFORMATION

It is difficult to explain and harmonize all of the court decisions about information dissemination. Even the courts have had to scramble to distinguish them. The principal differences among these cases are in the details of the plans and the degrees to which the courts claim they succeeded in rigging the market.[19]

For some time antitrust students, DJ, and FTC tried to make "oligopoly interdependence," *plus* something, equal to a Section 1 or Section 2 offense—collusion or like collusion. The "plus factors" seem to have included various ingredients:

Meetings and other contacts with competitors

Opportunities and motive to conspire

"Invitations" to conspire

Conduct inconsistent with or contrary to independent business self-interest or "normal business methods"

Refusal or inability, at trial, to rebut or explain uniform behavior. This, oddly enough, seems to be one of the more important factors that courts have relied upon to infer an agreement.

So far, it appears, structure and "interdependence" have not yet been taken by courts as sufficient in themselves to establish antitrust violations. Indeed, the cases point in various directions.

The notion of "conscious parallelism" goes pretty far back, really beginning in full-blown form with Count II in the *Triangle Conduit & Cable Rigid Steel Conduit* case (1948), often discussed as a basing point case.[20] Others say it begins with *Eastern States Lumber* (1914) or *American Tobacco* (1946). Then comes *Interstate Circuit* v. *U.S.* (1939), and *Theater Enterprises* v. *Paramount* (1954). *GE-Westinghouse* has already been discussed above.

Interstate Circuit (1939)[21]

Interstate, a chain of motion picture theaters, wrote identical letters to eight motion picture distributors. Interstate wanted the distributors to set minimum admission prices and to limit the use of their films for double features. Each of its letters showed that copies were going to all eight film distributors.

In that case, the Supreme Court majority said:

> It was enough that, knowing that concerted action was contemplated and invited, the distributors gave their adherence to the scheme and participated in it. Each distributor was advised that the others were asked to participate; each knew that cooperation was essential to successful operation of the plan. They knew that the plan, if carried out, would result in the restraint of commerce, which we will presently point out, was unreasonable within the meaning of the Sherman Act, and knowing it, all participated in the plan. The evidence is persuasive that each distributor early became aware that the others had joined. With that knowledge they renewed the arrangement and carried it into effect for the two successive years.[22]

The Court looked on this as an invitation to conspire, and concluded that the distributors had accepted it. Although the Court did not call them "plus-factors" they noted that:

> Each distributor was listed as an addressee
>
> There was a strong motive for concerted action
>
> There was evidence of meetings and negotiations among distributors and exhibitors before the letter went out
>
> There was no other plausible explanation than agreement for the distributors' parallel behavior (the Court leaned hard on this one)
>
> Adoption of the parallel restrictions represented a far-reaching change in past business methods.

Theatre Enterprises (1954)[23]

A film exhibitor outside the central city tried unsuccessfully to obtain first-run films for his theater. Distributors turned him down, one after another, on grounds that his location and clientele were not suitable for first-run showings, and that booking first-run films with him would reduce their profits. Defendants won. The Court held that notions of conscious parallelism had not yet read conspiracy completely out of the Sherman Act.

Container Corporation. (1969)[24]

Then came *Container Corporation* (1969), followed by *U.S.* v. *General Motors* (E.D. Michigan 1974), and by *Wall Products Co.* v. *National Gypsum* (N.D. Cal. 1971) 326 F. Supp. 295. In *Container* and *Gypsum*, defendants lost. GM won. At one point FTC seemed increasingly inclined to broaden the definition of "signalling" by including press releases; interviews; and publication of prices and other information in the *Wall Street Journal*, trade association journals, and the like. They are especially sensitive to discussions about *future* prices and *future* plans.[25]

Now for a closer look at *Container*. This Section 1 civil case charged a price-fixing agreement. A district court dismissed the complaint. Mr. Justice Douglas wrote the majority Supreme Court opinion. According to Douglas, this case is different from others previously decided: it involves exchange of price information among competitors, but without an explicit agreement to adhere to a price schedule. Douglas claims there was such agreement in *Sugar Institute* (297 U.S. 553) and *Socony-Vacuum* (310 U.S. 150), a claim that goes too far.

Here each defendant asked others for information about the most recent prices charged, bid, or quoted, and expected to give such information itself whenever asked. Mutuality or reciprocity resulted. Douglas said the result was "concert" and "conspiracy."

These exchanges were, according to Douglas, irregular and infrequent. Nevertheless, he says, from such sometimes "fragmentary" information, "each defendant had the manuals with which it could compute the price charged by a competitor on a specific order to a specific customer."

"Further, the price quoted was the current price which a customer would need to pay in order to obtain products from the defendant furnishing the data." Eighteen defendants (out of 51 producers) accounted for about 90 percent of shipments of corrugated paper containers from plants in the southeastern U.S. It is not easy for 18 sellers to cartelize a trade without explicit agreements. That may be why Douglas did not stress their number. Such containers are made to buyers' specifications, and—for given specifications—are "substantially identical" amongst different sellers and "fungible." *Price* matters; little else does.

According to Douglas, " . . . where a competitor was charging a particular price, a defendant would normally quote the same price or even [?!] a lower price."

Exchanging price information "seemed to have the effect of keeping prices within a fairly narrow ambit." The complaint period was 1955 to 1963, during which prices trended downward. Capacity exceeded demand. Nevertheless, there was entry into the industry, which does look peculiar. Southeastern producers grew from 30—with 49 plants—to 51—with 98 plants. It required only about $50,000 to $75,000 investment to enter, and entry was "easy."

"The result of this reciprocal exchange of prices was to stabilize prices though at a downward level."

Price-information exchanges need not cause price to exceed the competitive level; but "the continuation of some price competition is not fatal to the Government's case." Here, however: (1) "The corrugated container industry is dominated by relatively few [?!] sellers." (2) The product is fungible, and competition is in price. (3) "Demand is inelastic." At the competitive price? At going prices? (4) "Exchange of price data tends toward price uniformity." (5) "A lower price does not mean a larger share of the available business but a sharing of the existing business at a lower return." "Stabilizing prices as well as raising them is within the ban of Section 1 of the Sherman Act."

According to Douglas, "The inferences are irresistible that the exchange of price information has had an anticompetitive effect in the industry, chilling the vigor of price competition."

Mr. Justice Fortas concurred in a separate opinion. He saw enough evidence of an unlawful effect on prices to go along: "This evidence, although not overwhelming, is sufficient in the special circumstances of this case to show an actual effect on pricing and to compel us to hold that the court below erred in dismissing the Government's complaint." According to the district court, "In the majority of instances," defendants quoted the same price when they got the price information from competitors.

In Fortas's words, "In addition, there was evidence that, in some instances, during periods when various defendants ceased exchanging prices exceptionally sharp and vigorous price reductions resulted." That does seem to be relevant, if true.

Justices Marshall, Harlan, and Stewart dissented. Marshall wrote the dissenting opinion. Eighteen defendant companies, out of 51 competitors, produced about 90 percent of the corrugated containers in the southeastern U.S. It is not shown whether defendants alone exchanged such price information. Entry was easy, and the number of firms was growing. Mr. Justice Marshall's dissent said that, "Given the uncertainty about the probable effect of an exchange of price information in this context, I would require that the Government prove that the exchange was entered into for the purpose of or that it had the effect of restraining price competition."

Similar is the case brought in *Wall Products Co.* v. *National Gypsum Co.*, 326 F. Supp. 295 (N.D. Cal. 1971), where the court found unlawful an agreement to adhere to posted prices, but permitted price exchanges to verify prices to defend against suits brought under the Robinson-Patman Act, and to prevent "fraud."[26]

U.S. Gypsum Co. (1978)[27]

Like many others, this case confuses the economics by commingling several legal and economic problems. The legal problems are enough to create a muddle on their own. First, this is a *criminal* case, charging violation of Section 1 of the Sherman Act.[28] Criminal law is concerned with intent as well as with effects. This fundamental feature of our legal system causes all manner of complications, including insanity defenses and the like. According to Chief Justice Burger, in a criminal case a requisite intent must be found as *fact* by the trier of fact. It is not to be inferred as a matter of law from "an impact on prices." How important Burger's distinction is, is not clear. As Burger put it,

> . . . action undertaken with knowledge of its probable consequences *and* having the requisite anticompetitive effects can be sufficient predicate for a finding of criminal liability under the antitrust laws. Therefore, although it would be correct to instruct the jury that it may infer intent from an effect on prices, ultimately the decision on the issue of intent must be left to the trier of fact alone.

As a practical matter, this distinction may do little more than limit what lower court judges say in their instructions to juries.

The situation in civil antitrust cases is said to be different. In the absence of showing anticompetitive effect, establishing a violation requires showing that defendants acted with unlawful purpose. Given a demonstration of unlawful effects, however, there is no need to demonstrate any kind of intent, let alone a specific intent to violate the antitrust law.[29]

The second legal problem is that this Sherman Law case also directly involves the Robinson-Patman Act, which is basically hostile to competition anyway. Not only that: this case comes during a period in which the courts are emasculating the Robinson-Patman Act by reinterpreting the Section 2(b) meeting-competition defense.[30] For *Gypsum*, therefore, it seems *legally* relevant that defendants needed less information to defend against an emasculated Robinson-Patman Act. Once Robinson-Patman requires less, or amounts to less, there is less Robinson-Patman excuse for what *Gypsum* defendants had been doing.

As enacted, the Robinson-Patman Act offered defendants at least a procedural rebuttal if they could show that discrimination had been necessary to meet, but not beat, a competitive offer. There were ambiguities about whether the offer met had itself to be a lawful offer, and so on. Section 2(f) also put *buyers* at hazard if they accepted a deal they had reason to believe, or might have suspected, violated the Robinson-Patman Act, and so on. *Gypsum* defendants tried to use Robinson-Patman to excuse what they did, which was, basically, to check with one another regularly to verify who was charging what prices to whom.

As Burger put it,

> We are left, therefore, on the one hand, with doubts about both the need for and the efficacy of interseller verification as a means of facilitating compliance with Section 2(b) of the Robinson-Patman Act, and, on the other, with recognition of the tendency for price discussions between competitors to contribute to the stability of oligopolistic prices and open the way for the growth of prohibited anticompetitive activity. To recognize even a limited "controlling circumstance" exception for interseller verification in such circumstances would be to remove from scrutiny under the Sherman Act conduct falling near its core with no assurance, and indeed with serious doubts, that competing antitrust policies would be served thereby.

In short, defendants had gone too far, violating the Sherman Act in the process.

As usual, the case is not satisfying from an economist's perspective. Burger does not clearly tell us either what an unlawful ''impact on prices'' really is, or even what defendants had actually done to prices. Is the illegal impact a reduction in price variance, an increase in the lowest prices, a rise in the average price, or what? And, indeed, how did gypsum board prices actually behave?

Gypsum is about laminated wallboard that has a gypsum core. This product had been involved in a number of earlier antitrust cases, including the patent case discussed in Chapter 8. Burger says that there were nine to fifteen producers between 1960 and 1973, and that the industry was ''highly concentrated.'' The largest eight, all of them multiple-plant producers, sold 94 percent of the total. Most producers belonged to the Gypsum Association, a trade association formed in 1930.

Among other things, defendants were charged with exchanging current and future price information on a continuing, regular basis. Defendants claimed that they were merely trying to comply with the Robinson-Patman Act, and that ''no court had ever held that a mere exchange of information which had a stabilizing effect on prices violated the Sherman Act, regardless of the purposes of the exchange.''

According to Burger, ''exchanges of information do not constitute a *per se* violation of the Sherman Act.'' But, he said, ''we do not agree . . . that the prior case law dealing with the exchange of price information required proof of a purpose to restrain competition in order to make out a Sherman Act violation.'' Exactly where this leaves his exegesis of criminal law requirements is unclear, although—it is true—*Container* (1969) was a civil case. For Burger cites the *Container* rule as relevant to *Gypsum*, which *was* a criminal case:

> Certainly our decision in *United States* v. *Container Corp.* is fairly read as indicating that proof of an anticompetitive effect is a sufficient predicate for Civil liability. In that case, liability followed from proof that ''the exchange of price information had an anti-competitive effect in the industry,'' and no suggestion was made that proof of a purpose to restrain trade or competition was also required.

If price exchanges are, as Burger says, not unlawful per se, what more is needed for them to become unlawful? According to Burger,

> A number of factors including most prominently the structure of the industry involved and the nature of the information exchanged are generally considered in divining the pro or anticompetitive effects of this type of interseller communication [citing *Container*]. . . . Exchanges of current price information, of course, have the greatest potential for generating anticompetitive effects and although not *per se* unlawful have consistently been held to violate the Sherman Act.

This brief survey of cases about information exchanges has ignored important questions. For example, increasing international competition in electronics, autos, and basic manufacturing industries not only increased the clamor for protective tariffs and quotas. It also generated proposals to loosen antitrust strictures on joint ventures and information pools, on the theory that this could increase technological progress, improve products, and lower costs.

VERTICAL ARRANGEMENTS

Some objectives of vertical integration may be achieved short of ownership. In the 1930s oil refiners began selling off their filling stations because of state anti–chain store taxation and the costs of Social Security and other federal laws. Yet even stations run by "independent" operators, under lease-back arrangements or requirements contracts, are also quasi integrated with refiners. Similarly, it can be argued that purely vertical price fixing or resale price maintenance is similar to vertical integration.

Law may regard the *form* of vertical control as important. For example, agency arrangements of the sort claimed in the 1926 *General Electric* case got better legal treatment than did vertical price fixing by manufacturers.[31] Yet the economic effects may not differ. Law is also more hostile to vertical control of price than to vertical control of sales territories and the like. We are told that—in the absence of express statutory permission—vertical price fixing is prohibited per se, just as is horizontal price fixing of the cartel type.

When law imposes different rules for different business forms that have the same motives and effects, the forms tend to change. Justices Douglas, Hughes, and Brandeis noted this tendency in some of their opinions.

The law and economics of vertical integration and resale price maintenance need to be reconciled, as well as put right. Chapter 12 argued that we should not object to vertical integration unless it increases horizontal monopoly without giving consumers cost or value compensations. Horizontal monopoly should be attacked as a horizontal problem, if it needs to be attacked at all.

The economics of vertical integration suggests that resale price maintenance gets worse legal treatment than it deserves. A vertically integrated firm can use the mix of qualities and services that consumers prefer and charge the profit-maximizing price for it. A vertically integrated firm can tell its retail division how much to charge. It will not let that division act like a monopsonist, or otherwise let it take too much for providing distribution services.

Why, then, should the unintegrated firm be kept from doing the same thing, in this case by specifying the price and gross margin that independent retailers can get? The only obvious reason is that it might increase monopoly. A cartel of dealers or wholesalers, for example, would like legally enforceable contracts to maintain the monopoly prices they set. And a cartel of manufacturers could use resale price maintenance both to remove excuses for price cutting and to make price cutting less profitable. Bowman and Telser believe that's what was going on in the old *GE* light bulb case.[32]

But what are the affirmative arguments for resale price maintenance? They are that it provides the locations, qualities, and services that consumers prefer. Without resale price maintenance, price-cutting dealers will freeload on those who offer services, ultimately killing off the services and leaving only price competition. Or, without guaranteed margins, fewer and less convenient outlets will be provided, leaving consumers worse off. Getting less quality and service characteristics could in the long run hurt consumers, distributors, and manufacturers.

Albrecht v. Herald Co. (1968)[33]

In its astounding *Albrecht* decision, the Supreme Court held that a publisher violated the Sherman Law by firing a newspaper carrier for charging more for home delivery than its contract with the publisher provided. That, the Court said, was vertical price-fixing, which violates the Sherman Act. Posner likens this to preventing a firm from "searching out the lowest bidder—just the sort of conduct the antitrust laws are intended to foster."[34] If law were neutral, sellers could choose either vertical integration or resale price maintenance to provide what consumers want and would choose the more efficient way. Chapter 12 criticized Mueller's test for whether vertical integration lowers costs. There is an analogy in the case of resale price maintenance. That manufacturers do not become completely integrated vertically when resale price maintenance is unlawful does not prove that resale price maintenance was up to no good.[35]

Reynolds Metals Co. v. FTC (1962)[36]

Aluminum foil is sheet that is from .00065 to .006 inch thick, oil-free and dry. FTC said that household foil is about .0007 inch and that florist foil is "usually" .00065 inch, which is the lightest and cheapest available. Three fully integrated producers made foil: Reynolds, Kaiser, and Alcoa. Anaconda, Revere, and Olin-Matheson were partially integrated producers. There were several nonintegrated producers: Johnston, Republic Foil, Stranahan, R. J. Reynolds, and Aluminum Foils.

Relying on "peculiar characteristics and uses," and citing *Du Pont* (Cellophane),[37] FTC said the relevant line of commerce was "the production and sale of decorative aluminum foil to the florist trade." That recalls another case in which FTC defined a market narrowly: earth-moving equipment used only the Mesabi Iron Range. Prices of florist foil, it said, were "substantially less than, and fluctuated independently from, the price of aluminum foil of a similar gauge and quality sold by major producers in other markets." Perhaps so; but florist foil is the cheapest so far as aluminum content, and there are questions about the relevancy of volume purchases, packaging, and the cost of decorations.

Florists bought foil in 50 foot lengths, 20 inches wide, "wrapped in cellophane and attractively boxed." They could use other foils, including household foils. Florist foil is decorated. Florists also use lace, colored cellophane, chip mats, grass mats, and so on, in spite of which FTC said "there is no practical substitute for the florist foil."

Firms like Arrow Brands, Inc. bought foil, decorated it, and sold it to florist supply houses. Florists used foil to package cut flowers and decorate flower pots. Reynolds, the largest U.S. producer of aluminum foil, bought Arrow in August 1956. With this step, Reynolds integrated into the business of supplying foil to florist supply houses. As a result, FTC said, the "balance of power" shifted to Arrow after the acquisition.

In October 1957, Arrow "drastically" cut prices "across the board," maybe below Arrow's full cost. Prices stayed low from October 1957 to mid-1958—a recession period—but Arrow got a new $500 thousand plant. Low prices hurt and displeased its competitors, naturally enough. FTC says that low prices "virtually" ran some of them out of the business. When FTC asked them, Arrow's competitors said things were tough. Reynolds said that the price cuts were meant to meet low prices of imported foil.

Holding that "here, competition has been actually lessened as a result of the acquisition," FTC ordered Reynolds to divest itself of Arrow. That would "reestablish Arrow Brands, Inc. as a competitive entity in substantially the form it existed."

Later, FTC denied Reynolds's motion to reopen the case. Reynolds wanted to show that competition in the field had not disappeared. Kaiser entered the florist foil business in 1960, and R. J. Reynolds expanded its florist foil operations after 1958. The FTC had not been impressed by this argument: "Even though subsequent events may show that future competitive conditions are not as anticipated, this would not make legal that which was illegal * * * the new evidence could have no bearing on the outcome of this proceeding." But this proceeding was not a murder trial. It was an action for divestiture because of what might happen to competition! What *did* happen to competition is clearly relevant.

But the FTC wanted a particular kind of competition—the kind there used to be: "A new entry comparable in strength to Reynolds Metals Company could no doubt offer competition to respondent; it would not restore the kind of competition which has been reduced or eliminated." That argument presumably applies however high cost or sluggish the old kind of competition had been.

In an ironic turnabout, FTC rebuffed Reynolds when it tried to play the Commission's own game. Reynolds said that competitors had not been injured, and were still in business. FTC said that "The issue before the Commission in deciding the case was not one of probable injury to competitors, but of probable injury to competition."

Reynolds appealed, and the D.C. Circuit Court of Appeals reviewed the case. Judge Burger, later chief justice of the Supreme Court, wrote the opinion. He noted that Reynolds had 40.5 percent of the U.S. foil output; that, although there were about 200 foil "converters," all of whom could make florist foil, only about eight served the florist industry; and that Arrow had about one-third of the florist foil market.

Burger noted *Brown Shoe* and *Du Pont* theories of market definition, citing several relevant ways to decide whether one product differs from another: industry or public recognition of a separate economic entity; a product's peculiar characteristics and uses; unique production facilities; distinct customers; distinct prices; sensitivity to price changes; and specialized vendors. In the end, however, the court found florist foil to be the relevant line of commerce because of public and industry recognition, distinct customers, and distinct prices.

Of the 9.7 million pounds of decorative foil produced, the eight foil converters—including Arrow—that served florists shipped less than 1.5 million pounds to florists. Reynolds said that the same kinds of decorative foil were used for cheese wrap, coffee cup covers, meat, and so on. Nevertheless, said the court, the only purchasers of florist foil—perhaps defined as foil that florists buy—are the 700 wholesale florist outlets. And, "Substantial evidence discloses a markedly lower price for florist foil compared with the price of other colored or embossed aluminum foil sold in comparable weight units and gauged at approximately the same thickness.'' Burger's theory is that this stuff *must* somehow be different. Otherwise, businesses would have substituted it for the other kinds.

Burger says that he found against Reynolds not because competitors had been foreclosed from one-third of the florist foil market. The problem was that Arrow derived advantages from being owned by Reynolds. It got a rich parent, deep pockets, and staying power. FTC, after all, claimed to have found an *actual* anticompetitive effect. The circuit court sustained the divestiture, but only of those properties added at the time of the acquisition.

Brown Shoe Co. (1962)[38]

This merger case, under Section 7 of the Clayton Act, is partly about (horizontal) competition and partly about vertical integration. Among other things, the case shows how courts define markets. Much has been written about it.[39]

Chief Justice Warren wrote the majority opinion. This suit began in November 1955, when Brown undertook to buy Kinney. The complaint sought an injunction to prevent that. The companies were permitted to merge if they kept their businesses separate until the antitrust issues had been sorted out. The merger went into effect May 1, 1956.

Out of 1,230 ''Brown stores,'' Brown actually owned only 470; the others operated under exclusive dealing franchises. The Court lumps them together. The district court had defined the relevant ''section of the country'' as all cities of at least 10,000 population (plus their contiguous surrounding area) in which a Kinney store and a Brown store were located. That court concluded that: (1) Combining Brown and Kinney shoe manufacturing facilities—4 percent plus 0.5 percent—would not lessen competition. (2) vertical foreclosure *would* hurt other shoe manufacturers; (3) three distinct ''lines'' of shoes are relevant—men's, women's, and children's; (4) merger of retailing—1.6 percent by number of pairs and 1.2 percent by dollar volume—would tend to lessen competition.

Citing the district court (DC) opinion, Warren said that '' . . . a small number of large companies occupied a commanding position.'' What a position! Four companies produced only 23 percent of the shoes made in U.S.; and the largest 24 (!) produced only 35 percent. That does not even count imports. There were at least 70,000 retail outlets selling shoes, only 22,000 of which the Census classifies as ''shoe stores.'' Department stores, for example, sell a lot of shoes; but they are not classified as ''shoe stores.''

The DC discerned what it called a ''trend'' toward acquiring retail outlets, from which ''foreclosure'' tended to follow. There was also a downward trend in the number of shoe plants and firms. In 1947, for example, there had been 1,077 firms manufacturing shoes in the U.S. In 1958, there were 872—not merely a few by any standard. The court made the amazing discovery that every time Brown bought retail outlets, it increased sales of Brown shoes to them!

Kinney operated the largest ''family-style shoe store'' chain in the U.S., more than 400 stores in more than 270 cities. It did a whopping 1.2 percent of the total dollar volume. Kinney stores had bought 20 percent of their shoes from Kinney's four manufacturing plants, which made men's, women's, and children's shoes. At the time of the merger, Kinney bought no shoes from Brown.

Warren's version of the legislative history of Section 7 is depressing, citing among other things the "threat to other values a trend toward concentration was thought to pose." Section 7 was meant to apply to vertical, horizontal, and conglomerate mergers.

Interchangeability in use—cross-elasticity of demand—enters into the question of market definition; but how? Definition of submarkets, Warren said, depends upon "industry or public recognition"; "peculiar characteristics and uses"; unique production facilities; distinct customers; distinct prices; sensitivity to price changes; specialized vendors—and heaven only knows what else. Brown urged distinctions based on "price/quality" and "age/sex"; but the DC disagreed. A footnote mentions that the cross-elasticity of production facilities is relevant, at least where vertical integration is involved, and cites *Bethlehem* and *Columbia Steel*.

To evaluate the vertical aspects, Warren says, the whole U.S. is the right geographic market, and " . . . foreclosure of a *de minimis* share of the market will not tend 'substantially to lessen competition'." But, he says, the percentage is not decisive. What is? "The present merger involved neither small companies nor failing companies." Brown was the fourth-largest U.S. manufacturer of shoes, with assets of $72 million. Kinney's assets were $18 million. "Thus, in operation this vertical arrangement would be quite analogous to one involving a tying clause."

Other factors were the "trend toward concentration"; effects on an "economic way of life," "local control of industry," and "small business." In spite of what the data show, Warren sounds convinced that a "cumulative" series of vertical mergers was under way. He says that it may foreclose competition from a substantial *share* of markets "without producing any countervailing competitive, economic, or social advantages." It is not clear how he could possibly know that.

What about the horizontal aspects of the case? The government did not contest that the merger was insignificant on the manufacturing level; Brown contested findings about the retail level. Warren agreed with the DC that shoe stores on the outskirts compete with those in central downtown areas. This is a good example of how biases differ with respect to market definitions in merger cases as compared with monopoly cases. In monopoly cases, the government tends to argue that geographic markets are small, for example that downtown stores do not compete with those in the suburbs. In merger cases, the government tends to argue that markets are broad enough to include both merger partners, since otherwise the merger could not diminish competition between them. In that tradition, Warren held the broader market against the merger. Brown objected because the DC confined detailed study to St. Louis, a city in which Kinney did not even operate! Warren says that didn't matter: the Record supports the lower court's findings anyway.

Warren emphasized cities with high combined shares of Brown and Kinney shoe stores. In 1955, the combined shares of women's shoes exceeded 20 percent in 32 cities. In 31 cities, the combined share of children's shoes exceeded 20 percent. In 6 cities, the combined stores sold more than 40 percent of children's shoes. And—horror of horrors—in Dodge City, the combined stores sold more than 57 percent of women's shoes. It is worth repeating that these shares are based on sales by what Census defines as shoe stores—that is, stores in which shoes are the most important contributor to total sales. That leaves out department stores. It also implicitly assumes that manufacturers of women's shoes can't switch to children's shoes, and it seems to say that the number of retail stores is difficult to expand.

This Court, like many laymen, seems to have had a gang-fight or weight-division theory of what competition is. This made it possible to use *against* Brown the *unconcentrated* character of the shoe business. As Warren put it, "In an industry as fragmented as shoe retailing, the control of substantial shares of the trade in a city may have important effects on competition." Besides, said Warren, we don't want to permit "oligopoly" to be created by merger.

Warren said that chains are dangerous. They can—somehow—insulate themselves from competition and "set and alter styles in footwear." They also "can market their own brands at prices below those of competing independent retailers," which seems to be the real rub. Nevertheless, Warren said the Court had not overlooked consumers:

> A third significant aspect of this merger is that it creates a large national chain which is integrated with a manufacturing operation. The retail outlets of integrated companies, by eliminating wholesalers and by increasing the volume of purchases from the manufacturing division of the enterprise, can market their own brands at prices below those of competing independent retailers. Of course, some of the results of large integrated or chain operations are beneficial to consumers. Their expansion is not rendered unlawful by the mere fact that small independent stores may be adversely affected. It is competition, not competitors, which the Act protects. But we cannot fail to recognize Congress' desire to promote competition through the protection of viable, small, locally owned businesses.

> Congress appreciated that occasional higher costs and prices might result from the maintenance of fragmented industries and markets. It resolved these competing considerations in favor of decentralization. We must give effect to that decision.

Here, the Court starts by bowing ceremoniously towards low costs, low prices, and competition, but ends by shielding competitors and abandoning consumers.

Mr. Justice Clark concurred, although he said the line of commerce should have included *all* shoes. Justice Harlan concurred in part and dissented in part. He would have dismissed the appeal for want of jurisdiction: the judgment was not yet final. And he was not pleased by the way the markets had been defined:

> . . . the history of Brown's own factories reveals that a single plant may be used in successive years, or even at the same time, for the manufacture of varying grades of shoes and may, without undue difficulty, be shifted from the production of children's shoes to men's or women's shoes, or vice versa.

Harlan thought the line of commerce ought to be the "wearing apparel shoe industry generally," and he saw no trend to oligopoly. From 1948 through 1954, chains of eleven or more stores held a constant 19.5 percent of dollar volume. And the market shares of the largest four, eight, and fifteen manufacturers were all going *down* from 1947 to 1955.

To Harlan, vertical integration was the real menace. It would result in significant foreclosure: some shoe manufacturers sold more than 40 percent of their production to Kinney in 1955 and the merger might force them to find other customers. Like the Supreme Court in the 1916 *Can* case and the lower court in *Alcoa,* Harlan emphasized the "open" part of the shoe market, which is the part not tied up contractually or affiliated. As he saw it, "displaced manufacturers have no choice but to enter some other market or go out of business." Why? So what? If monopoly margins were set in retailing, there would be more room for competitors than ever before—unless it is efficiency that is the real issue. He thought the chains had too great an advantage at retail: they can outlast smaller, unaffiliated competitors.

No one had shown what effects earlier integration had on manufacturers, retailers, or competition.

PRICE DISCRIMINATION

The relationship of price discrimination to monopoly and monopolization is somewhat ambiguous. First, price theory specifies conditions in which sellers will systematically discriminate in price to increase profits from whatever monopoly power they happen to have. Second, many believe that price discrimination can be used to increase monopoly power as well as to exploit a given amount of it. Correctly or not, many believe that price discrimination lowers the cost of monopolizing through predation to kill or predation to merge. And, if delivered-pricing systems are really collusive, the conspirators use price discrimination to make their delivered prices identical.

Third, however, price theory recognizes that secret, discriminatory price cutting undermines cartels and frustrates live-and-let-live oligopoly.[40] There is evidence to support the theory. Secret, discriminatory price cutting has undermined many a real-world cartel. References cited in Chapter 18 discuss early railroad cartels and the Interstate Commerce Commission, both of which made cartels more effective by prohibiting price discrimination. The same thing shows up in other cartel cases, such as *Board of Trade*, *Trenton Potteries*, and *Sugar Institute*.[41] The Sugar Institute's private "Code of Ethics" anticipated a common feature of government-enforced NRA codes when it abolished all "discriminations." Preventing price discrimination was also a goal in many of the information-collection and distribution cases.

Given all this, it is not surprising that trying to obey the Robinson-Patman Act has actually been used as an excuse for conspiracies themselves.

Fourth, in countless markets that are hotly though not *perfectly* competitive, information is so thin that prices differ significantly among buyers—as they do in public markets and bazaars. Some firms have no price systems at all, but offer whatever price is necessary to obtain an order and contribute something to fixed costs.[42] And, as Telser once pointed out, even in organized exchanges it is not unheard of for transactions prices to differ at the same time on different sides of the same trading pit.

Fifth, economics recognizes that many price *differences* are not discriminatory at all. Some price differences recognize differences in costs of manufacture or sale; some evaluate differences in risks. None of these differences is easy to measure, and some are impossible.[43] And convincing FTC and courts about such differences proved difficult, indeed. It is worth remembering that many Robinson-Patman cases are about sellers claimed to be discriminating among their own dealers, allegedly damaging some of them dreadfully. But why should they discriminate against and ruin dealers they will need for survival; or create monopsony positions and inflated margins for those few dealers they allegedly favor?

These ambiguities notwithstanding, there is remarkable consensus about the Robinson-Patman Act of 1936. Many economists and lawyers now believe that this statute is inherently and profoundly anticompetitive, not merely clumsily written and perversely enforced.[44]

The Robinson-Patman Act catered to those who claimed that chains would ruin small business by buying and selling cheap. The courts never overthrew the fatal conception of competitive injury with which the act was born. On the contrary, that conception eventually contaminated the Sherman Act itself.

Morton Salt (1948)[45]

In 1948, in *Morton Salt*, the Supreme Court ratified the FTC's boldest conceptions of what competitive injury is. As the Court put it, "In a case involving competitive injury between a seller's customers, the Commission need only prove that a seller had charged one purchaser a higher price for like goods than he had charged one or more of the purchaser's competitors."

It is curious that this case is famous distinguished between a probability and a possibility of competitive injury. The Court said that the Commission need show "only that there is a reasonable possibility that discriminatory prices . . . may have such an effect." This is a relatively trivial distinction once competitive injury has been defined as the Court did in the language just quoted. From that point on, definitional identity completely dominates whatever practical difference there may be between possibilities and probabilities.

Utah Pie (1967)[46]

A much later case showed little improvement. Utah Pie Co., apparently the only Salt Lake City manufacturer of frozen desserts, including pies, sued Pet Milk, Carnation Milk, and Continental Baking. Utah Pie charged that defendants had injured it by selling frozen pies in Salt Lake City at discriminatory and low prices, in violation of Section 2(a) of the Robinson-Patman Act. It sought treble damages.

Before Utah Pie entered the business, most of the Salt Lake market had been supplied by national food manufacturers whose plants were outside Utah. Utah Pie, a local baker, entered the frozen pie business in 1957 and built a new plant in 1958. The frozen pie market expanded rapidly, growing 368 percent between 1958 and 1961. With location and freight on its side, Utah Pie cut prices and grabbed off two-thirds of the Salt Lake market in 1958.

Defendants then cut their prices in Utah, where they were occasionally lower than in other markets. Utah Pie continued to grow and prosper. Its market share fell, it is true, from 66.5 percent (1958) to 34.3 percent (1959); then rose to 45.5 percent (1960) and stood at 45.3 percent in 1961. In 1961 Pet sold 29.4 percent; Carnation, 8.8 percent; and Continental, 8.3 percent. Other firms sold less than 10 percent.

Although the jury found no conspiracy, it did conclude that defendants had individually violated the statute by this "area discrimination." The circuit court of appeals overturned their verdict, finding no adverse effect on competition.

The Supreme Court reversed again, because plaintiff's market share and the whole price structure in Utah had fallen. As Mr. Justice White put it,

> The major competitive weapon in the Utah market was price. The location of petitioner's plant gave it a natural advantage in the Salt Lake City marketing area and it entered the market at a price below the then going prices for the respondents' comparable pies. For most of the period involved here [1958-1961] its prices were the lowest in the Salt Lake City market. There was ample evidence to show that each of the respondents contributed to what proved to be a deteriorating price structure over the period covered by this suit, and each of the respondents in the course of the ongoing price competition sold frozen pies in the Salt Lake market at prices lower than it sold pies of like grade and quality in other markets considerably closer to their plants.

The rule here seems to be that you should not compete in price unless you do it everywhere equally. That slows, and may stop, price movements toward marginal costs. The opinion establishes no guidelines for the maximum kind of competition that is legal, though rigid uniform delivered or F.O.B. prices would presumably have been just fine.

Utah Pie and Pet Milk made large private-brand sales to Safeway at lower prices. Pet Milk's cost justification failed to satisfy the Court. The Safeway episode was particularly serious, White said, because "private-label sales influenced the general market, in this case depressing overall market prices."

According to Ward Bowman, this opinion is outrageous but "not very serious to pie-eaters in Utah. They can eat cake."[47]

SUMMARY AND CONCLUSIONS

Taft's *Addyston* decision is widely admired. When fundamental problems show up even in the best-of-breed, however, we know we've got trouble. Remember that one of Taft's contributions was to explain and establish a per se rule against "naked" trade restraints, defined as those that do nothing else but increase prices and reduce outputs. With respect to such arrangements, there was to be no rule of reason to set us adrift upon a "sea of doubt."

But there is a problem with even a per se rule: someone must decide what is a naked restraint and what is not. And there are at least two reasons why this is not so easy. First, we should not expect firms candidly to admit that their contracts, understandings, and arrangements tend to reduce competition at all, let alone that they are *purely* output-reducing. Second, many arrangements that are suspect under the antitrust laws may actually increase values as consumers perceive them. They could do so if they increase the *value* of output as well as merely increasing its price. Suppose, for example, that a manufacturer contractually restrains price competition among retailers to encourage them to provide the convenience, information, and services that some consumers prefer to somewhat lower prices. Since about 1912, the U.S. antitrust laws have struck down any such arrangements that were not explicitly exempt.

Chapter 9 discussed tie-in and requirements contracts, some of which no doubt serve consumers. The "loyalty" contracts that ocean freight-rate cartels used may also have been benign. Shippers who did not use competing steamship lines got lower rates. Though there is no doubt that these contracts were meant to exclude competitors, they may have provided benefits as well as repelling entrants and raising rates. It is conceivable, for example, that they helped provide the kind of regular, frequent service that many shippers want. Otherwise, the story goes, outsiders would move their ships in just ahead of scheduled sailings, leaving no cargo for scheduled ships. If such restraints are necessary to provide customers what they want, why consider them restraints of trade? On the other hand, the restraints may go farther than necessary to accomplish good results. For example, could the shipping companies have provided scheduled services merely by selling cargo space in advance, thereby collecting for and assuring both shipping space and schedule?

Other examples are the antitrust problems that arise in professional sports. If a whole sports league is the relevant firm, how can the teams be considered members of a cartel? But is it necessary or desirable to suppress competition as much as the leagues do, geographically and for players, for example?

Practices such as resale price maintenance and loyalty contracts pose important analytic questions and policy problems. It is not easy to determine what these arrangements do and whether alternative arrangements could produce better results. On net balance, do the restraints raise consumer benefits, for example, by increasing outputs of the same thing, or by producing even better things? Could alternative arrangements produce what consumers want without burying competition quite so deep? In short, do the complained-of restrictions clearly produce highest net benefits?

It is dangerous to accept arrangements just because they claim to offer consumers better qualities than can be gotten with no restraints at all. Yet commanding law to find the "optimal" arrangement may be totally infeasible, plus destructive even in principle. How can courts tell whether a more restrictive alternative really is better, let alone optimal?

Most of the vertical integration and vertical price fixing decisions make little sense from a consumer point of view. Chapter 12 argued that vertical integration in itself is not a threat to consumers, and probably the best thing courts can do is to ignore it. This chapter shows that they have not done that. Vertical price fixing is no threat, either, unless it is used to facilitate horizontal agreements amongst manufacturers, wholesalers, or retailers.

Robert Bork observed, first, that it is legally inconsistent (and odd) to permit a vertically integrated firm to set its own resale prices but not permit a nonintegrated firm to do what amounts to the same thing.[48] This is the point that Taft made when he referred to the old *Pullman* case. Second, neither monopolist nor competitor would conspire against its own best interests, and vertical price fixing can not therefore really be price fixing in the value reducing sense. According to this logic, resale price maintenance would become a vice only if it were turned into horizontal price fixing among manufacturers; or were (coercively?) imposed upon manufacturers by dealers seeking to increase *their* horizontal monopoly power. But what room does this leave for quid pro quo agreements between conspiring manufacturers and conspiring dealers? It can be argued that cooperating bilateral monopolies, established in both cases by conspiracy, are not the ideal form of industrial organization unless they are sanctified by cost savings.

For good reason, most economists dislike the Robinson-Patman Act. It has probably reduced more competition than it ever protected and should be repealed. Some economists still believe that *predatory* price discrimination is a threat and should be prohibited. The Sherman Law already does that.

QUESTIONS

1. The Clayton Act is an "incipiency" statute that is supposed to catch monopoly in the seed before it comes to flower. What practical and theoretic problems does such a statute pose?
2. What does *restraint of trade* mean? How did Judge Taft differentiate between restraints of trade and business forms and practices that are legal?
3. What does *per se* mean? What per se rule applies in Sherman Law cases?
4. What happened in the cast-iron pipe industry after the government won in *Addyston*?
5. Think back to the welfare trade-off analysis developed in Chapter 13. In principle, how would you use that analysis to decide which arrangements should be legal under the Sherman Law and which should not?
6. In what sense did *American Tobacco* (1946) outlaw pricing and other practices because they reduced profits and market shares of competitors? Is that a good idea in general? Explain. Is that *ever* a good idea? Explain.
7. What unanswered questions remain from *Arizona* v. *Maricopa County Medical Society*?
8. The per se rule against price fixing caused some grief in *Maricopa* and *Albrecht*. Explain. Do you see any way around this problem?
9. Enumerate and comment on standards courts use to decide whether disseminating information is lawful or unlawful.
10. Present the basic facts of *Brown Shoe* and analyze how the decision trades off between efficiency and industrial structures.
11. "The relationship of price discrimination to monopoly and monopolization is somewhat ambiguous." Explain and comment.
12. What standards of competitive injury did the Court use in *Morton Salt*? In *Utah Pie*?

NOTES

1. George J. Stigler, "The Economic Effects of the Antitrust Laws," *Journal of Law & Economics* (1966), reprinted in Stigler's *The Organization of Industry* (Homewood, Ill.: Richard

D. Irwin, Inc., 1968), pp. 259–95; Thomas W. Ross, "Winners and Losers Under the Robinson-Patman Act," *Journal of Law & Economics*, 27 (October 1984), pp. 243–71.

2. B. Espen Eckbo and Peggy Wier, "Antimerger Policy Under the Hart-Scott-Rodino Act: A Reexamination of the Market Power Hypothesis," *Journal of Law & Economics*, 28 (April 1985), pp. 119–41.

3. Outlines of McGee's views about antitrust can be seen in "Patent Exploitation: Some Economic and Legal Problems," *Journal of Law & Economics*, 9 (October 1966), pp. 135–62; *In Defense of Industrial Concentration* (New York: Praeger Publishers, 1971); "Efficiency and Economies of Size," in Goldschmid, Weston, and Mann, eds., *Industrial Concentration: The New Learning*, (Boston: Little, Brown & Company, Inc., 1974), pp. 55–97; "Predatory Pricing Revisited," *Journal of Law & Economics*, 23 (October 1980), pp. 289–330; *The Robinson-Patman Act and Effective Competition* (New York: Arno Press, Inc., 1979); "The Decline and Fall of Quantity Discounts," *Journal of Business*, 27 (July 1954), pp. 225–34; "Some Economic Issues in Robinson-Patman Land," *Law and Contemporary Problems*, 30 (Summer 1965), pp. 530–51; and "Why not De-Regulation for Antitrust?", in American Bar Association, *Antitrust Law Journal*, 46, no. 3 (Summer 1977), pp. 777–92 (reprinted in American Bar Association, *Industrial Concentration and the Market System* (1978), pp. 53–68.

4. 15 *United States Codes Annotated*, Sections 1–11.

5. 15 *United States Codes Annotated*, Sections 12–27.

6. R. A. Posner and F. H. Easterbrook, *Antitrust: Cases, Economic Notes, and Other Materials*, 2nd ed. (St. Paul, Minn.: West Publishing Co., 1981), pp. 457–61; and Posner and Easterbrook, *1982–83 Supplement* to *Antitrust* (St. Paul: West Publishing Co., pages 35–50. See also U.S. Department of Justice, Antitrust Division, *U.S. Department of Justice Merger Guidelines* (Washington, D.C., June 14, 1984), pp. 1–31.

7. *United States* v. *Aluminum Co. of America*, 148 F.2d 416 (2nd Cir. 1945).

8. *Brown Shoe Co.* v. *United States*, 370 U.S. 294 (1962).

9. R. H. Bork, "Legislative Intent and the Policy of the Sherman Act," *Journal of Law & Economics*, 9 (October 1966), pp. 7–48; and *The Antitrust Paradox: A Policy at War with Itself* (New York: Basic Books, Inc., Publishers, 1978).

10. See J. S. McGee, *The Robinson-Patman Act and Effective Competition*.

11. *U.S.* v. *Addyston Pipe & Steel Co.*, 85 F.271 (1898).

12. *U.S.* v. *E.C. Knight Co.*, 156 U.S. 1 (1895).

13. *U.S.* v. *Trans-Missouri Freight Association*, 166 U.S. 290, 17 S. Ct. 540 (1897).

14. *American Tobacco Co., et al.* v. *U.S.*, 328 U.S. 781 (1946).

15. Several sources discuss these cases: John Fuller, *The Gentlemen Conspirators* (New York: Grove Press, 1962); John Herling, *The Great Price Conspiracy* (Washington, D.C.: Robert B. Luce, Inc., 1962); Clarence C. Walton and Fred. W. Cleveland, Jr., *Corporations on Trial: The Electric Cases* (Belmont, Calif.: Wadsworth Publishing Co., Inc., 1964); U.S. Senate Committee on the Judiciary, Subcommittee on Antitrust and Monopoly, Hearings on Administered Prices, *Price Fixing and Bid Rigging in the Electric Manufacturing Industry*, pts. 27 and 28, 87th Cong., 1st sess. (Washington, D.C., 1961); *Ohio Valley Electric, et al.* v. *GE, et al.*, 244 F. Supp. 914 (1965); *U.S.* v. *GE and Westinghouse* (1976), Plaintiff's Memorandum, Civil No. 28288; and D. F. Lean, J. D. Ogur, and R. P. Rogers, *Competition and Collusion in Electric Equipment Markets: An Economic Assessment* (Washington, D.C.:

Bureau of Economics Staff Report to the Federal Trade Commission, July 1982), hereinafter referred to as FTC, *Assessment*.

16. *Arizona* v. *Maricopa County Medical Society*, 102 S. Ct. 2466, 73 L.Ed. 2d 48 (1982).

17. *Ball Memorial Hospital et al.* v. *Mutual Hospital Insurance, Inc.*, No. 85–1481 (C.C.A. 7th, decided March 4, 1986).

18. Phillip Areeda, *Antitrust Analysis: Problems, Text, Cases*, 2nd ed. (Boston: Little, Brown & Company, 1974), pp. 224–26. See also Wesley J. Liebeler, "Market Power and Competitive Superiority in Concentrated Industries," *UCLA Law Review*, 25 (August 1978), pp. 1231–1300.

19. The best review of early cases on these subjects is George W. Stocking, *Workable Competition and Antitrust Policy* (Nashville, Tenn.: Vanderbilt University Press, 1961), pp. 18–118. Stocking studied the trial transcripts, rather than secondary sources.

20. *Triangle Conduit & Cable Co.* v. *Federal Trade Commission*, 168 F. 2d 175 (C.C.A. 7th 1948). Also see the discussion in Chapter 6 of this book.

21. *Interstate Circuit, Inc.* v. *United States*, 306 U.S. 208 (1939).

22. 306 U.S. at 226–27.

23. *Theatre Enterprises, Inc.* v. *Paramount Film Distributing Corp.*, 346 U.S. 537 (1954).

24. *U.S.* v. *Container Corp. of America*, 393 U.S. 333 (1969).

25. For example, see "FTC Expands Interpretation of Antitrust Law: Agency Rules Dupont, Ethyl Effectively Set New Prices with Illegal 'Signalling'," *The Wall Street Journal*, 4 April 1983, p. 8.

26. See also *Webster* v. *Sinclair*, 338 F. Supp. 248 (1971); and *Gray* v. *Shell Oil*, 469 F.2d 742 (1972). *Cert. denied*, 412 U.S. 943 (1973).

27. *United States* v. *U.S. Gypsum Co.*, 438 U.S. 422 (1978).

28. This *Gypsum* criminal case imposed fines of $50,000 for each corporate defendant and $1,000 to $5,000 fines for individual defendants. No one went to jail. In an earlier *civil* action defendants had to pay around $100 million in judgments and settlements, demonstrating that civil actions, like criminal actions, punish.

29. See *U.S.* v. *Socony-Vacuum Oil Co.*, 310 U.S. 150 (1940).

30. See, for example, *A&P* v. *FTC*, 440 U.S. 69 (1979); and compare with the earlier RP cases: *Morton Salt* (1948), *Staley* (1945), and the dissent in *Standard Oil Co.* v. *Federal Trade Commission*, 340 U.S. 231 (1951).

31. *U.S.* v. *General Electric Co.*, 272 U.S. 476 (1926).

32. Ward S. Bowman, Jr., "Prerequisites and Effects of Resale Price Maintenance," *University of Chicago Law Review*, 22 (Summer 1955), pp. 825–73; and Lester G. Telser, "Why Should Manufacturers Want Fair Trade," *Journal of Law & Economics*, 3 (October 1960), pp. 86–105.

33. 390 U.S. 145 (1968).

34. Richard A. Posner, *Antitrust Law: An Economic Perspective* (Chicago: University of Chicago Press, 1977), p. 157.

35. Several studies on resale price maintenance, and vertical integration, have recently come out of the Federal Trade Commission. See Thomas R. Overstreet, Jr., *Resale Price Maintenance: Economic Theories and Empirical Evidence* (Washington, D.C.: Bureau of Economics Staff Report to the FTC, November 1983); Edward C. Gallick, *Exclusive Dealing and*

Vertical Integration: The Efficiency of Contracts in the Tuna Industry (Washington, D.C.: Bureau of Economics Staff Report to the FTC, August 1984); and R. N. Lafferty, R. H. Lande, John B. Kirkwood, eds., *Impact Evaluations of Federal Trade Commission Vertical Restraints Cases* (Washington, D.C.: Bureau of Competition, Bureau of Economics, FTC, August 1984).

36. 309 F. 2d 223 (1962).
37. *U.S.* v. *E.I. du Pont de Nemours and Co.*, 351 U.S. 377 (1956).
38. *Brown Shoe Co.* v. *U.S.*, 370 U.S. 294 (1962).
39. For example, see John Peterman, "The Brown Shoe Case," *Journal of Law & Economics*, 18 (April 1975), pp. 81–146; and "The FTC v. Brown Shoe Co.," *Journal of Law & Economics*, 18 (October 1975), pp. 361–419.
40. See, for example, the discussion of Stigler's theory of oligopoly in Chapter 5.
41. *Chicago Board of Trade* v. *U.S.*, 246 U.S. 231 (1918); *U.S.* v. *Trenton Potteries Co.*, 273 U.S. 392 (1927); *Sugar Institute* v. *U.S.*, 297 U.S. 553 (1936).
42. Several FTC cases show just these kinds of situations, in which the discriminations complained of could not possibly have reduced competition or promoted monopoly. For example, see *National Grain Yeast*, 33 FTC 684 (1941); *Republic Yeast*, ibid., p. 701; *Federal Yeast*, ibid., p. 1372; *Samuel H. Moss*, 36 FTC 640 (1943); *Samuel H. Moss* v. *FTC*, 148 F.2d 378 (1945); *Williams and Wilkins*, 29 FTC 678 (1939); *Nutrine Candy*, 30 FTC 115 (1939); *National Numbering Machine*, ibid., p. 139.
43. McGee, "Some Economic Issues in Robinson-Patman Land," pp. 538–43.
44. The Robinson-Patman literature is large. For an impression of how it evolved, see, for example, Morris A. Adelman, "Effective Competition and the Anti-Trust Laws," *Harvard Law Review*, 61 (September 1948), pp. 1289–1350); Adelman, "Anti-Trust Upside-Down Cake and Eat It Too," *Fortune*, 41 (March 1950), pp. 57–58; Adelman, "The Large Firm and Its Suppliers," *Review of Economics and Statistics*, 31 (May 1949), pp. 113–18; Adelman, "The A&P Case," *Quarterly Journal of Economics*, 63 (May 1949), pp. 238–57; Ward S. Bowman, Jr., "Restraint of Trade by the Supreme Court: The Utah Pie Case," *Yale Law Journal*, 77 (November 1967), pp. 70–85; Kenneth Elzinga and Thomas Hogarty, "Utah Pie and the Consequences of Robinson-Patman," *Journal of Law & Economics*, 21 (October 1978), pp. 427–34; Richard Posner, *The Robinson-Patman Act* (Washington, D.C.: American Enterprise Institute, 1976); R. H. Bork, *The Antitrust Paradox*, Chapter 20; J. S. McGee, *The Robinson-Patman Act and Effective Competition*; McGee, "Some Economic Issues in Robinson-Patman Land"; McGee, "Price Discrimination and Competitive Effects: The Standard Oil of Indiana Case," 23 *Chicago Law Review* 3 (1956), pp. 398–473; McGee, "The Decline and Fall of Quantity Discounts." Thomas W. Ross, "Winners and Losers Under the Robinson-Patman Act," *Journal of Law & Economics*, 27 (October 1984), pp. 243–71 estimates the quantitative effects of the Robinson-Patman Act.
45. *F.T.C.* v. *Morton Salt Co.*, 334 U.S. 37 (1948).
46. *Utah Pie* v. *Continental Baking Co.*, 386 U.S. 685 (1967).
47. Ward S. Bowman, Jr., "Restraint of Trade by the Supreme Court: The *Utah Pie* Case," pp. 70–85.
48. Robert H. Bork *The Antitrust Paradox*, pp. 280–96.

20 ANTITRUST POLICY AND THE LARGE FIRM

INTRODUCTION

The preceding chapter concentrated on three categories of antitrust problems: agreements among legally separate firms; vertical integration; and practices that the Clayton Act discourages (price discrimination and mergers, for example).

This chapter discusses how antitrust law deals with absolutely or relatively large firms, sometimes called tight-knit combinations to distinguish them from looser arrangements among separate firms. The cases discussed in the next section involve allegedly dominant firms and single-firm monopolies. Some of them achieved large market shares by combining previously independent firms. The following section briefly assesses the overall contribution that antitrust policy makes to consumer welfare.

THE CASES

E. C. Knight (1895)[1]

In 1892 the American Sugar Refining Co., a corporation that owned most of the sugar refineries in the U.S., obtained control of four of the five remaining independent refining companies. President Searles of American Sugar exchanged shares of American Sugar Company for the stock of these companies. No ancillary agreements prohibited re-entry into the refining business.

These companies were all in business in Pennsylvania and before the acquisition had vigorously competed among themselves, with the American Sugar Company, and with a fifth concern, Revere, of Boston. The output of sugar was said to have increased after the acquisitions. After the consolidation, the American Sugar Co. produced and sold about 98 percent of the sugar sold in the U.S. The price advanced somewhat above the preacquisition level, but was not as high as it had been some years earlier.

The government sought to cancel the agreements under which the stock was transferred, and to prevent further performance of the agreements and further violations of the Sherman Act. After the lower court dismissed the suit on the grounds that the facts did not show an unlawful restraint of interstate commerce, the government appealed.

Mr. Chief Justice Fuller wrote the Supreme Court opinion. This case hinged on constitutional law and Sherman Act jurisdiction, not economics. As Fuller put it,

> The relief of the citizens of each state from the burden of monopoly and the evils resulting from the restraint of trade among such citizens was left with the States to deal with. * * * The power of Congress to regulate commerce among the several States is also exclusive. * * * Commerce succeeds to manufacture and is not a part of it.

As authority, Fuller quoted from Justice Lamar's *Kidd* v. *Pearson* opinion:

> No distinction is more popular to the common mind, or more clearly expressed in economic and political literature, than that between manufacture and commerce. Manufacture is transformation—the fashioning of raw materials into a change of form for use. . . . The buying and selling and the transportation incidental thereto constitute commerce.

The contracts and acts of the defendants related altogether to the acquisition of the Philadelphia refineries and the business of sugar refining in Pennsylvania. Because they did not have the direct relation to interstate or international commerce that the Court thought our Constitution required for federal regulation, the Sherman Act was powerless to reach them.

Some believe that *E. C. Knight* was one of the great disasters in Sherman Act history. The merger movement of 1895 to 1904 may thereby have been accelerated. There is no doubt that the concept of interstate commerce is much broader now than Fuller made it. Fuller saw clearly that a broad notion of commerce would lead to large government and expanding regulations. Imagine what regulation would be like today if his conception of interstate commerce had prevailed.

Standard Oil of New Jersey (1911)

This case and its companion are credited with creating a "rule of reason" for the Sherman Act.[2] They also created what may be a legend about abusive and predatory competition.[3] Mr. Chief Justice White delivered the majority opinion.

Section 1 of the Sherman Act deals with restraints of trade; Section 2 deals with attempts to monopolize and monopolization. But what did they mean? In White's words,

> . . . it was intended that the standard of reason which had been applied at the common law— was intended to be the measure used for the purpose of determining whether in a given case a particular act had or had not brought about the wrong against which the statute provided.

White's version of New Jersey Standard's history is interesting, though some of it is wrong. In 1867, the partnership of Rockefeller, Andrews, and Flagler united several large oil refineries. In 1870 the Standard Oil Co. of Ohio, capitalized at $1 million, succeeded the partnership. The company is supposed to have done 10 percent of the U.S. refining at that point; in 10 years it did around 90 percent. It also controlled every important crude oil pipeline in the oil fields, except for the Tide Water Pipe Line Co., which White (incorrectly) said SONJ eventually acquired. In 1882, the Standard Oil interests formed the Standard Oil Trust, which held the entire stock of 14 companies and majority interest in 26 others. The trust was capitalized at $70 million, of which $46 million was held by nine of the trustees. The State of Ohio in 1892 brought a suit that declared the trust illegal. The trust form of organization was succeeded by a "community of interest" that, Ohio claimed, illegally evaded the court decree.

In 1899, a holding company, the Standard Oil Co. of New Jersey (SONJ), was created to avoid an Ohio action for contempt. SONJ was capitalized at $100 million. In the U.S., the company owned 11 refining companies and 14 pipeline companies. Another 7 pipeline and refining companies were closely affiliated with or controlled by Jersey. Overseas, it did business through 16 companies.

Although SONJ owned only about one-sixth of the wells in U.S. oil fields, its pipelines made it the only crude purchaser in many fields. Its refineries, everyone conceded, were well located and efficient. In 1904, it produced about 86.5 percent of the "refined illuminating oil" (kerosene), still the leading product. SONJ accounted for 84 percent of U.S. exports of oil products. It was an enormously profitable concern. In 1906, the government brought suit to break it up.

The "bad practices" alleged in this case may have been crucial to the Court's decision; but it is debatable whether, if they took place at all, they played a significant part in achieving Standard's monopoly position. Mergers and efficiency accounted for its size: it bought more than 100 small refineries, and had the largest and most efficient refineries of the time. In any case, White pictures SONJ as an abusive and predatory competitor (local price cutting, "bogus independents," spying); and a user of railroad rebates and its own pipelines to get a monopoly position and to exclude competitors.

From the railroads, the opinion says, Jersey Standard got rebates on its own shipments and drawbacks on competitors' shipments; received better service; got rates manipulated for its own purposes; got lower rates on oil in tanks than in barrels; and obtained information about the business of competing companies.

According to the opinion, Jersey's pipelines did not perform like legitimate common carriers. It earned excessive profits. It sold its products more cheaply abroad than at home. It used discriminatory, predatory price competition to kill off competitors whenever they appeared. It used bogus companies—which it secretly owned but disavowed—to fight and kill competitors. It used novel and dangerous business forms—holding companies, for example—to accomplish its ends. It was (what we now call) vertically integrated. It appeared to want a *perpetual* monopoly, and it looked as though it might manage to get it.

White found Jersey had unreasonably restrained trade in violation of the Sherman Act, and affirmed the lower court's dissolution decrees

. . . because the unification of power and control over petroleum and its products which was the inevitable result of the combining in the New Jersey corporation . . . , gives rise, in and of itself, in the absence of countervailing circumstances, to say the least, to the prima facie presumption of intent and purpose to maintain the dominancy over the oil industry not as a result of normal methods of industrial development, but by new means of combination . . . [massive mergers, holding company] the whole with the purpose of excluding others from the trade and thus centralizing in the combination a perpetual control of the movements of petroleum in the channels of interstate commerce.

In an ideal world a decision such as *SONJ* should make the kinds of trade-offs between concentration and size that Chapter 13 presents. Jersey was an efficient and innovative firm that appeared to have substantial power to determine price. Part of its superior efficiency came from size economies; part from a superior management and work force. At the very least, Jersey grew more *quickly* because of its wholesale mergers and acquisitions. What is not so clear is whether, because of its relative efficiency, it would ultimately have grown to as commanding a position by internal growth alone.

Whatever their preferences and beliefs, it is reasonable that judges should welcome concepts like bad practices, good and bad trusts, and rules of reason. Cloaked in notions like those, courts can ignore explicit trade-offs like those discussed in Chapter 13, accomplishing a bold simplification if nothing else. The economic trade-offs are difficult to make. Even today, more than 75 years after dissolution, who knows whether Jersey's efficiency outweighed its power to fix price?

The simplest economic argument for dissolution is that it costs less than the amount by which it increases consumer benefits. That is not so simple as it sounds, among other things because a law strong enough to break up firms imposes risks and incentive effects on all firms, not just those directly involved in dissolution suits.

Neither the *SONJ* case nor any other can create atomistic competition. Because of the size, number, and location of Jersey's refineries, it was not even feasible to reduce market concentration in one stroke. Dissolution cut the Standard Oil companies apart, leaving each with a regional near-monopoly. The Indiana company, for example, emerged from dissolution with 75 to 100 percent of midwestern markets.

Since the New Jersey companies' positions had already eroded somewhat, and—in the absence of further mergers and acquisitions—would have continued to erode as oil markets grew, it is debatable how much dissolution accomplished. Two effects are discernible. First, the suit discouraged large-scale mergers by Jersey, by other oil companies, and by other firms in other industries. Second, though dissolution left each successor company with a large market share in its regional market, the successor companies eventually entered one another's markets and competed.

This case made a lot of noise and dust, and possibly did some good. But most of the reasons that White gives for dissolving Standard are debatable as fact and theory. At least some of the Court's aversion was to absolute firm size and to the abuses that giantism is supposed to make possible. It is doubtful that absolute size has anything to do with such abuses, if that's what they are.

As usual, judicial rhetoric and practical remedy were different things. Much had been made of Jersey's strong position and abusiveness in pipelines. Antitrust can do little useful about that. There are large size-economies in pipelining; and there is no such thing as cutting an existing pipeline system into several *competing* systems. Perhaps regulation could do something useful. This case and *American Tobacco* also contributed to the body of strange theories about vertical integration.

Jersey's competitors did not seem to want dissolution at all, for they feared that would increase competition and lower prices. They did want law to bar Jersey from their markets—as had been done earlier in state suits that ousted Jersey companies from Texas and Missouri—or at least to blunt its competitive edge. The Court's early emphasis on improving competitors' comfort and well-being is unfortunate.

When, in *Tobacco*, White summarized his *Standard Oil* opinion he said that the rule of reason simply prevents destruction of "the individual right to contract" and preserves "movement of trade in the channels of interstate commerce—the free movement of which it was the purpose of the statute to protect." This sounds like policy directed against abusive, predatory exclusion that rests on large size. It does not sound anything like the cost-benefit economics of Chapter 13.

American Tobacco Company (1911)

The Supreme Court decided this case and *Standard Oil* in the same term and White wrote both majority opinions as well.[4] American Tobacco was another monopoly, another "bad trust." It allegedly sold 86 percent of the cigarettes and 91 percent of the small cigars sold in the U.S. American was formed in the late nineteenth century by James Buchanan Duke, used mergers and every other form of combination known at the time, was hugely profitable, and allegedly used predatory price cutting and other unfair methods to get and keep its monopoly.[5] Of legal significance were the findings that American had intended to monopolize, that is, to exclude competitors.

The Court's decision relied as much or more upon how this monopoly had been achieved as upon what it did. That is odd in more ways than whether predatory tactics were used successfully. For example, the Court relied upon a rule of reason to strike the combination down. Yet, oddly, although the majority of the Court concluded that the combination had produced economic benefits, it also seems to have concluded that merging competitors had in and of itself restrained competition. Perhaps there was no rule of reason after all.

It is worth noting that although the 1911 dissolution produced a much less concentrated tobacco industry, the Department of Justice claimed later that this restructured industry did not compete either. See the discussion of the 1946 *Tobacco* case in Chapter 19.

U.S. Steel (1920)[6]

This case, unlike *Standard Oil* and *Tobacco*, is about a "good trust." United States Steel (USS) was formed in 1901 to acquire stock in 12 operating companies. This was in fact "a combination of combinations" and was at the time the largest industrial corporation in the world.

USS capitalization was $1.4 billion. Promoters' profits reached $62.5 million. The first great merger wave (1895 to 1904) was notable for combinations of absolutely and relatively large firms into firms that had large shares of national markets. Even so, the consolidation eventuating in USS accounts for 23 percent of the total capitalization of firms involved in that whole merger wave.

In the beginning, USS had about 60 to 70 percent of the nation's basic steel ingot capacity. By the time of this suit, its market share had eroded to about 50 percent. By 1958, to 28 percent; and by the 1980s, to less than 18 percent, even ignoring imports. In the early part of this history, at least, the corporation was highly profitable, which is not what Chapter 4 leads us to expect of a dominant firm unless it is more efficient than its competitors.[7]

Mr. Justice McKenna wrote the Supreme Court opinion. The Court voted 4 to 3 against dissolution. The majority found an intent to monopolize; but decided that USS had never succeeded in doing it. It had, it's true, avoided competition through pooling agreements and, later, the notorious Gary Dinners. It is also true that the industry used the infamous Pittsburgh-Plus basing-point system.

The Court applauded USS for never having been accused of abusive or predatory practices. Its competitors admired it. The industry worked in a harmonious atmosphere of live and let live; not aggressive competition, let alone warfare. Perhaps the worst things about this decision, and the lower court's opinion, are criticisms of price competitors such as Andrew Carnegie and praise for "industrial statesmen," including Elbert Gary, chief executive officer of USS.

The Court concluded USS did not "abuse" such power as it may have had, and did not have enough power to control the market unilaterally. That it had needed, even at its peak market share, to conspire with competitors showed that it lacked monopolistic power on its own. The improper exercise of monopoly power consists in fixing a monopoly price and in excluding competitors. The Court concluded that USS had done neither. And

> The law does not make mere size an offense, or the existence of unexerted power an offense. It, we repeat, requires overt acts and trusts to its prohibition of them and its power to repress or punish them. It does not compel competition nor require all that is possible.

The Court said that the whole case came down to a question of size: is it illegal for a firm to have 50 percent of an industry's output, when it no longer intends to monopolize and does not restrain the competition of its rivals? This Court said no.

Alcoa (1945)[8]

The lower court had found for Alcoa and the government appealed. So many justices disqualified themselves that the Supreme Court couldn't get a quorum of six. Chief Justice Stone withdrew because he had recommended prosecution; three others because they had participated in the case while serving in the Department of Justice. Following special enabling legislation, this circuit court of appeals decision has the status of a Supreme Court decision. Judge Learned Hand wrote the opinion after reviewing 40,000 pages of evidence.

The Aluminum Company of America (Alcoa), a Pennsylvania corporation, was organized in 1888 under the name of Pittsburgh Reduction Co. It became Alcoa in 1907. It produced and sold ingot aluminum and, after 1895, fabricated the metal into finished and semifinished articles. Until February 2, 1909, Alcoa had either a monopoly in manufacture of new ("virgin") aluminum ingot, or monopoly over a patented process that eliminated all competition.

Aluminum production uses enormous quantities of electrical power, which Alcoa got by building its own power plants and dams, and by contracting with water power companies.[9] In three cases, it made exclusive contracts preventing the power company from selling to any other manufacturer of aluminum.

Either on its own or through a subsidiary, Alcoa also entered into four successive cartels with foreign manufacturers of aluminum. They set up foreign market quotas in return for a domestic monopoly or near-monopoly. On May 16, 1912, the U.S. government filed suit against Alcoa, charging that these cartels violated the Sherman Act. A decree, handed down June 7, declared most of the agreements to be illegal.

According to Learned Hand,

> None of the foregoing facts are in dispute, and the most important question in the case is whether the monopoly in "Alcoa's" production of "virgin" ingot, secured by the two patents until 1909, and in part perpetuated between 1909 and 1912 by the unlawful practices, forbidden by the decree of 1912, continued for the ensuing twenty-eight years, and whether, if it did, it was unlawful under § 2 of the Sherman Act.

The government had contended that Alcoa, as the sole producer of virgin ingot in the U.S., was an unlawful monopoly. Be that as it may, the government said that Alcoa had certainly used unlawful exclusionary practices to preserve a dominant market position, which might have been lawful if retained only by "natural growth" rather than by illegal monopolistic expansion. Some or all of these practices, it asserted, were per se restraints of trade under Section 2 of the Sherman Act.

Alcoa, by contrast, said its virgin aluminum competed with imports and with reclaimed scrap ("secondary") aluminum and, in any case, that its market position was due to natural growth and did not violate the Act.

Hand saw three issues: the amount and character of competition; the extent of monopoly; and the legality of such monopoly as Alcoa had. Alcoa's ingot production, including that of Aluminium Ltd., its Canadian subsidiary, was nearly always more than 80 percent of the total virgin ingot produced in the U.S. From 1934 to 1938 it exceeded 90 percent.

In computing Alcoa's market share, the lower court had included secondary ingot and excluded the part of Alcoa's production that it fabricated itself. It therefore concluded that Alcoa had only 33 percent of the market. As Hand noted, other ways to define the market put Alcoa's share far above the lower court's finding of 33 percent:

If, on the other hand, "Alcoa's" total production, fabricated and sold, be included, and balanced against the sum of imported "virgin" and "secondary," its share of the market was in the neighborhood of sixty-four percent for that period. The percentage we have already mentioned—over ninety—results only if we both include all "Alcoa's" production and exclude "secondary." That percentage is enough to constitute a monopoly; it is doubtful whether sixty or sixty-four percent would be enough; and certainly thirty-three percent is not.

To the extent that Alcoa controlled primary aluminum production it was able, by regulating this production, to exercise some control over future secondary production. It would recognize and use that control, given the shrewd business foresight that the record shows and counsel for Alcoa stressed.[10] Thus, said Hand, "We conclude . . . that 'Alcoa's' control over the ingot market must be reckoned at over ninety percent; that being the proportion which its production bears to imported 'virgin' ingot."

Even that large a share, of course, did not mean Alcoa could raise price without limit:

> It is entirely consistent with the evidence that it was the threat of greater foreign imports which kept "Alcoa's" prices where they were, and prevented it from exploiting its advantage as sole domestic producer; indeed it is hard to resist the conclusion that potential imports did put a "ceiling" upon those prices. Nevertheless, within the limits afforded by the tariff and the cost of transportation, "Alcoa" was free to raise its prices as it chose, since it was free from domestic competition, save as it drew other metals into the market as substitutes. Was this a monopoly within the meaning of § 2?

It appears that Alcoa had not been especially profitable. In deciding the monopoly question, however, whether Alcoa received more than a fair profit over the past "is irrelevant anyway, for it is no excuse for 'monopolizing' a market that the monopoly has not been used to extract from the consumer more than a 'fair' profit." Many think that more progress is made when there are many producers in a field. In any case, Congress "did not condone 'good trusts' and condemn 'bad' ones; it forbade all." Hand acknowledged that

> Not all contracts which in fact put an end to existing competition are unlawful. Starting, however, with the authoritative premise that all contracts fixing prices are unconditionally prohibited, the only possible difference between them and a monopoly is that while a monopoly necessarily involves an equal, or even greater, power to fix prices, its mere existence might be thought not to constitute an exercise of that power. That distinction is nevertheless purely formal; it would be valid only so long as the monopoly remained wholly inert; it would disappear as soon as it began to . . . sell at all—it must sell at some price and the only price at which it could sell is a price which it itself fixed. Thereafter the power and its exercise must needs coalesce. Indeed it would be absurd to condemn such contracts unconditionally, and not to extend the condemnation to monopolies; for the contracts are only steps toward that entire control which monopoly confers: they are really partial monopolies. . . .
>
> We hold that "Alcoa's" monopoly of ingot was of the kind covered by § 2. It does not follow because "Alcoa" had such a monopoly, that it "monopolized" the ingot market: it may not have achieved monopoly; monopoly may have been thrust upon it.

Monopoly may result from natural growth and if so, "The successful competitor, having been urged to compete, must not be turned upon when he wins." However, in this case, " 'Alcoa's' size was 'magnified' to make it a 'monopoly'; indeed, it has never been anything else; and its size not only offered it an 'opportunity for abuse,' but it 'utilized' its size for 'abuse' as can easily be shown."

Aside from some abortive attempts to enter the industry, which Alcoa forestalled, there had been no competition from domestic producers. Nevertheless, "we need charge it with no moral derelictions after 1912; we may assume that all it claims for itself is true." Hand found much evidence that Alcoa had done business skillfully, energetically, and resourcefully.

> The only question is whether it falls within the exception established in favor of those who do not seek, but cannot avoid, the control of a market. It seems to us that that question scarcely survives its statement. It was not inevitable that it should always anticipate increases in the demand for ingot and be prepared to supply them. Nothing compelled it to keep doubling and redoubling its capacity before others entered the field. It insists that it never excluded competitors; but we can think of no more effective exclusion than progressively to embrace each new opportunity as it opened, and to face every newcomer with new capacity already geared into a great organization, having the advantage of experience, trade connections and the elite of personnel.

Thus Alcoa did monopolize the market within the meaning of Section 2 of the Sherman Act. The lower court decision was reversed.

The government had challenged a variety of other practices and conduct, the legality of which depended upon intent. Alcoa had allegedly preempted bauxite deposits and water power, purchased two Norwegian aluminum companies and a power plant in Canada, and bought out prospective competitors. But the government had not proved that Alcoa had intended thereby to tie up resources beyond its legitimate future needs. Alcoa's suspicious activity in making finished products consisted of three practices. First, it acquired two makers of cooking and other utensils. The government proved no wrongful intent. Second, Alcoa was alleged to have discouraged competition by "squeezing" the margin between the price of its ingots and the price of its fabricated aluminum products, which its market control enabled it to do. Alcoa cut its ingot price in 1932 when it feared action by the Department of Justice. The lower court held this was not an attempt to monopolize the sheet market. But, Hand said, "we hold that at least in 1932 it had become a wrong." Regarding patent misuses that involved agreements, the lower court held there was insufficient evidence on two charges and, in the third case, the patents had expired. For that reason, no ruling was made.

"The arrangement involving the 'cartel' was found to be violative of the Sherman Act, although silent as to sales in the United States, since it obviously affected imports." Aluminium Co. of Canada was enjoined from entering into cartel agreements that restricted sales in the U.S.

What about remedies? According to Hand, "Dissolution is not a penalty but a remedy; if the industry will not need it for its protection, it will be a disservice to break up an aggregation which has for so long demonstrated its efficiency.''[11] As part of the remedial decree following this decision, Alcoa in essence agreed not to compete too hard with the new companies that were created out of government aluminum capacity built during World War II, and promised to supply them with bauxite whenever they might need it.

Hand's *Alcoa* opinion was hailed as single-handedly creating a new and powerful law against monopoly power in and of itself, however genteelly that power had been acquired and used. It was supposed to have shed the legal distinction between good and bad trusts and to have embraced economists' notions of monopoly power. In the process, we were told, *Alcoa* had created a bold new law that was strongly procompetitive. Both of these claims went too far, and the opinion has lost much of its luster over the years.

One reason was that, to support his monopoly diagnosis, Hand reached to get as high a market share as he could, and he misdefined the market to do it. To get a 90 percent share, Hand had to ignore reclaimed scrap (secondary), a highly doubtful procedure. Whenever firms sell, rather than lease, durable goods, their past production reduces current demand. This does not mean that a monopoly of a durable good has no monopoly power when it begins. It means that, for given conditions of final demand, its monopoly will tend to erode as time goes by. To tell how much monopoly power it has at any future point, we must consider how much competition its previous production poses for its current production.

Nor could Alcoa's share conceivably have been as high as 64 percent, for that completely writes off competition from aluminum substitutes. There is neither novelty nor boldness in holding that a 90 percent share *of a well-defined economic market* would be a ''monopoly.'' If Hand really wanted to make bold new law, he should have defined the market properly and urged a lower percentage standard for ''monopoly.''

Hand made a big thing of demolishing the old legal distinctions between cartel monopoly and single-firm monopoly power. He shouldn't have done it in the name of economics or logic. Taft's 1898 distinction made a great deal of sense: naked price fixing by cartels is often quite different from what large firms do. The latter often benefit consumers. An even more serious criticism is that Hand's standards of conduct are anticonsumer and anticompetitive. His famous conclusion that ''doubling and redoubling capacity'' illegally excludes entry is anticompetitive and anticonsumer. He is really saying that large, efficient firms must not expand to satisfy markets they serve. Instead, they must drag their feet, encouraging newcomers to enter or smaller existing firms to expand. In the meanwhile, consumers will have paid more than need be for what they want.

Sharp criticisms of Hand's *Alcoa* decision have reduced enthusiasm for the principles it enunciated. The worst of *Alcoa* principles may now be buried, though even older antitrust ghosts than those have returned to haunt us from time to time.

Du Pont Cellophane (1956)[12]

In this civil suit, the U.S. charged that Du Pont had monopolized interstate commerce in cellophane, in violation of Section 2 of the Sherman Act. Mr. Justice Reed wrote the majority opinion, which for better or worse remains the authoritative legal guide for market definition in Sherman Act and Clayton Act cases. Chapters 10 and 11 are good background for analyzing the *Cellophane* case, which is a potent example of what judges can do to economic concepts as they explain and apply them.

Although Du Pont produced about 75 percent of the cellophane sold in the U.S., one question was whether cellophane itself, or something called flexible wrapping material, was the relevant market. According to Reed,

> What is called for is an appraisal of the "cross-elasticity" of demand in the trade. The varying circumstances of each case determine the result. In considering what is the relevant market for determining the control of price and competition, no more definite rule can be declared than that commodities reasonably interchangeable by consumers for the same purposes make up that "part of the trade or commerce," monopolization of which may be illegal. . . .
>
> The "market" which one must study to determine when a producer has monopoly power will vary with the part of commerce under consideration. The tests are constant. That market is composed of products that have reasonable interchangeability for the purposes for which they are produced—price, use and qualities considered.

The court had concluded that ". . . cellophane shares the packaging market with others. The over-all result is that cellophane accounts for 17.9 percent of flexible wrapping materials, measured by the wrapping surface." Therefore, "Du Pont should not be found to monopolize cellophane when that product has the competition and interchangeability with other wrappings that this record shows."

Economists have provided few objective, scientific guides to market definition, and the courts often misuse the relevant economics that does exist. Learned Hand murdered market definition by *completely* writing off both reprocessed aluminum and obvious substitutes for aluminum. Reed murdered economic theory by ignoring that own- and cross-elasticity coefficients can be expected to be high *because* a good has been monopolized. He ended by expanding the market almost without limit.

In any case, however, why shouldn't Du Pont have won on the basis of its patent rights alone?

After studying the *Du Pont* transcript, Stocking and Mueller wrote an interesting analysis of the *Cellophane* case.[13] Du Pont became acquainted with cellophane through its production of rayon. The two processes are very closely related.

Before 1923, only the French firm, La Cellophane, made cellophane. In 1923, Du Pont bought rights from it, realizing this gave it a monopoly in markets for which it bought rights, and anticipating that it could retain its monopoly principally through knowhow rather than patents. Before buying the rights, it made a market survey showing a prospective annual return on capital of some 31.6 percent. Du Pont became the only U.S. producer of cellophane.

Du Pont got a tariff increase from 25 percent to 60 percent ad valorem. Would it have sought higher tariffs on cellophane unless cellophane is a distinctive product? The tariff stopped the cut-price competition of a Belgian cellophane manufacturer, which had begun in 1925. Du Pont started to wage a patent suit, but wisely decided against it: patent strength was problematical; if it lost, entry into cellophane would be wide open. In 1928, Du Pont had 76 percent of the U.S. market. By 1929, it had 91.6 percent. Between 1930 and 1947, imports never reached 1 percent of the U.S. market. By 1930, French, German, and U.S. cellophane producers had pretty well carved up world markets in an orderly fashion. The British came in 1935.

In 1925, two employees of La Cellophane defected and started a new firm. In 1929 they established Sylvania Industrial Corporation of America, an American subsidiary. La Cellophane sued Sylvania for patent infringement, and took stock in Sylvania as settlement. La Cellophane thus became Du Pont's competitor in the U.S., contrary to their 1923 agreement. In exchange, La Cellophane gave Du Pont certain rights in new foreign markets.

By 1927, Du Pont had discovered a process for moisture-proofing cellophane, for which a patent issued in 1929. Du Pont's total research expenditures on this process were only $19,503! Although getting large results from small expenditures is consistent with efficiency or good luck, Stocking and Mueller said it shows that the discovery was trivial. In 1930, Sylvania completed its Virginia plant, and started "inventing around" Du Pont's moistureproof cellophane patent. Du Pont filed an infringement suit, settled by a patent exchange and licensing agreement. If Sylvania had won, the field might have been wide open. The agreement restricted Sylvania's share of the market. Until mid-1951, Sylvania and Du Pont were the only U.S. producers of cellophane. Olin began producing in June, 1951. From 1933 to 1950 shares of the U.S. market worked out at 76 percent for Du Pont, and 24 percent for Sylvania. Their list prices were generally identical; but Sylvania offered trade discounts that Du Pont didn't meet.

According to Stocking and Mueller, the record clearly shows that Du Pont *thought* it had monopoly power in cellophane. Was it wrong and Judge Leahy right? Several hundred firms produced other kinds of flexible wrapping materials. How close were these substitutes? The lower court found that in 1949 Du Pont cellophane accounted for only 17.9 percent (physical volume) of all flexible wrapping materials, excluding Kraft paper. Du Pont's own market analysts concluded in 1948 that cellophane had no close competition in the major markets, and Olin analysts agreed. To be truly competitive with cellophane, said the experts, a substitute should be low cost and transparent; work well on high-speed packaging equipment; and print speedily and well. In wrapping cigarettes, cellophane was king. In 1949, 80 percent of Du Pont's sales were for packaging food products. In no one of the more important food packaging fields did cellophane supply as much as 50 percent of the total area of packing materials used.

The Court's appraisals of demand elasticities were loose, not systematic. Stocking's and Mueller's were no better. They noted that, when Du Pont lowered its price to broaden the market—1924 to 1940—the *prices* of other wrappers didn't follow a similar pattern. But what about *quantities*? To Stocking and Mueller, this "independence of prices" suggested that cellophane was a distinct product, as indeed it might have been.

Du Pont's annual rate of earnings (after taxes) declined from a high of 52 percent in 1928; but from 1923 through 1950 it never fell below 20 percent. Operating earnings were very much higher (58.3 percent in 1925, 45.3 percent in 1950). A comparison of rates of return in cellophane and rayon is interesting because rayon stems from the same raw materials. Rayon began as a monopoly, but entry was rapid. In 1949 there were 15 rayon producers. When Du Pont first produced rayon, the American Viscose Corp. realized 64.2 percent on its investment. Du Pont's earnings were 38.9 percent in 1923; by 1929, 19 percent. In 1930—after six entrants came in—Du Pont lost .9 percent. During the next 8 years, Du Pont averaged 7.5 percent on its rayon investment. From 1929 to 1938 Du Pont averaged 29.6 percent on cellophane, before taxes. During those same years, Du Pont averaged 6.3 percent before taxes on rayon.

IBM (1982)

Although Franklin Fisher, John McGowan, and Joen Greenwood, consultants who worked on IBM's most recent case make it sound like a *unique* antitrust "disaster," to use their characterization,[14] it was not unique.[15] It was a protracted, extremely costly, and a probably wrong-minded Section 2 case; but it embodies the same inconsistencies and anticompetition biases that figure prominently in many earlier cases, including some already analyzed in this chapter.

The government filed its original complaint on January 17, 1969, then amended it. In 1975, the case went to trial. It went on for more than six years, accumulating more than 100,000 pages of testimony and thousands of exhibits and documents on top of that. As the government's case ground on, various private damage suits were also making their way through the courts.[16]

The Antitrust Division of the Department of Justice began reviewing its case in June 1982, and William F. Baxter, who had become its head, signed a Stipulation of Dismissal on January 8, 1982. Perhaps the most novel thing about *IBM* is the most uncommon assistant attorney general who dismissed the case in 1982. If bringing and continuing to press the *IBM* case was not a unique disaster, neither does its dismissal guarantee that the string of anticompetitive antitrust cases stops there.

IBM's predecessor company started in 1911, and changed its name to IBM in 1924. It became highly successful making and leasing patented electromechanical tabulating machines, including devices to punch, sort, and tabulate cards. In a civil antitrust suit filed in 1932, the U.S. charged that IBM and Remington Rand had restrained and monopolized trade by agreeing to lease only, and not to *sell*, tabulating machines; to fix minimum rental prices; and to require each customer to buy its tabulating card requirements from the firm that leased it machines. Before that case came to trial, defendants consented to a decree that cancelled their agreements, which were dropped as an issue in the case.

Legality of the tie-in (or requirements) contracts themselves remained at issue. In *IBM* v. *U.S.*, the U.S. Supreme Court struck them down as violations of Section 3 of the Clayton Act, sustaining the district court.[17]

IBM's card sales brought in about one-third as much as it got from leasing machines, and IBM stipulated that card profits were "substantial." IBM made cards out of stock that it bought from outside manufacturers. The federal government made its own cards under terms of a special lease. It paid a 15 percent lease premium in exchange for the right to use cards it made itself. According to the Supreme Court, the government would recoup the premium if it could make cards for less than 55 percent of what IBM charged for them.

IBM argued that its contracts were lawful because they did not extend or enlarge its legitimate patents on machines and cards. It also stressed that tabulating cards had to be made right to work right. Defective cards would not only cause its machines to falter or fail; they would also cause serious computational errors that are hard to find and correct. Bad cards would hurt customers, which would also hurt IBM's reputation and business. IBM serviced the machines it leased. Its tie-in assured that cards and machines would work properly together.

Aaron Director may have been the first economist to say that IBM tied cards to measure how much different lessees used the machines and to charge more to those who used them more.[18] In effect, he said, IBM charged a royalty for machine use by raising the price of its cards substantially above what it cost to produce them. The machines were worth less to those who used fewer cards because they used the machines less. Under this scheme, those who used the machines less would pay less for them each month, including what they paid for cards. According to this argument, IBM was simply making the most of its machine patents, and not enlarging that monopoly at all. Though increased monopoly in machines tends to *lower* output, IBM's exacting different card plus machine rental charges from different users discriminated according to the value of machine use and could increase total machine output and use.

In 1896 and 1912, courts had actually used that argument to explain and justify tie-ins,[19] and IBM tried to use it here. In Justice Stone's words, "It argues that the condition of its leases is lawful because it does not enlarge the monopoly secured by the patents, and the trial court erred in refusing to consider appellant's patent monopoly as a defense to this suit." This Supreme Court cited the earlier cases that had established that defense; but it wanted nothing more to do with them. Indeed, the Court said, Section 3 of the Clayton Act had been passed to bury just that kind of defense, for patented as well as unpatented goods. Stone's argument is not very satisfying. Read literally, Section 3 does not establish a per se rule against tie-ins and requirements contracts. As the Court specifically recognized, Section 3 proscribes only such arrangements as "may . . . substantially lessen competition or tend to create a monopoly in any line of commerce." It therefore seems clearly relevant to inquire whether the arrangement extended monopoly or merely charged for a legal patent monopoly. Chapter 9 discusses this, in a section about compound pricing.

Although, as Director claimed, the 1936 IBM case may not really have been about monopolizing and increasing the price of *cards*, the Court seemed to think it was. As Justice Stone put it,

> The agreed use of the "tying clause" by appellant and its only competitors, and the agreement by each of them to restrict its competition in the sale of cards to the lessees of the others, have operated to prevent competition and to create a monopoly in the production and sale of tabulating cards suitable for appellant's machines, as the District Court found. The commerce in tabulating cards is substantial.[20]

If this case was not properly about monopolizing, at least it was about a significant (patent) monopoly. Judge Lurton's, Aaron Director's, and Justice Stone's theories about tie-ins all describe firms with substantial and enduring monopoly power. That is more than can be said for theories of monopoly that the government embraced in its most recent *IBM* case.

In 1956, the government settled by consent judgment another civil suit against IBM.[21] This decree obliged IBM to sell, as well as lease, its machines, and to reduce its share of the card market to 50 percent or less.

Prototype and experimental electronic computers came onto the scene in the 1940s; but as a practical matter the industry began when Remington Rand, later to become Sperry Rand, introduced its models in 1951. In late 1952, IBM introduced its computers. These first-generation machines, large, costly, and slow, used hosts of short-lived, unreliable vacuum tubes. By the end of the decade, solid-state machines had completely transformed the market.

The government complained that what followed was not beneficial competitive evolution. Instead, they claimed, it was a history of monopolization and attempted monopolization by IBM. IBM (and other successful manufacturers) plunged into a dynamic competitive process, displacing their own and competitors' machines with a parade of new and better models. One result was that the cost of data processing fell dramatically. Another result was that IBM got sued.

In 1964, following its successes with both large ''scientific'' computers and the very popular 1400 series of smaller ones, IBM announced its System/360 family of computers, with which it planned both to replace its own most popular lines and to compete against a stream of improved models from competitors. The 360s were designed for versatility and for compatibility with other members of that family, making them suitable for a wide range of business and scientific applications.[22] Major components of the 360s were modular boxes that could be interchanged within the family and—as it turned out—replaced by compatible competitive substitutes offered by what came to be called plug-compatible manufacturers (PCMs).

Like other models to come, the 360s encountered competition on all dimensions and fronts: used machines; different new models offering different specialization, size, power, price, and add-on memories; complementary appurtenances, including printers; and so on. Nevertheless, ''The *Alcoa* decision made it possible to attack an entire course of conduct, and the Justice Department did just that until nearly every act of IBM was seen as anticompetitive—not excluding the introduction of System/360 itself.''[23] And, although IBM ultimately won them all, a rash of private antitrust actions followed the government suit and later influenced it.[24]

As is not rare in antitrust, the government's attempts at market definition were flawed in concept and execution, inconsistent, and trouble all around. Their ''submarkets'' were not subsets of their ''market.''[25] They ignored or distorted facts about substitutability for IBM products, on both the demand and supply sides of the market. They excluded foreign suppliers; ''nonmanufacturers,'' including firms in the business of creating systems from components they bought in the open market; those that leased and sold used machines; and those, including the PCMs, who competed with IBM without offering complete ''general purpose'' data processing ''systems.''[26] By the early 1970s, '' . . . peripheral equipment accounted for roughly 50–70 percent of the value of the average system.''[27] How the government dealt with competitive products offered by the PCMs is truly incredible. It would have been bad enough to ignore the PCMs altogether. Instead, the government proposed that the PCM peripherals sold by its competitors should be counted as part of *IBM's* share because, one day, IBM might offer better products or a better deal and earn that business for itself. Of course it might, as it might win other business on the merits, including other business that it had never had before. To count PCM peripherals in IBM's share before it wins that business is premature, to put it mildly.[28] According to one of several market definitions that IBM proposed, its market share fell from around 78 percent in 1952 to about 33 percent in 1972.[29]

There can be no doubt that IBM tried to stay ahead of its competition by offering new and better equipment and services at declining real prices.[30] Withington, a government witness, reported that "With the introduction of their System/360 equipment, IBM established the new price-performance standard for equipment within the computer industry for the next several years."[31] The government's theory, however, was that all this improvement was anticompetitive and vicious. Among other things, the government asserted that IBM's monopoly was protected by various "barriers to entry," an impoverished theoretical construct criticized at length in chapters 7 and 9. In any case, it is a fact that entry had been very substantial by any reasonable reckoning and that IBM's share declined significantly over time. The appraisal of Fisher and associates is that this decline in market share is affirmatively a virtue, a doubtful proposition. What is not debatable is that large-scale entry undermines the theory that entry was barred.

It is also undeniably true—and presumably a virtue—that competition was so stiff that several well-known firms gave up on the trade and withdrew. This list includes RCA, GE, and Xerox. No student of antitrust history should, however, have been surprised when the government claimed that competition had been *too* stiff; that is, had been predatory and monopolizing. IBM's products were too good, improved too fast, and were simultaneously too cheap and too dear. This seems to have been the government's principal vision.

There is no denying that IBM tried to take business from its competitors, and they from it. That sounds like competition; and, since the dimensions of the competition were quality and price, it is a competition that served consumers well. There is evidence that IBM meant its pricing and new product introductions to be profitable, in the normal sense, and that it did not attempt to achieve a monopoly position through predation of any kind. And as a matter of fact, IBM did not manage to monopolize the business, whatever its intentions may have been.

Indeed, it is striking that virtually all of the government's complaints were that IBM had reduced prices and increased outputs, not exactly the stuff of which real monopolizing and consumer injury is made.[32]

For various reasons, including those discussed in chapters 6 and 9, the decline in IBM's market share is not virtuous in itself. Another reason for reserving judgment on declining shares is that antitrust doctrine is flexible enough to cut both ways. If, for example, IBM proceeds to build a big market share of some specific type of computer, someone is bound to claim that it has monopolized that market and must be turned back. It would hurt consumers if IBM, or anyone else, holds its share down to cultivate political opinion or avert collision with the antitrust laws.

AT&T (1982) _____

The government dropped the *IBM* suit and settled *AT&T* by consent decree. Cases that are not fully litigated in the courts are hard to analyze: outsiders lack published full court opinions and summaries of the facts. It is difficult for anyone who did not work on the cases to study the testimony and exhibits that accumulated before legal proceedings stopped. About all we do have are materials that participants in *AT&T* published.[33] This is particularly troubling in the case of *AT&T*, one of the most complicated antitrust cases of all.

In 1876, Alexander Graham Bell filed his basic telephone patent claims just a few hours before Elisha Gray filed a competing application. Unlike most patents, Bell's established and preserved a major monopoly until they expired in 1893 and 1894. After that, the Bell system[34] still held hundreds of improvement patents; but they proved to be weak.[35] Although Bell filed many patent infringement suits (many of which it lost), and refused either to connect their systems or sell them equipment, many new companies entered after the basic patents expired. According to one source, "By the turn of the century, direct competition between local exchanges was common. Of 1002 cities that had telephone service and populations greater than 4000, 41% were served exclusively by Bell, 14% were served exclusively by an independent, and 45% were served by two or more competing telephone systems."[36]

In the early days, telephone companies operated under city franchises, some of which turned out to be exclusive.[37] Whether because of franchise policies or something else, most towns served by competing telephone companies had only two, and they typically overlapped only in the main business sections, in which telephone demand was heaviest. Even in competitive towns, only 8 to 13 percent of telephone customers subscribed to more than one system. Nevertheless, competitive alternatives seem to have lowered rates and increased telephone use. In at least some cases, subscribing to two services cost less than the rates Bell had charged for one much smaller system before competitors appeared.[38]

By 1902, more than 4,000 independent telephone companies operated 44 percent of the telephones in the U.S. Although the independents operated a lot of toll lines, neither individually nor collectively did they establish a long distance network connecting the largest business centers. That mattered little when it was infeasible to send an intelligible message more than 20 miles. It mattered more once it was feasible to send clear messages across the continent.

More than any other individual, Theodore Vail created Bell's ethos and management system. He became president of AT&T in 1907, when independent companies operated 51 percent of the telephones. Vail abhorred competition in the telephone business and welcomed regulation as the best alternative going. From 1907, Bell turned to merging and interconnecting with independents, reducing their share of total telephones to 45 percent by 1912. Companies not interconnected with Bell operated 17 percent. The Mann-Elkins Act of 1910 gave the ICC authority to regulate interstate telephone communications and, in 1912, it began to investigate Bell. Following independents' complaints, the government also threatened a Sherman Act suit. In 1912, the British nationalized their telephone system and in 1913 the postmaster general of the U.S. urged that we deal with ours in the same way. In a successful response, Bell agreed to connect noncompeting independents and to buy only companies with which it was not competing directly. By 1921, when the Willis-Graham Act permitted Bell to buy independents with which it *did* compete, the independents' share had already fallen to around 36 percent. By 1915, most states regulated the telephone business to some degree. And, "by 1920, AT&T was firmly entrenched as a regulated monopoly. All but three states regulated telephone rates and practices. . . . Most state regulatory commissions opposed local telephone competition. Thus, in return for accepting regulation, AT&T gained tacit approval for its monopoly over the telephone industry."[39]

From 1921, Bell could, with regulatory approval, buy competing companies, and "by 1934, there was no direct competition with the Bell System."[40] The Federal Communications Act of 1934 created a Federal Communications Commission (FCC) to regulate the interstate telephone business, including rates, entry, and interconnection.[41] One avowed objective of the Act was to promote the widest possible use of a national telephone system. Whether in pursuit of this legislative purpose, or its own interests, or both, Bell evolved a discriminatory rate structure that encouraged even those with relatively small demand to get a phone. Relative to costs, household rates were low and business rates were high. And long-distance rates were high relative to local rates.

Almost from the beginning, Bell and its regulators, as well as many economists, claimed that the telephone business is the kind of monopoly that must be both protected and regulated. To achieve maximum efficiency, the monopoly must be protected against entry; but rate and rate-of-return regulation are necessary to protect consumers from the monopoly. Available history does not appear to be adequate to evaluate those claims.[42] Neither, apparently, are the many cost studies that have been made.[43] Whenever a monopoly has been preserved by law, it is difficult to tell whether it is, or ever was, either a natural monopoly or one that must be protected against competition to benefit consumers most. Deciding whether telephone service is a natural monopoly is more difficult than it sounds. Those who do remember textbook diagrams of the demand and costs faced by a natural monopoly may need to reinterpret them. According to such diagrams, a natural monopoly's average cost declines with output size over the relevant range. But there is evidence that large telephone systems have higher average costs than small ones. If all telephones in a system are interconnected, the number of required interconnections rises much more rapidly than the number of telephones in an exchange. Two telephones require one connection; three telephones require five; and so on. One problem is whether the relevant output (or scale) is the number of telephones, the number of message minutes, or something else. A related issue is how to compare equivalent qualities of service. One way to ask the question therefore seems to be whether, if service were provided at cost, consumers would choose to have one firm, or more than one, provide it. Yet starting with local monopoly everywhere, Bell's completely interconnected local monopoly services did not everywhere dominate, even at what were sometimes equal rates.[44]

In the case of single-product firms, natural monopoly means that one firm can satisfy the market at lower cost than two or more firms. Natural monopoly in the provision of two or more products requires that two conditions apply over the relevant range of demand. First, it costs less to produce those products together than separately. That is, the products are complementary in production. And, second, when the firm expands the output of all its products proportionally, total costs rise less than proportionally. Among other things, this means that a firm that is permitted to produce one of the goods but is prevented from producing one or more of the others will not be able to produce at lowest cost.

Without settling the claim that local telephone services are naturally monopolistic, we can say that the claim looks weaker for long-distance than for local service. New technologies, including microwave transmission, permitted entry without tearing up streets, stringing wire on new posts or towers, or otherwise duplicating expensive and durable fixed assets—assuming that the new long-distance companies could use Bell's local services and facilities on reasonable terms. Bell's regulated monopoly was besieged by technological, political, and regulatory changes.

After World War II, in small steps at first, competitors and would-be competitors began appearing at Bell's heels.[45] Having earlier restricted entry into the television business, FCC in 1959 decided that there was enough room in the (microwave) frequency spectrum above 890 megacycles so that it could license new *private*-line (as opposed to general common-carrier) communications systems between specific cities.

In 1969 FCC licensed MCI to establish what was supposed to be a limited private-line microwave service between Chicago and St. Louis, and—in its *Specialized Common Carriers* decision (1971)—said it would license other qualified firms to provide private-line systems in competition with Bell. When MCI began offering traditional common-carrier, long-distance service in 1975, Bell protested, claiming that MCI was unlawfully exceeding what it had been licensed to do. FCC agreed and ordered MCI to stop offering general long-distance service. MCI appealed that order and got it overturned in federal court on grounds that, in the absence of showings that it would damage the public, more competition is better than less. For better or worse, legal theory and regulatory practice had changed fundamentally. Although FCC had itself eased entry and grown to favor more competition, courts would not support even the less stringent entry restrictions that FCC *was* trying to impose. Entry into general long-distance service, traditionally reserved to Bell, was now open.[46]

Thus, in a surprising reversal of long-established regulation and law, FCC had permitted entry into general or common-carrier long-distance markets. But Bell kept its local-service monopolies and the new entrants were soon suing Bell for predatory pricing of its long-distance services and for denying them access to its local exchanges on what they thought were appropriate terms. Then, on November 20, 1974, the Department of Justice filed suit, claiming that Bell had monopolized telecommunication markets, and demanding that AT&T divest its operating companies and that Western Electric be divested and dissolved. The proceedings moved, though slowly, until,

> On January 7, 1982, . . . the parties reached a settlement. AT&T agreed to divest the local exchange facilities held by the Bell operating companies . . . The Justice Department agreed to release AT&T from a 1956 Consent Decree. . . . Unfettered by this decree, AT&T will be able to offer various computer and information services. The Court approved the settlement, with some minor modifications, on August 24, 1982.[47]

The history of the Bell system includes patent-law, technological, and economic complications aplenty. As much as anything else, however, it is telephone regulation that makes the *AT&T* case difficult to understand and appraise. After years of protecting multiproduct, multimarket telephone monopoly, regulators and courts admitted entrants into more and more markets; but not into all. To compete effectively, entrants needed to use parts of the telephone system that Bell still operated under monopoly franchise. That put FCC, Bell, and the entrants onto unstable new ground. It became difficult to tell whether Bell was hurting competition and consumers by obstructing access to its monopoly system, by pricing too low in the competitive markets, or by other means. And it became increasingly difficult for Bell either to compete or to defend itself against charges that it was stamping out competition.

In justifying the tariffs and services that Bell offered in response to competition, FCC and Bell's rivals called on it to price its *individual* services no lower than average total costs—"fully allocated costs." This called for suspending economics and logic to allocate the unallocable by apportioning joint and common costs among several products. Quixotic pursuit of this dream promised to shelter entrants and distort competition. This regulatory evolution complicated and limited what antitrust law could do. The government complained that Bell had excluded entry by misusing the regulatory process. There is little doubt either that "AT&T consistently argued before the FCC that entry was neither necessary nor desirable"; or that regulation imposed costs upon those who were trying to get in.[48] Those flaws seem more a result of regulation than monopolizing behavior under the antitrust laws.[49] In some ways, the major issue was whether Bell had given entrants access to its local facilities on appropriate terms: regulation prevented new entry on the local level. Dissolution surely must have seemed a tempting way out.

Whatever else it did, dissolution might eventually shorten the costly regulatory tournaments in which accountants and other experts chopped away at one another under the gaze of FCC and the courts.[50]

ANTITRUST POLICY AND CONSUMER WELFARE

It is common to approach antitrust policy for the first time with high hopes; then, after experience with how it works, to lose faith in how much good it does. One difficulty is that many serious monopoly problems in the U.S. seem to come from government policies that are, for the most part, beyond the reach of antitrust law. They require other approaches. Second, a good case can be made that antitrust law has itself become a threat to competition.

Third, the quality of economic analysis used in antitrust proceedings is and is likely to remain problematic, or worse. Most cases that economists read, analyze, and cite are not about defendants caught red-handed doing well-specified things that unquestionably violate antitrust law and hurt consumers. In most of the cases that people do cite, there are serious questions about the facts or law or both. Many of what lawyers and judges call facts are inferences at best, and some are rank speculation. It is disturbing when courts infer one thing, while the facts are at least as consistent with a very different hypothesis.

Fourth, the nature of the laws themselves, the enforcement process, and the kinds of cases brought, make antitrust policy an unreliable, slow, and costly way to protect consumers.

As Posner put it,

> . . . a recent study found that a high level of concentration in an industry tends to dissipate by natural forces within an average period of 10 years. Yale Brozen, The Antitrust Task Force Recommendation for Deconcentration, 13 J. Law & Econ. 279 (1970). My table 29 discloses that the average length of a divestiture proceeding in a monopolization case involving a major regional or national market is 8 years, so assuming that a proceeding will not normally be brought immediately upon the attainment of monopoly, it seems unlikely that administrative methods of deconcentration will work significantly more rapidly than the market. Kenneth G. Elzinga, The Antimerger Law: Pyrrhic Victories?, 12 J. Law & Econ. 43, 74–75 (1969) makes a similar point with respect to divestiture in merger cases.[51]

One scholar has argued that, ''however its amount is determined, the antitrust budget should be allocated to maximize the satisfaction of consumers and not that of agency staffs, businessmen, and other special interests,''[52] and wondered whether a random allocation would have done at least as well as the allocations we got.

In an interesting 1975 article, John Siegfried used multiple-regression analysis to try to explain the number and types of antitrust suits brought by the Department of Justice.[53] He included as possible explanatory variables industry profits, concentration, and the estimated welfare loss due to monopoly. Anyone considering antitrust law as a policy alternative should be aware of the results that Siegfried got. Siegfried concluded ''that there is apparently *no* consideration of economic benefits in the decision process for allocating antitrust cases. . . . we must conclude that economic benefits, in the form of efficiency gains and income redistributions, do not play any discernible role in the allocation of Antitrust Division resources.''[54]

He notes, as McGee did in 1965, that ''Perhaps this is not too surprising if we consider the reward structure confronting decision makers in the Antitrust Division. It is probably more important to win cases than to reduce economic losses or inequities in order to move up the success ladder in the Justice Department.''[55] The kinds of cases that show up in court are affected by business practices of the time, the state of the law, and the tastes of antitrust enforcers. If prosecutors want to extend the law, they can push theories that oligopoly *is* monopoly, and bolster them with inference and circumstantial evidence. When courts are sympathetic, this approach wins cases. If, on the other hand, prosecutors think the law is punishing beneficial practices and competitive firms, they can concentrate on explicit conspiracies, including the bidding rings in road building and construction that the Department of Justice ferreted out in the 1980s.

On the whole, however, there is little reason to suppose that antitrust policy will do better work and do it faster and cheaper in the future.

Fourth and worst of all, antitrust laws, even the Sherman Act, which started well, may have protected competitors more effectively than they have protected competition:

Whether it is economists or lawyers who should be blamed, two closely related, and highly mischievous, notions about competition came to prominence both in economics and antitrust law. They are, respectively, the structural theory, and the cast-of-characters theory, of competition. According to the first, concentrated markets do not produce ''competitive'' results. One fatal flaw of this theory, of course, is that it ignores that concentration itself may result from a beneficially competitive process. According to the second theory, involving a cast-of-characters fixation, the law should preserve the health and comfort of individual competitors, especially smaller ones. * * * Once anyone accepts such theories, bizarre results follow in due course. Anything that a relatively large and successful firm does to hold or increase its business; anything that increases concentration, discomfits or makes individual competitors jittery; and anything that displaces individual competitors is at least suspect. Ultimately, it comes to be presumptively illegal. In all of this no one seems to be asking whether consumers really benefit . . . . ''Competition'' must not be interpreted so as to compel, guarantee, or favor a place for anyone, except consumers.[56]

Perhaps some other kind of antitrust policy would do a better job than the one we have. It might conceivably have only two parts. The first would pursue cartels and punish those who participate in them. One way or another, the second part would formulate merger policy, a much harder and more debatable problem. Some would prefer to permit all mergers; others would be quite tough on them. Probably most authorities would want at least to prohibit industry-wide mergers resulting in *national* market shares as high as, say, 45 or 50 percent.[57] As Brozen sees it: ''A case can be made against horizontal mergers of industry-wide proportions when there are high entry barriers. A merger of firms holding competing process patents or patents on competing products with no close substitutes and few distant substitutes could achieve sufficient control over supply to yield monopoly rents.''[58]

Bork would prohibit horizontal mergers ''that leave fewer than three significant rivals in any market.''[59]

This is not the place to spell out detailed proposals for antitrust policies that would genuinely protect consumers. Such a change in emphasis would in any case provoke long debate and a hard fight: many lawyers, consultants, and other special interests have much to gain by keeping the antitrust laws and processes pretty much as they now are.

SUMMARY

Antitrust policy toward large firms has changed several times and in various ways. Taft's *Addyston* (1898) decision gave us a per se rule against naked or unalloyed price fixing, which raises price and reduces consumer welfare.

What the law would be for large firms that act unilaterally was more complicated. Congress evidently did not intend the Sherman Act to jeopardize efficiency and hurt consumers. In *E. C. Knight* (1895), the Court declined to do anything about massive mergers in the sugar industry. Something called the rule of reason—which almost everybody confidently claims to understand—came in with White's *Standard Oil* (1911) and *American Tobacco* (1911) decisions. It is commonly said that the rule of reason did not make size alone an offense, but added abusive and exclusionary practices to monopoly power as ingredients making the offense. This, we are told, ushered in a long period during which courts differentiated between good and bad trusts. One trouble with that, of course, is *how* it differentiates. Some of what passed for bad practices and exclusion can increase consumer welfare; some of what passed for industrial statesmanship and good practice hurts consumers.

Many thought Learned Hand's 1945 *Alcoa* decision ended an era by scrapping the old rule of reason. Some thought it made *all* large firms look like "bad trusts." Hand's notion of illegal monopolizing and abuse included rapid capacity expansion to clear the market at prices that yielded modest profits.

Hand's view has lost ground. *IBM* (1982) may indicate at least a change of tide. Hostility to concentrated industries and firms with large market shares has waned.

QUESTIONS

1. "Since the market share of the sugar trust declined sharply after it *won* the *E. C. Knight* case in 1895, it is not clear whether we need an antimerger policy at all. No matter how big they are, firms that are not innovative and efficient cannot hold their position." Discuss.

2. The old Standard Oil and American Tobacco "trusts" are legendary for having used predatory pricing to create monopoly. Did the Supreme Court say much about that?

3. Discuss and evaluate the *United States Steel* case (1920). What kind of conduct did the Court seem to favor? Oppose?

4. Explain and evaluate Hand's definition of Alcoa's market, including how he dealt with secondary aluminum and substitutes for aluminum.

5. How, exactly, did Hand say Alcoa excluded competition? Draw diagrams showing what he said they actually did, and what they might or ought to have done.

6. How did the Court define Du Pont's cellophane market? What did Stocking and Mueller say about that, including the relevancy of an import tariff?

7. How did IBM price cards for its tabulating machines? What are the main theories about why they did that? How, in principle, could you decide which theory is right?

8. How did the government propose to treat plug-compatible peripheral products in defining IBM's computer market? Do you agree? Discuss.

9. Do you find any similarity between Hand's theory of exclusion in *Alcoa* and the government's theory of excessive and premature product introduction in *IBM*? Explain.

10. Using consumer welfare as your standard, decide whether you agree or disagree with the outcome (lawful, or unlawful) in each of the 8 cases analyzed in this chapter. Explain your answer.

NOTES

1. *U.S.* v. *E. C. Knight Company*, 156 U.S. 1 (1895).
2. *Standard Oil Co.* v. *U.S.*, 221 U.S. 1 (1911); and *U.S.* v. *American Tobacco Co.*, 221 U.S. 106 (1911).
3. For a discussion of different views on this, see Chapter 9.

4. *U.S.* v. *American Tobacco Co.*, 221 U.S. 106 (1911).

5. Chapter 9 discusses Malcolm Burns's conclusion that American Tobacco did use price cutting to reduce the cost of acquiring competitors.

6. *U.S.* v. *U.S. Steel Corporation*, 251 U.S. 417 (1920).

7. G. J. Stigler, "The Dominant Firm and the Inverted Umbrella," *Journal of Law & Economics*, 8 (October 1965), pp. 167–72; D. Parsons and E. Ray, "The United States Steel Consolidation: The Creation of Market Control," *Journal of Law & Economics*, 18 (April 1975), pp. 181–219.

8. *U.S.* v. *Aluminum Company of America*, 148 F.2d 416, Circuit Ct. of Appeals of the U.S. (2d Cir. 1945).

9. In 1925, James B. Duke, of *Tobacco* fame, sold Alcoa a water-power site on the Saguenay River in Canada. Donald H. Wallace, *Market Control in the Aluminum Industry* (Cambridge, Mass.: Harvard University Press, 1937), pp. 73–74, 132–37.

10. It is true that a durable-good monopoly should try to take into account how its present production will affect future demands for its stuff. But it is also true that it eventually does compete against its own previous output, which reduces its real market share and power. That is, once its previous output is in the market, it is and should be counted as a competitive factor.

For detailed discussions of this point, see Peter L. Swan, "Durability of Consumption Goods," *American Economic Review*, 60 (December 1970), pp. 884–94; and Swan, "The Durability of Goods and Regulation of Monopoly," *Bell Journal of Economics and Management Science*, 2 (Spring 1971), pp. 347–57; and Ronald H. Coase, "Durability and Monopoly," *Journal of Law & Economics*, 15 (April 1972), pp. 143–49.

11. For what happened afterwards, see Simon Whitney, *Antitrust Policies*, vol. II (New York: The Twentieth Century Fund, 1958), Chapter 13; and Leonard W. Weiss, *Economics and American Industry* (New York: John Wiley & Sons, Inc., 1961), Chapter 5.

12. *U.S.* v. *E.I. du Pont de Nemours and Co.*, 351 U.S. 377 (1956).

13. G. W. Stocking and W. F. Mueller, "The Cellophane Case and the New Competition," *American Economic Review*, 45 (March 1955), pp. 29–63, reprinted in Stocking and Heflebower, eds., *Readings in Industrial Organization* (Homewood, Ill.: Richard D. Irwin, Inc., 1958), pp. 118–50.

14. F. M. Fisher, J. J. McGowan, and Joen E. Greenwood, *Folded, Spindled, and Mutilated: Economic Analysis and U.S. v. IBM* (Cambridge, Mass.: MIT Press, 1983).

15. *U.S.* v. *IBM*, U.S. District Court for the Southern District of New York, Civil Action No. 69 Civ. 200.

16. Fisher, McGowan, and Greenwood, *Folded, Spindled, and Mutilated*, p. 1.

17. *IBM* v. *U.S.*, 298 U.S. 131 (1936); 13 F. Supp. 11 *aff'd.* See the discussion of compound pricing, in Chapter 9.

18. See the discussion of his theory in Chapter 9.

19. "Interestingly enough, Judge Lurton used almost precisely this reasoning in deciding both *Heaton-Peninsular Button-Fastener Co.* v. *Eureka Specialty Co.*, 77 Fed. 288 (6th Cir. 1896), and *Henry* v. *A.B. Dick Co.*, 224 U.S. 1 (1912)." Ward S. Bowman, Jr., *Patent and Antitrust Law* (Chicago: University of Chicago Press, 1973), p. 104, note.

20. *IBM* v. *U.S.*, 56 S. Ct. 701 (1936).

21. The U.S. filed suit on 21 January 1952; consent judgment entered on 25 January 1956 (Civil Action 72–344).

22. By *360*, IBM apparently meant that these machines could cover 360 degrees—all points of the electronic data processing "compass." Fisher, McGowan, and Greenwood, *Folded, Spindled, and Mutilated*, p. 53.

23. Ibid., p. 12.

24. Ibid., p. 13.

25. Ibid., pp. 68–69.

26. Ibid., pp. 60, 61, 64, 89, 92.

27. Ibid., p. 68.

28. Ibid., p. 127.

29. Ibid., p. 110.

30. Ibid., Chapter 5.

31. Ibid., p. 163.

32. Ibid., p. 328.

33. An important source for the following discussion is David S. Adams, ed., *Breaking Up Bell: Essays on Industrial Organization and Regulation* (New York: North-Holland Press, 1983). Adams and his contributors were government consultants in the *AT&T* case. The book does not tell where, in the transcript of record, their facts come from.

    For more general industry history, see also Richard Gabel, "The Early Competitive Era in Telephone Communications, 1893–1920," *Law and Contemporaty Problems* (Spring 1969), pp. 340–69; John Brooks, *Telephone: The First Hundred Years* (New York: Harper & Row, Publishers, Inc., 1975); and Gerald W. Brock, *Telecommunications Industry* (Cambridge, Mass.: Harvard University Press, 1981).

34. The text refers to the Bell system simply as "Bell." In fact, however, in 1899 Bell transferred its securities to its New York subsidiary, AT&T.

35. According to Adams, the rate of return on investment declined dramatically, from an average of 46 percent a year 1876–1894, to 8 percent 1900–1906. Adams, *Breaking Up Bell*, p. 25.

36. Ibid., pp. 17–18.

37. Independents failed to get franchises in Chicago, and failed to get subway rights in Boston and New York. For example, see ibid., p. 22 and p. 36, note 54.

38. Ibid., p. 18.

39. Ibid., p. 42.

40. Ibid., p. 14.

41. Ibid., p. 42.

42. There is no shortage of opinions. To Kahn it was "clear" that local telephone service was a natural monopoly. A. E. Kahn, *The Economics of Regulation*, vol. II (New York: Wiley & Sons, Inc., 1971), p. 123. Bornholz and Evans argue that, although "Few markets could have supported more than two competing exchanges. . . . Sunk costs of entry were not effective deterrents to entry" and that contracts and franchises "prevented Bell from lowering prices today in the hopes of raising prices tomorrow." *Breaking Up Bell*, p. 34.

43. For example, see Adams, *Breaking Up Bell*, Chapter 6, "Natural Monopoly," and Chapter 10, "Multiproduct Cost Function Estimates and Natural Monopoly Tests for the Bell System," pp. 253–82. Also see D. S. Evans and J. J. Heckman, "A Test for Subadditivity of the Cost Function with an Application to the Bell System," *American Economic Review*, 74 (September 1984), pp. 615–30.

44. Adams, *Breaking Up Bell*, p. 31. Using Bell System data for 1947–1977, Evans and Heckman estimated its multiproduct cost function. They concluded that it did not have a natural monopoly. D. S. Evans and J. J. Heckman, "A Test for Subadditivity of the Cost Function with an Application to the Bell System," *American Economic Review*, 74 (September 1984), pp. 615–23.

45. Adams, *Breaking Up Bell*, pp. 42–43.

46. There was more competition on other margins as well. For example, "The 1968 *Carterfone Decision* ruled that AT&T could not unreasonably prohibit the connection of terminal equipment manufactured by AT&T's competitors to the telephone system." Ibid., p. 2.

47. Ibid., pp. ix–x.

48. Ibid., p. 46. "In order to obtain permission to construct a microwave system which cost $2 million and took 7 months to complete, MCI spent $10 million in regulatory and legal costs and waited 7 years." Ibid.

49. *Breaking Up Bell* seems to agree with this view: pp. 47–49.

50. This assumes that local Bell companies will continue to be kept out of the long-distance (and some other) markets. If not, tournaments contesting access to local networks will resume, this time with AT&T jousting against the Bell operating companies and Bell operating companies jousting against one another as well as against other entrants, and with state regulatory commissions and the Antitrust Division sitting in the judges' tent.

51. Richard A. Posner, "A Statistical Study of Antitrust Enforcement," *Journal of Law & Economics*, 13 (October 1970), pp. 365–420, at p. 417, note.

52. John S. McGee, "Some Economic Issues in Robinson-Patman Land," p. 532.

53. John Siegfried, "The Determinants of Antitrust Activity," *Journal of Law & Economics*, 18 (October 1975), pp. 559–74.

54. Ibid., pp. 567–68.

55. Ibid., p. 573.

56. John S. McGee, "Why Not 'Deregulation' for Antitrust?" *Antitrust Law Journal*, 46, no. 3 (Summer 1977), p. 778.

57. Compare Bork, *The Antitrust Paradox: A Policy at War with Itself*; and Yale Brozen, *Concentration, Mergers, and Public Policy* (New York: Macmillan Publishing Co., Inc., 1982).

58. Yale Brozen, *Concentration, Mergers, and Public Policy*, p. 402.

59. Bork, *The Antitrust Paradox*, p. 406. Bork would also prohibit horizontal "non-ancillary agreements of rivals or potential rivals to fix prices or divide markets"; and "deliberate predation" *not* including "predatory" price cutting, but including predatory misuse of the courts and regulatory agencies.

INDEX